Communications in Computer and Information Science 334

Editorial Board

Simone Diniz Junqueira Barbosa
Pontifical Catholic University of Rio
Rio de Janeiro, Brazil

Phoebe Chen
La Trobe University, Melbourne, Aus

Alfredo Cuzzocrea
ICAR-CNR and University of Calabria, Italy

Xiaoyong Du
Renmin University of China, Beijing, China

Joaquim Filipe
Polytechnic Institute of Setúbal, Portugal

Orhun Kara
TÜBİTAK BİLGEM and Middle East Technical University, Turkey

Tai-hoon Kim
Konkuk University, Chung-ju, Chungbuk, Korea

Igor Kotenko
St. Petersburg Institute for Informatics and Automation
of the Russian Academy of Sciences, Russia

Dominik Ślęzak
University of Warsaw and Infobright, Poland

Xiaokang Yang
Shanghai Jiao Tong University, China

Ruchuan Wang   Fu Xiao (Eds.)

Advances in Wireless Sensor Networks

6th China Conference, CWSN 2012
Huangshan, China, October 25-27, 2012
Revised Selected Papers

 Springer

Volume Editors

Ruchuan Wang
Fu Xiao

Nanjing University of Posts and Telecommunications
College of Computer
Mailbox 157, 66 Xin Mofan Road
Nanjing 210003, China
E-mail: {wangrc, xiaof}@njupt.edu.cn

ISSN 1865-0929   e-ISSN 1865-0937
ISBN 978-3-642-36251-4   e-ISBN 978-3-642-36252-1
DOI 10.1007/978-3-642-36252-1
Springer Heidelberg Dordrecht London New York

Library of Congress Control Number: 2012955854

CR Subject Classification (1998): C.2.0-6, C.5.3, F.2.2

© Springer-Verlag Berlin Heidelberg 2013
This work is subject to copyright. All rights are reserved, whether the whole or part of the material is concerned, specifically the rights of translation, reprinting, re-use of illustrations, recitation, broadcasting, reproduction on microfilms or in any other way, and storage in data banks. Duplication of this publication or parts thereof is permitted only under the provisions of the German Copyright Law of September 9, 1965, in its current version, and permission for use must always be obtained from Springer. Violations are liable to prosecution under the German Copyright Law.
The use of general descriptive names, registered names, trademarks, etc. in this publication does not imply, even in the absence of a specific statement, that such names are exempt from the relevant protective laws and regulations and therefore free for general use.

Typesetting: Camera-ready by author, data conversion by Scientific Publishing Services, Chennai, India

Printed on acid-free paper

Springer is part of Springer Science+Business Media (www.springer.com)

Preface

This volume of *Communications in Computer and Information Science* contains the proceedings of the *6th China Conference of Wireless Sensor Networks* (*CWSN* 2012), which was held in Huangshan, China, during October 25–27, 2012. CWSN represents the highest research level of sensor networks in China. CWSN 2012 served as a forum for researchers, developers and users to compare their experiences of sensor network research and applications, and to discuss the key challenges and research directions facing the sensor network community.

CWSN 2012, with its focus on sensor network design and implementation, aimed to promote the exchange of the theories and applications surrounding sensor networks. In addition, the conference provide the opportunity to consider research on CPS and the Internet of Things. Some well-known experts were invited to attend and present keynote speeches. Related sensor networks enterprises demonstrated their state-of-the-art products and technologies. A total of 458 papers were submitted to CWSN 2012, of which 272 were in English. Eighty high-quality papers, focusing, amongst other things, on node systems, infrastructures, communication protocols, data management, etc., were recommended by the Program Committee to be presented at the conference and included in this volume of CCIS.

On behalf of the Organizing Committee, we would like to thank Springer for publishing the proceedings of CWSN 2012. We would also like to express our gratitude to the reviewers for providing extra help in the review process, and the authors for contributing their research results to the conference. We would like to express our appreciation and to profusely thank them for making CWSN 2012 a success.

We look forward to seeing all of you next year at CWSN 2013. With your support and participation, CWSN will continue its success for a long time.

October 2012

Ruchuan Wang
Fu Xiao

Organization

The 6th China Conference of Wireless Sensor Networks (CWSN 2012) was held in Huangshan, China, and was organized by Nanjing University of Posts and Telecommunications, Nanjing, China.

General Chairs

Zhen Yang	Nanjing University of Posts and Telecommunications
Jianzhong Li	Harbin Institute of Technology

Honorary Chair

Hao Dai	Chinese Academy of Sciences

PC Co-chairs

Lijuan Sun	Nanjing University of Posts and Telecommunications
Limin Sun	Chinese Academy of Sciences
Huadong Ma	Beijing University of Posts and Telecommunications
Min Sha	Technology Research Center of National RFID System Engineering

Organizing Chair

Ruchuan Wang	Nanjing University of Posts and Telecommunications

Organizing Vice-Chair

Geng Yang	Nanjing University of Posts and Telecommunications

Local Chair

Fu Xiao	Nanjing University of Posts and Telecommunications

Organizing Committee

Aiqun Li	Nanjing University of Posts and Telecommunications
Zhihong Zhu	Nanjing University of Posts and Telecommunications
Haiping Huang	Nanjing University of Posts and Telecommunications
Jian Guo	Nanjing University of Posts and Telecommunications
Chao Sha	Nanjing University of Posts and Telecommunications
Lingyun Jiang	Nanjing University of Posts and Telecommunications
Linfeng Liu	Nanjing University of Posts and Telecommunications

Sponsoring Institutions

China Computer Federation, Beijing, China.
China Computer Federation Technical Committee on Sensor Network, Beijing, China.
Technology Research Center of National RFID System Engineering, Nanjing, China.

Table of Contents

Design and Implementation
of Cooperative Platform for Multiple Devices
Based on Multi-Agent System
in Ubiquitous Networking Environment

Hanzhen Cao[1], Weijun Qin[2], Jiadi Zhang[1], Qiang Li[2], and Yan Liu[1]

[1] School of Software and Microelectronics, Peking University,
Beijing, 102600, China
`caohanzhen@is.iscas.ac.cn`, `dedezhang@gmail.com`, `ly@ss.pku.edu.cn`
[2] Institute of Information Engineering, Chinese Academy of Sciences,
Beijing 100195, China
`qinweijun@iie.ac.cn`, `liqiang@is.iscas.ac.cn`

Abstract. With the development of embedded and communication technology, along with the rapid popularization of smart mobile devices in recent years, the communication techniques in ubiquitous networking becomes more and more mature and variety, ranging from wireless communication techniques in long distance such as WiMAX and 3G to wireless communication techniques in moderate distance such as WiFi, as well as wireless communication techniques in short distance such as Bluetooth and ZigBee. Smart mobile devices can take advantages of various communication techniques in ubiquitous networking to connect, discover and communicate to each other, forming into groups to realize cooperation among multiple devices in ubiquitous networking environment. Combined with the application context of cooperation among multiple devices on entertainment in the scene of smart home, ubiquitous networking techniques and smart mobile devices are adopted while a method of group management for multiple devices in ubiquitous networking is put up. And a cooperative platform in ubiquitous networking based on a multi-agent framework, named JADE, is designed and implemented. Last but not least, a prototype system is given to validate the feasibility and the performance.

Keywords: Ubiquitous Networking, Cooperative Platform, Multiple Devices, Multi-Agent.

1 Introduction

Ubiquitous Networking is characterized by wide application, range and ability. It regards the smooth communication as the target whenever it is, wherever you are, whoever you are and whatever it is. Ubiquitous Networking composed of wireless communication technology, such as long distance wireless communication technology WiMAX and 3G,medium distance wireless communication technology WiFi and short distance wireless communication technology Bluetooth

R. Wang and F. Xiao (Eds.): CWSN 2012, CCIS 334, pp. 1–13, 2013.
© Springer-Verlag Berlin Heidelberg 2013

and ZigBee. The development of embedded technology and computer communication technology, for one thing, makes more and more physical terminal devices connected to the ubiquitous network environment. For another, it endows these terminal devices more powerful ability, storage ability, expression ability of media, computing and communication abilities. All the abilities can be collectively referred to as the Terminal Capability.

On the one hand, these increasingly Terminal Capabilities the terminal devices share remains to be digged and make full use of by the researchers and developers. On the other hand, signal terminal device can't meet the increasingly complicated functional demand and experiential demand from users. The so-called experience demand refers to the user in the function demand, expects to obtain better user experience demand except for the functional demand. The reality of these two aspects reflects the Necessity and urgency of multiple devices cooperation .

Recently, researchers pay much more attention to particular application based on the particular terminal device concerning on the Multiple Devices Cooperation. However, they rarely can provide a universal platform, which is limited by the hardware and software technology the previous terminal device carried on .With the development of the intelligent device, the effects caused by the technological difference are increasingly more and more small.so researchers will have the conditions and abilities to build up the universal cooperative platform to implement the cooperation among different devices. CSCW (Computer-Supported Cooperative Work) means that a group of devices complete a common task in the cooperative way under the environment supported by computer. Some characteristics of CSCW are as followed. Perception, individual of the group can get other individual information if it is in the cooperative group. Task clarity, individuals in the cooperative group have clear responsibility on task division, completion and integration. Adaption, individuals in cooperation and group can adjust their technology to different scene. However, these features are still the goals that the cooperative platform for multiple devices pursuits.

This paper of the first part, first of all, provides a method of group management based on the ubiquitous network technology and intelligent mobile terminal technology. At the same time, it designs and implements the cooperative platform for multiple devices. In addition, based on the foundation of cooperative platform and association with requirement of family entertainment, it gives the design and implementation of a prototype system. In the end, experiments are carried out to prove the feasibility of cooperative platform for multiple devices based on multi-agent system in ubiquitous networking environment in logic and performance. The second part briefly describes the domestic and foreign related work. The third part describes the requirement, concept and process of group management method based on the ubiquitous network technology. The fourth part describes the design and implementation about the cooperative platform for multiple devices based on multi-agent system in ubiquitous networking environment. The fifth part, associated with family entertainment scene, makes an experiment and describes the experimental setting, methods, results and conclusions. At the end of this paper, we make a conclusion about current work and propose the next research direction and content.

2 Related Work

In recent years, researchers have carried out some work in the terminal cooperation field. Eric K [1] etc. proposed the concept of Capability Reconciliation. In their paper, the service was regarded as a black box process and separated from a group of input/output stream. Then, on the basis of input/output flow type and attribute, match for the appropriate mobile devices and get the optimum solution. ZHANG X [2] etc. put forward the concept of distributed mobile terminal. In this paper, it presented a system structure of distributed mobile terminal and designed the control process of polymerization reconstruction. WANG X [3] etc. proposed distributed terminal technology based on the ubiquitous environment. Compared with the concept of distributed mobile terminal, this paper focused on the mobile environment and discussed the model and process of mobile terminal polymerization reconstruction. HU Z [4] etc. proposed the concept of best experience. Actually, he nature of their view is to add the optimal solution concept and process to the concept of distributed mobile terminal.

Getting the optimum solution in the terminal polymerization process provides a theoretical basis for improving the performance of the terminal polymerization. WANG X [5] etc. presented the concept of using the structure and organization of deconcentration in the distributed mobile terminal system. That is to say, they proposed a model and process of deconcentration based on the concept of distributed mobile terminal. The model of deconcentration is much more appropriate for polymerization and control management among mobile terminals and also complicated. JIN Y.H. [6] etc. proposed how to build a satisfaction optimal model in the ubiquitous service terminal system. Their paper discussed the dynamic aggregation mechanism and the optimal model of the mechanism and implementation based on service experience. Most of the work above involved in building theoretical model, however, lacking in the implementation of combining practical problems with specific technology.

3 Group Management Method Based on Multi-Agent System in Ubiquitous Networking Environment

3.1 Application Scene

With the development of economy and technology, a user or a family with multiple terminal devices (personal computer, notebook computer, intelligent TV, panel computer, intelligent mobile phone and so on) are not uncommon. In the following scene shown in Fig. 1, user connects the family WiFi network by the smart mobile phone, panel computer, Smart TV and other terminal devices, and experiences entertainment applications in the family synergy entertainment environment.

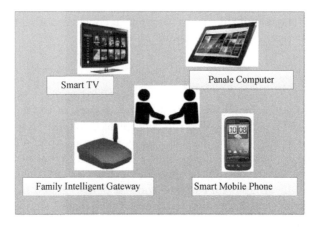

Fig. 1. Scene of family synergy entertainment environment

In this scene, there are several issues to be resolved. The first problem is how terminal devices can find entertainment applications. The second is how the terminal devices can find each other. The last is how the terminal devices communicate and cooperate with each other to implement the entertainment applications. To solve all the problems above, this paper puts forward a method of group management based on ubiquitous network.

3.2   Group Management Method

In some scenes, a number of terminal devices is closely linked to because of some entertainment applications, which is called a group. The so-called group management method is on these groups' management .group management method should maintain a terminal device and a task queue. All terminals devices of the scene are in the device queue and all the tasks are in the task queue.

One group only has a business application and a business can only be in one group. Therefore, the task queue is equal to the group queue, which maintains the task information devices information of the group. Group management is responsible for tasks in the task queue. In the practical scene, group management method appears in the form of service, so it is called group management service. The following three stages describe the process of group management, the initialization phase, group stage and exit the stage respectively.

3.2.1   Initialization Phase

Group management method for the initialization phase is shown in Fig. 2(a). First of all, the management service started (Step 1). The process also has relation to the initialization of terminal device queue and task queue and restoration of persistence data. Persistent data can be the service configuration information and can also be the persistent information when the group management services exited last time. Then the terminal device A and B in the practical scene start (Step 2) and register in the group management service (Step 3). After group management service has gotten the registration request, it adds terminal device A and B into the terminal device queue (Step 4).

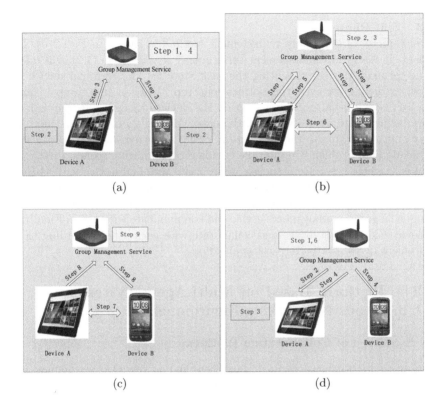

Fig. 2. Group management method

3.2.2   Group Stage
The group stages of the group management method is shown in Fig. 2(b) and 2(c). At a moment, terminal device A sends request to the group management service to create a new task (Step 1). Group management service receives the request, generates new task, adds it into the task queue and associate the terminal device with task just created (Step 2). Then the group management services will select the appropriate terminal device which can participate in the task from the device queue, such as B, associate the selected device with the task (Step 3) and give the device a notification (Step 4). When all the terminal devices the task required have been matched, the group management service notice these terminal devices to start (Step 5). The terminal device A and B execute the task through communication (Step 6). After having completed the task(Step 7),

they inform the group management services of the condition of the process(Step 8).The group management service deal with the following task after having receiving the notification from the devices. It will cancel the task whenever it receives the notification. If there is no terminal devices associated with the task, the whole task will be canceled.

3.2.3 Exit Phase

The exit phase of the group management method is shown in Fig. 2(d). In a moment, If the group management service need to exit(Step 1), it will inform all the terminal devices executing the task(Step 2). The terminal device will exit when having received the notification(Step 3). Then the group management service will send notification to all the devices (Step 4). In the end, the group management service will deal the data which is should be persistent and finally quit. According to the description, group management method can solve the encountered problems in multiple terminal collaboration scenes. Firstly, the group management service associate appropriate terminal device with the task so that they can find the existence of task application. Secondly, after the start of the task, the involved terminal device can find other devices in the same task through the group management service and communicate with them. Finally, all the devices can communicate and collaborate with each other according to the requirement of the particular task application.

4   The Platform Based on Multi-Agent System in Ubiquitous Networking Environment

4.1   Structure of Collaboration Platform

The previous section has described the concept and process of group management method. The structure and implementation of the collaboration platform as followed based on the group management method. The structure collaborative platform adopts is as followed in Fig. 3. The architecture of the collaboration platform based on Multi-Agent system in ubiquitous networking environment is divided into three levels. The lowest layer is the terminal device queue and task queue, which is the foundation of the group management method. The middle layer is a collection of functional module and packages many kinds of operation of the terminal device queue and task queue. The topmost layer contains zero or more agents, which is called agent layer. Agent is the image of the terminal device in the collaboration platform. That is to say, the agent corresponding to the registered terminal device can communicate with it directly.

The terminal device communicates with each other through agents, which is shown in Fig. 4 below. Firstly, the terminal device2 sends a message to its corresponding agent—agent2 (Step 1). Secondly, agent2 sends the message to the agent the target terminal device correspond to (Step 2)—agent1 and agent3. Thirdly, agent1 and agent3 sends the message to its corresponding terminal device (Step 3)—device1 and device3. Finally,After having receiving the request,

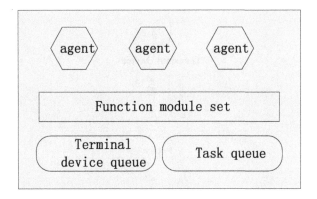

Fig. 3. Structure of collaboration platform

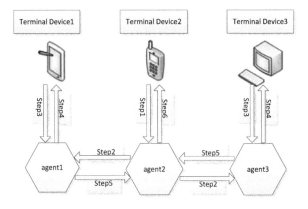

Fig. 4. Communication among Terminal devices

device1 and device3 will complete the corresponding task and then return results in the reverse order.

Collaboration platform communicate with the terminal device through agent too, which is shown in Fig. 5. Firstly, the terminal device sends a message to its corresponding agent(Step 1). Secondly, after having receiving the message, the agent will send the message to the function module set(Step 2). Thirdly, the function module set will deal with the data structure to implement the practical service function(Step 3). Finally, it will return results in the reverse order(Step4, 5, 6).

As the procedure described above, a terminal device only communicates with its corresponding proxy, while the proxy is communicating or interacting with other proxies or functional module(s) of the Cooperative Platform. The terminal device needs not to care about the condition of other proxies or functional module cluster, as all the messages are transmitted or received by the corresponding proxy. The communication between terminal devices only requires the

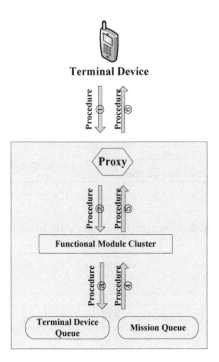

Fig. 5. Communications between Cooperative Platform and Terminal device(s)

communication between proxies, instead of the communication between terminal devices and the functional module cluster; while the communication between terminal device(s) and the functional module cluster requires the communication between corresponding proxies and the functional module cluster, instead of the communication between proxies.

4.2   Design and Realization of the Cooperative Platform

Corresponded to the architecture design, the Cooperative Platform is divided into 3 layers as shown in Fig. 6: Data Structure Layer, Functional Module Layer and Process Layer. The bottom layer is Data Structure Layer, including Terminal Device Queue, Mission Queue and Backup Data Structure. The first two queues are used to group management; Backup Data Structure is mean to persistent data of Cooperative Platform and backup/restore data when the Platform is powering up/off. The second layer is functional module Layer, including functional modules which operate and maintain the bottom-layer data structure. The Functional Module Layer includes Terminal Log in/Log out/Check Module, Mission Log in/Log out/Query Module, Platform Power up/off Management Module, Terminal/Mission Matching Module, Terminal/Mission Status Management Module and System Log/Exception Record Module. The top layer is Process Layer, including proxy Component, Process Engine and Exception

Handler. Proxy Component manages all proxies of terminal devices; Process Engine is in charge of the running of Cooperative Platform; Exception Handler is responsible to handling the encountered exception during the running process of Process Engine.

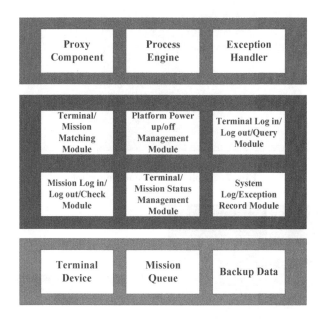

Fig. 6. Design of the Cooperative Platform

5 Experiment Verification

5.1 Scene

As the Fig. 7 shown below, 3 terminal devices are connected to router in home environment; two devices are held as application controller, while the other one as the application display. The controller is private and the display is shared to the family members. In the experiment, two smartphones are used as controller and a Tablet PC is used as the display.

5.2 Prototype System Realization

The prototype system is realized as an Android application, using JADE (Java Agent Development) Framework. As the core of the Cooperative Platform, the JADE Framework is deployed on the Platform and 3 terminal devices; the JADE host program is deployed on Cooperative Platform while the JADE mobile-client is deployed on terminal devices. The prototype system is developed and deployed a Tetris application based on the Cooperative Platform; the controller is deployed

Fig. 7. Application Scene Snapshot

(a) Smartphone Application Screen-   (b) Tablet PC Application Screenshot
shot

Fig. 8.

on smartphones, and the display is deployed on a Tablet PC. The application screenshots of the smartphone and the Tablet PC are shown below.

Fig. 8(a) is the screenshots of the smartphone, which show the controller of the Tetris application. As the diagrams show, the control message can be sent to Cooperative Platform through two different ways. The diagram on the left shows how Gesture Mechanis5.3m works in sending control message to Cooperative Platform: when user finish drawing gestures on the board, the application would translate the gestures into corresponding commands. The diagram on the right shows how Screen Touching Mechanism works in sending control message to Cooperative Platform: while user freely touching and moving their fingers on the screen, the application will translate the movement into corresponding commands by identifying the direction and distance of a Screen Touching action.

Fig. 8(b) is the screen shot of the tablet PC, which indicates that the Tetris application supports single player or two players. And the gesture and screen touching action on the smartphone would be translated to the corresponding commands (move left, move right, fall down, transform, exit, etc.) and sent to Cooperative Platform. After processing the commands, Cooperative Platform sends data to tablet PC to display. The two-dimensional code shown in Diagram 8b contains configuration information, which is used to terminal devices matching.

5.3   Result

5.3.1   Feasibility Test
Firstly a feasibility test is run on Cooperative Platform Based on Multi-Agent System in Ubiquitous Networking Environment. Table 1 shows the interactive time delay when the Cooperative Platform loads two terminal devices. The sample data demonstrates that the interactive time delay of the terminal device cooperation is within 20 milli-seconds, with an average below 10 milliseconds, which could be completely ignored for a human-computer interaction application.

Table 1. Time Delay (Time in Millisecond)

16	5	12	17	8	1
2	5	8	0	5	5
14	7	1	2	13	19
1	1	7	2	4	2
0	2	2	2	17	9
Average: 6.3		Median: 5, 5		Standard Deviation: 5.8	

5.3.2   Performance Test
Secondly a feasibility test is run on Cooperative Platform Based on Multi-Agent System in Ubiquitous Networking Environment. The message data transmission is the only concern of the performance test, regardless of the business logic process before or after the data transmission. Note that this performance test only focuses on the performance of Cooperative Platform under stress test, regardless of the restriction of one-to-one correspondence between terminal device and proxy which described above. Test cases are divided into two groups, thrice testing and sample, and then calculate the average. The result is shown in Table 2 below.

In the first group of test cases, 1 sending proxy and 50 receiving proxies are joined Cooperative Platform. The sending proxy sends a message to all receiving proxies every 50 milliseconds; the receiving proxy receives the message and calculates the time delay. The result indicates that the average time delay of a message is far below 1 millisecond. The second group of test cases increases the

Table 2. Four Cases under Stress Test

	Case 1	Case 2	Case 3
Sending Proxy	1	1	1
Receiving Proxy	50	50	100
Sending Interval	50ms	100ms	50ms
Average Time Delay	<<1ms	<<1ms	<<1ms
	Case 4	Case 5	Case 6
Sending Proxy	2	1 + 1	2 + 2
Receiving Proxy	50	50 + 50	50 + 50
Sending Interval	50ms	50ms	50ms
Average Time Delay	Unstable	$O(1)$ ms	Unstable

sending interval from 50 milliseconds to 100 milliseconds, and the third group increases the number of receiving proxies from 50 to 100. The test results of these two groups have no obvious difference compare to the first group. However, the forth group has an obvious different result. There are 2 sending proxies are used instead of 1 sending proxy in first three groups, and these 2 sending proxies are deployed on a same terminal device. The result shows that the average time delay would increase as time passes by. The fifth group also uses 2 sending proxies, but they are deploying in two different terminal devices. Although the test result shows the time delay is at the same level as 1 millisecond, it is remarkably increased compared to the first 3 groups. The sixth group of test cases uses 4 sending proxies deployed on two different terminal devices. The result is just the same as the group 4, which the average time delay increases as time passes by.

Judging from the six groups of test cases above, Cooperative Platform Based on Multi-Agent System in Ubiquitous Networking Environment has a good adaption in relation to the variation of receiving proxy number and message sending intervals. Cooperative Platform can keep high performance under stress test only when there is one sending proxy in each one terminal device. Otherwise the performance of the system would become unpredictable and become unusable as time passes by.

6   Conclusion and Further Research

This paper introduces a Cooperative Platform for Multiple Devices Based on Multi-Agent System in Ubiquitous Networking Environment, which fully utilizes the capability of multiple terminal devices and provides functional and experience requirements that cannot be provided with single terminal device. It is proved feasible in logic and performance through experiment verification and can be built with existing technology.

Further research will be focused on extracting a general develop framework base on the present research results and distributing a universal development kit. Multi-device distributed applications could be developed based on this develop framework.

Acknowledgments. The work has been funded by National High Technology Research and Development Program of China (2012AA050804), State Key Program of National Natural Science Foundation of China (61073180) and National Science and Technology Major Project (2010ZX03006-001-01).

References

1. Eric, K., Amiya, N.: Capability Reconciliation for Virtual Device Composition in Mobile Ad Hoc Networks. In: Proc. of 2010 IEEE 8th International Conference on Wireless and Mobile Computing, Networking and Communications, pp. 27–34. IEEE, NJ (2010)
2. Zhang, X., Su, F., Ji, Y.: Research on Distributed Reconstruction Terminal Technology. Journal of Beijing University of Posts and Telecommunications 28(3), 65–67 (2005) (in Chinese)
3. Wang, X., Ji, Y.: Distributed Terminal Technology for Mobile Ubiquitous Environments. Rado Communications Technology 33(6), 36–39 (2007) (in Chinese)
4. Hu, Z., Shi, J.W., Tang, X.-S.: Study and implementation of terminal aggregation based on ABE. Application Research of Computers 25(6), 1864–1866 (2008) (in Chinese)
5. Wang, X., Yang, J., Tang, X.S., et al.: Decentralized Architecture and Organizing Mechanisms for Distributed Terminal System. In: Proc. of Wireless Communications and Networking Conference, pp. 236–241. IEEE, NJ (2006)
6. Jin, Y.H., Tian, H., Liu, Z.M.: An Optimal Satisfaction Model for Universal Service Terminal System. In: Proc. of Vehicular Technology Conference, pp. 1–5. IEEE, NJ (2008)

Research on Data Fault Tolerance Mechanism Based on ECT in Cloud Storage

Danwei Chen* and Xiaojuan Ping

Nanjing University of Posts and Telecommunications,
Nanjing 210007, China
chendw@njupt.edu.cn

Abstract. In cloud storage, the user's data is no longer locally stored. So the key issue we are facing now is to ensure the reliability and validity of data storage. Due to this problem, erasure codes and token mechanism have been adopted, and then a fault-tolerant method named Ensure Codes token (ECT) has been designed to make sure the correctness of data and rapid position of errors. The result shows that this method can improve the reliability of data storage.

Keywords: cloud storage, fault tolerance, erasure codes, reliability.

1 Introduction

In cloud data storage, data is stored into a set of cloud servers, which are running in a cooperated and distributed manner. Cloud servers finish accessing or retrieving the data and then execute some operations such as block update, delete, insert and append [1–4]. In order to ensure the security and dependability of cloud data storage, an efficient security mechanism has been designed for dynamic data verification and management, and the main goals are as follows:

1. Storage correctness: to ensure that users' data files are indeed stored appropriately and kept intact all the time in the cloud.
2. Fast localization of data error: to effectively locate the malfunctioning server when data corruption has been detected.
3. Dynamic data support: to maintain the same level of storage correctness assurance even if users modify, delete or append their data files in the cloud.

In cloud data storage system(as Fig. 1), there are two methods including complete copy and erasure code copy [5], which are adopted to employ redundant technology and ensuring the data correctness. Storage systems, such as GFS, Atmos and Ceph, all adopt complete copy redundancy method. For the Google File System (GFS) in Google [6], three copies are generated through completely replicating data block in cloud storage system. However, Atoms system of EMC

---

* Danwei Chen is a professor in College of Computer, Nanjing University of Posts and Telecommunications. His research interests are focused on Information Security, and Computer Application.

R. Wang and F. Xiao (Eds.): CWSN 2012, CCIS 334, pp. 14–25, 2013.
© Springer-Verlag Berlin Heidelberg 2013

provides more copy services to pay users than free users. To ensure the security of data, S3 system of Amazon [7] produces multiple copies for data of each user. What's more, although complete copy guarantees the data correctness, it needs larger storage space and more cost for large amount of data. While ECT mechanism not only saves storage space, but also improves the efficiency of error detection.

2   The Architecture of ECT System

The principle of ECT system architecture is shown in Fig. 1 and the data redundancy backup is through RS erasure code [8, 9]. RS erasure code is a multi-system BCH code with strong error correction ability, which not only corrects burst error but also random error. According to the principle, the origin data is firstly divided into m data blocks which are RS encoded and then generate n data blocks. Among the n data blocks, $n - m$ data blocks are the verification data blocks. Finally, the encoded data is stored in n servers. When there exist bad data blocks in storage files, RS erasure code can be used to recover data blocks and obtain the recovering data. On the base of guaranteeing the efficiency, this code may provide more abundant storage strategies and save a lot of storage space. It may also reduce the data storage cost, through the number of backups and the setting of encoding parameters. The principle is shown in Fig. 1.

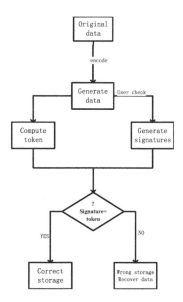

Fig. 1. Principle of ECT architecture

In addition, the system can ensure the rapid and effective detection of the data that is changed and destroyed according to the failure in the servers or random error of Byzantine. When errors are detected, it is the most important thing to confirm the server in which the data error is occurred, and then you can quickly recover data. Meanwhile, in order to make sure the correctness of data and rapid position of errors, ECT mechanism introduces a kind of tokens. Token's computing function is a hash function. Before storing the distributed files, the user precalculates a certain number of checking tokens. Each token corresponds to a random subset of the data block. So in order to confirm the correctness of the data in the cloud, users can check the block index of randomly generated string of data in the cloud on the server. After receiving challenge value from the user, the cloud server returns a short signature by specifying the data block index. The signature value should be equal to the corresponding checking token, otherwise, data storage should be abnormal. In addition, all servers are running on the basis of a subset of the same index, so the response to a request by the integrity check value must be determined by the encoding matrix $\mathbf{P}$. Furthermore, ECT model's simple steps will be described in Fig. 2.

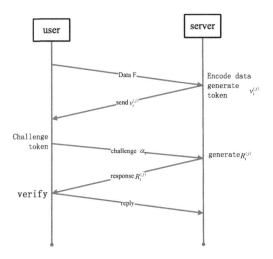

Fig. 2. Steps of ECT

The preparation is as follows:

$\mathbf{F}$ the data file $\mathbf{F}$;
$\mathbf{A}$ the generator matrix of R-S Erasure code;
$\mathbf{G}$ file encoding matrix, vector $n = m + k$, each vector is composed of data blocks;
$\mathbf{f_{key}}(\cdot)$ pseudo-random function (PRF), defined as $f : \{0,1\}^* \times key \rightarrow GF(2^p)$;
$\phi_{\mathbf{key}}(\cdot)$ pseudo-random permutation (PRP), defined as $\phi : \{0,1\}^{\log_2(l)} \times key \rightarrow \{0,1\}^{\log_2(l)}$;
$\mathbf{ver}$ the version number of file blocks, recording the number of times that each data block modified. All beginning versions of the data blocks are 0.

$\mathbf{S_{ij}^{ver}}$ the key in the PRF. The value depends on the file name, block index i, the server's location j and file version number ver.

The ECT steps are as follows:

1. The data file $\mathbf{F}$ is decomposed into m data blocks, recorded as a matrix composed by the same size of the data vectors $\mathbf{F} = (F_1, F_2, \cdots, F_m)$. Each data vector has l data blocks. Each data block is included in the Galois field $GF(2^p)$, to ensure uniqueness and speed of operation. In order to facilitate the calculation, p is 8;
2. $\mathbf{F}$ is stored in the $m + k$ servers $\mathbf{G} = \mathbf{F} \cdot \mathbf{A}$, where $\mathbf{A}$ is the changing Vandermonde matrix, which is to ensure effectively restoring the original data when the data error is occurred.
3. Calculate each $G^{(j)}$ and token value $v_i^{(j)}$ according to $\mathbf{G}$, and compare it to the response value $R_i^{(j)}$ that server gives. If they are the same, storage is correct, otherwise an exception occurs, and you need to restore the original data.

3   ECT's Implementation

3.1   Erasure Code

In cloud storage, data files F are redundantly distributed and stored on the n servers. Construct k redundancy checks vectors from m data vectors by using RS erasure codes. The original m data vectors can be recovered by m random vectors from $m + k$ data vectors. $m + k$ vectors are stored in the different cloud servers with the number of $m + k$, even if there are k servers occurring errors, the raw data files will still be intact and preserved. In order to ensure that the raw data input and output, file distribution must be regular, and m data file vectors and k check vectors are stored in the different $m + k$ servers.

Assume $\mathbf{F} = (F_1, F_2, \cdots, F_m), F_i = (f_{1i}, f_{2i}, \cdots, f_{li})^T, (i \in \{1, \cdots, m\})$, where $l \leq 2^p - 1$. Note all these blocks are elements of $GF(2^p)$. The systematic layout with parity vectors is achieved with the information dispersal matrix A, which is derived from $m \times (m + k)$ Vandermonde matrix [10]:

$$\begin{pmatrix} 1 & 1 & \cdots & 1 & 1 & \cdots & 1 \\ \beta_1 & \beta_2 & \cdots & \beta_m & \beta_{m+1} & \cdots & \beta_n \\ \vdots & \vdots & \ddots & \vdots & \vdots & \ddots & \vdots \\ \beta_1^{m-1} & \beta_2^{m-1} & \cdots & \beta_m^{m-1} & \beta_m^{m-1} & \cdots & \beta_n^{m-1} \end{pmatrix}$$

where $\beta_j, \quad (j \in \{1, \cdots, n\})$ are distinct elements randomly picked from $GF(2^p)$.

After a sequence of elementary row transformations, the desired matrix $\mathbf{A}$ can be written as:

$$\mathbf{A} = (\mathbf{I} \mid \mathbf{P}) = \begin{pmatrix} 1 & 0 & \cdots & 0 & p_{11} & p_{12} & \cdots & p_{1k} \\ 0 & 1 & \cdots & 0 & p_{21} & p_{22} & \cdots & p_{2k} \\ \vdots & \vdots & \ddots & \vdots & \vdots & \vdots & \ddots & \vdots \\ 0 & 0 & \cdots & 1 & p_{m1} & p_{m2} & \cdots & p_{mk} \end{pmatrix}$$

where I is a $m \times m$ identity matrix and $\mathbf{P}$ is the secret parity generation matrix with size $m \times k$. Noting that $\mathbf{A}$ is derived from a Vandermonde matrix, thus it has the property that any out of the $m + k$ columns forms an invertible matrix.

By multiplying $\mathbf{F}$ by $\mathbf{A}$, the user obtains the encoded file $\mathbf{G}$: $\mathbf{G} = \mathbf{F} \cdot \mathbf{A} = (G^{(1)}, G^{(2)}, \cdots, G^{(m)}, G^{(m+1)}, \cdots, G^{(n)}) = (F_1, F_2, \cdots, F_m, G^{(m+1)}, \cdots, G^{(n)})$, where $G^{(j)} = (g_1^{(j)}, g_2^{(j)}, \cdots, g_l^{(j)})^T$, $(j \in \{1, \cdots, n\})$. The first m vectors are determined by the identity matrix $\mathbf{I}$, so they are the same to the original data. The rest part $(G^{(m+1)}, \cdots, G^{(n)})$ is generated based on the k parity data vectors $\mathbf{H}$ from $\mathbf{F}$.

The parity vector $\mathbf{H}$ from the generator matrix makes $GH^T = 0$. This equation can be used to test whether an n-vector is correct. If the equation has been set up, it is the correct code word, otherwise it is certainly not the correct code word. Therefore, we can use these redundancy messages which is generated by the error correction to improve data's reliability and availability.

3.2   Token Generation

In order to ensure the correctness of the data storage and rapid position of errors at the same time, before the file prior to the distribution of storage, the user should pre-calculate checksum token of a single vector based on a certain number $G^{(j)}$, $(j \in 1, \cdots, n)$. Each token corresponds to a random subset of the data block. To confirm the correctness of the data on the cloud, the user can view the block index of randomly generated string of data in the cloud servers. After receiving challenge value from the user, the cloud servers specify the data block index to return a short signature. The signature value shall be equal to the corresponding checksum token, or data storage is abnormal. In addition, all servers are running on the basis of a subset of the same index, so the response to a request by the integrity check value must be determined by the encoding matrix $\mathbf{P}$ yards.

If the users want to check correctness of data for t times, they must pre-compute t checksum tokens for each individual $G^{(j)}$, $(j \in 1, \cdots, n)$, which relates to a PRF $f(\cdot)$, a PRP $\phi(\cdot)$, a challenge key and a universal replacement key K_{PRP}. To generate the ith token in sever j, it needs the following approach:

1. Random challenge value $\alpha_i = f_{k_{chal}}^{(i)}$ within the $GF(2^p)$, and one replacement key $k_{prp}^{(i)}$ based on the K_{PRP}.
2. Calculate the r index selected randomly: $\{I_q \in [1, \cdots, l] \mid 1 \leq q \leq r\}$, where $I_q = \phi_{k_{prp}^{(i)}}(q)$.
3. Get the token

$$v_i^{(j)} = \sum_{q=1}^{r} \alpha_i^q \times G^{(j)}[I_q], \text{where} \quad G^{(j)}[I_q] = g_{I_q}^{(j)}$$

where $v_i^{(j)}$ is not only the element of $GF(2^p)$, but also the server's response value the user expect when he challenges a specific data block. Therefore, after the token is generated, the user decides whether to keep the token pre-calculated or store it encrypted in the cloud server. Once all the tokens are generated, the final step before distributed storing files is to encrypt each calibration data $g_i^{(j)}$ from $(G^{(m+1)}, \cdots, G^{(n)})$, using the formula $g_i^{(j)} \leftarrow g_i^{(j)} + f_{k_j}(s_{ij})$, $(i \in \{1, \cdots, l\})$, where k_j is the encryption key of checksum vector $G^{(j)}$, $(j \in \{m+1, \cdots, n\})$, in order to protect the coding matrix. Finally, all the n encoding vectors $G^{(j)}$, $(j \in \{1, \cdots, n\})$ are stored and distributed in the cloud server.

Algorithm to calculate the token:

1. Set the parameters l, n and functions f, ϕ.
2. Select calibration code number t.
3. Set the number of indexes for each verification.
4. Generate the master key K_{prp} and the challenge value k_{chal}.
5. For vector $G^{(j)}, j \leftarrow 1$, n do.
6. For round $i \leftarrow 1$, t do.
7. Derive $\alpha_i = f_{k_{chal}}^{(i)}$ and $k_{prp}^{(i)}$ from K_{PRP}.
8. Compute.
9. End for.
10. End for.
11. Store all v_i locally.

The position of errors is a prerequisite for eliminating errors in the storage system. The challenge server not only includes if the distributed storage is correct or not, but also contains a potential data error location. For example, the ith response process of the review of the n servers challenge is as follows:

1. The user will send α_i and the ith replacement key to each server.
2. r row index in the storage vector $G^{(j)}$ is arranged in a linear combination in sever:

$$R_i^{(j)} = \sum_{q=1}^{r} \alpha_i^q \times G^{(j)}[\phi_{k_{prp}^{(i)}}(q)]$$

3. With $R_i^{(j)}$ received from all the servers, users get the hidden value of $R_i^{(j)}, (j \in \{m+1, \cdots, n\})$ by using the formula:

$$R_i^{(j)} \leftarrow R_i^{(j)} - \sum_{q=1}^{r} f_{kj}(S(I_q, j)) \cdot \alpha_i^q, \text{where} \quad I_q = \phi_{k_{prp}^{(i)}}(q).$$

4. User verifies the effectiveness of the received encodes by coding matrix $\mathbf{P}$:

$$(R_i^{(1)}, \cdots, R_i^{(m)}) \cdot P \stackrel{?}{=} (R_i^{(m+1)}, \cdots, R_i^{(n)})$$

The challenge response algorithm (the ith challenge):

1. User sends the calculation $\alpha_i = f_{k_{chal}}(i)$ and $k_{prp}^{(i)}$.

2. Receives

$$R_i^{(j)} = \sum_{q=1}^{r} \alpha_i^q \times G^{(j)}[\phi_{k_{prp}^{(i)}}(q)]$$

from server.

3. For $(j \leftarrow m+1, n)$.
4. Do

$$R_i^j \leftarrow R_i^j - \sum_{q=1}^{r} f_{kj}(S(I_q, j)) \cdot \alpha_i^q$$

5. End for.
6. If.
7. Then complete the response and make the next challenge.
8. Else.
9. For $(j \leftarrow 1, n)$.
10. Do if $R_i^{(j)} \neq v_i^{(j)}$.
11. Then return server j abnormal behavior.
12. End if.
13. End for.
14. End if.

The servers are using the same subset index, specific r-row linear collection $(R_i^{(1)}, \cdots, R_i^{(n)})$ must be coded by the code file matrix. If the equation above is equal, it shows a successful challenge. Otherwise, the file data block is destroyed in these provisions.

Once the inconsistency among the storage has been successfully detected, we can rely on the pre-computed verification tokens to further determine where the potential data error(s) lies in. Noting that each response $R_i^{(j)}$ is computed exactly in the same way as token $v_i^{(j)}$, thus the user can simply find which server is misbehaving by verifying the following equations:

$$R_i^{(j)} \stackrel{?}{=} v_i^{(j)}, \quad j \in \{1, \cdots, n\}$$

After verification exception occurs in the server, we can download data from the front of m in the servers to reconstruct the original data. While the verification is based on random checks by selecting the appropriate system parameters (eg: r, l, t) and controlling sufficient time for verification, we can ensure the successful recovery of the files with high probability. In addition, when corrupt data is detected, with pre-computed token and get the response value compared in order to ensure the identification of abnormal server. Therefore, as long as there is at least k abnormal servers to identify them can re-generate the correct block, through removing the corrective newly restored data block which can be re-assigned to the abnormal server, thus maintaining the correctness of storage.

3.3 Data Storage and Procession

Assume that the matrix $\mathbf{F}$ describes the static or archived data. But there will be a dynamic data storage in the cloud data storage, such as electronic documents, photographs, or log. So the key is to take the dynamic case into consideration and to ensure that users at all levels of the files perform the update to delete the correctness of the data modification operations. The most direct and tedious way is to download all data from the cloud server and re-compute the checksum of the data block and the verification token, which is obviously very inefficient. In this section, we will show you how to effectively deal with dynamic data storage operations.

Update. In the cloud data storage, sometimes the user will need to modify some data blocks or change the value. This situation ranges from f_{ij} to $f_{ij} + \Delta f_{ij}$ is called the data updates. Because of the linear characteristics of the RS erasure codes, the user can only use Δf_{ij} to complete updating and producing the latest calibration data block, without considering other unchanged data blocks. So we can create a completed revision of the matrix:

$$\mathbf{\Delta F} = \begin{pmatrix} \Delta f_{11} & \Delta f_{12} & \cdots & \Delta f_{1m} \\ \Delta f_{21} & \Delta f_{22} & \cdots & \Delta f_{2m} \\ \vdots & \vdots & \ddots & \vdots \\ \Delta f_{l1} & \Delta f_{l2} & \cdots & \Delta f_{lm} \end{pmatrix} = (\Delta F_1, \Delta F_2, \cdots, \Delta F_m)$$

Noting that we use zero elements in $\mathbf{\Delta F}$ to denote the unchanged blocks. To maintain the corresponding parity vectors as well as be consistent with the original file layout, the user can multiply $\mathbf{\Delta F}$ by $\mathbf{A}$ and thus generates the update information for both the data vectors and parity vectors as follows:

$$\mathbf{\Delta F} \cdot \mathbf{A} = (\Delta G^{(1)}, \cdots, \Delta G^{(m)}, \Delta G^{(m+1)}, \cdots, \Delta G^{(n)})$$
$$= (\Delta F_1, \cdots, \Delta F_m, \Delta G^{(m+1)}, \cdots, \Delta G^{(n)})$$

Because the data update operation inevitably affects some or all of the remaining verification tokens, after preparation of update information, the user has to amend those unused tokens for each vector $G^{(j)}$ to maintain the same storage correctness assurance. In other words, for all the unused tokens, the user needs to exclude every occurrence of the old data block and replace it with the new one. Thanks to the synchronization of our verification token, the user can perform the token update efficiently. To give more details, supposing a block $G^{(j)}[I_s]$ is covered by the specific token $v_i^{(j)}$, which has been changed to $G^{(j)}[I_s] + \Delta G^{(j)}[I_s]$, where $I_s = \phi_{k_{prp}^{(i)}}(s)$. To maintain the usability of token $v_i^{(j)}$, it is not hard to verify that the user can simply update it by $v_i^{(j)} \leftarrow v_i^{(j)} + \alpha_i^s \times \Delta G^{(j)}[I_s]$ without retrieving any other $r - 1$ blocks required in the pre-computation of $v_i^{(j)}$.

After relation of the token, in order to hide the encryption matrix $\mathbf{P}$, we hide updated information in each data block checksum with formula $\Delta g_i^{(j)} \leftarrow \Delta g_i^{(j)} +$

$f_{k_j}(s_{ij}^{ver})$, $(i \in 1, \cdots, l)$, by using a subset of the random function PRF. Ver is the number of hidden information specific calibration data block. The user will correct information is sent to the cloud server and cloud server will renew such information.

Delete Processing. Sometimes, after being stored in the cloud, certain data blocks may need to be deleted. The delete operation we are considering is a general one, in which user replaces the data block with zero or some special reserved data symbol. From this point of view, the delete operation is actually a special case of the data update operation, where the original data blocks can be replaced with zeros or some predetermined special blocks. Therefore, we can rely on the update procedure to support delete operation, i.e., by setting Δf_{ij} in $\mathbf{\Delta F}$ to be $-\Delta f_{ij}$. Besides, all the affected tokens have to be modified and the updated parity information has to be blinded through the same method specified in update operation. Δf_{ij} in $\mathbf{\Delta F}$ is $-\Delta f_{ij}$ and all the affected token must be modified and updated using the update processing to hide updated parity information.

Same to the update operation, only need $-\Delta f_{ij}$ to complete the removal process and generate new parity data blocks, the establishment of a complete revision of the matrix is:

$$\mathbf{\Delta F} = \begin{pmatrix} -\Delta f_{11} & -\Delta f_{12} & \cdots & -\Delta f_{1m} \\ -\Delta f_{21} & -\Delta f_{22} & \cdots & -\Delta f_{2m} \\ \vdots & \vdots & \ddots & \vdots \\ -\Delta f_{l1} & -\Delta f_{l2} & \cdots & -\Delta f_{lm} \end{pmatrix} = (\Delta F_1, \Delta F_2, \cdots, \Delta F_m)$$

Similarly, in $\mathbf{\Delta F}$, the unchanged data blocks are tagged as 0. Multiply $\mathbf{A}$ by $\mathbf{\Delta F}$ to get the updated information of the each data vector and the parity vector to make sure that parity vector and the original documents consistent with the distribution:

$$\mathbf{\Delta F} \cdot \mathbf{A} = (\Delta G^{(1)}, \cdots, \Delta G^{(m)}, \Delta G^{(m+1)}, \cdots, \Delta G^{(n)})$$
$$= (\Delta F_1, \cdots, \Delta F_m, \Delta G^{(m+1)}, \cdots, \Delta G^{(n)})$$

The checksum token which did not be updated may also change, so they will have to be modified. Assuming that a data block $G^{(j)}[I_s]$, $(I_s = \phi_{k_{prp}^{(i)}}(s))$, whose particular token $v_i^{(j)}$ changes the data block to be $G^{(j)}[I_s] + \Delta G^{(}j)[I_s]$. To ensure the availability of the token, the token can be revised to $v_i^{(j)} \leftarrow v_i^{(j)} + \alpha_i^s \times \Delta G^{(j)}[I_s]$. After relating the relevant token, hide the updating information $\Delta g_i^{(j)}$ of each checksum data block with the formula $\Delta g_i^{(j)} \leftarrow \Delta g_i^{(j)} + f_{k_j}(s_{ij}^{ver})$, $(i \in 1, \cdots, l)$.

Addition Process. Users may add data blocks in the end of data files, which increase the storage space, and this is the addition of data. It is expected that the addition in cloud data storage is bulk adding, and users can upload a lot of data blocks.

According to steps in the distribution process of the file matrix $\mathbf{F}$, adding data blocks in the end of the file is equal to adding corresponding row number under the matrix of file $\mathbf{F}$. File matrix has l rows at the beginning. Supposing users add m data blocks in the end of file $\mathbf{F}$ and mark those as $(f_{l+1,1}, f_{l+1,2}, \cdots, f_{l+1,m})$, then add 0 if the number of data blocks is no more than m. We can compute coding vectors $(f_{l+1,1}, f_{l+1,2}, \cdots, f_{l+1,m}) \cdot P = (g_{l+1}^{(m+1)}, \cdots, g_{l+1}^{(n)})$ of adding data blocks by encryption matrix $\mathbf{P}$, directly.

In order to better furnish add process, we need to do a little change for token pre-computation. Firstly setting the size of each data block and labeling as l_{max}, computing each token parameter $r_{max} = [r \times (l_{max}/l)]$ at the same time, then the computation of the token i in server j can be modified to

$$v_i = \sum_{q=1} \alpha_i^q \times G^{(j)}[I_q]$$

In this expression,

$$G^{(j)}[I_q] = \begin{cases} G^{(j)}[\phi_{k_{prp}^{(i)}}(q)] & [\phi_{k_{prp}^{(i)}}(q)] \leq l \\ 0 & [\phi_{k_{prp}^{(i)}}(q)] > l \end{cases}$$

The above equation ensures that there are average r index in the existed data blocks. Server checks the token values according to the above steps when receiving challenge request of users. When users want to add data blocks, file data blocks and the corresponding verified data blocks change, and the length of each vector $G^{(j)}$ also increase in the range of $[l, l_{max}]$. Adding $\alpha_i^q \times G^{(j)}[I_q]$ $(G^{(j)}[I_q] \neq 0, I_q > l)$ and $I_q = \phi_{k_{prp}^{(i)}}(q)$ to the origin v_i. The next hiding and updating of data block verification are the same.

Insertion. Insertion is to add applications to handle additional data file index in the desired position, to maintain the original data block structure of the data files, and insert data from the index $j + 1$ location of data blocks $F[j]$. Inserted to deal with the many rows of the matrix will affect the logical data file $\mathbf{F}$, which is followed by data blocks have to re-encoding, and the challenge response tokens should be recalculated.

Because $\mathbf{\Delta F} = (F_1, F_2, \cdots, F_m),$

$$F_i = (f_{1i}, f_{2i}, \cdots, f_{li})^T$$

So $\mathbf{F} = \begin{pmatrix} f_{11} & f_{12} & \cdots & f_{1m} \\ f_{21} & f_{22} & \cdots & f_{2m} \\ \vdots & \vdots & \ddots & \vdots \\ f_{l1} & f_{l2} & \cdots & f_{lm} \end{pmatrix}$

Assumptions insert the data are recorded as:
$$F' = (F_1', F_2', \cdots, F_m'), \quad F_i' = (f_{1i}', f_{2i}', \cdots, f_{li}')^T$$

Data encoding vector encoding matrix $\mathbf{P}$ calculated directly inserted:
$(F_1', F_2', \cdots, F_m') \cdot P = (G^{(1)'}, G^{(2)'}, \cdots, G^{(m)'}, G^{(m+1)'}, \cdots, G^{(n)'})$, among the
above equation $G^{(j)'} = (g_1^{(j)'}, g_2^{(j)'}, \cdots, g_l^{(j)'})^T$, $j \in \{1, \cdots, n\}$. Perhaps need
to count the token which is expected to make changes, the first preset the size
of each data block, in the calculation of server j first token to change:

$$R_i^{(j)} = \sum_{q=1}^{r} \alpha_i^q \times G^{(j)'} [\phi_{k_{prp}^{(i)}}(q)]$$

4   Conclusion

4.1   Redundancy

The redundancy discussed in this paper is based on the same error correction
capability. For a Maximum Distance Separable (MDS) Erasure Code of (n, m, k),
the fault tolerant capability is t $(t = n - m)$, which is to say the failure of any
t nodes does not lead the loss of data. However, for the completely copy of
correcting n errors, $n + 1$ copies are needed and the redundancy becomes $n + 1$
which is clearly larger than that of Erasure Code. Therefore, the Erasure Code
has great superiority in storage space.

4.2   Intrusion Tolerance Capacity

Suppose there are n data blocks, the former m nodes store the user's data and
the later n nodes store the redundant data. The data would loss only when all the
data stored in the nodes which are larger than m nodes was stolen. Meanwhile,
the intrusion tolerance capacity is $m - 1$ for the system based on completely copy,
apparently. The two mechanisms are almost the same in the intrusion tolerance
capacity. And the comparisons of completely copy and Erasure Code are listed
in Table 1.

Table 1. Comparisons of Completely Copy and Erasure Code Technologies

Redundancy mechanisms	Storage costs	Fault-tolerant numbers	Complexity
Completely copy	Higher	Number of backup:n, The worst tolerant:n-1	Simple
Erasure code	Economic	n/m	More complex

If we set the same checked files and the same condition of modified data, the
results are shown in Fig. 3 when comparing our model and completely copy.

The successful detection probability changes with the detection row number
when the proportion of the modified data is 10 percentages. In Fig. 3, the detection probability of Completely Copy is higher than that of ECT model when the

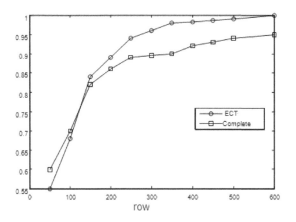

Fig. 3. Probability of Normal Error

files are few. However, the advantage of our model (ECT model) is revealed with the increase of the files. Generally, the storage data is extensive in cloud storage. So our scheme has powerful advantage in cloud storage. In addition, the Completely Copy is a method for completed replicate, while our scheme carries out redundant storage by generating verified data. The storage space of Completely Copy is much more than that of our model.

References

1. Chen, Y., Paxson, V., Katz, R.H.: What's New About Cloud Computing Security? UCB/EECS (May 2010)
2. Sotto, L.J., Treacy, B.C., McLellan, M.L.: Privacy and Data Security Risks in Cloud Computing. Electronic Commerce & Law Report (February 2010)
3. Huang, X.: Based the HDFS cloud storage service system. Dalian Maritime University (2010)
4. Borthakur, D.: HDFS architecture. The Apache Software Foundation (2008)
5. Flag hearing data backup and recovery and security. China Railway Publishing House, Beijing (2008)
6. Ghemawat, S., Gobioff, H., Leung, S.-T.: The Google file system. In: Proc. of the 19th ACM SOSP, pp. 29–43. ACM Press, New York (2003)
7. Amazon Simple Storage Service (S3), http://www.amazon.com/s3
8. Jia, W., Chen, W.: Based on the information is scattered RS erasure code algorithm. Computer Applications (30), 3197–3200 (2010)
9. Plank, J.S., Ding, Y.: Note: Correction to the 1997 Tutorial on Reed-Solomon Coding. University of Tennessee. Tech. Rep. CS-03-504 (2003)
10. Niu, H.: Vandermonde determinant in the determinant calculation. Education Innovation Review (17) (2008)

Live Migration of Virtual Machines Based on DPDT

Danwei Chen[1,*], Hanbing Yang[1], Qinghan Xue[1], and Yong Zhou[2]

[1] College of Computer, Nanjing University of Posts and Telecommunications,
Nanjing, Jiangsu 210003, China
chendw@njupt.edu.cn, icyice1989@gmail.com, xqh_George@163.com
[2] Faculty of Engineering Science and Technology, Norwegian University of Science
and Technology, Trondheim 7491 Norway
yongzho@stud.ntnu.no

Abstract. Virtualization is a hot topic in current research. As one of
the important applications of cloud computing, the live migration of virtual machine(VM) can move a VM from one host to another without
shutting it down. The key of live migration is to reduce the total migration time and its downtime. This paper focuses on the optimization of
live migration in Xen environment due to the default algorithm does not
work well when memory pages are dirtied rapidly. Base on Xen source
code, a DPDT(dirty page delayed transfer) algorithm has been designed.
Later experiments show that the improved algorithm reduces the total
migration time and downtime efficiently with a high dirtying page rate
environment.

Keywords: Virtual Machine, Live Migration, Delayed Transfer.

1 Introduction

Virtualization refers to computing elements on a virtual basis, rather than running on a real basis, which is a solution to simplify the management and optimization of resources . In computer science, a virtual machine(VM) is a completely
isolated guest operating system installation within a normal host operating system. Through the virtual machine monitor (VMM), hardware can be shared by
each running VM operating system and application. Besides virtualization allows one physical machine to run multiple operating systems at the same time,
thus can be an effective way to allocate resources and separate the individual
services.

Live migration allows a server administrator to move a running virtual machine or application between different physical machines without disconnecting
the client or application. Admittedly live migration is very meaningful. In order to maintain the continuity of service in the migration process, the overall
migration time and downtime of VMs should be reduced as much as possible.

---

* Corresponding author.

R. Wang and F. Xiao (Eds.): CWSN 2012, CCIS 334, pp. 26–33, 2013.
© Springer-Verlag Berlin Heidelberg 2013

However in the case of high dirty page rate, the effect of existing pre-copy algorithm is relatively poor. So an improved dirty page delayed transfer algorithm is proposed in this paper with the help of analyzing the live migration of VMs and pre-copy algorithm. Later experiments show that, in the case of the high rate of dirty pages, the algorithm can effectively reduce total migration time and downtime.

2   Related Work

The major role of live migration is to migrate memory information of a VM. The authors in [1] proposed a pure stop-and-copy method which involves stopping the original VM, copying all the original VM memory pages to the target and then starting the target VM. This method is simple to achieve. However, system downtime and overall migration time are proportional to the amount of physical memory allocated to the VM. If a VM running a real-time service, the cost of downtime is unacceptable.

Xen [2] is a Hypervisor developed by the University of Cambridge.It is widely supported in the Linux community. In literature [3], Christopher Clark et designed and implemented live migration of virtual machines based on Xen. It works as follows: in the first phase, all the memory pages are copied to destination; in the second phase, several rounds of incremental synchronization are employed, and all the pages that are modified during last round are migrated; in the last phase, the VM is suspended on the source node, and all the remaining memory image and VCPU context are copied, then VM is resumed on the destination node.[4] Basically by using pre-copy algorithm can reduce the downtime of the system to less than 1s. However, these tests are based on the simple web server. With existing algorithms, there is a high risk of service interruption when migrating VMs with high workloads and/or over low-bandwidth networks. In these cases, VM memory pages are dirtied faster than they can be transferred over the network, which leads to extended migration downtime.[9].

VMware is one of the most widely used virtual machine software. Michael Nelson proposed a V motion program based on VMware[7]. And its algorithm is also similar to the Pre-copy.

The authors in [6], [9] propose the incremental compression (Delta Compression) methods to improve the efficiency of migration in the case of the high rate of dirty pages, but this algorithm may consume more resources of the system's CPU and memory.

3   Current Pre-copy Memory Migration

Pre-copy [2], [3] means to take several rounds of incremental synchronization when migrate VM of host A to host B, thus ensuring the memory of both ends is the same. Memory pages are iteratively copied from the source to the destination. Within pre-copy algorithm, they are three types of bitmap:

to_send: dirty pages in the last round of iteration;

to_skip: frequent changes pages, will be skip in the current round of iteration;

to_fix: the page has not been mapped and would be translated in the final round.

Pre-copy algorithm steps are as follows:

Step1. Because all pages will be sent in the first round of the iteration, all to_send should be set 1;

Step2. At the beginning of every round of iteration, bitmap of dirty pages would be copied to to_skip. Transmit the page only if the value of its to_send and to_skip are separately 1,0;

Step3. After the transmission is complete, determine whether it meets the requirement to go into the final round of iteration or not. At the same time copy the dirty page bitmap to to_send and empty the dirty page bitmap. If it meets the requirement, go to Step4, otherwise go to Step2;

Step4. In the final round, stop the VMs and transfer the rest pages in to_send and to_fix.

Table 1. Pre-copy Algorithm Dirty Page Bitmaps

to_send	0	0	1	1
to_skip	0	1	0	1
transfer or not	NO	NO	YES	NO

4   Dirty Page Delayed Transfer Memory Migration

In pre-copy algorithm, memory pages are transferred iteratively. Iterative means that pre-copying occurs in rounds, in which the pages to be transferred during round n are those that are modified during round n-1. The more frequently the pages are modified, the higher possibility they are sent. So the total amount of transmission is increasing. The total migration time, network burden would also be greatly affected especially when VMs with high memory loads. Although to_skip bitmap is used to identify the page of frequent changes, it is just determined by a short time which varies from the end of the last round of iteration to the start of the next round(see Fig 1). If the page is judged changing frequently in the last round, but not changing during the judgment of to_skip in the current round then it may be sent again. In fact, it has the large probability that these pages continuing to change in the current round. Therefore pre-copy algorithm does not work well for situation when pages are frequently changed.

In response to these problems, this paper proposes the dirty page delayed transfer algorithm. The algorithm adds a new bitmap named to_delay to mark those pages which are changed both in the last round and current round of the beginning. These pages would be transferred later.Therefore, there are four types of bitmap within the improved algorithm, to_send, to_skip, to_delay and to_fix.

The steps of dirty page delayed transfer algorithm are as follows:

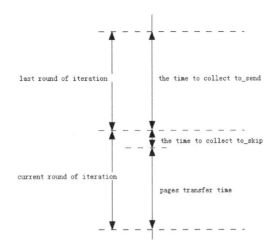

Fig. 1. The Timeline of Pre-copy Algorithm

Step1. Because all pages will be sent in the first round of the iteration, all to_send should be set 1;

Step2. At the beginning of each round of iteration, bitmap of dirty pages would be copied to to_skip.

1)If both the value of a pages to_send and to_skip are 1, its to_delay should be set 1.

2)Transmit the page if the value of its to_send, to_skip and to_delay are separately 1,0,0.

3)Transmit the page if the value of its to_send, to_skip and to_delay are separately 0,0,1. Then the value of corresponding to_delay should be restored to zero.

4)The other cases are not allowed to transfer.

Step3. After the transmission is completed, determine whether it meets the requirement to go into the final round of iteration or not. At the same time copy the dirty page bitmap to to_send and empty the dirty page bitmap. If it meets the requirement, go to Step4, otherwise go to Step2;

Step4. In the final round, stop the VMs and transfer the rest pages of to_send, to_delay and to_fix.

Table 2. DPDT Algorithm Dirty Page Bitmaps

to_send	0	0	0	0	1	1	1	1
to_skip	0	0	1	1	0	0	1	1
to_delay	0	1	0	1	0	1	0	1
transfer or not	NO	YES to_delay=0	NO	NO	YES	NO	NO to_delay=1	NO to_delay=1

After add the to_delay bitmap, the page whether to be transferred in each round is judged by Table 2. When both the values of to_send and to_skip are 1, set the value of corresponding to_delay to 1. If a pages to_delay is 1, only both the values of to_send and to_skip are 0 can the page be sent. The value of a pages to_delay is restored to zero when the page is sent. That is when a page is marked as to_delay, it can only be transmitted if there is no change during the last round and current round at the beginning. This can effectively reduce the frequent transfer of dirty pages, lessen the total amount of migration, and diminish the total migration time and downtime. This algorithm is not only easy to implement, but also has no additional loss of system resources such as memory and CPU. Moreover it does not need to modify migration destinations.

5   Experiments and Results Analysis

5.1   Experimental Environment

Migration is operated between two computers in the LAN node. The configuration of these two computers is Intel Celeron E3400 2.6Hz and 4G memory. Virtual platform is Xen-3.1.2 and virtual machine is ubuntu-10.04-destop-amd64. The memory of the VM is set to 512M. In addition, there is a NFS server and the experimental network environment is Fast Ethernet.

5.2   Experimental Results and Analysis

Migration under the low workloads. The experimental results are as follows:

Table 3. Migration under Low Workloads

	Total Rounds	Downtime(ms)	Total Time(ms)
Original Algorithm	5	420	47940
Improved Algorithm	5	410	48037

As can be seen From the Table 3 and Fig. 2, the live migration is completed within several rounds of iterations because of the low dirtying rate under low workloads. Besides the decrease of the overall migration time and downtime is less obvious by using the improved algorithm.

Migration under the high dirtying rate. The experimental results are as follows:

Table 4. Migration under High Dirtying Rate

	Total Rounds	Downtime(ms)	Total Time(ms)
Original Algorithm	30	1883	59147
Improved Algorithm	28	1381	50964

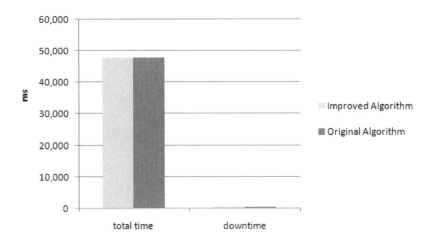

Fig. 2. Migration under Low Workloads

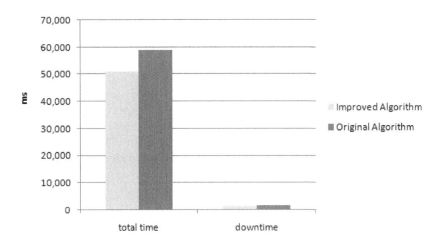

Fig. 3. Migration under High Dirtying Rate

It can be seen through the comparison of Table 4 and Fig. 3,, under the high dirtying rate, the original pre-copy algorithm reaches the maximum number of iterations which is 30 times and then exits. Yet the improved dirty page delay transfer algorithm proposed in this paper can be controlled to enter the downtime copy of the final round before reaching the maximum number of iterations. The system overall migration time and downtime are somehow reduced.

The Fig. 4 above shows the number of pages transferred per-iteration in the case of high dirtying rate. Because it will send all the pages in the first round of iteration, so the transfer time of the first iteration is approximately the same. Meanwhile from the figure above, it can be found that the number of the transmission pages is reduced within each iteration by applying the improved

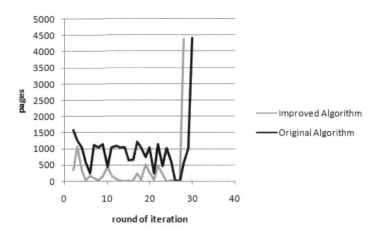

Fig. 4. The Number of Pages Transferred Per-iteration under High Dirtying Rate

algorithm. This can not only shorten the migration time, but also effectively reduce the network bandwidth. From the second round of the iteration to the final round, the original algorithm and the improved pre-copy algorithm are separately transferred 27634 and 9606 pages. It can be seen that the dirty page delay transfer algorithm greatly reduces the amount of the dirty pages which are frequently changed in the transmission.

6   Conclusion

This paper proposes a dirty page delayed transfer algorithm which is used to reduce the number of pages transferred during the live migration of virtual machine. The experiment shows that this algorithm is perfectly decreasing the overall migration time and downtime.

It can be found through experiments that the time of the first round of iteration occupies relatively large proportion of the overall migration time. With the help of the compressed thought, further work is to optimize the first round of iteration and avoid the transmission of a large number of blank pages, so that the migration time can be reduced further.

References

1. Sapuntzakis, C.P., Chandra, R., Pfaff, B., Chow, J., Lam, M.S., Rosenblum, M.: Optimizing the migration of virtual computers. In: Proceedings of the 5th Symposium on Operating Systems Design and Implementation, OSDI 2002, pp. 377–390 (2002)
2. Barham, P., Dragovic, B., Fraser, K., Hand, S., Harris, T., Ho, A., Neugebauer, R., Pratt, I., Warfield, A.: Xen and the art of virtualization. In: SOSP 2003 Proceedings of the Nineteenth ACM Symposium on Operating Systems Principles, pp. 164–177 (2003)

3. Christopher, C., Keir, F., Steven, H., Jacob, G.H., Eric, J., Christian, L., Ian, P., Andrew, W.: Live migration of virtual machines. In: Proceedings of the 2nd Conference on Symposium on Networked Systems Design and Implementation, Boston, vol. 2, pp. 273–286 (2005)
4. Zhang, X., Huo, Z., Ma, J., Meng, D.: Exploiting Data Deduplication to Accelerate Live Virtual Machine Migration. In: IEEE International Conference on Cluster Computing, Cluster 2010, pp. 88–96 (2010)
5. Xen Open Source Project, http://www.xen.org
6. Hacking, S., Hudzia, B.: Improving the live migration process of large enterprise applications. In: Proc. ACM International Workshop on Virtualization Technologies in Distributed Computing, VTDC 2009, New York, pp. 51–58 (2009)
7. Michael, N., Lim, B.H., Greg, H.: Fast transparent migration for virtual machines. In: Proceedings of the USENIX Annual Technical Conference 2005 on USENIX Annual Technical Conference, Anaheim, p. 25 (2005)
8. VMWARE. Vmware vmotion: Live migration of virtual machines without service interruption datasheet (2007),
http://www.vmware.com/files/pdf/VMware-VMotion-DS-EN.pdf
9. Svard, P., Hudzia, B., Tordsson, J., Elmroth, E.: Evaluation of Delta Compression Techniques for Efficient Live Migration of Large Virtual Machines. In: Proceedings of the 7th ACM SIGPLAN/SIGOPS International Conference on Virtual Execution Environments, VEE 2011, pp. 111–120 (2011)
10. Akoush, S., Sohan, R., Rice, A., Moore, A.W., Hopper, A.: Predicting the performance of virtual machine migration. In: The 18th Annual IEEE/ACM International Symposium on Modeling, Analysis and Simulation of Computer and Telecommunication Systems, MASCOTS 2010, Florida, pp. 37–46 (2010)
11. Liu, Z.B., Qu, W.Y., Yan, T., Li, H.T.: Hierarchical Copy Algorithm for Xen Live Migration. In: 2010 International Conference on Cyber-Enabled Distributed Computing and Knowledge Discovery (CyberC), pp. 361–364 (2010)
12. Liu, Z.B., Qu, W.Y., Liu, W.J., Li, K.Q.: Xen Live Migraion with Slowdown Scheduling Algorithm. In: 2010 International Conference on Parallel and Distributed Computing, Applications and Technologies, PDCAT, pp. 251–221 (2010)

Storage and Management Strategy for Heterogeneous Data Stream Based on Mutation Information

Jianxin Chen, Tao Liu, and Linjun Li

Nanjing University of Posts and Telecommunications,
Nanjing, 210046, China
{chenjx,1010041302,llj}@njupt.edu.cn

Abstract. mutant information For the internet of things(IoT), how to effectively store heterogeneous data streams is a new challenge. Currently random sampling is generally used for data stream storage. Additionally $B+$ tree is widely used to for quickly indexing. Such data in store are random, and it ignores the users' interest. In addition, $B+$ tree is applicable for one-dimension data, which is not feasible for multiple heterogeneous data streams. Herein, in this paper we propose a new sampling method to satisfy the users' interest according to the mutant information. Besides that an extended $B+$ tree structure is designed for multiple heterogeneous data stream so that the user can quickly index the interested data. Extensive experiment results show that the new sampling method and the extended $B+$ tree work efficiently than current sampling methods and storage mechanisms.

Keywords: heterogeneous data streams, mutation data, real-time, multi-dimensional $B+$ tree.

1 Introduction

Recently data streams are appearing in wide applications, which absorb a growing number of scholars concerning on their sampling and storing. The real time monitoring human motion with body sensor network is one of data stream application. Different from the traditional data stored, the data stream appears in the form of fast and unlimited stream [1]. The system that manages and processes is is known as a data stream system.

Data stream can be regarded as infinite multiple collections. Each element of the collection has a form of $< s, t >$, where s is a tuple, and t is a timestamp [2]. Due to the limited memory, in data stream system a sliding window is defined to filter the recently stream data so as to support real-time query. As data stream entering in the sliding window, some past data will leave out of the sliding window [3], which is called historical data [4].

In realistic applications, queries of the data stream are quite common. Since the memory capacity is limited and the date stream is continuous, the online query is limited in the current sliding window. But when the query data is outside

R. Wang and F. Xiao (Eds.): CWSN 2012, CCIS 334, pp. 34–43, 2013.
© Springer-Verlag Berlin Heidelberg 2013

of the current window, the current online query techniques are not feasible. In most situations, to satisfy the requirement of real time, an approximate querying results with errors to some extent are enough for data stream querying. To combat the above problems, sampling the data stream is a feasible approach to resemble the original data [5]. [5][6][7] list the current sampling methods for data stream system, including reservoir sampling, accurate sampling and count sampling. But all these methods are based on random sampling. For supporting real-time querying, $B+$ tree and its variants are used to index the historical data. [8] uses reservoir sampling method on historical data for data stream sampling, and index sampling data by using $B+$ tree. [4] uses multi-layer recursive sampling method and HDS-Tree structure to release the storage pressure.

Giving the storage space and effectiveness of sampling, and considering the numbers of heterogeneous data streams, this paper proposes a sampling method depending on the mutation information, and extends the $B+$ tree to multi-dimensional B+ tree. The sampling method based on the mutation information considers the inherent features of data stream, extracting the interested data as the samples to ensemble the original data. Multi-dimensional B+ tree fits to the unified management for heterogeneous data streams, and improve the storing and indexing efficiencies.

Other part of this paper is organized as follows. Section II introduces the definition of the mutation information. Section III gives the sampling method based mutation information and the storage strategy of multi-dimensional B+ tree. Section IV discusses the performance of the sampling strategy. Finally part gives the next step of research work.

2   Problem Formulations

2.1   Definition of Mutation Information for Data Stream

The data stream is a large, continuous, rapid and time-varying data sequence, and the information is usually contained in data sequence. So it is almost impossible for a single data to carry all the information contained in sequence. The Shannon information entropy could carry statistics information of data, but it cant reflect mutation in data stream. So we give a function that could measure the mutation information of data stream (Fig.1).

Definition 1: Suppose the data sequence can be expressed as x_1, x_2, x_i, the data elements information is related to its context. On the timeline, the status of current element can be described as smooth or mutation compared with its neighbors. The mutation information measure function is given as follow

$$I_i = H(, x_{i-1}, x_i, xi + 1,), , \tag{1}$$

where x_i is element data at time i. If the mutation of x_i is greater, it means that the mutation information I_i is greater and the data stream is mutant. On the contrary, if $I_i is smaller$, the data stream is more smooth. The definition has a special meaning for abnormal event monitoring. Herein we can store the user-related interesting data according to the mutation information.

2.2   Computation Calculation of Mutation Information

The above description is a definition of mutation information, and in order to calculate the value of mutation information, we use the heuristic segmentation algorithm in [9][10].

Assume there is a time series $x(t)$ with N items. At time i, we define a **left sub-sequence** and a **right sub-sequence**. The left sub-sequence contains N_1 elements which come before x_i, while the right sub-sequence contain N_2 elements which come after the element x_i. $u_1(i)$ and $u_2(i)$ is the mean value of left and right sub-sequence. $s_1(i)$ and $s_2(i)$ is the standard deviation of the two sequences. $s_d(i)$ is combined deviating of data x_i. $T(i)$ is the mean difference of the two sequences. Herein we have

$$s_d(i) = (\frac{s_1(i)^2 + s_2(i)^2}{N_1 + N_2 - 2})^{1/2} \bullet (\frac{1}{N_1} + \frac{1}{N_2})^{1/2} \qquad (2)$$

$$T(i) = |\frac{u_1(i) - u_2(i)}{s_d(i)}| \qquad (3)$$

After calculating every data for $x(t)$, we obtain a series of statistic values T_i. Here T_i denotes the difference between the left and right sequence. The greater T_i means the more observable of difference between the two sequences. It also illustrates that mutation could have happened and the current element data carries more information.

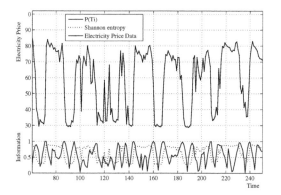

Fig. 1. Shannon Entropy and Mutation Information

The method to calculate the statistical significance of T_i is given as follow:

$$P(T_i) = Prob(T \leq T_i). \qquad (4)$$

It is accumulative probability density function of T_i, which is obtained by counting all received data or data comes recently. $P(T_i)$ is the probability of T that is less than or equal to T_i. If $P(Ti) \geq P0$ (P_0 is a threshold), the difference of the two sequences is greater than the given threshold. That means x_i is a mutant data, which is an interesting point we may sample.

For example, we take electricity price data as our experimental data. Fig.1 shows the Shannon entropy and mutation information of the experimental. We can see from the graph that the Shannon entropy almost matches our experimental data. So it cannot reflect the mutation of data. At the same time, the mutation function we give can effectively describe the mutation situation at mutation data. Usually, the abnormal data is our interesting data. Therein we define Eq.4 to determine mutational probability that we can obtain these interesting points.

2.3   Storage for Data Stream

The current method to store and index historical data of the data stream is $B+$ tree or its variants. A $B+$ tree is a type of tree data structure. It represents sorted data in a way that allows for efficient insertion and removal of elements. It is a dynamic, multilevel index with maximum and minimum bounds on the number of keys in each node. In a B+ tree, all data are saved in the leaves. Internal nodes contain only keys and tree pointers. All leaves are at the same lowest level. Leaf nodes are also linked together as a linked list to make range queries easy and fast. Due to these advantages, it can be used to store and index historical data in data stream system.

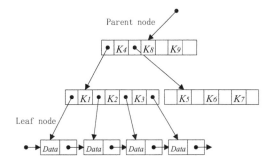

Fig. 2. The structure of B+ tree

Fig.2 depicts the structure of B+ tree. The Internal node of B+ tree can be described as $(P_1, k_1, P_2, k_2, \cdots, P_j, k_j)$. k_i is keyword (here it is timestamp), and P_j is a tree pointer which point to its child node. This kind of storage mechanism can be only used for one-dimensional data storage management. While for multiple heterogeneous data stream in the Internet of Things, such as temperature, humidity, pressure and wind strength etc, this one-dimensional storage scheme will result in low storage efficiency and indexing efficiency. Therein we propose a multi-dimension $B+$ tree structure, which is applicable for multi-dimensional heterogeneous data stream storage.

3   Storage Mechanism for Heterogeneous Data Stream

3.1   Data Stream Sampling

In order to improve the storage efficiency, we prefer to retaining the data which users are interested in, namely mutational data rather than storing the whole incoming data. Therefore, we will use the mutant information defined in Eq.4 to store the mutant data. According to the definition, the left sub-sequences and right sub-sequences should be predefined in order to compute the mutant significant information. Without loss of generality, we use a sliding window mechanism to determine the size of sub-sequences.

Define a window as $(a_s, ..., a_e)$, where s and e denote the start time and end time respectively. Data in the sliding window updates continuously, with new data entering in and first data leaving out. Define the window with a size as N, where N must be greater than the sum of the length of the left and right sub-sequences. Assumption that there are m heterogeneous data streams, for each data stream we use the sampling method based on mutant information, and then we use index structure based $B+$ tree and multidimensional B+ tree respectively to store and index the sampled data.

Sampling approach follows:

(1) Assume that the left sub-sequence length and right sub-sequence length, respectively, N_1 and N_2;

(2) Select the number i point of the window as the current calculate data, the selection of the point i must make sure that it has left sub-sequence and right sub-sequence in the sliding window;

(3) Calculate the left sub-sequence $u(i)$ and right sub-sequence $s(i)$ of data x_i; get the combined error $s_d(i)$ by the Eq.2 and Eq.3, and then calculate T_i;

(4) According to the statistic properties, we obtain the approximate cumulative probability density function of T. Compute the information of point x as $P(T_i)$;

(5) Choose the appropriate critical value P_0, if $P(T_i) \geq P_0$, choose the point x_i as a sample; If $P(T_i) < P0$, skip this point.

(6) Update the sliding window data, entry and output one data respectively, then perform step (1).

3.2   Storage Mechanism for Heterogeneous Data Stream

In order to retrieve heterogeneous data streams rapidly, we expand the $B+$ tree structure. Fig.3 is the multi-dimensional $B+$ tree structure. The structure of leaf layer remains the storage structure of the $B+$ tree. Leaf node index layer is added to the multi-dimensional $B+$ tree, it is the lowest level of the multi-dimensional $B+$ tree index structure which points to the metadata node layer. There are pointers between the index layers nodes, the index nodes are arranged in accordance with the keyword order. This structure can show the difference of the underlying multidimensional data, make indexing files fast and efficiently.

Metadata node layer, a multi-dimensional space which is expanded from a one-dimensional, is used to record the metadata which corresponded by the summary sampled data of the different types of data stream in the current period.

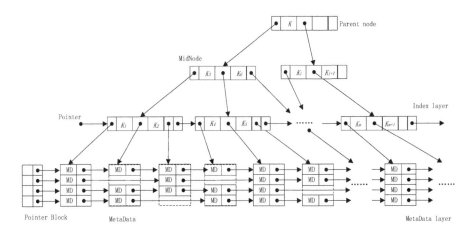

Fig. 3. The Structure of Multi-dimensional B+ tree

Metadata is the core of the multi-dimensional B+ tree; it is also the bridge which connect different types of data, its structure is shown in Fig. 4, mainly consists of aggregate values, sampling number n, the sampling rate f ,window starting time ts and ending time te ,as well as storage address of sampled data. The same type of data forms a sampling data sequence in accordance with the chronological order, different types of data are independent of each other, but they stay at the same time period. Thus we can query and manage heterogeneous data stream by the time attribute.

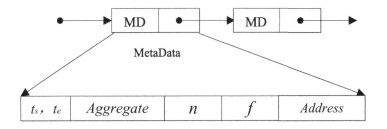

Fig. 4. The metadata structure of multi-dimensional B+ tree

From Fig.4 it can be noted that it still likes a B+ tree structure except that the leaf nodes point to an object which is constituted by multi-dimensional data stream. This object contains the sample metadata of all different types of data in the corresponding period. Additionally, multi-dimensional B+ tree structure is also conducive to the mutual index between the different dimensions, which makes adding or deleting operation more flexible.

4   Experiment Analysis

The experimental environment is using Windows 7 OS, Intel Core 2 Duo T6570 2.1GHz. The experimental data is electricity price data from the IESO[11] and cosine data mixed with noise. The experiment mainly analyses sample rate, sample error about the new sample method. Otherwise, it also analyses the basic characteristics of the multi-dimensional B+ tree.

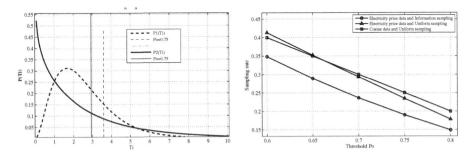

Fig. 5. T-value Distribution Curve   **Fig. 6.** Comparison of sampling rate

4.1   Sampling According to the Mutant Information

The sampling method of mutation information is sample and store data which contains more mutation information in data sequence. Thus the original data sampling rate is mainly affected by the size of the data sequence which contains mutant information. The information of each data series point is measured by T according to Eq.3. Fig.5 shows the T-value distribution derived by Eq.3 which uses two types of experimental data mentioned above. The point A and B in the figure representatively shows $P_1(A) = P_0 P_2(B) = P_0$. Here $P_0 = 0.75$. The value of T_i corresponding with the data that should be sampled must be greater than that corresponding with P_0. Fig.6 depicts the sample rates of two sampling methods under the same threshold P_0.

Under the same threshold, the sampling rate of the electricity price data using the sampling method based on mutation information is lower than the uniform sampling. Meanwhile the sampling rates of electricity price data and cosine data with additive noise both using the sampling method based on mutation information are quite different from each other. It is mainly because that the different data flow sequences contain different mutation information, which results in the difference of T_i distribution, the difference is also reflected in the sampling rate.

The sample method based on mutation information is sensitive to abnormal data in sequence. So it is more effective to sample non-stationary series and has

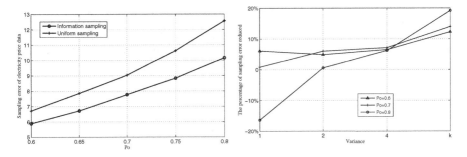

Fig. 7. Sampling Errors

Fig. 8. Influence of Instability on Sampling Errors

lower error than uniform sampling. Fig.7 compares the two different sampling errors by different sampling method. It can be seen that, with the increase of threshold, the proportion of the sample decreases, the sampling data error also increased. However, sampling error on mutation information sampling is less than the uniform sampling. Combination of Fig.6, when the sampling rate is small, the sampling error based on the mutation information is less than uniform sampling. Thus it could be used for generating summary data in the management of data stream.

Fig. 8 displays sampling errors of two kinds of sampling method. The horizontal axis shows instability of data sequence. The vertical axis indicates the reduced percentage of mutation information based sampling errors combining to uniform sampling. In Fig.8, the mutation information sampling method has a great advantage than uniform sampling when processing unstable data series. The more unstable it is, the sampling error produced by mutation information sampling method is less than uniform sampling.

The threshold also has an effect on sampling error. The experiment compares the errors on different thresholds. Fig.9 shows us that the new sampling methods sampling error is smaller than uniform sampling. But for stable data series, the accuracy of the new sampling method reduced.

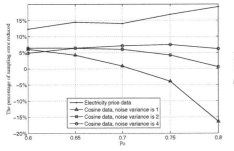

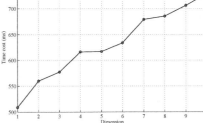

Fig. 9. Influence of Threshold

Fig. 10. Dimension and Insert Time

4.2   Characteristics of Multi-dimensional B+ Tree

Assume that we sample and save the results of m heterogeneous data stream. Traditionally, we use one-dimensional $B+$ tree for each category of data storage. The establishment of the $B+$ tree is as follows: they have same order and consistent index time period, we denote c as the space of the $B+$ tree index layer. n_i is meta-data layer space. d_i $(i = 1, 2, \cdots, m)$ as external space occupied by sampling data, and t is the index time.

(1) Space Complexity

For m heterogeneous data streams, the memory and disk space to establish B+ trees for each kind of data are $\sum_{i=1}^{m}(c+n_i)$ and $\sum_{i=1}^{m} d_i$ respectively.. While using multi-dimensional $B+$ tree to store all this m-dimensional data, the memory and disk space needed are $\sum_{i=1}^{m} n_i + c$ and $\sum_{i=1}^{m} d_i$. Thus it could lessen the memory space .

(2) Time Complexity

Then considering the retrieval time, establishing each independent $B+$ tree for m heterogeneous data stream, it takes $m \bullet t$ to search data on a particular period of time. While using multi-dimensional B+ tree, it only takes t, the query speed can be increased by m times.

(3) Impact of Dimension

Multi-dimensional $B+$ tree is the expansion of the B+ tree, it also has the advantages of B+ tree such as highly balance and fast index. The efficiency of $B+$ tree index is mainly influenced by the height of $B+$ tree, the height determines the $B+$ tree indexing times, namely $B+$ tree indexing time. For multi-dimensional $B+$ tree, it only extends the one-dimensional $B+$ tree on the space, and it has little effect on indexing time. But it will definitely increases the building time. Fig.10 shows the time that spent for establishing different dimensions of multidimensional B+ tree with 10,000 leaf nodes. Obviously, the more the dimension is, the more complex the building metadata node layer is. Therein building metadata structure costs more time.

5   Conclusions

By analyzing the features of heterogeneous data streams, we propose a mutant sampling and storing mechanism for multiple data streams according to the mutant information. It satisfies the requirements in which the users are more interested in the abnormal information. In addition, we extended one-dimensional $B+$ tree, so that it is applicable for heterogeneous data streams storage in the IoT. Such design of the multi-dimensional $B+$ structure can improve the setting up time m times and save the cache space (m is the dimension). Experiment results show that the multi-dimensional $B+$ tree has a greater advantage than that with one-dimensional for heterogeneous data streams in terms of storing and indexing, making it more suitable for the storage management of heterogeneous data streams in IoT. In future, we will consider the size of sliding window further so as to improve the sampling accuracy.

Acknowledgements. This work was finished under the support from Chinese National 973 Funding: 2011 CB302903; Nanjing University of Posts and Telecommunications Funding: NY207021, NY211063.

References

1. Babcock, A.K., Babu, S.: Data Model and issues in data stream systems. In: Popa, L. (ed.) Proc. of the 21st ACMSIGACT-SIGMOD-SIGART Symp. on Principles of Database Systems, pp. 1–16. ACM, Madison (2002)
2. Araru, A., Babu, S., Widom, J.: An abstract semantics and concrete language for continuous queries over streams and relations. Technical Report, Stanford University Database Group, pp. 1–6 (2002)
3. Jin, C.Q., Qian, W.N., Zhou, A.Y.: Analysis and Management of Streaming Data: A Survey. Journal of Software 15(8), 1172–1182 (2004)
4. Zhang, D.D., Li, J.Z., Wang, W.P., Guo, L.J.: Algorithms for Storing and Aggregating Historical Streaming Data. Journal of Software 16(12), 2089–2098 (2005)
5. Cormode, G., Muthukrishnan: An Improved Data Stream Summary: The Count-Min Sketch and its Applications. Journal of Algorithms 55(1), 58–75 (2005)
6. Wu, C.T.: The research and realization synopsis data structure in the data stream management system. Southeast University, 12–14 (2006)
7. Zhuang, W.: The research and realization of the data stream management system. Nanjing University of Aeronautics and Astronautics, 5–23 (2006)
8. Ge, J.W., Gong, P.Q., Liu, Z.H.: Method of Storing and Indexing Historical Streaming Data. Application Research of Computers 43(8), 149–153 (2007)
9. Feng, G.L., Gong, Z.Q., Dong, W.J., Li, J.P.: Research of climate mutation detection of based on heuristic segmentation algorithm. Acta Physics Sinica 54(11), 5494–5499 (2005)
10. Garofalakis, M., Gehrke, J., Rastogi, R.: Querying and mining data streams: You only get one look. In: Proceeding of the ACM SIGMOD International Conference on Management of Data (2002)
11. Independent Electricity System Operator (IESO), www.ieso.ca

A Data Gathering Approach
for Wireless Sensor Network
with Quadrotor-Based Mobile Sink Node

Yuanyuan Chen, Jianxin Chen, Liang Zhou, and Yuelin Du

Nanjing University of Posts and Telecommunications,
Nanjing, 210046, China
{b09040606,chenjx,liang.zhou,duyl}@njupt.edu.cn

Abstract. In this paper, we use a quadrotor-based mobile sink to gather sensor data from the terrestrial wireless sensor network. By analyzing the features of the mobile sink node, we theoretically studied the constraints of trajectory, velocity, height and data amount which the mobile sink can send. According to these analysis results, we propose a data acquisition strategy bases on the trajectory, speed and height of the controlled mobile sink. A plenty of simulations showed that the relationships between the sojourning time, transmission delay, packet loss rate and the mobile trajectory, velocity, etc under this approach, which founded a theoretical basis for such applications.

Keywords: mobile sink node, quadrotor, length of stay, data acquisition.

1 Introduction

Wireless sensor network is a network information system which includes the distributed information gathering, information transmission and processing. The purpose is to effectively sense, acquire and transport data from sensor nodes. Such a network can be widely used in national defense, security, environmental monitoring, traffic management, health care, manufacturing and anti-terrorism disaster and etc..Since the wireless sensor nodes are powered by batteries, the energy efficiency is the key for their wide applications. The mobile sink node strategy using one-hop transmission policy is one of the main solutions for such energy consumption and prolonging the network lifetime [1][2]. In such scenario, one or more mobile sink nodes travel in an statically deployed network to collecting data, which not only improves the energy efficiency, but has other advantages: no special concerning on the network connectivity, low cost of deployment, high reliability [3][2].

The previous research about data acquisition strategy of mobile sink node focuses on the node discovery, data forwarding, routing algorithms and mobile control. The travel way of mobile sink node affects the network data gathering efficiency. The greatest effect of mobile feature is the controllability, i.e. whether

R. Wang and F. Xiao (Eds.): CWSN 2012, CCIS 334, pp. 44–56, 2013.
© Springer-Verlag Berlin Heidelberg 2013

the mobile sink nod is controllable [4] or uncontrollable [5]. The controllable mobile sink node may change the location by controlling of travel trajectory and the speed, which can weaken some problems during data acquisition. For example, the mobile sink node is set to access some sensor nodes in some pre-defined time, which can simplify the node discovery procedure. Additionally, as the mobile sink node is controlled to stay within the communication range for some duration, the connection with the static node become easy too. However, a new challenge appears, e.g. how to control the mobile sink node gathering data under the energy constraint while satisfying some specific quality of service [6].

For the trajectory controllability of mobile sink node, there divided into two categories: the static controllability [1] and the dynamic controllability [8][13]. In the static controllability, the travel path of mobile sink node does not change with time. In the dynamic controllability, the mobile trajectory may change so as to satisfy some constraints, e.g. delay. For those mobile sink nodes whose speeds are controllable, they use stop-and-communication strategy. Specifically, the mobile sink node moves according to the predefined trajectory, when it enters the communication range of sensor node, it determines whether the sensor node has data to send. If so, it stops and move till all data are acquired [9][14]. In [10], by controlling the mobile routine and speed of mobile sink node, a linear programming problem was defined in the uniform 2-demision grid network, in which the mobile sink node starts from some specific sensor node, and uses stop-sojourn scheme to gather data so as to maximize the network lifetime. In [11], the problem was extended for the non-uniform network, and the delay of routing releasing/establishing and the energy consumption are also concerned. For these problems, they proposed a heuristic algorithm based on the greedy sojourning energy. In [13], the problem concerns both the scheduling and routing, and solve the linear programming problem in a distribution manner.

Different from the previous studies, the mobile sink node in this paper flies in the air, which is not only affected by the trajectory and moving speed, but also highly relevant with the flying height. In this paper, we discuss the constraints of movement trajectory, speed, altitude of the controllable mobile sink node, and propose a data collection strategy for such scenario. Other parts of this paper are organized as the following: Section II formulates the problem in terms of the moving speed, height, the amount of data and delay; Section III gives the data gathering strategy for such network environment; Section IV analyzes the performance of the mobile sink node data acquisition strategy in detail, such as the packet loss rate, the travel speed and flying height; The final section concludes this paper and shows the future work.

2   Problem Formulation

We concern the cases in which the wireless sensor networks are deployed in the scenarios where human are difficult to reach, such as virgin forest, the forest monitoring, the flood, and lake monitoring. In such networks, sensor nodes are chosen to be the cluster head, and others are all cluster members. All cluster members communicate with the nearby cluster heads. A mobile sink node carried by a quadcopter is controllable to fly above the deployed sensor networks. The mobile sink node collects the data from the cluster head when it enters the communication range of cluster head node. Therein, the problem is that how to control the trajectory, speed and altitude of the quadcopter since it affects the validity and reliability.

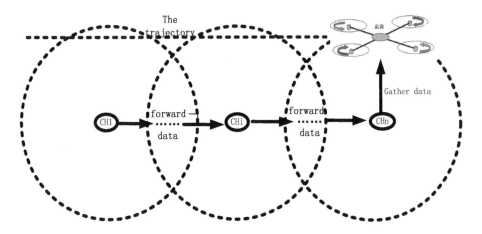

Fig. 1. Cluster Heads in Line

We chose a quadcopter to carry the mobile sink node since the quadcopter is more flexible than other kinds of aircrafts to move, stay, lift and descent. For easy analysis, we simply the problem, let all cluster heads are deployed in line and the quadcopter flies above the cluster heads as in Fig.1. Here *CH* denotes the cluster head, and the spherical dotted line represents the communication range and adjacent nodes are annexed in the communication range of each other. We first analyze the mobile sink node communicates with one cluster head, then extend to more than one cluster head.

2.1   One Cluster Head

Here we study the features of sojourning time of mobile sink node, average data transmission delay and the amount of data which might be sent.

1. Conversation time
    The time for a mobile sink node stay in the communication range of the cluster head depends on the flying speed and the movement pattern. Assume that the mobile sink node flies with a fixed velocity v from the left to the right and communication range of the cluster head (spherical) is D. As a result, the conversation time for the mobile sink node and the cluster head node is:

$$0 < t < 2D/v. \tag{1}$$

2. Data transmission delay Assuming that in each cluster head, there are L bits data to send, the transmission rate of the cluster head is R. Thus, the time for the data transmission from the cluster head is t_t, i.e.

$$t_t = L/R. \tag{2}$$

3. Data amount, height and flying speed Consider the flying speed and the height of mobile sink node in the realistic scenario, we analyze the maximum data amount which can be sent during the conversation between the mobile sink node and cluster head. Assume the time for the mobile sink node passes through the fixed communication range is T, the data amount L might be transmitted is constrained by:

$$L/R + T_p + T_c T, \tag{3}$$

where T_p and T_c denote the propagation delay and processing delay. As $T_p = h/c$ (where h denotes the height, c denotes the propagation rate of electromagnetic wave). Therein the maximum amount data which might be transmitted is :

$$L_{max} = R(2D/v - h/c - Tc). \tag{4}$$

If the data amount which might be directly collected from the cluster head is fixed (L is a const value), the allowed maximum flying rate of mobile sink node is:

$$V_{max} = \frac{2D}{L/R + h/C + T_c}. \tag{5}$$

Herein, the maximum height of mobile sink node is:

$$h_{max} = c \bullet (\frac{2D}{v} - \frac{L}{R} - T_c). \tag{6}$$

2.2 Multiple Cluster Heads in Line

In above, we analyze the mobile sink node gather data from a single cluster head. Now we extend to multiple cluster heads. Fig.2 depicts the communication ranges of adjacent cluster heads. The whole area is divided into three sub-regions: a, b and c. The distance between two adjacent nodes is d, and the number of cluster heads is n.

In Fig.2, G, H and I denote the location of the cluster head nodes i, $(i+1)$ and $(i+2)$ respectively. M is the intersection point of communication ranges of the cluster heads i and $(i+1)$, and N is the intersection point of communication range of the cluster heads i and $(i+2)$. Assume that all cluster heads have the same communication ranges. Therein there are $MG=MH=D$, $GH=d$, $NG=NI=D$, $GI=2d$. Here H, D, R and v are explained in above. Therefore the heights of points M and N follow:

$$m_h = \sqrt{D^2 - d^2/4}, \tag{7}$$

$$n_h = \sqrt{D^2 - d^2}. \tag{8}$$

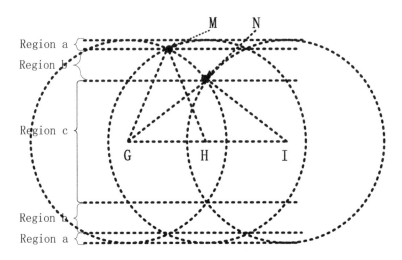

Fig. 2. Communication Ranges of Multiple Cluster Heads

According to the above analysis, the sub-region a has $m_h < h < D$, the sub-region b has $n_h < h < m_h$, and the sub-region c has $0 < h < n_h$. Herein we discuss the data amount which might be sent in these three sub-regions.

(1) Sub-region a $(m_h < h < D)$

In sub-region a, the mobile sink node can only communicate with one cluster head. At this time, the data amount of each cluster head which can be sent depends on the duration in which the mobile sink node stays in the communication range of the cluster head. We use a theorem to show the data amount which can be transmitted in one cluster head.

Theorem 1: When a mobile sink node in sub-region a moves with a uniform speed, the maximum data amount can be transmitted in the cluster head is $L_1 = R \cdot (\frac{2\sqrt{D^2-h^2}}{v} - T_a)$, where T_a denotes the sum of the processing and propagation delay.

Proof: In sub-region a, the duration in which the mobile sink node stays in the communication range of cluster head is T, i.e. Consider the delay of data transmission, propagation and processing delay, we obtain Eq.9. Herein Theorem 1 is proved.   ∎

(2) Sub-Region b $(n_h < h < m_h)$

Data gathering procedure in sub-region b can be divided into two phases. In phase 1, the mobile sink node can only communicate with one cluster head; in phase 2, the mobile sink node might communicate with two cluster heads. Herein, the data amount to be transmitted should contain these two phases. Theorem 2 shows the maximum data in this sub-region.

Theorem 2: When a mobile sink node in the region b, the maximum data for the first cluster head or the last cluster head node is $L_2 = \frac{R}{2} \cdot (\frac{2\sqrt{D^2-h^2}+d}{v} - T_a)$. Besides that, the data amount for other cluster heads is $L_2 = R \cdot (\frac{d}{v} - T_a)$.

Proof: In order to analyze, we detailed Fig.2 into Fig.3. When the mobile sink node is located in PQ and ST segments, it can communicate with two cluster heads nodes. When the mobile sink node is located in OP and QS segments, it can only communicate with one cluster head. According to the plane geometry principle, we can obtain $QS = 2d - 2\sqrt{D^2 - h^2}$. If the mobile sink node can communicate with two cluster heads, we use a fair strategy, i.e. each cluster head sends the same data. Then the total data amount can be computed. Therein, it is possible to obtain the the above solution. ∎

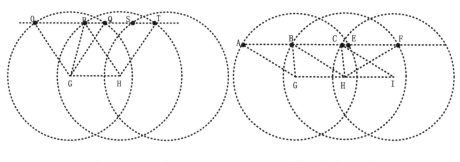

Fig. 3. Sub-region b **Fig. 4.** Sub-region c

(3) Sub-region c $(0 < h < n_h)$ Data communication in sub-region c includes three phases: in phase 1, the mobile sink nodes only communicate with one cluster head; in phase 2, the mobile sink node can communicate with two cluster heads; in phase 3 the mobile sink node can communicate with three cluster heads. Theorem 3 shows the data amount that can be sent by each cluster head nodes within communication range.

Theorem 3: When a mobile sink node in sub-region c, the data amount of the end cluster heads(the first and the last cluster head nodes) can transfer is L_3, i.e. $L_3 = \frac{R}{6} \cdot (\frac{4\sqrt{D^2 - h^2} + 5d}{v} - T_a)$. Besides that, other cluster heads can transfer data amount as $L_3 = \frac{R}{3} \cdot (\frac{2\sqrt{D^2 - h^2} + d}{v} - T_a)$.

Proof: Fig.4 depicts the sub-region C in detail. For the short of space, we do not list it here. ∎

3   Data Gathering Approach

In this section, according to the above analysis we will propose a data gathering approach for the wireless sensor network with a mobile sink node in the quadrotor. The mobile sink node flies over the sensor network with a constant speed, and in the above of the last cluster head the mobile sink node will stay for a short time till all of data are acquired. When the mobile sink node flies over the sensor network, it advertises own identification periodically. When the cluster head in the cluster head on the ground receives this advertisement, it acknowledges and starts to transmit data to the mobile sink node. If the cluster head can not complete all data transmission during the period when the mobile sink node in its own communication range, other data will be sent through the terrestrial routing algorithm to the last cluster head. The last cluster head is in charge of transferring all of these data to the mobile sink node.

This data collection approach transmits data as much as possible to the mobile sink node. Therein few data will be sent through the terrestrial network to the last cluster head node, which could save the energy in of each sensor node, and prolong the network lifetime.

3.1   Advertisement from Mobile Sink Node

The mobile sink node periodically advertises its position to the cluster heads. Constrained by the wireless communication range, flying speed of the mobile sink node, the period of advertisement should be less than D/v, where D is the communication range, and v is moving speed of sink node. This period can not be defined too short which might result in that most network bandwidth is used for sending the broadcast packet. This period also can not be too long otherwise it will result in that the node can not get enough information to predict the direction of movement and the amount of data the sink node can be transmitted. As the mobile sink node has a GPS module, it has the positioning function. Advertisement message includes velocity vector and height of the mobile sink node as $< velocity(v_x, v_y), height >$. If a cluster head receives a notice message from the mobile sink node and has data to sent, it immediately responses with a message including node ID to inform the mobile sink node to prepare to receive data.

After the cluster head responses to the mobile sink node, it also broadcasts some information about the mobile sink node to the adjacent nodes so as to building routing in the terrestrial sensor network. The broadcast message includes the source node ID, mobile sink node velocity vector v_x, v_y and height.

When the adjacent cluster heads receive the broadcast packet, they are able to determine whether the mobile sink node will pass through their communication range according to the position and movement speed, direction of the mobile sink node. Assume the current cluster head which is communicating with the mobile sink node has a position of (x, y) and the position of adjacent cluster head which receives a broadcast packet is (x', y'). Therein, if $(x - x') \times v_x > 0$, it can decide that the mobile sink node will pass by the cluster head (in this case, all cluster heads are deployed in line, so $y = y'$). If the mobile sink node passes by the cluster head, this cluster head continues to send broadcast message after modifying the source node ID in flooding way, otherwise the packet is discarded.

3.2   Linear Network Data Acquisition

We need to determine the period in which the ground cluster head may send data when the mobile sink node is within its communication range. If during this period, the data in the cluster head may be transmitted completely, there is no need to use the terrestrial sensor network to forward data. Otherwise, the remaining data will be forwarded to the final cluster head node by using a terrestrial routing algorithm. Mobile sink node stay in the communication range of the last cluster head for some time till all data in the current network are gathered.

When the mobile sink node flies over the sensor network, the related cluster head compute the data amount which can be sent according to the information received from the mobile sink node. The cluster head sends data after the transmission of response message. If the data amount which might be transmitted is too short (less than a threshold), this cluster head will not send data. Otherwise, the data in the sensor network are gathered according to the following procedure. Assume there are L bits in the cluster head to be sent:

(1) When the mobile sink node ranges in sub-region a, if $L \leq L1$(Theorem 1), the cluster head can transmit all data within time of T without forwarding by terrestrial network. If $L > L1$, not all data can be transmitted. Therein, the cluster head sends L1 bits to the mobile sink node, the remaining data of $(L - L1)$ bits will be forwarded to the final cluster head according to the routing algorithm.

(2) When the mobile sink node ranges in sub-region b, if $L \leq L2$ (Theorem 2), the cluster head can transmit all data to the mobile sink node directly. If $L > L2$, not all data can be transmitted. Therein, the cluster head sends $L2$ bits to the mobile sink node, the remaining data of $(L - L2)$ bits will be forwarded to the final cluster head according to the routing algorithm.

(3) When the mobile sink node in sub-region c, where $L \leq L3$(Theorem 3), the cluster head node can transmit all data within time of T without need to be forwarded. If $L > L3$, not all data can be transmitted. Therein, the cluster head sends $L3$ bits to the mobile sink node, the remaining data of $(L - L3)$ bits will be forwarded to the final cluster head according to the routing algorithm.

3.3   Terrestrial Routing Algorithm for Cluster Heads

We have analyzed the data collection strategy for the mobile sink node with the cluster heads. When the mobile sink node can not collect the data in the current cluster head, the remaining data will be sent to the last cluster head by using the straight-line routing. The last cluster head node forwards all data to the mobile sink node.

Within each cluster, consider the random distribution of general nodes and the system energy efficiency, not each sensor node in the cluster can communicate with the cluster head directly. That is to say, some nodes need to forward data through intermediate nodes. At this time, we need routing algorithm. The detailed procedure of routing algorithm could be referred to [16].

3.4   Non-linear Network

In above, we analyze the sensor network in which the cluster heads in line. In this section, we extend to general case non-linear network. In such situation,

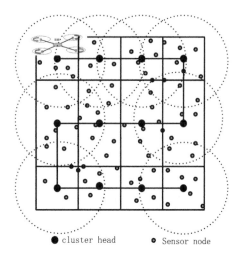

Fig. 5. Non-linear Sensor Network

we divide the entire area into sub-areas with equal size. All senor nodes in in each sub-area form a cluster. The cluster head is chosen according to the energy. All cluster members communicate with the cluster head. Cluster head nodes communicate with the adjacent cluster head and mobile sink node. Fig.5 gives an example of 12 sub-areas. Here we divide the whole sensor network into several linear networks. The cluster heads in different lines can not communicate with each other. In our example, 12 cluster heads are divided into three rows of four columns. In each row there are four cluster heads.

4   Simulation Analysis

Here we use the simulations to see the proposed data gathering approach. Simulation platform is Omnet++ [15]. In our simulations there are 30 nodes arranged in three lines, each line with five equal distant cluster head. Other 5 nodes randomly deployed around these cluster heads. The communication range of each cluster head is assumed to 100 meters. The communication range of general nodes is set to 50 m. In each sensor node there are 640 bits data waiting for gathering. Each packet length is defined as 128 bits or 16 bytes. The cluster heads which are not in the same line can not communicate with each other. We assume that CSMA/CA is used in MAC layer. According to the previous analysis, we mainly discuss the performance such as the moving speed, altitude, the sojourning time and the data packet loss rate.

4.1   Move Speed and Sojourning Time

(A) The mobile sink node files with different heights

Fig.6 gives that when mobile sink node located at different heights the relationship between moving speed and data acquisition time. It can be seen, when the height is constant, the sojourning time gradually reduces to a certain extent with the move speed increasing of sink node. In such cases the mobile sink node mainly locates in sub-area a. When increasing the moving speed of mobile sink node, data gathered from the cluster heads are relatively small. Most of them are forwarded by the terrestrial routing. Therein, the sojourning time of mobile sink node almost does not change. In terms of fixed flying speed, the sink node can collect more data from the cluster heads directly with the height decreasing, thereby reducing its sojourning time.

The right of Fig. 6 shows the mobile sink node flies with lower height. It is noted that when the sink node movement speed is less than 40 m/s, the sojourning time decreases with the increasing of the movement speed. When the movement speed is greater than 40m/s, the sojourning time increases with the movement speed of the mobile sink node. Since in this scenario, the mobile sink node mainly flies in sub-area b and c, most of data in the cluster head can be transmitted directly to the mobile sink node. After the movement speed is increased, some cluster heads node can not communicate with the sink node, which results in that more data will be transmitted by the terrestrial sensor network.

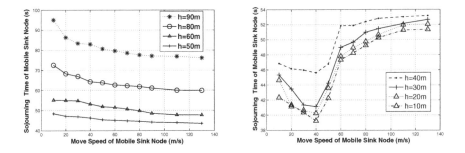

Fig. 6. Sojourning Time, Gathering time and Mobile rate

(B) Changing Network Size

Here we discuss the performance of the average transmission time per packet. Fig.7 depicts the average transmission time of each packet when we change the movement speed of the mobile sink node in terms of network size. It is noted that changing the movement speed of the mobile sink does not reduce the average data transmission time. The main problem is that when increasing the movement speed of sink node, it might reduce time in which the mobile sink node travels through the network. Thus it reduces the time which can be used for the communication between each cluster head and the mobile sink node. Herein, more time is required for the data transmission from each non-last cluster head to the last cluster head, which results in the average packet delivery delay increasing.

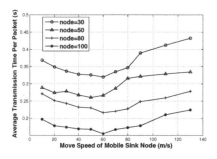
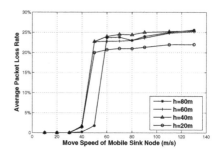

Fig. 7. Average transmission time   **Fig. 8.** Average Packet Loss Rate

4.2 Packet Loss Rate

Here we analyze the packet loss rate in terms of the movement speed of mobile sink node, the data amount in each sensor node, and network size.

(A) Move speed of the mobile sink node

Fig.9 depicts the packet loss rate in terms of movement speed, and flying height. It is noted that when the flying speed of mobile sink node is greater than 40m/s, the average packet loss rate suddenly increases. This is due to that the movement speed of mobile sink node is too fast, only few data in the cluster heads which might be transmitted to the sink node directly. And the remaining data have to be transferred to the end of the cluster head node. If the forwarded packet did not reach the end of the cluster head node, and all packets in the last cluster head have been transmitted to the mobile sink node, the mobile sink node thought that all data in this network have been gathered. Therefore it will fly away. As a result, the packet loss rate increases substantially. From this point, the height of the mobile sink node has a little effect on the packet loss rate.

(B) Average data transmission per node

Fig.10 shows the packet loss rate in terms of data transmission per node with different flying heights. It can be noted that when the data amount in each node is greater than (9 128) bits, the average packet loss rate increases significantly. When the flying speed and height of the mobile sink node do not vary, we can compute the data amount of each cluster head which can be delivered directly to the mobile sink node following Theorem (1-3). When each node sends few data, most or all of the packets are sent to the sink node directly. When the data amount is greater than the threshold, it results in most of the data have to be transferred by the terrestrial routing algorithm. Even the mobile sink node completes collecting the data in the last cluster head, in fact, there are other data in the intermediate cluster headers, which increases the packet loss rate significantly. On the other hand, from the figure, it can be found that the flying height of sink node has little effect on the packet loss rate.

(C) Move speed and the network size

Fig.11 gives the packet loss rate in terms of network size and the move speed of the mobile sink node. It can be seen that there is a sudden increase of the

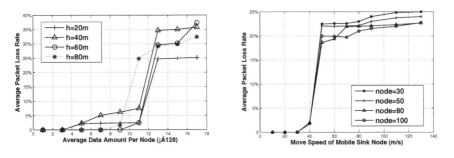

Fig. 9. Average Packet Loss Rate   **Fig. 10.** Average Packet Loss Rate

average packet loss rate when the speed of mobile sink node is greater than 40 m/s. The main reason is that mobile sink node moves too fast. So there will be part of the packet in each cluster head which can not be transmitted to the mobile sink node. The data which has not been transmitted will be forwarded to the last node following the terrestrial routing algorithm. If the forwarded packet does not reach the last node and the mobile sink node has finished the data gathering in the last node, the mobile sink node will fly away, which results in the packet loss rate increasing. On the other hand, the network size has a little effect on the packet loss rate.

5   Conclusion

A new data gathering approach is proposed for the wireless sensor net-works where a mobile sink node is located in the quadrotor. We studied the flying trajectory, speed, height, sojourning time and the data amount to be transmitted explicitly. After that, we propose a novel data gathering approach for such applications where the mobile sink node is carried in the aircraft. A plenty of simulation results show that the main features under this approach such as sojourning time, average transmission time per packet, packet loss rate, etc. in terms of flying speed, height, and network size. In future work, we will further explore the data gathering strategy from the point of energy efficiency, to control the movement trajectory, speed and altitude of mobile sink node, so as to prolong the network lifetime.

Acknowledgements. This work was finished under the support from Chinese National Funding: No. 61201165); Nanjing University of Posts and Telecommunications Funding: NY207021, NY211063, STITP funding.

References

1. Rao, J., Wu, T., Biswas, S.: Network-assisted sink navigation protocols for data harvesting in sensor networks. In: Proceedings of the IEEE Conference on Wireless Communications and Networking, WCNC 2008, pp. 2887–2892. IEEE Press, New York (2008)

2. Di Francesco, M., Das, S.K., Giuseppe, A.: Data Collection in Wireless Sensor Networks with Mobile Elements: A Survey. ACM Transactions on Sensor Networks 8(1), 7:1–7:31 (2011)
3. Anastasi, G., Conti, M., Di Francesco, M., Passarella: Energy conservation in wireless sensor networks: A survey. Ad Hoc Network 7(3), 537–568 (2009)
4. Poduri, S., Sukhatme, G.S.: Achieving connectivity through coalescence in mobile robot networks. In: Proceedings of the 1st International Conference on Robot Communication and Coordination, RoboComm 2007, pp. 1–6 (2007)
5. Chatzigiannakis, I., Kinalis, A., Nikoletseas, S.: Sink mobility protocols for data collection in wireless sensor networks. In: Proceedings of the 4th ACM International Workshop on Mobility Management and Wireless Access, MobiWac 2006, pp. 52–59 (2006)
6. Yao, Z., Gupta, K.: Backbone-based connectivity control for mobile networks. In: Proceedings of the IEEE International Conference on Robotics and Automation, ICRA 2009, pp. 2420–2426 (2009)
7. Rao, J., Biswas, S.: Network-assisted sink navigation for distributed data gathering: Stability and delay-energy trade-offs. Comp. Comm. 33(2), 160–175 (2010)
8. Tseng, Y.-C., Wang, Y.-C., Cheng, K.-Y., Hsieh, Y.-Y.: IMouse: An integrated mobile surveillance and wireless sensor system. IEEE Comp. 40(6), 60–66 (2007)
9. Sugihara, R., Gupta, R.K.: Optimal speed control of mobile node for data collection in sensor networks. IEEE Trans. Mob. Comp. 9(1), 127–139 (2010)
10. Wang, G., Cao, G., La Porta, T., Zhang, W.: Sensor relocation in mobile sensor networks. In: Proceedings of the 24th IEEE Conference on Computer Communications, INFOCOM 2005, vol. 4, pp. 2302–2312 (2005)
11. Basagni, S., Carosi, A., Melachrinoudis, E., Petrioli, C., Wang, Z.M.: Controlled sink mobility for prolonging wireless sensor networks lifetime. Wirel. Netw. 14(6), 831–858 (2008)
12. Gatzianas, M., Georgiadis, L.: A distributed algorithm for maximum lifetime routing in sensor networks with mobile sink. IEEE Trans. Wirel. Commun. 7(3), 984–994 (2008)
13. Hao, S.H.: Sink track fixed sensor networks and efficient data collection mechanism. Journal of Software 21(1), 147–162 (2010)
14. Gao, S., Zhang, D.: Delay constrained sensor networks Mobile Sink path selection method. Acta Electronica Sinica 39(4), 1–6 (2011)
15. Omnet++ Simulation, http://www.omnetpp.org
16. Sun, L.M., Li, J., Chen, Y., et al.: Wireless Sensor Network, pp. 29–36. TungHua University Publishing House (2010) (in Chinese)

A Node Design for Intelligent Traffic Monitoring Based on Magnetic Sensor

Zhen Fang, Zhan Zhao, Yundong Xuan, Lidong Du, Xianxiang Chen,
Xunxue Cui, Huaiyong Li, and Lili Tian

The State Key Laboratory of Transducer Technology,
Institute of Electronics, Chinese Academy of Sciences, Beijing 100190, China
{zfang,zhaozhan}@mail.ie.ac.cn

Abstract. In order to meet the real-time demand of the intelligent traffic system for traffic information, this paper have presented an intelligent traffic monitoring method based on magnetic sensor, and have analyzed the principles of magnetic sensitive detection and wireless node design, and have developed a practical detection node. Based on experimental test, the success rate vehicle detection is over 95%, and can avoid the iteration count of vehicles. We also have carried out on the speed and length measurement. The results show that the designed node can meet the demand of intelligent transportation system of the vehicle flow, vehicle speed and length parameters real-time monitoring needs. The test results show that the intelligent traffic monitoring method based on magnetic sensor has high accuracy, low cost, easy to deploy, and provides a new practical method and solution for intelligent transportation system.

Keywords: wireless sensor networks, intelligent traffic monitoring, magnetic sensor, node.

1 Introduction

Traffic congestion and traffic safety is an important factor in restricting the current social and economic development, and this can bring a serious impact on people's normal life. Intelligent Transportation Systems (ITS) can realize the efficient integration of advanced information technology, data communications technology, the sensor technology and electronic control technology and computer processing technology applied to the entire ground traffic management system, which can improve the operating efficiency of the transport system, reduce traffic accidents and reduce environmental pollution, in order to establish an efficient, convenient, safe, environmentally friendly, comfortable integrated transport system [1-4].

Accurate traffic information is the basis of traffic management and control. Existing traffic monitoring techniques have commonly used by the camera, radar, and inductance coils and other techniques, which there are some restrictions in terms of deployment of the convenience, cost, and environmental adaptability, and thus there are not conducive to large-scale deployment of intelligent transportation systems. The traffic monitoring technology, which can monitor the

R. Wang and F. Xiao (Eds.): CWSN 2012, CCIS 334, pp. 57–67, 2013.
© Springer-Verlag Berlin Heidelberg 2013

vehicle through the disturbed magnetic field that measured by use of magnetic sensors, has simple deployment, low cost, but also conducive to the integration with existing wireless sensor networks [2-4].

In this paper an intelligent traffic monitoring method based on magnetic sensor have been presented. We have analyzed the principles of magnetic sensitive detection and developed a practical detection node. The rest of paper is organized as follows: section 2 describes the magnetic sensitive principles of traffic monitoring and then designs the sensor node in section 3, the experimental verification is presented in section 4, and the last section is conclusion.

2   The Principles of Traffic Monitoring

The Earths field provides a uniform magnetic field over a wide area, which is about several kilometers2 [2]. The left part of the Fig. 1 shows how a ferrous object, creates a local disturbance in this field whether it is moving or standing still. Appealing to the fact that almost all road vehicles have significant amounts of ferrous metals in their chassis, magnetic sensors are a good choice for detecting vehicles. Today, most magnetic sensor technologies are fairly miniature in size, and thanks to solid state technology, both the size and the electrical interfacing have improved to make integration easier. The right part of the Fig. 1 shows a good graphical example of the lines of flux from the earth between the magnetic poles, and the bending they receive as they penetrate a typical vehicle with ferrous metals.

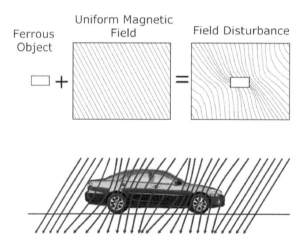

Fig. 1. The schematic diagram of the perturbed magnetic field due to the existence of the ferrous objects and the vehicle, respectively

Two magnetic sensors were distributed in the sensor node at both ends with a known separation of 20cm along the traveling direction. When the vehicle is passing on the top of the node, the magnetic sensor A first monitor the perturbation of the magnetic field, followed by the magnetic sensor B. Assuming the vehicle has negligible lateral offset and acceleration within these 20cm, the vehicle signature measured by node A should be identical to the one measured by node B. Moreover, the detection flag should change virtually at the same point within the vehicle signature. As a result, the time difference between A and B at which the detection flags change is the travel time across the separation distance. The vehicle speed and their lengths are estimated by the following equations:

$$V = L_{separation}/T_{difference}; L = V * T_{occupancy} \tag{1}$$

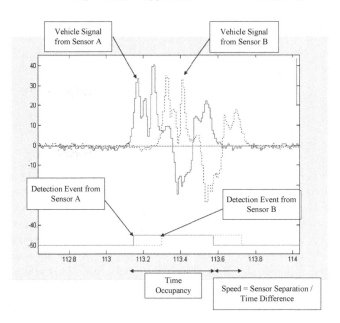

Fig. 2. The principle of the vehicle detection event by the magnetic sensor node and the vehicle speed estimation by a pair of magnetic sensor distributed in the node at both ends

3   The Magnetic Sensor Node Design

The main innovative hardware features are its ability to explore the possibilities of a practical and novel WSN-based magnetic sensing system, using IC based sensor. The overview of sensor node architecture and the insightful power characterization of different operational modes are also discussed in this section.

The intelligent traffic monitoring node architecture is depicted in Fig. 3, which includes four function modules, i.e. main control, power, communication, sensor subsystem. Each hardware sub-circuit is isolated; power to the circuit can be turned on or off independently of the rest of the platform. This isolation provides a degree of robustness-in the event of a failure; faulty modules can be disabled to minimize their impact on the system. Since the failure can be recognized in software, the ability to cut power to that section of the board may have saved the system as a whole.

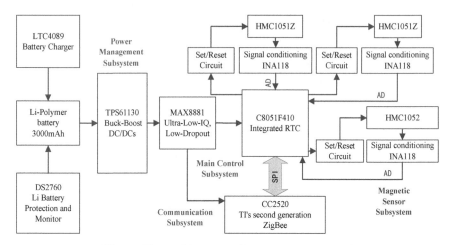

Fig. 3. The architecture of magnetic sensor node

Fig. 4 shows the assembled sensor node object. Two Z-axis Magnetic sensors were distributed in the sensor node at both ends, and one X-axis was set up in the middle of the sensor board. From analysis of the empirical magnetic signal of an urban traffic stream, we know that there is a chance that a stop-and go vehicle stays on top of the sensor node with its Z-axis measurements below the threshold level. In order to avoid double-counting, the X-axis measurements are also introduced into the decision of vehicle numbering. This effectively filters out the double-counting error as it is very unlikely that both the Z and X-axis measurements are below the threshold when a vehicle is present. Z-axis magnetic measurements are used as the major source for vehicle detection because of its localized characteristic, so that it can isolate detections from vehicle in adjacent lanes. The Li-polymer battery and power management subsystem was distributed in the right part of the board.

For the practical convenience, the package illustrated in Fig. 5, is designed for our sensor node by using PTFE material, which measures 230mm (L) * 130mm (W) * 30mm (H). The sensor board was embedded in the bottom of the package. There is a power switch in the sidewall. Including the Li-Polymer battery pack and package, the finished sensor node weighs 652 grams.

3.1   Microcontroller Subsystem

Each sensor node is equipped with a microcontroller (MCU) which acts as a local control centre for collecting and processing data, arbitrating sensor behavior, maintaining communication with the RF module, and timing events.

Since lots of WSN node was released in recent years, a number of new microcontroller have been introduced offering lower power consumption, more on-chip peripherals, and various RAM and flash sizes. To realize the lower power

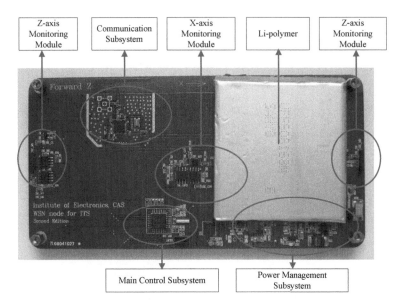

Fig. 4. Assembled sensor node board and battery pack

consumption, principle focuses on sleep current, wakeup time of the system and energy-efficient. It is important to differentiate low power from energy-efficient. Low power is a quality of a device that consumes low power per clock and energy-efficient is a device that consumes low energy per instruction. The series of the MCU from Silicon Labs have the highest efficiency and the fastest wakeup time among the industry. In the current design, the C8051F410 from the Silicon Labs has been adopted. This is a low-power, 50 MIPS, 8-bit device with 24-channel, 12-bit ADC, which is ideal for those small sensor systems, The more important topic is that there integrates smaRTClock, and multi-flexible low power management mode, which can keep track of time corresponding to the monitoring operation and support long-term monitoring task.

3.2   Power Subsystem

Power is supplied by a 3.7V 3000mAh lithium polymer battery pack. This chemistry is chosen as it is lightweight, compact, and rechargeable. The battery charger and protection circuit are designed on macro node in order to integrate the mass of the device, thereby making it more convenient to use. We select the LTC4089 as the power management, which includes a high efficiency current limited switching power path manager with automatic load prioritization, a battery charger and an ideal diode. The DS2760 was adopted to monitor the remaining capacity estimation, and safety of the lithium polymer battery, which have battery protection circuit and current-sense resistor, so it is easy integrated in the sensor board.

Fig. 5. The package of magnetic sensor node

The subsequent power management was designed to achieve the goal: high efficiency, low quiescent current and low noise. The buck-boost converter excels at efficiently converting a 4.2- to 3.0-V Li-ion battery to a certain output voltages. The TPS61130 from TI with a peak efficiency of 96% was used in our designed. However, the DC/DC converter has relatively high electromagnetic interference inevitably, which is bound to affect the performance of the magnetic signal acquisition and wireless communication. Unfortunately, the low dropout regulator (LDO) connected to the output of the DC/DC converter can provide noise filtering and maintain the high efficiency, as well as a constant and stable output voltage. The quiescent current and dropout voltage are two more important indexes to select the appropriate element. The MAX8881 from the MAXIM with low 3.5A supply current and 2Ω PMOS (the dropout voltage is 2Ω multiplied by the load current), was select to used in our design.

3.3   Communication Subsystem

The CC2520 is used in macro node, which is TI's second generation IEEE 802.15.4 RF transceiver for the 2.4 GHz band. Compared with CC2420, it has extensive IEEE 802.15.4 MAC hardware support, more superior performance on quality of radio signal, more abundant functions, more reliability and stabilization and less power consumption, which can reduce the load on the host controller and is more proper to use in the sensor node. The CC2520 radio is wired to a hardware interrupt that can wake up the processor upon the arrival of an incoming packet. In order to facilitate the integration and practicality of the node system, the Inverted-F PCB board antenna was used in the node, which is a linear monopole antenna, the top folded back to the PCB flat parallel to the ground. So it can reduce the antenna height at the same time to ensure that the resonant length of the antenna, but the parallel structure of a parasitic capacitance to the antenna make the input impedance not conducive to the antenna impedance matching design.

3.4 Sensor Subsystem

The Honeywell HMC1051X or HMC1052 magneto resistive sensor is at the core of the magnetic sensing subsystem. This sensor was chosen because of its two-axis orthogonal sensing, small size, low-voltage operation, low-power consumption, high bandwidth, low latency, and miniature surface mount package. Internally, the magnetometer is configured as a Wheatstone bridge whose output is differentially amplified by an instrumentation amplifier with a gain $G1 = 247$. The output of this instrumentation amplifier is low pass filtered using an RC-circuit with cutoff frequency $fc = 19Hz$. The output of the low pass filter is fed into the non-inverting input of a second instrumentation amplifier with gain $G2 = 39$, for a combined gain approaching 10,000. The inverting input of the second instrumentation amplifier is connected to the wiper terminal of a digital potentiometer configured as a voltage divider. The instrumentation amplifiers inverting input is the only user-adjustable parameter in the magnetometer subsystem and varying it adjusts the bias point of the amplifier.

3.5 Power-Consumption Analysis

The estimated power consumption of the various subsystems is shown in Table 1. The key point to note is that the magnetometer subsystems draw 3mA during high frequency operation. One popular approach to lowering the power consumption of sensor circuits is to duty-cycle the sensor. The magnetometer is a predominantly resistive element with a bandwidth of 5MHz and nanosecond-scale latencies, so it is well suited to duty-cycled operation. However, the signal conditioning circuit is not suited to duty-cycled operation because of the phase delay of a low pass filter used for anti-aliasing. To address the problem of a low startup-latency, high-power sensor coupled with a high-latency, low-power signal conditioning circuit, we propose the use of a mixed signal, multi-phase clocked, sample-and-hold control circuit as the interface between the sensor and signal conditioning electronics. Under the magnetic signal acquisition frequency of 1000Hz, the current consumption of our designed sensor system comes down to 3.26mA at average, so our system can last: $3000mAh/3.26mA/24h = 38.3days$, which is over one month.

4 Node Performance Measurement

4.1 Vehicle Detection Algorithm

To verify the performance of the design nodes, a series of experimental validation have been carried out, shown in Fig. 6. The node was placed in a line perpendicular to the direction of travel. The node will be collected traffic parameter

Table 1. The estimated power consumption of the various subsystems

Subsystem	State	Current (at 3V)	Units
Magnetometer	off	1	uA
Magnetometer	on	9	mA
Radio	off	<1	uA
Radio	Receive	18.5	mA
Radio	Transmit	25.8 (0dBm)	mA
Processor	Sleep	11 (32KHz)	uA
Processor	Active	7.5 (50MHz)	mA
Quiescent Current	on	15.5	uA

information, and transmitted to the master node located at the side of the road by wireless, and then enter the back-end platform.

The captured original magnetic signals have much fluctuation, which is not conducive to vehicle monitoring algorithm. So the window moving average algorithm was put forward to process the signals, as shown in the following equation. The r(k) is the raw signal and M is the pre-defined running average buffer size.

$$a(k) = \begin{cases} (r(k) + r(k-1) + \cdots + r(1))/k & \text{for } k < M \\ (r(k) + r(k-1) + \cdots + r(k-M+1))/M & \text{for } k \geq M \end{cases}$$

Due to limited processing capacity of the sensor node, vehicle monitoring algorithms require the computation to be as simple as possible. The system needs to be deployed in different environments, so the algorithm needs sufficient

Fig. 6. The scenarios of the magnetic system

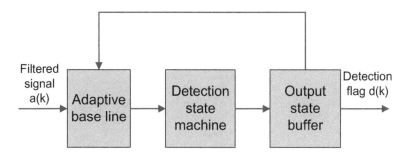

Fig. 7. The block diagram of the adaptive threshold detection algorithm

robustness to achieve accurate detection of vehicles in different working environment. Also the drift of the magnetic field itself and temperature coefficient, the adaptive threshold detection algorithm has been designed in the algorithm, the algorithm block diagram is shown in Fig.7.

The detection state machine is shown in Fig. 8. Assuming there is no vehicle near the sensor node when it is being reset. It will go into state S1 and start initializing the baseline with the environmental measurements. After a pre-defined initializing time, it will jump to the state S2 where the baseline is updated adaptively. It will jump to state S3 when a Z-axis measurement larger than the adaptive threshold is recorded. It was found that a vehicle signature produces a successive sequence of state with over the threshold and this state is used to track such a sequence. Within this state, it will jump back to state S2 after the number of successive state with less than threshold has reached a critical value. In order not to lose potential vehicle detection, it will jump back to the state S3 again in case there is any state with over the threshold emerging. Staying in state S5 implies the magnetic fluctuation is strong as the vehicle is still traveling over the sensor node. Such a situation is identified by the detected timer when it exceeds a predefined value of longest reasonable detected time. It will jump back to S1 and reset the whole state machine. Finally, the detection flag d(k) is generated according to the output state of this state machine. This computationally simple detection algorithm can be executed in the senor node.

4.2   Experimental Results and Analysis

One sensor node sampling at 1 KHz was placed in the middle of a lane on the Zhongguancun North First Street, Beijing. The setup was located on a section right after a traffic light-controlled intersection, as shown in Fig. 6. Ground truth was established by a visual count. A total of 98 vehicles were observed, most of which are small vehicles. Detections were generated at real time by the magnetic sensor node without any post processing. A total of 96 out of 98 (98%) vehicles were detected by magnetic sensor node. However, the numbers detected by the sensor node are 101, which are more than the actual vehicles passed near the node, and the reason is bike passing the sensor.

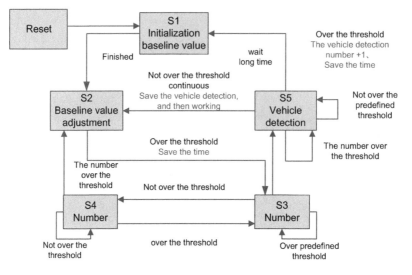

Fig. 8. The block diagram of the detection state machine

For estimating speed with the magnetic sensor node approach, a vehicle was driving above the sensor node according to the predefined velocity. Summary statistics of the speeds estimated by the magnetic sensor node and the predefined are shown in Table 2. The overall statistics of the vehicle speeds from the estimated and the predefined agree with each other. Due to lack of the dataset of various vehicles lengths, the experiments of vehicle length have not conducted in the paper.

Table 2. Comparison of estimated speeds from a sensor node and predefined.

Subsystem	Predefined (kmh)	Estimated(kmh)
Average	48.5	48.1
Minimum	15.2	14.7
Maximum	80.3	78.9
Median	47.8	47.2

5   Conclusion

In this paper, a new practical method and solution for intelligent transportation system based on magnetic sensor has been designed, and the test results show that this method has high accuracy, low cost, easy to deploy, and provides more traffic parameter information. With this promising result from an urban traffic intersection with heavy traffic flow, one may confidently predict that such a robust wireless sensor network can detect vehicles and estimate speeds as well as a highly calibrated inductive loop detector and video.

Acknowledgments. The paper is based on research funded through 973 Program under project no. 2011CB302100, 863 Program under Grant no. 2009AA045300, through NSFC under Grant no. 60971071 and 61170252.

References

1. Guo, J.F., Quan, Y.S., et al.: Study on the Traffic Flow of the Expressway. Urban Transport 11, 42–44 (2000)
2. Cheung, S.Y., Varaiya, P.: Traffic Surveillance by Wireless Sensor Networks: Final Report. Technical report, American: California PATH (2007)
3. Zhang, Y.H., Huang, X., Cui, L.: WSN Nodes for Real-Time Traffic Information Detection. J. Com. Res. Dev. 45(1), 110–118 (2008)
4. Lin, G., Dong, J., Pascal, V., Ting, Y., et al.: Lightweight detection and classification for wireless sensor networks in realistic environments. In: Proc. of the 3rd International Conference on Embedded Networked Sensor System, pp. 205–217. ACM Press, San Diego (2005)

A Lightweight RFID Mutual Authentication Protocol with Ownership Transfer

Xiaotong Fu and Yandong Guo

National Key Lab of Integrated Service Networks, Xidian University,
Xi'an710071, China
xtfu@mail.xidian.edu.cn, yandong803@126.com

Abstract. By analyzing Jin et al's protocol, we find it doesn't resist replay attack and man-in-the-middle attack. And then , based on the improvement of the Rabin encryption scheme (SQUASH function), a new lightweight RFID mutual authentication protocol is proposed,which satisfies security requirement: untraceability, denial of service(DoS) resistance, man-in-the-middle attack resistance, replay attack resistance and forward security etc. And the new proposed protocol can support secure ownership transfer between the current tag owner and the new one.

Keywords: RFID, Ownership transfer, Lightweight, Man-in-the-middle attack, Forward security.

1 Introduction

The earliest RFID protocols using Hash function is Sarma et al's Hash-Lock protocol[1,2]. A lot of protocols[3,4,5] using Hash function and without updating tag ID have been proposed from then on. However, if the tag ID is not updated, there is usually an obvious flaw that the tag can be traceable. Meanwhile, if DB does not store previous authentication data, a simple interruption will make DB and Tag into desynchronization state. Thus the Hash function and previous data storage in the DB have been applied to RFID authentication protocols, such as Henrici's protocol [6]. Sometimes, a tag can be traceable by continuing to query the tag with a constant number, so Lee et al introduced the pseudo-random number generator $(PRNG)$into their protocol [7]. But Deursen et al, according to their algebraic replay attacks theory, made an effective man-in-the-middle-attack[8]against the protocol. The lightweight RFID protocol was firstly proposed in RFIDSec in 2006. In the Chien et al's scheme[9], the dynamic update mechanism and CRC and $PRNG$ are introduced. However, Deursen et al pointed out the protocol didn't resist replay attack[10]. In the Chien et al's scheme[11], tag does not update its ID, and $PRNG$ and cyclic operation are used to hide the secret information, but the protocol is still subjected to the man-in-the-middle attack[8].

All protocols above do not support the secure ownership transfer, but in the practical application secure ownership transfer is required[12]. Ng et al proposed a practical RFID ownership transfer scheme. But it is necessary to change the

R. Wang and F. Xiao (Eds.): CWSN 2012, CCIS 334, pp. 68–74, 2013.
© Springer-Verlag Berlin Heidelberg 2013

current tag key before and after the completion of ownership transfer between current tag owner and new tag owner. In the future, all of the RFID authentication protocol should be able to simply implement secure ownership transfer, because it is easy for the current tag owner to get the tag ID and other tag secret information, and this is a great threat to the new tag owner.

The remainder of the paper is organized as follows. In Section 2, Jin et al's scheme is analyzed and its flaws will be pointed out. The new protocol with ownership transfer is proposed in Section 3.Its security and efficiency analysis is made in Section 4.Finally, we conclude the paper in Section 5.

2   Jin et al's Protocol and Its Security Analysis

The protocol[13] involve the definitions as follows.

T_i: Tag R_i:Reader DB_i: The database of the T_i

k: A security parameter,$1200 < k < 1300$

n: The product of unknown prime factors (at least two),$n = 2^k - 1$

s_i: A string of l bits assigned to T_i t_i: T_i's identifier of l bits $t_i = s_i^2 \ mod \ n$

u_i: The previous identifier of l bits assigned to T_i

v_i: T_i's previous identifier of l bits,$v_i = u_i^2 \ mod \ n$

U_i: The detailed T_i's information $[x]_t$: Obtain t bits of x

$\oplus$: XOR operator $\|$: Concatenation operator

$x \gg l$: The right circular shift operator, which rotates all bits of x to the right by l bits, as if the right and left ends of x are joined

2.1   Jin et al's Protocol

In the initialization phase, s_i is chosen for each T_i as its initial identifier,$t_i = s_i^2 \ mod \ n$.At the same time,DB_i stores the following value for the corresponding tag:$[(s_i, t_i), (u_i, v_i), U_i]$. The detailed protocol description is as follows:

1. $R_i \rightarrow T_i$: Reader queries the tag.

2. $T_i \rightarrow R_i \rightarrow DB_i$: When the tag receives query from R_i , T_i selects a pseudo-random number r_T ,and computes $M = t_i \oplus r_T, N' = r_T^2 \ mod \ n$ and $N = [N']_t$ and sends M, N to R_i ,then R_i forwards$M$,N to DB_i . If an adversary forges a new message f_M by M and f_N by N , he needs to compute r_T and solve SQUASH scheme[14], which is proved at least as secure as Rabin's public key encryption scheme.

3. $DB_i \rightarrow R_i$: When DB_i receives the request from R_i,for each tuple (s_i, t_i),computes $N' = (M \oplus t_i)^2 \ mod \ n$ and $N = [N']_t$,and verifies the equation $N(computed) = N(received)$ .If DB_i can find a match t_i which makes the equation true, then the tag T_i is successfully identified and authenticated. And DB_i will forward s_i , r_T ,U_i to R_i , at the same time, DB_i will update its database, $u_i \leftarrow s_i$, $v_i \leftarrow t_i, s_i \leftarrow t_i$,$t_i \leftarrow t_i^2 \ mod \ n$.

4. $R_i \rightarrow T_i$:R_i computes $P = s_i \oplus (r_T \gg l/2)$and forwards P to T_i .

5. T_i : When T_i receives the feedback information from R_i ,it will obtain s_i by computing $s_i = P \oplus (r_T \gg l/2)$ and verify $t_i = s_i^2 \ mod \ n(computed)$ .If okay, T_i will update its t_i , $t_i \leftarrow t_i^2 \ mod \ n$.

2.2   Security Analysis

The authors claim that the scheme satisfies forward security, replay attack resistance, denial of service(DoS) resistance and man-in-the-middle attack resistance. However, by analyzing the scheme, we find it can't resist replay attack and man-in-the-middle attack.

Replay Attack. In the authentication process, adversary obtains(M, N) and then interrupts the communication:$R_i \rightarrow T_i$, in this case, T_i can't update t_i . Later, the adversary only needs simply to replay(M, N), and thenDB_i will find a match using (u_i, v_i), thus, the adversary will be regarded as a legal tag.

Man-in-the-Middle Attack. An adversary queries a tag, T_i will response (M, N),$M = t_i \oplus r_T$,$N' = r_T^2 \bmod n$, and$N = [N']_t$ to him. When the real Reader R_i queries T_i ,the adversary only needs simply to forward (M, N) to R_i,where R_i will send (M, N) to DB_i and then DB_i will find a match using (u_i, v_i), thus, the adversary will be also regarded as a legal tag.

3   The Mutual Authentication Protocol with Ownership Transfer

The notations Jin et al defined are used in the new scheme and two notations are added as follows:

k_i: The secret value of the tag T_i, which stored in the DB_i, is not stored in T_i. It is used to support secure ownership transfer.

$x \ll a$ or $x \gg a$: The left or right circular shift operator, which rotates all bits of x to the left or right by the Hamming weight of a, as if the right and left ends of x are joined.

$CRC(x)$: Cyclic redundancy code of x.

3.1   Setup

In the initialization phase, s_i is chosen for each T_i as its initial identifier, $t_i = s_i^2 \bmod n$. At the same time, DB_i stores the following value for the corresponding tag: $[(s_i, t_i), (u_i, v_i), k_i, U_i]$.

3.2   Protocol Description

1.$R_i \rightarrow T_i$: R_i generates a pseudo-random number r_R and queries T_i with r_R and $query$.

2.$T_i \rightarrow R_i \rightarrow DB_i$: When T_i receives the query,it generates pseudo-random number r_T and computes $M_1 = CRC(t_i \gg r_R) \oplus r_T$,$M_2 = [r_T^2 \bmod n]_t$, then sends M_1,M_2 to R_i, where R_i will forwards M_1,M_2 to DB_i. In the scheme. we also use SQUASH scheme[14], which is proved at least as secure as Rabin's public key encryption scheme.

DB_i	R_i	T_i
$[(s_i,t_i),(v_i,u_i),k_i,U_i]$		$[t_i]$
searh(s_i,t_i)	r_R,query	r_T
$r_T^{'}=$	$\xrightarrow{\hspace{1cm}}$	$M_1=$
$M_1\oplus CRC(t_i\gg r_R)$ $\quad r_R,M_1,M_2$	M_1,M_2	$r_T^{'}\oplus CRC(t_i\gg r_R)$
$M_2^{'}=[r_T^{'2}modn]_t=M_2 \quad \longleftarrow$	$\longleftarrow$	$M_2=[r_T^2modn]_t$
$k_i\leftarrow r_R$		
$M_3=s_i\oplus r_T^{'}$		$s_i^{'}=M_3\oplus r_T$
$M_4=(k_i\gg r_T^{'})^2modn$		If $t_i=s_i^{'2}modn$
$M_5=k_i\gg (r_T^{'}\|s_i) \quad M_3,M_4,M_5,U_i$	M_3,M_4,M_5	$k_i=M_5\ll (r_T\|s_i^{'})$
$u_i\leftarrow s_i, s_i\leftarrow t_i$ $\quad\longrightarrow$	$\longrightarrow$	$(k_i^{'}\gg r_T)^2modn=M_4$
$s_i\leftarrow t_i\|k_i$		$t_i\leftarrow (t_i\|k_i)^2modn$
$t_i\leftarrow (t_i\|k_i^{'})^2modn$		

Fig.1. The Proposed Protocol

3.$DB_i\rightarrow R_i$: When DB_i receives the request from R_i, it will operate as follow:

(1) DB_i firstly retrieves (s_i,t_i) field, computes $r_T^{'}=M_1\oplus CRC(t_i\gg r_R)$ and verifies the equation $M_2^{'}=[r_T^{'2}\bmod n]_t=M_2(received)$. If the equation above is true, it means DB_i finds a match and the tag T_i is successfully identified and authenticated ,and then k_i will be updated r_R:$k_i\leftarrow r_R$. Meanwhile, DB_i computes $M_3=s_i\oplus r_T^{'}$, $M_4=(k_i\gg r_T^{'})^2\bmod n$ and $M_5=k_i\gg (r_T^{'}\|s_i)$, and sends M_3,M_4,M_5,U_i to R_i and updates its database as follows: $u_i\leftarrow s_i$, $s_i\leftarrow t_i$, $s_i\leftarrow t_i\|k_i$, $t_i\leftarrow (t_i\|k_i)^2modn$.

(2)If DB_i can't find a match in (1), this may mean data between T_i and DB_i are not updated synchronously. So DB_i will retrieve (u_i,v_i) and compute $r_T^{'}=M_1\oplus CRC(v_i\gg r_R)$, verify the equation $M_2^{'}=[r_T^{'2}\bmod n]_t=M_2(received)$. If the equation above is true, it means DB_i finds a match and the tag T_i is successfully identified and authenticated, and data between T_i and DB_i is not updated synchronously. Now, DB_i and k_i won't be updated. DB_i Computes $M_3=u_i\oplus r_T^{'}$, $M_4=u_i\oplus r^{'}$ and $M_5=k_i\gg (r_T^{'}\|u_i)$, send M_3,M_4,M_5,U_i to R_i. If DB_i can't find a match in(1) or (2), DB_i will reject the authentication request.

4. $R_i\rightarrow T_i$: R_i send M_3,M_4,M_5, to T_i.

5. T_i: When T_i receives M_3,M_4,M_5 from R_i ,it computes $s_i^{'}=M_3\oplus r_T$ and verifies the equation $t_i=(s_i^{'})^2\bmod n(computed)$. If the equation above is true, T_i computes $k_i^{'}=M_5\ll (r_T\|s_i^{'})$ and verifies the equation $(k_i^{'}\gg r_T)^2\bmod n=M_4$. If the two equations above are both true, T_i will update its t_i: $t_i\leftarrow (t_i\|k_i^{'})^2modn$. The detailed protocol description is in the Fig.1.

4 Security and Efficiency Analysis

4.1 Security Analysis

Untraceability:The full information:M_1,M_2,M_3,M_4,M_5 transmitted in the insecure channel $R_i\leftrightarrow T_i$ contains r_T,which assures each interaction is fresh. Even in the case of interruption of M_3, M_4, M_5 transmission, adversary can't obtain the unique attribute of T_i by continuing to query T_i with a constant bits string.

Replay Attack Resistance: If an adversary simply replays M_1, M_2, T_i won't be authenticated.Even if adversary obtained previous several groups of r_R, M_1, M_2, the adversary can't compute the real response of the new query r'_R because of r_T's randomness.

Denial of Service (DoS) Resistance: Because DB_i stores the previous authentication data (u_i, v_i),T_i will be successfully authenticated in the next authentication request even if T_i's data is not updated but DB_i because of the interruption of M_3, M_4, M_5 transmission or sudden-loss-of-Power of T_i in this request.

Man-in-the-middle Attack Resistance: The adversary queries T_i with r_1 chosen by himself and can obtain $M_1 = CRC(t_i \gg r_1) \oplus r_T$ and $M_2 = [r_T^2 \bmod n]_t$.When the legitimate Reader R_i queries T_i with r_R,the adversary forges M'_1, M_2 using r_1, M_1, M_2, r_R and sends M'_1, M_2 to R_i.If DB_i can find a match, the scheme can't resist man-in-the-middle attack. If the attack succeeds, there will be equation $M'_1 \oplus CRC(t_i \gg r_R) = r_T$,thus $M'_1 = CRC(t_i \gg r_R) \oplus r_T = M_1 \oplus CRC(t_i \gg r_1) \oplus CRC(t_i \gg r_R)$.According to the equation, if the adversary wants to be successfully authenticated, he must have access to t_i,which is impractical. So the scheme can resist man-in-the-middle attack.

Forward Security: According to the security of SQUASH scheme, if adversary obtains the t_i of the tag T_i by tampering or other means, he can not pose a threat to the RFID system security of the moment $t' < t$.

Secure Ownership Transfer: Because t_i is updated using the pseudo-random number r_T,the new owner only needs to successfully perform an authentication process, which can ensure that the previous owner does not pose a threat to his security.

The following Table 1 shows the comparison in the sense of security discussed in this section.

Table 1. Security Comparison

Schemes	DoS	MA	FS	RA	LW	OT
Wei et al.[2]	Y	N	N	N	N	N
Henrici et al.[6]	N	Y	Y	Y	N	N
Lee et al.[7]	Y	N	Y	Y	N	N
Chien et al.[9]	Y	N	Y	Y	Y	N
Chien et al.[11]	Y	N	Y	Y	Y	N
Jin et al.[13]	Y	N	Y	N	Y	N
Ours scheme	Y	Y	Y	Y	Y	Y

MA:MAn-in-the-middle Attack   FS:Forward Security   RA:Replay Attack
LW:Lightweight   OT:Ownership Transfer   Y:Yes,can resist such an attack
N:can't protect against such an attack

4.2   Efficiency Comparison with Other Protocols

In the new scheme, T_i needs l bits of non-volatile memory to store its secret information. Now, we do the following assumptions: l is the length of the pseudo-random number and secret value of tag T_i; z is the length of the tag T_i's ID; q is the length of the Hash value; n is the number of total tags in the RFID system; c is the cost of CRC operation; p is the cost of $PRNG$ operation; h is the cost of Hash function; r is the cost of Rabin encryption;$r \ll n$;The cost of XOR, etc operation is negligible. The following Table 2 shows the performance comparison between the new scheme and the existing scheme.

Table 2. Performance Comparison

Schemes	TC	TS	DBC	DBS	CC
Wei et al.[2]	h	$q+z$	h	$l+z+q$	$l+z+q$
Henrici et al.[6]	$3h$	$2l+z$	$2h+p$	$4l+2z+2q$	$2l+3q$
Lee et al.[7]	$3h+p$	$2l$	$2h$	$2l+2z$	$l+2q$
Chien et al.[9]	p	$2l+z$	$2p+c$	$2l+z$	$3l$
Chien et al.[11]	p	$2l+q$	p	$2l$	$3l$
Jin et al.[13]	$3r+p$	$l+q$	$2r$	$z+4q$	$2l+t$
Ours scheme	$4r+p+c$	$l+q$	$3r+c$	$l+z+4q$	$4l+t$

TC: Tag Computation Cost   TS: Tag Storage Capacity Needed
DBC: DB Computation Cost   DBS: DB Storage Capacity Needed
CC: Communication Complexity

According to 4.1 and 4.2, we can conclude that our scheme satisfies security requirement: untraceability, denial of service(DoS) resistance, man-in-the-middle attack resistance, replay attack resistance and forward security etc, but our scheme still needs to improve its efficiency as high as possible.

5   Conclusions

In the paper, Jin et al's protocol is analyzed and pointed out that it doesn't resist replay attack and man-in-the-middle attack. A new lightweight RFID mutual authentication protocol with secure ownership transfer is proposed. The new scheme's security and efficiency are also analyzed and the comparison with other schemes is also given.

In the future, as a part of work, the low-cost, secure and efficient RFID protocols with secure ownership transfer will be deeply researched. Meanwhile, in designing the kind of scheme, the performance efficiency will be given a special attention.

References

1. Zhou, Y.-B., Feng, D.-G.: Design and analysis of cryptographic protocols for RFID. Chinese Journal of Computers 29(4), 581–589 (2006)
2. Weis, S.A., Sarma, S.E., Rivest, R.L., Engels, D.W.: Security and Privacy Aspects of Low-Cost Radio Frequency Identification Systems. In: Hutter, D., Müller, G., Stephan, W., Ullmann, M. (eds.) Security in Pervasive Computing 2003. LNCS, vol. 2802, pp. 201–212. Springer, Heidelberg (2004)

3. Ohkubo, M., Suzuki, K., Kinoshita, S.: Hash-chain based forward-secure privacy protection scheme for low-cost RFID. In: Proceedings of the 2004 Symposium on Cryptography and Information Security, SCIS 2004, Sendai, pp. 719–724 (2004)
4. Molnar, D., Wagner, D.: Privacy and security in library RFID: Issues, practices, and architectures. In: Proceedings of the 11th-ACM Conference on Computer and Communications Security, CCS 2004, pp. 210–219 (2004)
5. Rhee, K., Kwak, J., Kim, S., Won, D.: Challenge-Response Based RFID Authentication Protocol for Distributed Database Environment. In: Hutter, D., Ullmann, M. (eds.) SPC 2005. LNCS, vol. 3450, pp. 70–84. Springer, Heidelberg (2005)
6. Henrici, D., Muller, P.: Hash-based enhancement of location privacy for radio-frequency identification devices using varying identifiers. In: Proceedings of the 2nd IEEE Annual Conference on Pervasive Computing and Communications Workshops, PERCOMW 2004, pp. 210–219 (2004)
7. Lee, S., Asano, T., Kim, K.: RFID mutual authentication scheme based on synchronized secret information. In: Symposium on Cryptography and Information Security (2006)
8. Deuresen, T., Radomirovic, S.: Attacks on RFID protocols (Version 1.1). Technical report (2009), http://eprint.iacr.org/2008/310
9. Chien, H.-Y., Chen, C.-H.: Mutual authentication protocol for RFID conforming to EPC Class 1 Generation 2 standards. Proceedings of Computer Standards Interfaces 29(2), 254–259 (2007)
10. van Deursen, T., Radomirović, S.: Algebraic Attacks on RFID Protocols. In: Markowitch, O., Bilas, A., Hoepman, J.-H., Mitchell, C.J., Quisquater, J.-J. (eds.) WISTP 2009. LNCS, vol. 5746, pp. 38–51. Springer, Heidelberg (2009)
11. Chien, H.-Y., Huang, C.-W.: A Lightweight RFID Protocol Using Substring. In: Kuo, T.-W., Sha, E., Guo, M., Yang, L.T., Shao, Z. (eds.) EUC 2007. LNCS, vol. 4808, pp. 422–431. Springer, Heidelberg (2007)
12. Ng, C.-Y., Susilo, W., Mu, Y.: Practical RFID ownership transfer scheme. Journal of Computer Security 19, 319–341 (2011)
13. Jin, Y., Sun, H., Xin, W., Luo, S., Chen, Z.: Lightweight RFID Mutual Authentication Protocol against Feasible Problems. In: Qing, S., Susilo, W., Wang, G., Liu, D. (eds.) ICICS 2011. LNCS, vol. 7043, pp. 69–77. Springer, Heidelberg (2011)
14. Shamir, A.: SQUASH – A New MAC with Provable Security Properties for Highly Constrained Devices Such as RFID Tags. In: Nyberg, K. (ed.) FSE 2008. LNCS, vol. 5086, pp. 144–157. Springer, Heidelberg (2008)

Network Topology Effects on Reachback Firefly Algorithm in Slot Synchronization

Can Guo and Yanliang Jin

School of Communication and Information,
Shanghai University, Shanghai
guocan1989@gmail.com

Abstract. This paper reviews the classic Reachback Firefly Algorithm (RFA) and cites all the problems when applying the RFA to realistic slot synchronization. To make the RFA feasible in slot synchronization, this paper proposed a novel slot modification to overcome the influences from random package arrivals and half-duplex mode. Whats more, a self-developed simulation tool for the RFA in slot synchronization is presented in this paper. Then, based on the simulation tool, simulations are done and impacts from network topologies and network size are thoroughly analyzed. Simulation results show that, considering the same connection rate, mesh topology is the best choice for the RFA in slot synchronization. Moreover, when connection rate stays constant, the performances of the RFA in slot synchronization get worse while the network size increasing.

Keywords: RFA, slot synchronization, firefly algorithm, wireless sensor networks.

1   Introduction

As WSNs consist of sensor nodes, whose storage, power and computational ability are limited, conventional time synchronization mechanisms [1-3] would be inappropriate and nonhierarchical distributed algorithms should be more preferable. Fireflies, in South-East Asia, distributed in trees with low intelligence, can flash in a perfect synchrony within a huge range from a chaotic situation. This striking phenomenon has been delved for a long run. Buck et al. investigated fireflies reaction to external flashings and studied their behaviors in more details [4].

The RFA proposed in [5] alleviates the burden on computation ability of sensor nodes and neutralizes parts of the impact from delays by using MAC layer timestamping. However, direct applications of the RFA in wireless communications can hardly achieve satisfactory results. Realistic radio effects, such as propagation delays, channel attenuation and noise, place a huge effect on their performances. Whats more, in realistic wireless communication scenario, a synchronization word is composed of a sequence of pulses with several bytes or even more but not an ideal pulse, thus the reception and parsing of synchronization

R. Wang and F. Xiao (Eds.): CWSN 2012, CCIS 334, pp. 75–82, 2013.
© Springer-Verlag Berlin Heidelberg 2013

words shall also bring in delays. Half-duplex transmission in the physical layer and random packet arrivals in the MAC layer also lead to a huge difference from ideal situations. As for the M&S model [6], lots of works [7-10] have been done based on slot synchronization to make it more applicable in WSNs and the authors have proposed several methods to make the M&S model compatible with the half-duplex and random arrivals of data packets. Even though the RFA has been utilized in realistic scenarios in [11], there are no details which indicate how the RFA could overcome the influences from half-duplex transmission and random packet arrivals.

This paper presents a novel slot modification method to apply the RFA to slot synchronization in WSNs. To make the RFA compatible with the half-duplex working mode and the random package arrivals, the transmission slot is inserted into the refractory period. Moreover, a novel self-developed simulation tool built on MATLAB for RFA in slot synchronization is proposed in this paper. This tool integrates almost all key factors of slot synchronization and vastly facilitates the simulation work of RFA in slot synchronization. Based on this tool, simulations are done with different topologies, such as mesh, star, line and ring. It is clear that the mesh topology, given a certain connectivity rate, mesh topology is the best choice for synchronization comparing with other topology shapes and the network shall finally be unable to be synchronized when the network size increases to a certain degree.

This paper is structured as follows: Section 2 reviews the RFA and refractory period at first, then introduces how to apply the RFA to realistic slot synchronization. Section 3 thoroughly introduces our self-developed simulation tool. In Section 4, simulations are done considering different topologies and thorough analysis is given. Finally, Section 5 draws the conclusions.

2   RFA in Slot Synchronization

2.1   RFA

By the theory of the RFA, oscillators use MAC layer timestamping to record and queue up the firing messages from neighbors without responding in phase adjustment immediately. At the beginning of the next period, oscillators calculate the overall phase adjustment from the firing messages in queue and update the phase. The phase adjustment is also decided by phase-state function:

$$\phi_i' = f^{-1}[f(\phi_i) + \epsilon] = f^{-1}\{\frac{1}{b}\ln[1 + (e^b - 1) \cdot \phi_i] + \epsilon\} \qquad (1)$$

The curvature of the curve is proportional to dissipation factor b, and the time to synchronicity is inversely proportional to $b \cdot \epsilon$. Fig.1 plots how the RFA works: when the oscillator receives flashings at t1, t2 and t3, it does not adjust its phase immediately but updates its phase at the very beginning of next period. Compared with the M&S model, the RFA avoids frequent phase adjustment to alleviate the computation burden. MAC-layer timestamping is also used in the RFA to avert two unpleasant conditions caused by propagation delays in WSNs:

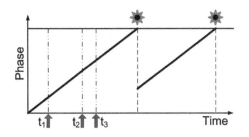

Fig. 1. The RFA diagram

1) The firing message of node A arrives just right at the firing instant of node B. 2) Unpredictable delays may cause disordered firing message arrivals. Timestamping is a valid method that makes the RFA more applicable in a realistic situation.

2.2 Refractory Period

Refractory period [12] is proposed to prevent the occurrence of an infinite feedback in a network with delays. In refractory period, oscillators do not update their phase state. The value of refractory period T_{ref} in a certain network varies with the largest transmission delay in a network: $T_{ref} \geq 2 \cdot max(v_{ij})$, where v_{ij} is the transmission delay between two nodes. Apparently, given a certain network, refractory period shall always be a key variable which should be allocated carefully.

2.3 Slot Synchronization

Comparing with the ideal RFA, several cardinal differences should be taken into account when it comes to realistic slot synchronization situations:

1) The RFA alone cannot decide whether or when shall a data frame be transmitted. As a matter of the MAC strategy, nodes may not always transmit a data frame at their firing instant, namely the random package arrival.
2) Multiple delays exist in the entire process of transmission and reception as the sync-word is not just an ideal pulse without length and processing delay.
3) To a certain node, at one time, the reaction to one node or a cluster of synchronized nodes is the same, for the sync-word detector can only detect a wave crest at one time no matter high or low.
4) Half-duplex mode makes the utilization of the RFA even more complicated, because nodes are deaf while transmitting and nodes which are receiving can only be scheduled to transmit mode after a whole data frame is completely received.

Delays from processing firing messages would not be a problem as the RFA could use MAC layer timestamping to overcome them. However, synchronization can hardly be achieved with the existence of random package arrival and half-duplex mode, because they would destroy the synchronization rhythm by randomly inserting a transmission slot and interrupting the continuous listening state. To deal with the half-duplex mode and random package arrivals, a novel slot modification is made by inserting the transmission slot into the refractory period. As there is no phase update in either refractory period, data frame could be transmitted within these slots. Therefore, the continuous listening state would not be interrupted and the data frame could be transmitted normally. We call this the fake full-duplex mode. To compare the performances of the RFA in slot synchronization with and without such slot modification, simulations are done in MATLAB. Fig2 plots the simulation results.

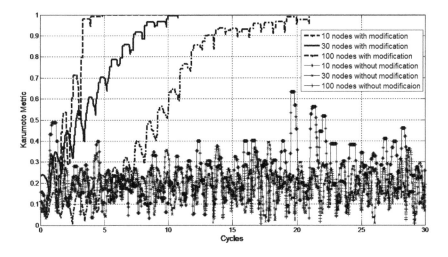

Fig. 2. RFA in slot synchronization with and without slot modification.

It is clear that the networks can hardly get synchronized without the modification. Within 30 cycles, no synchronization trends could be found in any of the three network sizes without slot modification. However, with the rearrangement of slot for the transmission slot, the networks would get synchronized within an acceptable time. Both the implement and the generalization of this method seem quite appealing.

3   A Self-developed Simulation Tool

In this section, a self-developed simulation tool, built on MATLAB, for the RFA in slot synchronization is introduced. In this paper, a concept named connection rate is utilized to characterize topological properties of a network. Given a certain graphic:

$$G = G(V, E) \tag{2}$$

Connection rate L_G is defined with the number of existing links E and the number of nodes N in a network:

$$L_G = \frac{2 \cdot |E|}{|V| \cdot (|V| - 1)} \tag{3}$$

where $|E|$ and $|V|$ are the number of edges and nodes respectively in the graphic. Connection rate is a simple way to characterize the density of a network. Moreover, with a given L_G and certain number of nodes, it is easy to generate and handle a network. Especially, $L_G = 1$ means a fully-connected network.

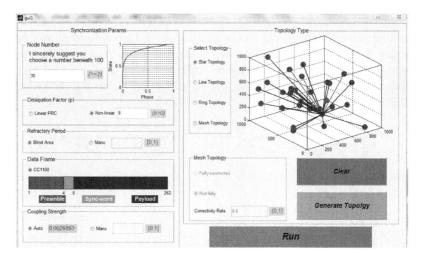

Fig. 3. Self-developed simulation tool

Fig. 3 plots the user interface of this simulation tool. The tool mainly consists of two parts, the topology generator part and the parameter control part respectively. The two parts can be operated separately, but only if both of the two are set appropriately can this tool work well. When the Node Number panel in parameter control part is set, a specific topology type can be selected in the topology generator part. So far, only star, line, ring and mesh topology are taken into consideration. Hit the Generate Topology button, a random topology shape can be generated correspondent to the topology selected. The Clear button can erase the topology already generated before. Especially, if the mesh topology is chosen, a connectivity rate should be given in the Mesh Topology panel. Except for the Node Number panel, parameter control part has four other panels to be considered with. Because the data frame structure is stationary so far, the Data Frame panel is frozen. Now there are only three parameters to deal with. Dissipation factor can be set or chosen as linear, refractory period can be set or chosen as Blind Area for convenience and the coupling strength can be set or chosen as auto if you cannot allocate an appropriate value. If the coupling strength is chosen as auto, the tool shall auto-adaptively calculate a proper value for the users. After all the parts are set, the simulation result can be obtained by pressing the Run button.

Simulation results of the RFA in slot synchronization are influenced by multiple parameters. This tool integrates almost all the key factors and facilitates the simulation work vastly. The tool is only the first version developed to be an executable application which could be installed on a Windows OS. Other versions, even powerful, which support the M&S model, customizable data frame structure and so forth have also been developed.

4   Topology Simulations and Analysis

The simulations are done based on the simulation tool introduced above, mainly accounting for topologies like line, ring, star and mesh with varying connection rate. Simulation results are shown in Fig. 4. Mesh-n means this topology is generated with a connection rate which equals n and Mesh-fully means the connection rate is 1.

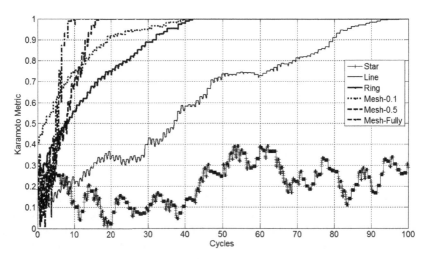

Fig. 4. Simulation results for different topologies

For Mesh Topology, three different connection rates are taken into consideration. It is easy to tell from Fig. 4 that the synchronization time is inversely proportional to the connection rate, which is reasonable. A higher connection rate means that a node could have a larger neighbor set and phase adjustment could happen more frequently in one cycle. In mesh topology, therefore, the performance of the RFA, applied to slot synchronization, is mainly affected by the connection rate. However, the same connection rate does not lead to the same topology shape, and different topology shapes could lead to unexpected results even with the same connection rate, such as star, line and ring.

Star Topology, in which every node is connected to a center node, may lead to the worst performance when the RFA is applied, shown in Fig. 4. The reason that causes such a bad condition is that the center nodes phase is always synchronized by its neighbors randomly and its neighbors cannot communicate each other. This situation, however, is not permanent. After a number of experiments, it is interesting to find out that a network with star topology could be synchronized when the number of nodes in it decreases below about 10.

In Line Topology, nodes are connected one by one, but the head and tail are not connected. Except for the head and tail only has one neighbor, each node has only two neighbors. Clearly, this kind of shape does no good to synchronization. A longer line makes it harder to achieve an overall rhythm. Given a certain connection rate, when the number of nodes if greater than 3, a mesh topology always leads to a better performance than what a line topology does.

Ring Topology can be generated by connecting the head and the tail of a line topology. Although the connection rate increases only a little bit, as shown in Fig. 4, the performance is improved vastly comparing with the line topology.

5 Conclusions

This paper proposed a novel modification on transmission and reception slot is proposed to make the RFA compatible with slot synchronization in WSNs, where half-duplex working mode and the random arrivals of data packets could vastly destroy the rhythm of synchronization. By inserting the transmission slot in refractory period, the RFA could perfectly overcome the influences from half-duplex and MAC layer strategy. Moreover, a self-developed simulation tool for RFA in slot synchronization is proposed in this paper. This tool integrates almost all key factors of slot synchronization and vastly facilitates the simulation of RFA in slot synchronization. Based on this tool, simulations are done with different topologies, such as mesh, star, line and ring. It is shown in Fig4 and Fig5 that the mesh topology, given a certain connectivity rate, a randomly generated mesh topology is the best choice for synchronization comparing with other topology shapes and the network shall finally be unable to be synchronized when the network size increases to a certain degree.

References

1. Jiang, W., Sun, L., Lv, J., Zhu, H.: An opportunistic time synchronization algorithm for mobile sensor networks. In: IET International Conference on Wireless Sensor Network, pp. 243–247 (2001)
2. Elson, J., Girod, L., Estrin, D.: Fine-grained network time synchronization using reference broadcasts. In: OSDI (2002)
3. Maroti, M., Kusy, B., Simon, G., Ledeczi, A.: The flooding time synchronization protocol. In: ACM SenSys (2004)
4. Buck, J., Buck, E., Case, J., Hanson, F.: Control of Flashing in Fireflies. V. Pacemaker Synchronization in Pteroptyx cribellata. J. Comparative Physiology A 144, 630–633 (1981)

5. Werner-Allen, G., Tewari, G., Patel, A., Welsh, M., Nagpal, R.: Firefly-inspired sensor network synchronicity with realistic radio effects. In: SenSys (2005)
6. Mirollo, R., Strogatz, S.: Synchronization of pulse-coupled biological oscillators. SIAM 50, 1645–1662 (1990)
7. Tyrrell, A., Auer, G., Bettstetter, C.: Fireflies as Role Models for Synchronization in Wireless Networks. In: Intl Conf. Bio Inspired Models of Network, Information and Computing Systems (2006)
8. Tyrrell, A., Auer, G.: Decentralized Slot Synchronization for Cellular Mobile Radio. NTT DoCoMo Technical Journal 10, 56–44 (2008)
9. Tyrrell, A., Auer, G., Bettstetter, C.: Emergent Slot Synchronization in Wireless Networks. IEEE Transactions on Mobile Computing 9, 719–732 (2010)
10. Tyrrell, A., Auer, G.: Self-organized slot synchronization in time and frequency. In: Proceedings of the 4th International Symposium on Applied Sciences in Biomedical and Communication Technologies, Barcelona, Spain, pp. 1–5 (2011)
11. Leidenfrost, R., Elmenreich, W.: Firefly clock synchronization in an 802.15.4 wireless network. EURASIP Journal on Embedded Systems 17 (2009)
12. Mathar, R., Mattfeldt, J.: Pulse-Coupled Decentral Synchronization. SIAM J. on Applied Math. 56, 1094–1106 (1996)

Opportunistic Routing in Multi-Power Wireless Sensor Networks

Yahong Guo[1], Xiaohang Guo[2,3], Yanqing Zhang[2,3], Jinghua Zhu[2,3], and Jinbao Li[2,3]

[1] School of Information Science and Technology, Heilongjiang University
Harbin, Heilongjiang, China, 150080
[2] School of Computer Science and Technology, Heilongjiang University
Harbin, Heilongjiang, China, 150080
[3] Key Laboratory of Database and Parallel Computing of Heilongjiang Province
Harbin, Heilongjiang, China, 150080

Abstract. In this paper, we investigate on the opportunistic routing in Multi-Power Wireless Sensor Networks (MP WSNs). We first propose a routing metric called METT of opportunistic routing in MP WSNs, and model the power selecting process as a Markov decision process for computing the METT metric. We describe the METT-based opportunistic routing problem, and design a polynomial time optimal algorithm for getting the optimal routing and power selection scheme. Theory analysis and experiments show that the proposed multi-power opportunistic routing can improve the data transmission efficiency, significantly reduce the energy consumption and the end-to-end transmission delay.

Keywords: multi-power, wireless sensor networks, opportunistic routing.

1 Introduction

In wireless sensor networks, it is one of the challenges faced by sensor networks to design a routing protocol to meet the communication demand. The traditional routing protocols do not take characters of wireless broadcasting into account. For wireless networks, when the node sends data to a neighbor node, all nodes within the communication radius of the sending node may overhear the data because of the nature of wireless broadcast. Therefore, if the specified neighbor node does not receive the data, whether do other nodes which overhear the data continue to forward the data in order to reduce the cost of data retransmission?

Based on the above discussions, in recent years, many researchers put forward some opportunistic routing protocols [12 − 14] in wireless networks. In opportunistic routing protocols, each forwarding node needs to determine the node set of the next hop, called forwarding set, which replaces the only node of the next hop selected by the traditional routing methods. According to the characters of wireless broadcasting and spatial multiplexing, every node in the forwarding set could receive the data when a node sends data. In order to prevent data redundant transmission, a node which is selected from the forwarding set and

R. Wang and F. Xiao (Eds.): CWSN 2012, CCIS 334, pp. 83–96, 2013.
© Springer-Verlag Berlin Heidelberg 2013

with the highest priority continues to forward the data. Forwarding priority is based on the routing standard, for example, in the shortest path routings, the closer node distance from the target node, the higher the priority of the node is. So, the data packet is lost only in the case that all nodes in the forwarding set fail to receive it. Therefore, the probability of successfully forwarding a packet is higher than the probability that the node select only a node of the next hop to successfully forward a packet in traditional route. Consequently, the opportunistic routing protocols improve routing reliability and throughput. However, the current study of the opportunistic routing does not consider that the node can take a multi-level transmitted power.

In recent years, the studies about multi-level transmitted power show that the method that nodes adopt multiple powers can effectively reduce the average power of the network, improve network performance [1 − 4].For the design of routing protocols, the different powers result in different communication radiuses, which will directly lead to the different nodes of the next hop. The increase of transmitted powers will increase the paths from the source node to target node, which can lead to have more opportunities to select the optimal path. However, the communication and interference radius will increase with the node power increasing, which will exacerbate the confliction of network communication. Therefore, in the design of routing protocols, how to properly control the multiple powers will become an important research in wireless sensor networks.

In this paper, we investigate on the opportunistic routing in multi-power wireless sensor networks (MP WSNs), and propose a routing metric called METT in MP WSNs. The METT standard takes various choices of transmitting power and the transmission quality of wireless links, etc. into account. We model the power selecting process as a Markov decision process for computing the METT metric to gain more chances of selecting powers. Then, we provide the definition of the routing problem based on the METT metric and mathematical model. Finally, we design an optimal routing algorithm, called DAOR, and proof the algorithm optimality. The theoretical analysis and experimental results show that the opportunistic routing strategy proposed in MP sensor networks, can effectively reduce the end-to-end transmission delay.

2   Related Work

Transmitted power control has been widely studied in wireless networks. Many researchers study the impact of transmitted power on the capacity of wireless networks and show that multiple powers perform better than single power [1 − 4] Wang et al.[5]proposed a distributed game-theory-based formulation to solve the optimal routing and power assignment problem, which considers both the benefits of the source node and the relay nodes. Wang et al.[6] discussed how power control, link scheduling and routing have mutual influence in the actual environment, and proved that effective power control can improve network throughput, and theoretically analyzed the number of throughput enhanced.

How to design routing standards directly affects the routing efficiency. De Couto et al.[7] firstly proposed the ETX routing standard, which considers retransmission mechanism of MAC layer to calculate the expected number of transmissions Based on the ETX, we can find a path with of the minimum number of expectations of transmission. On the basis of the ETX standard, Koksal *et al.*[8]considered the link quality changing over time, and proposed ENT routing standard, while Jakllari *et al.*[9] considered the link location which may impacts on the routing, and proposed ETOP routing standard. In order to select an efficient route, a good routing metric WCETT was proposed in [10] for MR-MC wireless networks, capturing the interference and channel diversity. Moreover, some interference-aware routing metrics such as WEED [11] were proposed, which take the end-to-end transmission delay or throughput as the path metric. However, the concurrent transmission schedule in MR-MC routing is still not considered, so they cannot compute the real transmission time or throughput.

In recent years, based on the characters of wireless broadcasting and spatial multiplexing, etc., a new routing, called opportunistic routing becomes a hot research topic. Biswas *et al.*[12] proposed a classic opportunistic routing algorithm, called ExOR. ExOR chooses ETX as routing standards. ExOR starts from the target node, and adopts the dynamic programming method to calculate the ETX values of each node in the whole network, each node in the forwarding set was determined priority based on the ETX value.

In order to improve network throughput, Zeng *et al.*[13] consider the opportunistic routing problems in multi-rate wireless networks. Considering the same channel confliction, they proposed the conflict graph for opportunistic routing, and turned the maximum throughput of the opportunistic routing problem into the maximum flow of the linear programming problem, based on the conflict graph. Based on the above problem, Zeng *et al.*[14]consider the multiple paths with more concurrent transmission links, and formulate the capacity of opportunistic routing in MR-MC networks as a LP problem.

From above routing and power assignment schemes, there is no cross-layer protocol joint routing, scheduling and power assignment in multi-power multi-radio WSNs. Therefore, this paper researches the problem of the opportunistic routing in multi-power multi-radio WSNs.

3   System Model

This chapter firstly introduces the basic theories of the opportunistic routing in wireless networks[12], and then specifically describes the model of the MP wireless sensor networks, as well as opportunistic routing in the MP WSNs.

3.1   Opportunistic Routing

In the opportunistic routing, there are two important definitions: Forwarding Set (FS) and Forwarding Priority (FP). When a node is forwarding the data, the nodes that are allowed to receive the packet consist of the forwarding set, and sort the forwarding nodes in accordance with the forwarding priority. When the nodes in the multiple forwarding sets receive the packet, the node with the highest

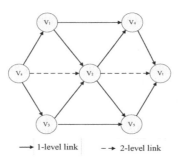

Fig. 1. The topology of MP WSNs

priority is considered as an intermediate node to continue forwarding packets, while other nodes discard the packet. Therefore, the opportunistic routing is to determine the forwarding set and the forwarding priority for each node.

The following describes the idea of opportunistic routing in detail using Figure 1. In figure 1, the source node v_s transmits data packets to the destination node v_t. The directed graph in figure 1 represents the topology of wireless networks. From the diagram, we know the set of neighbor nodes for each node, for example, the set of neighbor nodes for v_s represents as $\mathcal{N}_s=\{v_1, v_2, v_3\}$. Suppose the forwarding set of v_s determined by the opportunistic routing algorithm is v_2, v_3, where F_s denotes the forwarding set of v_s. $\mathcal{F}_s \subseteq \mathcal{N}_s$, and $\mathcal{F}_s$ is an ordered set according to the forwarding priority, namely the priority of v_2 is higher than the priority of v_3 in the forwarding set. When node v_2 has received the packet, it continues forwarding the packet; if not and v_3 receives the packet, then v_3 continues to forward the packet. When all the nodes in the forwarding set fail to receive the packet, v_s retransmits the data, and the transmission fails when exceeding the number of retransmission. Therefore, the opportunistic routing makes full use of wireless broadcasting to improve the transmission efficiency.

3.2 MP Wireless Sensor Network Model

We consider a MP WSNs with N nodes, where there are n transmitted power levels $P_1, P_2, \ldots, P_n$ ($P_1 < P_2 < \ldots < P_n$) for each node each node v_a ($1 \leq a \leq N$) to choose, and the transmission ranges are $R_1, R_2, \ldots, R_n$ and interference ranges are $IR_1, IR_2, \ldots, IR_n$, respectively. Let $d(a,b)$ denote the Euclidean distance between node v_a and v_b. The link l_{ab} exists, if and only if $d(a,b) \leq R_n$, namely when v_a uses the highest level of transmitted power, v_b is in the communication radius of v_a. Let l_{ab}^k denote when l_{ab} exists, and v_a uses k-level of transmitted power, v_b is in the k-level of communication radius of v_a. Therefore, in this paper, the MP WSNs can be abstracted as a directed graph $G = (V,L)$, where V denotes the set of all sensor nodes, L denotes the set of all links.

Definition 1 Minimum Choice Power of link l_{ab} MCP(a, b). When the link l_{ab} exists, For a node v_b, define the power P_k ($1 \leq k \leq n$) as the minimum choice power of v_a, if and only if $R_{k-1} < d(a,b) < R_k$. Denote MCP$(a,b) = P_k$.

Definition 2 Neighbor set of node v_a, N_a. The neighbor set of node v_a in the k-level power can be represented as N_a^k, and for $\forall\, b \in N_a^k$, $d(a,b) \le R_k$. So $N_a^k \subseteq N_a^c$, $\forall\, k \le c \le n$.

Definition 3 Transmission Time on link l_{ab}^k, t_{ab}^k. By Shannon formula, the bandwidth of link l_{ab}^k is defined as follow:

$$C_{ab}^k = W\log_2(1 + P_k d(a,b)^{-\sigma}/N_0 W)$$

Then, the transmission rate of the link l_{ab}^k is defined in Eq.(1)

$$R_{ab}^k = p_{ab}^k C_{ab}^k = p_{ab}^k W\log_2(1 + P_k d(a,b)^{-\sigma}/N_0 W) \tag{1}$$

Where p_{ab}^k denotes the probability of successful forwarding data for the link l_{ab}^k, and it is a function related to the transmitted power. Assume that a packet size is b Byteso the delay of sending a packet for l_{ab}^k is defined in Eq.(2)

$$t_{ab}^k = b/R_{ab}^k \tag{2}$$

4   Routing Metric of Opportunistic Routing

This chapter firstly introduces opportunistic routing in MP WSNs, and then pro-poses a routing metric for the MP WSNs, called Multi-power Expected Transmission Time (METT for short). The METT considers that 1) the selection diversity of transmitting power for each sending node; 2) retransmission mechanism based on the MAC layer; 3) transmission quality of wireless links; 4) the broadcasting character of the wireless networks.

4.1   Optimal Forwarding Power

This paper describes the basic idea of opportunistic routing in detail in chapter 3.1, where the two important concepts have been provided, the forwarding set (FS) and forwarding priority (FP). The METT metric depends on forwarding priority, therefore, the smaller METT is, the higher the priority of the nodes. In opportunistic routing in MP WSNs, because of the diversity of power selection and the neighbor sets in different power, the forwarding set may also be different. Let $\mathcal{F}_a^k$ donate the forwarding set of the node v_a in the k level forwarding power. Because different forwarding powers lead to the different forwarding sets, the successful forwarding probability and transmission rate, how to choose forwarding power directly impacts on efficiency and result of the routing, when each node sends data. Therefore, opportunistic routing is determined by three elements: the forwarding set, forwarding priority and forwarding power in MP sensor networks.

In the opportunistic routing, the power selecting process can be modeled as a Markov decision process (MDP for short).We know a MDP consists of five parts: decision-making period, state set, action set, income value and transition probability[18]. In each decision-making period, MDP remains in a state

S Decision-makers select an action from the action set of the current state S, which makes MDP transfer from the current state S to the next state S in a certain transition probability, and in this transfer process, we can calculate the corresponding value of the income. An important feature of the Markov process is that in each decision period, the calculation of income value and transition probabilities only depends on the current state S and the action selection, and is independent on the previous state and action. The goal of the MDP is that decision-makers decide the action selection in every decision-making period, obtaining the maximum or minimum sum of the income value in the whole process.

For opportunistic routing in MP sensor networks, each forwarding node is regarded as a state, and also a decision-maker. For each forwarding node, its action set is regarded as the forwarding power set which can be selected. Therefore, the decision-making process of the forwarding power is an MDP. The initial state of the MDP is the source node, the end state is the destination node. This paper will design the opportunistic routing scheme with the minimum expected transmission delay, therefore, in the MDP, the income value of each action is the expected transmission delay which is calculated by transition probabilities, and the goal of MDP is to find a series of state and action, making the income value minimize, that is, finding routing scheme with the minimum delay.

Definition 4 Optimal Forwarding Power of Sending node v_a, Π_a . For any forwarding node v_a, according to the MDP model, Only using the power $P_k (1 \leq k \leq n)$ as the transmitted power, it makes the expected transmission delay minimize, namely we can obtain the optimal routing scheme. So, P_k is the optimal forwarding power of sending node v_a, denoted by Π_a .

4.2   METT Routing Metric

Given the source node v_s and the destination node v_t, assume the for-warding set of the sending node v_a in n different forwarding power is $\mathcal{F}_a^1, \ldots, \mathcal{F}_a^n$. Based on the MDP model in chapter 4.1, for the nodes of any state v_a and v_b, the transition probability from the state v_a to v_b at the k-th action is:

$$\begin{cases} P_{a,k,b} = 0, & \text{if } v_b \notin \mathcal{F}_a^k; \\ P_{a,k,b} = p_{ab}^k \displaystyle\prod_{v_c \in \mathcal{F}_a^k \wedge v_c \prec v_b} \left(1 - p_{ac}^k\right), & \text{otherwise}; \end{cases} \tag{3}$$

where $v_c \prec v_b$ represents the forwarding priority is higher than the forwarding priority of v_b in forwarding set, so the formula (3) represents that the node v_b is as the node to continue forwarding data, if and only if v_b is in the forwarding set of v_a using k-level forwarding power, and the nodes that forwarding priority is higher than that of the node v_b do not receive the packet. If The state v_a transfers to its state in the k-th action, it represents that all nodes in forwarding set do not receive the packet, so the transition probability is as follows.

$$P_{a,k,a} = \prod_{v_c \in \mathcal{F}_a^k} \left(1 - p_{ac}^k\right); \tag{4}$$

So the increase value transferred from the state v_a to the state v_b at k-th action is the transmission delay t_{ab}^k that node v_a successfully forwards a data packet to node v_b using k-level forwarding power (see Definition 3). The increase value transferred to itself is $\max\limits_{v_c \in \mathcal{F}_a^k} (t_{ac}^k)$, denoted by t_{amax}^k.

We know that METT_a denotes the minimum expected transmission delay that node v_a successfully sends a packet to the destination node v_t. According to the above theory, the following gives the formula to calculate METT:

$$\text{METT}_a = \min_k \left(P_{a,k,a} \left(t_{amax}^k + \text{METT}_a \right) + \sum_{v_b \in \mathcal{F}_a^k} P_{a,k,b} \left(t_{ab}^k + \text{METT}_b \right) \right)$$
(5)

where $\text{METT}_t = 0$.

From organizing mathematical formula (5), solving the equation (5) is equivalent to solving the following equation:

$$\max \text{METT}_a$$

$$\text{s.t.} \text{METT}_a \leq P_{a,k,a} \left(t_{amax}^k + \text{METT}_a \right) + \sum_{v_b \in \mathcal{F}_a^k} P_{a,k,b} \left(t_{ab}^k + \text{METT}_b \right), \forall 1 \leq k \leq n$$

After organizing the equation, we get:

$$\max \text{METT}_a$$

$$\text{s.t.} \text{METT}_a \leq \frac{P_{a,k,a} t_{amax}^k + \sum\limits_{v_b \in \mathcal{F}_a^k} P_{a,k,b} \left(t_{ab}^k + \text{METT}_b \right)}{1 - P_{a,k,a}}$$

Therefore, we get the equation that computes METT:

$$\text{METT}_a = \min_k \frac{P_{a,k,a} t_{amax}^k + \sum\limits_{v_b \in \mathcal{F}_a^k} P_{a,k,b} \left(t_{ab}^k + \text{METT}_b \right)}{1 - P_{a,k,a}}$$
(6)

Node va calculates METT according to the formula (6), and obtains the optimal transmitted power:

$$\Pi_a = P_{k^*}.$$
(7)

Where $k^* = \arg\min\limits_{k} \dfrac{P_{a,k,a} t_{amax}^k + \sum\limits_{v_b \in \mathcal{F}_a^k} P_{a,k,b} \left(t_{ab}^k + \text{METT}_b \right)}{1 - P_{a,k,a}}$.

Finally, we can calculate the minimum expected transmission delay from the node v_s to the node v_t, called METT_s, using the formula (6). Each node can calculate the optimal transmitted power by the formula (7). We can obtain the opportunistic routing with minimum transmission delay by computing METT_s.

5 Model and Algorithm of Opportunistic Routing

In order to gain the opportunistic routing scheme, METT-based routing standards proposed in Chapter 4 can calculate the optimal forwarding power of each forwarding node. However, the condition of computing METT is that assume we know which the forwarding set each forwarding node belongs to, then, how to determine the forwarding set for each forwarding node that can get the optimal opportunistic routing scheme? This chapter firstly proposes the definition of opportunistic routing problem based on METT and a mathematical model, then, proposes the optimal routing algorithms.

5.1 Definition of Opportunistic Routing Problem Based on METT

In order to obtain the optimal opportunistic routing algorithms, we propose the routing metric of METT, and show the definition of the optimal opportunistic routing with minimum multi-power expected transmission time as follows:

Input: Given a source-destination node pair (v_s, v_t), $G= (V, L)$.

Output: A opportunistic routing scheme $\mathcal{P} = \{V_{\mathcal{P}}, \Pi_{\mathcal{P}}, \mathcal{F}_{\mathcal{P}}, \text{FP}\}$, where $\mathcal{P}$ consists of four parts, (1) $V_{\mathcal{P}}$: all of node set consisted of this scheme; (2) $\Pi_{\mathcal{P}}$: the optimal forwarding power set of each node in $V_{\mathcal{P}}$; (3) $\mathcal{F}_{\mathcal{P}}$: the forwarding set of each node in the optimal forwarding power; (4) FP: the forwarding priority of the nodes in the forwarding set.

Objective: Minimize end-to-end transmission delay, that is, to get the minimum delay METT_s from v_s to v_t. According to the above definition, solving METT_OOR problem is to obtain the four parts of routing scheme.

This paper takes the strategy that the smaller METT is, he higher the priority of the node is, so we calculate the METT of each node to get forwarding priority. All of node set $V_{\mathcal{P}}$ for (1) are determined by the result of (2) and (3). Because if the source node determines the optimal forwarding power $\Pi_s = P_{k^*}$ and the optimal forwarding set $\mathcal{F}_s^{k^*}$ in P_{k^*}, then, all the nodes in $\mathcal{F}_s^{k^*}$ also determines the optimal forwarding power, and so on, until reach the target node. All nodes of the routing consist of the forwarding nodes. So, it gets the optimal opportunistic routing algorithms. Therefore, the key to solve METT_OOR is to solve (2) and (3) $\Pi_{\mathcal{P}}$ and $\mathcal{F}_{\mathcal{P}}$ in the four parts.

5.2 Model of METT_OOR Problem

According to the above definition of METT_OOR problem and the method of METT calculation, here is a METT_OOR problem model based on METT to solve METT_OOR. Firstly, given the definition of two variables:

$$x_{ab}^k = \begin{cases} 1, \text{if} v_b \notin \mathcal{N}_a^k; \\ 0, \text{otherwise}; \end{cases}$$

$$y_{ab}^k = y_{ab}^k \cdot x_{ab}^k == \begin{cases} 1, \text{if} v_b \notin \mathcal{F}_a^k; \\ 0, \text{otherwise}; \end{cases}$$

Let the variable x_{ab}^k donate whether v_b is the neighbor node of v_a in the k-level power or not, and the variable y_{ab}^k donate whether v_b belongs to forwarding set of v_a in the k-level power or not, and the results that multiplies with the variable x_{ab}^k is to meet the constraints $\mathcal{F}_a^k \subseteq \mathcal{N}_a^k$. So, the model to solve METT_OOR based on METT as follows:

$$\min \text{METT}_s \qquad (8)$$

$$\text{s.t.} \text{METT}_a = \frac{P_{a,k,a} t_{amax}^k + \sum\limits_{v_b \in V} y_{ab}^k P_{a,k,b} \left(t_{ab}^k + \text{METT}_b\right)}{1 - - P_{a,k,a}} \forall v_a \in V \qquad (9)$$

$$\text{METT}_t = 0 \qquad (10)$$

The objective function (8) is to minimize end-to-end expected transmission delay from v_s to v_t. The recursive equation (9) is to compute METT of any node, while equation (10) gives the export of the recursive equation. The above model shows that in order to solve the optimal routing scheme $\mathcal{P}$,if we solve the variable y_{ab}^k ($\forall v_a, v_b \in V, 1 \leq k \leq n$), that is, calculate the forwarding set for each node in the different forwarding power. Then, it can obtain the optimal forwarding power and the optimal forwarding set ($\Pi_\mathcal{P}$ and $\mathcal{F}_\mathcal{P}$) to minimize METT$_s$ using formula (6) and (7), so as to solve the problem.

How to solve y_{ab}^k? The above METT_OOR model provides a plain algorithm: in order to solve the forwarding set $\mathcal{F}_a^k$ of v_a in the k-level forwarding power, we can traverse 0 and 1 combinations of all the variables y_{ab}^k ($v_b \in \mathcal{N}_a^k$), and choose a combination to minimize METT$_a$. Finally, we get the forwarding set$\mathcal{F}_a^k$. For METT_OOR problems, this paper uses the idea of Dijkstra algorithm, and puts forward the optimal opportunistic routing algorithm.

5.3 Optimal Routing Algorithm for METT_OOR

To solve the METT_OOR problem, and minimize METT in opportunistic routing scheme,this paper proposes a **D**ijkstra-**A**dvanced **O**pportunistic **R**outing Algorithm (**DAOR**). Given a directed topology $G = (V, L)$ and a destination node v_t, The DAOR algorithm can calculate the expected transmission delay of all nodes to the destination node, namely METT$_a$ ($\forall v_a \in V$). In order to describe the DAOR algorithm better, METT$_a^k$ denotes the minimum transmission delay of v_a in the forwarding power P_k, and $\mathcal{F}_a^k$ denotes the corresponding forwarding set. In DAOR algorithm, define two set of nodes: S and Q, where S denotes the set of nodes that have calculated the minimum METT in the process of DAOR algorithm, while $Q = V\text{-}S$ denotes the set of nodes that have not yet calculated the minimum METT. DAOR algorithm is algorithm 1. It takes a time complexity of $O(Nn)$ in the initial work with 10 steps in algorithm 1, where N stands for the number of node in G, n is the different level of power. In the 11th step, it takes a time of $O(N)$ to all-node coverage, a run time in the 12th step of $O(N)$, therefore, the total time we need in the 11th-12th step is $O(N^2)$ the

Algorithm 1. Dijkstra-Advanced Opportunistic Routing.

Input: $G = (V, L)$, v_t;
Output: METT_a ($\forall v_a \in V$)
1: **for** $\forall v_a \in V$ **do**
2:     $\text{METT}_a = \infty$
3:     $\Pi_a = P_{k^*} = -\infty, k^* = 0$
4:     $\mathcal{F}_a^{k^*} = NULL$
5:     **for** $\forall k 1 \le k \le n$ **do**
6:         $\text{METT}_a^k = \infty$
7:         $\mathcal{F}_a^k = NULL$
8:     **end for**
9: **end for**
10: $\text{METT}_t = 0$
11: $S = NULL$
12: $Q = V$
13: **while** $(Q! = NULL)$ **do**
14:     search the node v_b with the minimum METT in Q
15:     $S = S \cup v_b$
16:     **for** $l_{ab} \in L$ **do**
17:         $\text{DOMCP}(a, b) = P_m$
18:         **for** $\forall k\ m \le k \le n$ **do**
19:             **if** $\text{METT}_a^k \text{METT}_b$ **then**
20:                 $J = \mathcal{F}_a^k \cup v_b$
21:                 compute $\text{METT}_a^k(J)$ in the forwarding set J according to the formula(6)

22:                 **if** $\text{METT}_a^k\ \text{METT}_a^k(J)$ **then**
23:                     $\text{METT}_a^k = \text{METT}_a^k(J)$
24:                     $\mathcal{F}_a^k = J$
25:                     **if** $\text{METT}_a^k\ \text{METT}_a$ **then**
26:                         $\text{METT}_a = \text{METT}_a^k$
27:                         $\mathcal{F}_a^{k^*} = \mathcal{F}_a^k$
28:                         $k^* = krt$
29:                     **end if**
30:                 **end if**
31:             **end if**
32:         **end for**
33:     **end for**
34: **end while**

---

time complexity in the 14th-16th step is $O(En)$, E is the number of links. So the time complexity of algorithm 1 is $O(Nn + N^2 + En)$.

Theorems 1. According to the problem of METT_OOR, DAOR is the best routing algorithm, when given a directed graph $G = (V, L)$ and the target node v_t, we can get the minimum expected transport delay METT_a of any node v_a in graph G by running the DAOR algorithm.

Prove: The optimal prove of DAOR algorithm is equivalent to the following factsIn any time, set S and set $Q = V - S$, when node v_a from set Q add into set S, node v_a has calculated the minimum expected transmit delay METT_a.

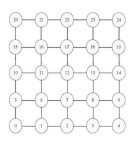

Fig. 2. Grid topology of 1-level power

This fact needs to prove two aspects: (1) after adding the node va into S, METT_a will not be changed since any node is added into S; (2) it gains the best forwarding set when then node v_a is added into S. For (1), if $\text{METT}_b \geq \text{METT}_a$, the METT_a not become smaller when the node v_b is added into the optimal forwarding set of the node v_a, and because the METT of any node in Q is greater than METT_a, so it does not change METT_a when any node is added into S after the node v_a is added into S. For (2), based on DAOR algorithm, the nodes that are added into the optimal forwarding set $\mathcal{F}_a^{k^*}$ of the node v_a, are added according on the METT value from small to large. It is because DAOR algorithm selects the node with the smallest value of the METT to add into S each time, and it can guarantee that DAOR algorithm has obtained the optimal forwarding set when the node v_a is added into S. The theorem is proved. The detailed proof for DAOR algorithm can be found in the proof of the Dijkstra algorithm [19].

6   Performance Evaluation

Simulation environment settings are as follows: the sensor nodes are distributed in grid network topologies, and the distance between adjacent nodes is 20m. We investigate the impact of changes in network size on the experimental results, respectively test the 5 groups of size : 5*5, 10*10, 15*15, 20*20 and 25*25. We select node v_0 at the left corner of the network as the destination, and the other nodes as sources, so there are 24 different source-destination pairs considered to compute the average of METT.We first consider a grid setting as illustrated in Fig.2. There are 25 nodes uniformly distributed in a square region of 100m100m. In addition to achieve the performance of DAOR algorithm in the multi-level power and the single-level power, we compare them against the shortest transmission delay routing algorithm (STTR). From the following two aspects compared:1) multi-power routing algorithm vs.single-power routing algorithm;2) opportunistic routing algorithm vs.traditional routing algorithms.

We implement the simulator by C++, and the main parameters involved in the experiment are set as follows: the test takes three transmitted power P_1, P_2 and P_3, the communication radius corresponding to the power are $R_1=25$,

R_2=50m and R_3=60m, the size of a packet is b=32Byte. The successful forwarding probability p_{ab}^k is a function related to the transmitted power in the formula (1). Therefore, the test sets successful forwarding probability in the three transmitted power respectively are p^2=0.5, p^1=0.4 and p^3=0.25. In contrast, the delay to send a packet in a different power is t^1=2ms, t^2=2.5ms and t^3=4ms.

6.1 Multi-Power vs. Single-Power

This set of experiments investigates the end-to-end transmission delay of DAOR algorithm in multi-power and single-power, and experimental results are represented in Figure 3. In Figure 3, MP_DAOR denotes DAOR algorithm that each node can choose three different transmitted powers, namely multi-power DAOR algorithm, and 3P_DAOR denotes DAOR algorithm that each node only chooses P3 as the transmitted power, namely a single-power DAOR algorithm.

From Figure 3, we know MP_DAOR algorithm is better than 3P_DAOR algorithm. Compared single-power DAOR algorithm, 2P_DAOR algorithm is superior to 1P_DAOR and 3P_DAOR algorithm, because nodes use P_1 as the transmitted power, and the transmitted power is small, the radius of the corresponding communications small, resulting in increasing path hops, and the path transmission delay; but nodes use P_3 as the transmitted power, and the transmitted power is greater than P_1, the radius of the corresponding communications becomes greater, resulting in reducing path hops, but the power becomes greater, leading that interference becomes larger, so, it makes the transmission quality of each link lower, and increases the path transmission delay. Therefore, it makes the minimum transmission delay using moderate transmitted power P_2.

In multi-power routing algorithm, in order to investigate the optimal power of each node, Figure 4 shows the optimal power of each node for DAOR algorithm and STTR algorithm. From the figure 4, we know the nodes which select the power P_1 as the optimal power account for 8%, the nodes which select the power P_2 as the optimal power account for 92%, but there are no nodes to select power P_3 as the optimal power. This shows that the transmitter power is too small or too large that will increase transmission delay, therefore, it is essential to select the appropriate transmitted power.

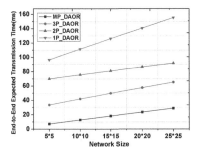

Fig. 3. multi-power vs.single-power

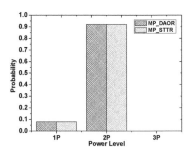

Fig. 4. the optimal power

N

6.2 Opportunistic Routing vs. Traditional Routing

In order to reflect the advantages of the opportunistic routing compared to the traditional routing, this paper realizes the shortest expected transmission delay of the traditional routing algorithm (STTR), and experimental results are represented in Figure 5. From MP_DAOR and MP_STTR in Figure 5, we know the delay of opportunistic routing is less than the delay of traditional routing, because opportunistic routing chooses multiple nodes as forwarding nodes, effectively improves successful forwarding probability, and reduces the transmission delay, but traditional routing, chooses only one node as forwarding node, reduces the successful forwarding probability, and increases the transmission delay. Comparing the MP_STTR and 1P_STTR in Figure 5, whether it is the opportunistic routing or traditional routing algorithm, the node to take multi-level transmitted power can effectively reduce end-to-end transmission delay.

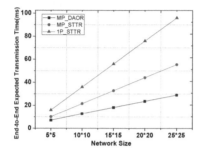

Fig. 5. Opportunistic Routing vs. Traditional Routing

7 Conclusion

In this paper, we study opportunistic routing in MPMR WSNs. In order to minimize expectations of the end-to-end transmission delay, we propose a opportunistic routing algorithm, called DAOR. The experimental results show that compared to traditional routing algorithms, DAOR can gain smaller end-to-end transmission delay, and significantly reduce the end-to-end transmission delay.

Acknowledgments. This work is supported in part by the National Natural Science Foundation of China (NSFC) under Grant Nos.61070193, Nos.61100048, the Foundation of University Science and Technology Innovation Team Building Program of Hei-longjiang Province under 2011PYTD002, Heilongjiang Province Founds for Distinguished Young Scientists under Grant Nos.JC201104, Heilongjiang Province Science and Technique Foundation under Grant Nos.GC09A109.

References

1. Gomez, J., Campbell, A.T.: Variable-Range Transmission Power Control in Wireless Ad Hoc Networks. IEEE Transactions on Mobile Computing, 87–99 (2007)

2. Zhang, X., Gong, H.G., Liu, M., Lu, S.L., Wu, J.: Quantitative analysis of the effect of transmitting power on the capacity of wireless ad hoc networks. In: ACM MOBIHOC, pp. 231–240. IEEE Press, New York (2010)

3. Bhatia, B.R., Kashya, A., Li, L.: The Power Balancing Problem in Energy Constrained Multi-hop Wireless Networks. In: INFOCOM, pp. 2553–2561. IEEE Press, New York (2007)

4. Shila, D.M., Cheng, Y., Anjali, T., Wan, P.J.C.: Extracing More Capacity from Multi-Channel Multi-Radio Wireless Networks by Exploiting Power. In: IEEE ICDCS, pp. 858–867. IEEE Press, New York (2010)

5. Wang, B., Han, Z., Liu, K.J.R.: Distributed relay selection and power control for multiuser cooperative communication networks using buyer-seller game. In: INFO-COM, pp. 544–552. IEEE Press, New York (2007)

6. Wang, Y., Lui, J.C.S., Chiu, D.: Understanding the paradoxical effects of power control on the capacity of wireless networks. IEEE Transactions on Mobile Computing, 406–413 (2009)

7. De Couto, D.S.J., Aguayo, D., Bicket, J., Morris, R.: A High-Throughput Path Metric for Multi-Hop Wireless Routing. In: ACM MOBICOM, pp. 134–142. ACM Press, New York (2003)

8. Koksal, C., Balakrishnan, H.: Quality-Aware Routing Metrics for Time-Varying Wireless Mesh Networks. IEEE J. Select. Areas Commun., 1984–1994 (2006)

9. Jakllari, G., Eidenbenz, S., Hengartner, N., Krishnamurthy, S.V., Faloutsos, M.: Link Positions Matter: A Noncommutative Routing Metric for Wireless Mesh Network. In: INFOCOM, pp. 744–752. IEEE Press, New York (2008)

10. Draves, R., Padhye, J., Zill, B.: Routing in Multi-Radio, Multi-Hop Wireless Mesh Networks. In: ACM MOBICOM, pp. 114–128. IEEE Press, New York (2004)

11. Li, H.K., Cheng, Y., Zhou, C., Zhuang, W.H.: Minimizing End-to-End Delay: A Novel Routing Metric for Multi-Radio Wireless Mesh Networks. In: INFOCOM, pp. 46–54. IEEE Press, New York (2009)

12. Biswas, S., Morris, R.: Exor: Opportunistic multi-hop routing for wireless networks. In: SIGCOMM, pp. 133–137. IEEE Press, New York (2005)

13. Zeng, K., Yang, Z.Y., Lou, W.J.: On End-to-end Throughput of Opportunistic Routing in Multirate and Multi-hop Wireless Networks. In: INFOCOM, pp. 1490–1498. IEEE Press, New York (2008)

14. Zeng, K., Yang, Z.Y., Lou, W.J.: Opportunistic Routing in Multi-radio Multi-channel Multi-hop Wireless Networks. In: INFOCOM, pp. 3512–3521. IEEE Press, New York (2010)

15. Zorzi, M., Rao, R.R.: Geographic random forwarding for ad hoc and sensor networks: energy and latency performance. IEEE Transactions on Mobile Computing, 349–365 (2003)

16. Fussler, H., Widmer, J., Kasemann, M., Mauve, M., Hartenstein, H.: Contention-based forwarding for mobile ad-hoc networks. Elseviers Ad Hoc Networks, 351–369 (2003)

17. Jain, S., Das, S.R.: Exploiting Path Diversity in the Link Layer in Wireless Ad Hoc Networks. Ad Hoc Networks, 805–825 (2008)

18. Puterman, M.L.: Markov Decision Processes: Discrete Stochastic Dynamic Programming. John Wiley & Sons, New York (1994)

19. Cormen, T.T., Leiserson, C.E., Rivest, R.L.: Inroduction to algorithms. MIT Press, Cambridge (2001)

Improved DV-Hop Localization Algorithm Based on RSSI Value and Hop Correction

Zhengwei Guo[1], Lin Min[2], Hui Li[3], and Wenjian Wu[1]

[1] School of Computer and Information Engineering, Institute of Image Processing and Pattern Recognition,Henan University, Kaifeng, Henan, 475001, China
[2] Network Information Center Office, Henan University, Kaifeng, Henan, 475001, China
[3] Henan University Minsheng College, Kaifeng, Henan, 475004, China

Abstract. On the basis of the analysis of the relation between network's topologyand localization precisionan improved DV-Hop algorithm based on hop correction is put forward. Firstly, RSSI value is used to correct the distance between unknown node and reference nodes in the range of single hop; secondly, a certain amount of correction value is added to the original hop between unknown node and reference nodes to further reduce the distance error between them. Simulation result shows that improved algorithm improves the localization precision.

Keywords: WSN, DV-Hop, correction.

1 Introduction

Currently, existing wireless sensor network algorithms can be roughly divided into range-based algorithm and range-free algorithm.The former has a high requirement of hardware because of the measurement of distance or angle between unknown node and reference nodes. The latter has a low requirement of hardware because of it's relying on network connectivity for the localization of unknown node. DV-hop is a typical range-free localization algorithm, which localization error is reflected in the estimation of network's average hop-distance and the distance between unknown node and reference nodes [1], [2]. As for classic DV-Hop algorithmnetwork' average hop-distance gained by unknown node is transferred from the nearest reference nodewhose single calculation of network's average hop-distance might not reflect the average hop-distance of the whole network truly.Therefore improved algorithm aimed at correcting network's average hop-distance is put forward by paper [3], according to which each reference node not only broadcasts its own hop and coordinate, but also broadcasts the network's average hop-distance calculated by it. Literature [4] and [5] add a certain amount of value to different network's average hop-distance to correct the one calculated by different reference nodes. Literature [6] utilizes the minimum mean square error to to correct network's average hop-distance.

R. Wang and F. Xiao (Eds.): CWSN 2012, CCIS 334, pp. 97–102, 2013.
© Springer-Verlag Berlin Heidelberg 2013

2   DV-Hop Localization Algorithm

As for range-free localization algorithm, centroid algorithm and DV-Hop algorithm is typical and commonly used. Centroid algorithm can attain a high precision of localization in the circumstance of high density of reference nodes, while the localization effect is bad when reference nodess are sparse. DV-Hop is a kind of localization algorithm based on distance-vector and hop information. Compared to centroid algorithm, DV-Hop utilizes distance-vector value and acquires the hop information of the node beyond its communication range through routing and switching. Its localization processing is as bellow

1. Each node broadcasts its information of location,hop and node's sequence number(unknown node broadcasts only hop information).Through distance-vector informationnode receives the broadcast and adds 1 to certain hop, then, unknown node can acquire the whole hop information between it and reference nodes while the network is stable.
2. Reference node calculates average hop-distance according to the distance and hop information between it and other reference nodes, that is it can be expressed as the equation below

$$hopdistance = \frac{\sum\limits_{i \neq j} \sqrt{(x_i - x_j)^2 + (y_i - y_j)^2}}{\sum\limits_{i \neq j} hop_j} \qquad (1)$$

in this equation(x_i, y_i) is the coordinate of reference node i, (x_i, y_i) is the coordinate of reference node j, hop^j represents the hop between reference nodes i and j .Thenthis node broadcasts again this average hop-distance information and unknown node receives the average hop-distance transfered from the nearest reference nodethat is the first broadcast information.At this pointthe distance between unknown node and reference node can be expressed by getting average hop-distance multiplied by hop.
3. When the distance values between unknown node and reference nodes are gained by unknown nodeits coordinate can be calculated through trilateration or least squares.

3   Improved DV-Hop Localization Algorithm Based on RSSI Value and Hop Correction

Existing localization algorithmes are mainly aimed at correcting the hop and distance between reference nodes to improve network's average hop-distance and get it much closer to the value calculated in real network topology. However, these algorithmes don't take the relation between unknown node and reference nodes into account, which results to the larger error value between them. Based on this consideration, this paper puts forward a DV-Hop localization algorithm based on hop correction.

3.1 Hop Correction between Unknown Node and Reference Nodes

The paths between reference nodes are usually not straight lines, so, mthe network's average hop-distance calculated under this condition usually has a larger error compared to the network's average hop-distance under the condition that reference nodes are evenly distributed.Therefore, through the correction of network's average hop-distance calculated by different reference nodes, this paper adds this correction value to the average hop-distance of the whole network to acquire the ultimate network's average hop-distance of each reference node. This can reduce localization error to a certain degree, but, the correction of network's average hop-distance of reference nodes increases the complexity of algorithm. This paper begins from the the hop between unknown node and reference nodes, the more the hops between them, the path between them is more deviant from straight line, then, estimation distance attained by getting network's average hop-distance multiplied by hop has a certain amount of error compared to the real value between them. Therefore, this paper adds a certain amount of correction value to the real hop between unknown node and reference nodes, that is

$$weight = k \cdot \frac{hop_{ij}}{hopdis\tan ce_{ave}} \qquad (2)$$

in this equation, hop_{ij} is the hop between unknown node i and unknown node j, $hopdistance_{ave}$ is the average hop-distance of the whole network, k is adjustment coefficient. The more the hop_{ij} value, the more the hop between unknown node and reference nodes, and the path is more unreliable, which means that more correction value should be added. The corrected distance value between unknown node and reference nodes is expressed as below

$$distance_{ij} = hopdistance_{ave} \cdot (hop_{ij} + k\frac{hop_{ij}}{hopdistance_{ave}}) \qquad (3)$$

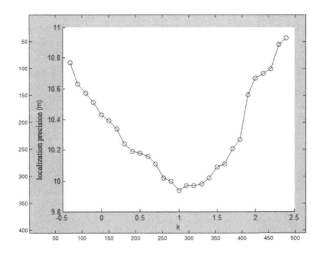

Fig. 1. The relation between k value and localization precision in equation (4)

that is

$$distance_{ij} = hopdistance_{ave} \cdot hop_{ij} + k \cdot hop_{ij} \qquad (4)$$

in this equation, $distance_{ij}$ is the estimation distance between unknown node i and unknown node j, hop_{ij} is the hop between unknown node i and unknown node j, $hopdistance_{ij}$ is the average hop-distance of the whole network, k is adjustment coefficient. According to experiment simulation, the localization error of improved localization algorithm has a close relation with the value of k. For example, under the condition that node communication radius is 30m, number of nodes is 100, the proportion of reference nodes is 10%, the relation figure between k value and localization precision is shown as figure 1. According to figure 1, the localization error is close to the least value when k approaches 1. In localization process, k value can be specifically selected on the basis of real application scene.

3.2   Single Hop Handling between Unknown Node and Reference Node

When the hop between unknown node and reference node is 1, the calculated distance value between them is usually accompanied by larger error. As shown in figure 2 Assuming unknown node A has a communication radius of R, within which node B and node C are included. However, error is caused because A utilizes the same hop 1 to calculate its distance to B and C. As reference node C is much closer to A, the estimation distance value between A and C calculated by unknown node through getting network's average hop-distance multiplied by hop 1 might be larger than the real value between them. Thus, with this inaccurate distance value, larger localization error might be caused. So, this paper puts forward single-hop correction method based on RSSI value.Unknown node receives the radio signal of reference node and compares its intensity value to the received intensity value under the circumstance that the distance between unknown and reference node is $\frac{R}{2}$ (this method involves only the comparision of signal intensity, ranging is not involved). If the former value is larger than the latter value, the hop between unknown node and reference node is 1, otherwise the hop is 0.5. This method gets hop value discreted to correct the distance value between unknown node and reference nodes when the hop between them is 1 and improves its credibility.

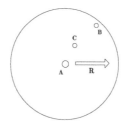

Fig. 2. Distance calculation(hop between unknown node and reference nodes is 1)

4   Algorithm Simulation

We utilize MATLAB to simulate the algorithm, which is performed in a square zone that is 100m × 100m. The number of nodes is 100, in which reference nodes have a proportion of 8% to 16%. The communication radius is 30m,40m and 50m. To attain a better statistics result, we perform a 500 times simulation calculation.With node communication radius that is 30m, 40m and 50m, also under the circumstance that reference nodes' proportion is changed gradually, the error statistics of classic DV-Hop localization algorithm, algorithm put forward by literature [6] and algorithm put forward by this paper is as shown in figure 3-5

Simulation result shows that when node communication radius is 30m, the improved algorithm put forward by this paper attains respectively a increase of 9.4%-13.7% and 2.9%-5.2% compared to classic DV-Hop localization algorithm and the improved localization algorithm in literature [6]; when node communication radius is 40m, the improved algorithm put forward by this paper attains respectively a increase of 10.4%-14.3% and 2.4%-5.6% compared to classic

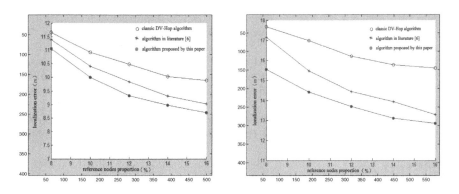

Fig. 3. communication radius: 30m   **Fig. 4.** communication radius: 40m

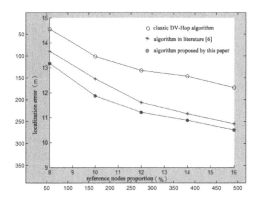

Fig. 5. communication radius: 50m

DV-Hop localization algorithm and the improved localization algorithm in literature [6]; when node communication radius is 50m and the reference nodes proportion is changed gradually, the improved algorithm put forward by this paper attains respectively a increase of 12.1%-17.7% and 3.3%-9.4% compared to classic DV-Hop localization algorithm and the improved localization algorithm in literature [6].

4.1   Conclusion

DV-Hop is a typical and commonly used range-free localization algorithm, which has a drawback of low localization precision. Through the research of network's topology, this paper gets the distance between unknown node and reference nodes much closer to real value by correcting the hop between them. And the simulation result shows that the improved algorithm improves the localization precision.

References

1. Luo, W., Jiang, X.-Z., Sheng, M.-M.: Selective DV-Hop localization algorithm for wireless sensor networks. Transducer and Microsystem Technologies 31(3), 71–77 (2012)
2. Xiao, M.-H., Zhou, Z.-P.: Weighted average hop-distance localization algorithm for wireless sensor nodes. Computer Engineering and Design 31(1), 78–85 (2010)
3. Peng, G., Cao, Y., Sun, L.: Study of Localiczation Schemes for Wireless Sensor Networks. Computer Engineering and Applications 40(35), 27–29 (2004)
4. Li, H., Xiong, S., Liu, Y., Duan, P.: An Improvement of DV-Hop Localization Algorithm for Wireless Sensor Network. Chinese Journal of Sensors and Actuators 24(12), 1782–1786 (2011)
5. Zhang, J., Wu, Y.-H., Shi, F., Geng, F.: Localization algorithm based on DV-HOP for wireless sensor networks. Journal of Computer Applications 30(2), 323–326 (2010)
6. Ji, W.-W., Liu, Z.: Study on the Application of DV-Hop Localization Algorithms to Random Sensor Networks. Journal of Electronics and Information Technology 30(4), 970–974 (2008)

A Candidate Forwarder Set Based Channel Assignment for Opportunistic Routing in Multi-radio Wireless Mesh Networks

Shiming He[1], Dafang Zhang[1], Kun Xie[1], Xiaan Bi[1], Hong Qiao[1], Ji Zhang[1], and Bin Zeng[2]

[1] College of Information Science and Engineering
Hunan University, HNU, Changsha, China
[2] China Mobile Group Hunan Company Limited, Changsha, China
{smhe,dfzhang,cskxie}@hnu.edu.cn

Abstract. Opportunistic routing (OR) involves multiple forwarding candidates to relay packets by taking advantage of the broadcast nature and multi-user diversity of the wireless medium. Compared with Traditional Routing (TR), OR can evidently improve the end to end throughput of Wireless Mesh Networks (WMNs). At present, there are many achievements concerning OR in the single radio wireless network. However, the study of OR in multi-radio wireless network stays the beginning stage. In this paper, we focus on OR in multi-radio multi-channel WMNs. Directly using the existing channel assignment leads to decreasing the number of candidate forwarder and the performance of OR. According to OR with one-to-more transmission mode, the Candidate Forwarder Set based Channel Assignment (CFSCA) for OR is proposed. Firstly, according to the candidate forwarder selected by routing, we bound the sender node and its candidate forwarders as a Candidate Forwarder Set(CFS). Then we calculate the interference among all the CFSs. Then the channel assignment for OR is described as a minimum CFS interference optimization problem, which must obey the constraints of the channel number of CFS and the number of radio interfaces. The evaluation results show that CFSCA improves 25.2%, 10%, 19% of the aggregative throughput than random, uniform and tradition channel assignment, respectively.

Keywords: wireless mesh networks, multi-radio and multi-channel, opportunistic routing, channel assignment.

1 Introduction

Opportunistic routing (OR) has been recently proposed as a radically new paradigm, which exploits the broadcast nature and multi-user diversity of the wireless channel to increase the reliability of packet transmissions. When a packet is transmitted, the sender broadcasts it directly without pre-selecting next-hop node as traditional routing (TR). It is possible to be received by multiple neighbor nodes of the sender. Among the nodes that receive the packet, the node

R. Wang and F. Xiao (Eds.): CWSN 2012, CCIS 334, pp. 103–116, 2013.
© Springer-Verlag Berlin Heidelberg 2013

"closest" to the ultimate destination should be the one that forwards the packet. OR defers the selection of the next hop for a packet until it has learnt the set of nodes which have actually received that packet. In a large dense network there is a penalty to using too many nodes as potential forwarders, since the costs of agreement grow with the number of participants. Thus OR must choose only the most useful nodes as participants called candidate forwarders. Since OR involves multiple candidate forwarders into routing packets, it is more suitable for unreliable wireless link, especially long distance and high loss links. And recent researches [1-5] have validate that OR can evidently promote the end to end throughput of multi-hop wireless network, especially Wireless Mesh Networks (WMNs)[6].

In single-radio and single-channel wireless networks the gain of OR is exploited fully, but the performance of OR in multi-radio multi-channel wireless networks is still unknown. Previously suggested opportunistic protocols [1-5] take account of neither possible concurrent transmission over 12/3 orthogonal channels in 802.11a/b or the wireless nodes equipped with multi-radio interface in WMNs. Equipping each node with multiple radios is a promising approach for improving the capacity of WMNs. The availability of cheap, off-the-shelf commodity hardware also makes multi-radio solutions economically attractive. Hence OR in multi-radio multi-channel WMNs become a concerned field recently.

There are preliminary progresses [7-10] to the multi-channel opportunistic routing, which can be classified to two kinds. i) The nodes are equipped with one radio [7] which can switch to different orthogonal channels. It's not suitable for multi-radio network. ii) The nodes are equipped with multi-radio [8-10]. However, [8,9] are only for single flow, and [10] is for multiple flows but assume that the number of radio and channel are equal. Neither of them proposes is feasible solution for OR in multi-radio multi-channel WMNs. On the other hand, the performance of opportunistic routing depends on candidate forwarder. Directly using the existing channel assignment [11-16] leads to decreasing the number of candidate forwarder and the performance of OR.

In this paper, we focus on OR in multi-radio multi-channel WMNs. Given the routing path from source to destination, we design the Candidate Forwarder Set based Channel Assignment (CFSCA) for OR, according to the one-to-more transmission mode of OR and the overhear opportunity of multiple candidate forwarders, Firstly according to the candidate forwarder selected by routing, CFSCA bound the sender node and its candidate forwarders as a Candidate Forwarder Set. Then we calculate the interferences among all the Candidate Forwarder Sets. Then the channel assignment for OR is described as a minimum Candidate Forwarder Set interference optimization problem, with constraints of the channel number of Candidate Forwarder Set and the number of radio interfaces. The evaluation results show that CFSCA improves 25.2%, 10%, 19% of the aggregative throughput than random, uniform and tradition channel assignment, respectively.

The rest of this paper is organized as follows. Section 2 briefly reviews the concepts of OR and related works. The system model and problem analysis are introduced in Section 3 and Section 4. We propose the new channel assignment for opportunistic routing in Section 5. Section 6 discusses the performance of the new channel assignment. Conclusions are drawn in Section 7.

2   The Concepts of OR and Related Works

2.1   The Concepts of Opportunistic Routing

Let's describe the concepts of OR via a simple example. There are five wireless nodes in a chain WMNs as shown Figure 1. The digit above the edge between two nodes represents the packet delivery ratio(PDR) of the link between them, that is a packet through this link can be correct decoded with PDR probability. The PDR is equal the total number of sending packet divided by the number of correct receiving packet. The longer the distance is, the lower the PDR is. In the example, there is a session from node 0 to node 4.

Fig. 1. The concepts of OR

Traditional routing (TR) could forward data through some sub-sequence of the chain, for example 0-4 or 0-1-2-3-4. Every packet need transmit several times for packet loss and multi-hop respectively. In the former case, if a packet transmission falls short of node 4, node 1, 2 and 3 overhear the packet due to the broadcast nature of wireless channel. Retransmission of the packet from node 1, 2or 3 is better than from node 0. In the latter case, if a packet from node 0 to node 1 is correctly overheard by node 2, 3 or 4, it is wasteful of channel resource that node 1 forwards the packet to node 2. Whichever path is chose, the transmission unit is one link, from one node to one node. Figure 2(a) presents the transmission unit of the four hops path.

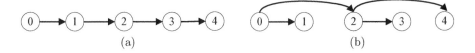

Fig. 2. The transmission mode:(a)Traditional Routing (b)Opportunistic Routing

OR exploit the diversity of multi-user and use multiple candidate forwarders instead of pre-selected one next-hop. OR defers the selection of the next hop for a packet until the packet has been actually received. The closest node to the destination among the candidate forwarders which received the packet should forward this packet. OR can reduce the number of transmissions and improve throughput. In Figure 1, node 4, 3, 2 and 1 are the candidate forwarders of node 0. If a packet transmission from node 0 falls short of node 4, reaching only node 1 and 2, then node 2 which is the closest node to node 4 become the real forwarder and forward the packet. If a packet from node 0 is received by node 4, 2, and 1, node 2 and 1 don't forward the packet since node 4 is the ultimate destination. Compared with TR, OR is more suitable for the unreliable wireless link. Due to the multiple candidate forwarders, each sender may have multiple receivers. Although only one of the receivers will forward the packet, its one-to-more transmission mode. The transmission unit is a set of links which share the same sender, as the Figure 2(b).

2.2   Related Works

We begin with a brief survey of prior work on multi-channel opportunistic routing and a summary of channel assignment.

i)Multi-channel OR

There are preliminary progresses [7-10] on the multi-channel opportunistic routing. MCExOR[7] solves the problem of selecting candidate forwarders under single-radio multi-channel environment. In MCExOR, channel assignment and routing policy are independent respectively, so it can be used together with any channel assignment. However, since MCExOR only fits the single radio network and lacks specific channel assignment method, it is essential to find out OR suitable for multi radio multi channel network.

Reference [8] builds a model for opportunistic routing and concurrent sets of multi-radio multi-channel, and gains the theoretical upper bound of single flow throughput by linear programming. After determining the candidate forwarders, also called the routing path, [8] try to find the best method of channel assignment and scheduling to gain the optimal throughput. Wu. et al. present a simple extension for MORE[3] (EMORE) to work in a multi-radio multi-channel setting in [9]. And a Workload-Aware Channel Assignment algorithm (WACA) for OR is designed. WACA identifies the nodes with high workloads in a flow as bottlenecks, and tries to assign channels to these nodes with high priority. Assuming that the number of radio and channel are equal, SCAOR [10] selects channel for each flow. Reference [8] needs strict time synchronization and neglects the delay of switching channel, leading to hardly extending to realistic network. WACA is the first static channel assignment for OR. However it is only suitable for the kind of OR with network coding like MORE. Those OR without network coding are incompatible with WACA. Further WACA deals with channel assignment for single flow. SCAOR is for multiple flows but assume that the number of radio and channel are equal. Neither of them proposes is feasible solution for OR in multi-radio multi-channel WMNs.

ii)Channel assignment

Although there are lots of progresses in channel assignment [11-13] field, these methods always are based on two kind of interference mode: Protocol Interference Model [14, 15] and Physical Interference Model [16].

In spite of the node-based nature of the interference, this interference criterion of protocol model and physical model are modeled through an edge-based or link-based constraint. [11-13] base on the link interference and assign channel to link to minimize the total interference among all links. They are suitable for tradition routing because the transmission mode of tradition routing is one-to-one or one link. But the transmission mode of OR is one-to-more or a set of link sharing the sender, the link based constrain is against the overhear opportunity of multiple candidate forwarders. Directly using the existing channel assignment [11-16] leads to decreasing the number of candidate forwarder and the performance of OR. Hence, how to design a new channel assignment for OR with taking advantage of OR and multi-channels is an urgent problem.

3   System Model

Figure 3 depicts a simple WMN architecture which consists of a lot of mesh routers. Our model of the previously described mesh architecture is a extension weighted undirected graph denoted by G=(V,E,P), where V is the set of n nodes, E is the set of l links, and P is a weight function such that $P(e) = P(i,j) > 0$ is the PDR of link $e = (i,j) \in E$ according to the propagation model. Every node is equipped with R radio interfaces. There are K orthogonal wireless channels. A node i is said to be a neighbor of node j if i can correctly decode the packets transmitted by j at least with the possibility $P0(P0 << 1)$, that is the P(i,j) is greater than P0. We assume that P is symmetrical and independent, that is $P(i,j) = P(j,i)$. The neighbor set of node j is denoted by $\Re(i)$. The PDR between j and other node i which doesn't belong to $\Re(i)$ is zero, that is $P(j,i) = 0$.

Fig. 3. The Wireless Mesh Networks

Given a static WMN with multi-radio interfaces, multiple flows and the paths of flows, we wish to assign channels to each node in the WMNs. The objective of the channel assignment problem for WMNs is to maximize the throughput of multiple flows.

4   Problem Analysis

In the following example, we analyze the problem of channel assignment for OR. As shown in Figure 4, we consider a WMN with four nodes, in which every node has 2 radio interfaces, the number of available orthogonal channels is 3, and the loss probability is labeled by each link. In the examples, there is a session from source S to destination D. Two intermediate nodes A and B are between S and D. In the examples, colored lines show data flows on different channels. Red solid line is channel C1, green dashed line with one point is channel C2, and blue dashed line with two points is channel C3. We show the optimal channel assignment computed by traditional channel assignment algorithm [11] that does not consider opportunism as shown in Figure 4(a), and the uniform channel assignment in which all nodes use the same channels as shown in Figure 4(b). The value above node is the channel assigned to node. For example, in Figure 4(a), node S is assigned channel C1 and C3.

We also compare the throughput achieved by the two channel assignments with EMORE [9]. The total normalized throughput of the traditional and uniform channel assignment is 0.5 and 0.6475 respectively. The traditional channel assignment use all channels, the uniform channel assignment only use channel 1 and 2. The traditional channel assignment use more channel resource, but the performance of traditional channel assignment is worse than that of uniform channel assignment.

Traditional channel assignment aims to exploit more concurrent transmissions to gain high performance, but some issues exist after traditional channel assignment in OR: i) The link between sender and its candidate forwarder is cut off, such as link AB, because they don't share a common channel. ii) The number of candidate forwarders will decrease when a node sends with some channel, such as when S sends with channel C1, B isn't the candidate forwarder of S leading to the overhear opportunity diminishing. The reason is that traditional channel assignment minimizes the interference among links to increase the concurrent transmissions and performance. It's suitable for tradition routing with the one-to-one transmission mode. But OR exploits the broadcast nature of wireless media and is the one-to-more transmission mode. A transmission unit of OR includes a set of links. It is against the overhear opportunity of multiple candidate forwarders.

In uniform channel assignment, all nodes use the same channel. Although it includes more interferences and less concurrent transmissions than traditional channel assignment, it reserves the candidate forwarder and the overhear opportunity. In this example, uniform channel assignment is better than traditional channel assignment, but they are only focus on multi-channel or OR. Hence, need to design new channel assignment for OR.

Reference [8][17] proposed node conflict graph for OR, when analyzing the performance of OR. For traditional routing, we first construct the link conflict graph as shown in Figure 5(a). In the conflict graph, each vertex corresponds to each link in the original connectivity graph Figure 4. There is an edge between two vertices when these two links conflict each other. According to the protocol

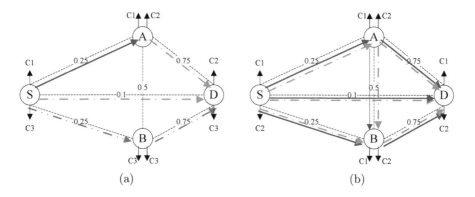

Fig. 4. Optimal channel assignment computed by different channel assignment.(a)the traditional channel assignment algorithm (b)the uniform channel assignment algorithm.

model any two links can not be scheduled simultaneously. Traditional channel assignments [11-13] are based on the link interference and assign channel to link to minimize the total interference among all links. For OR, we construct the node conflict graph. Assume S chooses nodes D, A and B as its candidate forwarders, A's candidate forwarders are node D and B, and B's candidate forwarder is just the destination D. The node conflict graph is constructed in Figure 5(b). Each vertex corresponds to a set of links between sender and its candidate forwarder. There is an edge between two vertices when any two links which belong to the two vertices conflict each other. In traditional routing with link conflict graph, link SA and SB, AB and AD conflict. But in opportunistic routing, needing multiple candidate forwarders, link SA and SB, AB and AD allow to transmit concurrently.

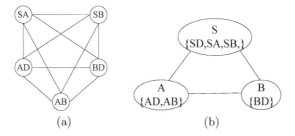

Fig. 5. Conflict graph (a) Link conflict graph for TR (b)conflict graph for OR

Inspired by the node conflict graph for OR, channel assignment for OR is able to bind the sender and its candidate forwarders as a unit named Candidate Forwarder Set. Then the channel assignment problem for OR replaces assigning channel to links with assigning channel to Candidate Forwarder Set. It aims to minimize the interference between Candidate Forwarder Sets. According to this idea, we design a Candidate Forwarder Set based channel assignment.

5   Algorithm Designing

Considering the one-to-more transmission mode and the overhear opportunity of multiple candidate forwarders, taking the send and its candidate forwarders as a unit, we propose the Candidate Forwarder Set based Channel Assignment (CFSCA). As a whole, CFSCA includes three steps.

Step 1, calculating the Candidate Forwarder Set(CFS). Given the source, destination and route of flows, we can get all Candidate Forwarder Sets by binding the sender nodes in route and its candidate forwarders.

Step 2, calculating the interference among the CFSs. According to the link interference relationship and the link and Candidate Forwarder Set relationship, we can obtain the interference among the Candidate Forwarder Sets.

Step 3, assigning channel by the interference among the CFSs. Channel assignment aims to minimize Candidate Forwarder Set interference, with the constraints of the channel number of Candidate Forwarder Set and the number of radio interfaces.

5.1   Calculating the Candidate Forwarder Set

In OR, each node i has multiple candidate forwarders denoted by FN(i), then node i and it's candidate forwarders FN(i) compose to a Candidate Forwarder Set(CFS). A CFS contains a set of links between the sender and it's candidate forwarders. As shown in Figure 6(c), node i's candidate forwarders are node 1 and 2, and node p's candidate forwarder is node 3 and 4. Node i, 1 and 2 compose to a CFS, node p, 3 and 4 compose to another CFS. All CFS is a set of Candidate Forwarder Sets (CFSs). Assuming that there are M CFS, we denote the relationship between nodes and CFS as an N*M matrix S. If node i belong to CFS m, we denote $i \in m$ and S_i^m is 1; Otherwise $i \notin m$ and S_i^m is 0.

5.2   Calculating the Interference among the CFSs

Interference exists among the Candidate Forwarder Sets. More concurrent transmission and overhear opportunity can be gotten when channel assignment decrease the interference among CFSs. Firstly, we define the interference of CFSs. Then, we propose the expression and calculating algorithm of interference of CFSs.

1)The definition of the CFSs interference

We give the definition of the CFSs interference, at the same time similar interference definition are given in order to compare them.

Neighbor. Node i and p are neighbors if they are in the transmission range of each other, or i can correctly decode the packets transmitted by q at least with the possibility $P0(P0 << 1)$, that is the P(i,p) is greater than P0, as shown in Figure 6(a). All the neighbors of node i compose of the neighbor set of node i, denoted by $\Re(i)$.

$$\Re(i) = \{p \in V : P(i,p) \geq P0\} \tag{1}$$

Link interference. Link (i,j) and (p,q) conflict if the sender or receiver of links are neighbors, that is, node i and p, node i and q, node j and p, or node j and q are neighbors, as shown in Figure 6(b). All the conflict links of link (i,j) compose of the link interference set of link (i,j), denoted by $\Gamma(i,j)$.

$$\Gamma(i,j) = \{(p,q) \in E : i \in \Re(p) \| i \in \Re(q) \| j \in \Re(p) \| j \in \Re(p)\} \qquad (2)$$

CFS interference. Two CFSs conflict when any two links of them conflict each other, as shown in Figure 6(c). Node i, 1 and 2 compose a CFS, node p, 3 and 4 compose another CFS. If only link (i,1)or (i,2) and (3,p)or(4,p) conflict, the two CFS conflict. All the conflict CFSs of CFS u composes of the CFS interference set of CFS u, denoted by $H(u)$.

$$H(u) = \{v \in CFSs : \exists i \in u, j \in u, \exists p \in v, q \in v, (i,j) \in \Gamma(p,q)\} \qquad (3)$$

Node interference. If only the links between the two node and its neighbor conflict, the two nodes conflict, as shown in Figure 6(d). All the conflict nodes of node i compose of the conflict nodes set of node i, denoted by $F(i)$.

$$F(i) = \{p \in V : \exists j \in \Re(i), \exists q \in \Re(p), (i,j) \in \Gamma(p,q)\} \qquad (4)$$

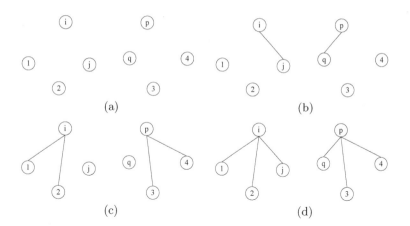

Fig. 6. Interference mode: (a) node neighbor (b) link interference (c) Candidate Forwarder Set interference (d) node interference

As shown in Figure 6, the neighbor is a relationship of node. The link interference is a relationship of link. The CFS and node interference is relationship of links set. The strict of definition gradually increased: neighbor < link interference < CFS interference < node interference.

2)Expression and calculating algorithm of interference of CFSs

The relationship among CFSs is expressed by M*M matrix I. If CFS u and v interfere, we denote I_{uv} is 1; Otherwise I_{uv} is 0.

According to the link interference relationship and the Candidate Forwarder Set, we can obtain the interference among the Candidate Forwarder Sets.

We implement it by C++. The interferences information is took as input to channel assignment.

5.3   Assigning Channel by the Interference among the CFSs

After get the interference of CFSs, channel assignment must obey two constraints of the channel number of Candidate Forwarder Set and the number of interface.

i) At least assigning a channel to a CFS. Otherwise the sender and its candidate forwarder can't communicate each other.

ii) The number of channels assigned to one node is less than the number of radios, because each node is only equipped with R radios.

Following we describe the optimal object and constrains. Every CFS can use its assigned channels for packet transmission and reception. Let $A_m^k \in \{0, 1\}$ which is an M*K matrix denoting whether a radio of CFS $m \in M$ is assigned to channel k. According to the constraints of the channel number of CFSs, we have the following constraint.

$$\sum_{k=1}^{K} A_m^k \geq 1 \tag{5}$$

One node can belong to multiple CFSs. If only one CFS including the node is assigned to a channel k, the node must be assigned to the channel k. Therefore we can obtain the node channel assignment according the relationship between nodes and CFS matrix S and channel assignment of CFSs matrix A.

$$X_i^k = \begin{cases} 1, & \sum_{m=1}^{M} S_i^m A_m^k \geq 1 \\ 0, & \sum_{m=1}^{M} S_i^m A_m^k = 0 \end{cases} \tag{6}$$

For simplicity, we use a linear inequality to replace it.

$$0 \leq X_i^k - \frac{1}{L} \sum_{m=1}^{M} S_i^m A_m^k < 1 \tag{7}$$

where L is a digital lager than M. If $\sum_{m=1}^{M} S_i^m A_m^k >= 1$, at least than one CFS including the node i are assigned to a channel k. Due to $\sum_{m=1}^{M} S_i^m A_m^k =< M$, according to the equation, $X_i^k = 1$; Otherwise, none of CFSs including the node i is assigned a channel k, according to the equation, $X_i^k = 0$.

According to the constraints of the channel number of radio interfaces, we have the following constraint.

$$\sum_{k=1}^{N} X_i^k \leq R \tag{8}$$

We denote the interference after channel assignment as an M*M matrix I'. Only if CFS u and v interfere and are assigned a same channel, they interfere under assignment A.

$$I'uv = \sum_{k=1}^{K} A_u^k A_v^k * Iuv \tag{9}$$

The problem of channel assignment is a minimum the interference between CFSs.

$$\min \pi = \sum_{u}^{M} \sum_{v}^{M} I'uv \tag{10}$$

subject to:

$$\sum_{k=1}^{K} A_m^k \geq 1, 1 < m < M$$

$$0 \leq X_i^k - \frac{1}{L} \sum_{m=1}^{M} S_i^m A_m^k < 1, 1 < i < N, 1 < k < K$$

$$\sum_{k=1}^{K} X_i^k \leq R, 1 < i < N \tag{11}$$

$$I'_{uv} = [\sum_{k=1}^{K} A_u^k A_v^k] * I_{uv}, 1 < u, v < M$$

$$A_m^k \in [0, R], A_m^k \in, 1 < m < M, 1 < k < K$$

Where variable is A. It's an integer linear quadratic program problem which can be solved by convex optimal theory. Now It's solved by LINDO API.

6   Performance Evaluation

We evaluate the performance of CFSCA from two aspects, interference and throughput. In the aspect of interference, we compare the interference of CFSs. In the aspect of throughput, we extend the performance model named Dice [18] to support multi-radio and multi-channel networks and exploit this extend model to evaluate CFSCA.

There are 4 schemes with different channel assignment. We compare the throughput of the following schemes.

Rand: Random channel assignment which assign channel to node randomly.

Unif: Uniform channel assignment which uniformly allocate the same set of channels to all nodes[10].

Trad[11]: This is a minimize links interferences based centralized channel assignment algorithm.

CFSCA: The candidate forwarder set based channel assignment.

The scenario consists of 16 nodes randomly in a terrain area of 400*400 meters. Every node is equipped with 2 radios since the number of radio in a wireless station is limited by the cost of commodity radios and the size of wireless station in real-world WMNs. There are 3 orthogonal channels. In each run, we examine Rand, Unif, Trad, CFSCA sequentially between the same source-destination pair. The Shadowing model is used in which frame losses are proportional to the distance between wireless nodes. Note that this model assumes that losses between the source and different forwarders are independent. Therefore, intra-path and inter-path collisions occur in a random manner.The Channel Bit Rate is 11 Mbps. The packet sizes are 1000 bytes.

We consider the interferences value among all CFSs. We define two CFSs interfere with each other when they conflict and are assigned a same channel, and set the interference value to one, otherwise zero. Interferences value among all CFSs is the sum of the interferences value between any two CFSs. In Random

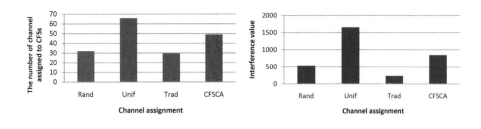

Fig. 7. The average number of channel assigned to CFSs

Fig. 8. The interference value

and Traditional channel assignment, nodes in a CFS may be assigned with no common channel, and the sender can't use all candidate forwarders in a CFS. Figure 7 presents the average number of channel assigned to CFSs. Hence, we calculate the average channel number and interference value of CFSs. In Uniform channel assignment, all CFSs are assigned two channels. The number of channel assigned to CFSs in Random and Traditional channel assignment is half less than that in Uniform channel assignment. That means there are some CFSs aren't assigned any channel. Hence, in Figure 8, the interferences values of them are small, but isn't satisfy the need of OR. CFSCA makes sure all CFSs at least are assigned a channel with smaller interference value.

We present the End-to-End performance with different sources and destination. We fix the number of flows at 8 where all nodes can be sources or destination to create heavy loads on the network. We randomly choose nodes as sources and destinations from 16 nodes and run 6 times with different random seeds in a random network topology.

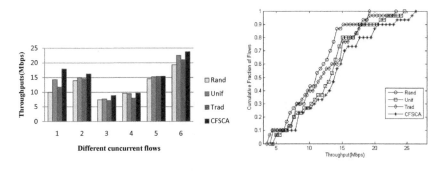

Fig. 9. The total throughput with heavy load

Fig. 10. The CDF of the total throughput

Firstly, we present the total throughput with different run in a same network topology. In Figure 9, generally, the throughput of applying CFSCA is higher or equal that of using other channel assignment. Uniform channel assignment is no worse than traditional channel assignment. Hence, we can exploit uniform channel assignment when node can't support complex computing.

Figure 10 presents the cumulative distribution function (CDF) of the achieved throughputs for 5 randomly network topology. The total throughputs achieved by Rand, Unif, Trad, CFSCA are 11.5, 13.1, 12.1, 14.4Mbps respectively. CFSCA improves 25.2%, 10%, 19% of the aggregate throughput than random, uniform and tradition channel assignment, respectively. The results show that SCAOR significantly improves the throughput compared with the other schemes.

7   Conclusion

In this paper, we have studied the problem of channel assignment in multi-radio WMNs, considering the support of OR technique. A candidate forwarder set based channel assignment(CFSCA), considering the one-to-more transmission mode and the overhear opportunity of OR, is proposed. Evaluation results show that CFSCA achieves higher throughput than existing channel assignment algorithms. Our future study will focus on designing efficient joint channel assignment and opportunistic routing algorithms/protocols.

Acknowledgments. This work is supported by the National Basic Research Program of China (973) under Grant No. 2012CB315801, the National Natural Science Foundation of China under Grant No. 61003305, 61173168 and 61173167.

References

1. Biswas, S., Morris, R.: ExOR: Opportunistic Multi-Hop Routing for Wireless Networks. In: Proceedings of SIGCOMM 2005, vol. 35, pp. 133–144 (2005)
2. Rozner, E., Seshadri, J., Mehta, Y., et al.: Simple opportunistic routing protocol for wireless mesh networks. IEEE Transactions on Mobile Computing Archive 8(12), 1622–1635 (2009)
3. Chachulski, S., Jennings, M., Katti, S., et al.: Trading Structure for Randomness in Wireless Opportunistic Routing. In: Proceedings of SIGCOMM 2007, vol. 37, pp. 169–180 (2007)
4. Katti, S., Katabi, D., Balakrishnan, H., et al.: Symbol-level Network Coding for Wireless Mesh Networks. In: Proceedings of SIGCOMM 2008, vol. 38, pp. 401–412 (2008)
5. Li, T., Leith, D., Qiu, L.: Opportunistic Routing for Interactive Traffic in Wireless Networks. In: Proceedings of ICDCS 2010, pp. 458–467 (2010)
6. Li, J., Blake, C., De Couto, D.S.J., Lee, H.I., et al.: Capacity of Ad Hoc Wireless Networks. In: MobiCom 2001, pp. 61–69 (2001)
7. Zubow, A., Kurth, M., Redlich, J.P.: An Opportunistic Cross-Layer Protocol for Multi-Channel Wireless Networks. In: IEEE PIMRC 2007, pp. 1–5 (2007)
8. Zeng, K., Yang, Z., Lou, W.: Opportunistic Routing in Multi-radio Multi-channel Multi-hop Wireless Networks. In: Proceedings of INFOCOM 2010, pp. 476–480 (2010)

9. Wu, F., Raman, V., Vaidya, N.: Being Opportunistic or Being Concurrent. In: Proceedings of SECON 2010 Poster (2010)
10. He, S., Zhang, D., Xie, K., Qiao, H., Zhang, J.: A Simple Channel Assignment for Opportunistic Routing in Multi-Radio Multi-Channel Wireless Mesh Networks. In: Proceedings of IEEE MSN 2011 (2011)
11. Subramanian, P., Gupta, H., Das, S.R.: Minimum interference channel assignment in multi-radio wireless mesh networks. In: SECON 2006 (September 2006)
12. Zhou, B., Zhao, Z., Huang, A., Chen, Q.: Optimization Model for Static Channel Assignment in Multi-radio Multi-channel Wireless Mesh Networks. IEEE Communications Society (2009)
13. Shao, B., Tao, J., Wang, F.: Static Channel Assignment with the Physical Interference Model for Maximum Capacity in Multi-radio Multi-channel Wireless Mesh Networks. IEEE Communications Society (2010)
14. Alicherry, M., Bhatia, R., Li, L.B.: Joint channel assignment and routing for throughput optimization in multiradio wireless mesh networks. IEEE J. Select. Areas Commun. 24, 1960–1971 (2006)
15. Kodialam, M., Nandagopal, T.: Characterizing achievable rates in multi-hop wireless mesh networks with orthogonal channels. IEEE/ACM Trans. Networking 13(4), 868–880 (2005)
16. Cruz, R.L., Santhanam, A.V.: Optimal routing, link scheduling and power control in multihop wireless mesh networks. In: ACM MobiHoc 2005, pp. 68–77 (2005)
17. Zeng, K., Lou, W., Zhai, H.: On End-to-end Throughput of Opportunistic Routing in Multirate and Multihop Wireless Networks. In: IEEE INFOCOM 2008 (2008)
18. Zhang, X., Li, B.: Dice: a Game Theoretic Framework for Wireless Multipath Network Coding. In: Proc. of ACM MobiHoc (2008)

The Analysis of Anchor Placement for Self-localization Algorithm in Wireless Sensor Networks

Liang Huang, Fubao Wang, Chao Ma, and Weijun Duan

School of Electronics and Information,
Northwestern Polytechnical University, 710072 Xi'an, China
huangliangnumber1@163.com

Abstract. In range-based localization systems of wireless sensor networks, a small fraction of nodes in the network have known locations while the remaining keep unknown. However, with the change of the anchors distribution, the positioning accuracy of the localization algorithm is quite different. Therefore, we use parameter estimation theory to analyze the node location problem, model the distance measuring with multiplicative normal noise model, and drive the Cramer-Rao lower bound of location. Through simulation we find an effective anchor placement strategy. Compared with random deployment, the proposed strategy provides higher positioning accuracy.

Keywords: Wireless sensor networks(WSN), Localization, Anchor Placement, Multiplicative normal noise model, Cramer-Rao Low Bound(CRLB).

1 Introduction

In recent years, wireless sensor networks technology has been rapid development and wide application. In most wireless sensor network applications, the location information of the sensors nodes is very important. GPS means to rely on external hardware support, and bring excessive cost. Therefore, the self-localization technologies of wireless sensor networks develop rapid recently, and appear a variety of different positioning methods. Self-localization technology in WSN is usually divided into rang-based and range-free according to whether rely on distance measuring[1]. The range-based approaches include RSSI[2], TOA[3]/TDOA [4], AOA[5], and TOF etc.

The range-free methods like as centroid algorithm[6], DV-hop [7], convex programming[8] and non-metric multidimensional scaling[9, 10] etc. The range-based WSN self-localization algorithms usually adopt ranging methods such as RSSI, TOA to measuring the distance between two nodes. Based on these distance information, the algorithms then perform positioning process in different ways such as trilateration/triangulation, maximum likelihood estimation, iterative approximation and so on. Therefore, the accuracy of the positioning system

R. Wang and F. Xiao (Eds.): CWSN 2012, CCIS 334, pp. 117–126, 2013.
© Springer-Verlag Berlin Heidelberg 2013

depends largely on the range measuring technology, which is not in the scope of this paper. WSN self-localization system needs to introduce anchor nodes that have known coordinate to help calculate others. In 2-D plane it is usually takes at least three anchors. It is worth noting that the studies have shown that the deployment of the anchors have a significant impact to the positioning result of the system[12, 13]. For example, when the anchors are collinear deployment the localization systems will not be able to perform the calculations, and when the anchor nodes distribution concentrated, the systematic positioning errors will get larger.

If the positioning problem is summarized as a parameter estimation problem, then the positioning error can be analyzed through the estimation theory. N. Patwari[10] use the Gaussian noise and logarithmic normal model to modeling the RSS and TOA distance measuring respectively, and estimate the node location to get the Cramer-Rao lower bound (CRLB) and the maximum likelihood estimator, which provide a means of quantitative analysis of the relevant parameters on the positioning accuracy. A. Catovic et al.[11] calculated the CRLB of the TOA/RSS and TDOA/RSS two different hybrid positioning mechanism to analysis the positioning accuracy. In addition, G. Latsoudas build the distance measuring model by multiplicative normal noise model and derive the CRLB of the positioning variance in [12].

H.C Shi et al[13] attribute quantized RSSI based Sensor network localization to a parameter estimation problem, to derive the CRLB of the positioning error variance estimation. Then study the impact of different network parameters on the positioning error variance CRLB, obtained by simulation that the anchors should not be deployed at the network edge but in the area near the border. Base on that, X.L.Li et al.[14] through exhaustive search algorithm to find the best location of the anchor nodes, and propose a selective mobile anchor placement scheme. The results show that the anchors distributed in an annular region close to the outer edge of the deployment area will get high positioning accuracy.

In this article, we firstly quantify estimated anchor node location error through statistical analysis methods. We modeling the distance measurement errors under the multiplicative normal noise model, and analyze the Cramer-Rao lower bound of the node positioning error parameter estimation. Then, we describe the relation between anchor distribution and positioning accuracy through simulation results. At last, we propose an effective anchor deployment strategy, and verify the validity of the proposed policy in MDS localization simulation experiment.

2   Relative Concepts

Network Model. A wireless sensor network with N nodes is deployed in a two-dimensional plane. Sensor node set S=$(s_1, s_2, \ldots, s_n)$ is uniform random deployed in the monitoring square area with side length L, which include a small amount (more than 3) anchor nodes. The anchor nodes have their absolute coordinate information. All nodes use the same type RF module, the node communication radius is R. All nodes can use the RF module for effective range measurement, and the ranging radius is R_t.

Multiplicative Normal Noise Model. The choice of measurement model dependent on many factors and is application-specific. In recent years, researchers generally use a multiplicative normal noise model, in which the ranging error and the actual distance are proportional[12]. Therefore, the measured values of the distance between nodes i and j can be expressed as:

$$d_{ij} \backsim \delta_{ij} + \delta_{ij} N(0, e_r^2) . \tag{1}$$

Where δ_{ij} is the actual distance between nodes i, j, and $N(0, e_r^2)$ denotes a zero mean normal random variable with variance e_r^2(range error variance). We also assume that the ranging results are symmetrical, i.e. $d_{ij} = d_{ji}$.

In the next section, we drive the CRLB for node localization using the above multiplicative normal noise model. The derivation of the CRLB in different noise model is available in literature [10–13].

3   The CRLB of the Position Error

In the range-based localization algorithm, the ranging methods itself exist some deviation, which making the measurement of distance is not accurate. As the ranging error introduced into the localization algorithm, the position error arise.

To estimate the position of the nodes, we define the parameter vector $r = [r_1, r_2, \ldots, r_n]$, in which r_i indicate the coordinates of node i, i.e. $r_i = (x_i, y_i)$. Assume that the network has three anchor nodes, then the other N-3 unknown coordinate vector can be defined as $R = (R_x R_y)$, where $R_x = [x_1, x_2, \ldots, x_{N-3}]$, $R_y = [y_1, y_2, \ldots, y_{N-3}]$. Assume the distance measurement value between the nodes i and j is d_{ij}, which is statistically independent. From the distance measuring model we can get the probability density function of the sample d_{ij} is $f(d_{ij}|r_i, r_j)$. Hence, their joint log-likelihood is estimated at [12]:

$$l(D, r) = \sum_{i=1}^{N} \sum_{j \in H(i), j < i} l_{i,j}, \\ l_{i,j} = \log f(d_{i,j}|r_i, r_j). \tag{2}$$

$H(i)$ represents the set of nodes within the working range of the node i.

Then we can get the Cramer-Rao lower bound of the positioning variance of R_i is $cov(R_i \geq [F_R^{-1}]_{ii})$, Where F_R is the Fisher information matrix (FIM):

$$F = \begin{bmatrix} F_{xx} & F_{xy} \\ F_{xy}^T & F_{yy} \end{bmatrix} . \tag{3}$$

Its sub-element matrix $F_{xx}(k, l)$ as follows:

$$F_{xx}(k, l) = \begin{cases} -\sum_{j \in H(k)} E\left[\frac{\partial^2}{\partial x_k^2} l_{kj}\right], k = l \\ -I_{H(k)}(l) E\left[\frac{\partial^2}{\partial x_k \partial x_l} l_{k,l}\right], k \neq l \end{cases} . \tag{4}$$

Where $I_{H(k)}(l)$ is the indicator function:

$$I_{H(k)}(l) = \begin{cases} 1 & if\ l \in H(k) \\ 0 & otherwise \end{cases}.$$ (5)

The other sub-elements $F_{xy}F_{yy}$ have the similar expressions.

For ranging model (1), we can deduce the following expression:

$$F_{xx}(k,l) = \begin{cases} \frac{1}{e_r^2}\sum_{j \in H(k)} \frac{(x_k - x_l)^2}{\delta_{kj}^4}, k = l \\ -\frac{1}{e_r^2}I_{H(k)}(l)\frac{(x_k - x_l)^2}{\delta_{kj}^2}, k \neq l \end{cases}.$$ (6)

$$F_{xy}(k,l) = \begin{cases} \frac{1}{e_r^2}\sum_{j \in H(k)} \frac{(x_k - x_j)(y_k - y_j)}{\delta_{kj}^4}, k = l \\ -\frac{1}{e_r^2}I_{H(k)}(l)\frac{(x_k - x_j)(y_k - y_j)}{\delta_{kj}^2}, k \neq l \end{cases}.$$ (7)

$$F_{yy}(k,l) = \begin{cases} \frac{1}{e_r^2}\sum_{j \in H(k)} \frac{(y_k - y_l)^2}{\delta_{kj}^4}, k = l \\ -\frac{1}{e_r^2}I_{H(k)}(l)\frac{(y_k - y_l)^2}{\delta_{kj}^2}, k \neq l \end{cases}.$$ (8)

4   Simulation Result

4.1   The CRLB of the Location

Assumptions $\delta_{x_k}^2$ and $\delta_{y_k}^2$ represent the variance of the estimated parameters x_k and y_k respectively, then we can calculate the position by the following formula to estimate the variance lower bound of R_k :

$$\theta_k^2 = \sigma_{x_k}^2 + \sigma_{y_k}^2.$$ (9)

Here, we illustrate through simulation. Assuming 1m * 1m square simulation area with an unknown node, its coordinates are (x, y). Then deploy four anchors in each corners of the square simulation region which is divided into 400 points in accordance with a grid. We need to use the above formula to calculate the CRLB of each point. Assume that each node in this area can perform distance measurement with anchor node, and then we get the CRLB distribution of location estimation variance as shown in Figure 1. The result shows that when the unknown node is located at the region central, the system gets the minimum positioning error.

Compared with the CRLB distribution under the RSS and TOA ranging model [10] as show in Figure 2, we can see that the multiplicative normal noise ranging model is very similar with RSS, but different with the TOA ranging model.

4.2   The Anchors Distribution and Position Accuracy

Also assume and represent the variance of the estimated parameters and , respectively. Then we can calculate the mean square error of the positioning variance in accordance with the following formula:

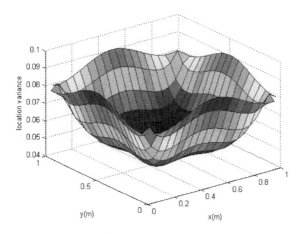

Fig. 1. Average CRLB distribution of location variance in multiplicative noise ranging model(With one unknown node and four anchors)

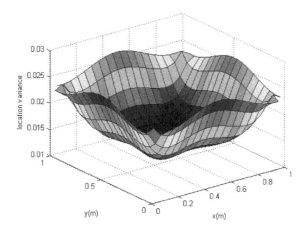

Fig. 2. Average CRLB distribution of location variance in RSS ranging model(With one unknown node and four anchors)

$$RMS(\sigma) = \sqrt{\frac{1}{N} \sum_{k=1}^{N} (\sigma_{x_k}^2 + \sigma_{y_k}^2)}. \tag{10}$$

RMS gives the reference for the position estimation performance. The smaller the RMS is, the more effective of the positioning algorithm, and the higher of the average positioning accuracy.

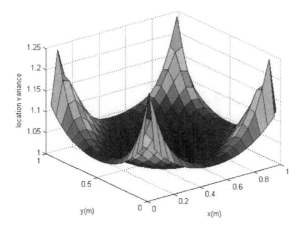

Fig. 3. Average CRLB distribution of location variance in TOA ranging model(With one unknown node and four anchors)

Some studies show that the deployment of anchors in the network boundary makes the positioning precision much higher [15]. In order to validate the conclusions or find a better deployment strategies, we simulate in a square region with side length $L = 1000m$, and deployment 400 unknown nodes and four anchor nodes in grid shape. Set nodes ranging radius $R_t = 300$ meters. Based on the distance of the anchors location to the nearest edge, divide the deployment region into 10 layers by 50 meters step from outside to inside, and deploy the anchor nodes in the four corners for each layer. Use the algorithm for solving $RMS(\sigma)$ while anchors are deployed in different layers, and then we get the simulation result as shown in Figure 3.

As can be seen from Figure 3, when the anchor is deployed to the inner of the area (x axis get large), the RMS of the system get large. The anchors are far from the border but close to the center of the deployment area, the positioning error fluctuates and the positioning performance is poor. When the anchor nodes deployed far away from the center but close to the border(x axis get small), the RMS show a downward trend, which indicating that performance improvement. In particular, RMS is smallest when anchors are deployed at the 3rd to 5th layers (100-200 m from the border), which means the system positioning performance is the best. But when the anchor nodes are deployed to the boundary (layer 1-2, 50-0 meters from the boundary), the system positioning RMS will increase, and the positioning accuracy will decline also. The analysis shows that the anchor nodes deploy at the boundary are not the best, but in the region from the border 0.1L   0.2L.

To further promote the above conclusions, we deploy the anchors randomly at different layers performing 100 experiments for each and get the average RMS in the same simulation scenarios (deployed in 1000m * 1000m square area with 400 unknown nodes). The experimental result is shown in Figure 3 (b).

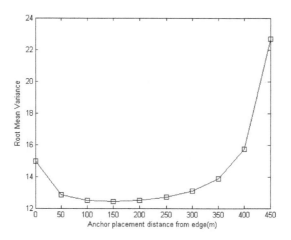

Fig. 4. The RMS that anchors distributed in the four corners at different layers with different distance from the edge. X axis represent the distance to the near edge, as $L = 1000, x < 500$.

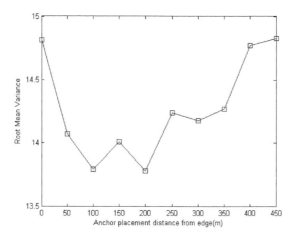

Fig. 5. The RMS that anchors random distributed at different layers. X axis represent the distance to the near edge, as $L = 1000, x < 500$.

The same with the conclusions above, we get the minimum RMS and the highest positioning accuracy when the anchor nodes are deployed at 3rd to 5th layers in the case of random anchor distribution.

4.3   The Random Deployment and Effective Deployment of the Anchors

Based on the above conclusions, we can get the anchor nodes deployment strategy:

1. Anchor nodes should be deployed in the area from the border 0.1L   0.2L , in order to ensure high positioning accuracy;

2. Anchor nodes should be evenly distributed in order to maintain balanced deployment and maximize the contribution of each anchor nodes;

We validate the performance of the deployment strategy by metric multidimensional scaling WSN localization algorithm. Random deployment of 25 nodes in 50 * 50 meters square area includes three anchor nodes. The anchors can be chose randomly. Using multidimensional scaling localization algorithm performs network self-localization by random deployment strategy and the proposed deployment strategy respectively. The result is shown in Figure 4.

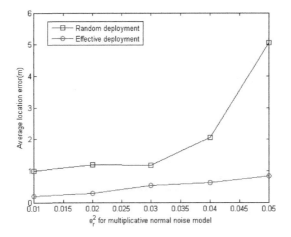

Fig. 6. Average positioning errors in anchor random deployment and effective deployment with the multiplicative normal noise model, in which the variance e_r^2 is set increase from 1% to 5%

Figure 4 indicate that compared to the anchor node random deployment, the proposed anchor deployment strategy significantly reduce the average location errors; in other words, improve the positioning accuracy of the localization algorithm. Besidesin multiplicative normal noise ranging model, the positioning error is decreased with reduction of the variance of the normal random variable.

5   Conclusion

Positioning is one of the basic problems of the wireless sensor network applications. The accuracy of existing range-based positioning algorithms is dependent on distance measuring technology, the network parameters and the algorithms itself. This paper research the relationship between the anchors deployment and the position accuracy. We build the ranging model in multiplicative normal noise model, use statistical estimation method for node location estimates, and derive the CRLB of the positioning variance. On this basis, through the simulation find the anchor node deployment which lead to high positioning accuracy, and give out the deployment strategy which is a more effective than random deployment strategy proved by experiments presented in this paper.

Future work includes analysis and modeling positioning error sources, and research on the mathematical relationships between the range measuring error, the anchor node location distribution and the positioning accuracy, and the transform of the relative location to the absolute one, etc.

References

1. Wang, F., Shi, L., Ren, F.: Self-Localization Systems and Algorithms for Wireless Sensor Networks. Journal of Software 16(5), 857–868 (2005)
2. Girod, L., Bychovskiy, V., Elson, J., Estrin, D.: Locating tiny sensors in time and space: A case study. In: Werner, B. (ed.) Proc. of the 2002 IEEE Int'l Conf. on Computer Design: VLSI in Computers and Processors, pp. 214–219. IEEE Computer Society, Freiburg (2002)
3. Harter, A., Hopper, A., Steggles, P., Ward, A., Webster, P.: The anatomy of a context-aware application. In: Proc. of the 5th Annual ACM/IEEE Int'l Conf. on Mobile Computing and Networking, pp. 59–68. ACM Press, Seattle (1999)
4. Girod, L., Estrin, D.: Robust range estimation using acoustic and multimodal sensing. In: Proc. of the IEEE/RSJ Int'l Conf. on Intelligent Robots and Systems, IROS 2001, vol. 3, pp. 1312–1320. IEEE Robotics and Automation Society, Maui (2001)
5. Niculescu, D., Nath, B.: Ad hoc positioning system (APS) using AoA. In: Proc. of the IEEE INFOCOM 2003, vol. 3, pp. 1734–1743. IEEE Computer and Communications Societies, San Francisco (2003)
6. Niculescu, D., Nath, B.: DV based positioning in ad hoc networks. Journal of Telecommunication Systems 22(1/4), 267–280 (2003)
7. Doherty, L., Pister, K.S.J., Ghaoui, L.E.: Convex position estimation in wireless sensor networks. In: Proc. of the IEEE INFOCOM 2001, vol. 3, pp. 1655–1663. IEEE Computer and Communications Societies, Anchorage (2001)
8. Shang, Y., Ruml, W., Zhang, Y., et al.: Localization from mere connectivity in sensor networks. In: Proc. of the 4th ACM Int'l Symp. on Mobile Ad Hoc Networking & Computing, pp. 201–212. ACM Press, New York (2003)
9. Shang, Y., Ruml, W., Zhang, Y.: Localization from connectivity in sensor networks. IEEE Trans. on Parallel and Distributed Systems 15(11), 961–973 (2004)
10. Patwari, N., Hero, A., Perkins, M., Correal, N., O'Dea, R.: Relative location estimation in wireless sensor networks. IEEE Trans. Signal Process. 51(8), 2137–2148 (2003)
11. Catovic, A., Sahinoglu, Z.: The Cramer-Rao bounds of hybrid TOA/RSS and TDOA/RSS location estimation schemes. IEEE Communications Letters 8(10), 626–628 (2004)
12. Latsoudas, G., Sidiropoulos, N.D.: A fast and Effective Multidimensional Scaling Approach for Node Localization in Wireless Sensor Networks. IEEE Trans. Signal Process. 55(10), 5121–5127 (2007)

13. Shi, H.C., Li, X.L., Shang, Y.: Cramer-Rao Bound Analysis of Quantized RSSI Based Localization in WSN. In: Proc. of the 2005 11th International Conference on Parallel and Distributed Systems, ICPADS 2005. IEEE (2005)
14. Li, X.L., Shi, H.C., Shang, Y.: Selective anchor placement algorithm for ad-hoc wireless sensor networks. In: Proc. of IEEE Int. Conf. Communications, ICC 2008, pp. 2359–2363 (2008)
15. Savvides, A., Garber, W., Adlakha, S., Moses, R., Srivastava, M.B.: On the Error Characteristics of Multihop Node Localization in Ad-Hoc Sensor Networks. In: Zhao, F., Guibas, L.J. (eds.) IPSN 2003. LNCS, vol. 2634, pp. 317–332. Springer, Heidelberg (2003)

Low-Cost VR System
Based on Wireless Accelerometer Sensor

Lingyun Jiang*, Ruchuan Wang, Wenxiang Qian, and Yachao Lv

College of Computer, Nanjing University of Posts and Telecommunications,
Jiangsu High Technology Research Key Laboratory for Wireless Sensor Networks,
Key Lab of Broadband Wireless Communication and Sensor Network Technology,
Ministry of Education Jiangsu Province, Nanjing, 210003, China
jianglingyun@njupt.edu.cn

Abstract. Virtual reality(VR) games have been popular in recent years, developed in the form of the games by capturing the body's various physiological activities, including the surrounding environmental factors to achieve a colorful variety of game features. This paper presents a system using acceleration sensor to capture the body movements to achieve gaming method. First the user's motion is captured by accelerometer sensor, then the signals collected by sensor can be processed and sent to computer. Finally the motion data of virtual character are synthesized to the VR game by the common interface processing these data. This motion-imitate system is diversity with combining various other appliances and the price and difficulty of development is reduced comparing with the recent mainstream VR games developing method.

Keywords: accelerometer sensor, wireless transmitter and receiver, virtual reality.

1 Introduction

Virtual reality game is a new and exciting field where the users experience benefit from the blending of real and virtual elements. In traditionally, the VR game makers usually built a virtual world in the game with some computer graphical programming tools, while the players are usually confined to the use of keyboards, mice, and joysticks to interact with the completely virtual environment. However, thanks to impressive technological advances, a lot of applications and systems had been developed to change this interaction[1] and various applications can be combined with VR game, to create a better virtual reality world.

Our proposed motion-imitate system consists of accelerometer, wireless communication sensor (data process algorithm included), and the common interface of VR game. Firstly, the user holds the motion capture node in the hand and performs the actions in six directs. Then the accelerometer measures the signals of acceleration and then wireless transceiver(plus a build-in processor) will

---

* Corresponding author.

R. Wang and F. Xiao (Eds.): CWSN 2012, CCIS 334, pp. 127–136, 2013.
© Springer-Verlag Berlin Heidelberg 2013

pre-process the signals like A/D conversion and send the processed data to the computer connected with $2.4GHz$ wireless sensor network. Finally the VR game computes the orientation of the sensor from the user by analyzing the data through the common interface. In this way, the VR game can imitate the user's motions, as shown in Fig. 1. The organization of this paper is as follows.

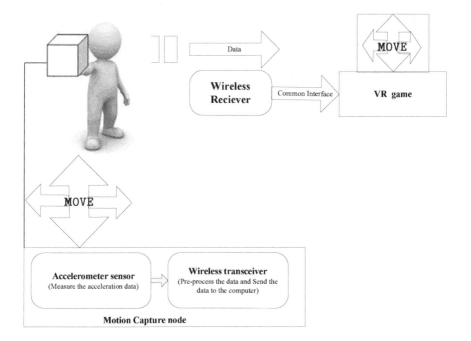

Fig. 1. system overview

Section 2 presents related works. Section 3 presents system hardware design and implementation. Section 4 shows the design and implementation of the embedded program and the common interface of VR game. Section 5 presents the experiment methods and results, and finally Section 6 concludes the paper.

2   Related Works

Dealing with the big challenge on the notion motion-aware application, sea of systems have been developed, such as the standard time difference of arrival technique, which was firstly systematically exposited of in the paper [2] and improved in the paper [3] which contains plenty of beacons, receiver and a center server and in the paper [4] which developed a VR game platform. These systems observe the time lag between the arrival of the $RF(radio\ frequency)$ and ultrasonic signals that sent from beacons, and combine these arrival times to compute the location of the receiver. T.Shiratori and his partners in their paper [5] also develop a method that based on an optical motion capture system, which can directly acquire the user's movements. However, methods above are always limited by the capture environment and lighting condition, especially in some board place, not only the standard time difference of arrival system but also the optical motion capture system will be highly disturbed. Furthermore, those devices usually are much more expensive than ordinary users can afford.

Using some tiny and cheap sensors attached to the user's body could be a good way to capture the motions of the user. There are more and more researchers use accelerometers to recognize human motions. K S Low and his partner use a board micro-controller and a micro machined accelerometer for human limbs monitoring[6]. Eric R.Bachmann and his partners use MAR(magnetic angular rate gravity) sensor to track human's motion[7]. It could be seen that the usage of accelerometer sensors is available to many modern game consoles, like $Sony$ PSV, $Nintendo$ $3DS$, etc. However, although it is true that these systems have managed to track the user's motion well, they cannot be widely used because of the expensive costs. If we want to attach these technologies into our everyday life, we must consider some cheaper alternatives.

We have designed and developed a low-cost VR system based on low-cost wireless Accelerometer sensor. It's advantages are: (a). The cost of the whole system is relatively low. (b). The system contains highly integrated devices which can provide a relatively stable data, and smaller volume. (c). The system is selected based on the CC2430 free ZigBee protocol module, simply and further reducing perational costs. (d). The system can be combined with various other appliances to satisfy other needs using the common interface.

3   System Hardware Design and Implementation

The hardware of the system is divided into two parts as shown in Fig. 1: motion capture node and motion receiver. Based on the motion-imitate application and some technical limitations, such as the lack of gyroscope [8][9], we consider user as a point easily, and the motion of user is also considered as six directions simply.

We choose MMA7260QT as accelerometer sensor, and it is a triple-axis accelerometer with adjustable sensitivity from $\pm 1.5g$ to $\pm 6g$. This design was recommend by other pages about MMA7260QT[10]. When user moves with the sensor on hand, the sensor can measure the linear acceleration and output three axis different magnitude of voltage. Then we should change this magnitude of voltage into magnitude of digital, and judge the direction based on this magnitude. For example, according to our experiment, the average magnitude of voltage of Z axis is approximately $2.51V$ when the user is motionless. After the user begin to jump, the output begin to change range from 1.47 to $3.09V$, so we can conclude that if output range between 2.51 to $3.09V$, the user must do UP motion at that time, and the more the magnitude is, the faster the user is moving.

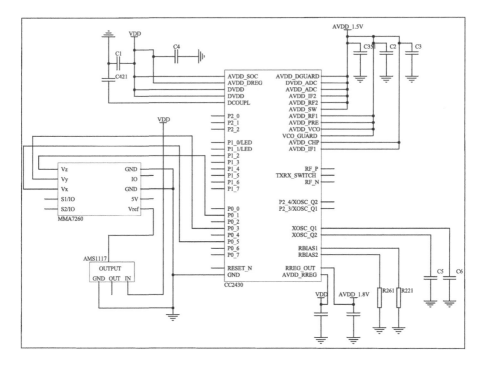

Fig. 2. The circuit of the motion capture node

We choose CC2430 as a transceiver. The CC2430 is a true System-on-Chip(*SoC*) solution specifically tailored for *IEEE* 802.15.4 and ZigBee applications. It enables ZigBee nodes to be built with very low total bill-of-material costs[11]. Compared with some other hot protocols, like Wi-Fi(using 208.11b) and Bluetooth (using 802.15.1), ZigBee(using 802.15.4) has its advantages on costs[12]. The networks based on ZigBee always have much longer battery life with an enough bandwidth for our system. On the other hand, the ZigBee protocol itself is also free, so CC2430 based on ZigBee protocol is a good choice for us to build a wireless network for our system.

The circuit design of the motion capture node is illustrated in Fig. 2(the circuit of the motion receiver is not given here because it is relatively simple). The demo of the motion capture node and the motion receiver is shown in Fig. 3.

4   System Software Design and Implementation

The system software is composed of the following parts: the build-in programs in the motion capture node and the motion receiver(the kernel algorithm of the build-in programs include the wireless data transmission and data receiving algorithm and the A/D conversion algorithm), the common interface of VR game. The A/D conversion model will change the analog signals to digit data as

Fig. 3. The demo of the motion capture node and the motion receiver

soon as MMA7260QT accelerometer sensor captures the motion analog signals and the digit data will be sent to the common interface through the wireless data transmission module and the data receiving module.

4.1 A/D Conversion Algorithm

The motion analog signals captured by MMA7260QT are sent to the input interface of CC2430 which could not be used unless these signals can be transformed to digit data. CC2430 contains a $ADC(Analog\ to\ Digital\ Converter)$ block in its build-in processor, it supports up to $14-bit$ analog-to-digital conversion,which is capable of converting an analog input into a digital representation with up to 13 bits resolution. The ADC uses a selectable positive reference voltage. The time required to perform a conversion depends on the selected decimation rate. When the decimation rate is set to 128 for instance, the decimation filter uses exactly 128 of the $4MHz$ clock cycles to settle in case the channel has been changed since the previous conversion. The 16 clock cycles setting time applies to all decimation rates. Thus in general, the conversion time is given by $equation(1)$

$$V = (decimationrate + 16) * 0.25us \tag{1}$$

In order to accurately describe the orientation of the accelerometer voltage changes in the relationship with their situation, the output voltage should be three-axis, in the form of the group (x, y, z) some time. The CC2430 has only one ADC, taking its handling of data at $2.4GHz$ into account. It is close to the mainstream PC processing frequency. Each group costs $1ns$ of magnitude. The processing speed is much larger than the body's reaction speed $0.1s$ for the human body feels. Thus, we take three steps for the three-axis data processing and output the data at the same time. The process of the A/D value conversion is shown in Fig. 4.

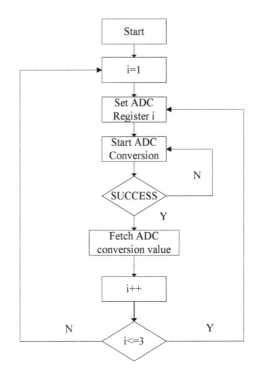

Fig. 4. A/D conversion process

We must find the relationship between ADC input voltage (that we define V, the value of MMA7260 transporting) and the output value N (14bit conversion result). Conversion result N is 14bit, when $N = 11111111111111$(binary), the output voltage should be maximum the reference voltage 3.3V(Because 14bit output is the complement of binary, the 14th bit is the sign bit. So from the view of absolute, the valid value only contains 13 bits. Therefore the maximum value is 2^{13}). Therefore, we have the following proportional relationship according to $equation(2)$.

$$N = V * 2^{13}/3.3 \tag{2}$$

4.2 Wireless Data Transmission and Data Receiving Algorithm

In the data transmitting phase, it is necessary to determine the data to be transmitted is greater than the predefined maximum length of the packet firstly. If the data is too large, it will be divided into several slices to transmit. The sliced data will be written to the RFD register after the $DMA(Direct\ Memory\ Access)$ channel is configured. It is necessary to determine the valid of $RSSI(Received\ Signal\ Strength\ Indicator)$ in cycles to verify the channel is free or occupied before the data is send. The channel is occupied and the $CSMA/CA$ mechanism shall be used to wait for a while to detect $RSSI$ again if $RSSI$ is invalid. If the $RSSI$ is valid ,the data can be sent.

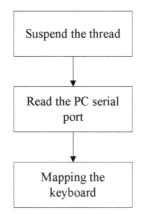

Fig. 5. The process of the common interface

The receiving algorithm is relatively simple. The frequency of channel in the motion receiver is configured the same with the data sender firstly, then the data source of DMA is set to RFD and the trigger signal of DMA is set to $RADIO$. When there are radio signals in the predefined frequency channel, the DMA channel will be trigged. The receiver determines whether to accept the data packet according to the destination address included in the packet. The receiver will send ACK frame to the sender if the data is send to itself(if the sender wants to receiver the ACK message, it will change to receive mode).

4.3   Common Interface Algorithm

The core feature of the common interface is its versatility, which can map the six direct movements to six keys in the keyboard, thus no matter what kind of VR games which use 6 direction keys can use the system. The process of the common interface algorithm is shown in Fig. 5. In order to make the results more intuitive and more convenient for statistics, the receive data received by the serial port which are saved in the array shall be transferred to analog voltage value using $equation(2)$, and the acceleration value can be calculated by $equation(3)(4)(5)$:

$$X_A = (V - 1.65)/0.8 * 10 \tag{3}$$

$$Y_A = (V - 1.65)/0.8 * 10 \tag{4}$$

$$Z_A = (V - 2.45)/0.8 * 10 \tag{5}$$

5   System Experiment and Testing

Firstly, we test the variation of the analog voltage value and the acceleration value in different motion mode, part of the sample data captured when the motion capture node in motionless and the node moves to the right direction are shown in Table 1 and Table 2 , from which we can distinguish the six direction movements.

Table 1. Sample data captured when the motion captures node is motionless

	acceleration value	voltage value
X	1.1097718	1.737817
Y	−1.701965	1.513843
Z	0.790862	2.513246

Table 2. Sample data captured when the motion capture node moves to the right direction

	acceleration value	voltage value
X	1.792602	1.793408
Y	2.598266	1.857861
Z	−1.706695	2.313464

Fig. 6. The tour of virtual countryside

Secondly, we develop a simple VR game, which builds a virtual scene about a mountain road, the player carries the motion capture node and moves, and sends the data to our VR game by the common interface which analyzes the data and judges the direction of the player's movement. Finally, the camera in VR game also moves to answer the data. For example, when a user holds the motion capture node and moves forward, the data about forward can be processed and sent to the computer, and then we can see the following scene changes, as shown in Fig. 6. In this way, the user can feel like walking in the virtual countryside road in the game. The VR system can imitate the player's motion and give the player into a good virtual reality enjoy. Also, we test other VR game just like '3D rotation Box', the system works well.

6 Conclusion

This paper introduces a virtual reality system using low-cost acceleration sensor to capture the body movements to achieve gaming method and using CC2430 as wireless transmitter and receiver. although the system is relatively simple but can can be applied to most VR games and improved by adding a lot of elements such as three-axis gyroscope.In this way, the system can adapt to more complex VR game environment.

Acknowledgments. The subject is sponsored by the National Natural Science Foundation of P. R. China ($No.6117006561100199$)Science and Technology Innovation Fund for higher education institutions of Jiangsu Province($CXLX12_0482$).

References

1. Youngho, L., et al.: Recent Trends in Ubiquitous Virtual Reality. In: International Symposium on Ubiquitous Virtual Reality, pp. 33–36. IEEE Press, New York (2008)
2. Friedman, J.S., King, J.P.: Time difference of arrival geolocation medhod. Signal Science 19(12), 342–387 (1989)
3. Rey, B., Lozano, J.A., Alcañiz, M., Gamberini, L., Calvet, M., Kerrigan, D., Martino, F.: Super-Feet: A Wireless Hand-Free Navigation System for Virtual Environments. In: Shumaker, R. (ed.) Virtual Reality, HCII 2007. LNCS, vol. 4563, pp. 348–357. Springer, Heidelberg (2007)
4. Eom, D.-S., Jang, J., Kim, T.-Y., Han, J.: A VR Game Platform Built Upon Wireless Sensor Network. In: Bebis, G., Boyle, R., Parvin, B., Koracin, D., Remagnino, P., Nefian, A., Meenakshisundaram, G., Pascucci, V., Zara, J., Molineros, J., Theisel, H., Malzbender, T. (eds.) ISVC 2006. LNCS, vol. 4292, pp. 146–155. Springer, Heidelberg (2006)
5. Shiratori, T., Hodgins, J.: Accelerometer-based user interfaces for the control of a physically simulated character. In: ACM Transactions on Graphics (TOG), pp. 1–9. ACM Press, New York (2008)
6. Low, K.S., Lee, G.X., Taher, T.: A wearable wireless sensor network for human limbs monitoring. In: International Instrumentation and Measurement Technology Conference, Singapore, pp. 1332–1336. IEEE Press, New York (2009)
7. Bachmann, E.R., McGhee, R.B., et al.: Inertial and Magnetic Posture Tracking for Inserting Humans Into Networked Virtual Environments. In: VRST 2001 Proceedings of the ACM Symposium on Virtual Reality Software and Technology, pp. 9–16. ACM Press, New York (2001)
8. Slyper, R., Hodgins, J.K.: Action capture with accelerometers. In: Proceedings of the 2008 ACM SIGGRAPH/Eurographics Symposium on Computer Animation, pp. 193–199. Eurographics Association, Aire-la-Ville (2008)

9. Li, Q., Jin, W., Geng, W.: Virtual Avatar Control Using Wireless Sensors. Journal of Computers 6, 184–189 (2011)
10. Ma, C., Wu, Y., Sun, K.: Wireless Sensor Data Acquisition System Based on CC2420 and MMA7260. Microcontrollers & Embedded Systems 4, 52–55 (2008)
11. Antifakos, S., Schiele, B.: Bridging the Gap Between Virtual and Physical Games using Wearable Sensors. In: Wearable Computers, ISWC 2002, pp. 139–140. IEEE Press, New York (2002)
12. Gislason, D.: Zigbee Wireless Networking. Newnes, Burlington (2008)

Using Sensor Web to Sharing Data
of Ocean Observing Systems

Yongguo Jiang, Zhongwen Guo, Keyong Hu, Feifei Shen, and Feng Hong

Department of Computer Science, Ocean University of China
266100 QingDao, P.R. China
{jiangyg,guozhw,hukeyong,shenfeifei,hongfeng}@mail.ouc.edu.cn

Abstract. Based on the OGC New Generation SWE-Sensor Web 2.0 and other related projects implementation, this paper gives the four layers architecture of ocean sensor web and details of every layer. The Information Model layer and Interface Model layer are illustrated in detail by the actual example. At last an ocean sensor prototype system sharing data is presented based on the real ocean sensor observing system of 20 nodes wireless sensor network, which is the middleware between ocean sensors and ocean sensor observing data usage. Though the SWE 2.0 standards can be applied in complex scenarios, most of the available deployments are providing data from in-situ sensors.

Keywords: Sensor Web, Ocean Observing System, Share data, SOS.

1 Introduction

A sensor [1][2] is defined from an engineering point of view as a device that converts a physical, chemical, or biological parameter into an electrical signal. Common examples include sensors for measuring temperature(i.e., a thermometer), wind speed(an anemometer), humidity, or barometric pressure, which are quickly becoming ubiquitous and can be found in a vast range of environments including the ocean observation domain as these little devices becoming smaller, cheaper, more intelligent, and more power efficient. However, according to sensor observation system, there are varieties of sensor data formats, parameters units, spatiotemporal resolution, application domains, data quality and sensors protocols etc. All of these differences affect the integration of data from varieties of sensor observation systems especially in the domain of Ocean Observing System. This has already lead to standardization efforts aiming at facilitating the so-called Sensor Web, which has been the driving force for the Open Geospatial Consortium (OGC) to start the Sensor Web Enablement (SWE) initiative back in 2003 [3]. SWE defines the term Sensor Web as "Web accessible sensor networks and archived sensor data that can be discovered and accessed using standard protocols and application programming interfaces", which leads to a powerful set of standards allowing the integration of sensors and sensor data into

R. Wang and F. Xiao (Eds.): CWSN 2012, CCIS 334, pp. 137–156, 2013.
© Springer-Verlag Berlin Heidelberg 2013

spatial data infrastructures. A Sensor Web can hence be seen as a huge internet based sensor network and data archive. To achieve the vision of the Sensor Web, the SWE initiative defines standards for encoding of sensor data as well as standards for service interfaces to access sensor data, task sensors or send and receive alerts.

1.1   Sensor Web and GEOSS

The concept of Sensor Web [4][5] is firstly described by Delin et al. in 1999, a Sensor Web was considered as an autonomously organized wireless sensor network which can be deployed to monitor environments. The term "Web" within Delins "Sensor Web" relates to the intelligent coordination of the network rather than the World Wide Web(WWW) [6]. The meaning of "Sensor Web" changed and it was more and more seen as an additional layer integrating sensor networks with the WWW and applications [7]. The Sensor Web [8-10] concept presents a vision of the (Geo-)Sensor Web is that access to (geo-)sensors as uniform and easy as access to resources on the World Wide Web today, which makes intra-communicating spatially distributed sensor pods that can be deployed to monitor and explore different environments.

Referring to earth observation domain of GEOSS(The Global Earth Observation System of Systems), the derived view of the Sensor Web as a concept in the context is an "open coordinated observation infrastructure composed of a distributed collection of resources that can collectively behave as a single, autonomous, task-able, dynamically adaptive and reconfigurable observing system that provides raw and processed data, along with associated meta-data, via a set of standards-based interfaces." [11][12] Being a system of system, GEOSS has to master the challenge of integrating heterogeneous systems across institutional and political boundaries. Timely delivery of earth observation sensor data is a key aspect in identifying potential natural and human threats, such as tornados, tsunamis, wild fires, or algae blooms.

1.2   OGC SWE

The OGC SWE working group was founded in 2003. As part of OGC's specification program, the SWE working group develops standards to integrate sensors into the Geospatial Web for enabling a specialized subtype, the Sensor Web. Therefore, SWE has specified a number of standards defining formats for sensor data(O&M) and metadata(SensorML) as well as service interfaces which enable the interoperable access to real and virtual sensor resources. The SWE 1.0 specifications have been approved as standards between 2006 and 2007. As the middleware between sensors and applications, the new generation SWE (SWE 2.0) [13] are divided into two informal subgroups. First, the information model includes the data models and encodings. Second, the interface model comprises the different web service interface specifications (the interface model was formerly called service model and to avoid naming confusion with the SWE Service Model standard, which is part of the new generation SWE).

1.3   Reality of the Existing Ocean Observing Systems' Sharing Data

A great wealth of ocean data exists, for a wide range of disciplines, derived from in-situ and remote sensing observing platforms, in real-time, near-real-time and delayed mode. These data are acquired as part of routine monitoring activities and as part of scientific surveys by a few thousand institutes and agencies all around the world. Both the means to acquire these data and the way in which they are used have changed greatly in the past ten years.

According to the Ocean Observing Systems, the variety of ocean data platforms needs to create seamless and coordinated access to ocean observation data and products from distributed and heterogeneous ocean observation system sources, which mainly depend on the on-the-fly ocean sensors observation. But in fact, for the reasons of different ocean groups often represent, transport, store and distribute their data in different ways, even if the simplified data exchange between the ocean data centers become difficult. So methods must be introduced to improve the way scientists observe the oceans and manage the ocean observation data.

For the bad ocean environments, the ocean observing sensor and platform often do not work normally, So Quality Controlling of observing data is needed. At the same time we must make in mind of the poor buoy or other platform data bandwidth by any communication mode such as Satellite, CDMA, GPRS and so on. Thinking of the above issues, we must concern the practical and efficient design and implementation of sensor web in sharing the ocean observing data, which is based on the New SWE 2.0 sensor web standards. In other words, we must think of the actual ocean observing systems. In fact, we make use of a sensor web system which sharing the ocean observing data between the data producers and data consumers. Combining the sensor web 2.0 standards and the ocean observing data user requirements, we design and develop the ocean sensor web prototype system, which can supply the required ocean data that ocean scientists wanted.

The remainder of the paper is organized as follows: Section 2 introduces background and related work of ocean sensor web, while our representational approach based on framework of Ocean Sensor Web is proposed in Section 3. We introduce the ocean sensor web prototype system in Section 4. Finally, we discuss and conclude our work in Section 5.

2   Related Work

2.1   Sensor Device and Sensor Network for Ocean Observing System

Satellites, monitoring buoys, research vessels, and autonomous underwater vehicles carry a wide range of sensors. Though some sensors are application-specific, in many cases sensors measure phenomena that are useful to a wide variety of research and user communities. Sensors measuring a host of interdisciplinary variables from moorings and other platforms. Some parameters of general interest include surface water temperature, atmospheric pressure, cloud cover, salinity, wind speed, wave height, plankton count, and ocean current speed and direction. There is great value in sharing ocean sensor data for most ocean sensors are expensive. And for the reason that the oceans are huge and inhospitable to electronics, the cost of fielding, maintaining and communicating with sensors makes sharing ocean observation data an attractive proposition.

The ocean sensors and systems are constantly evolving. Ocean Observing systems comprise a collection of sensor and non-sensor marine environment measurements. The observing subsystem data collectors transmit their data from the sensor to data providers such as ocean data assembly centers and ocean data archive centers.

There are many Ocean Observing Sensor Platform. The sensors in observing devices or instruments can be classified as Physical, Chemical, Biological, Geophysical measuring parameter. Different Ocean Observing Systems, which consist of the ocean sensor devices, can improve our physical understanding in offshore zone and seabed, where data gathered locally by an underwater sensor network.

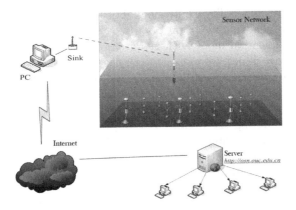

Fig. 1. Our Sensor Network Configuration Model

In fact, we deployed surface wireless sensor networks in the ocean experiment field of HuangHai area of China.(see Fig.1) The wireless sensor networks were made up of 20 floating nodes which were deployed on the sea surface of about 500 square meters. Every node was TelosB node(see Fig.2), and had a waterproof floating package. The sensor networks measured light intensity, temperature and wireless signal strength among the nodes in its location, which were used to estimate ocean depth and tidal conditions. The wireless sensor node was fixed by a anchor, we can get the radius by node's active range, and measure the depth of water according to the length of rope and radius.

We deployed some nodes, every node acquired the temperature of water, light information and so on, every node would send a signal every 10

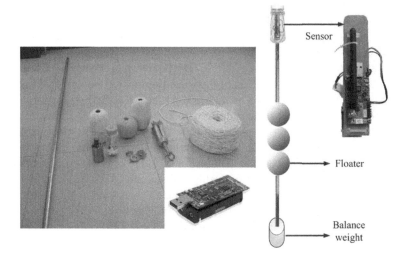

Fig. 2. Our TelosB Sensor Node

minutes, and its neighbor node received the signal and sent the information package including the signal and the information acquired by itself to the base-station by "multi-hop" protocol, at last, the base-station node received all signals and transmitted them to the PC linked with the base station directly. The PC would show the information of signals by networks in the website (http://osn.ouc.edu.cn/SensorData/exp_pic.html). At present, we can receive data in our laboratory, and we can express the degree of the data signals and do analysis of data.

2.2   The New Generation SWE-Sensor Web 2.0

Due to the large number of different sensor manufacturers and differing sensor communication protocols, integrating diverse sensors into observation systems is not straightforward. A coherent infrastructure is needed to treat sensors in an interoperable, platform-independent and uniform way. Sensor Web reflects such a kind of infrastructure for sharing, finding, and accessing sensors and their data across different applications. It hides the heterogeneous sensor hardware and communication protocols from the applications built on top of it. The Sensor Web Enablement initiative of the Open Geospatial Consortium standardizes web service interfaces and data encodings which can be used as building blocks for a Sensor Web.

The Sensor Web layer stack of The OGC SWE Group is mainly divided into three main architectural layers, that is, the sensor layer, the intermediary Sensor Web layer and the application layer. And the three main layers are further divided into sub-layers depending on the architectural design of middleware systems.

The SWE information model comprises a set of standards which define data models primarily for the encoding of sensor observations as well as sensor metadata. For this purpose, the first generation of SWE contained three specifications: Observations&Measurements(O&M), the Sensor Model Language(SensorML) and the Transducer Markup Language (TML). In the new generation SWE2.0, O&M 1.0 which is used for the description of measured sensor data evolves to O&M2.0. Also, the SensorML 1.0 standard advances to version 2.0. TML supports the encoding of sensor data as well as metadata by focusing on data streaming. TML has only been rarely used in practice and has not been further evolved so far. In the new generation of SWE specifications, TML is not referenced anymore and recent conversations in OGC's SWE working group showed that there is no urgent demand in TML and a retirement of the standard is in discussion.

The SWE interface model comprises standards that specify the interfaces of the different Sensor web services. Four service interfaces were defined for the first generation of SWE: The Sensor Observation Service(SOS) offers pull-based access to sensor measurements as well as metadata. The Sensor Alert Service(SAS) allows subscribing to alerts in case of a sensor measurement event that fulfills certain criteria. The Sensor Planning Service(SPS) can be used for tasking sensors and setting their parameters. The Web Notification Service (WNS) is, unlike the other three services, not directly sensor related. It is a supportive service which provides asynchronous notification mechanisms between SWE services and clients or other SWE services (e.g., delivery of notifications) including protocol transducing capabilities. While the SAS has evolved to the more powerful Sensor Event Service (SES), the WNS has not yet been further developed since an approved standard for eventing needs to be in place first.

Standardized access to sensor observations and sensor metadata is provided by the Sensor Observation Service(SOS). The service acts as a mediator between a client and a sensor data archive or a real-time sensor system. The heterogeneous communication protocols and data formats of the associated sensors are hidden by the standardized interface of the SOS. Sensor data requested by a client are returned as observations. The interface of the SOS supports access to heterogeneous sensor types, stationary as well as mobile sensors which gather their data in-situ or remotely. Currently, the development of the second version of the SOS specification has finished the public comment phase, and is about to be submitted to the standard approval process.

In recent years, SWE based Sensor Web infrastructures have been deployed in various projects and applications which demonstrated the practicability and suitability of the SWE standards. Many diverse sensor data management application frameworks were compared, such as:

1)The 52°North Sensor Web framework (http://52north.org/swe) provides implementations for the different SWE services. An implementation of the Sensor Observation Service (SOS) enables querying as well as inserting measured sensor data and metadata. Discovery of sensors is supported by implementations of Sensor Instance Registry (SIR) and Sensor Observable Registry (SOR). To integrate sensor resources with the SWE service implementations, the 52°North framework comprises an intermediary layer, called the Sensor Bus , to which sensor resources and SWE services can be adapted to establish communication.

2)Other middleware systems for building Sensor Web infrastructures based on SWE are GeoSWIFT and its successor GeoSWIFT 2.0. The latter redesigns the GeoSWIFT system to optimize its scalability by introducing a peer-to-peer based spatial query framework. The PULSENet framework, which reuses and amends the open source components of the 52°North Sensor Web framework, allows the implementation of a SWE-based Sensor Web. An important aspect of the system is to accommodate legacy and proprietary sensors (e.g., IEEE 1451 or CCSI) in SWE-based architectures. NASA's Sensor Web 2.0 system incorporates SWE services and combines them with Web 2.0 technology. It envisions an easy creation of mash-up applications which integrate data from multiple sources. This includes for example the creation of composite maps overlaying data from sensor sources with data from other sources such as weather or traffic. The mash-up functionality is realized by incorporating the representational state transfer (REST) approach to access data. However, it remains unclear how the system provides REST access to sensor resources by leveraging SWE services.

3)Non-standardized approaches for building a Sensor Web are for example Hourglass, the Global Sensor Network(GSN), the Sensor Network Services Plat-form(SNSP), or SOCRADES. GSN focuses on a flexible integration of sensor networks to enable fast deployment of new sensors. SNSP defines a set of service interfaces usable as an application programming interface for wireless sensor networks. SOCRADES comprises multiple services providing functionality such as data access, eventing or discovery. Further, only SOCRADES provides push-based delivery of sensor data, as offered by the SAS or SES.

The applications above have been implemented several types of SWE services for selected sensor data sources, then combined these services in different ways to develop or implement the prototype of a variety of data processing and management applications. But the frameworks of these applications are different due to different actual domains, it soon become obvious that these application frameworks provide only localized interoperability and that a standards-based framework is necessary.

3   The Design of Ocean Sensor Web

3.1   Architecture of Ocean Sensor Web

Fig. 3 shows the four layers architecture of Ocean Sensor Web. The Ocean Sensor Web is divided into four layers. First is Ocean Sensor Source Layer, which mainly refer to the varieties of ocean observing sensors source, such as Satellites, buoys, research vessels, Gliders, AUV/ROV and Seabed observing network node. Second is Information Model Layer, the sensor data and metadata is described by O&M 2.0 and SensorML 2.0. Third is Interface Model Layer(Service Model Layer), which consists of SOS, SPS, WNS, SES, SIR, SOR. Last is the Application Layer, also the destination of sensor web, depending on the variety of user requirements.

There are several benefits that this kind of integration has brought to the ocean community. First of all, the heavy load of ocean sensor observation processing can be moved from sensor networks to the distributed ocean computer systems which belong to the ocean data centers. The separation is either saving a lot of energy and power of sensor networks just concentrating on sensing and sending information or accelerating the process for processing and fusing the huge amount of information by utilizing distributed systems.

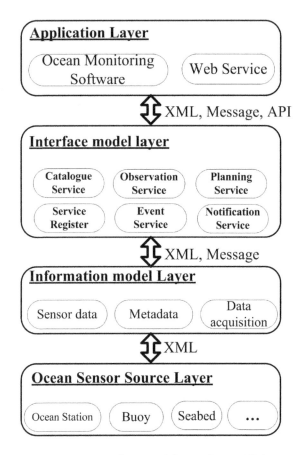

Fig. 3. Four Layers of Ocean Sensor Web

Actually, the various sensors defined in Ocean Sensor Web are from the various platform of ocean sensor source such as Ocean Station, Seabed, Buoy and Sensorchain etc. For the different sensor data format, protocols and so on, we designed the Sensor Network Access Module as illustrated in Fig. 4. We added the Network module in the sensor node, which can hide the different communication protocols, easy linked to the Information Model Layer of Ocean Sensor Web.

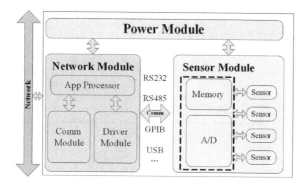

Fig. 4. Sensor Network Access Module

We also need to think and determine the relevant use possibilities: Data provider annotates Sensor Observation Datasets with references to semantic definitions; User(or software agent) searches for data providers and observation data via service queries; User(or software agent) gets data and then navigates (linked) metadata elements in associated vocabularies. So the Ocean Sensor Web needs to support the following functions: 1)Service query support-by using background service capability, our application has the opportunity to only expose coherent query (portal and services); 2)Semantic integration-in the past users had to remember (and maintain codes) to account for numerous different ways to combine and plot the data whereas now semantic mediation provides the level of sensible data integration required, now exposed as smart web services understanding of coordinate systems, relationships, data synthesis, transformations, etc. 3)Return independent variables and related parameters-A broader range of potential users(ocean scientists, students, professional research associates and those from outside the fields).

3.2   Ocean Sensor Web Service Based on SOA

The SOA is the essential infrastructure that supports the Ocean Sensor Web Layer and plays a very important role to present the core middleware components as services for clients to access. The reason why Ocean Sensor Web heavily relies on SOA is quite obvious since SOA is a loose coupling distributed architecture and can make interoperability of the heterogeneous systems possible. Moreover, SOA allows the services to be published, discovered and invoked by each other on the network dynamically. All the services communicate with each other through predefined protocols via messaging mechanism, which supports both synchronous and asynchronous communication model. As the sensor networks basically differ from each other, trying to put different sensors on the web through uniform operations to discover and access them requires the adoption of SOA.

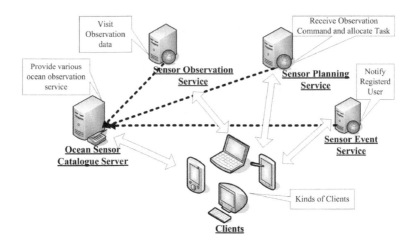

Fig. 5. Ocean Sensor Web Services Based on SOA

We are currently developing a prototype application for the Ocean Sensor Web (see Fig. 5 for a screenshot of Ocean Sensor Web Services).

4   Prototype System of Ocean Sensor Web

When successfully implemented, the prototype system of Ocean Sensor Web in our ocean sensor information exchange platform can be applied to many other industry information resources. We propose using it as early as possible to be the recommended standard of ocean sensor surveillance networks integration, providing the researchers a better way of tracking ocean sensor data throughout its life history. The development of ocean sensor data for publish, query and get ocean data will prove useful as data centers moving towards web services for sensor data distribution. Additionally, the ability to give the ocean sensor data directory service will allow researchers to collaborate on global observational data issues.

4.1   The Sensor Metadata and Data Format of Observation

An observation is an event that estimates an observed property of a feature of interest, using a procedure, and generating a result. Sometimes "observed property" and "feature of interest" are conflated in describing geophysical parameters, e.g. sea surface temperature. We take Davis Weather Station System as the example of sensor observation, which is an common outdoor electronic device that not only measures temperature, but also gives a reading for wind speed, wind direction, rainfall, humidity, and barometric pressure.

Davis weather station is setup to measure and record atmospheric measurements at 15 minute intervals. Davis weather station can provide temperature,

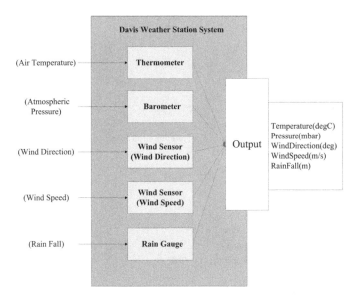

Fig. 6. The Davis Weather Station Logic Chart

barometric pressure, wind speed and direction and rainfall, measured by sensors attached to the station either through cables, or wirelessly, as illustrated in Fig. 6.

According to the SensorML(Sensor Model Language) 2.0 of OGC standards, we adopt only core elements and attributes of SensorML 2.0 for the reason of readability and efficient bandwidth management. Davis:Thermometer is described as follows:

```
<sml:Sensor
xmlns:swe="http://www.opengis.net/swe"
xmlns:xlink="http://www.w3.org/1999/xlink"version="1.0"
xmlns:sml="http://www.opengis.net/sensorML"
xmlns:xsi=http://www.w3.org/2001/XMLSchema-instance
id="OSN-Davis:Thermometer">
<sml:identification>
  <sml:IdentifierList>
    <sml:identifier name="manufacturer">
      <sml:Term qualifier="urn:ogc:identifier:manufacturer">Davis Corporation
      </sml:Term>
    </sml:identifier>
  </sml:IdentifierList>
</sml:identification>
<sml:inputs>
  <sml:InputList>
    <sml:input name="electricalsignal">
```

```
      <swe:Quantity definition="urn:ogc:phenomenon:frequency"
      uom="urn:ogc:unit:hertz"/>
    </sml:input>
  </sml:InputList>
</sml:inputs>
<sml:outputs>
  <sml:OutputList>
    <sml:output name="Temperature">
      <swe:Quantity definition="urn:ogc:phenomenon:temperature"
      uom="urn:ogc:unit:degC"/>
    </sml:output>
  </sml:OutputList>
</sml:outputs>
<sml:referenceFrame>
  <sml:LocalTimeCRS id="SensorTime">
    <sml:srsName>GMT</sml:srsName>
    <sml:usesCS xlink:href="urn:ogc:crs:GMT"/>
  </sml:LocalTimeCRS>
</sml:referenceFrame>
</sml:Sensor>
```

According to the O&M encodings proposed in the OGC Observations and Measurements draft proposal, the two following formats were designed: The first is FullObservation, which includes the sensor parameter metadata and sensor observation data as illustrated in Fig. 7, the second is SimpleObservation, that is, only the sensor observation data, which is illustrated as the following XML descriptions. Referring to the bandwidth restriction, SimpleObservation is the best format of sensor observation data.

```
<om:Observation gml:id="SimpleObservationOfDavisWeather"
xmlns:swe=http://www.opengis.net/swe
xmlns:xst=http://www.seegrid.csiro.au/xml/st
xmlns:xsi=http://www.w3.org/2001/XMLSchema-instance
xmlns:xlink=http://www.w3.org/1999/xlink
xmlns:gml=http://www.opengis.net/gml
xmlns:schemaLocation="http://www.opengis.net/om ../om.xsd">
<gml:description>Simple Observation of Davis Weather Station</gml:description>
<gml:name>Simple Observation</gml:name>
<om:time>
  <gml:TimeInstant >
   <gml:timePosition>2008-10-11T17:22:25.00</gml:timePosition>
  </gml:TimeInstant>
</om:time>
<om:location xlink:href="http://osn.ouc.edu.cn/coord?rec=Laoshan1"/>
<om:observedProperty xlink:href="urn:x-ogc:def:phenomenon:weather"/>
<om:featureOfInterest xlink:href=" http://osn.ouc.edu.cn/coord?rec=Laoshan1"/>
<om:resultDefinition xlink:href="DavisWeatherRecordDefinition.xml"/>
```

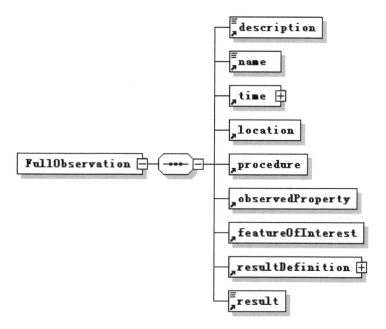

Fig. 7. The Definition of FullObservation Root Node

```
<om:result>
  <swe:Record>
    <swe:item>25.4</swe:item>
    <swe:item>770</swe:item>
    <swe:item>176</swe:item>
    <swe:item>12.2</swe:item>
    <swe:item>200</swe:item>
  </swe:Record>
</om:result>
</om:Observation>
```

4.2   The Ocean Sensor Observation Service

The Ocean Sensor Observation Service mainly provides the following Web Service interfaces: GetCapabilities( ), DescribeSensor( ), GetObservation( ), RegisterSensor( ), InsertObservation( ).

The GetCapabilities( ) provides the description of Sensor(s) and all available Web Service interfaces - the source of Ocean Sensor Observation Service instance metadata , which has the XML format of capabilities as illustrated in Fig. 7. Essentially, the GetCapabilities( ) describes the types of sensors, the operations to gain remote access to sensor data, and the logical sensor grouping available to the consumer.

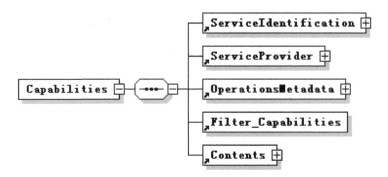

Fig. 8. XML model of Capabilities Root Element

From Fig. 8 you can see that the Capabilities root element mainly consists of four sub-elements:ServiceIdentification,ServiceProvider,OperationsMetadata and Contents. The "ServiceIdentification" tag means the information of Sensor Observation Service being offered, which mainly consists of service keywords, version type and other identification information. The "ServiceProvider" tag provides the information of provider, a person or organization, which provides the service and can be contacted. The "OperationsMetadata" tag mainly referred to the operations and URL for HTTP Get and Post. The Contents tag contains the details of sensor observation service.

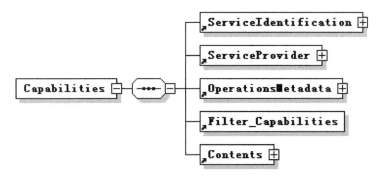

Fig. 9. XML Node of ServiceIdentification Element

Just as Fig.9, ServiceIdentification Node is the instance of ocean sensor observation service, which is mainly illustrated by Title, Abstract, Keywords, ServiceType and ServiceTypeVersion nodes, and in the application of ocean observation domain, such as the example of Davis Weather Station Service.

GetCapabilities( ), DescribeSensor( ) and GetObservation( ) mainly consist of the sequence of between the Data User and Sensor Observation Service as

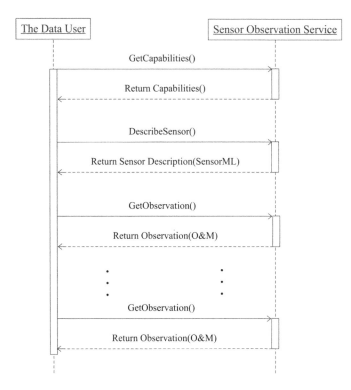

Fig. 10. UML Sequence Diagram

illustrated in Fig. 10. Firstly, the data user interact with the Sensor Observation Service, which returns a metadata listing in the form of the format as illustrated in Fig. 8. The Capabilities document consists of sensors involved, locations, phenomena, etc. especially, the Sensor ID of the next DescribeSensor( ) is provided by the Capabilities document. Secondly, when the DescribeSensor( ) is invoked, the SensorML document which describes the sensors is returned. And the next step is GetObservation( ), which can return the O&M format observed sensor data.

Ocean Sensor Data Provider has the operations of RegisterSensor( ), InsertObservation( ) and ReturnRequest( ). If the data of Ocean Sensor Data User in not in the server of Ocean Sensor Observation Service(SOS), SOS server will help the user to get the needed data from Ocean Sensor Data Provider by the interface of RequestObservation( ). So the data provider sends the data to SOS server by the interface of ReturnRequest( ). All these can be illustrated in Fig. 11.

The data provider must register the sensor by the RegisterSensor() function. if a new sensor is to be observed by interface of the Sensor Observation Service, which is aware of the new sensor information by the GetCapabilities function.

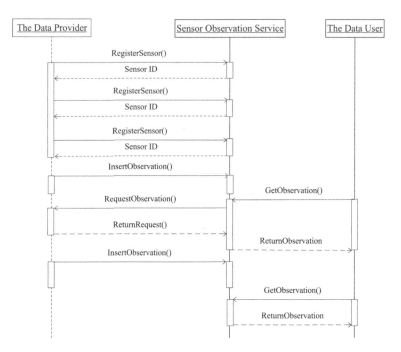

Fig. 11. UML Sequence Diagram of SOS

After being registered in the Sensor Observation Service, the new sensor can perform the InsertObservation() function to insert new sensor observed data.

The RequestObservation( ) is responded to the GetObservation( ) of the data user, when the request is not immediately serviced by the Sensor Observation Service(i.e. the required sensor data have not reached the site of Sensor Observation Service).

The ReturnRequest( ), just like the function of "InsertObservation( )", except that this function is invoked by RequestObservation( ). In other words, we can say that the distinction between "push" data mode of InsertObservation( ) and "pull" data mode of ReturnRequest( ).

4.3   The Ocean Sensor Web Prototype System

We create the Ocean Sensor Observation Service prototype using Microsoft C#.Net 2005 for developing the Ocean Sensor Web Prototype System as Fig. 12, which displays the sensor data of Fig.1's sea area.

Thinking of the GUI interface of GoogleEarth mode, we provide two ways of displaying the sensor data: GoogleMap and GoogleEarth, which are based on the Web Service Interface of Google.

Fig.12 shows the displaying page of 20 ocean sensors in the sea area of Huanghai of China near the mountain of LaoShan.

Fig. 12. Ocean Sensor Web Prototype System

If you click the sensor node in the page, the details of this sensor node can be seen from the next page illustrated in Fig.13.

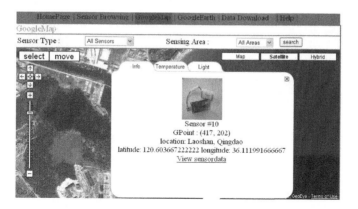

Fig. 13. Details of Ocean Sensor Node10

So through the "Info","Temperature" and "Light" selection you can get the details of this sensor #10 node. Because this type sensor only detect the environment temperature and light value near the sea, you can view the current data curve as illustrated in Fig.14 and Fig. 15.

At last, through the prototype system of ocean sensor web we can query the required metadata information and sensor data through the GUI interface of ocean sensor service system.

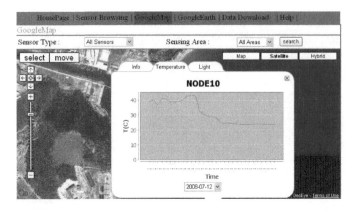

Fig. 14. Temperature Curve of Sensor Node 10

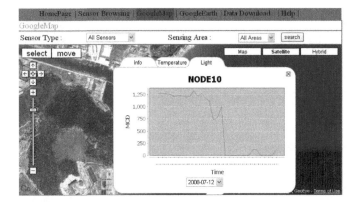

Fig. 15. Light Curve of Sensor Node 10

4.4   Conclusions

By incorporating the standardization efforts of the OGC and W3C into a robust Ocean Sensor Web, we are able to provide an environment for the effective discovery and retrieval of ocean sensor data. Beyond ocean sensor data on the Web, this framework could play an important role in many domains. We see great potential for the Sensor Web in many different domains, including weather forecasting, biometrics, emergent applications, and EventWeb.

In fact, we expect to implement the integration of new technologies into the Ocean Sensor Web concept, like mass market sensors and tools like Google Earth, Microsoft Virtual Earth, and NASA World Wind. Such framework could then be used to query and retrieve similar sensor data or share this experience with the world. We believe that the expressivity and accessibility provided by such an integrated vision is essential to realizing sensors as a first-class citizen of the Web.

Acknowledgments. This work was supported by the open fund project "Research on key technology of information service of marine sensor web" by the Shandong Provincial Key Laboratory of Marine Ecology and Environment&Disaster Prevention and Mitigation(Grant No. 2011002) and the Chinese Marine public welfare project-"Ocean environment information integration and dynamic management of Bohai Sea"(Grant No.200905030). Altova generously provided a free copy of XML Spy 2008 to JIANG Yongguo that was used in ocean Sensor XML and ocean sensor service capabilities in this paper. The authors thank Drs. Zhengbao Li, Lu Hong and Tong Hu for their reviews, which improved the quality of the manuscript.

References

1. Bermudez, L., Delory, E., O'Reilly, T., del Rio Fernandez, J.: Ocean Observing Systems Demystified. In: Proceedings of OCEANS 2009, Marine Technology for Our Future: Global and Local Challenges, Biloxi, MS, USA, pp. 1–7. IEEE, New York (2009)
2. Gross, N.: The earth will don an electronic skin, BusinessWeek (August 1999)
3. Botts, M., et al.: OGC Sensor Web Enablement: Overview and High Level Architecture (OGC 07-165). Open Geospatial Consortium white paper (December 28, 2007)
4. Delin, K., Jackson, S., Some, R.: Sensor Webs. NASA Tech. Briefs 23, 90 (1999)
5. Delin, K.: The Sensor Web: A Macro-Instrument for Coordinated Sensing. Sensors 2, 270–285 (2001)
6. Gibbons, P., Karp, B., Ke, Y., Nath, S., Seshan, S.: Irisnet: An Architecture for a Worldwide Sensor Web. IEEE Pervasive Comput. 2, 22–33 (2003)
7. Shneidman, J., Pietzuch, P., Ledlie, J., Roussopoulos, M., Seltzer, M., Welsh, M.: Hourglass: An Infrastructure for Connecting Sensor Networks and Applications. Technical Report. Harvard University, Columbia, MA, USA, EECS (2004)
8. Nittel, S.: A Survey of Geosensor Networks: Advances in Dynamic Environmental Monitoring. Sensors 9, 5664–5678 (2009)
9. Liang, S.H.L., Crotoru, A., Tao, C.V.: A Distributed Geospatial Infrastructre for Sensor Web. Computers & Geosciences 31(2), 221–231 (2005)
10. Balazinska, M., Deshpande, A., Franklin, M.J., Gibbons, P.B., Gray, J., Nath, S., Hansen, M., Liebhold, M., Szalay, A., Tao, V.: Data Management in the Worldwide Sensor Web. IEEE Pervasive Computing, 30–40 (2007)
11. GEO Group. GEOSS Sensor Web Workshop 2009 invitation, May 21-22 (2009)
12. Teillet, P.: Sensor Webs: A Geostrategic Technology for Integrated Earth Sensing. In: Kooistra, L., Ligtenberg, A. (eds.) Proceedings of International Workshop Sensing a Changing World, Wageningen, The Netherlands, pp. 10–14 (November 2008)
13. Bröring, A., Echterhoff, J., Jirka, S., Simonis, I., Everding, T., Stasch, C., Liang, S., Lemmens, R.: New Generation Sensor Web Enablement. Sensors 11, 2652–2699 (2011)
14. Sheth, A., Henson, C., Sahoo, S.S.: Semantic Sensor Web. IEEE Internet Computing, 78–83 (July/August 2008)
15. Francois, A.R.J., Nevatia, R., Hobbs, J., Bolles, R.C.: An ontology framework for representing and annotating video events. IEEE MultiMedia 12(4), 76–86 (2005)

16. Hayes, J., O'Connor, E., Cleary, J., Kolar, H., et al.: Views from the coalface: chemo-sensors, sensor networks and the semantic sensor web. In: Proceedings of the 1st SemSensWeb 2009 Workshop on the Semantic Sensor Web, Collocated with ESWC 2009 (2009)

17. Henson, C.A., Neuhaus, H., Sheth, A.P., Thirunarayan, K., Buyya, R.: An Ontological Representation of Time Series Observations on the Semantic Sensor Web. In: Proceedings of the 1st SemSensWeb 2009 Workshop on the Semantic Sensor Web, Collocated with ESWC 2009 (2009)

18. Isenor, A.W., Robert Keeley, J.: Modeling Generic Oceanographic Data Objects in XML. Computing in Science and Engineering 7(4), 58–66 (2005)

19. Gruber, T.: Towards Prineiples for the Design of ontologies Used for Knowledge Sharing. International Journal of Human-Computer Studies 43(5-6), 907–928 (1995)

20. Gibbons, P.B., Karp, B., Ke, Y., Nath, S., Seshan, S.: IrisNet: An Architecture for a Worldwide Sensor Web. IEEE Pervasive Computing 2(4), 22–33 (2003), doi:10.1109/MPRV.2003.1251166

21. Chen, N., Di, L., Yu, G., Min, M.: A flexible geospatial sensor observation service for diverse sensor data based on Web Service. ISPRS Journal of Photogrammetry and Remote Sensing 64, 234–242 (2009)

22. Chen, N., Di, L., Yu, G., Gong, J., Wei, Y.: Use of ebRIM-based CSW with sensor observation services for registry and discovery of remote-sensing observations. Computers & Geosciences 35, 360–372 (2009)

A Survey on Event Processing for CPS

Fangfang Li, Jia Xu, and Ge Yu

College of Information Science and Engineering,
Northeastern University,
110004, Shenyang, China
{lifangfang,xujia,yuge}@ise.neu.edu.cn

Abstract. Cyber-Physical System (CPS) is an important research area
which promotes the progress of IT revolution and digital life in the 21st
century. As a vital element in CPS, event plays an important role in
transforming physical data into our semantic model. Therefore, the event
processing scheme is of importance to guarantee the usability of the
CPS. In this survey, we at first represent the notion, characteristics and
research significance of the events in CPS. Then, we summarize event
processing techniques under the context of CPS and its related research
fields separately, with pointing out the deficiencies of existing technologies when to support CPS applications. Finally, we discuss the challenges
of event processing in CPS as well as its future research directions.

Keywords: Cyber-Physical System (CPS), event processing, interactive.

1 Introduction

A Cyber-Physical System (CPS) is a system featuring a tight combination of
the systems computational process and its physical elements. CPS is known as
the next generation intelligent system, for it successfully integrates the computation, communication and system control together [33][20]. In CPS, the interactions to physical elements are achieved by defining the human-computer
interaction interfaces, with which the remote physical elements can be operated
reliably and safely at real-time. Due to the good properties of CPS, CPS applications will doubtlessly promote the IT industry revolution in the 21st century
and hence have a wide application prospect [1]. As a new research field, CPS
is developed with the supporting of the mature techniques in wireless sensor
networks and RFID systems. It thus requires the system to have the abilities
of "sensing", "communicating", "knowing" and "controlling". Specifically, the
"sensing" ability of CPS stems from the utilization of the sensor networks or
the RFID system that can "sense" data from the physical world. The "communicating" ability of the CPS system is to transform the sensing data to
the sink node in sensor networks or other types of data-collecting servers. The
"knowing" ability of the CPS system means it can derive the relative infor-
mation/knowledge from those collected sensing data. At last, the "controlling"
ability in CPS makes it powerful enough to control the physical world from the

R. Wang and F. Xiao (Eds.): CWSN 2012, CCIS 334, pp. 157–166, 2013.
© Springer-Verlag Berlin Heidelberg 2013

cyber world or vice verse. Although there are some similarities between the concept of CPS and the definition of Internet of Things, the Internet of Things differs from CPS in that it emphasizes the global connectedness while CPS pays more attention to the interactions between the cyber world and the physical world [18].

An application scenario of CPS is the intelligent medical monitoring system which is shown in Figure 1. Patients in the hospital are equipped with various kinds of intelligent medical devices, which sense a patients body temperature, blood pressure, heart rate and blood sugar level. These sensing data are immediately transformed to some remote monitoring service center with the aid of wireless communication techniques, such as blue teeth or WiFi. Based on those remote collected sensing data, doctors can give an instant diagnosis and adopt some necessary medical treatment to the patient [19][12]. Another example of the CPS application is the Future Transportation System, within which CPS makes a safe, clear unobstructed, reliable and efficient guarantee for the system [39][6]. Under the context of web-based building control system, the utilization of CPS apparently improves the power usage effectiveness by reducing the emission of fuel and greenhouse gases. Financial network that embeds the CPS greatly boosts the accuracy and the real-time capability of the system. In a nut shell, CPS brings new vitality into the areas of process control, environmental control, aviation equipment development, basic equipments control, distributed robot technology, national defense system, and intelligent building. All these applications will make great impact to the national economy [33].

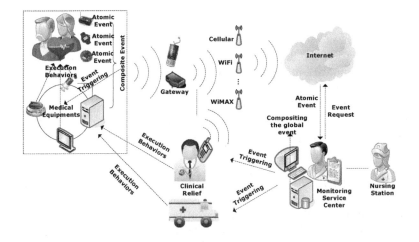

Fig. 1. The basic structure of medical monitoring system applying CPS

2   Properties of Event Processing in CPS

CPS applications have been bringing great changes to our daily life. Meanwhile, it also poses many challenges to research scientists. Each physical element in CPS integrates the functionalities of sensing, computing and communicating. By embedding a large amount of such physical elements, the CPS system aims to monitor the changes in the physical world, based on which the system will make intelligent reply and takes necessary actions following some established procedure. The computer processing system in CPS handles the information coming from the physical world in the form of "events" [9]. Taking the medical system shown in Fig. 1 as an example again, sensing equipments transfer sensing data (which is also known as the *"atomic events"*) to servers on which middleware systems integrate those atomic events into several local composite events. Those local composite events will then be transferred to a monitoring center to help doctors make timely diagnosis. Meanwhile the doctors can also issue a command to the CPS system, e.g., increasing the sampling rate to the patients heart rate. Such command will be delivered from the monitoring center to the bottom sensing equipments. This example indicates that interactions between the physical layer and the computing layer in CPS are achieved with the help of event middleware, and thus the CPS applications are known as *"event-driven"* applications. Since there are a great deal of equipments in CPS, *"heterogeneity"* becomes a key property of CPS. The heterogeneity comes from the differences between any two sensing devices or from the diversity in communication mode (by wireless or by wired network). The following summarizes the distinct properties of event processing in CPS compared with that in traditional event-handling systems.

Interactivity and Dynamic Feedback. One important property of CPS is the interactions between the cyber world and the physical world. The collected information from the physical world can infect the decision-making process in the cyber world, and on the other hand, the decision made in the cyber world will in return impact the physical world. The interactivity in CPS comes from the interoperability between different physical participants in CPS. Those interactivities are transferred to the back-end system which takes necessary actions to impact the physical participants. This completes one feedback loop between cyber and physical worlds.

Context Correlation. A judgment towards an event is usually made by combining the concrete context of the event. Specifically, the semantic of events is highly correlated to the concrete applications which provide the context of those events. In the example of medical monitoring system, our monitoring parameters can include body temperature, heart rate and ratio of white blood cells. However, when the context tells us that the patient has the heart disease, we need to pay more attentions to the heart rate.

Streaming Events. The physical elements in CPS sense data from the physical world and those sensing data generate the basic atomic events in CPS. For the sensing activities are really uninterrupted, and this produces a large amount of atomic events in a streaming pattern. Hence, the event processing scheme in CPS needs to ensure the efficiency of the event detection.

The Uncertainties in Event Composition Rules. The time and space of an event are multi-scale variables that may be uncertain, which leads to the uncertainties in event composition rules. With the help of event semantics, we can sometimes decrease such uncertainties [7]. The event composition rules are continually updated based on the feedback of events occurring in the physical world [9].

3   Research Status

CPS has been widely concerned at home and aboard. US National Science Foundation puts forward the development plan of CPS project in 2008 and invests 30 million to fund its related projects [4]. The European Community starts the CPS research project called "Advanced Research and Technology of Embedded Intelligent Systems". It invests 700 million in succession from 2007 to 2013 and hopes to achieve "the leader of intelligent electronic system in world" in 2016. The Korean Information Industry Association also puts forward a research plan which is "Embedded System Projects" for providing CPS services. China is also actively involved in the study of CPS. With a subsequent aim of "Experience China", the CPS is widely concerned. Jifeng He raises the significance and necessity of the CPS study in China National Computer Congress in 2009 [15]. China Computer Federation also organizes a special academic discussion [25] that is a preliminary study [31] about the data management [36] and the relationship of the CPS and the Internet of Things [18]. In addition, China Computer Federation Technical Committee on Sensor Network regards CPS as a major research area, which causes interest and concern of scholars in 2011.

The development of embedded technology, network technology, sense technology and control technology lays the advantageous foundation for the study of CPS. But there are many techniques needed to be studied. For example, we need to consider the intersection and integration of different kinds of digital parts and physical parts. We can set up a reasonable model that computers use to simulate the physical action. As another example, the physical interface and man-machine interface also need to be studied. Amongst all subjects needed to be explored, event processing is an important research topic.

3.1   Research Status of Event Processing in CPS

At present, the study of the CPS is at the beginning stage. The research of the CPS event processing is also at the discussion and embryonic stage. In 2008, the CPSweek [2] arranges the workshops [3] of the CPS event processing, in which the content of discussion includes the semantic of events and the challenges. These challenges are: 1) The support of many event types including discrete events and continuous events; 2) The recognition, modeling and reasoning of the event dependence; 3) The reasoning and integration of different scales based on the event semantic; 4) The method of the interactive event synthesis and interactive event constraint; 5) The model and method of the event monitoring, inspection and control. The CPSweek in 2010 still discussed the application of CPS of data-centric. The CPSweek in 2011 discussed the relationship between the calculation and control. Some projects are being studied:

The Architecture of Cyber-Physical Space. [17] describes the Information Cyber-Physical System (ICPS) that uses calculating interaction and bases on the event semantic. They establish a two layer "observation-analysis-adjustment" framework. The main techniques include the integration of executable system components, the model of the simulation and system monitoring. These techniques can support the analysis and parameter adjustment of crossing layers and crossing nodes.

SATWare System [16]. University of California, Irvine, carries the rescuing and responding project. At present, about a third of California universities have a variety of sensor equipment. In this system, they design the middleware of event streaming processing called SATware to allow programming sensors.

Multi-dimension Analysis of Atypical Events. [27] considers the CPS integrates physical device with cyber components to form analysis system with the situation. It can respond and change dynamically according to the real world. These responses and changes can be described by complex atypical events. They cluster the data obtained from sensors by spatio-temporal contacting. And then, they judge if the an atypical event happens.

3.2 Research Progress of Event Processing in Related Fields

In recent years, there are many studies of the event processing in related fields such as Wireless Sensor Networks (WSNs), RFID systems and etc, which can provide important references for us. The typical event streaming processing system includes: 1) University of California, Berkeley, develops the SASE system [14]; 2) Cornell University develops the Cayuga system [10]; 3) University of California, Berkeley, develops the HiFi system [8]; 4) University of Washington develops the Cascadia system [32]; 5) University of Texas, Arlington develops EStream system [28]; 6) University of Massachusetts develops real-time medical monitoring prototype system based on active CEP [30]; 7) University of Worcester Polytechnic develops the complex event query language called NEEL [22]; 8) Worcester Polytechnic Institute puts forward a new E-Cube model [23].

The studies on the event detection mainly focus on improving the reliability of data and the accuracy of forecasting events. We should take measures to get rid of the false data. The main event detection methods are classified into space-based clustering methods, geometry and the approaches based on probability model. The main idea of space-based clustering methods [29][5] is clustering the sensor network. They take the "K-out-of-N" [37] voting strategy which belongs to the judgment rules to judge the space correlation. Because there are correlations amongst nodes in each cluster, he distributed detection methods based on the geometry of fault tolerance can take advantages of existed geometrical theory. It can determine the error node information [26] effectively. For example, it can use the feature that the area of events taking place meets the convex polygon, or use the detection method based on triangle. The methods based on the probability model design a conversion model to calculate the probability on each attribute of the distributed function using the correlations among different attributes, because the spatial correlations [11] are accompanied on the sensing data. Events can be abstracted into spatial-temporal patterns of sensing data, and then the patterns can be matched through the contour map method effectively [34][24].

In China, according to incomplete reports, there are some researches about the complex event processing in universal applications in some Universities and research institutes such as Peking University [38][35], Institute of Software Chinese Academy of Sciences [21], and the Northeastern University [13].

3.3   Research Status Analysis of Event Processing

As the representatives [14]-[22] of complex event processing systems, for mass events in event streaming, they combine different applications and show different schemes of complex event detection. Those schemes offer important technology foundation for our research. But the versatile event streaming processing system only aims at the complex event matching and detection. The CPS event is the interaction ties between the physical world and computers. After the events from physical world are synthesized into complex events, they need to give feedback to the physical world. Then they guide the physical executors' behaviors or get more event information. So the CPS event processing has its own characteristics. The existing techniques still have limitations, and they are mainly reflected in creating event patterns and rules dynamically. The event pattern of event detections is predefined in the past database, the RFID and the sensor network. The fundamental models of the complex event detection includes the model based on finite automata, the model based on Petri nets, the model based on matching tree and the model based on directed graph. These models all use a kind of organization structures (such as automates, Petri nets, trees and acyclic graph, etc) to express the known rules. They make use of basis units of structures to stand for atomic events or the immediate results of composite events. According to the semantic rules that the structures express, they can detect the contained composite events from the event streaming. Those composite event detecting systems and typical prototype systems are only applicable to the known and fixed semantic rule set. And they regard the detected composite events as the final results, not considering the uncertain of rule set and the impact of feedback information for the event processing. Because of the interactivity of CPS system, just using the existing models cannot meet the demand. Therefore we need to establish a new event processing model to meet the interaction and feedback. Also how to build the dynamic event model based on the interaction and feedback needs to be studied.

4 Major Research Problems and Challenges for Interactive Event Processing in CPS

In this section, we present some vital research problems and challenges when we design interactive event prossing schemes in CPS.

4.1 Interactive Event Processing Model

As a summarization, we list some open research problems and challenges for interactive event processing in CPS.

Interactive Event Processing Model. Due to the interactivity of event in CPS, partial composite event usually can be used as the input of producing new event composition rules. Furthermore, it is necessary to produce new event composition rules in different scenarios. Therefore, solving the interactivity in CPS needs to build a feedback control model instead of utilizing the existing models for CPS running in real time and more accurately.

Expansive Methods of the Event Instance Consuming Strategies under Full Context Semantics. In event processing of CPS, the abstracts of events need some additional constraints to reflect the relationship of context semantic in the real world better. And this is called the event instance consuming strategies. There are some existing strategies of event instance consuming, such as *Recent, First, Chronicle, Cumulative, Continuous* and so on. There is still a pressing need for expanding event instance consuming strategies to express the full context semantics and support mixed-mode applications.

4.2 The Construction and Optimization of Adaptive Rule Sets

Due to the interactivity of CPS, the rules of event composition should be dynamically adaptive. There are some new challenges in building the rule sets. The key points of building and optimizing CPS event rules set is expressed as follow.

Building Dynamic Rule Set. In CPS, every complex semantic can be expressed as a composite event which is derived by matching rules in a certain rule set. To ensure the rule set can reflect the real-time properties of events in the physical world, the rule set should be built and adjusted dynamically on the basis of events in the physical world.

Rule Adjustment Based on Context Information. Event patterns in CPS are often changed by outside factors and individual differences, so context correlation is a factor of affecting event patterns. Context correlations should be taken as the important feedback information in the designing of event model, which are used to improve the composite event rules. It also ensures suit for the changes of physical world.

Elimination of Event Pattern Conflicts. According to event rules, create the corresponding physical objects. Those objects may meet some other rules again and then create objects again. Therefore, the interactive event processing system is feedback-driven. In the process of feedback-driven system, there are some rules improved or created at the same time, which may cause the confliction between the original rules and new rules or among the new rules. It will not make the system terminate in a state at a time. Thus, event conflict resolution should be one of the researches.

Elimination of Redundant Rules. Some additional rules can be redundant rules though deduced in adding event rules dynamically of CEP. Because redundant rules lead to low efficiency of event matching, they should be eliminated.

4.3 Event Detection Schemes for Interactive Events

Interactive event information in CPS is one of the important symbols. And detecting events method in an interactive way is one of the core researches. The main research points include:

Interactive Event Detection Based on Context Semantics. In the process of compositing atomic events in CPS, atomic events may meet different semantics at the same time, which asks event composition method work in an interactive way based on context semantics. Therefore, event composition method with introducing the context semantics is one of the research topics.

Adjustment of Event Pattern Utilizing Feedback Control Strategy. Feedback control is an important characteristic of CPS system. Event composition rules in a CPS system should be adjusted based on the feedback knowledge from the physical world. Therefore, designing an effective and efficient feedback control function to adjust event composition rules at real-time is an important research topic.

Optimized Event Composition Based on Shared Semantic Segments. Different queries registered in a CPS system may share some basic events. To enhance the efficiency of event composition process, techniques to handle the shared semantic segments is very necessary, which includes data sharing and operation sharing.

5   Conclusions

CPS is an emerging subject and rapidly becomes a hot research area. Event processing scheme is the most important link between the cyber world and the physical world. This paper introduces properties of events in CPS and makes an overview over some related research areas. The new research problems and challenges for event processing in CPS are also pointed out.

Acknowledgment. This work is supported by the National Natural Science Foundation of China under Grant No. 60973018.

References

1. CPS Steering Group. Cyber-physical systems executive summary, http://varma.ece.cmu.edu/summit/
2. http://www.CPSweek.org
3. http://blackforest.stanford.edu/eventsemantics/
4. Cyber-physical systems (cps) programm solicitation. Technical Report NSF 08-611, National Science Foundation (February 2009)
5. Abbasi, A., Ghadimi, E., Khonsari, A., Yazdani, N., Ould-Khaoua, M.: A Distributed Clustering Algorithm for Fault-Tolerant Event Region Detection in Wireless Sensor Networks. In: Thulasiraman, P., He, X., Xu, T.L., Denko, M.K., Thulasiram, R.K., Yang, L.T. (eds.) ISPA Workshops 2007. LNCS, vol. 4743, pp. 493–502. Springer, Heidelberg (2007)
6. Atkins, E.M.: Cyber-physical aerospace: Challenges and future directions in transportation and exploration systems. In: National Science Foundation Workshop on Smart Transportation and Aviation (2006)
7. Baker, D., Georgakopoulos, D., Nodine, M., Cichocki, A.: Requirements in providing awareness from events (2007)
8. Cooper, O., Edakkunni, A., Franklin, M.J., Hong, W., Jeffery, S.R., Krishnamurthy, S., Reiss, F., Rizvi, S., Wu, E.: Hifi: A unified architecture for high fan-in systems. In: VLDB, pp. 1357–1360 (2004)
9. Talcott, C.: Cyber-Physical Systems and Events. In: Wirsing, M., Banâtre, J.-P., Hölzl, M., Rauschmayer, A. (eds.) Software-Intensive Systems. LNCS, vol. 5380, pp. 101–115. Springer, Heidelberg (2008)
10. Demers, A.J., Gehrke, J., Panda, B., Riedewald, M., Sharma, V., White, W.M.: Cayuga: A general purpose event monitoring system. In: CIDR, pp. 412–422 (2007)
11. Fasolo, E., Prehofer, C., Rossi, M., Wei, Q., Widmer, J., Zanella, A., Zorzi, M.: Challenges and new approaches for efficient data gathering and dissemination in pervasive wireless networks. In: InterSense, p. 25 (2006)
12. U. S. Government: High-Confidence Medical Devices: Cyber-Physical Systems for 21st Century Health Care: A Research and Development Needs Report. Books LLC (2005)
13. Gu, Y., Yu, G., Zhang, T.: Rfid complex event processing techniques. Journal of Computer Science and Frontiers 1(3), 255–267 (2007)
14. Gyllstrom, D., Wu, E., Chae, H.-J., Diao, Y., Stahlberg, P., Anderson, G.: Sase: Complex event processing over streams (demo). In: CIDR, pp. 407–411 (2007)
15. He, J.: Cyber-physical systems (cps). China's Computer Assembly 2009 Special Report (2009)
16. Hore, B., Jafarpour, H., Jain, R., Ji, S., Massaguer, D., Mehrotra, S., Venkatasubramanian, N., Westermann, U.: Design and implementation of a middleware for sentient spaces. In: ISI, pp. 137–144 (2007)
17. Kim, M., Massaguer, D., Dutt, N., Mehrotra, S., Ren, S., Stehr, M.-O., Carolyn Talcott, N.V.: A semantic framework for reconfiguration of instrumented cyber physical spaces. In: Second Workshop on Event-based Semantics (WEBS 2008) in conjunction with IEEE Real-Time and Embedded Technology and Applications Symposium (RTAS 2008) in part of CPSWEEK, St. Louis, MO, USA (April 2008)
18. Kong, L., Wu, M.: The information industry for new revolution: Internet of things or cps. Communications of the CCF (CCCF) 6(4), 8–17 (2009)
19. Kornerup, J.: A vision for overcoming the challenges of building cyber-physical systems. In: National Science Foundation Workshop on Critical Physical Infrastructures, pp. 1–3 (2006)

20. Lee, E.A.: Cyber physical systems: Design challenges. In: Proceedings of the 11th IEEE International Symposium on Object Oriented Real-Time Distributed Computing (ISORC 2008), pp. 363–369. IEEE (2008)
21. Li, X., Qiao, Y., Wang, H.: A flexible event-condition-action (eca) rule processing mechanism based on a dynamically reconfigurable structure. In: ICEIS (1), pp. 291–294 (2009)
22. Liu, M., Rundensteiner, E.A., Dougherty, D.J., Gupta, C., Wang, S., Ari, I., Mehta, A.: High-performance nested cep query processing over event streams. In: ICDE, pp. 123–134 (2011)
23. Liu, M., Rundensteiner, E.A., Greenfield, K., Gupta, C., Wang, S., Ari, I., Mehta, A.: E-cube: multi-dimensional event sequence analysis using hierarchical pattern query sharing. In: SIGMOD Conference, pp. 889–900 (2011)
24. Liu, Y., Li, M.: Iso-map: Energy-efficient contour mapping in wireless sensor networks. In: ICDCS, pp. 36–47 (2007)
25. Ma, H.: Internet of things technology preliminary study. Communications of the CCF (CCCF) 6(4), 6–7 (2010)
26. Ould-Ahmed-Vall, E., Riley, G.F., Heck, B.S.: A geometric-based approach to fault-tolerance in distributed detection using wireless sensor networks. In: IPSN, pp. 211–218 (2006)
27. Tang, L.A., Yu, X., Kim, S., Han, J., Peng, W.-C., Sun, Y., Gonzalez, H., Seith, S.: Multidimensional analysis of atypical events in cyber-physical data. In: ICDE, pp. 1025–1036 (2012)
28. Vihang, G.: Estream: An integration of event and stream processing (2005)
29. Vuran, M.C., Akyildiz, I.F.: Spatial correlation-based collaborative medium access control in wireless sensor networks. IEEE/ACM Trans. Netw. 14(2), 316–329 (2006)
30. Wang, D., Rundensteiner, E.A., Ellison, R.T., Wang, H.: Active complex event processing: Applications in real-time health care. PVLDB 3(2), 1545–1548 (2010)
31. Wang, Z., Xie, L.: Cyber-physical systems: a survey. Journal of Tsinghua University 37(10), 1157–1166 (2011)
32. Welbourne, E., Khoussainova, N., Letchner, J., Li, Y., Balazinska, M., Borriello, G., Suciu, D.: Cascadia: a system for specifying, detecting, and managing rfid events. In: MobiSys, pp. 281–294 (2008)
33. Wing, J.M.: Cyber-physical systems research charge. Presentation at Cyber-Physical Systems Summit, St. Louis, MO, April 24 (2008)
34. Xue, W., Luo, Q., Chen, L., Liu, Y.: Contour map matching for event detection in sensor networks. In: SIGMOD Conference, pp. 145–156 (2006)
35. Ye, W., Zhao, W., Huang, Y., Hu, W., Zhang, S., Wang, L.: Formal Definition and Detection Algorithm for Passive Event in RFID Middleware. In: Li, Q., Feng, L., Pei, J., Wang, S.X., Zhou, X., Zhu, Q.-M. (eds.) APWeb/WAIM 2009. LNCS, vol. 5446, pp. 538–543. Springer, Heidelberg (2009)
36. Yu, G., Li, F.: Data management of internet of things. Communications of the CCF (CCCF) 6(4), 30–34 (2010)
37. Zhang, W., Wang, G., Xing, Z., Wittenburg, L.: Distributed stochastic search and distributed breakout: properties, comparison and applications to constraint optimization problems in sensor networks. Artif. Intell. 161(1-2), 55–87 (2005)
38. Zhu, J., Huang, Y., Wang, H.: A formal descriptive language and an automated detection method for complex events in rfid. In: COMPSAC (1), pp. 543–552 (2009)
39. Zobel, D.: Autonomous driving in goods transport. In: National Science Foundation Workshop on Smart Transportation and Aviation (2006)

MND: An Information of Detected Neighbors Based Multi-channel Neighbor Discovery Protocol for Wireless Sensor Networks

Jinbao Li, Zhigang Wang, Liang Yao, and Longjiang Guo

School of Computer Science and Technology, Heilongjiang University, Harbin, 150080
Key Laboratory of Database and Parallel Computing of Heilongjiang Province

Abstract. Multi-channel neighbor discovery protocol based on information of detected neighbors for wireless sensor networks is proposed in this paper, called MND. To make sure that the discovery among nodes is as quick as possible, MND uses the schedule mechanism in which the nodes compute the potential neighbors set so as to calculate the sleep and wake schedule of the node. To minimize the influence of channel conflict to the performance, MND uses multi-channel mechanism and calculates the required total number of channels according to the duty cycle and network density. Through analysis, we can get how to choose the total number of channels for each node and the fact that the common neighbor node of the neighbors of a node is the neighbor of this node in a large probability. The simulation and test-bed experiment results show the discovery rate and discovery latency of MND is higher and lower, respectively.

Keywords: Neighbor Discovery, WSNs, Multi-Channel.

1 Introduction

Recently, the requirement of communication in time between many nodes increases with the development of mobile devices and the applying of sensor nodes[1,2,3,4,5]. Using protocols without duty cycle mechanism can make sure that nodes can be discovered as quickly as possible. However, these protocols are not realistic due to the energy constraint of nodes. Therefore, in WSNs with dense deployment, designing a protocol that can ensure the energy efficiency and satisfy the delay requirement becomes a challenge. To save energy, some protocols like Birthday[7], Disco[8], U-Connect[9] and Searchlight[10] adopt duty cycle mechanism. These protocols can guarantee the discovery delay between nodes to be low by overlapping their wake-up slot when the network density is small. However, the performance of them may be affected by the increasing of channel conflicts caused by the increasing of network density.

To solve the problem above, we analysis the relation between the node density and the required total number of channel and design a multi-channel neighbor discovery protocol for WSNs called MND which is short for multi-channel neighbor discovery. In MND, to reduce the probability of beacon conflicts, nodes

R. Wang and F. Xiao (Eds.): CWSN 2012, CCIS 334, pp. 167–180, 2013.
© Springer-Verlag Berlin Heidelberg 2013

randomly choose a channel from the channel list and send a beacon message at this channel when they are in wake up procedure. Meanwhile, the nodes execute the sleeping schedule according to the information of discovered nodes in order to ensure energy efficiency and quick speed of discovering nodes. The main contribution of this paper is as follows: We proposed a multi-channel neighbor discovery protocol based on information of detected neighbors. A duty cycle mechanism is used to save energy and the discovery latency is guaranteed to be low by utilizing discovered neighbors. Through theoretical analysis, we can get that the multi-channel neighbor discovery mechanism and the predicting mechanism based on information of detected neighbors can be more efficient in densely deployed sensor networks. The good performance of MND is verified through simulation and real test-bed experiments.

2   Related Work

In recent years, many neighbor discovery protocols are proposed, such as Birthday, Quorum, Disco, U-Connect, SearchLight, WiFlock[5] and SWOPT[6].

In [7], McGlynn proposed the asynchronous neighbor discovery protocol in a static ad hoc network. In this protocol, nodes send, listen and sleep in a different probability. The protocol supports the asymmetric node duty cycle and its perfor-mance of discovery is not bad, but it cannot guarantee the timeliness of the neighbor discovery. In [11] and [12] two probability-based neighbor discovery protocols are proposed. In these two protocols, time is divided into slots. Without considering the conflicts, any two nodes can discovery each other in m^2 slots. However, subject to the consistency of the m, these two protocols cannot be applied to application in which the duty cycle of nodes is different from each other.

According to the Chinese Remainder Theorem[13], the Disco protocol is proposed in [8]. In Disco, in order to ensure nodes discover each other in a timely manner, each node selects two different prime p_1 and p_2 and wake up periodically according to these primes. For any two nodes, assuming that their prime pairs are (p_1, p_2) and (p_3, p_4) respectively, the maximum delay for them to discovery each other is $min\{p_1p_3, p_1p_4, p_2p_3, p_2p_4\}$ in the case of no channel conflict. In [9], a protocol called U-Connect is proposed. Each node using this protocol is required to choose only one prime p according to the duty cycle. To make sure that nodes with same duty cycle can discover each others, each node not only wake up once every p slots, but also wake up $\frac{p+1}{2}$ slots every p^2. By using the power energy product parameters proposed in [8] to evaluate the performance, we can get that Disco and the U-Connect are 2-approximate optimal algorithm and 1.5-approximate optimal algorithm respectively when the duty cycle of all nodes are same. Since these protocols do not have a good average performance, M. Bakht proposed SearchLight protocol in [10]. SearchLight uses duty cycle mechanisms as well. However, when all nodes choose the same duty cycle, each node is no longer need to choose a prime number. In SearchLight, each node computes the fixed wake-up time slot interval t in accordance with the duty cycle. Besides waking up every t time slots, each node choose a slot to wake up between two fixed waking up slots. Through analysis by using the PL metric proposed in [8] SearchLight is 1.41-approximate optimal algorithm.

Aveek et al [5] proposed a protocol called WiFlock in mobile sensor networks. WiFlock combines the neighbor discovery and group maintenance and its performance of discovering is good. However, synchronized listening consumes more energy. Meanwhile, WiFlock does not use multi-channel so that it is vulnerable by changes of network density. To reduce the impact of conflict increasing partly caused by density increasing to the protocol, the multi-channel neighbor discovery protocols for wireless network are proposed in [6], namely OPT and SWOPT. They use linear programming to solve the node sleep scheduling and the scheduling of the channel. However, the protocols are not suitable for energy-constrained sensor networks, so is the protocol proposed in [14].

3   Theoretical Analysis

In the mechanism based on duty cycle, the channel conflict is determined by network density, duty cycle of nodes and required channel m. Meanwhile, the channel conflict will affect the discovery probability of nodes within a certain time. Some symbols used in the analysis are shown in Table 1.

Table 1. Symbol and Meaning

Symbol	Meaning
p^i_{succ}	The probability node i received the beacon form node k in one time slot
p^i_s	The probability that node i is awake in some slot
p^i_t	The probability that node i is in sending state
p^i_l	The probability that node i is in listening state
CUC_i	The channel number that nodes i is using
RS_c	node i successfully received the beacon form node k at channel c
$RSU^c_{i\_k}$	node i received the beacon form node k at channel c
$\overline{RSU^c_{i\_N^{i\backslash k}}}$	node i does not receive the beacon form the nodes except k at channel c
$\overline{SS^c_{N^{i\backslash k}}}$	The nodes does not send beacon at channel c except k
$CIS^c_{i\_k}$	node i and node k are using the same channel c
NT_i	node i is on the sending state
NL_i	node i is on the listening state
STL_{i_k}	node i is on the listening state while node k is on the sending state
m	the required total number of channel
d	average node density in the networks
N_i	neighbor set of nodes i
$N^{i\backslash k}$	$N_i - \{k\}$
$CA(i)$	communication coverage area of node i

3.1 Multi-Channel Neighbor Discovery

Assume that node i and node k using the same channel c, then

$$Pr(CIS_{i\_k}^c) = Pr(CUC_i = c \cap CUC_k = c) = \frac{1}{m^2}. \tag{1}$$

The event that node i is in a listening state and the event that node k is in the sending state are independent of each other, so

$$Pr(STL_{i\_k}) = Pr(NT_k \cap NL_i) = Pr(NT_k)Pr(NL_i) = p_t^k p_l^i. \tag{2}$$

Node i can received the beacon form node k at channel c means that node i and node k are using the same channel c and node i is on the listening state while node k is on the sending state, namely

$$Pr(RSU_{i\_k}) = Pr(CIS_{i\_k}^c \cap STL_{i\_k}). \tag{3}$$

For any two nodes, the event that they are in sending or receiving state and the event that whether they are at a same channel are independent of each other, therefore,

$$Pr(CIS_{i\_k}^c \cap STL_{i\_k}) = Pr(CIS_{i\_k}^c)Pr(STL_{i\_k}). \tag{4}$$

From (1), (2), (3) and (4), we can know that

$$Pr(RSU_{i\_k}^c) = Pr(CIS_{i\_k}^c \cap STL_{i\_k}) = \frac{p_t^k p_l^i}{m^2}. \tag{5}$$

The event node i does not receive the beacon form the nodes except k at channel c is equivalent to that node i is not on the listening state at channel c or other nodes are not on sending state at channel c, namely $\overline{RSU_{i\_N^{i\backslash k}}} = \cup \overline{SS_{N^{i\backslash k}}^c} NL_i$. Meanwhile, the event other nodes are not on sending state at channel c means that the event that these nodes are not using channel c or not on the sending state. Assume that $p_t^i = p_t^j$ is satisfied for any i and j, and any j nodes ($0 \le j < d$) among the $d-1$ neighbors of nodes i are on the sending state except k, then it can be inferred that

$$Pr(SS_{N^{i\backslash k}}^c) = \sum_{j=0}^{d-1} C_{d-1}^j p_t^{kj} (1 - p_t^k)^{d-1-j} (1 - 1/m)^j. \tag{6}$$

In a time slot, node i can successfully receive the beacon form node k at channel c only if node k is sending beacon at channel c and the other neighbor nodes of nodes i are not sending packets at this channel, it means that

$$Pr(RS_c) = Pr(RSU_{i\_k}^c)Pr(\overline{RSU_{i\_N^{i\backslash k}}^c}). \tag{7}$$

As $RSU_{i\_k}^c = CIS_{i\_k}^c \cap STL_{i\_k} = CIS_{i\_k}^c \cap NT_k \cap NL_i$ and $\overline{RSU_{i\_N^{i\backslash k}}^c} = \overline{SS_{N^{i\backslash k}}^c} \cup \overline{NL_i}$, $RSU_{i\_k}^c \cap \overline{RSU_{i\_N^{i\backslash k}}^c} = CIS_{i\_k}^c \cap NT_k \cap NL_i \cap (\overline{SS_{N^{i\backslash k}}^c} \cup \overline{NL_i})$, substituted into (7), therefor

$$Pr(RS_c) = Pr(CIS_{i\_k}^c \cap NT_k \cap NL_i \cap (\overline{SS_{N^{i\backslash k}}^c} \cup \overline{NL_i})) = Pr(RSU_{i\_k}^c \cap \overline{SS_{N^{i\backslash k}}^c}). \tag{8}$$

The event node i received the beacon form node k at channel c and the event other nodes are sending beacon at channel c is independent of each other, thus equation (8) changes into the following form:

$$Pr(RS_c) = Pr(RSU_{i\_k}^c)Pr(\overline{SS_{N^{i\backslash k}}^c}). \tag{9}$$

From (5), (6) and (9), we can get that

$$Pr(RS_c) = \frac{p_t^k p_l^i}{m^2} \sum_{j=0}^{d-1} C_{d-1}^j p_t^{kj}(1-p_t^k)^{d-1-j}(1-1/m)^j. \tag{10}$$

In MND, the node i can receive a beacon message sent by node k through any channel, thus

$$p_{succ}^i = \sum_{c=1}^{m} Pr(RS_c). \tag{11}$$

$m > 1$, (10) is substituted into (11), therefore,

$$p_{succ}^i = \frac{p_t^k p_l^i}{m} \sum_{j=0}^{d-1} C_{d-1}^j p_t^{kj}(1-p_t^k)^{d-1-j}(1-1/m)^j. \tag{12}$$

3.2   Single Channel Neighbor Discovery

In single channel neighbor discovery, all nodes use the only one channel, that means $m = 1$. Because of (5) and $m = 1$, $Pr(RSU_{i\_k}^c)$ can be given by:

$$Pr(RSU_{i\_k}^c) = p_t^k p_l^i. \tag{13}$$

All nodes use the same channel c in single channel neighbor discovery, so the nodes other than node k are not on the sending state at channel c means that $d - 1$ nodes are not on sending state, namely

$$Pr(\overline{SS_{N^{i\backslash k}}^c}) = (1-p_t^k)^{d-1}. \tag{14}$$

From Equation (9), we know that $Pr(RS_c) = Pr(RSU_{i\_k}^c)Pr(\overline{SS_{N^{i\backslash k}}^c})$. When m=1, $p_{succ}^i = Pr(RS_c)$ can be derived by (11), thus

$$p_{succ}^i = Pr(RSU_{i\_k}^c)Pr(\overline{SS_{N^{i\backslash k}}^c}). \tag{15}$$

p_{succ}^i can be derived by (13) (14) and (15). The result is:

$$p_{succ}^i = p_t^k p_l^i(1-p_t^k)^{d-1}. \tag{16}$$

3.3 Comparative Analysis

Equation (16) shows that in the single-channel neighbor discovery protocol, when p_t^k and p_l^i is given, p_{succ}^i is only related with d which is equal to $n + 1$. With the increase of node density, channel conflict intensified, the value of p_{succ}^i decreased significantly. However, equation (12) shows that, for the multi-channel neighbor, p_{succ}^i is not only related to the node density, but also with the desired m. Therefore, the downward trend of p_{succ}^i can be controlled by properly selecting the value of m.

If the p_{succ}^i in multi-channel neighbor discovery is no less than the p_{succ}^i in single channel neighbor discovery, then the following inequation can be derived by equation (12) and (16):

$$(1 - p_t^k)^{d-1} \le \frac{1}{m} \sum_{j=0}^{d-1} C_{d-1}^j p_t^{kj} (1 - p_t^k)^{d-1-j} (1 - 1/m)^j. \tag{17}$$

Let $n = d - 1$, then above inequation can be changed into the following form:

$$(1 - p_t^k)^n \le \frac{1}{m} \sum_{j=0}^{n} C_n^j p_t^{kj} (1 - p_t^k)^{n-j} (1 - 1/m)^j \le \frac{1}{m}. \tag{18}$$

p_t^k is related to the duty cycle of the nodes. In MND, p_t^k is equal to half of the node duty cycle. When p_t^k is given and does not change again, the above inequality relations depend only on m and d. To satisfy the inequality relations, m needs to be changed with the changes of d. That is to say, the total number of the desired channel should be changed as the node density changes. To get high value of p_{succ}^i, MND computes the desired m for each node according to inequation (18) when node density changes.

3.4 Spatial Correlation

Assume that the communication range of each node in the network is circular, the following theorems and corollaries are satisfied. Due to the space limitations, the proofs are not given in this paper.

Theorems 1. For any three nodes s, a and b, assume that the distance between a and b is g, r is the communication radius and $\alpha = \arcsin(\frac{g}{2r})$. If $CA(a) \cap CA(b)$ is not empty, namely $g < 2r$, a and b is in the communication range of s, $\frac{(CA(s) \cap CA(a) \cap CA(b))}{(CA(a) \cap CA(b))} \ge \frac{4 - \frac{3}{\sqrt{3}} - 6\alpha}{6(\pi - 2\alpha - \sin 2\alpha)}$ is thus satisfied.

Corollary 1. For any three nodes s, a and b, assume that the distance between a and b is g, r is the communication radius and $\alpha = \arcsin(\frac{g}{2r})$. If $CA(a) \cap CA(b)$ is not empty, a and b is in the communication range of s, $\frac{(CA(s) \cap CA(a) \cap CA(b))}{(CA(a) \cap CA(b))} \ge \frac{4 - \frac{3}{\sqrt{3}}}{6\pi}$ is thus satisfied.

Corollary 2. For any three nodes s, a and b, assume that the distance between a and b is g, r is the communication radius and $\alpha = \arcsin(\frac{g}{2r})$. If $CA(a) \cap CA(b)$ is not empty, a and b are not neighbors with each other, a and b is in the communication range of s, node q is any one node in the area $CA(a) \cap CA(b)$, then the probability that node q is the neighbor of node s is satisfied the following inequality: $Pr(q \in N_s | (q \in N_a \cap N_b) \cap (\{a, b\} \in N_s)) > \frac{3\pi - 3\sqrt{3}}{4\pi - 3\sqrt{3}}$.

4   MND Design

4.1   Sleep Scheduling and Channel Selection

Theorem 3.4 shows that a neighbor of neighbors of node s is the neighbor of node s in a large probability. To simplify the description, any node that is in the neighbor sets of neighbors of node s is defined as the potential neighbor of node s. Corollary 1 and Corollary 2 in Section 3.4 shows that whether the neighbors of node s are neighbors affects the probability that the common neighbor of neighbors of node s is the neighbor of s. That is to say, whether the neighbors of node s are neighbors has an impact on the probability that the potential neighbor of node s is the neighbor of s. Therefore, in MND, to discover the neighbors in advance and do not consume more energy, the potential neighbor of a node is set to different priority according to whether the neighbors of this node are adjacent, and the probability that the node wakes up at the time slot in which the potential neighbor wakes up is set according to the priority.

Algorithm 1 shows the calculation of the potential neighbor sets and the method of setting the priority.

Algorithm 2 shows the specific sleep scheduling and channel selection algorithm. In Algorithm 2, DCR represents the duty cycle of the nodes, wt represents the total number of wake-up time slots since the initial state, $rtDC$ stands for the average duty cycle of node so far, $wakeFlag$ and P_{wake} represent whether a node is in the wake-up state and the probability of being in wake-up state.

In Algorithm 2, Algorithm 1 is executed and the required total number of channel is computed by formula (18) at first. Then wake-up time-slot scheduling (including wake-up time slots at regular intervals and random wake-up time slots) is generated on the basis of the DCR and potential neighbor set obtained in Algorithm 1. Finally, node s makes a uniform random selection of the channel among all the m channels, sends beacon at the selected channel, and listens on it.

4.2   Instance of MND

The network topology and working mechanism are shown in Figure 1 and Figure 2, respectively.

In the MND shown in Figure 3, assume that only node s, a, b and c choose the same channel l during the first 15 slot. In this instance, A represents the fixed wake-up time slot, R and P represent two random wake-up time slots with

---

Algorithm 1. An example for format For While Loop in Algorithm.

Require: N_s, newly discovered node v and N_v;
Ensure: Set_s^{pn};

1: **if** N_s is empty and N_v is not empty **then**
2:     Add the next wake-up node not discovered by s to Set_s^{pn}, and set it to low priority;
3: **else**
4:     **if** N_v and N_s are all not empty **then**
5:         **while** N_s is not empty **do**
6:             Compute the intersect set $setI$ of N_v and N_b which is the neighbor set of any node b
7:             in N_s;
8:             **if** $setI$ is not empty **then**
9:                 **if** node v and node b are not neighbors **then**
10:                    Set elements in $setI$ to high priority based on corollary 2;
11:                **else**
12:                    Set elements in $setI$ to high priority;
13:                **end if**
14:                $Set_s^{pn} = Set_s^{pn} \cup setI$;
15:            **end if**
16:            $N_s = N_s - b$;
17:        **end while**
18:    **end if**
19: **end if**
20: Remove the nodes in N_s from the Set_s^{pn} and add v into N_s;
21: **if** v belongs to Set_s^{pN} **then**
22:     Remove the v from the Set_s^{pn};
23: **end if**

---

differ-ent probability, and other time slots are sleep slots; The duty cycle (DCR) of node s, a, b and c are 40%, 66.67%, 40% and 28.57%, the neighbor set and potential neighbor set of these node are empty in the initial state. To simplify the description of the MND instance, the elements in the neighbor set and potential neighbor set of any node x are defined as the triples $< r, s, p >$ and the quad $< r, s, p, t >$, where r represents the id of neighbors or potential neighbors, s represents the clock skew between the node x and the node (denoted by node y) whose id is r, p represents the fixed wake-up period of node y, t is the time slot of discovering node y.

Node b and node c discover each other in their first time slot. Because they have not found any other nodes before this time slot, based on Algorithm 1, the information of detected nodes only need to be added into the neighbor set of nodes and the potential neighbor set should not be changed. Their neighbor sets are updated, namely $N_b = \{< c, 0, 7 >\}$ and $N_c = \{< b, 0, 5 >\}$, and their potential neighbor set are empty. In the 4th time slot of node a (ie, the 6th time slot of node b), node a and node b discovered each other. They record information with each other and compute the potential neighbor set and neighbor set of them

---

Algorithm 2. Sleep Scheduling and Channel Selection.

Require: DCR;
Ensure: Sleep Scheduling and Channel Selection of node s;
1: $rtDC = DCR$; //real time DC;
2: $wakeFlag = FALSE$;
3: **while** t is less than the time slot set **do**
4:      **if** v is a newly discovered node **then**
5:          Execute Algorithm 1 and compute the required m according to formula 18;
6:      **end if**
7:      $rtDC = \frac{wt}{t}$;
8:      **if** $t\%(\frac{2}{DCR}) == 0$ **then**
9:          $P_{wake} = 1$; //Wake up at regular interval (A)
10:     **else**
11:         **if** Set_s^{pn} is not empty **then**
12:             **if** node b in Set_s^{pn} is awake at this time slot **then**
13:                 Set P_{wake} according to the priority of node b;
14:             **end if**
15:         **else**
16:             **if** $rtDC \leq DCR$ **then**
17:                 $P_{wake} = \frac{1}{\frac{2}{DCR}-1}$; //Wake up randomly (R)
18:             **end if**
19:         **end if**
20:     **end if**
21:     Execute $wakeFlag$=TRUE with the probability P_{wake};
22:     **if** $wakeFlag$=TRUE **then**
23:         $wt = wt + 1$;
24:         choose channel l randomly from m channels, send messages and listen at l;
25:     **end if**
26:     $t = t + 1$; //update time slot;
27: **end while**

---

according to Algorithm 1. The computing results are $Set_a^n = \{< c, 2, 7, 0 >\}$, $Set_b^n = \phi$, $N_a = \{< b, 2, 5 >\}$, $N_b = \{< c, 0, 7 >, < a, -2, 3 >\}$. Node a wakes up at its 6th time slot (P slot) according to Set_a^n, and discovers node c (node c also detected node a). As $N_a \cap N_c = b$, that is to say there is only one common neighbor node between node a and node c, thereby according to Algorithm 1, the information of node c is move from Set_a^n to N_a, namely $Set_a^n = \phi$ and $N_a = \{< b, 2, 5 >, < c, 2, 7 >\}$; the information of node a is added into N_c, namely $N_c = \{< b, 0, 5 >, < a, -2, 3 >\}$. Similarly, node s and node a detect each other in the 7th time slot of node a and record the related information; node a and node b detect each other again in the 8th time slot of node a and record the related information. Finally, node s and node b discovery each other at the 13th slot of node s on the basis of the potential neighbor set of node s and record information required. We can see from the above example, if MND do not use the information of neighbors discovered, node a will not wake up in the 6th slot (a P-slot), node a and node c will not discover each other, node s will not detect node b in its 13th slots.

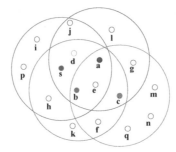

Fig. 1. Network Topology

Fig. 2. Instance of MND

5   Performance Evaluation

5.1   Simulation

In this section, MND is compared with representative protocols including Disco,
U-connect, SearchLight and the simplified version of MND (MND-SC, MND-
AS). MND-SC did not use the multi-channel mechanism. MND-AS use the same
required total number of channels m for all nodes. In all experiments below, the
discovery latency requirement denoted by DLR is 10000. When DD changes,
$DCR=0.05$; When the DCR changes, $DD=10$.

Average Discovery Latency. In this section, the discovery latency means the
average delay of discovery any one node for each node; the average detection
latency represents the average discovery latency of all nodes in whole network.
The trend of the average delay is as Figure 3(a) and Figure 3(b) shown. the average delay of MND-SC, MND-AS and the MND is lower than that of the other
three protocols, which validated the discovery mechanism based on information
of neighbor discovered can speed up the speed of neighbor discovery and reduce
the average discovery delay. MND outperforms other protocols in most cases

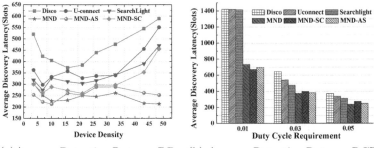

(a) Average Detection Rate vs. DD   (b) Average Detection Rate vs. DCR

Fig. 3. Results of Average Detection Latency

indicates that MND has good scalability and adaptability. Meanwhile, MND protocol outperforms the MND-SC and MND-AS, indicating that the average detection latency is reduced by the calculation of desired m according to the local information in MND.

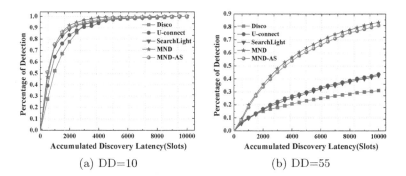

(a) DD=10   (b) DD=55

Fig. 4. CDF of Nodes Detected

CDF of Nodes Detected. Figure 4 shows the CDF of nodes detected when $DCR = 5\%$. The percentage of nodes detected of MND and MND-AS is larger than other protocols at the same accumulated discovery latency. This is because the discovery mechanism of MND can play an important role with the increasing of total number of discovered node. Compared Figure 4(a) with Figure 4(b), we can get that MND is comparative for dense deployed sensor networks.

5.2 Test-Bed Experiments

We implemented MND on a test-bed of TelosB and conducted experiments to evaluate the real performance of MND.

The node 0 in the center has nine neighbors. When the discovery is over in each experiment, node 0 sends the data received to the sink node. In order to ensure that the neighbors of neighbors of node 0 are not all the neighbors of node 0, two nodes are deployed outside the communication range of node 0. Therefore, the total number of neighbor node of node 0 is always 9 in all the experiments, namely $DD=9$. Meanwhile, to test the different performance of under different duty cycle, the duty cycles of all nodes are not the same. However, the average duty cycle of all nodes in the network is kept at 5% or 10% during the experiments.

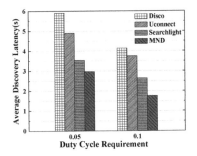

Fig. 5. Average Detection Latency

Figure 5 shows the experimental results of the average discovery latency under the duty cycle of 5% and 10%. The figure shows that, compared with the other three protocols Disco, U-Connect and SearchLight, when $DCR = 5\%$, average discovery latency of MND is reduced by 49.7%, 39.4% and 16.0% respectively; when $DCR = 10\%$, the average discovery latency of MND is shortened 57.5%, 53.2% and 33.5%. The results verify the efficiency of the MND, indicating that when energy consumption of protocols are same, MND can use neighbor discovery mechanism to speed up neighbor discovery rate, thus shortening the average discovery delay. Meanwhile, the gap of average discovery latency between MND and other protocol is higher when $DCR = 10\%$ indicates the speed of detecting new neighbor node can be speeded up by the increasing of discovered nodes.

Figure 6 shows the trends of percentage of nodes detected. Compared with other protocols, using MND, the node discovered other nodes quickly under both duty cycle of 5% and 10%. Meanwhile, as the duty cycle increased from 5% to 10%, the discovery speed of all protocols is improved and the speed of MND is higher than that of other protocols clearly. This is because that, for other protocols without using the information of detected nodes, the information acquired has no effect on the discovery of new neighbors although the neighbors detected in the duty cycle of 5% are increased compared to that in the duty cycle of 5%. In contrast, the discovery speed of nodes using MND is increased significantly due to the use.

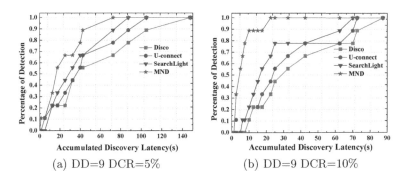

(a) DD=9 DCR=5%   (b) DD=9 DCR=10%

Fig. 6. CDF of Nodes detected

6   Conclusion

We analyzed how to use the multi-channel mechanism and detected neighbor nodes at first, and then proposed a multi-channel neighbor discovery protocol called MND. In MND, potential neighbor node is computed according to the information of nodes detected so that it can be detected in advance; the required total number of channel is adjusted according to the variation of node density. To evaluate the performance of MND, simulation and test-bed experiments are conducted. The results show that, MND can adapt to the changing of node density; the discovery speed of MND is improved and the average discovery latency is reduced significantly when the energy consumption is the same to other protocol.

Acknowledgments. This work is supported in part by the National Natural Science Foundation of China (NSFC) under Grant Nos.61070193, the Foundation of University Science and Technology Innovation Team Building Program of Heilongjiang Province under 2011PYTD002, Programs Foundation of Ministry of Education of China for New Century Excellent Talents in University(NCET-11-0955), Heilongjiang Province Founds for Distinguished Young Scientists under Grant Nos.JC201104, Heilongjiang Province Science and Technique Foundation under Grant Nos.GC09A109.

References

1. Liu, T., Sadler, C.M., Zhang, P., Martonosi, M.: Implementing software on resource-constrained mobile sensors: experiences with impala and zebranet. In: 2nd International Conference on Mobile Systems, Applications, and Services, pp. 256–269. ACM Press, New York (2004)
2. Eisenman, S.B., Miluzzo, E., Lane, N.D., Peterson, R.A., Ahn, G.-S., Campbell, A.T.: The bikenet mobile sensing system for cyclist experience mapping. In: 5th International Conference on Embedded Networked Sensor Systems, pp. 87–101. ACM Press, New York (2007)

3. Miluzzo, E., Lane, N.D., Fodor, K., Peterson, R., Lu, H., Musolesi, M., Eisenman, S.B., Zheng, X., Campbell, A.T.: Sensing meets mobile social networks: the design, implementation and evaluation of the cenceme application. In: 6th ACM Conference on Embedded Network Sensor Systems, pp. 337–350. ACM Press, New York (2008)

4. Huang, J.H., Amjad, S., Mishra, S.: Cenwits: a sensor-based loosely coupled search and rescue system using witnesses. In: 3rd International Conference on Embedded Networked Sensor Systems, pp. 180–191. ACM Press, New York (2005)

5. Purohit, A., Priyantha, B., Liu, J.: WiFlock: Collaborative group discovery and maintenance in mobile sensor networks. In: 10th International Conference on Information Processing in Sensor Networks, pp. 37–48. ACM Press, New York (2011)

6. Karowski, N., Viana, A.C., Wolisz, A.: Optimized Asynchronous Multi-channel Neighbor Discovery. In: 30th IEEE International Conference on Computer Communications, pp. 536–540. IEEE Press, New York (2011)

7. McGlynn, M.J., Borbash, S.A.: Birthday protocols for low energy deployment and flexible neighbor discovery in ad hoc wireless networks. In: 2nd ACM International Symposium on Mobile Ad Hoc Networking and Computing, pp. 137–145. ACM Press, New York (2001)

8. Dutta, P., Culler, D.E.: Practical asynchronous neighbor discovery and rendezvous for mobile sensing applications. In: 6th ACM Conference on Embedded Network Sensor Systems, pp. 71–84. ACM Press, New York (2008)

9. Kandhalu, A., Lakshmanan, K., Rajkumar, R.R.: U-connect: a low-latency energy-efficient asynchronous neighbor discovery protocol. In: 9th International Conference on Information Processing in Sensor Networks, pp. 350–361. ACM Press, New York (2010)

10. Bakht, M., Kravets, R.: SearchLight: A Systematic Probing-based Asynchronous Neighbor Discovery Protocol. ACM SIGMOBILE Mobile Computing and Communications Review 14(4), 31–33 (2010)

11. Lai, S., Ravindran, B., Cho, H.: Heterogenous quorum-based wakeup scheduling in wireless sensor networks. IEEE Transactions on Computers 59(11), 1562–1575 (2010)

12. Tseng, Y.C., Hsu, C.S., Hsieh, T.Y.: Power-saving protocols for IEEE 802.11-based multi-hop ad hoc networks. In: 21st Annual Joint Conference of the IEEE Computer and Communications Societies, pp. 200–209. IEEE Press, New York (2002)

13. Ivan Niven, H.L., Zuckerman, H.S.: An Introduction to the Theory of Numbers. John Wiley and Sons, Oxford University (1991)

14. Zhang, P., Sadler, C.M., Lyon, S.A., Martonosi, M.: Hardware design experiences in zebranet. In: 2nd International Conference on Embedded Networked Sensor Systems, pp. 227–238. ACM Press, New York (2004)

Research on Network Malicious Code Dendritic Cell Immune Algorithm Based on Fuzzy Weighted Support Vector Machine

Peng Li[1,2,3], Ruchuan Wang[1,2,3], Yanting Zhou[4], and Qiuyu Dai[1]

[1] College of Computer, Nanjing University of Posts and Telecommunications,
Nanjing, Jiangsu 210003, China
[2] Jiangsu High Technology Research Key Laboratory for Wireless Sensor Networks,
Nanjing, Jiangsu 210003, China
[3] Key Lab of Broadband Wireless Communication and Sensor Network Technology
(Nanjing University of Posts and Telecommunications), Ministry of Education
Jiangsu Province, Nanjing, Jiangsu 210003, China
[4] College of Telecommunications and Information Engineering, Nanjing University of
Posts and Telecommunications, Nanjing, Jiangsu 210003, China
lipeng@njupt.edu.cn

Abstract. According to the significant impact on the accuracy rate of detection of current immune algorithms brought by incorrect classification of signal, it proposes network malicious code dendritic cell immune algorithm based on fuzzy weighted support vector machine. It summarizes and compares the pros and cons of the four methods, which are basic artificial intelligence immune algorithm, detection of unknown viruses based on immunity theory, malicious code immunity based on cryptography and automated intrusion response based on danger theory. It elaborates the process of the algorithm of the proposed immune algorithm, discusses a variety of input and output signals, gives the samples of the actual input signals, applies the coefficient of variation method to determine the values of the weights so as to enhance the discrimination ability of signal processing results, describes the principle and algorithm steps of fuzzy weighted support vector machine clustering method within immune algorithm proposed. By comparing the fuzzy aggregation before and after the immunization program experiments, it draws the conclusion that the proposed immune algorithm can optimize the input signal, fuzzy clustering the signal and the antigen, so as to bring down the number of immunization strategies and reduce the immune response time, as a result it improve the efficiency and performance of the immune system.

Keywords: Network Security, Artificial Intelligence Immune, Dendritic Cell Immune Algorithm, Fuzzy Weighted Support Vector Machine, Network Malicious Code.

1 Introduction

Computer immunity is one of the new methods to solve the network security problem. Its inspiration is derived from the nature biosystem. [1,2] There are

R. Wang and F. Xiao (Eds.): CWSN 2012, CCIS 334, pp. 181–190, 2013.
© Springer-Verlag Berlin Heidelberg 2013

many similarities between the biological immune system and the computer security systems.

Biology immune system is a complex system. The core elements include cells, signal, antigen and organizational environment. Cells enter the organizational environment by signal and antigen, signal provides cell characteristic information in substance, and antigen provides cells information of substance structure. If the characteristics of cells change, features of the corresponding antigen will change.[3] Such immune procedure is used for immunity of network malicious code for computers, which is the basic idea of Dendritic Cell Immune Algorithm (DCIA) in this paper. [4]

The corresponding researches show that, DCIA is based on the situation that the system with the types known of input signal, while it hardly considers about judging the types of signal and assumes that signal is detected and judged by 'professional' cells. However, experiments in [5] demonstrate that incorrect classification of signal will impact the accuracy rate of detection. This paper puts forward malicious code DCIA which adopts Fuzzy Weighted Support Vector Machine (FWSVM), aiming at optimizing input signal and classifying signal and antigen in order to improve the efficiency and performance of Immune System (IS).

2   Related Studies

Some related studies of malicious code immune algorithms have been generated and used to some practical immune systems. The paper classifies the current immune algorithms studies into four types, which are basic artificial intelligence immune algorithm[6-7], detection of unknown viruses based on immunity theory[8-10], malicious code immunity based on cryptography[11] and automated intrusion response based on danger theory[12].

Table 1 shows the comparison of the said four immune technologies. It ranks the degree of the comparison from 1 to 4, of which 1 stands for the worst and 4 stands for the excellent degree.

Table 1. Comparison of the Four Immune Technologies

Comparison method	Mature Degree	Comp.	Reli.	Stab.	Univ.
Basic Artificial Intelligence Immune Algorithm	4	4	2	1	2
Detection of Unknown Viruses based on Immunity Theory	3	3	1	3	3
Malicious Code Immunity based on Cryptography	2	1	4	3	1
Automated Intrusion Response based on Danger Theory	1	2	3	3	3

3   Models and Key Technologies

3.1   Algorithm Model

This paper uses immune biological imitation for the immune technology of network malicious code, the following points are taken into account. [13-15]

(1) Antigen processing: including two stages, one is antigen uptake, where antigen enters the interior of cells from peripheral organization, the other one is antigen presentation, where interior antigen appears on cellular surface. Antigen presentation cell is responsible for implementing antigen processing.

(2) Signal processing: generating characteristic influence ability at signal level, such as cell factor or of peripheral organization hormone level. Pathogen Associated Molecular Pattern (PAMP) or Danger Signal (DS) controls Dendritic Cell (DC), and DC controls T cell, both of them are signal processing.

(3)Cell bond: cells bond to each other by adhesion molecule on their surface and the effect of acceptors.

(4) Antigen matching: the procedure where a certain type acceptor is activated by specific antigen, specific antigen makes cells generate response. Such response has impact on tissue, leading cells to change their specialties and structures.

This paper puts forward malicious code DCIA based on FWSVM, and the flow chart of its algorithm is shown as Figure 1.

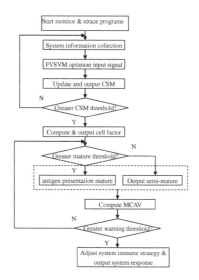

Fig. 1. Flow Chart of Malicious Code DCIA based on FWSVM

3.2   DCIA

The immunologist Polly Matzinge [16] puts forward danger theory: in immune system, the fundamental is not from the exterior but the interior. IS doesn't generate response to all exterior antigens but to 'danger' signal. The input signal and output signal of dendritic cell algorithm are presented in Table 2.

Table 2. The Input Signal and Output Signal of Dendritic Cell Algorithm

$Type$	$Name$	$Symbol$
$Input Signal$	$Pathogen Associated$ $Molecular Pattern$	$PAMP$
	$Danger signal$	DS
	$Safety signal$	SS
	$Inflammation Cytokines signal$	IS
$Output Signal$	$Co-Stimulatory Molecules$	CSM
	$semi-mature cell$	$semi-mature$
	$mature cell$	$mature$
$Result$	$Mature Context Antigen Value$	$MCAV$

Signal processing formula is as follows:

$$C_i = (\omega_1 * P_i + \omega_2 * D_i + \omega_3 * S_i) * (1 + IS) \tag{1}$$

In Formula 1, P_i, D_i, S_i are the ith signal of PAMP, DS and SS. IS represents inflammation cytokines signal, ω_i is associated weight of PAMP, DS and SS, respectively, the corresponding output C_i of may be semi-mature or mature. This paper determines the value of weight by coefficient of variation method (CVM).

Definition 1: weight depends on the order of the value measured many times, coefficient of variation of P_i, D_i, S_i are the ratio between the standard deviation of the order of their value and mean value and absolute value, presented in Formula 2 to Formula 4.

$$v = \frac{\sigma}{|\mu|} \tag{2}$$

$$\mu = \frac{1}{n} \sum_{i=1}^{n} P_i \tag{3}$$

$$\sigma = \sqrt{\frac{1}{n-1} \sum_{i=1}^{n} (P_i - \mu)^2} \tag{4}$$

Each P_i, D_i, S_i sequence assigns weight v_1, v_2, v_3, so that coefficient of variation ω_i represents in Formula 5.

$$\omega_i = \frac{v_i}{\sum\limits_{j=1}^{3} v_j}, i = 1, 2, 3 \tag{5}$$

Such coefficient of variation takes the specialties of P_i, D_i, S_i into account, highlights relative rangeability and reflects the target ability to distinguish signal and antigen. The bigger P_i, D_i, S_i is, the larger the range of variation of will be, making the ability to distinguish results increase.

3.3 FWSVM Cluster Algorithm

Definitions of FWSVM Problems. Support vector machine is a new machine learning method proposed by Vapnik. [17] It can be very successful to deal with the Classification and regression problems. The paper adopts fuzzy weighted support vector machine method to deal with the clustering problem, which seems to be a good solution to the input signal of immunization program. [18]

Definition 2: fuzzy membership. Define membership θ.

$$\theta = \begin{cases} [-1, -0.5), fuzzynegativeclass \\ (0.5, 1], fuzzypositiveclass \\ \theta = 0.5 or \theta = -0.5, fuzzyneutralclass \end{cases} \tag{6}$$

Definition 3: triangular fuzzy function. According to the membership in Definition 2 ,it calculates the corresponding fuzzy number $\overline{y}$ with Formula 7.

$$\overline{y} = \begin{cases} (\frac{2\theta^2+3\theta-2}{\theta}, 2\theta - 1, \frac{2\theta^2-3\theta+2}{\theta}), 0.5 \le \theta \le 1 \\ (\frac{2\theta^2+3\theta+2}{\theta}, 2\theta + 1, \frac{2\theta^2-\theta-2}{\theta}), -1 \le \theta \le -0.5 \end{cases} \tag{7}$$

Definition 4: fuzzy training set. Suppose fuzzy training set $\overline{S}$

$$\overline{S} = \{(x_1, \overline{y}_1), (x_2, \overline{y}_2), ..., (x_s, \overline{y}_s)\} x_j \in R^n, j = 1, 2, ..., s \tag{8}$$

$\overline{y}$ is triangular fuzzy function, which reflects the corresponding fuzzy category of the sample x. When the degree of membership where the sample belongs to degree of membership with positive class is higher than that belongs to degree of membership with negative class, it is called fuzzy positive class. While the degree of membership where the sample belongs to degree of membership with negative class is higher than that belongs to degree of membership with positive class, it is called fuzzy negative class. If the degree of membership where the sample belongs to degree of membership with positive class equals to that belongs to degree of membership with negative class, it is called fuzzy neutral class.

According to Definition 2 to Definition 4, the definition of optimization problem of FWSVM is put forward in Definition 5.

Definition 5: the presentation of FWSVM problems. It is supposed that training point comes form the totality of the model of category k, kernel cluster can be developed to search optimal k-1 separating hyperplanes and such hyperplanes can separate the model of category k. The target is to obtain a hyperplane that is corresponding to a minimum distance and maximize the distance. In Formula 9, C is a given constant number, $\varepsilon_i \succ 0$ represents the point of cluster error. [19] The constant $\lambda_i(i = 1, ..., s)$ is given in advance to weight cluster error variable, the optimization problems is Formula 9, α_i in the formula is a parameter of kernel function. Approximation programming approximation programming is used to answer the question.

$$
\begin{cases}
\min \frac{1}{2}(\omega, \omega) + C \sum_i \lambda_i \varepsilon_i^2 \\
s.t.(\alpha_i \cdot K(x_i, x_j) - b_j + \varepsilon_i)^2 = 1, \varepsilon_i \geq 0 \\
i = 1, ..., s; j = 1, ..., k - 1
\end{cases}
\tag{9}
$$

Credibility Weight Value λ_i. Order $x_i \in [u, v](i = 1, ..., s)$, if $x = i, \rho(x) = \alpha_i$; or $\rho(x) = 0$ and a unascertained number $[[u, v], \rho(x)]$ will be formed. For credibility weight value λ_i, the solution can be in accordance with the following steps. Its comprehensive mean $\mu_i(i = 1, ..., m)$ is obtained by analyzing multi-indexes during sampling period and measured weight value β_i, so that

$$
\gamma = \sum_{i=1}^{m} \beta_i \cdot \mu_i
\tag{10}
$$

The expected value and credibility weight value λ_i is caculated by Formula 11.

$$
E(\gamma) = \left[\left[\frac{1}{\alpha} \sum_{i=1}^{m} x_i \cdot \alpha_i, \frac{1}{\alpha} \sum_{i=1}^{m} x_i \cdot \alpha_i \right], \rho(x) \right]
\tag{11}
$$

Then it is calculated that the expected value γ of is $\frac{1}{\alpha} \sum_{i=1}^{m} x_i \cdot \alpha_i$ with the credibility $\lambda_i = \sum_{i=1}^{m} \alpha_i$.

4   Analyses of Experimental Data

4.1   Experimental Introduction

(1) Experimental platform: experimental mainframe adopts Intel processor with 2GB internal storage, Red Hat Linux operating system is used for the original DCIA. And while Microsoft Windows 7 operating system and MATLAB R2009b is used for process the input data with FWSVM Algorithm.
(2) Experimental item
Experiment 1 collects input signal by systematic supervisory program and strace program;
Experiment 2 optimizes the signal of immune procedure by FWSVM algorithm;
Experiment 3 compares and analyzes the performance of Libtissue immune procedure before and after being optimized.

4.2   Experimental Procedure and Data Analysis

The input data of Libtissue [20] program comes from correct systematic supervisory program and the result of strace program information gathering, which is submitted to IS as antigen and signal after data processing and regularization, shown in Table 3. thereinto, systematic supervisory program can collect information of specific process and all child processes; strace program can collect detailed information of system call and parameter of operational program.

Table 3. Input Data of Libtissue Program

$Collecttime$	$Signaltype$	$IDnumber$	$Parameternum$	$value$
1.1091	$signal$	0	4	$0; 0; 0; 0$
2.0509	$antigen$	355	1	$execve$
2.0956	$antigen$	355	1	brk
2.1757	$signal$	355	4	$1; 0; 1122304; 323584$
2.2004	$antigen$	358	1	$close$
3.3960	$signal$	358	4	$1; 0.395683; 1683456; 782336$

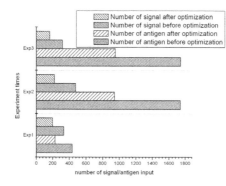

Fig. 2. Comparison between Signals before and after Optimization

The signal that is used in this algorithm is data source of presort and prenormalization. When it is used in malicious code computer immunity, the degree of duplication of data is quite high with many repetitive input data, for the processing is only according to the acquisition time of antigen and signal without consideration of data aggregate. Figure 2 shows the comparison between signals before and after optimization, form which, it is concluded that data after optimization is more concise.

This paper makes experiments on input signal of immune procedure by FWSVM algorithm and gives a probable value to each signal, for the category of know signals can't be determined completely. This paper adopts FWSVM method to cluster signals and the clustered results are shown in Fig. 3. According to this, it is found

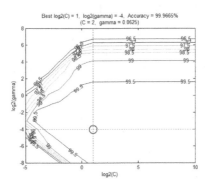

Fig. 3. Schematic Plot of FWSVM Algorithm Cluster

that over 99% signals can be clustered by FWSVM algorithm, which provides basis for the implementation of follow-up immune algorithm.

After implementing the optimization of FWSVM algorithm of signals, scanning tools are used to carry out scan attack on experimental machine and implement the comparison between immune strategy and response time observed by immune procedure. This paper compares immune strategy and response time before and after fuzzy cluster. According to the experimental results, it is found the performance of immune system after signal optimization is more optimized. Immune strategy is a strategy of strace based on collected systematic calls, while response time is the interval from the time when commence starts to the time when immune procedure begins to adopt immune strategy.

Table 4. Comparison Table of Signal before and after Fuzzy Cluster

$Type$	$Comparison$	$Exp1$	$Exp2$	$Exp3$
	$immune strategy number$	38	56	56
$Original Data$	$immune response time (second)$	14	14	17
	$immune strategy number$	23	31	29
$FVSVM cluster$	$immune response time (second)$	7	9	4

Table 4 compares response time, from which, it can be concluded that, on the one hand, systematic call strategies of immune procedure supervision are relatively concise after signal cluster, on the other hand, the response time of immunity can be reduced after the processing of immune data.

5   Conclusions

Adopting DCIA to imitate immune mechanism of biosystem to realize immune effect on network malicious code is featured by relatively small calculating scale and favorable ability to distinguish specialties. This paper optimizes and simplifies its signals based on FWSVM algorithm and verifies the improvement of its performance by experiments. Of course, Libtissue offers a new frame aiming at malicious code immune mechanism, although it has simplified biosystem immune mechanism significantly, more favorable analog simulation should be implemented to achieve better immune effect. Meanwhile, the fusion between the methods of signal optimization and immune procedure put forward in this paper is the key point of further researches.

Acknowledgment. This work was supported by the National Natural Science Foundation of China (No.60973139, No.61170065, No.61171053, No.61100199, No.60903181, No.61003 039, No.61003236); the Hi-Tech Research and Development Program of China (2007AA01Z404, 2007AA01Z478); the Natural Science Foundation of Jiangsu Province (No.11KJA520001, No.10KJB520013, No.10KJB520014); Science and Technology Innovation Fund for Higher Education Institutions of Jiangsu Province ((No.CX10B-196Z, No.CX10B-199Z); Foundation of National Laboratory for Modern Communications (9140C1105040805); Postdoctoral Foundation (0801019C, 20090451240, 20090451241); and the Six Kinds of Top Talent of Jiangsu Province (2008118).

References

1. Aickelin, U., Bentley, P., Cayzer, S., Kim, J., McLeod, J.: Danger Theory: The Link between AIS and IDS? In: Timmis, J., Bentley, P.J., Hart, E. (eds.) ICARIS 2003. LNCS, vol. 2787, pp. 147–155. Springer, Heidelberg (2003)
2. Dasgupta, D.: Advances in Artificial Immune Systems. Computational Intelligence Magazine 1(4), 40–49 (2006)
3. Twycross, J., Aickelin, U.: Towards a Conceptual Framework for Innate Immunity. In: Jacob, C., Pilat, M.L., Bentley, P.J., Timmis, J.I. (eds.) ICARIS 2005. LNCS, vol. 3627, pp. 112–125. Springer, Heidelberg (2005)
4. Kim, J., Bentley, P., Aickelin, U., Greensmith, J., Tedesco, G., Twycross, J.: Immune system approaches to intrusion detection - a review. Natural Computing 6(4), 413–466 (2007)
5. Al-Hammadi, Y., Aickelin, U., Greensmith, J.: DCA for detecting bots. In: IEEE World Congress on Computational Intelligence, WCCI 2008, Hong Kong, China, pp. 1–10 (2008)
6. Sun, F.-X., Jin, X.-T.: Immune danger theory based quantitative model for network security situation awareness. Application Research of Computers 28(7), 2680–2686 (2011) (in Chinese)
7. Zheng, J.-Q., Chen, Y.-F., Zhang, W.: A Survey of artificial immune applications. Artificial Intelligence Review 34(1), 19–34 (2010)
8. Jain, P., Goyal, S.: An Adaptive Intrusion Prevention System Based on Immunity. In: International Conference on Advances in Computing, Control, and Telecommunication Technologies, Trivandrum, Kerala, India, pp. 759–763 (2009)
9. Zeng, Li, T.: A Novel Computer Virus Detection Method from Ideas of Immunology. In: International Conference on Multimedia Information Networking and Security, Wuhan, China, pp. 412–416 (2009)

10. Wei, Y., Zhang, J., Xu, H.: The Application of Immune Theory to Virus Detection. Computer Applications and Software 25(9), 52–54 (2008)
11. Chen, Z., Shen, C., Wu, X.: A Crypto-based Immunization Model against Malicious Code. Computer Science 82(1), 288–289 (2008) (in Chinese)
12. Peng, L.-X., Xie, D.-Q., Fu, Y.-F., Xiong, W., Shen, Y.-L.: Automated intrusion response system model based on danger theory. Journal on Communications 33(1), 136–144 (2012) (in Chinese)
13. Aickelin, U., Cayzer, S.: The Danger Theory and Its Application to Artificial Immune Systems. In: Proceedings of the 1st Internet Conference on Artificial Immune Systems, ICARIS 2002, Canterbury, UK, pp. 141–148 (2002)
14. Kim, J., Greensmith, J., Twycross, J., Aickelin, U.: Malicious Code Execution Detection and Response Immune System inpired by the Danger Theory. In: Proceedings of Adaptive and Resilient Computing Security Workshop, ARCS 2005, Santa Fe, USA, pp. 1–4 (2005)
15. Meng, Q., Zhao, W.: Study on fault diagnosis algorithm based on artificial immune danger theory. In: International Conference on Mechanic Automation and Control Engineering, MACE 2010, Hangzhou, China, pp. 5997–6000 (2010)
16. Matzinge, P.: The Real Function of the Immune System or Tolerance and Four D's (Danger, Death, Destruction and Distress),
http://cmmg.biosci.wayne.edu/asg/polly.html
17. Deng, N., Tian, Y.: Support Vector Machine: Theory, Algorithm and Continuation, pp. 81–111. Science Press, Beijing (2009) (in Chinese)
18. Li, P., Wang, R.-C., Gao, D.-H.: Research on Rootkit Dynamic Detection based on Fuzzy Pattern Recognition and Support Virtual Machine Technology. Acta Electronica Sinica 40(1), 115–120 (2012) (in Chinese)
19. Yang, Z., Liu, G.: Thoery and Application of Unascertained Support Vector Machine, pp. 191–193. Science Press, Beijing (2007) (in Chinese)
20. Twycross, J., Aickelin, U.: Libtissue - implementing innate immunity. In: IEEE Congress on Evolutionary Computation, Sheraton Vancouver Wall Centre, Vancouver, BC, Canada, pp. 499–506 (2006)

Ant Colony Based Routing Strategy in UAV Delay Tolerant Networks

Xuanya Li[1], Linlin Ci[1,2], Bin Cheng[1],
Chengping Tian[1], and Minghua Yang[2]

[1] School of Computer Science and Technology,
Beijing Institute of Technology, Beijing, China
xuanya.li@gmail.com
[2] Beijing Institute of Information Technology, Beijing, China

Abstract. Flying a swarm of unmanned aerial vehicles (UAVs) with mutual sense and communication capability in the air space, a late-model airborne perceptive network accordingly takes shape. Among all research issues about it, routing strategy is the prior problem that significantly blocks the whole efficacious communication, because this three-dimensional architecture features randomly violent topological changes and usable paths generate in an unpredictable moment. In this paper, we consider an exploration-exploitation trade-off in this specific delay tolerant network (DTN). The pivotal conception is the resultant of heuristic information and ant pheromone based on the ant foraging behavior. A fuzzy inference system is introduced to calculate the heuristic information using approximate reasoning, which helps ant routing. The simulation witnesses the effectiveness of the proposed mechanism in the end.

Keywords: unmanned aerial vehicle, delay tolerant network, heuristic information, ant routing, fuzzy inference system.

1 Introduction

Flying a swarm of unmanned aerial vehicles (UAVs) with mutual sense and communication capability in the air space, a late-model airborne perceptive network accordingly takes shape. The tight combination of sensing and free navigation in three-dimensional space draws the attention of many exciting applications in multifarious areas: exploring the depopulated zone that men could hardly reach for the purpose of some idiosyncratic data; studying the rate of dispersion of pollutant, or distribution of CO_2 in the atmosphere and its relation to global warming; modeling the local weather produced by wildfires to better predict their evolution and improve the deployment of the firefighting resources; investigating, deploying and adversary target positioning in an execrable battlefield environment by carrying out the command from ground stations.

Among all research issues about UAV networks including three-dimensional deployment and target positioning, routing strategy is the prior problem that significantly blocks the whole efficacious communication. Traditional routing protocols assume that there has already existed an end-to-end path between a pair of

R. Wang and F. Xiao (Eds.): CWSN 2012, CCIS 334, pp. 191–203, 2013.
© Springer-Verlag Berlin Heidelberg 2013

source/destination nodes before the message forwarding starts which, however, is not always available in the aerial network featuring randomly violent topological changes. Most UAV individuals navigate at a three dimensional inertial velocity independently which readily makes the previous reliable links no longer used. In addition, under the control of distributed and task driven algorithm, UAV individuals may get isolated to each other. Therefore usable paths generate in an unpredictable moment. And then an adaptive and dynamic routing strategy is required here to maintain the network communication.

Delay Tolerant Network (DTN) is used here to solve the routing problem. Fall [9] proposes this new network architecture and application interface where nodes are deployed sparsely in the scenario and opportunity for end-to-end link is awfully low. Many researchers have advanced new routing algorithms such as Direct Delivery [10], First Contact [11], Epidemic [12], Spray and Wait [13], Prophet [15] and MaxProp [16] to address this specific issue. One common characteristic is the utilization of store-and-forward mechanism to the frequently-disconnected problem. These approaches assume that the topology is disconnected and partitioned as a rule rather than an exception. However, our circumstance seems not so wicked. Depending on specific phases, the complete links may hold steadily during a period due to temporarily relatively stable topology. Epidemic protocol, for example, is not applicable under such moment on account of its unnecessary transmission cost. Our goal is to find a balance solution between the sparse connectivity situation and temporal quiescence scenario.

In this paper we consider this kind of exploration-exploitation trade-off issue. Exploration, here, is defined as the ability to explore diversified routes, using current local situation as much as possible, to find a possible neighbor node to relay the forwarding message. On the contrary, exploitation is explained as the process to focus on a promising group of solutions, taking advantage of historical experience as much as possible, to exploit a best candidate. DTN is more like an exploration problem, in which the paramount objective is to make use of every contact opportunity to forward the messages. Traditional networks, however, intend to find an optimum route based on the long-time cumulative routing table, which appears to be an exploitation topic.

On the other hand, in the last decade, technology inspired by ant colony has been broadly implemented in the network routing problems [2-6] due to the appealing analogies between mobile computing networks and dynamic biological systems. Muhammad and Di Caro [1] present an overview of swarm intelligence based routing protocols, more specifically, taking inspiration from ant foraging behaviors. In [4], Rosati emphasizes the simplicity as the true nature. Ant-like agents, carrying out very simple rules, find the optimal way between the nest-like source and food-like destination, through a no-supervisor collective behavior. In fact, we also believe that simplicity is the design objective of our airborne perceptive network.

In our research we propose a novel routing strategy, which is based on the ant foraging behavior, to balance the exploration-exploitation capability. The pivotal conception is the resultant of heuristic information and ant pheromone.

An approximate reasoning based fuzzy inference system is introduced to calculate the heuristic information, in which the inputs are Crowd Density (CD) and Relative Velocity Direction (RVD), two parameters easily acquired without complex computational cost.

The remainder of this paper is organized as follows. In the next section, related researches are presented. Section three describes the general ant routing model. In the following section, proposed fuzzy inference system and ant routing algorithm will be given, followed by experimental results in section 5, and the last section will make a conclusion for the paper.

2   Related Works

UAV delay tolerant networks enable communication in intermittent environments where communication opportunities appear and disappear frequently. When two nodes get into each other's RF coverage, there is a chance to exchange message packets. All routing modules first check if they have already received the messages or they are destinations of the neighbor's data packets. Then, the rest of the messages, if any, transfer depending on the routing strategies.

Direct Delivery [10], First Contact [11] and Epidemic [12] are the simplest ideas. Direct Delivery [10], as implied by the name, complies with the only rule that any transaction does not happen merely when the sender is in contact with the receiver. This method greatly reduces the bandwidth overhead but is evidently not the preferred solution in many cases.

First Contact [11], equivalently with zero knowledge to the overall situation, makes a further step. Among all current contacts, a deliverer randomly selects a neighbor to transfer the message as it has time. If no neighbor is currently available, the node waits until the first useful connect. Unfortunately, there is no evidence that the first node is a better candidate than the previous one, so First Contact is not a prior suggestion either.

Epidemic [12], on the contrary, using quite distinct approach, is another extreme instance. A relay node sends copies of a message to its neighbors unless the buffer filled or link disconnected, and then its neighbor nodes do the same procedure like flooding. Ideally, Epidemic can get the highest delivery probability considering no buffer space and bandwidth limited. Practically, we cannot bear that worthless messages occupy too much resources. These simplest protocols, however, provide fundamental views about DTN routing.

Spray and Wait [13], derived from Epidemic, includes two phases. Initially, each message has a fixed number of copies. In the spraying phase, a node with more than one copies, meets another node and transfers one copy (normal mode) or half of the copies (binary mode). If one node has only one copy, it comes into the second waiting phase. In this stage, the node does nothing until it meets the final recipient.

Prophet [15] and MaxProp [16] take the delivery predictability into account. If two nodes have met before, they are assumed to meet again. They maintain a list showing which node has met which node, and calculate the delivery predictability after each contact according to several regulations. Historical connection conditions are used as heuristic information to make forwarding decisions consequently. While Prophet places emphasis on the opportunities to meet the final recipient, MaxProp considers the whole path from source to destination through Dijkstra's algorithm. It introduces an incremental averaging method to estimate the delivery probability.

Good performance appears in Prophet and MaxProp in a regular movement case. However, our airborne network may be in irregular topology changes when each vehicle takes a random walk movement model. New solution should be found in our requirement.

3   Bio-inspired Routing Modeling

In the society of ants, individuals are real simple in morphology, but the swarm can carry out very complex foraging behaviors. The colony's ability to converge on the shortest way connecting the nest to food source as quickly as possible is amazing. The explanation for this is called trail-laying trail-following mechanism. Ants search for a way to the food and deposit a hormone called pheromone while roaming preferentially towards path with highest pheromone density. Shorter paths would be completed earlier and attracted by more ants, which will increase the concentration degree turn and turn about. By selecting the direction probabilistically the best alternative from a collection of alternatives appears. This emergence is a consequence of interactions between the individuals of the ant colony over time.

The ant colony, actually, do solve routing issues. Available path should be explored and established from nest to the food source through a series of back and forth creeping ants. Individuals make their decision on each crossroad according to accumulative pheromone level in optional directions, irrespective of future conditions. One ant is insignificant to the conformation of the path, which, instead, depends on the whole swarm. Moreover, concerning the features of a routing network, exact similarity exists astonishingly. Available route should be discovered and determined from a source node to an ultimate destination through intermediate nodes. Each message packet is forwarded according to the routing algorithms. The delivery probability, transmission delay and other relational metrics of relayed packets are used as heuristic information to route. Besides, tasks in ant foraging behavior and network routing are both dynamically distributed, without any central controller.

Inspired by the appealing analogies, we try to model this sort of swarm intelligence. However, modeling is quite different from observing the natural system. Since in modeling, we would attempt to explore what actually exists in the ant colony system. In [1] a novel taxonomy for routing protocols is presented and used to classify the existed ant colony based algorithms. Essentially, all the strategies almost mimic the similar following rules:

(1) There exist two kinds of packets: the data packets, which signifies traditional intended datastream, and ant agents (control packets), which imitate physical insect individuals to find a feasible route to the final recipient.

(2) Each node maintains different entries for its known destinations through its neighbors, where each entry implies a pheromone variable, a measure of priority of stepping over that neighbor to the destination.

(3) Ant agents are used to establish the routing tables, called pheromone tables. A forward ant travels from a source to a destination while gathering the whole route quality. By turns, a backward ant retraces the way back to the source and updates the routing tables at intermediate nodes by the collected information.

(4) Next hop routing is used by data packets and forward and agents. At each node they choose the next relay node by means of a stochastic or deterministic rule, using the integration of pheromone variables and local heuristic information. Separately, backward ants make use of source routing in which all path information is encapsulated in the packet datagram.

(5) Additionally, a pheromone evaporation mechanism is executed sometimes to balance the exploration-exploitation problem. The topology is volatile, so pheromone evaporation on every link at regular intervals can favor exploration ability and prevent over-constrained by the previous exploitation decisions.

4 Fuzzy Control Based Ant Colony Routing

4.1 Problem Description

Traditional ant colony based routing modeling is not suitable for UAV delay tolerant network immediately. These approaches are capable of dealing with occasional disconnection error, but not treat the dynamic topology as a rule rather than an exception. Additional, since the ant routing has quick convergence, precocity and stagnation, it is expert in exploiting rather than exploring, which is in great demand of the specific network.

Figure 1 shows a specific use case. Eight vehicles hover over two different heights with two groups as in Fig.1(a). This square structure would take a conversion after receiving a "circle" command from the base station. Fig.1(b)-Fig.1(f) show this transformation clearly, which is a self-regulation and self-deployment process essentially . However, the deployment strategy is not the emphasis here and we just concentrate our attention on the link availability which is the critical factor to dynamic routing. Practically, UAVs are not as controllable as vehicles on land and are more likely overstep the neighbors' communication range. The reasons are capable to divide into internal, such as the high speed and great inertia of UAVs, and external, such as the drifting characteristic of GPS and influence of sudden wind. From Figure 1 we could recognize that the irregular navigation makes the disconnected links extremely unpredictable. Moreover, the pictorial example is already the simplest use case. Added individuals and more complicated tasks both make the behaviors even more troublesome. Ant colony

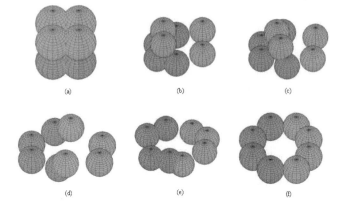

Fig. 1. A process that the airborne perceptive network transforms from square to circle. Each center of the ball denotes the hovering UAV, while the radius of each ball indicate half of UAV communication range, which is designed for comprehending easily. Once two balls interconnect, the distance of two vehicles satisfy the communication requirement and a usable link builds.

algorithm, therefore, should take uncertainty as its paramount consideration to solve the dynamic issue.

4.2   Fuzzy Inference System

Local heuristic information, to a certain degree, reflects more about the temporary link characteristic than historical experience sometimes. In ant routing, pheromone values in routing tables are the consequences of long time studying of the whole network graph from ants' actions while heuristic information of each node points out the local availability of every potential path.

When the neighbor node has better heuristic information, we say it has higher reliability, and vice versa. In fuzzy set theory initially introduced by Zadeh in 1965 [17], this "better", "higher" like linguistic description cannot simply belong to an element of a crisp set or not an element of this crisp set, but instead, it can be defined as a fuzzy value between 0 and 1 of a fuzzy set. Fuzzy set theory models the imprecise sensory circumstance as perceived by human brain. For proper decision making by fuzzy approximation reasoning, linguistic information should be incorporated into it. A precise model is hard to build as mentioned above in our airborne network situation. Therefore, fuzzy inference system is used as a tool to handle the problem that crisp set theory cannot process well. The steps involved in fuzzy inference system design are as follows:

Fuzzification of Inputs and Outputs. It would be best to satisfy several properties when choosing input variables to be fuzzified. First and foremost, the metric must represent the reliability of the selected node. That is, if we choose

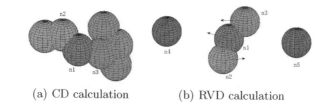

(a) CD calculation   (b) RVD calculation

Fig. 2. Examples of CD and RVD

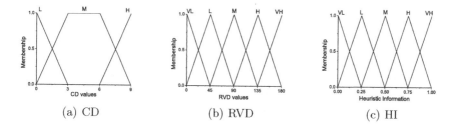

(a) CD   (b) RVD   (c) HI

Fig. 3. Membership functions

the node as a relay node, why do we believe that the node is a better candidate than myself and it has the higher probability to meet the recipient directly or indirectly. Secondly, the practical calculation methods of the metric must be as simple as possible. It is not wised to waste much computational cost on such a bitty step of fuzzy inference system, which is itself a component of the whole routing algorithm. Here we just use two parameters, Crowd Density (CD) and Relative Velocity Direction (RVD), which are locally acquired or estimated.

(1)Crowd Density (CD)

We consider Crown Density as the first parameter, which denotes the sum of neighbors (except the demander itself) of an intended candidate neighbor. Take Figure 2(a) as an example, n1 is a source node or relay node already. Now n1 has to pick a node to forward its carrying packet from two candidate neighbors, n2 and n3, colored by blue and green respectively. Naturally, we believe that the node with more neighbors have the higher probability to transmit the messages to destination, for the reason that more neighbors generally imply more choices. In Figure 2(a), the n2's CD value is 1 and n3's CD value is 3, which means from n1's standpoint, entry for n3 has better heuristic information.

The membership function of CD is divided into 3 sections, low, medium and high, entitled as L, M, H, correspondingly. We choose trapezoidal function as the membership function for its simplicity in formulas and computation. We run simulation with random walk and random waypoint model in different circumstances and define the suitable boundary conditions. And maximum number of CD is almost nine, for a 2000*2000 place with 90 nodes in our simulation. Figure 3(a) illustrates the degree of membership functions of CD for this scenario.

(2)Relative Velocity Direction (RVD)

Relative Velocity Direction is another great reference meaning and easily got parameter. The RVD value turns small when the intended candidate node navigates at approximately the same direction as the demander, and vice versa. This regulation bases on the hypothesis that if directions are the same, node that encountered by the candidate in the future is possibly also met by the demander. However, copies of forwarding messages are best to transmit to those who will encounter different nodes to increase the delivery probability. Figure 2(b) gives an expressive and readable example. n1 is the demander while n2 and n3 are the candidates. Evidently, n2 gets higher RVD value than n3. Then n1 transmit a copy of message to n2. Ultimately n4 and n5 both have opportunity to contribute to the message forwarding.

Make a translation of related velocity vectors to the same plane, and calculate their intersection angle, then we get the RVD values. The membership function of RVD is divided into 5 sections, very low, low, medium and high, very high, entitled as VL, L, M, H, VH respectively. We choose triangular function here due to the same simplicity, as shown in Figure 3(b).

(3)Heuristic Information (HI)

The output of fuzzy inference system is heuristic information, which is a considerable factor in routing selection. Heuristic information from highest to lowest are define as VH, H, M, L, VL, as illustrated in Figure 3(c), which stand for very high, high, medium, low, very low separately.

Fuzzy Rules and Reasoning

Fuzzy inference system models on the base of conditional sentences called linguistic rules rather than mathematical formulas. Each system is implemented in the form of "IF-THEN" rules, a simple form of logic such as:

IF "CD is H" and "RVD is VH", THEN "HI is VH".

The set of fuzzy rules which regulate the management of the process of interest from human's view are presented in Table 1.

Table 1. Fuzzy rules

CD \ RVD	VL	L	M	H	VH
L	VL	VL	L	M	H
M	VL	L	M	H	VH
H	L	M	H	VH	VH

Defuzzification

In this stage the outcome in the previous phase is converted into a nonfuzzy value, which is used as heuristic information. Many defuzzifiers exist and here we use center of area (COA) strategy as the defuzzification method to create this single number.

Figure 4 shows the surface-plot of our fuzzy inference system, which depicts the relationship between the inputs and output. In this figure, preferences of CD and RVD values are "High" and "Very High" separately. As a result, directions with closer costs to the favors generate better heuristic information. In the meantime, neighbor with Low CD and Very Low RVD values obtain the least heuristic information.

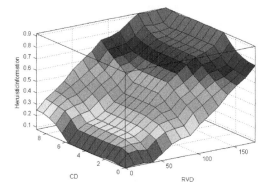

Fig. 4. Surface-plot of CD and RVD versus Heruistic information

4.3   Ant Colony Routing for UAV Delay Tolerant Network

In this part we describe our proposed strategy in detail. The most conspicuous difference between the proposed algorithm and traditional methods is the utility of fuzzy local situation. In the decision process of next hoping routing, path selecting is not only determined by pheromone value derived from forward and backward exploration ants, but also decided by heuristic information, which is computed by the fuzzy inference system. The sequence of the novel algorithm is described as follows:

(1)Initially, as mentioned in section 3, forward ants are launched to find a way to destination and backward ants are retraced to renew the possible pheromone table. Being c the current node, k the neighbor node of c, τ_k the pheromone value of entry of link $c \to k$. After one backward ant comes back from neighbor node d, the pheromone quantities of neighbors of c are updated as

$$\tau_k = \begin{cases} \tau_k + r(1 - \tau_k), if \ k = d; \\ \tau_k - r\tau_k, if \ k \neq d. \end{cases} \qquad (1)$$

where r is a constant value.

(2)Suppose N as the sum of neighbors of c, the probability that a data packet select node i as next hop is calculated as:

$$p_i = \frac{\theta\tau_i + (1 - \theta)HI_i}{\sum_{k=1}^{N}[\theta\tau_i + (1 - \theta)HI_i]} \qquad (2)$$

where θ balances the exploitation and exploration ability. Such calculation is reasonable, since if the network is completely partitioned and forward ants won't get to destination to generate backward ones, local heuristic information would dominate the choice and historical experience of pheromone would contribute less.

(3)In order to augment the delivery probability, a L copies mechanism is implemented. That is, each message carried on node c, whether it is a source node or a relay node, would be copied L times to transmit to L neighbors of c. If $N > L$, the nodes with L most highest probability calculated in equation (2) are selected as the relay nodes. Otherwise, every neighbor can get a copy and $L - N$ copies would temporarily remain until c meet new neighbors and distribute the left duplication. In simulation, we found L is very critical in the delivery ratio and overhead ratio. It is also determined by buffer size, number of nodes and messages.

5   Simulation

We choose ONE (Opportunistic Network Environment) simulator [18], which combines mobility modeling, routing, visualization and reporting modules in one package. It allows researchers to create scenarios based upon different movement models and offers a framework for implementing routing protocols. All modules are dynamically loaded when ONE is started using the Java reflection API. We implement our novel algorithm in a new file by overriding the update method and extending the MessageRoute class, and then the simulator automatically loads it when the scenario begins to run.

ONE simulator enables configuring different parameters. In our scenario, we consider 250M buffer and message size with the range of 10k and 100k. Additional, the message event generator randomly creates a message every 10 to 15 intervals, and each message's TTL is 5 minutes. Under such configuration, buffer size would be not issues for those multi-copies protocols such as Epidemic, which is a perfect method if enough buffer size and transmission bandwidth exist. RandomWaypoint model, which generates zig-zag paths, is used to here to provide the interface for requesting a new path for a node and asking when the next path is available. Each mobile node, with the transmission range of 100m, has a Simple Broadcast Interface with the transmission speed 250 kb per second.

Here we conduct several basic groups of simulations. Every result is taken from an average of 10 runs with different number generators of movement model. First, we set 90 nodes in the simulation world and run 6000 seconds to capture the interesting data. The performance of ant colony based routing (AC) is evaluated with other five existing protocols, i.e. Direct Delivery (DD), First Contact (FC), Epidemic (EP), Spray and Wait (SW) and Prophet (PR).

Figure 5 compares different aspects to witness AC's high performance. Due to enough buffer size and adequate transmission bandwidth, EP mostly provides an upper bound on achievable performance to measure other routing algorithms. Message generator creates about 500 messages altogether during 6000 seconds

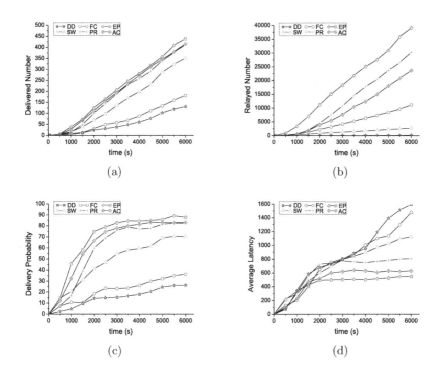

Fig. 5. Delivered Number, Relayed Number, Delivery Probability and Average Latency within 6000 seconds

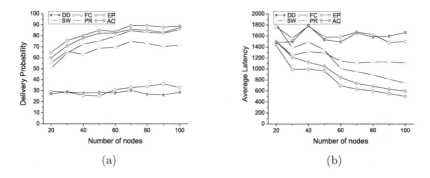

Fig. 6. Delivery Probability and Average Latency versus number of nodes

period and the numbers of delivered messages, the ones that have been accepted by the final recipients, are reflected in Figure 5(a). EP delivers uppermost number of 450 approximately and AC is the nearest to this level subsequently. PR follows closely and transmits about 400 messages. Bigger delivered number indicates higher delivery probability, which is a principal measuring criterion about delay tolerant networks shown in Figure 5(c). Another two considerable metrics are transmission overhead and average latency. Here, we count relayed number, which means copies to be transmitted successfully under all valid contacts, to denote the intractable communication overhead. Additional duplication will lead to higher arrival possibility of messages, and meanwhile, increase the overhead, necessarily or unnecessarily. From Figure 5(b) we obtain that DD outperforms all the other protocols and has the lowest overhead on account of its one-copy strategy, which, however, brings about the worst delivery probability. On the contrary, EP creates the best delivery probability at the expense of most relayed messages, which is not feasible practically. In the middle, AC achieves a good balancing among these methods and is more realizable. The other metric is named average latency, which contributes much to the quality of service (QoS). Figure 5(d) shows that AC has satisfactory transmission speed in contradistinction to others.

In the second group of simulations, we run different scales of networks while keeping identical environment mentioned above. All data are collected after running 6000 seconds and event intervals do not change, thus generating same number of messages. Compared with the whole simulation area, transmission coverage is about 0.79% (1 node) and 15.8% (20 nodes) to 79% (100 nodes) for all together. Figure 6 demonstrates that AC is the best protocol in terms of delivery probability and average latency, without consideration of unachievable EP strategy. Heuristic information and pheromone balancing methods will makes the AC protocol suitable for mobile network on all sizes, featuring sparse connectivity or fully connected.

6   Conclusion

In this paper we have looked at a late-model airborne perceptive network, a three-dimensional architecture featuring randomly violent topological changes and usable path generates in an unpredictable moment. Therefore, we have proposed the significance of local heuristic information in such UAV delay tolerant networks. To accomplish this, a fuzzy inference system is introduced to calculate the heuristic information using approximate reasoning, in which the inputs are Crowd Density and Relative Velocity Direction, two parameters easily acquired without complex computational cost. Thus the integration of heuristic information and ant pheromone would result in a good exploration-exploitation trade-off for ant colony based protocol. Compared to some existing well-known protocols, simulation results in Section 5 demonstrate the fairly good performance of our novel strategy, both in terms of delivery probability and average latency.

There still exist several research issues in the future. Owing to the limitation of simulation tool, we do not test the method in substantial three-dimensional space, in which our application background really consists. Unknown characteristics about three-dimensional routing deserve to study and discuss thoroughly. We could pay more attention to this point to improve the performance of intermittently connected networks.

References

1. Saleem, M., Di Caro, G.A.: Swarm intelligence based routing protocol for wireless sensor networks: survey and future directions. Information Sciences 181(20), 4597–4624 (2011)
2. La Richard, J., Priya, R.: Ant-based adaptive message forwarding scheme for challenged networks with sparse connectivity. In: IEEE Military Communications Conference, MILCOM (2009)
3. Mirabedini, S.J., Teshnehlab, M., Shenasa, M.H., Moraghar, A., Rahmani, A.M.: AFAR: Adaptive fuzzy ant based routing for communication networks. Journal of Zhejiang University Science A 9(12), 1666–1675 (2008)
4. Rosati, L., Berioli, M., Reali, G.: On ant routing algorithms in ad hoc networks with critical connectivity. Ad Hoc Networks 6, 827–859 (2008)
5. Goswami, M.M., Dharaskar, R.V., Thakare, V.M.: Fuzzy ant colony based routing protocol for mobile ad hoc network. In: International Conference on Computer Engineering and Technology, ICCET 2009, pp. 438–444 (2009)
6. Salehinejad, H., Talebi, S.: Dynamic Fuzzy Logic-Ant Colony System-Based Route Selection System. Applied Computational Intelligence and Soft Computing (2010)
7. Mathurapoj, A., Pornavalai, C., Chakraborty, G.: Fuzzy-spray: efficient routing in delay tolerant ad-hoc network based on fuzzy decision mechanism. In: 2009 IEEE International Conference on Fuzzy Systems, FUZZ-IEEE, pp. 104–109 (2009)
8. Li, X., Ci, L., Yang, M., Cheng, B.: Exploration-Exploitation Balancing Deployment Strategy in UAV Sensor Networks. INFORMATION-An International Interdisciplinary Journal 14(8), 2701–2710 (2011)
9. Fall, K.: A Delay-Tolerant Network Architecture for Challenged Internets. In: ACM SIGCOMM (August 2003)
10. Spyropoulos, T., Psounis, K., Raghavendra, C.S.: Single-copy routing in intermittently connected mobile networks. In: Proc. IEEE Conf. Sensor and Ad Hoc Communications and Networks, SECON (2004)
11. Jain, S., Fall, K., Patra, R.: Routing in a Delay Tolerant Network. In: Proc. ACM SIGCOMM, pp. 145–158 (August 2004)
12. Vahdat, A., Becker, D.: Epidemic Routing for Partially-Connected Ad Hoc Networks. Technical Report CS-2000-06, Duke University (July 2000)
13. Spyropoulos, T., Psounis, K., Raghavendra, C.S.: Spray and wait: Efficient routing in intermittently connected mobile networks. In: Proceedings of ACM SIGCOMM Workshop on Delay Tolerant Networking, WDTN (2005)
14. Spyropoulos, T., Psounis, K., Raghavendra, C.S.: Spray and Focus: Efficient Mobility-Assisted Routing for Heterogeneous and Correlated Mobility. In: Proc. PerCom Workshops apos, pp. 79–85 (March 2007)
15. Lindgren, A., et al.: Probabilistic Routing in Intermittently Connected Networks. Mobile Comp. and Commun. Rev. 7(3) (July 2003)
16. Burgess, J., Gallagher, B., Jensen, D., Levine, B.N.: MaxProp: Routing for Vehicle-Based Disruption-Tolerant Networks. In: Proc. IEEE Infocom, pp. 1–11. IEEE (April 2006)
17. Zadeh, L.A.: Fuzzy sets. Information and Control 8, 338–353 (1965)
18. Keranen, A.: The ONE Simulator for DTN Protocol Evaluation (2009)

Deploying Three-Dimensional Mobile Sensor Networks Based on Virtual Forces Algorithm

Xuanya Li[1], Linlin Ci[1,2], Minghua Yang[2],
Chengping Tian[1], and Xiang Li[3]

[1] School of Computer Science and Technology,
Beijing Institute of Technology, Beijing, China
xuanya.li@gmail.com
[2] Beijing Institute of Information Technology, Beijing, China
[3] North University of China, Taiyuan, Shanxi, China

Abstract. With the scientific and technological progress, new-style three-dimensional (3D) mobile sensor networks draw the attention of many exciting applications in multifarious areas, where the former two-dimensional (2D) assumptions do not make sense. Existing references were mostly restricted to 3D static sensor networks, featuring either random or deterministic, while basing on more realistic mobile conditions, the studies were rarely referred. In this paper, we, for the first time, apply the noted virtual force algorithm (VFA) to 3D space. Except for traditional virtual forces, central gravitation and equilibrium force are additionally introduced to get better sensor distribution. Then four groups of cases are presented to summarize various mobility patterns and two metrics are of particular interest to evaluate the performance of our proposed improvement, namely coverage ratio and homogeneous degree. The simulation witnesses the effectiveness of the improved mechanism in the end.

Keywords: three-dimensional, mobile sensor network, virtual force algorithm, deployment.

1 Introduction

In this paper, we, for the first time, focus on the problem of how to deploy a three-dimensional (3D) mobile sensor network in which each movable sensor can navigate freely in 3D space. Under the complete distributed manner, navigated sensors self-organize into the target region to perform tasks, while optimal coverage is achieved with least participants.

1.1 Background and Motivation

Currently most studies in the literature address the issues of sensor networks by modeling the region of interest as a two-dimensional (2D) plane. This is reasonable since a great variety of applications deploy the sensors on the flat plane and phenomenon to be monitored mainly takes place on the earth surface

R. Wang and F. Xiao (Eds.): CWSN 2012, CCIS 334, pp. 204–216, 2013.
© Springer-Verlag Berlin Heidelberg 2013

(a) Air pollution detection   (b) Fire fighting support

(c) Adversary target positioning   (d) Seawater pollution detection

Fig. 1. Typical application scenarios for 3D mobile sensor networks in which mobile sensors are denoted by cross mobile carriers

or nearby, which do not present the dimension of height as an attention. However, with the scientific and technological progress, new-style sensor networks are tried to perceive the real 3D world, where the previous 2D assumption does not make sense.

Airborne and underwater applications are such instances taking the dimension of height into consideration (Fig1). Airborne perceptive networks consisting of sensor integrated unmanned aerial vehicles are novel solutions for studying the rate of dispersion of air pollution, preventing the fire disaster and supporting fire fighting, and adversary target positioning in an execrable battlefield environment. On the other hand, underwater applications include seawater pollution detection, oceanic disasters prewarning, marine navigation, and underwater ordnance defending. All these scenarios must not ignore the importance of the dimension of height, the one not proposed in the planar model. Another common characteristic of these applications is the mobility of the individual unit. In 2D planar ground, sensors can be fixed on the earth surface, while in 3D space they are mostly embedded in moving carriers, unmanned aerial vehicles or inflatable float chambers for instance, which make autonomic three-dimensional movement possible, thus resulting in 3D mobile sensor networks.

In this paper, we focus on the deployment issue, also interpreted as a coverage problem here, which means the ability that each point in the 3D target region can be observed by the network. Unfortunately, the 3D puzzle becomes extremely troublesome comparing to its 2D counterpart. Similar sphere packing and covering problems, Kelvin's and Kepler's conjecture for examples, went through centuries to achieve breakthroughs [1]. Alam's research [1] can be seen as the milestone in the progress of 3D network design, which considered the node placement strategy as the main issue and indicated that the use of Voronoi tessellation of 3D space should be a good solution. Based on [1] for the past few years, researchers concentrated on theoretical studies, mostly restricted to 3D static wireless sensor networks. Considering the mobility premise, however, relative studies were much less referred.

Practically, 3D sensors are always impossible to stay still like its 2D counterparts for they should embed in moving carriers to navigate to 3D space. In other words, 3D sensor networks are essentially mobile networks, mostly. This brings about a large number of capabilities, such as the abilities to self-organize and self-deploy, which mean that starting from some compact initial configuration, the nodes can intelligently track the target region in a self-adaptive topology. The assumption of mobility offers unprecedented opportunities for observing the 3D physical world, and meanwhile, generates more technical puzzles. Here in this paper, we focus the deployment issue which is one of the fundamental problems in sensor networks.

1.2   Related Work

Effective deployment of sensor networks is often the fundamental premise of various desired design goals. Related studies in 2D assumption are fairly comprehensive, using either static or dynamic strategies respectively [2]. However, considering the 3D scenario, the papers are limited.

Huang [3] formulated the coverage problem as a decision problem and proposed an efficient polynomial-time distributed algorithm to determine if the service area is entirely α-covered, that is to say, every point in the volume is covered by α sensors. However, it referred to nothing about how a compact α-coverage network takes shape.

Fundamental characteristics of a random deployed set of sensors in 3D space were investigated in [9]. In the paper, different crucial transmitting/sensing ranges for deployment issue are analyzed. In [10], the author addressed the problem of selecting a minimum subset of sensors for complete coverage. Numerical simulations show that the optimized sensor network has better energy efficiency compared to the standard random deployment even when the sensors start to fail over time.

Compared to the random deployment mentioned above, deterministic strategies appear to be more attractive, for planned manners could achieve the designed goal more effectively with least cost. A major breakthrough was made in [1], which can be seen as the milestone in the progress of 3D network design. The authors showed that the use of Voronoi tessellation to create truncated octahedron units is the best strategy to achieve 100% coverage of 3D space while minimizing the number of sensors. In the paper, other contenders including rhombic dodecahedron, hexagonal prism and cube, were presented and corresponding placement strategies were designed correspondingly. Further, in [4], they developed their research into diverse situations featuring different ratios of communication range to sensing range.

In [5], the authors proposed a trade off ratio between the number of sensors and the volume of overlapping achieved. They believed that the detection of an event can be more relatively easy with more sensors covering the objective. The authors presented multi-factors and concluded that rhombic dodecahedron is the optimal model for 1-coverage deterministic deployment.

A new type Reuleaux tetrahedron model was shown to guarantee κ-coverage of a 3D region [6]. The authors deduced the minimum sensor spatial density of k-coverage attribute based on the geometric properties of Reuleaux tetrahedron. Then they also investigated the connectivity of homogeneous and heterogeneous structures.

Another series of studies was conducted in [7][8]. Bai and Zhang provided deployment patterns with proven optimality that achieves both coverage and connectivity issues for the first time. In the published papers, different connectivity patterns were analyzed in detail.

Accordingly, to summarize the points which we have just concluded, preceding references were restricted to 3D static wireless sensor networks, featuring either random or deterministic. Studies based on more realistic mobile conditions, to our knowledge, unfortunately, were rarely referred. Therefore, we have to look into 2D mobile strategies to seek for solutions. Here the noted 2D virtual force algorithm (VFA) [11] is introduced and extended into our 3D circumstance.

1.3   Our Contributions

In this paper, we, for the first time, apply the VFA algorithm to 3D space. Except for traditional virtual forces, central gravitation and equilibrium force are additionally defined to make the deployment process more reasonable and obtainable, resulting in better uniformity of sensor distribution. In simulation, four groups of cases are presented to summarize various mobility patterns and two metrics are of particular interest to evaluate the effectiveness of our proposed improvement. Concretely, coverage ratio is treated as the primary objective and homogeneous degree is used to measure the uniformity of sensor distribution.

2   Problem Statement

In this section, the main assumptions of our research are proposed. Even though some of these preconditions do not act in accordance with the practical situation, our work, to some extent, provide an illuminating theoretical foundation for the novel 3D scenario, which could be modified to accommodate to diverse function specific applications under respective circumstances. The main assumptions are defined as follows:

(1) The sensing and communication ranges are deterministic, omni-directional and spherical, which is the common assumption in all 3D researches, thus generating sensing ball and communication ball respectively.

(2) We use the binary sensor model, in which detection probability of the target is 1 if it happens in the sensor's sensing range, 0 otherwise. Probabilistic

sensor detection model is not adopted due to its uncertainty and complexity, in which the detection probability decreases while the target's relative distance increases.

(3) Each sensor could get its own absolute position information from global positioning system (GPS), or relative position from location protocols such as RSSI and TOA.

(4) Target region to be tracked or monitored stays still or moves slowly to remain in the network's sensing range, for fast moving target would lead the mobile network to a hard convergent status.

(5) Target region is initially already known to the full-connectivity networks. Moreover, mission planning and target positioning are not discussed in this paper. Otherwise, the actual sensor fusion and tolerant routing algorithm, while of enormous importance, are beyond the scope of the present work.

3   Three Dimensional Virtual Force Algorithm

3.1   Applying VFA to 3-D Space

Traditional virtual force algorithm (VFA) [11] is deduced from the ideas of potential field [12] and disk packing [13]. A balanced combination of attractive (positive) and repulsive (negative) forces is utilized between pairs of particles. Here, we first present a brief introduction about the virtual forces and then produce their derivative definition in 3D space.

For the purpose of maintaining a compact covering conformation in case an individual should escape the preferred region, each sensor is attracted by its neighbors when it is getting far away from the main swarm. Imitating the physical world, we call it the attractive force. With the assumption of locating in each other's communication range, the longer the relative distance between pairs appears, the more anxious they expect to approach each other, thus generating stronger attractive force. On the other hand, in case individuals should stray too close to produce unnecessary coverage overlap, so-called repulsive force is defined correspondingly, which ensures that the sensors are not overly crowded. Practically, it makes sense for that repulsive force could prevent the sensors from colliding, which benefits much from the economic and security perspectives.

Actually, this virtual forces mechanism treats the mobile sensor network as a virtual physical system involving force and velocity. For simplicity in the design, the direction of the composition of forces at one moment is the direction of velocity in the next time step. Ultimately, the virtual forces among sensors make the swarm indicative of considerable stability and collectivity. When certain sensor runs out of action for specific reasons, due to the local unbalance of forces, remaining sensors would spontaneously move until a new convergent status takes shape.

In our 3D space, each sensor makes contact with three balls with the same center of a sphere. First, each sensor is capable of perceiving the active targets within a certain distance in an omni-directional manner, which forms a spherical pattern. We name it S-Ball (sensing ball), and specify R_s as its radius. Secondly, each sensor has a direct contact with its partner through a wireless transmitter, which has a limited radius, namely communication radius R_c. Correspondingly, resulting sphere is distinguished as C-Ball (communication ball). Finally, the third is called B-Ball (balanced ball), with radius equal to $R_b(0 \leq R_b \leq R_c)$, the boundary between attractive force and repulsive force. A sensor exerts merely repulsive forces to those neighbors seated inside its B-Ball and only attractive forces, on the contrary, to those located outside the B-Ball while remaining inside the C-Ball.

Every sensor is assumed to be a potential field to exercise influence over its adjacent companions. Figure 2 shows such an instance of treating sensor B_1 as the calculation reference point. In the figure, three derivative ball of sensor B1 are colored by yellow, green, blue, and denoted by radius (convenient for non-color printed viewers) respectively. B_2, perched in B-Ball, is pushed by B_1 while B_3, suspended outside B-Ball, is pulled by the potential source. Notably, lying on the spherical surface of B-Ball, B_4 is in equilibrium and neither positive nor negative force is given by B_1. Furthermore, situated beyond B_1's C-Ball, B_5 is not even B_1's neighbor sensor, and it is of course not influenced by B_1's potential field. Due to the symmetry of forces simultaneously, B_1 is as well in its neighbors' fields and undergoes repulsive (attractive) force from B_2 (B_3). Every moment in VFA, each sensor computes relationships in different potential fields generated by its neighbors, and calculates the summation of vector forces, which determines the sensor where to navigate in the next time step in 3D space.

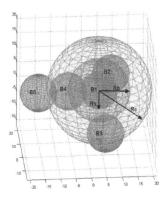

Fig. 2. An example shown that how a sensor B_1 exercises influence over its adjacent companions

We refine the acting force rules as follows. The closer (farther) the sensors are to each other, the bigger the repulsive (attraction) force appears. In other words, longer distance to the balance spherical surface means a stronger impact by the corresponding potential field. When the neighbor is exactly located on the R_b's range, both repulsive and attraction forces would decrease to zero. Any equation can be selected as the computing formula of mutual forces as long as it reflects above-mentioned properties. This paper introduces an uncomplex form as follows. For any two sensors s_1 at (x_1, y_1, z_1) and s_2 at (x_2, y_2, z_2), we denote their Euclidean distance as $d(s_1, s_2)$, i.e. $d(s_1, s_2) = \sqrt{(x_1 - x_2)^2 + (y_1 - y_2)^2 + (z_1 - z_2)^2}$. Let the virtual force exerted on s_1 by another sensor s_2 be expressed by $\overrightarrow{F_{12}}$. Note that $\overrightarrow{F_{12}}$ is a vector whose orientation is decided by the type of virtual force, and magnitude is determined by Equation (1):

$$|\overrightarrow{F_{12}}| = ((d(s_1, s_2) - R_b) * \alpha)^k \tag{1}$$

where k is the amplification exponent, used to magnify the influence of range differences to the balance point. α is used to make the equation as an increasing function, and here we assign α as 10. Equation (1) helps sensors push or pull their neighbors towards individual B-Ball surfaces. In this way, each sensor automatically adjusts its current position according to space distance relationships to its surrounding neighbors. A high coupling structure, consequently, takes shape depending on virtual forces between pairs. By means of different configuration of R_b, the whole deployment can be relatively sparse or compact.

3.2   Improvement

Traditional VFAs are always on the premise of high concentration of initial distribution, and then for the purpose of achieving an entirely uniform coverage in a diffusion manner. In fact, however, an initial random placement of mobile sensors in the 3D scenario is usually utilized to explore the search space with increased possibilities to catch the objective event. The resulting irregular topology would easily lead to network partitioning and coverage holes. Further adjustment is needed to make the compact region spread and sparse region shrink. Traditional VFAs do not act well under such cases. Because the relationships between sensors are equal and their prior knowledge is limited, they do not know deployment densities of various parts. Sensors would only make use of local situations to take decisions, not from a global perspective.

The shortage of overall coordination probably brings about two potential issues. Firstly, target region may not be covered effectively. Random placement and non-intervention self-deployment possibly produce, large or small, an offset to the target. Secondly, sensors are still likely to distribute non-uniformly even if the former issue is resolved. In extreme cases, multiple partitioning networks appear while the whole is balanced under virtual forces. Here in our research, apart from traditional virtual (TV) forces, central gravitation (CG) and equilibrium force (EF) are additionally defined to make the deployment process more reasonable and obtainable.

– Central gravitation (CG)

Central gravitation, which is as same as the positive force from preferential area mentioned in [11], represents the attraction to sensors exerted by target region.

Based on the last assumption in Section 2, target region is already discovered before the deployment process. Such presupposition is reasonable, for VFA algorithm runs after the objective is detected by randomly navigated mobile sensors. Once the target is assured, sensors are trended towards CG's direction and simultaneously inform other unwitting companions of information about target coordinates.

The magnitude of CG can be defined on the basis of traditional potential field [12], varying according to relative Euclidean distance between the target and the sensor itself. Computational methods of CG, together with other virtual forces, influence the final arrangement. Here in our research, to simplify, CG is configured as one unit constant with the same order of magnitude to TV. Because CG is not expected to contribute too much in the deployment process, and we only depend on it attracting sensors to the intended destination.

– Equilibrium force (EF)

There is no control center in distributed deployment, and the tight coupling conformation generated by TV possibly contains non-uniform areas due to the limited knowledge of individual. Uniform distribution, however, has considerably practical significance. Regular conformation can take advantage of valid coverage proportion of each sensor as much as possible, thus minimizing the number of participant mobile sensors.

The optimal distribution is of course under deterministic strategies, such as the rhombic dodecahedron model [5]. However, self-formed appearance based on virtual forces is rather unpredictable. Mobile sensors are not encouraged to calculate their desired locations dynamically in a Voronoi polyhedron model [1] and then moved to the proper position, which is not a self-adaption strategy essentially. The best solution should be in a totally distributed criterion to fit reality. Therefore, Equilibrium force (EF) is advanced.

During deployment, each sensor is assumed to be not only a potential field to produce TV forces but also a coordinator to equilibrate the self-centered local region, which is through EF designed as follows. Relative Euclidean distance is still exploited for its simplicity. Reference sensor obtains the average value of distances to its neighbors and compares it to the individual. Repulsive force comes into being if the average value is greater than individual and attractive force generates conversely. Making sensor i as the reference point, EF exerted by it to its neighbor j is denoted as $\overrightarrow{EF_{ij}}$. The magnitude of $\overrightarrow{EF_{ij}}$ is determined as follows:

$$|\overrightarrow{EF_{ij}}| = ((d(s_i, s_j) - \overline{D_i}) * \alpha)^k \tag{2}$$

where $\overline{D_i}$ signifies the average values of distances of i to all neighbors and α, k have the same meaning as Equation (1).

In each time step, each node calculates CG from the target region, TV and EF from all its neighbors, and makes a vector addition:

$$\overrightarrow{F_i} = \overrightarrow{CG} + \sum_{j=1}^{N_i} (\overrightarrow{TV_{ij}} + \overrightarrow{EF_{ij}}) \tag{3}$$

where N_i indicates the neighbors of sensor i, and $\overrightarrow{TV}$ is calculated by Equation (1). The direction of vector $\overrightarrow{F_i}$ determines the direction of motion of i in the next time step. Thus, a complete distributed method is accordingly operated.

4   Experiment

A series of simulation experiments is conducted aimed at applying the noted VFA algorithm to 3D space and evaluating the effectiveness of our proposed improvement. Two metrics are of particular interest: coverage ratio and homogeneous degree. Coverage ratio indicates the percentage of a target region covered by the network, and we only focus 1-coverage problem here. Coverage is the principal issue in WSN problems, for achieving bigger coverage with lesser sensors is very meaningful indeed. On the other hand, the coverage ratio cannot reflect the relationships of sensor locations, and we introduce the homogeneous degree to measure the uniformity of sensor distribution, which is reasonable strongly. Unlike deterministic strategies, the final conformation of self-deployment of mobile sensors is unknown, in which may contain both compact and sparse parts. That is why higher uniformity is expected to obtain and we define this metric correspondingly.

4.1   Simulation Setups

To our knowledge, there is a lack of appropriate simulation tools for 3D mobile sensor networks currently, and we use Matlab 7.10 for our simulation due to its excellent computational capabilities.

Based on the premise of homogeneous network, sensors have identical sensing and communication ranges, and we define R_s as 1 and R_c as 3. Concerning the coefficients in virtual forces, we do a series of simulations to compare the performances and establish R_b as 1.4 and k as 12 in Equation (1)(2), which is inspired by Van Der Waals' forces. Due to the lack of space, we have to omit this process and pay more attention to the comparison of performances between traditional VFA and improved VFA algorithms.

For the convenience of expression, $R\{(x_1, x_2), (y_1, y_2), (z_1, z_2)\}$ signifies the region of a cuboid with X coordinates between x_1 and x_2, Y coordinates between y_1 and y_2 and Z coordinates between z_1 and z_2. We assume the whole space as $R\{(-5, 5), (-5, 5), (-5, 5)\}$, and original point $O(0, 0, 0)$ as the center point of the target region. Four groups of cases, with different configurations of initial patterns, are brought forward to witness the effectiveness as follows.

(1) Case 1:
$R_1\{(-0.5, 0.5), (-0.5, 0.5), (-0.5, 0.5)\}$ is appointed as the initial room for sensors (Fig3(a)). This case studies the capability that sensors go spread to deploy when they gather together in the beginning.

(2) Case 2:
$R_2\{(-5, 5), (-5, 5), (-5, 5)\}$ is appointed as the initial room for sensors (Fig4(a)). This case studies the capability that sensors go shrink to deploy when they are randomly placed in the whole space.

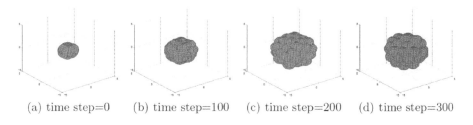

(a) time step=0   (b) time step=100   (c) time step=200   (d) time step=300

Fig. 3. Case 1 with 60 sensors

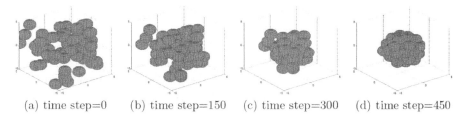

(a) time step=0   (b) time step=150   (c) time step=300   (d) time step=450

Fig. 4. Case 2 with 60 sensors

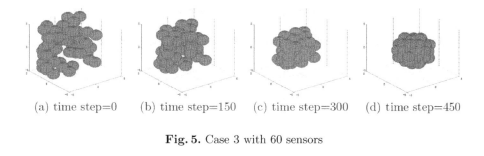

(a) time step=0   (b) time step=150   (c) time step=300   (d) time step=450

Fig. 5. Case 3 with 60 sensors

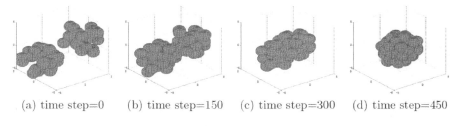

(a) time step=0   (b) time step=150   (c) time step=300   (d) time step=450

Fig. 6. Case 4 with 60 sensors

(3) Case 3:

$R_3\{(-5,5),(0,5),(-5,5)\}$ is appointed as the initial room for sensors (Fig5(a)). This case studies the capability that the swarm of sensors navigates to the target region to deploy as a whole when they are originally placed on one side of the destination.

(4) Case 4:

$R_4\{\{(-5,0),(0,5),(-5,0)\} \cup \{(0,5),(-5,0),(0,5)\}\}$ is appointed as the initial room for sensors (Fig6(a)). This case studies the capability that n swarms of sensors ($n = 2$ here) move to the target region together when they are located on different sides of the target in the beginning.

These four cases basically summarize all conditions in 3D scenarios. Correspondingly, Fig3-Fig6 are examples in our simulations using improved VFA and the number of sensors in which are assigned 60 for a better view. In these illustrations, each sphere denotes the sensing ball of a sensor. These processes are seemingly very perfect as estimation and further analysis need to be stated. We run each case with 100 sensors for 10 times for both traditional and improved VFA, and calculate the average value of the two metrics mentioned above, namely coverage ratio and homogeneous degree. Traditional VFA, we mentioned here, is the 3D extension of the basic version proposed by [11].

4.2   Coverage Ratio

Coverage ratio in our research denotes the ratio of regions covered by at least one sensor to a certain space, namely 1-coverage ratio. Computational method of the coverage ratio is always complicated, especially in the mobility model. Due to the efficient data processing ability of Matlab, Monte Carlo method [14] is introduced as the solution, which relies on repeated random sampling to compute their results. In each computation cycle, we give Monte Carlo method 105 random inputs to increase the accuracy.

According to repeated series of experiments, we found that with the above simulation configuration, improved VFA could always complete the 1-coverage task to the maximal region $R'\{(-2.68, 2.68),(-2.68, 2.68),(-2.68, 2.68)\}$ while traditional VFA cannot. So R' is treated as the target region to measure the performance. On the other hand, the whole space, namely $R^*\{(-5,5),(-5,5),(-5,5)\}$, is also selected as a reference.

Figure 7 shows the results for different cases. It is obvious that improved VFA can always achieve complete coverage for R' in the early time, while traditional VFA is continually trying hard. Adjustment from EF is uninterrupted to make the compact region spread and sparse region shrink, thus making the best use of every sensor's valid part. And then it makes easier for improved VFA to 1-coverage status.

Because less overlays have been produced to achieve a tight coupling structure to fill in R', traditional VFA generates more incompact volumes in R^* while not covering R'. Therefore, the coverage ratio for R^* would be higher in traditional VFA ultimately, which can be also verified in Figure 7.

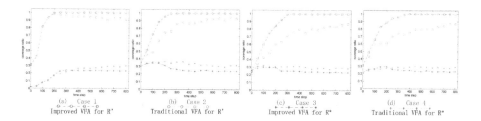

Fig. 7. Coverage ratios for different cases

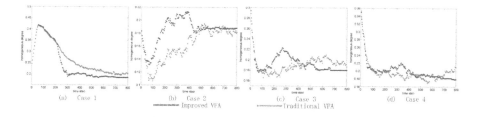

Fig. 8. Homogeneous degrees for different cases

4.3 Homogeneous Degree

Homogeneous degree is expressed by the average of local uniformities, which is represented by standard deviation of relative distances among neighbors:

$$HD = \frac{1}{n} \sum_{i=1}^{n} \sqrt{\frac{1}{N_i} \sum_{j=1}^{N_i} (d_{ij} - \overline{D_i})^2} \tag{4}$$

where n denotes the total number of sensors and N_i indicates the neighbors of sensor i. d_{ij} means the relative Euclidean distance between sensor i and j and $\overline{D_i}$ signifies the average values of distances of i to its all neighbors.

Lower HD signifies better uniformity of sensor distribution and Figure 8 depicts the comparisons in different cases. We obtain that HD with improved VFA is adjusted into a stability condition in an early time while its competitor fluctuates repeatedly. The change law of HD in the figure is truly influenced by EF. In a deployment process, equilibrium force constantly makes the individual sensor aware of local uniformity and adjusts the tendency exerted by TV force from a globe perspective. Without the help of EF, traditional VFA executes relatively poorly and is not easily gotten to a stability condition.

5   Conclusion

Increasing related works have been proposed in 3D sensor networks, which draw the attention of many exciting applications in various areas. In this paper, we first consider the problem of how to deploy in a self-adaptation pattern if all sensors are allowed to navigate freely in the space. Traditional virtual force algorithm is selected as a reference for its simplicity and distributed implementation. We extend its rules by introducing additional central gravitation and equilibrium force, which make the deployment process more reasonable and obtainable. Simulation results witness the effectiveness of improved VFA, both in coverage ratio and homogeneous degree metrics.

There still exist several research issues in the future. More realistic models should be considered to help us improve the proposed mechanism, such as a complex environment with obstacles and multi-objectives. Although the 3D mobile applications may not be possible nowadays, researches for it would pave the way for the developing prospect in the near future.

References

1. Alam, S., Haas, Z.J.: Coverage and connectivity in three-dimensional networks, pp. 346–357. ACM (2006)
2. Younis, M., Akkaya, K.: Strategies and techniques for node placement in wireless sensor networks: A survey. Ad Hoc Networks 6(4), 621–655 (2008)
3. Huang, C.F., et al.: The coverage problem in three-dimensional wireless sensor networks, vol. 3185, pp. 3182–3186. IEEE (2004)
4. Alam, S., Haas, Z.J.: Coverage and connectivity in three-dimensional underwater sensor networks. Wireless Communications and Mobile Computing 8(8), 995–1009 (2008)
5. Mishra, M.K., Gore, M.M.: On Optimal Space Tessellation with Deterministic Deployment for Coverage in Three-Dimensional Wireless Sensor Networks. In: Janowski, T., Mohanty, H. (eds.) ICDCIT 2010. LNCS, vol. 5966, pp. 72–83. Springer, Heidelberg (2010)
6. Ammari, H.M., Das, S.K.: A study of k-coverage and measures of connectivity in 3d wireless sensor networks. IEEE Transactions on Computers 59(2), 243–257 (2010)
7. Bai, X., et al.: Full-coverage and k-connectivity (k= 14, 6) three dimensional networks, pp. 388–396. IEEE (2009)
8. Bai, X., et al.: Low-connectivity and full-coverage three dimensional wireless sensor networks, pp. 145–154. ACM (2009)
9. Ravelomanana, V.: Extremal properties of three-dimensional sensor networks with applications. IEEE Transactions on Mobile Computing 3(3), 246–257 (2004)
10. Watfa, M.K., Commuri, S.: Coverage issues in wireless sensor networks. University of Oklahoma (2006)
11. Zou, Y., Chakrabarty, K.: Sensor deployment and target localization based on virtual forces, vol. 1292, pp. 1293–1303. IEEE (2003)
12. Howard, A., et al.: Mobile sensor network deployment using potential fields: A distributed, scalable solution to the area coverage problem, pp. 299–308. Citeseer (2002)
13. Locatelli, M., Raber, U.: Packing equal circles in a square: a deterministic global optimization approach. Discrete Applied Mathematics 122(1), 139–166 (2002)
14. http://en.wikipedia.org/wiki/Monte_carlo_method

A Module Harvesting Wind and Solar Energy for Wireless Sensor Node

Yong Li*, Xiaolong Li, and Ping Wang

Key Laboratory of Industrial Internet of Things and Network Control,
Chongqing University of Posts and Telecommunications,
Chongqing 400065, China

Abstract. This paper makes an introduction to a module harvesting wind and solar, it is designed for wireless sensor node to meet the need of power in outdoor application like forest monitoring. To get very long life, the module harvests wind and solar together, takes the super capacitor and alternate lithium battery as the energy store device to take advantage of their complementary nature. A wind MPPT (maximum power point tracking) circuit which is specifically designed for application in wireless sensor network and a solar tracking circuit are designed to increase the efficiency of energy harvesting.

Keywords: Wireless Sensor Node, Wind, Solar, MPPT.

1 Introduction

Wireless sensor network is characterized by low-speed and low power. Most of its nodes are supplied by battery. The survival time of the network depends directly on the battery life. However, the sensor nodes are required to survive for a long time, years or even ten years, once were deployed in some applications which is difficult to maintain (for example, environmental monitoring, intelligent agriculture and so on). This poses a huge challenge of power supply problem of the sensor nodes, especially aggregation node with higher duty cycle. Although these nodes are in a poor environment, and difficult to be maintained, most of them are in the open field area where sunshine and wind resources are abundant. The problem of limited power of the node would be resolved if these environmental resources could be used effectively.

The key problem of energy harvesting is efficiency[1][2], which directly affects the cost, size, and life of the energy harvesting system. Increasing the harvesting efficiency must address the maximum power point tracking (MPPT) problem

* This work was supported in part by Construction project of Chongqing Engineering Technology Research Center:research and industrialization for intelligent Substation and intelligent distribution automation system based on the EPA (KJzh10207) and The major projects of the National Science and Technology:Comprehensive testing and evaluation of the information gathering sensor networks(Comprehensive Perception)(2011ZX03005-002).

R. Wang and F. Xiao (Eds.): CWSN 2012, CCIS 334, pp. 217–224, 2013.
© Springer-Verlag Berlin Heidelberg 2013

which refers to the nature of solar battery[3] and wind turbine generator[4][5]. Solar panels and wind turbine generator have different value of output impedance when light intensity or wind speed changes. Only the node whose input impedance matches the value can get the most energy. The way to get the maximum power is called MPPT Technology.

In addition to the harvesting efficiency, power consumption of the system itself, the life of the storage device, the using efficiency of supply circuit should be all considered carefully to optimize the performance of the module.

2   Research and Background

Some energy harvesting platform have been designed for sensor network by the current research , such as WEH, Heliomote[6], Everlast[7],AmbiMax[8], PUMA[9],etc. Heliomote charges NIMH rechargeable battery in serials in use of solar energy without MPPT circuit. Everlast charges super capacitor by solar with a design of MPPT circuit, but it is inappropriate for WSN because its MPPT circuit need the real time controlling of the micro control unit (MCU) which will, however, sleep periodically. AmbiMax is a device harvesting multiple types of energy from environment, and has a MPPT circuit without MCU. But it needs for further improvement because of too much power consumption of MPPT circuit itself and lack of effective management circuit to manage the charging and discharging of super capacitor or Lithium battery. The MPPT circuit of PUMA and WEH is also in need of MCU .

3   System Analyses and Design

3.1   System Framework

Fig.1. shows the overall hardware architecture, it is composed of 3 sub-module : optimization module of harvesting, management module of charging and discharging, module of storage energy. Solar Tracking device and wind MPPT are

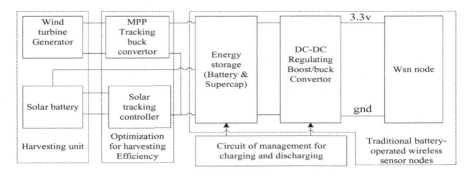

Fig. 1. Framework of system

contained in optimization module to improve the efficiency of harvesting. Management module is designed to guarantee the best performance of storage model, it charges super capacitor first, the battery begin to be charged after the energy in super capacitor is much enough, In the meanwhile, load connecting to output first consumes the energy of super capacitor , in order to protect the battery by reducing the times of recharging . The controlling function of system is all realized by analog circuit .it doesnt affect the sleeping of sensor node.

The energy of MPPT controlling circuit is directly provided by wind turbine generatorsolar tracking module and the sensor nodes are powered by regulator circuit , management circuit are directly supplied by battery .

3.2   Design of Optimization Module for Harvesting

Environment energy is extremely unstable, the key problem of using it is harvesting efficiency which directly affects the cost, size, and life of the energy harvesting system. In this paper, a solar tracking device and a wind MPPT circuit are designed to solve the problem.

Design of Solar Tracking Device. The solar tracking device uses a 180-degree vertical, horizontal 360-degree rotation mode to track solar in full range .System will obtain 30-40% more energy by realize the designation.

In this paper, a simple circuit is designed to realize the tracking as Fig.2. Four photo-resistors are used to sense the orientation of solar, two H-bridge driver circuit made in eight MOSFET control two geared Motor rotation around in real time, control circuit belong to two low-power operational amplifier comparator with hysteresis, to avoid Jitter and the resulting unnecessary energy consumption when motor rotate in the critical point.

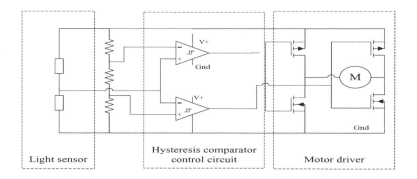

Fig. 2. Schematic of solar tracker

MPPT Design of Wind Energy. Traditional photovoltaic or wind application prefers to use microcontroller to search for the maximum power point in
real time. Modify the duty cycle of DC-DC converter firstly, watch the tendency
of converters output power change. If power grows up, modify the duty cycle
in the same direction, if not, modify it in opposite direction, until power reach
the maximum. Although this method have high controlling accuracy, it prevent
sensor nodes CPU from sleeping, In order to avoid the influence to the microcontroller of the sensor nodes, the paper design a MPPT module completely
realized by analog circuit , basing on the characteristic[4] that the maximum
power point of wind turbine is proportional to its rotation speed.

Firstly make the rotation speed of the wind turbine convert into a voltage
signal. By experimental methods, find the linear ratio between the signal and
the maximum power point voltage V_{mpp} and get the value of V_{mpp} in different
rotation speed, then compared it with the V_{wind}(output voltage of the wind
turbine). When the V_{wind} is larger than V_{mpp}, open the DC-DC module, output
filter capacitor begin to charge the energy storage, and then the voltage drops.
When the V_{wind} is less than V_{mpp} , close the DC-DC module, and then the output
voltage increases again. As shown in Fig.3. So this will make the output voltage
of the wind turbine follow the change of V_{mpp}. Fig.4 shows the schematic of the
MPPT control circuit, after processed by the square wave shaping circuit ,fixed
width pulse shaping circuit and RC integral circuit, the single-phase sinusoidal
AC wave produced by wind turbine will converts to a voltage signal which is
linearly varied with the speed of the wind turbine. This design does not need to
use the F-V (frequency transfer to voltage) chip which is expensive and has high
power consumption; therefore it has lower cost and higher energy efficiency.

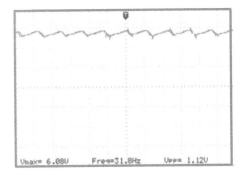

Fig. 3. Waveform of V_{wind}

3.3   Energy Storage Design

Energy storage scheme was used in this paper is super capacitor combined with
alternate lithium battery, super capacitor has the characteristic of a large number of cycles[10] (million of times) for charging and discharging , but the volume

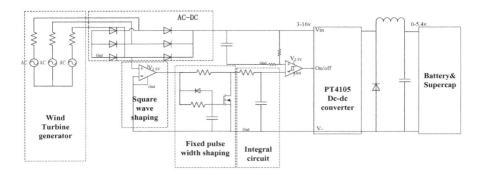

Fig. 4. Schematic of the MPPT control circuit

is too large. The capacity of lithium battery is great, but the number of recharge-able cycles is limited (300-500 times). So the storage module using them together would get a better performance for absorbing their respective advantages. Two 2.7v super capacitors are connected in serials while the leakage current is reduced and greater range of voltage (0-5.4v) is obtained. The design of charge and discharge circuit is also simplified by the greater range of voltage.

3.4 Management Module for Charging and Discharging

Management module gives priority to the super capacitor charging and discharging owing to super capacitors advantages for better rechargeable performance. Schematic shows in Figure 5, the circuit of Lithium battery for charging and discharging includes a current limiting chips and two threshold comparators .Compared to the current dedicated charging chip, this charging method can achieve higher conversion efficiency when the charge current does not exceed the limiting value. The module power supply circuit is designed based on the TPS63001 chip. The input voltage of TPS63001 chip is range from 1.8v to 5.5v,

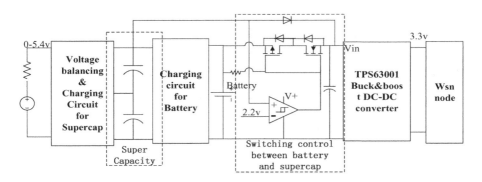

Fig. 5. Management design

its output voltage is 3.3v. When the output current is in the range from 10ma to 500ma, its conversion efficiency can reach more than 80%. These parameters make the chip very suitable for efficient use of harvested energy, and make it adapt to different power requirements of sensor nodes.

When the charging condition is ready (there are enough wind or sun), the harvesting module start to charge the super capacity until the voltage exceed 5.4v. The battery wont be charged before the capacitys voltage is bigger than batterys voltage.

When the capacitor voltage is lower than 2.2v, enable the battery-powered. If the battery voltage is also lower than 3.7v, the module will stop the output to protect the battery.

4   System Implementation and Verification

According to the design and analysis above, we made a real module for testing. As shown in Fig.6 .

(6.1)   (6.2)

Fig. 6. Module for testing

The power consumption of temperature and humidity sensor node which used for test is about 100mw when it works in sending or receiving mode. The table 2 and table 4 show that harvesting module could fully meet the needs of sensor nodes in good weather conditions. In fact, the size of wind turbine, solar panels, and energy storage devices could be reduced a lot due to the sensor nodes sleep mechanism.

Through the confrontation of table 2 and table 3, the conclusion is as follows: The output power of the wind turbine without MPPT module increase slowly with wind speed changing, and in the same wind speed, the output power of the wind turbine with MPPT module increased by 50-100%. That means the MPPT circuit can take much more energy for system. We also test the current consumed by control and management circuits and find that it is not more than 300 uA. This shows that the own power consumption of harvesting module is very low.

Table 1. Paraments for test module

	Power	Voltage	Current
Output of solar battery	Max 400mw	0-5.5v	130ma@short-circuit
Output of wind turbine	0.3w@3m/s	13v@3m/s no load	100ma@3m/s short-circuit
Output of Regulator	Max 1.5w	3.3v	Max 500ma
Range of supercap		2.2-5.4v	
Supercap	50F	2.7v	Charging <3A
Battery	600mah	3.7-4.2v	Charging <500ma
Switch voltage point		2.2v	

Table 2. Data for wind turbine with MPPT when voltage of supecap is 2.5v

Wind speed	Output current	Output voltage	Output power
2m/s	8ma	4.2v	33.6mw
3m/s	28ma	7.1v	198.8mw
4m/s	26ma	10.5v	273mw

Table 3. Data for wind turbine without MPPT when voltage of supecap is 2.5v

Wind speed	Output current	Output voltage	Output power
2m/s	10ma	2.5v	25mw
3m/s	36ma	2.5v	90mw
4m/s	51ma	2.5v	127mw

Table 4. Data for solar in different weather when output voltage of solar is 3.5v

Weather	Output power
Rainy	3-10mw
Sunny 11AM	250-340mw
Sunny 6PM	50-100mw

5   Conclusion

A micro wind and solar harvesting module was designed for wireless sensor systems for their outdoor applications. It succeeds in designing the MPPT circuit, management circuit to get better performance. Experimental results show that the module consumes low power. Under the action of the MPPT circuit, the harvesting efficiency increases a lot; the energy harvested by system can fully meet the needs of practical application.

References

1. Tan, Y.K., Panda, S.K.: Optimized Wind Energy Harvesting System Using Resistance Emulator and Active Rectifier for Wireless Sensor Nodes. IEEE Transactions on Power Electronics 26(1), 38–50 (2011)
2. Simjee, F.I., Chou, P.H.: Efficient charging of super capacitors for extended lifetime of wireless sensor nodes. IEEE Trans. Power Electron. 23(3), 1526–1536 (2008)
3. Dondi, D., Bertacchini, A., Brunelli, D., Larcher, L., Benini, L.: Modeling and optimization of a solar energy harvester system for self-powered wireless sensor networks. IEEE Trans. Ind. Electron. 55(7), 2759–2766 (2008)
4. Chen, Z., Guerrero, J.M., Blaabjerg, F.: A review of the state of the art of power electronics for wind turbines. IEEE Trans. Power Electron. 24(8), 1859–1875 (2009)
5. Islam, S.: Maximum power point tracking of wind turbine generators. In: Australasian Universities Power Engineering Conference, AUPEC 2005 (September 2005)
6. Raghunathan, V., Kansal, A., Hsu, J.: Design consideration for solar energy harvesting wireless embedded systems. In: IPSN 2005 (April 2005)
7. Simjee, F., Chou, P.: Everlast: Long-life, supercapacitor-operated wireless sensor node. In: Proceedings of the 2006 International Symposium on Low Power Electronics and Design, ISLPED 2006, pp. 197–202 (2006)
8. Park, C., Chou, P.H.: Ambimax: Autonomous energy harvesting platform for multi-supply wireless sensor nodes. In: 2006 3rd Annual IEEE Communications Society on Sensor and Ad hoc Communications and Networks, SECON 2006. IEEE (2006)
9. Park, C., Chou, P.: Power Utility Maximization for Multi-Supply Systems by a Load-Matching Switch. In: ISLPED 2004, pp. 168–173 (August 2004)
10. Jiang, X., Polastre, J., Culler, D.: Perpetual environmentally powered sensor networks. In: Fourth International Symposium on Information Processing in Sensor Networks, IPSN 2005 (2005)

Integrated Tracking Initiation Mechanism Based on Probability for Bearing-Only Sensor Networks

Yuanshi Li[1,2], Zhi Wang[1,*], Huajie Shao[1], Shengsheng Cai[1,2], and Ming Bao[2]

[1] State Key Laboratory of Industrial Control Technology, Zhejiang University,
Hangzhou 310027, China
[2] Institute of Acoustic Chinese Academy of Sciences, Beijing 100190, China
wangzhizju@gmail.com

Abstract. Tracking initiation issue under bearing-only sensor networks is studied. A mechanism for tracking initiation based on probability is proposed, aiming at solving problem under measuring environment with false alarm and undetected. The mechanism is achieved by two phases including target localization and target confirm. In target localization phase, Multiple Target Probability Localization algorithm is proposed to estimate target initial state, providing new thinking for multi-target localization under bearing-only measurements which distinguishes the true target localizations from the false ones relatively by probability. In target confirm phase, target probability is introduced as judgment for tracking initiation and a recursive algorithm under multi-sensor is provided. The simulation shows that the proposed mechanism can be well-work under different settings and the required computation is limited which is suitable for WSN.

Keywords: sensor networks, tracking initiation, multiple target probability localization, target probability.

1 Introduction

Target tracking has attracted much attention for its great application in certain civilian, military and scientific applications. The related theory and technology are numerous, especially in classical tracking systems like radar, tracking theory has achieved great success in application. However, in some special cases, for example, a hostile environment, sensors in classical tracking system are easily located and destroyed by enemies for their active sensing pattern and cannot meet the requirement of stealthiness. In recent years, WSN-based tracking system provides new thinking in tracking field for its passive sensing pattern, distributed structure, self-organization and other advantages. At present, most of the studies on target tracking based on WSN are on the basis of energy sensing which faces great trouble in application: the energy sensing model is not reliable enough to provide accurate

---

* Corresponding author.

R. Wang and F. Xiao (Eds.): CWSN 2012, CCIS 334, pp. 225–236, 2013.
© Springer-Verlag Berlin Heidelberg 2013

measurement. Also, energy sensing is prone to be interfered and the valid sensing range is limited which leads to a failure in large-scaled or noisy environment. While array sensor networks based on phase sensing can avoid the problems above and is superior for target tracking in complex environment. Many researchers have focused on this field and a series of achievement have been obtained in both theory and practice [1], [2] [3]. The difficulty in target tracking based on array sensor networks mainly lies on the information processing under bearing only measurement, especially for the design of track initiation mechanism.

Track initiation concerns on problem for initializing a track when a new target appears. Since the core task for tracking is done under the assumption that target exists, track initiation is essential to the whole tracking process. Although there exists some researches on track initiation, few of them are appropriate for the case considering in this paper. Then we give a brief view on this problem. The idea behind classical track initiation algorithms is to form a tentative track and then confirm or terminate it according to a certain rule. Common methods include distance based method [4] and probability based method [5], [6]. The former adjudges track initiation by the quality of statistical distance for measurements in several consequent scans, such as the heuristic rule method, logic-based (LB) method and so on. Obviously, this category of methods can be hardly to make a credible decision in cluttered environment and it is also not appropriate for problems under bearing only sensor networks. The latter introduces conception of target probability and by calculating target probability via the process of track updating, decisions can be made to accomplish track initiation. This category of methods can tolerate undetected and false alarm in some degree and has clear advantages over distance based method but the methods are designed for classical tracking system and new problems under bearing only sensor networks. Moreover, some methods are designed by taking advantages of intelligent algorithms [11] [12]. However, the calculating time cannot be guaranteed in a constrained value and the computational resources needed cannot be satisfied in WSN.

In this paper, track initiation problems for bearing only sensor networks in complex environment is considered. Since bearing only measurements lack of immediate knowledge of target position, the initial state of the target is unknown leading to a failure by using common methods for the following two reasons: firstly, the measuring equation is nonlinear and the convergence for nonlinear filter is related with deviation of initial state; secondly, the data association problem exists, so it is hard to assign appropriate measurements to a track without initial state and the track initiation process can be hardly executed. As a result, it is essential to achieve target initial state estimation before track initiation. Unfortunately, the work in this field [11], [12], [13] has not paid much attention on target initial state estimation. The mechanism proposed in this paper is to solve the target initial state estimation problem and form an integrated track initiation workflow.

Initial state estimation is in fact the problem of multi-target localization under bearing only measurements. Single target localization under bearing measurements is not difficult [1] while few work has been done in multi-target localization.

Since the associations between target and measurement are unknown, we probably get the so-called ghost engendered by false measurement-target association, labeled as G1. The false measurement can also produce ghost, labeled as G2, see Figure 1. Enumerating all the intersections forming by two emitters from different sensors is not a good idea for the repeating localizations and false localizations are excessive which costs awful computational resource to the subsequent process. In addition, considering the measurement is not accurate, the localization error may be significant by using only two measurements which leads the convergence rate getting slower and the time for making track initiation decision getting longer. More complex and intelligent methods [7], [8], [9] focus on distinguishing target localizations from ghost localizations. By utilizing n-permutation, [9] provides a method to localize multiple targets but can be only applied in ideal measurements without error. Under the assumption that each measurement associates one target, [8] designs a mechanism with three-level gates to eliminate ghost localizations and can achieve an ideal localization result in high probability. However, this mechanism can be hardly effective in complex environment with undetected and false alarm also the number of sensors are fixed at 3. According to the analysis of the characteristics of ghosts and noise, method in [7] using frequency and bearing measurement can avoid common ghosts but still without considering undetected and false alarm cases. In fact, it is almost impossible to absolutely distinguish target localization and ghost in only one scan. Fortunately it is not necessary for initial state estimation part to provide a completely perfect target initial state. A feasible mechanism is proposed in this paper that initial state estimation is responsible for providing a try-best service but leaves more precise work to following process during several scans' iteration.

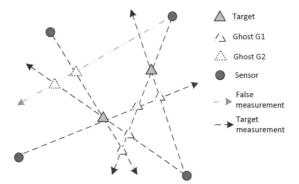

Fig. 1. Ghost problems in multiple target localization

The innovation and contribution of this paper mainly lies on the following items:

- Firstly, the design of a mechanism for track initiation under bearing only sensor networks in complex environment is a problem worthy of studying in both theory and application. The proposed mechanism provides a new idea to solve the problem. Under the two-phase workflow, the reliability of the algorithm can be surely guaranteed and the computational complexity can be limited in a foreseeable value.

- Secondly, the innovated MTPL algorithm introduces target probability to localization providing new thinking on multiple target localization under bearing measurement and can well combine the following process. Also, simplification in MTPL are carefully analyzed.
- Finally, by extending the track initiation algorithm based on probability to be applied in multiple sensors case, track initiation decision can be made under sensor network systems.

The rest of this paper is organized as following. Section 2 describes the basic model and assumptions for the considering problem. Section 3 introduces the integrated track initiation mechanism. The simulation and performance analysis are presented in Section 4 and Section 5 gives the conclusion.

2   Problem Formulation

The measuring model for bearing only sensor network is illustrated in Figure 2. Sensors are deployed randomly in surveillance field, labeled as S_i ($1 \leq i \leq N_s$, N_s is the number of sensors). The position of each sensors are known. The targets appear in the field, labeled as T_j ($1 \leq j \leq N_T, N_T$ is the number of targets). The measurement $z_{i,j}$ can be expressed as:

$$z_{i,j} = \tan^{-1}(\frac{Pos_y(T_j) - Pos_y(S_i)}{Pos_x(T_j) - Pos_x(S_i)}) + n_{i,j} \tag{1}$$

where $Pos(.)$ is the position of an object and $n_{i,j} \sim N(0, \sigma_i^2)$.

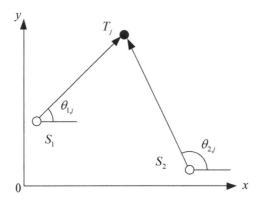

Fig. 2. Measuring model for bearing only sensor network

Considering the undetected case, we assumes detection of a target when the target exists is an independent event at each scan with detection probability

P_D, $0 \leq P_D \leq 1$. The false alarm can be modeled as a Poisson distribution. The probability that the number of false measurement is m can be expressed:

$$P_F(m) = \frac{(m_{ave})^m}{m!} e^{-m_{ave}} \qquad (2)$$

where m_{ave} is the prior average number of false measurement and it is common to assume that each false measurement is uniformly distributed in possible range, i.e.,

$$P_{FM}(z_{i,j}) = \frac{V_{dif}}{V_{all}}, \quad z_{i,j} \text{ is false measurement} \qquad (3)$$

where V_{all} is the volume of the measurement space and V_{dif} is the minimum differential value. Under the above model and assumptions, track initiation problem can be described. Assume that in N scans a measurement set $\mathbf{Z}^N = \{\mathbf{z}_1, ..., \mathbf{z}_N\}$ is obtained, where $\mathbf{z}_k$ is the measurement set in scan k, which can be denoted by $\mathbf{z}_k = \{z_{i,j}^k\}$. The task of track initiation is to distinguish target measurements from false measurements and form tracks corresponding to existing targets by using $\mathbf{Z}^N$.

3   Integrated Track Initiation Mechanism

Integrated track initiation mechanism based on probability consists of two phases: target localization phase and track confirm phase. In target localization phase, multiple target probability localization (MTPL) algorithm is proposed to obtain several possible localizations and give a relative distinguish between target localizations and ghosts by target probability, then tentative track can be formed based on the result of MTPL; in track confirm phase, by dealing with the tentative track, target probability can be updated at each scan and according to the variation of target probability, decision can be made to confirm or terminate the tentative track. In detail, tentative tracks are formed by localization and responding target probability calculated in target localization phase by one scan measurements $\mathbf{z}$ and the set of tentative tracks will be as input in following scans to obtain confirmed track set. The reason why we use only one scan localization as initial state estimation is that measurements from target are not stable in application and localization results are not accurate enough so that it is hard to estimate a valid target velocity by using localizations from multiple scans. Also, multiple scans process needs additional memory and time for computation which can be hardly achieved under the constrain of WSN, especially the on-line process requirements.

3.1   Multiple Target Probability Localization

Towards the goal of providing localization and its probability, MTPL can be achieve by localization process and probability analysis.

Localization Process

The main ideal of localization process is to translate the multiple target localization into multiple single-target localizations by measurement association. Enumerating all the possible associations is not advisable for the computation complexity will increase exponentially as the number of sensors and measurements increase. Also, it will produce a mass of repeated and wrong localizations which increase the system burden for the subsequent processing. A heuristic algorithm is proposed to obtain the possible associations. Intersection of two bearing measurements from different sensors is selected as association reference and measurements from other sensors can be associated by the residual to each intersection defined as:

$$Res_{t,i,j} = z_{i,j} - \tan^{-1}\left(\frac{Pos_y(I_t) - Pos_y(S_i)}{Pos_x(I_t) - Pos_x(S_i)}\right) \tag{4}$$

I_t denotes tth intersection and $Res_{t,i,j}$ is residual of $z_{i,j}$ to I_t Then we can do association by using nearest neighbor (NN) method and the result is denoted by measurement association indicator $\tau_{t,i,j}$ which indicates whether $z_{i,j}$ is associated with I_t , i.e.,

$$\tau_{t,i,j} \triangleq \begin{cases} 1 & if\, Res_{t,i,j}\ is\ the\ minimum\ in\ Res_{t,i}, and\ Res_{t,i,j} \leq Res_{Gate} \\ 0 & others \end{cases} \tag{5}$$

Res_{Gate} is the gate for valid association but it is considerably difficult to give its analytical formal, so we set it as $K\sigma_i$ for simplicity (K is a constant). Luckily, it is not necessary to obtain an optimal gate and the simplified gate can also work well. Clearly, NN association method is also a simplification and the feasibility can be in a qualitative analysis: if true target measurement is replaced by another measurement, the impact on localization result is not remarkable for the replaced measurement is surely close to true target measurement, so the error is limited and also it will not impact following association.

The association algorithm can be implemented by a recursive process, see Figure 3. The problem can be divided into 3 independent sub problems: Sub Problem One is the case when Sensor 1 faces undetected and it needs to do the association again among Sensor 2 to Sensor N; Sub Problem Two is the case that measurements from Sensor 1 and Sensor 2 contain the target measurement, so by enumerating all the intersections forming by measurements from these two sensors and using NN to associate the measurements from other sensors, we can solve this sub problem; Sub Problem Three is the case when Sensor 2 faces undetected and it needs to do the association again among Sensor 1 and Sensor 3 to Sensor N. Sub Problem One and Sub Problem Three is actually the same as the original problem and it can be solved by a recursive calling and when the number of associated sensors is below 3, it will return null. The computational complexity of the association algorithm is $O(N_s M)^3$, M is the number of measurements for each sensor. and it can practically contain the optimal associations with relatively few false associations. The only exception caused by NN is proved that it has little impact on subsequent processing. Considering

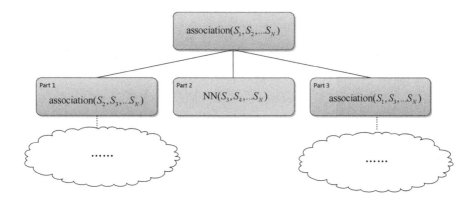

Fig. 3. Recursive implementation for heuristic association algorithm

the great decrease on computational complexity, the suboptimal algorithm can be accepted. By taking advantage of the result of association, the multi-target localization problem is simplified to multiple single-target localization problems. A pseudo-linear algorithm is adopted and the formula is expressed as:

$$\mathbf{X}_t = [\mathrm{H}^T(\mathbf{Z}_t)\mathrm{H}(\mathbf{Z}_t)]^{-1}\mathrm{H}(\mathbf{Z}_t)\mathrm{Y}(\mathbf{Z}_t) \tag{6}$$

where

$$\mathbf{X}_t = \begin{bmatrix} Pos_x(Loc_t) \\ Pos_y(Loc_t) \end{bmatrix}, \mathrm{H}(\mathbf{Z}_t) = \begin{bmatrix} -\sin(z_{\mathrm{ass}(t,1)}) & \cos(z_{\mathrm{ass}(t,1)}) \\ \vdots & \vdots \\ -\sin(z_{\mathrm{ass}(t,n)}) & \cos(z_{\mathrm{ass}(t,n)}) \end{bmatrix},$$

$$\mathrm{Y}(\mathbf{Z}_t) = \begin{bmatrix} -Pos_x(S_{\mathrm{ass}(t,1)})\sin(z_{\mathrm{ass}(t,1)}) + Pos_y(S_{\mathrm{ass}(t,1)})\cos(z_{\mathrm{ass}(t,1)}) \\ \vdots \\ -Pos_x(S_{\mathrm{ass}(t,n)})\sin(z_{\mathrm{ass}(t,n)}) + Pos_y(S_{\mathrm{ass}(t,n)})\cos(z_{\mathrm{ass}(t,n)}) \end{bmatrix}$$

Probability Analysis

Then we need to calculate target probability for each localization. The target probability PT_t is determined by sensing probability $PD(Nd_t)$ and localization probability $PM(X_t)$:

$$PT_t = PD(Nd_t)PM(\mathbf{X_t}) \tag{7}$$

Nd_t is the number of associated measurements. $PM(X_t)$ can be calculated by the residual of each associated measurement:

$$PM(\mathbf{X}_t) = \frac{1}{Nd_t} \sum_{z_{i,j} \in \mathrm{ass}_t} \exp(-\frac{Res_{t,i,j}^2}{2\sigma_i^2}) \tag{8}$$

and $PD(Nd_t)$ can be acquired by applying Bayes' rules:

$$PD(Nd_t) = P(\chi|Nd_t) = \frac{P(Nd_t|\chi)P(\chi)}{P(Nd_t|\chi)P(\chi) + P(Nd_t|\bar{\chi})P(\bar{\chi})} \tag{9}$$

where χ denotes the event that target exists and $\bar{\chi}$ denotes the event that no target exists. By a series probability analysis, we get $P(Nd_t|\chi)$ and $P(Nd_t|\bar{\chi})$ as:

$$P(Nd_t|\chi) = P(D|\chi)^{Nd_t-2}(1 - P(D|\chi))^{Ns-Nd_t} \tag{10}$$

$$P(Nd_t|\bar{\chi}) = P(D|\bar{\chi})^{Nd_t-2}(1 - P(D|\bar{\chi}))^{Ns-Nd_t} \tag{11}$$

where N_s is the number of sensors. $P(D|\chi)$ and $P(D|\bar{\chi})$ is the probability that the measurement from a sensor is associated when target exists or no target exists:

$$P(D|\chi) = P_D P_W + (1 - P_D)\hat{m}_{ave}V_{gate}/V_{all} \tag{12}$$

$$P(D|\bar{\chi}) = \hat{m}_{ave}V_{gate}/V_{all} \tag{13}$$

where P_W is probability that detected measurement can be associated and $V_{gate}/Vall$ denotes the ratio that a random bearing measurement is associated. Then by using the localization and its probability, new tentative track can be formed to come into track confirm phase.

3.2   Target Probability Iteration

Target probability iteration for track determination is executed accompany with the updating process of tentative track. Considering that track updating process is not the key problem concerned here, we will not repeat track updating process in this paper and the algorithm can be found in [5] [6]. Since the prior target state and probability are available, target probability iteration algorithm can follow track initiation algorithm based on probability: **Target probability forecast:** We can model the target probability as Markov process and then predicted target probability can be expressed:

$$PT_t(\chi_k|\mathbf{Z}^{k-1}) = C_{11}^1 P(\chi_{k-1}|\mathbf{Z}^{k-1}) + C_{21}^1(1 - P(\chi_{k-1}|\mathbf{Z}^{k-1})) \tag{14}$$

where $C_{i,j}^m$ is the Markov chain coefficients.

Target probability update: The update process can be achieved by:

$$PT_t(\chi_k|\mathbf{Z}^k) = \frac{1 - \delta_k}{1 - \delta_k P(\chi_k|\mathbf{Z}^{k-1})}PT_t(\chi_k|\mathbf{Z}^{k-1}) \tag{15}$$

where δ_k is a middle parameter which can be calculated by the prior probability density function $P(\mathbf{x}_t|\mathbf{Z}^{k-1})$

$$\delta_k = \begin{cases} P_D P_W (1 - \sum_{t=1}^{Nd_t} PN(ND_t)\frac{\sum_j^{m_k} P(\mathbf{x}_t|z_{t,j})V_k}{Nd_t\hat{m}_{ave}}) & Nd_t \neq 0 \\ P_D P_W & Nd_t = 0 \end{cases} \tag{16}$$

where V_k is the volume of the gate. $PN(Nd_t)$ is the sensing probability for track:

$$P(Nd_t|\chi) = P(D|\chi)^{Nd_t}(1 - P(D|\chi))^{Ns-Nd_t} \tag{17}$$

4   Simulation and Analysis

In order to evaluate the integrated track initiation mechanism proposed in this paper, we do several simulation experiments to test its performance. Considering networks with 5-7 sensors distributed deployed, the measuring qualities are the same for each sensor and wireless transmission error and delay are ignored here. The variance of measuring error is set to be a constant, i.e. $\sigma_2 = (3^o)^2$. The detection probability varies from 0.55 to 0.95 and the prior average number of false measurement varies from 0.2 to 2. Another important parameter, number of existing targets, is set to vary from 0 to 3. Then the performance of the proposed algorithm under different parameter cases is studied.

4.1   MTPL Performance Test

The localization performance of the proposed MTPL algorithm is evaluated. In the meanwhile, localization algorithm proposed in [8] is compared. Three groups simulation experiments are performed: Firstly, $\hat{m}_{ave} = 0.5$ and $N_T = 3$ are fixed and evaluate the performance while P_D varies. Then $P_D = 0.85$ and $N_T = 3$ are fixed and evaluate the performance while $\hat{m}_{ave}$ varies. Finally, $P_D = 0.85$ and $\hat{m}_{ave} = 0.5$ are fixed and evaluate the performance while varies. All the simulations are run 1000 times, and two indexes are compared: 1) number of target localizations characterizing the correction of localization process and the closer to actual number of targets the better; 2) number of total localizations implying the computational resources needed and the smaller the better. The results are shown as Figure 4-6. The number of ideal localizations is defined as targets with more than 2 corresponding measurements and it is the upper limitation of target localizations because that if the corresponding measurements of a target is less than 2, its probability will be zero.

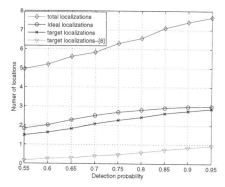
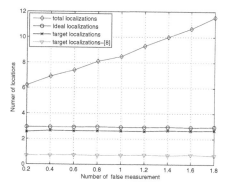

Fig. 4.   Number of localizations under different detection probability

Fig. 5. Number of localizations under different number of false measurements

Clearly, the compared algorithm can hardly deal with the complex environment with undetected and false alarm, most of the target will be lost while the number of target localizations using MTPL is close to the ideal localizations with relatively small number of false localizations. Also MTPL shows a fine performance on the requirement of computational resources for the number of total localizations is limited.

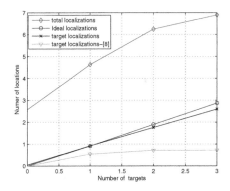

Fig. 6. Number of localizations under different number of targets

4.2   Track Initiation Performance Test

To evaluate the performance of target probability iteration algorithm consistent with localization performance, we check the indexes of tentative track forming in one scan and compare the IPDA algorithm by simply average the target probability obtained by each sensor. The special setting for track initiation performance test is as below: $\hat{m}_{ave} = 1$, $N_T = 3$, $N_s = 5$ and P_D varies.

The simulation shows that both the proposed method and IPDA can achieve well performance on deciding track initiation while the proposed method can be superior for the decision time is less. Figure 7 gives the track confirming and termination time. Whether the tentative track is to be confirmed or terminated, its lifetime is limited and the computational resource needed can be estimated by multiply the maximum number of tentative tracks and its maximum lifetime. As long as we can meet the computational resource requirement, the mechanism can be run normally. Since the computational resource needed is limited, the mechanism can be well applied in WSN. It is clear that the extended target probability iteration algorithm is superior to basic IPDA algorithm especially when the detection probability is low.

In order to give an overview of the whole process of track initiation, Figure 8 gives one simulation when $P_D = 0.85$. (a) is the localization results and (b) is that the locus of confirmed tracks which shows that the track initiation mechanism perfectly achieves expected tasks. Figure 8 is the target probability of confirmed

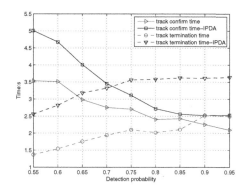

Fig. 7. Indexes of tentative track under different detection probability

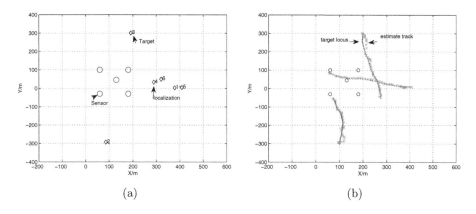

(a)   (b)

Fig. 8. Track initiation process

tracks which shows the variation of the iteration of target probability. Although target probability may be fluctuant at some time, track initiation decision can be made correctly.

5   Conclusion

In this paper, we proposed a novel integrated track initiation mechanism under bearing only sensor networks based on probability analysis. The key innovation lies on the new thinking on solving the problem that initial state is unknown under bearing only sensor networks. The proposed MTPL algorithm relatively distinguishes target localizations from ghost localizations by target probability which achieves success on track initiation process. Simulations show that the whole mechanism can work well under different measuring environment and it can be well applied in WSN.

Acknowledgments. This work was supported in part by the National Natural Science Foundation of China (NSFC) under Grant No. 61273079, in part by the Strategic Priority Research Program of the Chinese Academy of Sciences under Grant No. XDA06020300, in part by State Key Laboratory of Industrial Control Technology under Grant No.ICT1206 and ICT1207, and in part by Key Laboratory of Wireless Sensor Network & Communication of Chinese Academy of Sciences under Grant No.2011001.

References

1. Chen, J.C., Yip, L., Elson, J., Wang, H., Maniezzo, D., Hudson, R.E., Yao, K., Estrin, D.: Coherent acoustic array processing and localization on wireless sensor networks. Proceedings of the IEEE on Wireless Sensor Networks 91(8), 1154–1162 (2003)
2. Wang, H., Chen, C.E., et al.: Acoustic sensor networks for woodpecker localization. In: Proc. of SPIE (2005)
3. Li, Y., Wang, Z., Bao, M., et al.: The design and experiments for multi-target tracking platform based acoustic array sensor networks. Journal of Scientific Instrument 33(1), 146–154 (2012)
4. Hu, Z., Leung, H., et al.: Statistical performance analysis of track initiation techniques. IEEE Transactions on Signal Processing 45(2), 445–456 (1997)
5. Musicki, D., Evans, R., et al.: Integrated probabilistic data association. IEEE Transactions on Automatic Control 39(6), 1237–1241 (1994)
6. Li, N., Li, X.R.: Target perceivability and its applications. IEEE Transactions on Signal Processing 49(11), 2588–2604 (2001)
7. Naus, H., van Wijk, C.: Simultaneous localisation of multiple emitters. In: IEEE Proceedings on Radar, Sonar and Navigation, pp. 65–70 (2004)
8. Henrik, E.: Multi target tracking initiation with passive angle measurements. United States Patent No: US6292136B1 (2001)
9. Bishop, A.N., Pathirana, P.N.: Localization of emitters via the intersection of bearing lines: a ghost elimination approach. IEEE Transactions on Vehicular Technology 56(5), 3106–3110 (2007)
10. Doğancay, K.: Bearing-only Target Localization Using Total Least Squares. Signal Processing 85, 1695–1710 (2005)
11. Xu, B., Chen, Q., et al.: Ants for track initiation of bearings-only tracking. Simulation Modeling Practice and Theory 16(6), 626–638 (2008)
12. Zhu, J., Xu, B., Wang, Z.: Hybrid Method of Track Initiation for Bearings-Only Target Tracking. Information and Control 39(5), 596–600 (2010)
13. Chen, H., Li, X.R., et al.: On joint track initiation and parameter estimation under measurement origin uncertainty. IEEE Transactions on Aerospace and Electronic Systems 40(2), 675–694 (2004)

A Graph-Based Multi-hop Cooperative MIMO Scheme for Heterogeneous WSN

Zhetao Li[1,2,3], Da Xie[1,3], Tingrui Pei[1,3,*], Youngjune Choi[4], and Renfa Li[5]

[1] College of Information Engineering, Xiangtan University,
Xiangtan, 411105, China
[2] School of Computer, National University of Defense Technology,
Changsha, 410073, China
[3] Key Laboratory of Intelligent Computing and Information Processing of Ministry
of Education, Xiangtan University, Xiangtan, 411105 China
[4] Department of Information and Computer Engineering, Ajou University,
Suwon, 443749, Korea
[5] School of Computers and Communications, Hunan University,
Changsha, 410082, China
chu5044130@sohu.com, {xieda86,peitr}@163.com,
choiyj@ajou.ac.kr, lirenfa@vip.sina.com
http://www.springer.com/lncs

Abstract. A Graph-based multi-hop cooperative MIMO transmission scheme (GM-MIMO) aimed at optimizing the network lifetime and saving energy for heterogeneous wireless sensor networks (WSN) is proposed. In GM-MIMO, clusters are established based on geographical position. Graph theory is applied to find an optimal forwarding path. For taking the presence of node heterogeneity into consideration, GM-MIMO obtains maximum network lifetime. Simulation results show that GM-MIMO makes a significant performance improvement in terms of network lifetime and survival rate of nodes.

Keywords: WSN, graph theory, heterogeneous, cooperative MIMO, energy efficiency.

1 Introduction

Under the same Bit Error Rate (BER) requirement and Signal to Noise Ratio (SNR), multiple-input multiple-output (MIMO) systems outperform single-input single-output (SISO) systems and need less transmission energy [1,2]. Moreover, MIMO systems outperform SISO systems with respect to channel capacity

* This work is supported by National Natural Science Foundation of China under Grant No.61100215 and No.61173036, Science and Technology Planning Project of Hunan Provincial Science and Technology Department with Grant No.2011GK3200, Hunan Provincial Natural Science Foundation of China with Grant No.12JJ9021, Natural Science Foundation for Doctor, Xiangtan University with Grant No. 10QDZ30.

R. Wang and F. Xiao (Eds.): CWSN 2012, CCIS 334, pp. 237–247, 2013.
© Springer-Verlag Berlin Heidelberg 2013

in wireless fading channel transmission [3]. However, it is impractical to apply multiple-antenna technique to WSN directly. As constrained by the physical size and limited battery the sensor nodes is allowed to contain only one antenna. Fortunately some individual sensor nodes can cooperate for the transmission and reception in order to set up a cooperative MIMO scheme.

Strategies designed to minimize energy consumption in different layers of the protocol stack of WSN have motivate intensive research interest. X. Li [4] and Y. Yuan [5] etc. studied the multiple-input single-output (MISO) transmission scheme based on Low Energy Adaptive Clustering Hierarchy (LEACH). Q. H. Wang [6] etc. proposed cooperative MIMO protocol in sparse WSN. The schemes they proposed have some improvement in network lifetime. However, in various applications, such as area surveillance for agriculture or intelligent transportation systems, long range transmissions are often required because of the large covered area of the WSN [7]. W. R [8] and W. Cheng etc. improved the MISO system and proposed a multi-hop cooperative MIMO transmission scheme (M-MIMO) based on LEACH. M-MIMO has some improvements in network lifetime and survival rate of nodes. However, as the clusters re-established randomly after each round, the distribution of clusters may be non-uniform. Besides, distance vector routing algorithm is unstable as the clusters are changed every round. Besides, most of the analytical result for existing protocol obtained are based on homogeneous sensor networks (the nodes are equipped with the same amount of energy). Actually, in most applications, the sensor networks are heterogeneous. For example, sensor nodes could, over time, expend different amount of energy due to the radio communication characteristics.

In this paper, a clustering WSN model based on geographical position was build. Based on this model, we consider two factors i.e. the residual energy and node heterogeneity, and proposed a graph-based multi-hop cooperative MIMO Transmission scheme (GM-MIMO). Unlike prior schemes, clusters are established based on geographical position in GM-MIMO. Graph Theory is applied to find an optimal forwarding path. We assume that the nodes are equipped with different amount of energy. We show by simulation that GM-MIMO outperforms existing protocols in terms of network lifetime and survival rate of nodes.

The remainder of the paper is organized as followsSection 2 provides the system model and transmission schemes. In section 3, we address the energy consumption model. Section 4 presents the simulation results. In the end, we provide our conclusions in Section 5.

2   System Model and Scheme Design

In this section, we describe our model and transmission scheme of wireless sensor network. To simplify the problem, we assume that N nodes are randomly distributed in a square region with a dimension in $M \times M$, and they are static. All the nodes are assumed heterogeneous and energy constrained, where each node can transmit data to any other node and the sink. The sensor nodes are geographically grouped into clusters. Inside a cluster, a cluster head node (CH) and several cooperative transmission nodes (CTN) are reelected after each round of data transmission. The sink equipped with multiple antennas is located over the field. We also assume that the sink is of enough computing power and is not energy limited. The proposed multi-hop cooperative MIMO transmission model is illustrated in Fig. 1. Similarly to existing protocols, the transmission procedure of the proposed scheme was divided into rounds.

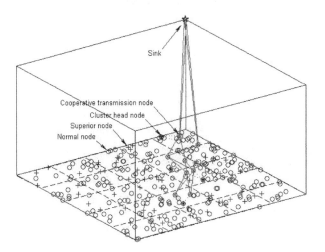

Fig. 1. Multi-hop cooperative MIMO transmission model

2.1 Cluster Formation

In GM-MIMO, sensor nodes are geographically grouped into clusters. We assume that some nodes are equipped with more energy resources than the rest of the nodes (we refer to these nodes as superior nodes and others are normal nodes).Let $\beta(0 < \beta < 1)$ be the fraction of the total N nodes, which are equipped with λ times more energy than the rest $(1 - \beta)N$ nodes. We use the result in Ref. [9], the weighted probabilities for normal nodes and superior nodes to be elected as cluster head are respectively given by:

$$P_{nrm}(i) = \left\{ \begin{array}{l} \frac{1}{1+\beta\lambda} \cdot \frac{k_c}{n-k_c[r \cdot mod(n/k_c)]}; if\, flag(i) = 1 \\ 0; otherwise \end{array} \right. \tag{1}$$

$$P_{sup}(i) = \left\{ \begin{array}{l} \frac{1+\lambda}{1+\beta\lambda} \cdot \frac{k_c}{n-k_c[r \cdot mod(n/k_c)]}; if\, flag(i) = 1 \\ 0; otherwise \end{array} \right. \tag{2}$$

The probability for superior nodes is $1 + \lambda$ times as the nodes, which effectively balance the energy load between superior nodes and normal nodes.

After the cluster heads are elected, each cluster head will broadcast an advertisement message (ADV) using CSMA protocol. The message contains the cluster heads ID and coordinate. If one CH received the advertisement message from another head j and the received signal strength (RSS) exceeds a threshold, it will take cluster head j as a neighboring cluster head and record its ID. As for the non cluster head in the local cluster, it will record the CH's ID and join the cluster by sending a join-request message (Join-REQ). This message contains the information of the nodes ID, the CH's ID. After the cluster head has received all the join-request messages, it will set up a TDMA schedule and transmit the schedule to its members as in the original LEACH protocol. If the sink receives the ADV messages, it records the coordinate and ID of each cluster head. Then, the sink calculates and stores the distances between any two adjacent cluster heads. On the other side, the sink selects the cluster head with the maximum RSS as the target cluster head (TCH) and record its ID.

After the clusters are formed, each cluster head will select M_t cooperative nodes and group them into a MIMO cell for cooperative MIMO communications with each of its neighboring cluster. For simplicity, we assume that the average distance between any two adjacent MIMO cells equal to that between corresponding CHs. In the end, the CH will broadcast a cooperate-request message (COOPERATE-REQ) to each cooperative node, which contains the ID of the cluster head itself, the IDs of the neighboring cluster heads, the IDs of the cooperative nodes of the neighboring cluster etc. When a cooperative node have received the cooperate-request message (COOPERATE-REQ), it will send back a cooperate-ACK message (COOPERATE-ACK) to the cluster head.

2.2   The Optimal Forwarding Path

We may use a graph of vertices and edges to represent the connective relationship among the MIMO cells (shows in Fig.2.). From this aspect, essentially finding an optimal forwarding path is to remove some of the vertices and edges while

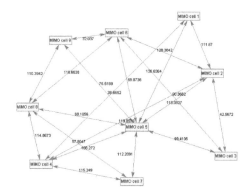

Fig. 2. Connective relationship among the MIMO cell

keep those remaining. Let $G = (V, E)$ be a weighted graph, the edges in G have weights. Let s be a special vertex, called source. Dijkstra algorithm suggests such an algorithm that for each vertex v it can always find the shortest path form v to s. Our contribution is to apply the graph theoretical concept on single-source shortest path into virtual MIMO to find the optimal forwarding path.

The basis ideas of the algorithm is:

Step 1: For each vertex v, Mark v as unvisited, and set $d(v) = \infty$ and set $d(v) = 0$;

Step 2: While (there is unvisited vertex) w=unvisited vertex with smallest d; Visit w, and *Relax* all its outgoing edges;

Step 3: return (V, d).

Where the *Relax* operation is:

When a vertex v can be reached from the source s with a certain distance, we examine an outgoing edge, say (v, w), and check if we can improve w.

Considering the sensor nodes' computational power is limited, the procedure of finding the optimal forwarding path is performed in the sink. After the clusters are formed the sink will compute the optimal forwarding path. Then the sink broadcast a polling message to the CHs which contains the TCH's ID and the optimal forwarding path (from each CH to the TCH) and the CHs' IDs. Each CH received the polling message will store corresponding optimal forwarding path. This guarantees that the CHs knows the forwarding path in real time and reduces the energy consumed to maintaining a routing table.

2.3   Data Transmission

The cluster members will transmit first their data to the cluster head by multiple frames during its allocated time slot, and sleeps in other slots to save energy. After the cluster head received data frames from its cluster members, the cluster head will perform data aggregation in order to remove the redundancy in the data.

After aggregated the received data frames, the cluster head will forward the data packet to the TCH by multiple hops routing. In each single-hop communication, if there exist cooperative MIMO nodes, the cluster head will add a packet header to the data packet, which includes the information of the optimal forwarding path (the IDs of the cluster heads in each hop). Then the data packet is broadcasted. Once corresponding cooperative nodes receive the data packet, they will encode the data packet by orthogonal STBC, and transmit it to the next hop.

3   The Energy Consumption Model

In this section, we will analyze the energy consumption of the proposed scheme. To simplify the problems, we make the following assumptions:

1) There are N nodes randomly distributed in an $M \times M(m^2)$ region.

2) An AWGN channel with squared power path loss is assumed for the intra-cluster communication.

3) A flat Rayleigh fading channel with k-th power path loss is assumed for the inter-cluster communication.

4) BPSK is used as the modulation scheme and the bandwidth is B Hz.

5) In each frame every node will send a packet with size S to the cluster head by probability P. The number of frames in each round is denoted by F_n .

6) The energy consumption for data processing is ignored.

Based on the above assumptions, there are three energy consuming operations in each round. i. The cluster members transmit data packets to the cluster head, whose energy consumption is denoted by $E_{CN}(k_c)$. ii. The cluster heads transmit aggregated data to corresponding cooperative nodes, whose energy consumption is denoted by $E_{CH}(k_c, M_t)$. iii. The cooperative nodes transmit the data to the adjacent MIMO cell in each single-hop transmission, whose energy consumption is denoted by $E_{CTH}(k_c, M_t)$.

3.1 $E_{CN}(k_c)$

The energy consumed by the cluster members to transmit one bit data to the cluster head node is given by:

$$Eb_{CN}(k_c) = -\frac{1}{\pi k_c}(1+\alpha)N_f\sigma^2 \ln(P_b)G_1M^2M_l + \frac{P_{ct} + P_{cr}}{B} \qquad (3)$$

where d_{max} is the distance from the node to the cluster head, α is the efficiency of the RF power amplifier, M_l is the link margin, N_f is the receiver noise figure, G_1 is the gain factor at $d = 1m$, P_b is the desired BER performance, P_{ct} and P_{cr} are the circuit power consumption of the transmitter and receiver. We use the result in Ref. [8] that $E(d^2) = M^2/(2\pi k_c)$. On the other hand, when the number of clusters is k_c, the average number of members for each cluster is N/k_c. Hence, the total number of bits transmitted to the cluster head for each cluster by each round is $S_1(k_c) = F_nPSN/k_c$. Therefore, the total energy consumed in cluster members is:

$$E_{CN}(k_c) = k_cS_1(k_c)Eb_{CN}(k_c) \qquad (4)$$

3.2 $E_{CH}(k_c, M_t)$

The energy per bit consumed by the cluster head to transmit the aggregated data to cooperative nodes is given by:

$$Eb_{CH}(k_c, M_t) = -\frac{1}{\pi k_c}(1+\alpha)N_f\sigma^2 \ln(P_b)G_1M^2M_l + \frac{P_{ct} + M_tP_{cr}}{B} \qquad (5)$$

The amount of data after aggregation for each round by cluster head node is given by:

$$S_2(k_c) = \frac{S_1(k_c)}{Pd_{agg}N/k_c - d_{agg} + 1} \qquad (6)$$

Where d_{agg} is the aggregation factor. The total energy consumed by cluster head to transmit the aggregated data to cooperative nodes is given by:

$$E_{CH}(k_c, M_t) = k_c S_2(k_c) E b_{CH}(k_c, M_t) \tag{7}$$

3.3 $E_{CTH}(k_c, M_t)$

On one hand, if the cooperative nodes of the cluster received the data from corresponding cluster head, they encode and transmit the sequence (according to orthogonal STBC) to the neighboring MIMO cell. On the other hand, if the cooperative nodes of the cluster received the data from pre hop, they forward the data packets to the next hop specified by the packet header. Suppose that the block size of the STBC code is F symbols, in each block pM_t training symbols are included and the block will transmitted in L symbol duration. $R = F/L$ is the transmission rate. Then, the actual amount of data required to transmit the $S_2(k_c)$ bits is given by:

$$S_2'(k_c) = S_2(k_c) F / R (F - pM_t) \tag{8}$$

The energy consumed by cooperative nodes to transmit MIMO data to the next hop cooperative nodes is given by:

$$E_{CTH}(k_c, M_t) \approx S_2'(k_c)[(1 + \alpha) \frac{N_0}{P_b^{1/M_t}} \frac{(4\pi)^2 (2M)^k M_l N_f}{G_t G_r \lambda^2 (\pi k_c)^{k_c/2}} + M_t \frac{P_{ct} + P_{cr}}{B}] \tag{9}$$

Based on the above analysis, the overall energy consumption in each round, can be described as:

$$E_{total}(k_c, M_t) = E_{CN}(k_c) + \bar{n}_k [E_{CH}(k_c, M_t) + E_{CTH}(k_c, M_t)] \tag{10}$$

Where $\bar{n}_k$ is the average number of hops.

4   Simulation Results

In this section, simulation was performed to evaluate the performance of the GM-MIMO scheme. an AWGN channel with squared power path loss is assumed for intra-cluster communications. For the inter-cluster communications, we assume the transmission from each cooperative nodes experiences frequency-nonselective and low Rayleigh fading. The rationale behind such channel assumptions is that the inter-cluster transmission distance is much larger than the intra-cluster transmission distance and the transmission environments are more complex in the inter-cluster communication. In the simulation, 300 nodes are randomly distributed on a $M \times M (M = 200m)$ field. The sink is located over the field. The size of the packet that cluster member send to corresponding CHN is set to 1 bit. Each normal node begins with 0.5 J of energy. Table 1 is the parameter in our simulations.

Table 1. System parameters

Parameters	Values	Parameters	Values
f_c	2.5GHz	G_tG_r	5dBi
B	10KHz	α	0.47
P_b	0.001	R	0.75
P_{ct}	98.2mw	F_n	2
P_{cr}	112.6 mw	P	0.8
F	200	p	2
R_{bt}	5	N_f	10dB
R_{ts}	100	σ^2	134dBm/Hz
M_l	40dB	k	[3,5]
β	0.1	λ	0.2

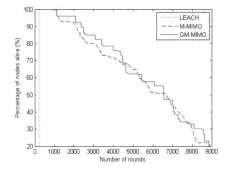

Fig. 3. Percentage of nodes alive over round

Fig.3 shows the percentage of nodes alive over round. If the network lifetime of WSN was defined as the duration of more than 80 percent of the nodes are alive, then we can observe that the network lifetime of WSN with the original LEACH protocol, the M-MIMO scheme, and the proposed GM-MIMO scheme is 230, 2820, and 3300 rounds. The improvement on network lifetime obtained by GM-MIMO scheme is significant. The reason is that in the fading channel environment, due to its single-hop transmission from the cluster heads to the sink, LEACH protocol consumes much more energy, which result in less network lifetime. On the other side, through assigning probabilities of cluster head node election weighted by the relative initial energy of nodes, GM-MIMO guarantees well balanced distribution of the energy load among nodes of the network. Besides, in GM-MIMO the sink provides the optimal forwarding path in real time, thus cluster heads are no need to expend energy to maintaining a routing table.

Fig.4 shows the number of effective packets received at the sink over time. During its lifetime the LEACH protocol can obtain better latency performance compared to the M-MIMO and GM-MIMO. The reason is that the multi-hop operation in the M-MIMO scheme and GM-MIMO scheme will increase the latency, and thus result in the number of data packets sent to the sink is less than

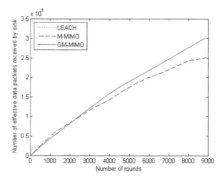

Fig. 4. Number of effective data packets received at the sink

LEACH for a given period of rounds. However, the better latency performance of the LEACH protocol benefits from the more energy consumption compared to the other two schemes. What's more, in the fading channel environment, due to its single-hop transmission from the cluster heads to the sink, LEACH protocol will consume much more energy which will result in less network lifetime.

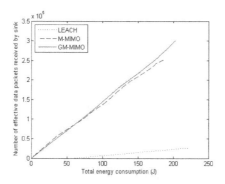

Fig. 5. Number effective data packets received at the sink per given amount of energy

Fig.5 shows that with the same amount of energy consumption, the GM-MIMO scheme can transmit much more data packets compared to the LEACH protocol and the M-MIMO scheme. From Fig. 4 and Fig. 5, we can find that the GM-MIMO scheme is more suitable for the application scenario which has large requirements on network lifetime but little requirements on latency.

Fig.6 shows the percentage of nodes alive per amount of effective data packets received at the sink. Fig. 6 exhibits that GM-MIMO needs less energy to transmit the same amount of data packets. Therefore, the improvement on network lifetime obtained by GM-MIMO is significant.

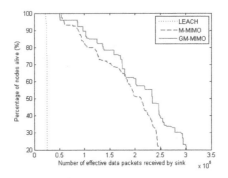

Fig. 6. Percentage of nodes alive per amount of effective data packets received at sink

5   Conclusion

In this paper, we proposed a GM-MIMO for the application of cooperative MIMO communication in the large scale energy heterogeneous WSN. GM-MIMO aims at optimizing the network lifetime and saving energy. It considers the presence of node heterogeneity. In GM-MIMO, clusters are established based on geographical position. Graph theory was applied to find an optimal forwarding path. Based on the scheme, we investigate the energy consumption of each operation, then the overall energy consumption model of the scheme is developed. Simulation results show that GM-MIMO outperforms existing protocols, and it dramatically prolongs the network lifetime.

References

1. Cui, S., Goldsmith, A.J., Bahai, A.: Energy-efficiency of MIMO and Cooperative MIMO Techniques in Sensor Networks. IEEE Journal on Selected Areas in Communications 22, 1089–1098 (2004)
2. Jayaweera, S.K.: Virtual MIMO-based cooperative communication for energy-constrained wireless sensor networks. IEEE Transactions on Wireless Communications 5, 984–989 (2006)
3. Marzetta, T.L., Hochwald, B.M.: Capacity of a mobile multiple-antenna communication link in Rayleigh flat fading. IEEE Transactions on Information Theory 45, 139–157 (1999)
4. Li, X., Chen, M., Liu, W.: Application of STBC-encoded cooperative transmissions in wireless sensor networks. IEEE Signal Processing Letters 12, 134–137 (2005)
5. Yuan, Y., He, Z., Chen, M.: Virtual MIMO-based cross-layer design for wireless sensor networks. IEEE Transactions on Vehicular Technology 55, 856–864 (2006)
6. Wang, Q.H., Qu, Y.G., Lin, Z.T., Bai, R.G.: Protocol for the application of cooperative MIMO based on clustering in sparse wireless sensor networks. The Journal of China Universities of Posts and Telecommunications 14, 51–57 (2007)
7. Ahmed, I., Peng, M., Wang, W., Shah, S.I.: Joint rate and cooperative MIMO scheme optimization in wireless sensor networks. Computer Communications 32, 1072–1078 (2009)

8. Heinzelman, W.B., Chandrakasan, A.P., Balakrishnan, H.: An application-specific protocol architecture for wireless microsensor networks. IEEE Transactions on Wireless Communications 1, 660–670 (2002)
9. Smaragdakis, G., Matta, I., Bestavros, A.: A stable Election Protocol for clustered heterogeneous wireless sensor networks. In: Proc. International Workshop on SANPA, Boston, vol. 1, pp. 662–670 (2004)

Research of Adaptive Frequency Hopping Technology in WIA-PA Industrial Wireless Network

Wei Liang[1], Shuai Liu[1], Yutuo Yang[1,2], and Shiming Li[1]

[1] Shenyang Institute of Automation, Chinese Academy of Sciences. 110016
Shenyang, P.R. China
[2] Graduate University of Chinese Academy of Sciences. 100039 Beijing, P.R.China
{weiliang,liushuai,yangyutuo,lishiming}@sia.cn

Abstract. WIA-PA (Wireless Networks for Industrial Automation - Process Automation) is IEC international standard. In order to solve the primary problem of wireless network in industrial applications, i.e. anti-jamming problem, WIA-PA support adaptive hopping technology. Two adaptive hopping methods based on WIA-PA standard are proposed in this paper. The proposed methods is realized and evaluated based on the experimental platform, the result indicates the feasibility and availability of the proposed methods.

Keywords: industrial wireless network, sensor network, adaptive frequency hopping technology, WIA-PA standard, reliability.

1 Introduction

Industrial wireless network technology emerges at the beginning of this century and aims the information interaction between industrial equipments, which can be applied in harsh industrial environment. As for the existing wireless technology, industrial wireless network technology is technical extension and innovation in the application of industry. Industrial wireless network technology is evolved from the emerging short-range wireless sensor network technology [1]. Compared with traditional wired process control system, the information transfer mode based on wireless technology of the industrial wireless network technology has the advantages of low cost, being easy to use and maintain, which provide it a broad application prospect in the industrial control area. And the industrial wireless network technology is becoming a hot technology after the field bus [2].

Standardization is the prerequisite for the extensive application and promotion of industrial technology. A number of industrial organizations, such as Chinese Industrial Wireless Alliance[3], ZigBee Alliance[4], HCF(Hart Communication Foundation)[5] and ISA(Instrument Society of America)[6] are actively promoting the application of wireless technologies and standards in the field of industrial automation.

In the year of 2007, Chinese Industrial Wireless Alliance, which was established in the leading of the Shenyang Institute of Automation, Chinese Academy

R. Wang and F. Xiao (Eds.): CWSN 2012, CCIS 334, pp. 248–262, 2013.
© Springer-Verlag Berlin Heidelberg 2013

of Science, proceeded to develop the industrial wireless network standard WIA (Wireless Network for Industrial Automation). WIA-PA (WIA-Process Automation)[7], which is first developed for the urgent needs of process industries, is a sub-standard of WIA. WIA-PA defines the WIA system architecture and communications specifications for process automation. WIA-PA standard has become the IEC international standard IEC 62601 and the Chinese National Standard GB / T 26790.1-2011. As an IEC standard, WIA-PA provides users with larger scale and lower cost network framework, more interoperability, and greater product and service quality, which can reduce the production risks of vendors and using risk of consumers.

The main problem of industrial wireless network technology, including WIA-PA, is the anti-jamming problem. Reasons are as follows: the physical layer and the MAC layer of most of the industrial wireless network standard are based on IEEE 802.15.4[8], which uses the public and open 2.4GHz ISM band. However, this band is also used by other wireless technologies, such as 802.11b/g and Bluetooth. And there is severe mutual anti-jamming problem among the wireless network technologies.

According to the different layers in the protocol stack, the solution to the problem of anti - jamming in industrial wireless network can be divided into the following three categories: using DSSS (Direct Sequence Spread Spectrum) communication technology in the physical layer to ensure reliable transmission of the broadband RF signal; applying Frequency Hopping Spread Spectrum (FHSS) in Data Link Layer(DLL)to fight the narrowband interference and ensure reliable point-to-point communication; taking MESH routing in network layer to ensure reliable end-to-end transmission through the space multiplex. The position of each method in the protocol stack is shown in Fig.1 [9-12].

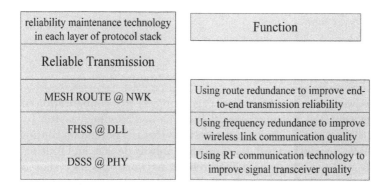

Fig. 1. Industrial wireless network reliability assurance techniques

In order to solve the anti-interference problem of the wireless network, WIA-PA standard adopt the mechanism of multi-channel communication, and introduced the thought of FHSS in data link layer on the basis of DSSS on physical layer [13]. On the basis of the state of the channel, adapting frequency hopping mechanism can reduce the blindness of time slot hopping, and can suppress the sudden interference, eliminate the frequency selective fading. Reliability assurance is the primary problem to be solved in WIA-PA, adaptive frequency hopping technology is one of the core technology features in WIA-PA industrial wireless network, and is the primary mechanism to guarantee reliability of wireless communication in WIA-PA. Therefore, researching and designing adaptive frequency hopping algorithm has broad application value.

Existing adaptive frequency hopping technology is based on the automatic channel quality analysis that is a combination of frequency hopping of frequency adaptive and power adaptive control. In order to realize frequency adaptive control, every node must have the receiving component for real-time channel signal quality evaluation and reverse communication link to real-time measure the received power and channel interference condition. Although this adaptive frequency hopping technology can maintain high quality communication for long time, but has a high requirement for processing capability of the node that requires every nodes have the function of channel quality measurement and self-adaption maintenance; On the other hand, adopting physical layer realizing method will make wireless transceiver very complex which belongs to typical "Expensive Transceiver" that is unfit for the low complexity requirement of embedded system in WIA-PA. In addition, most existing adaptive frequency hopping technology adopts centralized control which cannot suffice the distributed feature in WIA-PA network. According to the network feature of WIA-PA, the algorithm designed in this paper is more suitable for the network feature of WIA-PA, what's more, the algorithm has the feature of simply effective and applicable in the development of the embedded environment.

This paper works in the following two aspects: (1) Researching the detail design and implementation of adaptive frequency hopping technology in WIA-PA; (2) Experimental verification of the adaptive frequency hopping performance through test bed of adaptive frequency hopping.

2   WIA-PA

2.1   Introduction of WIA-PA

WIA-PA network consists of five types of equipment: host configuration computer, gateway device (GW), routing device, field device and handheld device. To improve reliability, there may be redundant gateway devices and redundant routing devices in the WIA-PA network, which backups the gateway devices and routing devices.

WIA-PA network supports a hierarchical network topology that combines star and mesh, as illustrated in Fig. 2. The first level of the network is in mesh topology, where routing devices and gateway devices are deployed. The second level of the network is in star topology, where routing devices, field devices, and handheld devices (if they exist) are deployed.

In order to facilitate management, this document specifies five kinds of logical roles:

– Gateway: Gateway handles protocol-translation and data-mapping between the WIA-PA network and other networks.

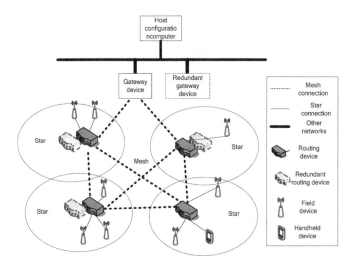

Fig. 2. Example of WIA-PA physical topology (combination of star and mesh)

– Network manager: Network Manager (NM) manages and monitors the entire network. There should be one and only one network manager per WIA-PA network.

– Security manager: Security Manager (SM) deals with security key management and security authentication of gateway devices, routing devices, field devices, and handheld devices (if they exist).

– Cluster head: Cluster head manages and monitors field devices and handheld devices (if they exist). Cluster head also merges and securely forwards packets from local cluster members and other cluster heads.

– Cluster member: Cluster member collects field data and sends the data to its cluster head.

The communication resource of WIA-PA is managed in the way of superframe. The WIA-PA superframe structure is shown in Fig. 3. The WIA-PA network extends the IEEE STD 802.15.4-2006 superframe structure. The inactive period defined in the IEEE STD 802.15.4-2006 superframe is used for intra-cluster communication, inter-cluster communication, and sleeping in the WIA-PA superframe, which can adapt to the management structure of WIA-PA.

2.2 Specification of Adaptive Frequency Hopping in WIA-PA

The WIA-PA network supports frequency hopping, and the hopping sequence is designated by the NM. Frequency hopping in the WIA-PA network includes three mechanisms: AFS, AFH, and TH.

Adaptive Frequency Switch (AFS): in the WIA superframe, the beacon, CAP and CFP use the same channel in the same superframe cycle, and change the channel according to the channel conditions in different superframe cycles. That is to say, bad channel condition triggers the operation of changing channels.

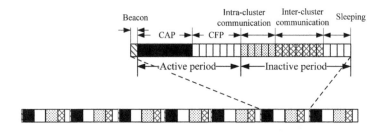

Fig. 3. The superframe of WIA-PA

Adaptive Frequency Hopping (AFH): irregularly changes communication channels per timeslot of the WIA superframe according to actual channel condition. The channel conditions are measured in retry times. If the cannel condition is bad, the device changes the channel. The sequence of frequency hopping is: (timeslot 1, channel 1) (timeslot 2, channel 2) (timeslot n, channel n).

Timeslot Hopping (TH): regularly changes communication channels per timeslot of the WIA superframe to combat interference and fading. The Inter-cluster period adopts the TH mechanism. The hopping structure is: (timeslot 1, channel 1) (timeslot 2, channel 2) (timeslot i, channel i).

3   AFS Method Based on WIA-PA Standard

The adaptive control resolution of AFS is one superframe cycle, the WIA-PA network can fastest respond in the next superframe cycle, AFS involved active period is mainly used for network management, which require higher accuracy and reliability of adaptive control that can enhance maintenance cost properly.

3.1   AFS Design

As shown in Fig. 4, AFS method mainly includes three sections: initialization, channel state monitoring and channel switching.

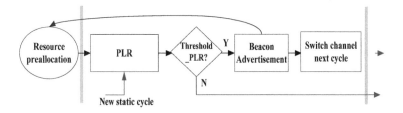

Fig. 4. Operation diagram of WIA-PA AFS

1) Initialization period includes the following details. Firstly, WIA-PA network manager allocate short address to the field device when field device joining the network. The network manager pre-allocate resource for cluster head, And then cluster head allocate communication resource for the new inner-cluster member. In addition, initializing the packet loss rate, packet loss rate threshold value, available channel list is done in this period.

2) Channel state monitoring and assessment. Channel state monitoring is the basic of AFS, this paper uses statistic value of successful message transmission count to monitor channel: in a cycle, continuously send specific messages in the monitoring channel, and then count the packet loss rate [14], when the packet loss rate reach the given threshold, switch the using channel to standby channel.

3) Channel switch method. After the packet loss rate reach the given threshold, cluster head allocate new standby channel for the link between cluster head and corresponding field device, and inform the relevant nodes. In the channel switch process, cluster head inform cluster members the standby channel and switch time by repeatedly broadcast beacon frame. the default work time of standby channel is the start of the next superframe.

3.2 AFS Implementation

AFS implementation is as Fig. 5:

4 AFH Method Based on WIA-PA Standard

The adaptive control resolution of AFH are timeslots of intra-cluster period, the WIA-PA network can responds channel status changing in the current super frame cycle and notifies the related equipment to change its working channel. AFS of intra-cluster period involved is mainly used for data transmission.

4.1 AFH Design

As shown in Fig. 6, AFS method mainly includes three periods: initialization, channel state monitoring and channel switch.

1) Initialization includes the following details. WIA-PA network manager allocate short address to the field device when field device joining the network. The network manager pre-allocate resource for cluster head. And then cluster head allocate communication resource for the new joining cluster member. In addition, initializing frame retry counter, frame retry threshold, and available channel list is done in this period.

2)Channel state monitoring and assessment: The channel conditions are measured in retry times in AFH. Cluster member uploads data during intra-cluster period of WIA-PA superframe and retransmission happens when the transmission

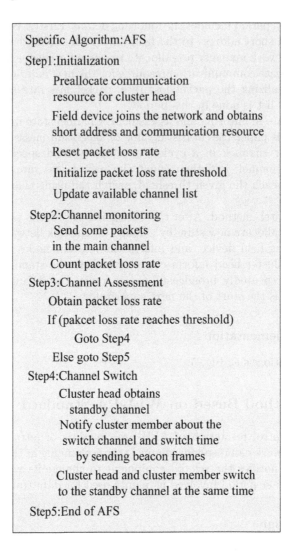

Fig. 5. AFS implementation

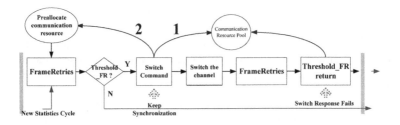

Fig. 6. Operation diagram of WIA-PA AFH

fails, if the retry times reaches threshold, the cluster head use the method in 3) to switch channel. Different from AFS, cluster head first caches the current link resources before actual channel switching, this is to insure that device can switch back to the main channel if the adaptive channel switch fails.

3) Channel switch method: If the channel condition is bad and the retry times of the sender reaches the threshold value, the sender chooses the next channel in sequence from standby channel set and notifies the receiver during the next retry timeslot by using the main channel. If the receiver does not receive the notification, it counts its retry times continuously. When the retry times of the receiver reach the threshold value, the receiver chooses the next channel from standby channel set and uses the chosen standby channel after 2 timeslot. If the receiver receives the notification of a channel switch, it changes the communication channel and returns acknowledge; otherwise, it does not change the communication channel and retry data by using the main channel. If the retry times of the sender reach maximal retry times, the sender discards the current packet and transmits the next packet by using the main channel. If the communication between the sender and the receiver is successful before the retry times of the sender reaches maximal retry times, the sender transmits the next packet by using the standby channel.

4.2   AFH Implementation

AFH implementation is as Fig. 7:

4.3   Channel Maintenance

As shown in the Fig. 8, when the network manager distributes the communication link for the receiving and sending nodes, according to the order of distributing the slot firstly and the channel secondly, it can get the slot resource from the slot matrix, then gets the channel resource from the channel matrix.

In order to meet the real-time maintenance requirement of the adaptive frequency hopping for the frequency channel, the channel resource matrix is divided into three parts: high quality channel set, inferior channel set and recycling channel set. The channel quality statistic module in the maintenance mechanism of the adaptive frequency hopping divides the channels into the high quality channels and inferior channels, according to the real-time statistic of the channel quality. When the high quality channel condition reaches to the lower limit of alarms, it is transfer to inferior channel set. The inferior channel is randomly selected to do a temporary test. If the selected inferior channel goes better , it will be transferred to the recycling channel set. The recycling channel will do another test, a more formal test. Once the channel in the recycling channel set pass the test and evaluation ,it will become the backup of the high quality channel. Otherwise, it backs the inferior channel set.

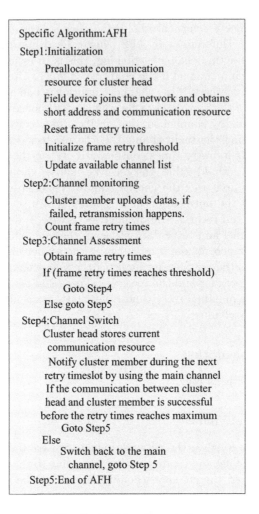

Specific Algorithm:AFH

Step1:Initialization

　Preallocate communication
　resource for cluster head

　Field device joins the network and obtains
　short address and communication resource

　Reset frame retry times

　Initialize frame retry threshold

　Update available channel list

Step2:Channel monitoring

　Cluster member uploads datas, if
　failed, retransmission happens.
　Count frame retry times

Step3:Channel Assessment

　Obtain frame retry times

　If (frame retry times reaches threshold)

　　Goto Step4

　Else goto Step5

Step4:Channel Switch
　Cluster head stores current
　communication resource
　Notify cluster member during the next
　retry timeslot by using the main channel
　If the communication between cluster
　head and cluster member is successful
　before the retry times reaches maximum
　　Goto Step5
　Else
　　Switch back to the main
　　channel, goto Step 5

Step5:End of AFH

Fig. 7. AFH implementation

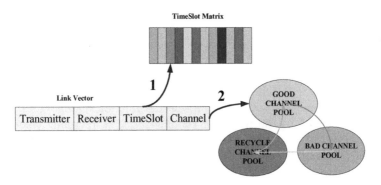

Fig. 8. The algorithm of the 2-step resource assignment in a cluster

5 Experimental Verification

5.1 The Adaptive Frequency Hopping Test Platform

The adaptive frequency hopping operation of WIA-PA runs in star network, therefore, we make a reasonable cutting and modification to the original network prototype to achieve a better research process and to facilitate the experiment for the adaptive frequency hopping operation of WIA-PA network. Generally, the adaptive frequency hopping test platform includes network manager, cluster head as well as cluster members. The physical structure of the network is shown in Fig.9. The network manager could be implemented on a host computer, with information exchanged between the host computer and cluster head device via a serial cable, meanwhile communicating with cluster members by RF radio [15].

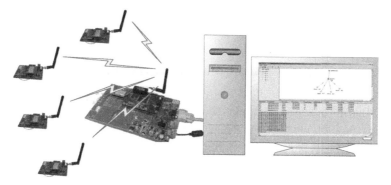

Fig. 9. WIA-PA adaptive frequency hopping test platform

Network Manager is the core device of the star cluster network in terms of management; it is responsible for maintaining the whole network, monitoring and storing data in disk, and displaying the topology. The Network Manager undertakes the management task of the entire network. In order to improve the efficiency of development and the locating the program errors, a modular modification idea should be resorted. The network management software consists of six major functional modules: initialization module, serial task module, device operation procedure management module, management information base module, GUI module and data storage module.

The network management software is implemented under MFC infrastructure and developed and debugged in Microsoft Visual C++ 6.0 environment. The overview of the network management software is shown in Fig. 10.

Cluster head is the star-cluster core management device, as well as central device connecting between star-cluster network and network manager, containing not only WIA-PA protocol stack but also serial port communication protocol, undertaking protocol translation, analysis and exchange of upstream and downlink data stream. The cluster head device mainly includes the following functional

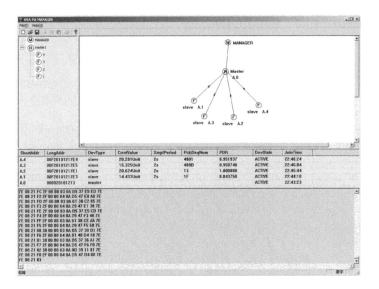

Fig. 10. Overview of the network management software

modules: the initialization module, the serial communication module, the protocol stack module, network management module, device management module, timing management module and channel quality detection module.

Cluster head device is implemented on ARM9 platform, the microprocessor is Atmel's AT91RM9200, with RF chip Chipcon CC2420 connected via SPI bus; Nucleus PLUS has been selected as real-time operating system, with task management, memory management, I/O management and interrupt management integrated for applications. Fig. 11 is the cluster head device.

Fig. 11. Cluster head device

Cluster members are the working nodes of a star-cluster network, which make use of sensors to obtain the relevant physical information; as for data acquisition method, convergence mode is selected, all cluster members send the data frame to the cluster head. And after protocol translation, the data is then sent to network manager by serial cable. The main functional modules of the cluster member device includes: the initialization module, the protocol stack module, device management module, timing management module, data acquisition module, and channel quality detection module and so on.

The implementation of cluster member devices is based on MSP430 embedded platforms, the microprocessor is TI MSP430F1611, with a Chipcon CC2420 RF chip welded via SPI. The embedded real-time operating system uC/OS-II has been ported to the platform, to facilitate relative management such as task management, memory management, I/O management and interrupt management for application programs. Fig. 12 is the cluster member device.

Fig. 12. Cluster member device

5.2 Experiment

In order to validate WIA-PA adaptive frequency hopping methods, two experiments are compared: the reliability of timeslot frequency hopping and the reliability of adaptive frequency hopping. The two experiments both are in the interference environment.

Referring to the setting of data update rate in the wireless industry, for example, in the Emerson Smart Wireless adapter, the data update rate is from 8s to 60 min [16]. In order to reflect the phenomena as quickly as possible, the field device at present is at the rate of 2s.

In order to evaluate the proposed algorithm of the adaptive frequency hopping, based on the existing interference environment, the proposed adaptive frequency switching algorithm (AFS) and the adaptive frequency hopping algorithm (AFH) will be compared with slot frequency hopping which is commonly used in the industry. The reliability of slot frequency hopping and AFS, in statistical cycle of 400s, within the test time of 3200s, is shown in Table 1.

Table 1. The comparison of AFS and FH

Comparison content	Network of FH	Network of AFS
Number of packets	1670	1670
PER (%)	14.25-15.15	4.6-5.4

The reliability of slot frequency hopping and AFH ,in statistical cycle of 400s, within the test time of 3200s, is shown in Table 2.

Table 2. The comparison of AFH and FH

Comparison content	Network of FH	Network of AFH
Number of packets	1600	1600
PER (%)	16.8-18.2	5.7-6.7

From the experiment, it can be concluded that the AFS is more reliable than the FH. AFS can guarantee the reliable transmission of the management frame. The AFH is more reliable than the FH, and the AFH can guarantee the reliability of data frame transmission. Therefore, WIA-PA adaptive frequency hopping technique can be against the interference and the destructive impact of the frequency selective attenuation , and guarantee the reliability of the network.

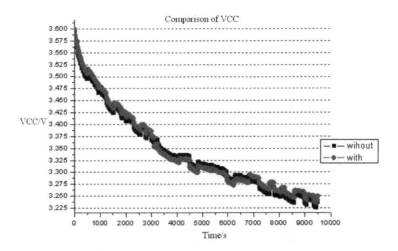

Fig. 13. VCC relation between networks with/without adaptive frequency hopping

Power consumption is an important performance. The power voltage VCC is adopted to evaluate the power consumption. Fig. 13 shows the comparison of power consumption between Networks with/without adaptive frequency hopping. The power consumption has no difference basically. The main reasons are as follows. Firstly, the energy consumption is increased a little bit because of the adaptive communication strategy, the additional protocol overhead and the processing of management frame. Meanwhile, the energy consumption is reduced, because the introduction of adaptive communication reduces the times of the failure of the retransmission. So the energy consumption of adaptive frequency hopping technology is almost equal to that of slot frequency hopping.

6   Conclusion

In order to solve the anti-jamming problem, WIA-PA support adaptive hopping technology. Two adaptive hopping methods based on WIA-PA are proposed in this paper. Experimental platform is built to verify the proposed methods and the experimental results show the feasibility and effectiveness.

Acknowledgments. This work was supported by the Natural Science Foundation of China under contact (61174026), the National High Technology Research and Development Program of China (863 Program: 2011AA040101), the Special Program for Key Basic Research Founded by MOST under contact 2010CB334705, Foundation of Chinese Academy of Sciences under contact (KGCX2-EW-104-2).

References

1. Wei, L., Xiaoling, Z.: WIA-PA: System Architecture and Communication Protocol of Industrial Wireless Network for Process Automation. Instrument Standardization & Metrology 2, 30–36 (2009)
2. Chinese Industrial Wireless Alliance [EB/OL],
   http://www.industrialwireless.cn
3. ZigBee Alliance [EB/OL], http://www.zigbee.org
4. HART Communication Foundation [EB/OL],
   http://www.hartcomm.org/protocol/wihart/wireless/technology.html
5. ISA100: Wireless System for Automation [EB/OL],
   http://www.isa.org//MSTemplate.cfm/MicrositeID=1134/CommitteeID=6891
6. IEC 62601. Industrial communication network - Fieldbus specifications - WIA-PA communication network and communication profile. IEC, Geneva (2008)
7. Wei, L., Xiaoling, Z., Yang, X.: Survey and Experiments of WIA-PA Specification of Industrial Wireless Network. Wireless Communications and Mobile Computing 11, 1197–1212 (2011)
8. IEEE Std 802.15.4-2006. Part 15.4: Wireless Medium Access Control (MAC) and Physical Layer (PHY) Specifications for Low-Rate Wireless Personal Area Networks (WPANs). IEEE, New York (2006)
9. Wei, L., Xiaoling, Z., Miao, Y.: WIA-PA Network and Its Interconnection with Legacy Process Automation System. In: 7th ACM Conference on Embedded Networked Sensor Systems, pp. 343–344. ACM Press, Beijing (2009)
10. Xiaoling, Z., Wei, L., Fuqiang, W., et al.: TDMA Channel Scheduling Algorithm Under Blacklist Technology. In: 2009 Asia-Pacific Conference on Computational Intelligence and Industrial Applications, pp. 263–266. IEEE Press, Wuhan (2009)

11. Xiaoling, Z., Wei, L., Haibin, Y.: Adaptive Timeslot Scheduling of Long Cycle Data in WIA-PA Network. In: 2009 Asia-Pacific Conference on Computational Intelligence and Industrial Applications, pp. 267–271. IEEE Press, Wuhan (2009)
12. Xiaoling, Z., Wei, L., Meng, Z.: Distributed and Dynamic TDMA Channel Scheduling Algorithm for WIA-PA. In: 2009 IEEE International Conference on Intelligent Computing and Intelligent Systems, pp. 462–466. IEEE Press, Shanghai (2009)
13. Wenbin, L.: Channel Model Introduction. Technical report, National Tsinghua University (2006)
14. Wenyuan, X., Wade, T., Yangyong, Z., et al.: The Feasibility of Launching and Detecting Jamming Attack in Wireless Networks. In: Proceedings of MobiHoc 2005. ACM Press, New York (2005)
15. Miao, Y., Wei, L., Weijie, X.: Design and Implementation of Industrial Wireless Network System Based on WIA-PA. In: 2010 8th World Congress on Intelligent Control and Automation, pp. 6799–6803. IEEE Press, Jinan (2010)
16. Emerson: Smart Wireless THUMTM Adapter Product Data Sheet. Emerson, Chanhassen (2009)

Novel Three-Party Password-Based Authenticated Key Exchange Protocol for Wireless Sensor Networks

Qiaomin Lin[1,2], Yangjunxiong Wang[3], Xing Shao[1,2],
Faxin Yang[4], and Ruchuan Wang[1,2]

[1] College of Computer, Nanjing University of Posts and Telecommunications,
Nanjing 210003 , China
[2] Jiangsu High Technology Research Key Laboratory for Wireless Sensor Networks,
Nanjing 210003, China
[3] Tongda College of Nanjing University of Posts and Telecommunications,
Nanjing 210003, China
[4] College of communications & arts, Nanjing University of Posts and
Telecommunications, Nanjing 210003, China
qmlin@njupt.edu.cn

Abstract. Despite recent improvements of the capabilities of wireless sensors, network protocol support for key exchange is still lagging behind. Three-party password-based authenticated key exchange protocols allow sensors communicate over an open network securely using high entropy session keys originated from a low entropy password. Due to their convenience in building a secure communication channel, many password-based key exchange protocols have been proposed and investigated over the years. Nevertheless, protocol must be designed carefully so as not to be broken using dictionary attacks in which an adversary tries all possible passwords in an attempt to figure out the correct one. Besides, protocol must be environment-friendly. That is say, the protocol should not pose too much loads on wireless sensors. And hence, a novel 3PAKE protocol is proposed for wireless sensor networks, which has better performance compared with similar protocols.

Keywords: Wireless Sensor Networks, Password-based Authenticated Key Exchange, Three-party, Elliptic Curve Cryptography.

1 Introduction

Wireless Sensor Networks are playing an important role in an ever-growing number of applications ranging from medical monitoring over home automation to environmental surveillance. Since wireless sensors are usually deployed in unintended or even hostile environments, they are prone to various malicious attacks, including the manipulation and personation of nodes. The establishment of a shared session key between sensor nodes is one of the vital security services needed to guarantee the proper functioning of wireless sensor networks.

R. Wang and F. Xiao (Eds.): CWSN 2012, CCIS 334, pp. 263–270, 2013.
© Springer-Verlag Berlin Heidelberg 2013

Despite some recent advances in this field, the efficient implementation of authenticated key exchange for wireless sensor networks remains a challenge due to the resource constraints of tiny sensor nodes. Password-based authenticated key exchange protocol is regarded as one of the most convenient mechanisms in an open environment to protect private network information. And hence, we intend to propose a secure and efficient password-based authenticated key exchange protocol for wireless sensor networks.

Password-based authenticated key exchange protocol is regarded as one of the most convenient mechanisms in an open environment to protect private network information [1, 2]. While two-party password-based authenticated key exchange (2PAKE) protocols are well suited for clientCserver architectures, they are inconvenient and costly for use in large-scale wireless sensor networks. And hence, various key exchange protocols were proposed [3-12] to tackle problems in 2PAKE protocols which keep a large number of shared passwords for communicating with other users. In three-party password-based authenticated key exchange(3PAKE) protocols, each user shares an easy-to-remember password with a trusted server. Each user can securely exchange information with other users via the trusted server. With the servers help, each user in 3PAKE protocols only shares one secret with the server, as seems to be more rational. Our proposed protocol is 3PAKE-based and efficiency-oriented. It has the following key features.

1.Firstly, the proposed protocol directly uses each participants unique id to accomplish mutual authentication. And hence, the server needs not to store a large public key table, which provides high scalability for the dynamic changes in large-scale wireless sensor networks.

2.The server in our proposed protocol cant extract information on the value of that session key in that the server is not supposed to be sheer honest.

3.The proposed protocol is very efficient in that it is based on elliptic curve cryptography. The remainder of this paper is organized as follows: Section 2 gives the detailed illustration of our protocol. Section 3 compares the proposed protocol with other protocols in terms of computational cost. Finally, a conclusion is brought in section 4.

2   The Proposed Protocol

2.1   Protocol Symbol Description

$< G, E, P, Q, q >$: G express the arithmetic multiplication bands finite cyclic group of prime q, E is elliptic curve on G, P is selected primitive, ensure that $nP = O$ minimum value of n is a large prime number,$P, Q \in E$;

X,Y,S: X and Y are both parties of the session key which shell be negotiated, S represents trusted server;

$pw_X, pw_Y, pw_X Q, pw_Y Q$: the former two denote respectively user password X,Y, and pw_X, pw_Y both selected from dictionary D; the latter two donate respectively password verified elements corresponding to the server-side;

t_1, t_2, x, y, r:random number from Z_q^* ;

$H_i : \{0,1\}^* \rightarrow \{0,1\}^{l_i}$:hash function, $i \in \{0,1,2\}$, A security parameter. H_1, H_2 For server authentication of X, Y (MAC). H_0 use negotiated Secret value to generate a session key;

2.2   Process of Implementation of the Protocol

Round 1:

Step 1 : $X \rightarrow S : X, Y$

   X send $< X, Y >$ to S, Request protocol began.

Step 2 : $S \rightarrow X : T_1^*, X, Y, S$

   S Selects a random value $t_1 \in Z_q^*$, calculate $T_1 = t_1 P$, using $pw_X Q$ encrypt T_1 for S authenticate X, obtained $T_1^*, T_1^* = pw_X Q$. Sending $< T_1^*, X, Y, S >$ to X

Step 3 :$S \rightarrow Y : T_2^*, X, Y, S$

   S Selects a random value $t_2 \in Z_q^*$, calculate $T_2 = t_2 P$, using $pw_Y Q$ encrypt T_2 for S authenticate Y, obtained $T_2^*, T_2^* = T_2 + pw_Y Q$. Sending T_2^*, X, Y, S to Y;

Round 2:

Step 4 :$X \rightarrow S : Auth_{1X}, U'$

   X Selects a random value $x \in Z_q^*$,calculate $U = xP$ Used to negotiate shared secret value, using pw_X decrypt T_1^* ,obtain T_1 ,calculate $K_1 = xT_1 = xt_1 P$ as the password for S authenticating X, using K_1, T_1, U, X, Y, S generating MAC $Auth_{1X} = H_1(X, Y, S, T_1, U, K_1)$,sending $< Auth_(1X), U' >$ to S

Step 5 : $Y \rightarrow S : Auth_{1Y}, V'$

   Y Selects a random value $y \in Z_q^*$,calculate $V = yP$ Used to negotiate shared secret value, using pw_Y decrypt T_2^* ,obtain T_2 ,calculate $K_2 = yT_2$ as the password for S authenticating Y, using K_2, T_2, V, X, Y, S generating MAC $Auth_{1Y} = H_1(X, Y, S, T_2, U, K_2)$,sending $< Auth_{1Y}, V' >$ to S.

Round 3:

Step 6 : $S \rightarrow X : Y^*, Auth_{2X}$

   S calculates $K_1 = t_1 U = t_1 xP$,obviously the key only X, S know seen by ECGDH difficult assumption, then can be used for the authentication of S to X. calculating $H_1(X, Y, S, T_1, U, K_1)$,if $Auth_{1X} \neq$

$H_1(X, Y, S, T_1, U, K_1)$,opponent is not X or the message has been tampered, S Terminate the protocolOtherwise, complete the authentication of X. Analogously, calculating $K_2 = t_2 V = t_2 y P$,obviously the key only Y, S know seen by ECGDH difficult assumption, then can be used for the authentication of S to Y. Calculating $H_1(X, Y, S, T_2, U, K_2)$,If $Auth_{1Y} \neq H_1(X, Y, S, T_2, U, K_2)$,opponent is not Y or the message has been tampered, S Terminate the protocolOtherwise, complete the authentication of Y. After finishing the authentication of X and Y,S Selects a random value $r \in Z_q^*$, calculating $X^* = rU$ Used to negotiate shared secret value, using K_1, Y^*, X, Y, S generating MAC $Auth_{2X} = H_2(X, Y, S, Y^*, K_1)$. Sending $< Y^*, Auth_{2X} >$ to X.

Step 7 : $S \rightarrow Y : X^*, Auth_{2Y}$

S Selects a random value $r \in Z_q^*$,calculating $Y^* = rV$ used to negotiate shared secret value, using K_2, X^*, X, Y, S generating MAC $Auth_{2Y} = H_2(X, Y, S, X^*, K_2)$,Sending $< X^*, Auth_{2r} >$ to Y.
X calculates $H_2(X, Y, S, Y^*, K_1)$,compared with the received $Auth_{2X}$,If not equal, opponent is not S or the message has been tampered, X Terminate the protocolOtherwise, complete the authentication of X to S. Then, X calculates shared secret value $cs = x \cdot Y^* = xryP$, using the shared secret value could calculate the Session key $sk = H_0(A, B, cs)$.
Y calculates $H_2(X, Y, S, X^*, K_2)$,compared with received $Auth_{2Y}$, If not equal, opponent is not S or the message has been tampered, Y Terminate the protocolOtherwise, complete the authentication of Y to S, Y calculates shared secret value $cs = y \cdot X^* = xryP$, using the shared secret value could calculate the Session key $sk = H_0(A, B, cs)$.

Now,X and Y have negotiated the shared session key sk.

2.3   Security Analysis

Now conducting special analysis of the security of the improved protocol in the environment of Server compromise attack, the Man-in-the-middle attack, offline password guessing attacks, online password guessing attacks:

(1)Resist server compromise attack:
Because the server does not store the user's password , but pwQ, even if the server leaks pwQ, know from ECGDHP, The attacker cannot calculate the user's password in polynomial time pw. So, the protocol can resist server compromise attack.
(2)Protocol achieved mutual authentication:
Because $T_1^* = T_1 + pw_X Q$,$T_2^* = T^2 + pw_Y Q$ and Y must use their own password to decrypt which encrypted by password verification meta sent separately to X, Y, respectively calculated once authenticated key K_1 and K_2 :Correspondingly, $Auth_{1X} = H_1(X, Y, S, T_1, U, K_1)$,$Auth_{1Y} = H_1(X, Y, S, T_2, V, K_2)$

calculated by S via K_1 and K_2 can achieve certification X and Y. In addition, by calculating $Auth_{2X} = H_2(X, Y, S, Y^*, K_1)$ and $Auth_{2X} = H_2(X, Y, S, Y^*, K_1)$,X and Y but also to realize the authentication of the server S. By certificating of S, X and Y are reasonable to believe the effectiveness of Y^* and X^* which sent from the trusted server.

(3) Resist to the Man-in-the-middle attack:

The man-in-the-middle attack in cryptography and computer security is a form of active eavesdropping in which the attacker makes independent connections with the victims and relays messages between them, making them believe that they are talking directly to each other over a private connection, when in fact the entire conversation is controlled by the attacker. However, the certification directly prevents such attacks. In such certification, MAC $Auth_{1X} = H_1(X, Y, S, T_1, U, K_1)$,$Auth_{1Y} = H_1(X, Y, S, T_2, V, K_2)$ provide the certification of X and Y to S, So can resist the Man-in-the-middle attack.

(4) Strong security of the session key:

Given $X^* = rU, Y^* = rV$ because have not found Polynomial algorithm which could solve ECGDH, and random number x, y, r are not given, attackers cannot get $cs = y \cdot X^* = xryP$ or $cs = x \cdot Y^* = xryP$ .The session key security is based on ECGDH, can be considered to be computationally infeasible.

(5) Resist to offline password guessing attacks:

Offline password guessing attack, the attacker to guess the password, then Offline confirmed their guess. In the protocol, because of the random number t_1 and t_2, no information can help directly confirmed the correctness of the guessed password. So the protocol can resist offline password guessing attacks.

(6) Resist to the imperceptible online guessing attacks:

In online guessing attacks, attackers try to confirm the correctness of the guessed password by the executing online protocol. In the protocol, S sends out $T_1^* = T_1 + pw_X Q$ and $T_2^* = T_2 + pw_Y Q$, and receives $Auth_{1X} = H_1(X, Y, S, T_1, U, K_1)$, $Auth_{1Y} = H_1(X, Y, S, T_2, V, K_2)$ from X and Y. So the server can realize the authentication of X and Y via calculating K_1 and K_2, checking $Auth_{1X} = H_1(X, Y, S, T_1, U, K_1)$, $Auth_{1Y} = H_1(X, Y, S, T_2, V, K_2)$. Obviously, when the attacker A guesses pw_X' as the password of X. If the guess failure, $pw_X' \neq pw_X$, A cannot be correctly decrypted T_1 , cannot correctly calculate the authentication key K_1 . By the collision of the hash function that A cannot certified through the S and will be perceived by S. The following will demonstrate the infeasibility of online attacks to the sever by Fig.1.

(7) Forward Security:

If long-term disclosure of secret value does not affect the previous session key, we say that a protocol has good forward security. In the protocol, because temporary multipliers x, y, r selected randomly, independent of the implementation of the protocol, the password leak cannot obtain negotiated session key. However, if a malicious attacker broken a weak passwords he will be able to successfully masquerade as the owner of the password to attack the system before the passwords owners aware.

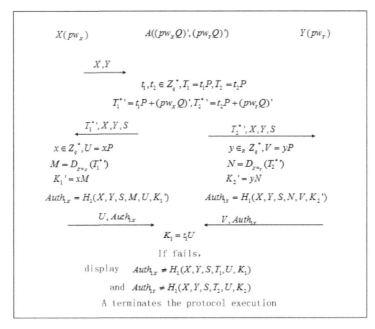

$X(pw_x)$ $\qquad$ $A((pw_xQ)',(pw_yQ)')$ $\qquad$ $Y(pw_r)$

$\xrightarrow{\quad X,Y \quad}$

$t_1,t_2 \in Z_q^*, T_1 = t_1P, T_2 = t_2P$

$T_1^{*\prime} = t_1P + (pw_xQ)', T_2^{*\prime} = t_2P + (pw_xQ)'$

$\xleftarrow{\quad T_1^{*\prime},X,Y,S \quad}$ $\qquad$ $\xrightarrow{\quad T_2^{*\prime},X,Y,S \quad}$

$x \in Z_q^*, U = xP$ $\qquad\qquad\qquad$ $y \in_R Z_q^*, V = yP$

$M = D_{pw_x}(T_1^{*\prime})$ $\qquad\qquad\quad$ $N = D_{pw_y}(T_2^{*\prime})$

$K_1{}' = xM$ $\qquad\qquad\qquad\qquad$ $K_2{}' = yN$

$Auth_{1x} = H_1(X,Y,S,M,U,K_1')$ $\quad$ $Auth_{1r} = H_1(X,Y,S,N,V,K_2')$

$\xrightarrow{\quad U,Auth_{1x} \quad}$ $\qquad\qquad$ $\xleftarrow{\quad V,Auth_{1r} \quad}$

$K_1 = t_1U$

If fails,

display $\quad Auth_{1x} \neq H_1(X,Y,S,T_1,U,K_1)$

and $\quad Auth_{1r} \neq H_1(X,Y,S,T_2,U,K_2)$

A terminates the protocol execution

Fig. 1. An example of online password guessing attacks

3   Performance Comparison

To the best of our knowledge, Lee[9] and Lin[10] proposed two similar 3PAKE protocols which is secure and more efficient than most of the previously ones. Here, the performance of our proposed protocol is compared with these two protocols in terms of computational cost. The detailed comparisons are shown in Table 1. In order to explain the computational cost, some notations and relationship are defined as below.

- T_{Exp}: time of modular exponentiation, $1T_{Exp} \approx 240T_{Mui}$.
- T_H: time of the Hash computation.
- T_{Xor}: time of the modular bit-XOR.

As shown in Table 1, our proposed scheme requires three modular exponentiations, three hash functions and one random number for both clients A and B, and three modular exponentiations, four hash functions, six modular multiplication computations, two XOR operations and three random numbers for the server S. However, in Lee and Hwangs proposal, there are four modular exponentiations, four hash functions, three modular multiplications, one XOR operation and one random number for both A and B, and four modular exponentiations, two hash functions, six modular multiplications, two XOR operations and four

Table 1. Comparisons between our protocol and [9],[10]

	[9]			[10]			Ours'		
Party	A	B	S	A	B	S	A	B	S
Exponentiation	$3T_{Exp}$	$3T_{Exp}$	T_{Exp}	$3T_{Exp}$	$3T_{Exp}$	$4T_{Exp}$	$1T_{Exp}$	$1T_{Exp}$	T_{Exp}
Hash function	$6T_H$	$6T_H$	$4T_H$	$7T_H$	$7T_H$	$8T_H$	$3T_H$	$3T_H$	$4T_H$
Multiplication	$3T_{Mul}$	$3T_{Mul}$	$6T_{Mul}$	0	0	0	$2T_{Mul}$	$2T_{Mul}$	$3T_{Mul}$
XOR operation	$1T_{Xor}$	$1T_{Xor}$	$2T_{Xor}$	$1T_{Xor}$	$1T_{Xor}$	$2T_{Xor}$	$1T_{Xor}$	$1T_{Xor}$	$2T_{Xor}$
Random number	1	1	2	1	1	2	1	1	2

random numbers for S. Its obvious that our proposed protocol has better performance than Lee and Hwangs proposal. Similarly, our proposals performance also prevails that of Ching-Ying Lins in terms of exponentiation, hash function and random number, as can be figured out from Table 1. Due to the low computational complexity our scheme may fit for the environment of wireless sensor networks.

4 Conclusions

We propose a novel 3PAKE protocol based on elliptic curve cryptography in this article. Our proposed scheme outperforms similar up-to-date 3PAKE protocols in terms of computational complexity. Therefore, we hope that our work will help specification designers build a secure and more efficient 3PAKE system for large-scale wireless sensor networks.

Acknowledgment. The subject is sponsored by the National Natural Science Foundation of P. R. China (No. 60973139, 61170065, 61171053, 61003039, 61003236, 61103195, 61202354), the Natural Science Foundation of Jiangsu Province(BK2011755), Scientific & Technological Support Project (Industry) of Jiangsu Province (No.BE2010197, BE2010198, BE2011844, BE2011189), Natural Science Key Fund for Colleges and Universities in Jiangsu Province (11KJA520001), Project sponsored by Jiangsu provincial research scheme of natural science for higher education institutions(10KJB520013, 11KJB520014, 11KJB520016, 12KJB520009), Scientific Research & Industry Promotion Project for Higher Education Institutions(JH2010-14, JHB2011-9), Postdoctoral Foundation (20100480048), Science & Technology Innovation Fund for higher education institutions of Jiangsu Province(CX10B-196Z, CX10B-200Z, CXZZ11-0405, CXZZ11-0406,CXZZ11-0409), Doctoral Fund of Ministry of Education of China(20103223120007, 20113223110002)and key Laboratory Foundation of Information Technology processing of Jiangsu Province(KJS1022), A Project Funded by the Priority Academic Program Development of Jiangsu Higher Education Institutions(PAPD) and Peak of Six Major Talent in Jiangsu Province(2010DZXX026)

References

1. Steiner, M., Tsudik, G., Waidner, M.: Refinement and extension of encrypted key exchange. ACM Operating Systems Review 29(3), 22–30 (1995)
2. Ding, Y., Horster, P.: Undetectable on-line password guessing attacks. ACM Operating Systems Review 29(4), 77–86 (1995)
3. Hamed, A.I., El-Khamy, S.E.: New Low Complexity Key Exchange and Encryption protocols for Wireless Sensor Networks Clusters based on Elliptic Curve Cryptography. In: 2009 National Radio Science Conference: NRSC 2009, vol. 1, 2, pp. 454–466 (2009)
4. Deng, M., Huang, Z., Lu, Z.: Authenticated key exchange protocol for medical sensor network. Huazhong Keji Daxue Xuebao (Ziran Kexue Ban)/Journal of Huazhong University of Science and Technology (Natural Science Edition) 38(8), 69–72 (2010)
5. Lee, T.F., Hwang, T., Lin, C.L.: Enhanced three-party encrypted key exchange without server's public keys. Computers and Security 23(7), 571–577 (2004)
6. Le Xuan, H., Lee, S., Lee, L.K.: A key-exchanging scheme for distributed sensor networks. In: Intelligence in Communication Systems, pp. 271–279 (2005)
7. Lu, R., Cao, Z.: Simple three-party key exchange protocol. Computers & Security 26(1), 94–97 (2007)
8. Chang, T.F.: A practical three-party key exchange protocol with round efficiency. International Journal of Innovative Computing, Information and Control 4(4), 953–960 (2008)
9. Lee, T., Hwang, T.: Simple password-based three-party authenticated key exchange without server public keys. Information Sciences 180(9), 1702–1714 (2010)
10. Lin, C., Hwang, T.: On a simple three-party password-based key exchange protocol. International Journal of Communication Systems 24(11), 1520–1532 (2011)
11. Tian, X., Wong, D.S., Zhu, R.W.: Analysis and improvement of an authenticated key exchange protocol for sensor networks. IEEE Communications Letters 9(11), 970–972 (2005)
12. Chang, T., Hwang, M., Yang, W.: A communication-efficient three-party password authenticated key exchange protocol. Information Sciences 181(1), 217–226 (2011)

TFA: A Scale-Free Network Approach to Topology Formation in Underwater Acoustic Sensor Networks

Linfeng Liu*, Ningshen Zhang, Fu Xiao, and Ruchuan Wang

Nanjing University of Posts and Telecommunications School of Computer,
Nanjing, China
liulinfeng@gmail.com
http://www.springer.com/lncs

Abstract. Underwater sensor networks will find many underwater applications in near future, and the topology formation problem in 3D sensor networks has not been paid enough attention at present. In order to maximize the network lifetime and shorten the propagation delay, a topology formation algorithm (TFA) for underwater sensor networks is proposed. TFA is based on a scale-free network approach (GLP model), and the generated topology has minor average path length and clustering coefficient, where node degree follows power law distribution as well. The simulation results suggest TFA can extend the UWSN lifetime and shorten propagation delay effectively.

Keywords: Underwater acoustic sensor networks, topology formation, scale-free network, propagation delay.

1 Introduction

Before the emergence of wireless sensor networks (WSNs) [1], the perception and collection of underwater data are generally accomplished through wired networks, which are very expensive and inconvenient. Underwater wireless acoustic sensor networks (UWSNs) [2] are the enabling technology for various underwater applications, and interest in UWSNs is growing interests. There are plenty of applications in underwater environments such as ocean resource exploration, pollution monitoring, and tactical surveillance. UWSNs consist of underwater sensors (anchored nodes and surface sinks) that perform collaborative monitoring tasks over a 3D space. Acoustic communications are the typical physical layer technology in underwater networks. Anchored nodes are equipped with floating buoys that are inflated by pumps. The depth of the anchored node is regulated by adjusting the length of the wire. The given phenomenon is observed by anchored nodes in charge of relaying data to surface sinks, which illustrates a 3D mobile UWSN. The measurements of environmental events are monitored by anchored nodes locally, and transferred to one of surface sinks by multi-hops.

---

* Corresponding author.

R. Wang and F. Xiao (Eds.): CWSN 2012, CCIS 334, pp. 271–279, 2013.
© Springer-Verlag Berlin Heidelberg 2013

Ultimately, the measurements are aggregated at a LEO satellite from all surface sinks for future processing. Due to the specificity and complexity of the water medium, UWSN and terrestrial wireless sensor networks are significantly different. The most distinct feature is the propagation delay because acoustic wave is much slower than that of the electromagnetic wave. Consequently, the propagation delay in UWSN cannot be neglected.

Network topology, as the important foundation of upper layer protocols, not only improves the performance of routing protocols and MAC protocols, which is the main objective of WSN, but also serves as the supportive groundwork for implementation techniques in synchronization, data aggregation and object localization. Hierarchical topology formation [4] is also suitable for the management of large scale UWSN. In order to save energy, a well-constructed topology backbone should be formed and the communication modules of non-backbone nodes should be shuttled down when idle. In the literature, UWSN lifetime [5] has often been defined as the time for the first node to die in the course of routing due to battery exhaustion. Scale-free network theory [6,7] is suitable for the hierarchical topology formation of UWSN, because the node degree follows the power law distribution.

2   Related Work

The problem of topology control for WSN has been extensively studied. Li et al. [8] proposed an MST-based topology control algorithm (LMST) that can effectively reduce transmission power while maintaining global connectivity. However, the topology obtained by LMST was fragile, and network lifetime was prone to termination. In a study by Li et al. [9], the topology control problem in heterogeneous ad hoc networks was formulated as an integer linear or a mixed integer linear programming problem. The study produced a network topology that minimized the maximum energy utilization of nodes. To maximize network life and ensure message delivery, a topology control algorithm EBC, which exploited the edge of the centrality concept, was proposed [10]. Forghani et al. [11] improved network life and decreased average energy consumption by reducing the transmission power of nodes and periodically choosing the active path. However, the approach ignored the extra overhead brought by the periodic regulation of active paths. Several topology control algorithms for UWSNs have been proposed by combining the characteristics of acoustic communication and underwater environments. A topology control algorithm FiYG designed for 3D UWSNs was proposed by Wang et al. [12], where it was proven that topology could be constructed locally and efficiently. In [13], Nazrul and Hass investigated the lifetime issue in 3D UWSNs and suggested that partitioning space into truncated octahedron shaped clusters can maximize the lifetime while maintaining full coverage. The result of Ref. [14] suggests truncated octahedron turned out to be the best choice, having the largest volumetric quotient of 0.68329 and the least active nodes, whereas the communication radius was required at least 1.7889 times the pre-determined sensing radius.

3   Problem Setting

Our work is based the scenario that a set of static sensor nodes in a special 3D underwater space: nodes carrying batteries of limited energy can obtain interest data, and forward for the neighbors in their communication range as well. Data aggregation and the signal interference of the MAC layer are ignored in this paper.

3.1   UWSN Model and Definitions

Suppose that a set of sinks are deployed on a horizontal plane of water, and plenty of anchored sensors are evenly deployed in underwater convex space $D \in IR^3$, whose volume is $L \times W \times H$.

Some cluster-heads should be selected from all sensors to construct a topology backbone, the non-cluster-heads monitor events periodically and turn off radio when idle. The topology of UWSNs can be represented as a graph $G(V,E)$, where V is the finite set of nodes. The set of surface sinks denotes as S. Static positions of nodes are known, whereas the positions after movement are unknown. Connectivity function is defined as connectivity(G).

1) Nodes: For any node(the kth node), its current communication radius, degree and residual energy are denoted as $RC(k)$, $deg(k)$ and $e(k)$, respectively. Any node can be in two kinds of status: *awake* or *asleep*. If the kth node is asleep, then $RC(k)=0$. We define the neighboring nodes set of Vk as $ne(k)$. The maximum communication radius is denoted by RC_χ.

2) Links: The link between Vk and Vk' is expressed as (k,k'). The propagation delay of (k,k') is denoted as $delay(k,k')$.

3) Average paths: Average path length is denoted as APL.

4) Consumption: $con(k)$ is defined as

$$con(k) = P_0 \cdot RC(k)^\beta \cdot 10^{RC(k) \cdot \alpha(f)/10} . \tag{1}$$

where P_0 is the least received power level to guarantee the required quality of reception [15], [16]. The energy spreading factor and absorption coefficient are denoted by $\beta(\beta \in [1,2])$, $\alpha(f)$, respectively.

5) Propagation delay: $delay(i,j)$ [17] is defined as

$$delay(i,j) = \frac{L}{B} + \frac{d(i,j)}{R_{uw}} . \tag{2}$$

where L is the length of every data packet, B is the channel capacity in bits per second, and R_{uw} is the propagation speed of underwater sound.

3.2   Assumptions

1) Sensor nodes are uniformly distributed in D, and the coordinates of every node have been informed.

2) If $V_k \in \mathbf{V}$, $RC(k)$ is the maximum range, therefore, $G(V,E)$ satisfies global connectivity.

3) The ordinary node can only communicate with the cluster-head to which it belongs, and the cluster-head can only communicate with the neighboring cluster-heads or the ordinary nodes in its own cluster.

3.3   Formal Objectives

1) $\mathbf{connectivity}(G)=1$;

2) $\min \sum_{V_k \in \mathbf{V}} con(k)$;

3) $\min \sum \sum delay(i,j)$.

Our early work [18] has proven that energy consumption will reduce under the topology with minor average path length (APL) and clustering coefficient. One has

$$\sum \sum delay(i,j) = \sum \sum \frac{L}{B} + \frac{d(i,j)}{R_{uw}} = \sum \sum \frac{L}{B} + \binom{n}{k} \cdot \frac{APL}{R_{uw}}. \qquad (3)$$

According to the formula (3), average path length is proportional to propagation delay approximately. Therefore, minor average path length will make short delay as well. The average path length is computed as

$$APL = \frac{1}{NM} \cdot \sum_{i \in \mathbf{V}, j \in \mathbf{S}} L_{ij} \qquad (4)$$

where L_{ij} denotes the shortest path length from sensor V_i to sink S_j. L_{ij} is expressed as follows

$$L_{ij} = \begin{cases} \sqrt{(x_i - x_j)^2 + (y_i - y_j)^2 + (h_i - h_j)^2} & \text{if } RC_\chi \gg \sqrt[3]{\frac{D}{N}} \\ |x_i - x_j| + |y_i - y_j| + |h_i - h_j| & \text{else} \end{cases} \qquad (5)$$

Thus, APL should be in the following value range

$$\sqrt{\frac{L^2}{12} + \frac{W^2}{12} + \frac{H^2}{3}} \le APL \le \frac{L + W + H}{2} \qquad (6)$$

4   Topology Formation Algorithm

GLP (Generalized Linear Preference) model [19] was proposed in 2002. It has been proved that GLP can generate a scale-free network with minor average path length and clustering coefficient. In this paper, we put forward a topology formation algorithm TFA, which is based on scale-free network approach. The following are the description and analysis of TFA algorithm.

Step 1. n_0 nodes (including the sink) will be selected and n_0-1 links will be added to maintain connectivity among these nodes. The n_0 nodes form set S.
Step 2. At the subsequent steps, one of the sub-steps will be operated randomly:
Sub-Step 2.1 $n(n \leq n_0)$ links are added with probability p_1. Node V_k is selected as the end of every link with probability $\Pi(deg(k))$, which can be expressed as

$$\Pi(deg(k)) = \frac{(deg(k) - \gamma)}{\sum(deg(i) - \gamma)} \tag{7}$$

where $\gamma \in (-\infty, 1)$, $p_1 \in [0, 1]$.
Sub-Step 2.2 With probability $(1 - p_1)$ a new node V_k is chosen and added into S according to formula (8).

$$P(V_k) = \frac{\frac{1}{\sum d(k,j)}}{\sum \frac{1}{\sum d(i,j)}} \tag{8}$$

where $P(V_k)$ denotes the selection probability of V_k. n links of the selected V_k should be added, and the other ends of these links are presented from formula (7).
Step 3. Repeat Step 2 until all nodes have been added into S. Step 4. n_1 cluster-heads are decided by formula (9).

$$P_C(V_k) = \frac{deg(k)}{\sum deg(i)} \tag{9}$$

where $P_C(V_k)$ denotes the probability of V_k becoming a cluster-head. Step 5. Every ordinary node determines their nearest cluster-head by signal strength. The time complexity of every step is shown in Table 1. If the accomplishment of Step 3 requires that all possible links must be added, then the worst complexity of TFA will be $O(N^2)$. Therefore, TFA has polynomial complexity.

Table 1. TFA Complexity

Step	Time Complexity
1	n_0
2.1	$n \cdot p_1$
2.2	$n \cdot (1 - p_1)$
3	N
4	n_1
5	$N - n_1$

5 Simulations

TFA is evaluated by observing the performance variation when adopting different model parameters and by comparing SAA with other algorithms. TFA is realized in OMNeT++. MAC Layer is outside the scope of this paper. The IEEE 802.15.4 is adopted for MAC, and the routing is FA [21]. The simulation environment is set as N-1 nodes evenly distributed in D, with one sink node selected randomly at the horizontal plane. Moreover, node mobility, delay from calculation, and energy consumption by receiving messages are neglected in simulations. Suppose the maximum communication radius is 30m, generated rate of data flow is 8 kbps, and energy consumption of monitoring is 0.1J. The values of other parameters are shown in Table 2.

Table 2. Simulation Parameters

Parameters	Value
N	2000
$|D|$	$100m \times 500m \times 200m$
E_0	$8000J$
β	1.5
$\alpha(f)$	$2 \times 10^{-3}dB/km$
L	50B
B	10kbps
R_{uw}	1500m/s
P_0	0.07
n	2
p_1	0.5
γ	0.6

5.1   Influence of v

UWSN lifetime variation with N exhibits five plots shown in Fig. 1. Shorter UWSN lifetime will be obtained with higher values of v. This because that the increase of v makes the traffic load become heavier. The lifetime has irregular fluctuation as N increases when v is determined. The phenomenon suggests the energy consumption may vary with deployment density even though generated rate of data flow is fixed.

5.2   Influence of *listen_cost*

From Fig. 2, UWSN lifetime gradually reduces as *listen_cost* increases. Furthermore, the plots *listen_cost*=0.12 and *listen_cost*=0.14 are very close, because the influence of monitoring consumption will be significantly weaken when *listen_cost* is large enough.

5.3   Comparison with Other Algorithms

This simulation compares UWSN lifetime and propagation delay in TFA, LEACH, FiYG and GAF. As shown in Fig. 3, TFA lifetime is apparently higher than those of LEACH, FiYG and GAF, which is attributed to the fact that TFA is more concerned about energy consumption. The differences of plots become more obvious

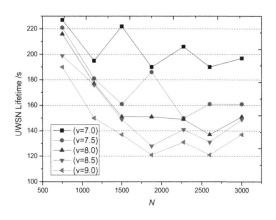

Fig. 1. Influence of v on the UWSN lifetime

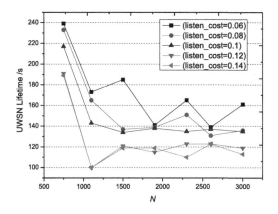

Fig. 2. Influence of *listen_cost* on the UWSN lifetime

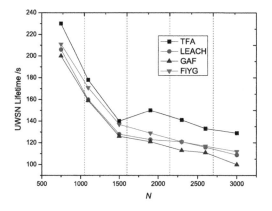

Fig. 3. Comparison of UWSN lifetime

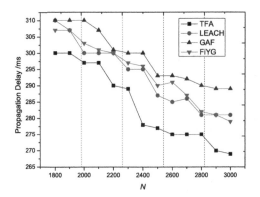

Fig. 4. Comparison of UWSN delay

as the increase of N, and the lifetime gap of TFA and GAF reaches 30.1s when N=3000. In Fig. 4, every plot decreases with the increase of N, and TFA gets the shortest propagation delay, because the topology generated has taken into account the average path length.

6   Conclusions

Aiming at the particularity of water medium and underwater acoustic communication, the topology formation problem was studied in this paper, and an algorithm TFA of scale-free network approach was designed accordingly. The topology exhibiting some favorable characteristics (such as power law distribution, minor average path length and minor clustering coefficient) is formed based on GLP model. The delay can be shortened and the lifetime can be prolonged by TFA. However, the UWSN model in this paper is idealistic, i.e., it prohibits node mobility, and delays from calculation, energy consumption by receiving messages are neglected. Furthermore, the communication range of nodes is irregular rather than spheres. Addressing the problem of topology formation in more real environments or scenarios is suggested for further study.

Acknowledgments. This research is supported by Open Research Fund from Key Laboratory of Computer Network and Information Integration in Southeast University, Ministry of Education, China, under Grant No. K93-9-2010-12, K93-9-2010-13; National Natural Science Foundation of China under Grants Nos. 60903181, 60973139, 61003236, 61003040; Postdoctoral Science Foundation of China under Grant No. 20100481168; Natural Science Foundation of Jiangsu Province under Grant no. BK2012833; Natural Science Foundation of Jiangsu Higher Education under Grant no. 12KJB520011.

References

1. Elson, J., Estrin, D.: Sensor Networks: a Bridge to the Physical World, pp. 3–20. Kluwer Academic Publishers, Norwell (2004)
2. Akyildiz, I.-F., Pompili, D., Melodia, T.: Underwater acoustic sensor networks: research challenges. Ad Hoc Networks 3(3), 257–279 (2005)
3. Jawhar, I., Mohamed, N., Agrawal, D.-P.: Linear Wireless Sensor Networks: Classification and Applications. Journal of Network and Computer Applications 34(5), 1671–1682 (2011)
4. Yun, Y.-S., Ye, X.: Maximizing the lifetime of wireless sensor networks with mobile sink in delay-tolerant applications. IEEE Transactions on Mobile Computing 9(9), 1308–1318 (2010)
5. Barabási, A.-L., Bonabea, E.: Scale-free networks. Scientific American 5, 50–59 (2003)
6. Bianconi, G., Barabási, A.-L.: Bose-Einstein condensation in complex networks. Physical Review Letters 24(86), 5632–5635 (2001)
7. Li, N., Hou, J.-C., Sha, L.: Design and analysis of an MST-based topology control algorithm. In: Proc. of Twenty-Second Annual Joint Conference of the IEEE Computer and Communications Societies, INFORCOM 2003, pp. 1702–1712. IEEE Press, San Francisco (2003)
8. Li, D.-Y., Jia, X.-H., Du, H.-W.: QoS topology control for nonhomogenous ad hoc wireless networks. EURASIP Journal on Wireless Communications and Networking (2), 1–10 (2006)
9. Cuzzocrea, A., Katsaros, D., Manolopoulos, Y., Papadimitriou, A.: EBC: A Topology Control Algorithm for Achieving High QoS in Sensor Networks. In: Bartolini, N., Nikoletseas, S., Sinha, P., Cardellini, V., Mahanti, A. (eds.) QShine/AAA-IDEA 2009. LNICST, vol. 22, pp. 613–626. Springer, Heidelberg (2009)
10. Forghani, A., Rahmani, A.-M., Khademzadeh, A.: QCTC: QoS-based clustering topology control algorithm for wireless sensor networks. In: Proc. of International Conference on Advanced Computer Theory and Engineering 2008, pp. 966–970. IEEE Press, Phuket (2008)
11. Wang, Y., Li, F., Dahlberg, T.-A.: Energy-efficient topology control for three-dimensional sensor networks. International Journal of Sensor Networks 4(1), 68–78 (2008)
12. Nazrul, S.M., Hass, Z.: Topology control and network lifetime in three-dimensional wireless sensor networks, http://arxiv.org/abs/cs.NI/0609047
13. Nazrul, S.M., Hass, Z.: Coverage and connectivity in three-dimensional networks. In: Proc. of ACM MobiCom 2006 (2006)
14. Sozer, E., Stojanovic, M., Proakis, J.: Underwater Acoustic Networks. IEEE Journal of Oceanic Engineering 25(1), 72–83 (2000)
15. Berkhovskikh, L., Lysanov, Y.: Fundamentals of Ocean Acoustics, 3rd edn. Springer, New York (2003)
16. Ibrahim, S., Cui, J.-H., Ammar, R.: Surface-level gateway deployment for underwater sensor networks. In: Proc. of Military Communications Conference 2007, pp. 1–7. IEEE Press, San Francisco (2007)
17. Liu, L.-F., Wu, J.-G., Xiao, F.: CFM: A Fitness-Model-Based Topology Control Algorithm for Wireless Sensor Networks. Sensor Letters (10), 1–4 (2012)
18. Bu, T., Towsley, D.: On distinguishing between Internet power law topology generators. In: Proc. of the IEEE INFOCOM 2002, vol. (2), pp. 638–647. IEEE, New York (2002)
19. Chang, J.-H., Tassiulas, L.: Energy conserving routing in wireless ad-hoc networks. In: Proc. of IEEE INFOCOM, pp. 22–31. IEEE Press, Tel Aviv (2000)

Full-View Coverage Algorithm in Camera Sensor Networks with Random Deployment

Wenyuan Liu, Juanjuan Liu, Lin Wang, and Yali Si

School of Information Science and Engineering, Yanshan University,
066004 Qinhuangdao, China
liujuanjuan996@126.com

Abstract. The full-view coverage ensures that the positive images of targets are obtained. In existing works, the topics only focus on whether a region is full-view covered or not, which needs too many nodes, and is less flexible for the change of surveillance environment. Therefore, full-view coverage for the targets is highlighted in this paper. Firstly, we derive the optimal observation angle between the sensing direction of nodes and the vector of target surface. We also prove that the full-view coverage is a NPC problem. Then the centralized and the distributed algorithms are proposed to maximize the number of full-view covered targets by scheduling the sensing directions of some sensors in the network. Simulation results show that local adjusting of the directional nodes will increase the full-view coverage for the global monitored objects in the condition of random deployment.

Keywords: Coverage, surveillance, greedy algorithm, directional sensor network, sensor network.

1   Introduction

Convergence of technology and application trends have resulted in exceptional levels of interest in wireless sensor networks (WSNs). Coverage is one of the basic problems of WSNs, which has answered the questions about quality of service, such as interest area or target point can be covered or the intrusion can be detected effectively. Optimizing the sensor network coverage is very important for rational allocation of space resources, better information acquisition, and extending the network lifework.

Most of the prior works have addressed the sensor coverage problem based on omni-directional sensors. The objective is to maximize coverage rate [1], duty-cycle mechanism to save energy [2], to optimize both coverage and connectivity [4] or tradeoff between some aspects of above. Recent years, with a combination of multimedia sensors and wireless network technology, the contradiction between the offset angles and coverage have become increasingly prominent.

In this article, we address the coverage problem in camera sensor network. Camera sensor has an inherent feature that one may generate very different views of the same object if they are from different viewpoints. However, the object is

R. Wang and F. Xiao (Eds.): CWSN 2012, CCIS 334, pp. 280–290, 2013.
© Springer-Verlag Berlin Heidelberg 2013

more likely to be recognized by computer vision system if the image is captured at or near the frontal viewpoint. In order to meet this special requirement of such application, the definition of full-view coverage is introduced in [15]. An object is full-view covered if there is always a camera covering it no matter which direction it faces and the cameras viewing direction is sufficiently close to the objects facing direction. Based on the model of full-view coverage, real-time positive image of the target can be obtained, but without coverage optimization it needs to deploy a large number of nodes, which inevitably leads to waste of resources with random deployment.

To deal with the problem, we present a method to full-view cover objects based on a rotating directional sensing model in camera sensor network. Our goal is adjusting the direction of sensor to guarantee target full-view covered as much as possible. First an important parameter is derived, which donates the lower bound of the angle between sensing direction and the target surface vector. Then we prove that the full-view coverage in camera sensor network of N nodes and M targets with random deployment is a NPC problem. Basis on this, the centralized and the distributed greedy algorithms are proposed, which maximize the targets of full-view coverage by scheduling the working directions of some camera sensors in the network. After Adjustment of camera sensor, it is much easier to obtain positive image for computer vision system, so that it laid the foundation of a variety of real-time applications.

This article is organized as follows. In Section 2, related works are reviewed. Notation and model are introduced, especially θ in Section 3. Section 4 shows that full-view coverage algorithm. In Section 5, a series of simulation experiments verify the effectiveness of the algorithm. Section 6 concludes the paper.

2 Related Works

The tradeoff between sensor coverage and network lifetime has been studied mainly in WSNs literature [1, 2]. With the combination of multimedia sensors and wireless communication technology in recent years, coverage in directional sensor network caused a lot of attention. Lots of research results emerged [3, 4].

Some works study coverage for region. Ma et al modeled first the directional sensor nodes as a sector of 4-tuple (P, r, v, β). Then a deployment strategy for satisfying given coverage probability and connectivity requirements is designed [5]. On this basis, Tao et al proposed an enhancement algorithm based on a direction adjustable sensing model. The concept of convex hull is introduced to model each sensing connected sub-graph in order to minimize the overlapping sensing area of sensors only with local topology information [6]. After then, a potential field based coverage-enhancing algorithm is presented [7]. Motivated by the traditional virtual potential fields local minimum may lead to path coverage-enhancing failure, Xiao et al designed an improved potential field function considering the joint coverage rate of adjacent sensor nodes to achieve path coverage-enhancing efficiently [8].

However, the extensive interests also concentrate on selecting a minimum number of sensors and assigning orientations such that the given target points is covered. Two closely related resolutions to the problem are integer linear programming problem [9, 10] and maximum coverage set problem [11–13]. Taking the network lifework into account, the authors designed some heuristic algorithm and greedy algorithm to avoid excessive consumption of a single node preventing network from failure. Beside, the delay because of the node density is considered by Wang et al [14]. However, the above literatures are concentrated on the coverage rate, without consider the relative position between the node and the monitoring targets for improving quality of coverage.

Meanwhile Wang et al first proposed the concept of full-view coverage, which brings new inspiration to the sensor network coverage. An object located in full-view coverage region always can be observed as a better positive image no matter which direction it faces [15]. However, the density of nodes needs too large and absence of inflexibility in [15]. Motivated by this fault, we will design scheme that adjusting sensing direction of nodes equipped with a video sensor nodes on a rotating platform, so as to achieve the goal of full-view coverage in camera sensor networks with random deployment. This is a very significant problem.

3   Definitions and Symbols

N camera sensors with random uniform Poisson distribution are deployed in the 2-dimensional region Ω. M monitoring objects can appear anywhere in the surveillance area. S_i donates the i-th node, P_j donates the j-th target, f_i is the vector of target surface.

For simplicity, we make the following assumptions for camera sensor networks: 1) All nodes are the same structure in the network. 2) The node position is known and fixed after deployed. 3) Communication radius R is 2 times the sensing radius r. 4) In order to eliminate the boundary impact, nodes deployed area is slightly larger than the range of targets distributing. If the targets distribute in Ω, nodes deployment range is $\Omega + r$, where r is sensing radius. When Ω is large, r can be neglected.

3.1   Sensing Model

The sensing area of a sensor S_i is a sector denoted by 4-tuple $< D(x_i,y_i)$, r, v_i, $\beta >$. Here $D(x_i,y_i)$ is coordinate of node S_i on plane Ω, v_i is the center line of

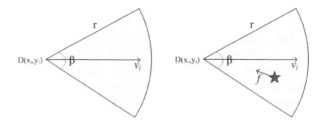

Fig. 1. (a) directional sense model (b) efficient coverage

sight of the camera sensing direction, β is the offset angle. Figure 1(a) illustrates the directional sensing model. Assuming that the sensor sensing model is the Boolean type, an object falling into the sensing region can be covered by the node, whose sensed probability is 1, otherwise, the value is 0.

Definition 1. (Effective Coverage) A target P_j is effective covered if P_j locates in the sensing area of node S_i. The angle between node sensing direction v_i and target surface vector f_j is greater than θ, as shown in Figure 1(b).

3.2   Full-View Coverage

Definition 2. (Full-View Coverage) A target P_j is said to be full-view covered if for any facing direction vector f_j, there always exists a sensor S_i, such that P_j is effective covered by S_i, shown in Figure 2(a).

Property 1. If the target P is full-view covered, to its position as the center, r is the radius of the circle, any two adjacent sensor nodes sensing direction of the number of folder angle not greater than δ, $\delta = 2(\pi - \theta)$. Shown in Fig.2(b).

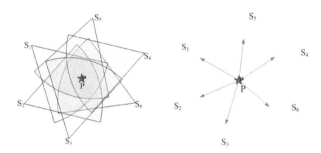

Fig. 2. (a)Full-view coverage (b)Angle between directions of neighbors

3.3 θ

The greater θ is, the finer monitoring granularity is, the higher probability to get a positive image is, the more service nodes need. However, the number of nodes is restricted according to the actual situation. Relationship between θ and $\alpha(f, v)$ for any targets:

$$\pi \geq \alpha(f, v) \geq \theta . \tag{1}$$

Suppose there are n nodes around target P, by the property 1 of full-view coverage:

$$\begin{cases} \alpha(v_i, v_j) \leq 2(\pi - \theta) \\ n\alpha(v_i, v_j) \geq 2\pi \end{cases} \tag{2}$$

Where n is 1, 2, ... Relationship between θ and n according to (1) and (2):

$$\theta \leq \frac{n-1}{n}\pi \tag{3}$$

When $n = 1$, $\theta = 0$, the target can be covered only by one node. When n is infinite, $\theta = \pi$, indicating that an infinite number of sensors are needed. When θ between 0 to π, the number of sensors has certain law, such as when $\theta = \pi/2$, at least 2 sensor nodes; $\theta = 2\pi/3$, at least 3 sensor nodes, and so on. We calculate the probability about at least n nodes per unit area with random deployment in the following context. Suppose the nodes obey the uniform random Poisson distribution, the unit area A is πr^2, λ is the density of nodes in the region, $\lambda = N/\Omega$, the distribution formula is

$$P(X = k) = \frac{(N\pi r^2/\Omega)^k}{k!}e^{-(N\pi r^2/\Omega)} \tag{4}$$

Because $\sum_{k=0}^{\infty}P\{X = k\} = 1$, the probability of more than n nodes in A is $P(X > n) = 1 - \sum_{k=0}^{n}P\{X = k\}$. For example, requiring the probability of 2 or more nodes per unit area is $P(X > 2) = 1 - P(X = 0) - P(X = 1) - P(X = 2)$. Suppose we requires at least half of the targets to achieve full-view coverage no less than θ in this article, we can determine n from equation (3) where $P(X > n) \geq 0.5$.

4   Full-View Coverage Algorithm

The node sensing directions usually random distribute in camera sensor network, so the targets can hardly achieve full coverage not less than θ. We need some coverage control algorithm scheduling node to complete the target of full-view coverage.

4.1   Full-View Coverage Is a NPC Problem

Theorem 1. Given a set of N nodes with fixed positions and M target points, assign their sensing direction, such that as much as possible target points are full-view covered. This assignment is a NPC problem.

Proof: We prove it as shown below using a reduction from 3-SAT problem.

Given a CNF paradigm A on a set of variables $X = \{x_1, x_2, ..., x_m\}$, where $A = C_1 \wedge C_2 \wedge ... \wedge C_i \wedge ... C_n$, C_i is 3-variable clause, each variable can be assigned 0 or 1, determine whether there is an assignment t, so that A is satisfied. This is 3-SAT problem, which plays an important role in the NPC problem tree. In full-view coverage issues, we create a target point for each clause, a node for each variable, the variable value is assigned 1 or 0 depends on whether coverage of the target in right spot. All targets are full-view covered equivalent to each clause value is 1. If A is satisfied, full-view coverage with $\theta = 2\pi/3$ is realized. It is easy to see that the above reduction is a valid Karp-reduction from 3-SAT to our decision problem. Thus, the assignment of full-view coverage is NPC. The theorem is proved.

Algorithm 1. Centralized Full-View Coverage (CFV)

1: Nodes rotate 360° to record the targets covered and pass the information to the base station
2: Divide nodes into M groups $\{T_1, T_2, , T_M\}$
3: Count group T_j numbers $\omega(P_i)$, the largest one donates W
4: **for** i to M **do**
5:     $\max U \leftarrow 0; Set_i \leftarrow \phi;$
6:     **for** S_j in T_i **do**
7:         Calculate $U_{j,i};$
8:         **if** $U_{j,i} > \max U$ **then**
9:             $\max U \leftarrow U_{j,i}; S \leftarrow S_j;$
10:             A=1;
11:         **end if**
12:     **end for**
13:     $v \leftarrow \overrightarrow{SP}$, remove from the groups;
14: **end for**(i)
15: **for** $\omega = 1$ to W **do**
16:     **for** i=1 to M **do**
17:         **for** S_j in T_i **do**
18:             **if** v_j make angle get smaller in $group_i$ **then**
19:                 Repeat 12; break;
20:             **end if**
21:         **end for**
22:     **end for**(i)
23: **end for**(ω)

4.2 Centralized Full-View Coverage Algorithm

In this section, we present a centralized full-view coverage algorithm. The basic idea of algorithm is to run round by round and gradually assigns the node directions according to target, so as to the biggest angle between neighbors serving target get smaller. Before algorithm introduction, we define a conceptthe Utility of node.

Definition 3: (the Utility of Node) Utility of node for target P_k is the ratio of angle between sensing direction of S_i and S_{il} and sensing direction of S_i and S_{ir} within r and 4π. The S_{il} is counterclockwise adjacent nodes of S_i, and S_{ir} is clockwise adjacent node of S_i. The formula is:

$$U(S_i, P_k) = \frac{\alpha(\overrightarrow{P_k S_i}, \overrightarrow{P_k S_{il}}) + \alpha(\overrightarrow{P_k S_i}, \overrightarrow{P_k S_{ir}})}{4\pi} \tag{5}$$

where

$$\alpha(\overrightarrow{P_k S_i}, \overrightarrow{P_k S_{il}}) = \arccos \frac{||P_k S_i||^2 + ||P_k S_{il}||^2 - ||S_i S_{il}||^2}{2||P_k S_i|| . ||P_k S_{il}||}$$

$$\alpha(\overrightarrow{P_k S_i}, \overrightarrow{P_k S_{ir}}) = \arccos \frac{||P_k S_i||^2 + ||P_k S_{ir}||^2 - ||S_i S_{ir}||^2}{2||P_k S_i|| . ||P_k S_{ir}||}$$

During initialization, each node rotates 360° to find the targets covered sometimes, and then passes the information to the base station. According to various targets can be covered, base station divides nodes into M service group $\{T_1, T_2, ..., T_M\}$. Group members count for $\omega(P_i)$, which of the maximum recorded is W, and W is also the largest number of algorithm running round.

In the first round, every node calculates the utility. Each group confirms sensing direction for the node of largest utility. After the first round, the node removes from the group includes it. When all targets are selected, the second round of algorithm starts. The node calculates angle between neighbors sensing direction and targets to firm whether is less than the current biggest angle of the neighbor. If yes, the node determines its sensing direction, otherwise make no decision. If there is a node can also cover two or more targets, give a priority to this direction. After decision, the node is removed from associated groups. When all group members are 0 or all group members do not satisfy the condition to choose, the algorithm stops. Detailed description of the algorithm is shown as below.

4.3 Distributed Full-View Coverage Algorithm

Due to the difficulty of collecting global information, communication overhead and scalability in large scale sensor networks, a distributed greedy algorithm is proposed in this section, which makes decision only depend on the local neighbors message to achieve full-view coverage.

Theorem 2. The nodes covering the same target must be neighbors within 1-hop.

Proof: S_i, S_j is any two nodes that can cover target P_k, $||P_k S_i|| \leq r$, $||P_k S_j|| \leq r$, so $||P_k S_i|| + ||P_k S_j|| \leq 2r$. Triangle on both sides is greater than the third side, so $||P_k S_i|| + ||P_k S_j|| \geq ||S_i S_j||$, the communication radius R is 2 times of the sensing radius r, $R = 2r$, so the node distance $||S_i S_j|| \leq ||P_k S_i|| + ||P_k S_j|| \leq 2r \leq R$. The theorem is proved.

Theorem 2 shows that coverage information of targets can be obtained to make the right decisions according to message from 1-hop neighbors.

During initialization, each node records the targets covered, and then exchange the information among neighbors. After receiving this information, nodes can confirm the node sensing direction mapping table locally. According to various targets can be covered, nodes are divided into M service group $\{T_1, T_2, ..., T_M\}$.

In the first round, every node calculates the utility and exchanges this information within group. In each group the node of largest utility confirms its sensing direction. Then the node broadcasts the decision to the neighbors in groups. Once receiving information, neighbors update the targets and nodes mapping table. When the first round finished, the node removes from groups including it.

After then, nodes make decision by local targets and nodes mapping table. If angle between neighbors sensing direction and targets is less than the current biggest angle of neighbors, assign its sensing direction. After decision, the node broadcasts to the neighbors in groups and removes itself from associated groups.

Algorithm 2. Distributed Full-View Algorithm(DFV)

Initialization:
1: Nodes rotate to record the targets covered, exchange information and confirm the map between node sensing direction and targets;
2: Divide nodes into M groups $\{T_1, T_2, , T_M\}$
3: Count group T_j numbers $\omega(P_i)$
4: **for** i = 1 to M **do**
5:    $\max U \leftarrow 0$; $Set_i \leftarrow \phi$;
6:    **for all** T_i **do**
7:        Find $maxU_{ji}$, Orienting direction v_i is $\overrightarrow{SP}$, remove from the groups;
8:        Broadcast to all $S_i's$ neighbors;
9:    **end for**
10: **end for**(i)
On receiving a message from neighbor S_j
11: Update the target and node mapping table;
12: **for** S_j in T_i **do**
13:    **if** v_j make angle get smaller in $group_i$ **then**
14:        Repeat 7, 8;break;
15:    **end if**
16: **end for**

When all group members are 0 or all group members do not satisfy the condition to choose, the algorithm stops. Detailed description of the algorithm is shown as below.

5   Experiment and Analysis

In this section, through a set of simulation experimental results, we discuss how the parameters influence on the performance of full-view coverage algorithm. All experiments are implemented on MATLAB7.10. Nodes are scattered randomly and uniformly in a region of $1000m \times 1000m$. Every experiment is constructed 10 times independently and averaged.

Fig.3a shows 30 targets and 200 nodes are deployed in area while Fig.3b is the result after a full-view algorithm, where yellow vectors are sensing range of the sensors, the red points are monitoring targets.

We will change some parameters (the network size N, the number of targets M, the sensing radius r and the offset angle β) to observe influence on the full-view coverage performance in following 4 experiments. The definition of performance parameters is K, which is the ratio of the targets number full-view covered and the total number.

Experiment 1: the network size N

The number of monitoring target is 50. The node sensing radius is 100m. The offset angle β is 60°. The number of nodes changes from 100 to 300. θ is $3\pi/4$, $4\pi/5$, $5\pi/6$, respectively.

Fig 4 shows that K and network scale are related both in CFV and DFV. We use y-axle to denote K and x-axle to denote the sensor number. CFV and DFV

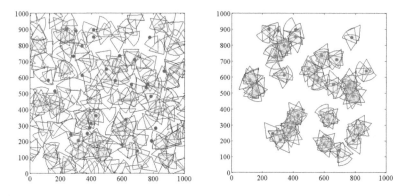

Fig. 3. (a)Full-view coverage (b)Angle between directions of neighbors

can nearly reach the same performance. The bigger network size is, the more incline K to be 1. On the other hand, the greater θ is, the smaller K is. That is the share of targets full-view covered in all targets for the smaller percentage. The results also show that when K requires to be above 0.8, θ is $3\pi/4$, $4\pi/5$, $5\pi/6$ needs 180, 220 and 260 nodes.

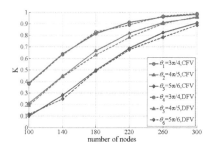 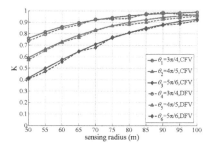

Fig. 4. number of the sensors vs K   **Fig. 5.** the sensing radius r vs. K

Experiment 2: the sensing radius r

The number of nodes is 300. The offset angle β is 60°. The number of targets is 50. The sensing radius r changes from 50m to 100m. Fig 5 is the line chart that K changes with the sensing radius r both in CFV and DFV. Along with the increasing of sensing radius, K is close to 1. Compared to network scale, r is influence of K more obviously. Of course, the same as network scale, the greater sensing radius is, the greater K is. When $\theta = 3\pi/4$, K is up to 0.8 requiring r=55, while $\theta = 5\pi/6$, it needs r=80 under the same request.

Experiment 3: the number of targets M

Node number is 300, the sensing radius r is 100m, the offset angle β is 60°, the number of targets changes from 20 to 200.

Fig 6 is the relationship of K and monitoring target number both in CFV and DFV. When θ is equal, K value is in a mean place fluctuate. This group of data shows that K and target number is less relationship. Because of the large target number, a node can serve several targets. Therefore the number of targets will not significantly effect on the performance of full-view coverage.

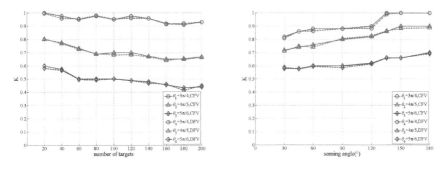

Fig. 6. number of targets vs. K   **Fig. 7.** the offset angle vs. K

Experiment 4: the offset angle β
    The number of nodes is 200, the number of targets is 50, the sensing radius r is 100m, the offset angle β changes from 30° to 180°.
    Figure 7 is offset angle β on the influence of K both in CFV and DFV. The data show that K is not sensitive to the node offset angle. This is because greater density of network nodes weakened the influence of node sensing angle. On the other hand, different θ to complete the targets covered vary significantly. The greater θ is, the smaller K is. When $\theta = 3\pi/4$, $4\pi/5$, $5\pi/6$, K is about 0.9, 0.8 and 0.65.

6   Conclusions

In this paper, we studied the problem of full-view coverage in camera sensor network with random deployment. Based on Possion distribution model, θ is derived, which is the greatest angle between camera sensors direction and target surface observations. Then we proved that full-view coverage is a NPC problem. After then, we designed a centralized and a distributed greedy algorithm to realize full-view coverage. A set of simulation results are performed to demonstrate various network parameters on the influence of the full-view coverage in proposed algorithm.

References

1. Liu, C., Cao, G.: Spatial-temporal coverage optimization in wireless sensor networks. IEEE Trans. Mob. Comput. 99, 465–478 (2011)
2. Liu, C., Cao, G.: Distributed Critical Location Coverage in Wireless Sensor Networks with Lifetime Constraint. In: IEEE INFOCOM (2012)
3. Guvensan, M.A., Yavuz, A.G.: On coverage issues in directional sensor networks: A survey. Ad Hoc Networks 97, 1238–1255 (2011)

4. Tao, D., Ma, H.D.: Coverage control algorithms for directional sensor networks. Journal of Software 22, 2317–2334 (2011)
5. Ma, H.D., Liu, Y.: On coverage problems of directional sensor networks. Mobile Ad-hoc and Sensor Networks 22, 721–731 (2005)
6. Tao, D., Ma, H.D., Liu, L.: Coverage-enhancing algorithm for directional sensor networks. Mobile Ad-hoc and Sensor Networks 22, 256–267 (2006)
7. Tao, D., Ma, H.D., Liu, L.: Virtual potential field based coverage-enhancing algorithm for directional sensor networks. Journal of Software 18, 1152–1163 (2007)
8. Xiao, F., Wang, R., Ye, X., Sun, L.: A path coverage-enhancing algorithm for directional sensor network based on improved potential field. Computer Research and Development 46, 2126–2133 (2009)
9. Cardei, M., Thai, M.T., Li, Y., Wu, W.: Energy-efficient target coverage in wireless sensor networks. In: IEEE INFOCOM (2005)
10. Cai, Y., Lou, W., Li, M., Li, X.Y.: Target-oriented scheduling in directional sensor networks. In: IEEE INFOCOM (2007)
11. Ai, J., Abouzeid, A.A.: Coverage by directional sensors in randomly deployed wireless sensor networks. Journal of Combinatorial Optimization 11, 21–41 (2006)
12. Cheng, W., Li, S., Liao, X., Changxiang, S., Chen, H.: Maximal coverage scheduling in randomly deployed directional sensor networks. In: IEEE ICPPW (2007)
13. Wen, J., Jiang, J., Dou, W.H.: Equitable direction optimizing and node scheduling for coverage in directional sensor networks. Journal of Software 20, 181–184 (2009)
14. Wang, Y., Cao, G.: Minimizing service delay in directional sensor networks. In: IEEE INFOCOM (2011)
15. Wang, Y., Cao, G.: On full-view coverage in camera sensor networks. In: IEEE INFOCOM (2011)

A Novel Real-Time Traffic Information Collection System Based on Smartphone

Xiang Liu[1], Zhibo Wang[1], Zhi Wang[1,*], Shugang Lv[1], and Tao Guan[2]

[1] State Key Laboratory of Industrial Control Technology,
Zhejiang University, 310027 Hangzhou, China
[2] Zhejiang Provincial Department of Land Resources
Information Center, 310027 Hangzhou, China
{wangzhi,liuxiang,zbwang}@iipc.zju.edu.cn

Abstract. The traffic information collection system is the underlying part of the intelligent transportation system. In this paper, we propose a novel real-time traffic information collection system, which recognizes driving status, detects the driving route, and updates the traffic condition accordingly. Specifically, we first model the roads as a virtual map, and then based on which we design a lightweight road topology relational database. Secondly, taking advantage of accelerometer and compass on the smartphone, we propose a lightweight driving status tracking algorithm that can accurately recognize users driving status. Finally the sensors readings is considered along with users driving status and the database to give real-time automatically route recognition. Meanwhile, in order to get accurate real-time information as well as protect users privacy, users driving speed is calculated in real-time manner and the encrypted driving route results are uploaded to the server. Experiments results show the effectiveness of our system.

Keywords: Intelligent Transportation System, GPS, algorithms, measurement, participatory sensing, smart phone.

1 Introduction

As the number of vehicles increases, the traffic problems such as traffic congestion and accidents become more and more serious. Recently, the Intelligent Transportation System (ITS) has been widely used to alleviate the traffic problems by providing a lot of functions. For instance, it can inform drivers the real-time condition of roads so that they can avoid terrible congestion. A fundamental issue for the ITS is that it requires the collection of high quality traffic information in real-time. Most of traditional ITS collect traffic data by the means

* This work was supported in part by the National Natural Science Foundation of China(NSFC) under Grant No. 61273079, in part by the Strategic Priority Research Program of the Chinese Academy of Sciences under Grant No. XDA06020300in part by State Key Laboratory of Industrial Control Technology under Grant No.ICT1206,No.ICT1207, and in part by Key Laboratory of Wireless Sensor Network & Communication of Chinese Academy of Sciences under Grant No.2011001.

R. Wang and F. Xiao (Eds.): CWSN 2012, CCIS 334, pp. 291–303, 2013.
© Springer-Verlag Berlin Heidelberg 2013

of sensors located along the roadside. Although the usage of traditional on-road sensors (e.g. inductive loops, cameras) for collecting traffic data is necessary and mature, however, they cant be used widely because of their limited coverage and expensive costs of implementation and maintenance [2–4].

Recently, the idea of using vehicles as probes to collect traffic data has become popular [5–7]. In this method, every vehicle should be equipped with GPS which can log the vehicles travelling time and location periodically and has the ability of sending these data to a server via wireless networks. On the server side, every probes track can be recovered by the map-matching algorithm [8–10], and then useful information (e.g., travelling time, traffic flow) can be extracted from them. Compared to the traditional way of using on-road sensors, this technology is much better since every vehicle behaves as a sensor which provides more rich and accurate information. However, this technology is still cost expensive as it requires every vehicle to equip with a GPS device and a wireless device.

With the development of mobile network and the popularity of smart phones, we have been witnessing the emergence of alternative data sources [11]. Because smartphones (e.g., iphone 4S, Galaxy Nexus) are equipped with a rich set of sensors including GPS, WiFi, cellular radio, accelerometer and digital compass, we are able to collect massive traffic data directly from end users [12, 13]. For example, GPS provides the location information and accelerometer provides the motion information of a vehicle. Using smartphone instead of equipping GPS on each vehicle has a lot of advantages: first, there is no additional cost because the system does not requires users to buy additional devices to collect data; second, the rich set of sensors could provide more rich information compared to using only GPS.

However, our challenge with real-time traffic information collection services is how to get accurate results from inaccurate sensors on smartphones. Most of the existing systems opt to directly upload GPS information to the server. Unfortunately, the results may not be accurate enough for reflecting the real-time traffic condition since both the vehicles track and traveling time need to be estimated in the server [14–17].

In spite of the powerful sensing capabilities of smartphone, there are still multiple challenges for collecting real-time traffic information by smartphones. First, although GPS can provide the highest accurate position estimate compared with WiFi and cellular radio, the GPS position error is still around 50 meters. If we only rely on the position estimated by smartphones, the accuracy of the traffic information cant be guaranteed. Second, when samrtphones are used in complex areas (e.g. small street, elevated road, side road), the map-matching algorithm may fail with a high probability without the status of vehicles. Meanwhile, the usage of map-matching algorithm increases server load and data delay.

In this paper, we design and implement a novel real-time information collection system on smartphones. GPS with accelerometer and compass on the smartphones are used to get the route information and driving status of vehicles. However, the GPS data would not be directly uploaded to the server. Instead, we argue that it is more efficient to know the road segment where the vehicle is on than the accurate location of the vehicle. Therefore, we propose a route detection algorithm to get the road segment information based on a virtual map model. A lightweight driving status algorithm are also proposed to improve the accuracy of route detection as well as filter out the invalid information. In summary, the main contributions of this paper are summarized as follows:

- We propose a virtual map model and design a lightweight road topology relational database.
- We design a lightweight driving status tracking algorithm to recognize users driving status accurately.
- We propose a route detection algorithm to get the road segment where the vehicle is on instead of the point locations of the vehicle.
- We implement the information collection system on android-based smartphones.
- We conduct experiments to evaluate the performance of our system. The experiments results show that our system can accurately recognize users driving status, track the vehicle as well as protect users privacy.

2   System Overview

In this section, we present the high-level overview of system architecture and also describe its components in details.

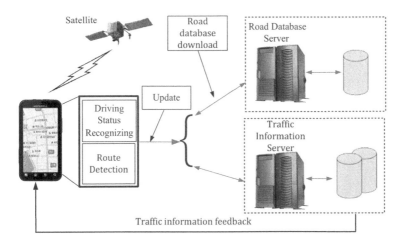

Fig. 1. System architecture

Figure 1 shows the architecture of our traffic information collection system. The system adopts a typical client-server mode, which consists of smartphones and a central server. Each smartphone performs driving status recognition and route detection, and uploads its traffic information to the server. The server can collect traffic information from smartphones and updates the traffic information database. The server can also response clients requests, such as downloading the road database.

2.1 Smartphone

Smartphone is the core of our traffic information collection system, which provides a rich set of sensors that can used to record motion information and location information. Users should first access to the server and download customized road topology database into their smartphones. Figure 2 illustrate the basic function performed on the smartphone. GPS and motion sensors (e.g., accelerometer and compass) are adopted to record location data and motion data when users are driving on the road. Based on the motion data, we propose a driving status recognition algorithm to recognize users driving status. The location data and driving status are combined with road database to provide real-time route recognition. Once the smartphone detects that the vehicle crosses an intersection, it updates its traffic information to the central server. Specifically, the traffic information need to be uploaded is defined as , where id is the path ID in the road database, d is the vehicles traveling direction, t is the traveling time, and v is the traveling speed.

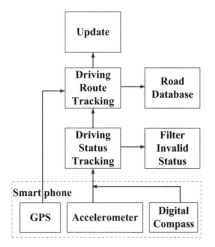

Fig. 2. Function flowchart of Smartphones

2.2 Server

Two kinds of servers are involved in our system: road database server and traffic information server. The first one is responsible for responding any download request from smartphones, while the latter one collects updates from smartphones and store them into the traffic information database for further analysis. The database is designed based on a virtual map model that gives each road a unique ID, so that the traditional location information can be uniquely encoded by IDs of roads. Considering that smartphone is resource limited, our system allows users to customize their road database for their smartphones.

3   Road Database Design

In this section, we present the virtual map model and describe the lightweight design of road database in details considering the limited resource on smart-phones. Furthermore, the privacy protection mechanism for our system is also provided.

3.1   Virtual Map Model

The virtual map model is the basis of our information collection system. It models the most important elements, roads and intersections, in real life as virtual paths and virtual intersections, respectively.

Virtual Path: virtual path is the smallest unit of road which uses traffic lights as its endpoints and does not contain other traffic light junctions. As shown in Figure 3, if each road is one-way street, cross road shown in Figure 3(a) has four virtual paths a, b, c and d, T roads has three virtual paths e, f and g, while straight road has only one virtual h since it does not have any other junction.

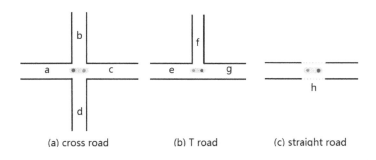

(a) cross road   (b) T road   (c) straight road

Fig. 3. Illustration of virtual paths in real life

The structure of virtual path is defined with five attributes: roadId, direction, length, startCrossingId and endCrossingId, where roadId is the id uniquely assigned to the virtual path, direction is the allowed travelling direction of the virtual path, distance is how long of the virtual path, startCrossingId is the id of the start crossing intersection and endCrossingId is the id of the end crossing intersection.

Virtual Intersection: virtual intersection is the endpoint of the virtual path. The structure of virtual intersection is defined as follows. The crossingId is the unique id assigned to the virtual intersection. The latitude and longitude is the location of point represented by the virtual intersection. We use a circle to denote the virtual intersection, which means that if the GPS reading follows in the circle, the vehicle arrives at the virtual intersection. Therefore, it also has a radius attribute.

3.2   Privacy Protection Mechanism Design

Traditional information collection systems upload GPS data directly to the server, which could reveal sensitive information of users, such as the locations of office and house. Therefore, another great advantage of uploading traffic information instead of GPS data is to protect users privacy. At the same time, because the road data downloaded from the road database server is dynamic generated, it further prevents deciphering road database through a large number of download request.

4   Driving Status Tracking Module

In this section, we present a lightweight module to efficiently recognize users driving statuses and filter out invalid driving statuses. Once the invalid driving status was recognized, the client application running on smartphones stop detecting the driving route and uploading the updates until a valid status was detected again. We first introduce the driving statuses and their characteristics, and then present our driving status tracking algorithm.

4.1   Driving Statuses

The objective of the module is to accurately recognize those driving status that can not reflect the real time traffic condition. Although different people have different driving habits, it can roughly reflect the real traffic information more or less. However, if a driver stops his car on the road for a short time because of some private reasons such as eating fast food or making an important phone, the calculated traffic information is totally wrong. Note that when drivers encounter a red light or get stuck in traffic, they may also drive with a stop-and-go behavior. Therefore, the status called temporary parking should be distinguished from traffic lights waiting status and traffic congestion status. Moreover, rather than update the traffic information until vehicle reached the next intersection, it can report the bad traffic condition to the server as soon as it recognized the traffic congestion status. Another objective of the module is to improve the accuracy of the route detection module. When a vehicle travels on the road, the route detection module needs to predict the next intersection the vehicle will pass through in advance. However, if the vehicle makes a turn before it reaches the next predicted intersection, the driving route tracking module needs to re-predict the next intersection. Therefore, the status called turning should be accurately distinguished from straight driving status. We do not consider the statuses that are not useful for vehicle tracking. For example, the parking status, it is not necessary to keep using the application on the smartphone when users get out of their cars.

Feature Extraction: typical feature should be extracted to distinguish these statuses. Since our module is running on the smartphone platforms, the most useful sensors are accelerometer and digital compass. Accelerometer can provide the acceleration information on three axles and compass can provide the direction information. Therefore, typical features can be extracted from the readings of accelerometer and compass in order to recognize the driving statuses. A smartphone can be put in a vehicle with its screen facing up.

Turning: In general, turning operation would result in a sudden direction change in the y-axis even when the turning speed is low. In our experiments, we find that the difference between the averages of two consecutive time windows is greater than 60 degrees for turning operation.

Braking: In general, braking operation would result in a sudden acceleration change in the y-axis even when the driving speed is low. We use braking detection method presented by Microsoft Research to recognize the obviously braking of vehicles in the acceleration decision tree [18].

Temporary parking: Drivers may park their cars on an on-street parking space for some personal reason. In this case, a vehicle would be entirely stopped for several minutes or even half an hour before it gets started again. That is, the time difference between stopping and starting is usually not very short. Therefore, the temporary parking status can be recognized once the difference of timestamp between braking and starting is larger than a specified time threshold.

Traffic congestion: In a traffic jam, vehicles are fully stopped for seconds of time. If the congestion is not particularly terrible, a vehicle behaves constantly slowing and accelerating. Therefore, the frequency of braking can be used to recognize the traffic congestion status.

Traffic lights waiting: When a traffic light turns red, every vehicle that has not passed through the crossroad should slow down and finally stop until green light appears. In this status, the vehicle behaves deceleration at first and is followed by acceleration. Therefore, the traffic lights waiting status can be recognized if frequency of braking is small.

4.2   Driving Status Tracking Algorithm

The proposed lightweight driving status tracking algorithm uses a multi-feature recognition technology and decision tree to recognize users driving status accurately. Multi-feature recognition refers to using the M features extracted from acceleration or direction to build a binary tree with M-1 depth. All the leaf nodes of the binary tree composed of the entire set of driving status space, while the path from root node to a leaf node represents a status judgment. The longer the path is, the more complex the judgment of the driving status can be decided.

The decision tree is shown in Figure 4. The entire matching process ensure that the status with obviously characteristics and high frequency can be recognized with a high priority while others need further matching. Therefore, we can recognize the driving status with the highest probability.

Each decision condition in Figure 4 is described as follows. Note that the time window is set to be 4 seconds, and the windows slides 1 second as time goes on.

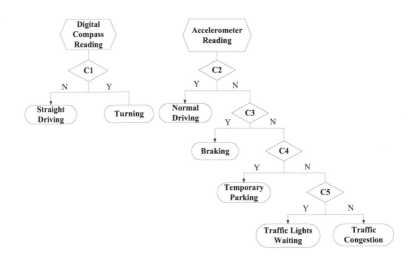

Fig. 4. The decision tree of the driving status tracking algorithm

$C1 : max((window(orientation)) - min(window(orientation)) > T1$

If the difference between the maximum reading and the minimum reading of the compass within a window is larger than the specified threshold T1, e.g., 60 degree, the vehicle is in turning status, otherwise, it is in straight driving status.

$C2 : abs(mean(window(acceleration_y))) < T2$

If the average value of the acceleration readings in the y-axis within a time window is between CT2 and T2, which is a specified threshold, e.g., -0.1g, it is normal driving.

$C3 : mean(window(acceleration_y)) > T3$

If the average value of the acceleration readings in the y-axis within a time window is larger than the specified threshold T3, e.g., -0.12g, it is braking.

$C4 : timestamp(start) - timestamp(brake) > T4$

If the difference between the starting timestamp and the braking timestamp of vehicle is larger than the specified threshold T4, e.g., 10 minutes, the vehicle is in temporary parking status.

$C5 : count(mean(window(acceleration)_y) > T3) < T5$

If the counts of the braking within a large window are smaller than the specified threshold T5, e.g., 3 times, the vehicle is in traffic light waiting status, otherwise, it is in traffic congestion status.

5   Route Detection Module

In this section, we present the route detection module in details. The objective of route detection is to get the traffic information of a vehicle, like which road segment the vehicle is on.

Previous information collection systems usually perform route detection on the server. That is, the server first receives the vehicles GPS track, and then uses map matching algorithm with a filter to estimate the route of vehicles. We have mentioned the drawbacks of this method in the introduction section. Therefore, instead of uploading GPS data, we choose to upload the traffic information of a vehicle. The traffic information is only uploaded to the server when it crosses a virtual intersection, which localizes a vehicle on a road segment instead of a point location.

The module first uses GPS data to determine which road segment the vehicle is on. Given the road segment information in the database, the module can predict the next intersection that the vehicle will pass through. Once the vehicle reaches the predicted intersection, the current position of the vehicle will be updated and the travelling time can be calculated accordingly. The process repeats when the vehicle is travelling. Note that once a turning status is detected, the module will recalculate the road segment the vehicle is travelling on. The pseudocode of the route detection algorithm is described in Algorithm 1.

6   Evaluation

In this section, we present the performance evaluation of our system on real experiments, where four volunteers help to drive their vehicles to contribute data and evaluate our system. Each of them carried a ME525 smartphone that has our system been installed. They were required to keep the application alive when they are driving on the road. The system on the smartphone uses SQLite database to store customized road database and communicates with the server through the HTTP protocol. Besides, they need to place their smartphones on a flat surface with the screen facing up, as shown in Figure 5. The server is composed of several modules. A MySQL Module stores the road database we create and the uploaded traffic information from mobile smartphones. A Java based Communication/Processing Module accepts the clients request or data and handles transaction.

The rest of this section is organized as follows. We first evaluate the performance of driving status tracking, and then present the performance of virtual intersection recognition and prediction. Finally, we present the evaluation of system measurement.

Fig. 5. The placement of the smartphone in a vehicle and the userface of smartphone

6.1 Driving Status Tracking Performance

We performed 50 experiments for each of the five driving statuses to test the driving status tracking algorithm. The performance results are shown in Table 1 and Table 2.

Table 1 shows the performance results of the straight driving status and the turning status based on compass readings. We can see that string driving status can be 100 percent recognized while only 2 of turning are not recognized correctly. The reason for this misclassification is because the turning speed is too slow. Table 2 shows the performance results of traffic lights waiting status, traffic congestion status and temporary parking status. We can see that the temporary parking achieves the highest recognition accuracy while the accuracy of traffic congestion is a little low. The reason is that the conditions of traffic congestion and traffic light waiting are very complicated. It is hard to extract very effective features for these two statuses. Specifically, the recognition accuracy of the traffic congestion status is 68% and 30% of them are recognized as the traffic lights waiting status, while the rest of 2% are recognized as the temporary parking status. We found that the reason for recognized incorrectly as the traffic lights waiting status is mainly because the vehicles drove very slowly without obviously braking and starting under the traffic polices commands. We also found that 10% of the traffic lights waiting status were incorrectly recognized as traffic congestion. This is mainly because the duration time of the green light was short, which makes the vehicles encounter two red lights before it passes through. Although the recognition rate of the traffic congestion is not very high, it does not affect the recognition and processing of the invalid status.

6.2 Virtual Intersection Recognition and Prediction Performance

In addition to the driving status experiments, we also let four volunteers drove randomly in the experimental area near Zhejiang University. The experimental

Table 1. The confusion matrix of the driving status based on compass readings

T/R	Straight driving	Turning
Straight driving	**50**	0
Turning	2	**48**

Table 2. The confusion matrix of the driving status based on acceleration readings

T/R	Traffic lights waiting	Traffic congestion	Temporary parking
Traffic lights waiting	**45**	5	0
Traffic congestion	15	**34**	1
Temporary parking	1	0	**49**

Table 3. The statistics of the virtual intersection recognition and prediction

	Accuracy Rate	False Rate	Misjudgment Source
Prediction	96%	4%	Compass was wrong
Recognition	98%	2%	Speed is too high

area contains 38 virtual intersections and 106 virtual roads. During the experiments, the ground truth data of speed, direction and travelling time of each road were also recorded.

As shown in Table 3, the virtual intersection recognition and prediction accuracy is very high. The intersection prediction accuracy achieves 96% and the recognition accuracy is even better. The analysis shows that the prediction of the virtual intersection failed because the direction data obtained from the digital compass was suddenly wrong. The data distortion is mainly due to the strong electromagnetic interference, but fortunately this situation rarely happened.

6.3   System Measurement Evaluation

In order to evaluate our system, the speedometers are also carried by volunteers for comparison. We use speedometers to sample the ground truth speed value.

The system measurements are shown in the left of Figure 6. We can see that the estimated speeds are very close to the ground truth speed value. We also find that the estimated speeds are large when vehicles were travelling on one-way streets and small when vehicles are travelling on heavy traffic road. The result is consistent with that in real life.

We also show the difference between estimated speeds and the ground truth speeds in the right of Figure 6. The average relative error of the measurements is only 0.91%. This implies that the traffic data calculated by our system can truly reflect the real-time traffic information. But at the same time we also noticed that a small part of measured value deviates a little large from the true value. Through analysis of these measured points, we found the traffic on these roads were usually very heavy and also with short length, which increased the probability of encountering red lights for vehicles.

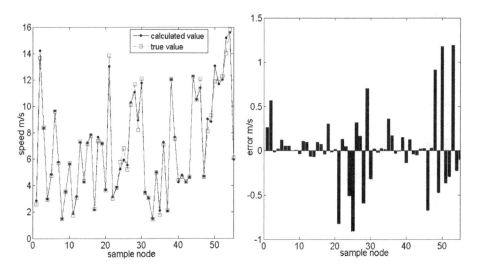

Fig. 6. The measurements and errors of the real-time traffic information collection system

7   Conclusion and Further Work

In this paper, we propose the design and implementation of a novel real-time traffic information collection system. A virtual map model is introduced to map roads into virtual paths and virtual intersections. Based on the virtual map model, we design an lightweight road database for our system. A route detection algorithm is proposed to accurately detect the traffic information of a vehicle. The traffic information uploaded to the server is the id of a road segment other than GPS location data. Moreover, a driving status tracking algorithm is proposed to improve the accuracy of route detection as well as filter out the invalid information. Experiments results show the effectiveness of our system.

Beyond the current prototype, the future work can be three folds: 1) we intend to obtain more real traffic data to verify the current system in large scale; 2) we want to involve more sensors on the smartphone and extract more significant features to achieve higher accuracy of driving status recognition; 3) we want to design a fast search algorithm that can quickly find the initial value of next crossing in the route detection algorithm.

References

1. Android, http://code.google.com/android/
2. ITS Unit Costs Database, http://www.itscosts.its.dot.gov/
3. Klein, L.A., Mills, M.K., Gibson, D.R.P.: Traffic Detector Handbook, 3rd edn. US Department of Transportation, Washington, DC, USA (2006)
4. Guillaume, L.: Road traffic data: Collection methods and applications. Technical report, Institute for Prospective Technological Studies, EU (2008)

5. Turksma, S.: The various uses of floating car data. Road Transport Information and Control, 51–55 (2000)
6. Schaefer, R.P., Thiessenhusen, K.U., Wagner, P.: A traffic information system by means of real-time floating-car data. In: Proc. ITS World Congress, Chicago, USA (2002)
7. Kerner, B.S., Demir, C., Herrtwich, R.G.: Traffic state detection with floating car data in road networks. In: Proc. 8th International IEEE Conference on Intelligent Transportation Systems, pp. 44–49 (2005)
8. Greenfeld, J.: Matching GPS observations to locations on a digital map. In: Proc. 81st Annual Meeting of the Transportation Research Board, pp. 164–173 (2002)
9. Quddus, M., Ochieng, W., Zhao, L.: A general map matching algorithm for transport telematics applications. GPS Solutions Journal 7(3), 157–167 (2003)
10. Quddus, M., Ochieng, W., Noland, R.: Current map-matching algorithms for transport applications: State-of-the art and future research directions. Transportation Research Part C: Emerging Technologies 15(5), 312–328 (2007)
11. Burke, J.A., Estrin, D.: Participatory sensing. In: ACM Sensys World Sensor Web Workshop, Boulder, CO, USA (2006)
12. The mobile millenium project, `http://traffic.berkeley.edu/`
13. The CarTel project, `http://cartel.csail.mit.edu/`
14. Wunnava, S., Yen, K., Babij, T.: Travel time estimation using cell phone for highways and roadways. Technical report, Florida Department of Transportation (2007)
15. Arvind, T., Lenin, R., Katrina, L.: VTrack: Accurate, Energy-AwareTraffic Delay Estimation Using Mobile Phones. In: Proc. 7th ACM Conference on Embedded Networked Sensor Systems, Berkeley, CA (2009)
16. Arvind, T., Lenin, R., Hari, B.: Accurate, low-energy trajectory mapping for mobile devices. In: Proceedings of USENIX NSDI (2011)
17. Hoh, B., Gruteser, M., Herring, R.: Virtual trip lines for distributed privacy-preserving traffic monitoring. In: MobiSys 2008: Proceeding of the 6th International Conference on Mobile Systems, Applications, and Services, pp. 15–28 (2008)
18. Mohan, P., Padmanabhan, V.N., Ramjee, R.: Nericell: Rich Monitoring of Road and Traffic Conditions using Mobile Smartphones. In: Proc. of 8th ACM Conference on Embedded Networked Sensor Systems, pp. 357–370 (2008)

Detection Performance Optimization Based Power Allocation between Sensing and Communication in Wireless Sensor Networks

Xiangyang Liu[1,*], Wenbin Bai[1], Peisheng Zhu[2], and Zheng Han[1]

[1] First Department, Xian Communications Institute, Xian, Shaanxi Province, China
liuxiangyangdr@gmail.com
[2] Institute of Acoustics, Chinese Academy of Sciences, Beijing China

Abstract. The design of wireless sensor networks for signal detection applications has to consider the limited battery power of the sensor nodes. Considering the scenario of using distributed radar-like sensors to detect the presence of an object through active sensing, we formulate the problem of power allocation between sensing and communication for signal detection under the Neyman-Pearson criterion. An allocation scheme of node's power budget between sensing and communication is presented. The objective is to maximize the global probability of detection under a fixed node's power constraint and a given global probability of false alarm. Simulation results show that the proposed method leads to a big gain in performance.

Keywords: Distributed detection, wireless sensor network, power allocation, cross-layer optimization.

1 Introduction

Distributed detection (DD) systems with multiple sensors have been investigated since 1980s. With the development of wireless sensor networks (WSNs), many authors have analyzed the performance of these DD systems in which transmissions from sensors to fusion center (FC) are prone to channel fading and noise[1–5], which may render the received decisions at the fusion center unreliable, especially in resource constrained networks. One prominent feature of a canonical WSN, however, is its limited node energy, which poses many challenges to network design and management.

The problem of optimizing detection performance with such imperfect communication brings a new challenge to distributed detection. Zhang et al.[6] considered the optimization of performance with individual and total transmitter power constraints on the sensors and the corresponding power allocation scheme

---

* The China National Science Foundation under Grant Nos. 61102160 and 61179002 and the project for postgraduates of military science (2010JY0423-241) support this work.

R. Wang and F. Xiao (Eds.): CWSN 2012, CCIS 334, pp. 304–312, 2013.
© Springer-Verlag Berlin Heidelberg 2013

strikes a tradeoff between the communication channel quality and the local decision quality. Considering the scenario of using distributed radar-like sensors to detect the presence of an object through active sensing, Yang et al.[7] formulated the problem of energy-efficient routing for signal detection under the Neyman-Pearson criterion. Moreover, they proposed a distributed and energy-efficient framework that is scalable with respect to the network size, and is able to greatly reduce the dependence on the central fusion center. Masazade et al.[8] evaluated the sensor thresholds of distributed signal detection system by formulating and solving a multiobjective optimization problem. Unfortunately, although the literature on energy-efficient communication or signal detection in WSNs is abundant, there is much less research on the power allocation between signal detection and communication, let alone the consideration of their joint optimization. Obviously, the energy consumption of the whole system can be lowered by jointly optimizing the signal detection of sensor node and the communication between sensor node and the fusion center. In another word, for a given node's power budget, we can find a power allocation scheme that strikes a tradeoff between the communication channel quality and the detection quality of local sensor with the objective of the optimum detection performance at the FC.

The remainder of this paper is organized as follows. In Section 2, the problem of distributed detection in parallel fusion networks with noisy channel, sensing model, link model, and fusion rule were stated, respectively. The power allocation strategy is introduced in Section 3. The numerical results are given in Section 4. Finally, Section 5 concludes the paper.

2   Problem Formulation

2.1   Distributed Detection Problem

Let us consider a scenario, where N sensors are scattered over an area to detect the presence of an object, for example people, vehicles, or military targets, using radar-like sensors that emanate specific electromagnetic signals into the region of interest. For this active sensing application, the monitored space is typically divided into many range resolution cells. Each range cell could be probed sequentially in turn to determine the presence of a target by using radar pulses that are possibly launched by directional antennas. Assume the position of k-th sensor node is (x_k, y_k). Sensors gathers information pertaining to a target in the position of (x_t, y_t) and makes a decision (for deciding the presence of the target and otherwise) and sends its binary decision to a fusion center through an unreliable communication channel. In a word, the parallel fusion model is adopted. The position of fusion center is assumed to be (x_{fc}, y_{fc}). Consider the following two hypotheses, the noise-only Hypothesis H_0 and the signal plus noise Hypothesis H_1.

2.2   Sensing Model

According to the freespace radar equation, the power of the echoes from the target with RCS σ at range R_k to the radar can be expressed as

$$P_r = P_t G^2 \lambda^2 \sigma (4\pi)^{-3} R_k^{-4} \tag{1}$$

where P_t is the radiated transmitted power, G is the gain of radar antenna, λ is the wavelength, and R_k is the range between the k-th radar and the target. For pulse radar with noise figure F and bandwidth B, the output signal-to-noise ratio $(SNR)_o$ of its receiver is

$$(SNR)_o = \tau P_t G^2 \lambda^2 \sigma / \left((4\pi)^3 k T_e B F L R_k^4 \right) \tag{2}$$

where k is Boltzmann's constant, T_e is the effective noise temperature, L is the system loss, and τ is the pulse duration. The minimum detectable signal S_{min} and the minimum output signal-to-noise ratio $(SNR)_{o_{min}}$ of a radar receiver is related by

$$S_{\min} = k T_e B F (SNR)_{o_{\min}} \tag{3}$$

The signal received by the k-th sensor is

$$y_k = \begin{cases} \sqrt{\tau P_r} + n_k , & H_1 \\ n_k , & H_0 \end{cases} \tag{4}$$

Assume that the k-th local sensor makes a binary decision $u_k \in \{+1, -1\}$, with false alarm rate $P_{lfk} = P[u_k = 1|H_0]$ and detection probability $P_{ldk} = P[u_k = 1|H_1]$, respectively. When n_k is Gaussian white noise with zero mean and variance σ_k^2, the return from the Swerling 0 target is constant. Therefore, the decision rule of the k-th sensor is

$$u_k = \begin{cases} 1 , & y_k \geq \tau_k \\ -1 , & y_k < \tau_k \end{cases} \tag{5}$$

where τ_k is decision threshold determined by the false alarm rate P_{lfk}. In this case, the P_{ldk} and P_{lfk} can be calculated as following,

$$P_{ldk} = \frac{1}{2} \operatorname{erfc} \left(\frac{\tau_k - \sqrt{\tau P_r}}{\sqrt{2\sigma_k^2}} \right) , \quad P_{lfk} = \frac{1}{2} \operatorname{erfc} \left(\frac{\tau_k}{\sqrt{2\sigma_k^2}} \right) \tag{6}$$

where $\operatorname{erfc}(x) = \frac{2}{\sqrt{\pi}} \int_x^{+\infty} e^{-t^2} dt$.

2.3   Link Model

Let P_t^{com} denote the radiated transmitted power of communication signal. Considering the path loss incurred during transmission, the power of signal received by the FC and from the k-th sensor is

$$P_{rk}^{fc} = P_{tk}^{com} / (\varepsilon_k d_k^{\alpha_k}) \tag{7}$$

where ε_k is a constant determined by the antenna characteristics, α_k is path loss exponent, and d_k is the range from the k-th sensor to the FC. Each local decision u_k is transmitted through a fading Rayleigh channel and the output of the channel for the k-th sensor is given by

$$r_k = \sqrt{P_{rk}^{fc}} h_k u_k + w_k \quad , \tag{8}$$

where w_k is zero mean Gaussian noise with variance $\sigma_{w_k}^2$, and h_k is the gain of a real valued Rayleigh fading channel with the PDF given by

$$f(h_k) = 2h_k e^{-h_k^2}, h_k \geq 0 \quad . \tag{9}$$

2.4   Fusion Rule

Based on the knowledge of channel statistics and local detection performance indexes, the LRT-CS (likelihood ratio test based on channel statistics)[1] is given by

$$\Lambda_{tot} = \log\left[\frac{f(r_1, r_2, \cdots, r_N | H_1)}{f(r_1, r_2, \cdots, r_N | H_0)}\right] = \sum_{k=1}^{N} \log \Big\{$$

$$\frac{\sqrt{\frac{\pi P_{rk}^{fc}}{2}}\left[2P_{ldk}-1+\mathrm{erf}\left(\sqrt{\frac{P_{rk}^{fc}}{2}}a_k r_k\right)\right]r_k a_k \exp\left(\frac{P_{rk}^{fc}}{2}a_k^2 r_k^2\right)+1}{\sqrt{\frac{\pi P_{rk}^{fc}}{2}}\left[2P_{lfk}-1+\mathrm{erf}\left(\sqrt{\frac{P_{rk}^{fc}}{2}}a_k r_k\right)\right]r_k a_k \exp\left(\frac{P_{rk}^{fc}}{2}a_k^2 r_k^2\right)+1} \Big\}, \tag{10}$$

where $a_k = 1/\sqrt{\sigma_{w_k}^2\left(P_{rk}^{fc}+2\sigma_{w_k}^2\right)}$, and $\mathrm{erf}(x) = \int_0^x \frac{2}{\sqrt{\pi}}e^{-t^2}dt$. The global probability of false alarm P_{ftot} and the global probability of detection P_{dtot} are determined by the conditional probabilities $P_{ftot} = P(\Lambda_{tot} > T | H_0)$ and $P_{dtot} = P(\Lambda_{tot} > T | H_1)$ where T is the detection threshold. The final decision at FC is given by

$$u_0 = \begin{cases} 1, & \Lambda_{tot} \geq T \\ 0, & \Lambda_{tot} < T \end{cases} \tag{11}$$

where $u_0 = 0$ denotes the hypothesis of no target and $u_0 = 1$ denote the hypothesis of target presence.

3   Power Allocation Algorithm

3.1   Power Consumption of Sensor Node

In general, the power consumption of sensor node can be divided into two kinds, range-related power consumption and range-free power consumption. Here, consider two kinds of range-related power consumption. One is consumed by target sensing, denoted by P_k^{sensing}, and is related to the drain efficiency of power amplifier and antenna gains. Assuming the total energy efficiency is η_k^{sensing}, the consumed power $P_{ktot}^{\text{sensing}}$ and the radiated signal power P_k^{sensing} has the following relation

$$P_{ktot}^{\text{sensing}} = P_k^{\text{sensing}} \left(\eta_k^{\text{sensing}} \right)^{-1} \quad . \tag{12}$$

For radar sensor, the larger P_k^{sensing}, the stronger the target's returns and correspondingly the higher local sensor's detection capability. Therefore, by adjusting P_k^{sensing}, sensor's target detection performance can be adjusted. Another kind of range-related power consumption is that consumed by the communication between sensor node and the FC. Assuming that the power of the signal radiated into wireless channel by sensor k is denoted by P_k^{com} and total efficiency of power amplifier and antenna is denoted by η_k^{com}, then the power used for radiating signal P_{ktot}^{com} can be denoted by

$$P_{ktot}^{com} = P_k^{com} (\eta_k^{com})^{-1} \quad . \tag{13}$$

Except for the range-related power consumption, the other power consumption, for example from low noise amplifier, A/D converter, D/A converter and so on, is range-free. Furthermore, it can be considered fixed or cannot be controlled freely. Besides, for maintaining the normal function of sensor network, sensor node will consume some energy, which may fluctuate. Therefore, the power allocation of sensor node, considered in this paper, is how to share the adjustable power budget by the target sensing power $P_{ktot}^{\text{sensing}}$ and communication power P_{ktot}^{com}. Assume that the total power budget is $P_k^{\text{sensing+com}}$ and then

$$P_{ktot}^{\text{sensing}} + P_{ktot}^{com} \leq P_k^{\text{sensing+com}} \quad . \tag{14}$$

For optimum system performance, the match between the communication capability and the detection performance index of local sensor node is needed. That is to say, the target sensing power $P_{kopt}^{\text{sensing}}$ and communication power P_{kopt}^{com} maximize the detection of total system. At this time, the following equation holds.

$$P_{ktot}^{\text{sensing}} + P_{ktot}^{com} = P_k^{\text{sensing+com}} \tag{15}$$

3.2 Objective Function

In general, performance indexes (probabilities of false alarm and detection) of local sensor are not equal for the system with maximum detection performance. However, when the number of sensors approaches infinity, the system with identical local detectors will have asymptotic optimum performance[9]. Therefore, we assume that every sensor node has identical sensing and communication performance and their power supplies have identical power. Furthermore, assume the power budget that can be distributed between sensing and communication is $P^{\text{sensing+com}}$. For given maximum false alarm rate α, the objective of system optimization is equivalent to finding the scheme of adjusting sensing power $P_{ktot}^{\text{sensing}}$ and communication power P_{ktot}^{com}, so as to maximize the total probability of detection P_{dtot}, expressed as the function of local sensor's performance indexes, sensing power, and communication power, as shown in

$$P_{dtot} \triangleq P\left(\Lambda_{tot} \geq T \mid H_1\right) = P_D\left(\tau_1, P_{1tot}^{\text{sensing}}, P_{1tot}^{com}, \cdots,\right.$$

$$\left.\tau_k, P_{ktot}^{\text{sensing}}, P_{ktot}^{com}, \cdots, \tau_N, P_{Ntot}^{\text{sensing}}, P_{Ntot}^{com}, T\right). \tag{16}$$

3.3   A Suboptimum Method

A simple method can be used to find a good allocation method. According to the total power budget P^{node}, a sufficient small power increase ΔP can be determined with the relation of $P^{node} = L\Delta P$. Let sensing power $P_{ktot}^{\text{sensing}}$ be ΔP, $2\Delta P$, $\cdots$, $L\Delta P$ successively and let communication power $P_{ktot}^{com} = P^{node} - P_{ktot}^{\text{sensing}}$. Next, compute P_{dtot}. The best sensing power is that with largest probability of detection.

4   Numerical Simulations

Consider a WSN with eight sensor nodes and a FC. The FC is with coordinate (0,300) and the target is at (0,-150). Assume that the Y-axis coordinates of all the sensors are 0 and their X-axis coordinates are given in Table 1. All units of coordinate are meters.

Table 1. X-axis coordinates of sensor nodes

Sensor's No.	1	2	3	4	5	6	7	8
X-axis coordinate	-60	-40	-20	0	20	40	60	80

Assume the false alarm rate α at the FC is 0.01. Each sensor has operating frequency 9375MHz, pulsewidth 10ns, and $\eta_k^{\text{sensing}} = 0.18$. Assume a noise figure $F = 8$ dB, effective noise temperature $T_0 = 290K$, antenna gain $G = 28$dB and total receiver loss $L = 4$ dB. Also assume that, for targets following the Swerling II fluctuations with average RCS of 5 square meters, a probability of detection 0.5 and radar returns' power of -93dBm are required at maximum range of 150 meters with false alarm rate 0.01 or better. Assume that communication system operates at 2.4GHz and adopts the following path loss model given by Shellhammer[10]

$$pl(d) = \begin{cases} 40.2 + 20\log_{10}(d), & d \leq 8m \ ; \\ 58.5 + 33\log_{10}\left(\frac{d}{8}\right), & d > 8m \ . \end{cases} \tag{17}$$

Assume that the signal-to-noise loss of the practical communication receiver compared with the ideal one is 5dB. Also assume that, for binary symmetric Rayleigh fading channel, a bit error rate of 0.001 is required at receiver sensitivity of -95dBm at maximum range of 102 meters with transmitted power 5 dBm. Let the drain efficiency of the power amplifier of communication module is 0.17. When $P^{\text{sensing}+com} = 30$mW, the plot of probability of detection at FC versus sensing power are given in Fig.1. Obviously $P_{ktot}^{\text{sensing}} = 21$ mW will maximize the

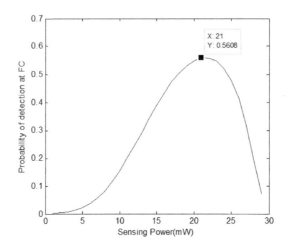

Fig. 1. Probability of detection versus sensing power of each node

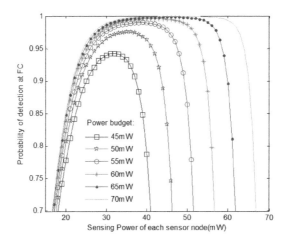

Fig. 2. Probability of detection versus sensing power under different power budget

P_{dtot} . A bad power allocation, for example $P_{\mathrm{ktot}}^{\mathrm{sensing}} = 5$ mW and $P_{\mathrm{ktot}}^{\mathrm{com}} = 25$ mW, will make the system's detection performance deteriorate sharply. Therefore, a reasonable allocation scheme of node's power is necessary.

When $P^{\mathrm{sensing+com}}$ varies from 45mW to 70mW, it can be found from Fig.2 that the maximum P_{dtot} makes steady increase, i.e. from 0.94 to 0.999. Moreover, the larger $P^{\mathrm{sensing+com}}$, the less the increased quantity of P_{dtot} . For the simulation, the maximum P_{dtot} is larger than 0.98 when $P^{\mathrm{sensing+com}} > 55$ mW. Therefore, for desired P_{dtot} , the minimum $P^{\mathrm{sensing+com}}$ can be obtained, as given in Table2. It can also be found that, for $P^{\mathrm{sensing+com}} > 55$mW, the curves of P_{dtot} versus sensing power are nearly in the shape of a trapezoid. Moreover, the larger $P^{\mathrm{sensing+com}}$, the longer the upper line of the approximate trapezoid.

Table 2. X-axis coordinates of sensor nodes

$P^{\text{sensing+com}}$ (mW)	45	50	55	60	65	70
maximum P_{dtot}	0.940	0.97	0.99	0.996	0.998	0.999

Furthermore, the desired $P^{\text{sensing+com}}$ can be lowered at the cost of slightly sacrificing detection performance. For example, letting the probability of detection at FC decreases from 0.998 to 0.996, the desired power budget can decrease from 65mW to 60mW.

5   Conclusion

Considering the scenario of using distributed radar-like sensors to detect the presence of an object through active sensing, we formulate the problem of power allocation between sensing and communication for signal detection under the Neyman-Pearson criterion. An allocation scheme of node's power budget between sensing and communication is presented to maximize the global probability of detection under a fixed node's power constraint and a given global probability of false alarm. Simulation results show that the proposed method can lead to a good power allocation. At the same time, without deliberate design of power allocation, the probability of detection at FC may deteriorate sharply. Overall, the joint optimization of sensing and communication is necessary and can lead to big gain in detection performance.

References

1. Niu, R., Chen, B., Varshney, P.K.: Fusion of decisions transmitted over Rayleigh fading channels in wireless sensor networks. IEEE Transactions on Signal Processing 54, 1018–1027 (2006)
2. Chen, B., Tong, L., Varshney, P.K.: Channel-aware distributed detection in wireless sensor networks. IEEE Signal Processing Magazine 23, 16–26 (2006)
3. Kanchumarthy, V.R., Viswanathan, R., Madishetty, M.: Impact of Channel Errors on Decentralized Detection Performance of Wireless Sensor Networks: A Study of Binary Modulations, Rayleigh-Fading and Nonfading Channels, and Fusion-Combiner. IEEE Transactions on Signal Processing 56, 1761–1769 (2008)
4. Wu, J.-Y., Wu, C.-W., Wang, T.-Y.: Channel-Aware Decision Fusion With Unknown Local Sensor Detection Probability. IEEE Transactions on Signal Processing 58, 1457–1463 (2010)
5. Lai, K.-C., Yang, Y.-L., Jia, J.-J.: Fusion of Decisions Transmitted Over Flat Fading Channels Via Maximizing the Deflection Coefficient. IEEE Transactions on Vehicular Technology 59, 3634–3640 (2010)
6. Zhang, X., Poor, H.V., Chiang, M.: Optimal Power Allocation for Distributed Detection Over MIMO Channels in Wireless Sensor Networks. IEEE Transactions on Signal Processing 56, 4124–4140 (2008)
7. Yang, Y., Blum, R.S., Sadler, B.M.: Energy-Efficient Routing for Signal Detection in Wireless Sensor Networks. IEEE Transactions on Signal Processing 57, 2050–2063 (2009)

8. Masazade, E., Rajagopalan, R., Varshney, P.K., Mohan, C.K., Sendur, G.K., Keski-noz, M.: A multiobjective optimization approach to obtain decision thresholds for distributed detection in wireless sensor networks. IEEE Transactions on Systems, Man, and Cybernetics, Part B: Cybernetics 40, 444–457 (2010)

9. Swami, A., Zhao, Q., Hong, Y.-W., Tong, L. (eds.): Wireless sensor networks: signal processing and communications perspectives. John Wiley & Sons Inc., Hoboken (2007)

10. Shellhammer, S.J.: Estimation of Packet Error Rate Caused by Interference using Analytic Techniques – A Coexistence Assurance Methodology. IEEE 802.19-05/0028r1 (2005)

A User-Oriented Resource Management Model for the Internet of Things

Yang Liu[1,2], Ye Tian[1], Ning Kong[1],
Yan Wang[1], Shuo Shen[1], and Wei Mao[1,2]

[1] Computer Network Information Center, Chinese Academy of Sciences, China
[2] University of Chinese Academy of Sciences, China
{liu-yang,tianye,nkong,ywang,shenshuo,mao}@cnnic.cn

Abstract. With the rapid development of Internet of Things (IoT), vast amounts of heterogeneous resources have been connected to the network. How to effectively manage these resources will become a critical issue. This paper first summarizes the current status of the resource management in different scenarios, like WSN, RFID, and RSN. Then from a user perspective, based on the resource name service, we propose a generic resource management model, which is composed of users, devices and resources. Two actual cases are introduced to describe how users can obtain the logical information and control the entity object through this theoretical model. Finally, the analysis shows that this model can meet the needs of ordinary users in compatibility, stability, real-time and flexibility for IoT resources management.

Keywords: Internet of Things, resource management, name service, compatibility.

1 Introduction

The Internet of Things is not entirely novel network architecture, but an extended concept, making the terminal of network from computers to sensors, RFID tags and other restricted resources, which have limited computing and storage capacity. Associated with these restricted devices, each object in the real-world can be mapped into the virtual network. Then some enabling IT technologies can be used to enhance the management of resources in the Internet of Things:

- *Identification technology* helps to uniquely identify the resource;
- *Sensing technology* helps to perceive the resource for obtaining surrounding information;
- *Naming service* helps to easily locate and retrieval the resource;
- *M2M communications technology* helps to communicate with the resource.

However, most resource management solutions for the Internet of Things are designed for administrators and specified applications. There is still no generic method

R. Wang and F. Xiao (Eds.): CWSN 2012, CCIS 334, pp. 313–324, 2013.
© Springer-Verlag Berlin Heidelberg 2013

at present. The rest of this paper is organized as follows: In Section 2, we will first analysis the users needs for resource management in the Internet of Things. Then we describe the current status in Section 3. In Section 4, we propose a user-oriented resource management model for the Internet of Things based on the resource name service. In Section 5, we will explain how to use this theoretical model through practical cases. A comprehensive analysis is given in Section 6. Finally, we will provide a summary of this paper and discuss the future work.

2   Requirements Analysis

Different from the traditional Internet, the connotation of resource in the Internet of Things becomes more abundant. Naturally, its new features also bring new challenges for management.

1) *Compatibility*: Not only a small chip but also a sophisticated server can both be addressing resource for the Internet of Things. Considering their own interests, many countries and organizations have made private rules for IoT resource management, which is certainly not conducive to the interoperability of the Internet of Things. While the ordinary users just want to shield the heterogeneity of resources, but access information and manage resources in a uniform way.

2) *Stability*: As an important identification tool, 2.88 billion RFID tags were sold in 2011 [1]. If fully deployed, the related information data is really surprising. Massive query for these data must make the name service platform under enormous pressure. This is just an example, the entire infrastructure and all public services for the Internet of Things need to have high stability.

3) *Real-time*: The Internet is mainly made up of static Web pages and their mutual links. But information in the Internet of Things is temperature, pressure, location, and so on, which can be changed at any time. In addition, the most important purpose for an Internet user is to get logical information, while an IoT user also wants to communicate with the entity object directly and even controls them.

4) *Flexibility*: Taking the search service as an example, a user may query for logistics information worldwide as well as traffic information locally. Such a disparate granularity asks the search engine of the internet of things for higher flexibility.

5) *Security*: On one hand, because most physical resource is private, authentication, access control, and other similar security problems will require much more attention. On the other hand, most underlying network of IoT depends on the wireless communication technology, which is easily to be illegal eavesdropped and disclose personal privacy [2].

3   State of the Art Review

WSN (wireless sensor network) and RFID (radio frequency identification) are the two most major network forms of IoT at present. The former mainly connect sensors to make up a local wireless network and interacts with external network through a special Sink node; the latter can be built a global system, but usually cannot perceive the surrounding information.

Against their respective inadequacies, some scholars have proposed the integration of RFID and WSN technology, which is called RSN [3] (RFID Sensor Network, also known as WSID network [4]). This section will describe the basic pattern of IoT resource management in these three different scenarios, and give a summary of the existing IoT resource management architecture.

3.1 WSN

WSN [5] usually consists of spatially distributed sensor nodes (groups), receivers and transmitters, etc. After constructing a wireless network autonomously, these distributed sensors can percept, collect, and process the surrounding information in the covering area coordinately in real time. The related information will be sent to the remote management center by sink nodes via multi-hop.

Users have two ways to obtain perceptive information and manage resources in WSN:

- When the user know the location of the sensor node or the remote management center it belongs to , he can communicates with gateway by TCP/IP first. As an agent, the gateway can help to achieve the interaction between the user and the sensor node.
- When the user does not know which sensor node can meet his needs, the user can use the search services to find resource. Kay. R [6] summarizes the main state-of-the-art research advances of search technology.

3.2 RFID

RFID system usually consists of tags, readers, middleware, and information server. With the increasing of applications, the closed-loop RFID systems gradually develop to the open-loop RFID networks, and distributed resource position technology is becoming increasingly important. According to different users need, the relevant query service can be divided into two categories, one is Resolution Services (RS) and the other is Discovery Service (DS) [7]. Currently, the mainstream resolution service is the Object Name Service [8] (ONS) brought by the Auto-ID lab, which can provide mapping service between the RFID tag's Electronic Product Code (EPC) and address of the EPC information Server. The basic principle of ONS is still the Domain Name Service (DNS), which is widely used by the Internet. Though several solutions were proposed, such as [9][10][11], Discovery Service has not yet reached a consensus.

3.3 RSN

Liu Hai et al. [12] summarize four types of integrations of RFID and WSN:

- integrating tags with sensors,
- integrating tags with wireless sensor nodes,
- integrating readers with wireless sensor nodes and wireless devices,
- mixing of RFID components and sensors.

Changing the hardware needs higher costs, while the idea of data aggregation is relatively more appropriate. Although RFID tags and sensor nodes exist independently in the physical layer, it is possible to integrate RFID data and WSN data through a unified control center in the software layer. Li Jie [13] proposed such a data integration module to filter the underlying differences. The sensor node is responsible for collecting the EPC of RFID tags and writes these data into WSN data packets.

3.4   Summary

A well designed architecture can contribute greatly to the practical application. But existing architectures of the Internet of things are mostly designed for a specified application, and not suitable for a unified resource management.

For example, the EPCglobal network architecture (EPC) [14], the uID architecture (ucode) [15], and the DIALOG system architecture (ID@URI) [16] are all proposed for RFID Resource Management and limited to a fixed coding structure, which is not compatible with each other.

An autonomic-oriented architecture was proposed by Guy Pujolle et al. [17] to support the self-organized and self-manageable STP/SP stack (replacing the existing TCP/IP stack). Simon Duquennoy et al. [18] proposed to create a Web of things, which will embed WWW service into every smart thing (smart card, sensor node and other embedded device). However, these two solutions only apply to the sensor node, which has a certain degree of computing and storage capacity.

Besides, some research effort has also been put on the abstract model of the Internet of Things. Luigi Atzori et al. [19] firstly summarized that the IoT paradigm shall be a convergence of three visions: a things oriented vision, an Internet oriented vision and a semantic oriented vision. Shen Su-bin et al. [20] further extended the analysis from technology level to the essence level, and proposed a concept model for the Internet of Things in three dimensions: things, networks and applications.

4   Design

The ultimate goal of the Internet of Things must achieve interoperability among all the resources through a unified addressing scheme, but not be limited to a particular network technology. From the perspective of a layered network architecture, the underlying perception layer will be bound to a variety of coexist autonomous networks. Just considering such a situation, this paper raises a common resource management model to meet all kinds of requirements introduced in Session 2.

4.1   Model

As is shown in Fig. 1, a user-oriented resource management model for the Internet of Things consists of users, devices and resources, relying on the existing network infrastructure and communication technologies to build networks and information exchange. As an important link service, Resource Name Service will be brought to locate and retrieval resources.

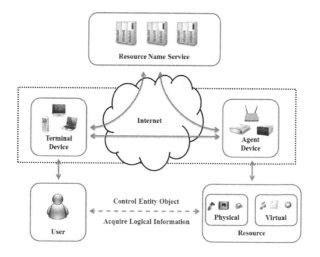

Fig. 1. A user-oriented resource management model

Definition 1: *user* is the human being who wants to interact with the resources in the Internet of Things.

Resource management by users is possibly two kinds of behaviors: one is to obtain the logical information, and the other is to control the entity object. The system administrator can be considered as a special user who has prior knowledge and certain privileges.

Definition 2: *device* is the physical equipment which can connect to the network and has a certain degree of computing and storage capacity.

In this paper, a device which will interact with users directly is named as a *terminal device*, such as personal computers, notebook computers, smart phones, et al. In contrast, a device which can help restricted resources to communicate with the Internet is named as an *agent device* [21], such as the WSN gateway, RFID reader, et al. However, a particular device may change its role. For example, when a smart phone is used to visit the remote server of a wireless sensor network for acquiring information, it is considered as a terminal device. But when the same smart phone is used to control local gravity sensor, it is considered as an agent device.

Definition 3: *resource* is any component of an IoT application that needs to be used or addressed, not only including physical resource, but also virtual resource.

Definition 4: *resource name service* is a mapping service from one kind of resource identifier to another, aiming at more direct or abundant name information.

4.2   RNS

The name of a resource can be used to uniquely identify it. A collection of names for the same type of resource form the corresponding name space. Unlike the traditional Internet, where seven-layer (OSI model) or five-layer (TCP/IP model) architecture have been the consensus, unified layer architecture of the Internet of Things has not yet formed. Accordance with current practice, we divide it into three layers and each layer protocol object has a variety of name space, as is shown in Fig. 2.

1) *Object identifier*: used to identify the various entity objects in the perceptual layer. For example, RFID tags can carry EPC codes to identify the attached items.

2) *Communication identifier*: used to identify the network nodes with communication capabilities (e.g., WSN gateway, RFID reader, smart phone, etc.). The source object and the target object must have the same class of communication identifier to establish a link.

3) *Application identifier*: used to identify the elements for various fields and service in the application layer. For example, the detailed information of the RFID tag is usually stored in the back-end server. We can assign it a URI to provide Web access service.

In the perception layer, RNS [22] provides a two-stage identification structure to be compatible with the heterogeneous IoT resources. Resource Identifier (RID) is used to uniquely identify the resource and Standard Identifier (SID) is used to define the naming rule. In application layer, RNS extends the traditional URI and adds resource name, resource type, and resource ownership to show abstract information in the name directly.

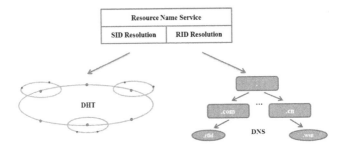

Fig. 2. Resource name service architecture

DNS has proven to be a mature distributed architecture in the current Internet, so we can make full use of existing DNS infrastructure for RIDs management to reduce the implementation difficulties. The situation of SID is different:

- Generally registered by organizations, SID is far less than the number of RID;
- Registration and management is private for RID, but it should be public for SID to allow the exchange of resources between countries and organizations;
- Queries to SIDs are far more frequent than RIDs, so that a pyramid-style of management mechanism may cause great stress on the root.

So a hierarchical P2P system will be used to ensure the resolution service of SID is decentralized and equitable.

RNS can provide service when the initial input is object identifier or application identifier, but cannot support communication identifier to be the initial input like Object Code Mapping Service (OCMS) [23]. If the initial input is object identifier, a naming scheme description will be returned after the first phase of SID resolution. With the help of such a description, the initial identifier can be transferred to an extended URI for the second phase of RID resolution. Name mapping information are all stored in the NAPTR record [24] corresponding to the extended URI.

According to different types defined in the Service domain, many kinds of expressions for name mapping information are allowed, so RID resolution may be a recursive process.

4.3   Management Mechanism

Based on the theoretical model presented in this paper, the concrete realization of resources management mainly includes the following steps:

1) *Registration Phase*: Standards organizations register the SID and the corresponding naming scheme description (usually a regular expression) to the SID name server. Agent devices register the RID and the corresponding resource name information to the RID name server.
2) *Query Phase*: Once a user wants to manage resource through the Internet of Things, application program installed in the terminal device will first call a resolver, which is a library program to query resource name service for allocating and retrieving the resource.
3) *Communication Phase*: Finally, the user can establish communication with the resource according to address obtained in phase 2).

Depending on the purpose of user management behavior, the concrete operation process is different:

- Management behavior is to obtain the logical information:
  During the registration phase, name mapping information between object identifier and application identifier can be directly stored in the NAPTR record corresponding to the RID, and record type is Inf. Then an application

identifier will be returned in the end, just like the URL of a Web page to describe the detailed information of the resource. Users can obtain these information through HTTP service.

– Management behavior is to control the entity object:
  During the registration phase, the agent device first assigned a virtual communication identifier to the resource and recorded such mapping information in local. After that, this agent will register the mapping information between the object identifier and the virtual communication identifier to the NAPTR record corresponding to the RID, and record type is Con. So a communication identifier will be returned in the end, just like a virtual IPv6 address of an active RFID tag with sensor unit, assigned by its reader. Users can send IP packets containing instruction to control how the tag works.

5   User Cases

A shopping guide application for a large furniture market will be introduced in this section to explain how to use this theoretical model to obtain the logical information and control the entity object.

5.1   Query Shopping Guide Information

The large furniture market attached a 13.56 MHz high-frequency RFID tags to all the furniture it sold. To name the RFID tag, EPC- SGTIN96 coding structure was adapted. Supposed that the object identifier of a sofa is $<sid_k, rid_k>$, and related information has been stored in the remote information server. Then, a complete process is shown in Fig. 3:

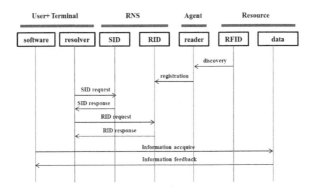

Fig. 3. Process to query shopping guide information

Step1. A customer can use the smart phone's NFC interface to read passive RFID tags and its object identifier $<sid_k, rid_k>$. Then the application program calls the resolver to query the local SID name server S_1 by sid_k.

Step2. S_1 forwards the request packet to the SID name server S_n, whose ID number is the Hash value of sid_k.

Step3. S_n returns the naming scheme description F_k corresponding to sid_k to the resolver. Here, F_k is a regular expression corresponding to EPC- SGTIN96.

Step4. The resolver maps the rid_k into URI_k according to F_k, and queries the RID name servers.

Step5. The responsible RID name server will return NAPTR record corresponding to the URI_k. The resolver can extract information server address and forward to the application program.

Step6. Finally, the application program using the address information to establish communication with the resource to obtained detailed information (e.g., attributes, logistics, security certificate, etc.).

5.2   Control Active RFID Tag

Considering the light issue in the building, many users express doubts about the visual furniture color. Deployment of mass active RFID tags containing a light sensing unit in the furniture market can help users to make decision. To name the active RFID tag, ucode-128 coding structure is adapted. Each reader has assigned virtual IPv6 addresses to the active RFID tags within its scope. Then, a complete process is shown in Fig. 4:

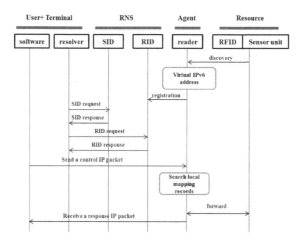

Fig. 4. Process to control active RFID tag

Step1. User queries the shopping guide software for light parameter. Supposing the nearest active RFID tags object identity is $<sid_t, rid_t>$.

Step2. The application program calls the resolver to query the local SID name server S_1 by sid_t.

Step3. S_1 forwards the request packet to the SID name server S_m, whose ID number is the Hash value of sid_t.

Step4. S_m returns the naming scheme description F_t corresponding to sid_t to the resolver. Here, F_t is a regular expression corresponding to ucode-128.

Step5. The resolver maps the rid_t into URI_t according to F_t, and queries the RID name servers.

Step6. The responsible RID name server will return NAPTR record corresponding to the URI_t. The resolver can extract the virtual IPv6 address of the active RFID tag and forward to the application program.

Step7. The application program uses the address to send an IP packet containing query or adjust command.

Step8. After receiving such a packet, the agent device (RFID reader) will forward the query and return the response in the end.

6   Discussion

In this section we will give a comprehensive analysis of the generic resource management model for the Internet of Things, which is proven to meet all kinds of requirements introduced in Session 2.

Firstly, because of the heterogeneity of the IoT resources, it is sure that various resources identify technology will co-exist. Any centralized and specific name services are not conducive to achieving real interoperability for the Internet of Things. Two-stage identification scheme can effectively maintain the compatibility between heterogeneous object identifiers. No matter what kind of resource identifier are taken as the original input, after the first stage of SID resolution, a naming scheme description is known. Then all various RID can be translated in to a unified resource name. So there is no need for an ordinary user to care about exactly what kind of naming schema is adapted for practical resource.

Secondly, as a third-party public service, name service will play an important role in the resource management model for the Internet of Things. In order to adapt to the different features of the RIDs and SIDs, we adopt a hybrid management mode, which can not only guarantees the efficiency of the frequent RID resolutions, but also ensure the equitability and fairness of the SID resolutions. Thirdly, in contrast to the traditional Internet, where users only care about accessing to logical information, users of the Internet of Things need to control entity object directly. Management mechanism proposed in this paper clearly focused the communication function on the agent device. Through assigning virtual IP addresses to the restricted resources which cannot run TCP/IP stack, a real-time communication will be ensured.

Finally, Internet of Things may have combination with various fields of human social life, so more and more heterogeneous resources will be connected to the network. Luckily, resource record has multiple service types, which is compatible with different levels of IoT resource name. According these name information, we can provide various service, just like location or retrieval.

7   Conclusion and Future Work

Acquiring information through the real-time interaction between ordinary users and various resources, and using this information to feedback to guide real-world decision-making behavior, in order to achieve optimal operation is just the major significance of the Internet of Things applications. Therefore, the resources management can be regarded as the foundation of all the Internet of Things applications.

Departure from the ordinary user's perspective, we analyze the requirements for IoT resource management and proposed a theoretical model to connect users, devices and resources together, based the resource name service (RNS) as a core. Resources are registered to the RNS through the devices, and users locate and query resources through RNS. This management mechanism can ensure users requirements on the compatibility, stability, real-time and flexibility for IoT resources.

Based on the ONS architecture, Wu et al. [25] first proposed a secure transmission model, using trusted computing technology and signcryption schemes from bilinear pairings to solve the security requirement in ONS query and information transmission. How to enhance the security, anonymity and trustworthy of the resource management model proposed in this paper is still need further exploration.

Acknowledgments. This work is supported by Knowledge Innovation Program of Chinese Academy of Sciences under Grant No.CNIC_QN_1208.

References

1. Raghu, D., Peter, H.: RFID forecast, players and opportunities 2011-2021. IDTechEx (2011)
2. Rolf, H.W.: Internet of Things - new security and privacy challenges. Computer Law & Security Review 26(1), 23–30 (2010)
3. Tomas, S.L.: RFID and sensor integration standards: State and future prospects. Computer Standards & Interfaces 33(3), 207–213 (2011)
4. Michael, B., Ben, G., Alanson, S., et al.: Revisiting smart dust with RFID sensor networks. In: Proc. of the 7th ACM Workshop on Hot Topics in Networks (Hotnets-VII), Calgary, Alberta, Canada. ACM (2008)
5. Li, C., Hailing, J., Yong, M., et al.: Overview of wireless sensor network. Journal of Computer Research and Development 42(1), 163–174 (2005)
6. Romer, K., Ostermaier, B., Mattern, F., et al.: Real-time search for real-world entities: A survey. Proceedings of the IEEE 98(11), 1887–1902 (2010)
7. Evdokimov, S., Fabian, B., Kunz, S., et al.: Comparison of discovery service architectures for the Internet of Things. In: Proc. of 2010 IEEE International Conference on Sensor Networks, Ubiquitous and Trustworthy Computing, Newport Beach, pp. 237–244. IEEE (2010)

8. EPCglobal: EPCglobal object name service (ONS) 1.0.1. The EPCglobal Standards Development Process (2007)
9. Kürschner, C., Condea, C., Kasten, O., Thiesse, F.: Discovery Service Design in the EPCglobal Network - Towards Full Supply Chain Visibility. In: Floerkemeier, C., Langheinrich, M., Fleisch, E., Mattern, F., Sarma, S.E. (eds.) IOT 2008. LNCS, vol. 4952, pp. 19–34. Springer, Heidelberg (2008)
10. Zhao, W., Liu, X., Ma, S., et al.: A distributed RFID discovery system: architecture, component and application. In: Proc. of the 14th International Conference on Computational Science and Engineering, Dalian. IEEE (2011)
11. Shi, J., Sim, D., Li, Y., et al.: SecDS: A secure EPC discovery service system in EPCglobal network. In: Proc. of the 2nd ACM Conference on Data and Application Security and Privacy, San Antonio, pp. 267–274. ACM (2012)
12. Hai, L., Bolic, M., Nayak, A., et al.: Taxonomy and challenges of the integration of RFID and wireless sensor networks. IEEE Network 22(6), 26–32 (2008)
13. Li, J.: Research method on data integration of wireless sensor node and RFID in IOT. Electronic Design Engineering 19(7), 103–106 (2011)
14. EPCglobal: The EPCglobal architecture framework 1.4. The EPCglobal Standards Development Process (2010)
15. Koshizuka, N., Sakamura, K.: Ubiquitous ID: standards for ubiquitous computing and the Internet of Things. IEEE Pervasive Computing 9(4), 98–101 (2010)
16. Framling, K., Harrison, M., Brusey, J.: Globally unique product identifiers - requirements and solutions to product lifecycle management. In: Proc. of the 12th IFAC Symposium on Information Control Problems in Manufacturing (INCOM), Saint Etienne. IFAC (2006)
17. Pujolle, G.: An autonomic-oriented architecture for the Internet of Things. In: Proc. of the IEEE John Vincent Atanasoff 2006 International Symposium on Modern Computing, Washington. IEEE (2006)
18. Duquennoy, S., Grimaud, G., Vandewalle, J.J.: Smews: smart and mobile embedded web server. In: Proc. of the 3rd International Workshop on Intelligent, Mobile and Internet Services in Ubiquitous Computing, Fukuoka, Japan. IEEE (2009)
19. Atzori, L., Iera, A., Morabito, G.: The Internet of Things: a survey. Computer Networks 54(15), 2787–2805 (2010)
20. Shen, S., Mao, Y., Fan, Q., et al.: The concept model and architecture of the Internet of Things. Journal of Nanjing University of Posts and Telecommunications (Natural Science) 30(4), 1–8 (2010)
21. Zhang, D., Wan, J., Liu, Q., et al.: A taxonomy of agent technologies for ubiquitous computing environments. KSII Transactions on Internet and Information Systems 6(2), 547–565 (2012)
22. Yang, L., Ye, T., et al.: Poster: A compatible and equitable resolution service for IoT resource management. In: Proc. of the 6th IEEE RFID, Florida. IEEE (2012)
23. Vladimir, K., Andrey, L., Dmitry, P.: EPC object code mapping service software architecture: web approach. MERA Networks Publications (2008)
24. Mealling, M., Daniel, R.: RFC2915: The naming authority pointer (NAPTR) DNS resource record. IETF (2000)
25. Wu, Z., Zhou, Y., Ma, J.: A security transmission model for Internet of Things. Chinese Journal of Computers 34(8), 1351–1364 (2011)

Distributed Joint Optimal Control of Power and Rate with Clustered Routing Protocol in Wireless Sensor Networks

Zhixin Liu, Lili Dai, Yazhou Yuan, and Jinfeng Wang

Institute of Electrical Engineering,
Yanshan University, Qinhuangdao, Hebei, China
lzxauto@ysu.edu.cn

Abstract. In clustered wireless sensor networks, to reduce the energy consumption and improve utility of network, it is proposed that cluster head is endowed with higher priority and a novel joint optimal model of power and rate is given. The distributed iterative algorithm is achieved by choosing the appropriate utility function, which is suit for variable separation and distributed computing. The dual decomposition method is adopted in the algorithm. Simulation results show that the joint optimal algorithm can prolong the lifetime of network and improve the comprehensive efficiency effectively.

1   Introduction

Wireless Sensor Networks is usually consisted of large number of sensors in the region of interest. WSN is a kind of flexible wireless communication network, which can perform collection, processing, transmission for sensing data in multi-hop self-organization manner. For the sake of the special working environment, the energy resource of sensor networks is unable to recharge or change. To save energy consumption and prolong the lifetime of networks, one of the hot topics in the researches of WSN is to design reasonable power control algorithm with the constraints of acceptable quality of service. For the lack of information of all other sensor nodes, it may result in the death of some nodes earlier and the deterioration of network performance, if every node only relay other nodes' data passively. It is an important problem to be solved how to allocate the energy of nodes, adjust the transmitting rate and balance the energy consumption [1]. In [2], to achieve the better performance in aspect of topology control and fault tolerance, a distributed adaptive power control scheme is proposed, which can guarantee the connectivity of networks and prolong the lifetime. Reference [3],[4] use the method of cross-layer optimization to solve the problem of power control and energy saving. However, it cannot avoid the extra overheads of information, which is from the frequently data calling in different protocol layers.

It is necessary to consider the demand of energy saving in the process of route design. There are two types of routing protocol algorithms [5]. One is flat routing algorithm, which is usually based on routing tree with redundancy and mobile

R. Wang and F. Xiao (Eds.): CWSN 2012, CCIS 334, pp. 325–334, 2013.
© Springer-Verlag Berlin Heidelberg 2013

sink node; the other is hierarchical routing based on cluster. In cluster routing algorithms, some nodes are selected as cluster head according to a certain of rules, and the other member nodes transport data to cluster. The flexible and adaptive multi-hop network can be formed with the relaying of clusters, which is favorable for stable topology and long lifetime of network [6]. Among clustering algorithms, LEACH protocol is one of the most representative algorithm. In LEACH, some nodes in a region can form cluster dynamically, and the cluster head is selected randomly. LEACH can make every node be cluster head with equal probability and balance the energy consumption among sensor nodes. The latter improved algorithms pay more attention on the energy saving, such as PEGASIS [9]HEED [10], EECF [11]. In the design of routing protocol for energy saving based on clustering, it usually focus on how to balance the energy consumption among nodes during the formation of cluster, and neglect that during the data transmission after the stable routing is set up. For the difference of roles, in the clustering networks, cluster head is in charge of data fusion, computation, storage, forwarding, and it will consume more energy [12]-[14]. In homogeneous network, cluster head and member nodes are with same features and energy constraints. Once the cluster head exhaust energy, the member nodes will lost the relay, and network reconfiguration and re-setup of routing are needed. Frequent change of routing and topology will increase the network overhead and decrease the network performance [15]-[16]. In this paper, the cluster head is endowed with higher priority, and the performance of cluster head is protected first by reducing the interference from member nodes. Based on the optimization model proposed in this paper, the cost function is design and the dual decomposition method is adopted to get distributed optimal iterative algorithm. The efficiency of cluster head is improved and the extra costs, caused by the performance deterioration or death of cluster head, is reduced. The network lifetime is prolonged effectively.

2   Network Model

It is assumed that there M sensor nodes in the sensing region, and according to some clustering rules, N clusters are set up, as shown in Fig.1. Ler N_n be the number of member nodes in cluster n . There are L links, the SINR in link l is γ_l , and its link capacity is c_l .

In clustering routing, cluster head is usually selected according to some rule. The cluster head CH_n can communicate with based station, and the member node s_i only exchange information with its cluster head. For that the cluster head take on more relay and forwarding task, it is rothole in the networks. The interference among different clusters cannot avoid, and this kind of interference will cause bad communication quality, even failure of communication. So the interference protection for cluster head is proposed. For cluster n , the protection for cluster head CH_n is described as

$$\sum_{i=1}^{N_n} p_i g_i < Q_n .$$ (1)

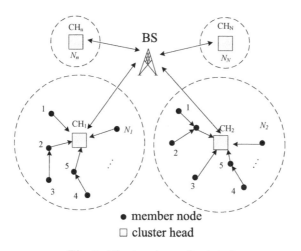

● member node
□ cluster head

Fig. 1. The topology of network

where, g_i is channel gain, p_i is transmission power of node s_i , Q_n is the demand of protection.

Assume that there are enough data to be sent at every node n , and the rate is r_i , which is larger than the minimum rate, i.e. $r_i > r_{\min}$. For the constraint of hardwire of node, the transmitting power is constrained, it is denoted as $p_i < p_{\max}$. In wireless communication, the link capacity satisfies the Shannon theorem. It is assumed that every node i in wireless networks transmits data independently, and the limit of transmitting rate c_l can be denoted as

$$c_l\left(p\right) = W\log_2\left(1 + \gamma\right) = W\log_2\left(1 + \frac{pK}{d^a W}\right) \ . \tag{2}$$

where, W is bandwidth, p is average power, d is the distance and K is a constant related to modulation, α is attenuation factor of channel and the typical value is 2 5. Denote $s\left(l\right)$ as the user set on link l , c_l as the capacity limitation. In fact, the actual rate is lower c_l , so we model the constraint the link capacity constrain as (3)

$$\sum_{j \in s(l)} r_j < \beta c_l \ . \tag{3}$$

where β is the efficiency factor, $0 < \beta < 1$

The object is to achieve the higher throughput with lower transmitting power, and the constraints on power, rate and capacity are satisfied. The optimization cost function is design as

$$U\left(r,p\right) = \sum_{i=1}^{M} F\left(r_i, p_i\right) \ . \tag{4}$$

where, $F\left(r_i, p_i\right)$ is increasing function of r_i , and decreasing function of p_i

According to above description, we give the power/rate joint optimal model based on clustering routing as shown in (5).

$$\max \sum_{i=1}^{M} F\left(r_i, p_i\right)$$

$$\begin{aligned} \text{s.t.} \quad & \sum_{j \in s(l)} r_j < \beta c_l\left(p\right) \, l = 1...L \\ & \sum_{i=1}^{N_n} p_i g_i < Q_n \qquad n = 1...N \\ & r_i > r_{\min} \qquad i = 1...M \\ & p_i < p_{\max} \qquad i = 1...M \end{aligned} \tag{5}$$

where, the first constraint is the rate constraint; the second is the protection constraint for cluster head; the third is the constraint of minimum transmitting rate; the forth is the power constraints. In general, the cost function is chosen as the nonlinear concave function of the variables of the sensor nodes, i.e. $F\left(r, p\right)$ is a second derivable function of r, p . The optimization object of the problem is to maximize the throughput utility with the low cost of energy consumption, i.e. achieve the joint optimization of power and rate. In the optimization model, the objective function is related to not only the rate of the node, but also of all other nodes' power level. That is difficult to execute in the real WSN. So we first construct an appropriate objective function, and separate the variables of power and rate. The distributed global optimization algorithm is achieved based on the dual decomposition method. To separate the effect of variables r, p on the objective function, here the cost function is chosen as the independent functions of two variables. Then the global optimization problem can be separated as two local optimization sub-problems. Therefore, we select the cost function as

$$F\left(r_i, p_i\right) = \alpha f\left(r_i\right) - \left(1 - \alpha\right) g\left(p_i\right) \tag{6}$$

where, $f\left(r_i\right)$ is a concave function of r_i , which can be regarded as the throughput benefit; $g\left(p_i\right)$ is a convex function of p_i , which can be regarded as the payment of power consumption. α is weighted factor, which can reflect the emphasis of rate utility and power utility.

3   Design of Optimization Strategy

As mentioned above, the joint optimization problem is formulated as nonlinear optimization problem. To fit for the feature of distributed operation in WSN, dual decomposition method is used. The Lagrangian dual function of problem (5) is

$$\begin{aligned} L\left(\mathbf{r}, \mathbf{p}, \lambda, \mu\right) = & \sum_{i=1}^{M} \left[\alpha f\left(r_i\right) - \left(1 - \alpha\right) g\left(p_i\right)\right] \\ & - \sum_{l=1}^{L} \lambda_l \left(\sum_{j \in s(l)} r_i - \beta c_l\right) - \sum_{n=1}^{N} \mu_n \left(\sum_{j=1}^{N_n} p_j g_j - Q_n\right) \end{aligned} \tag{7}$$

where, $\mathbf{r} = [r_1, r_2, \cdots r_n]$ is the vector of user power, $\mathbf{p} = [p_1, p_2, \cdots p_n]$ is the vector of transmitting rate, $\lambda = [\lambda_1, \lambda_2, \cdots \lambda_n]$ and $\mu = [\mu_1, \mu_2, \cdots \mu_n]$ are vectors of Lagrangian multiplier. Then the dual problem can be described as

$$\min_{\lambda, \mu} \varphi(\lambda, \mu) \tag{8}$$

where, $\varphi(\lambda, \mu) = \max_{r, p} L(\mathbf{r}, \mathbf{p})$ For the given λ, μ , the optimal power and rate can be achieved by solving the dual problem. To separate the variables, rewrite $L(\mathbf{r}, \mathbf{p})$

$$L(\mathbf{r}, \mathbf{p}) = \left[\sum_{i=1}^{M} \alpha f(r_i) - \sum_{l=1}^{L} \lambda_l \sum_{j \in s(l)} r_i \right]$$
$$- \left[\sum_{i=1}^{M} (1-\alpha) g(p_i) - \beta \sum_{l=1}^{L} \lambda_l c_l - \sum_{n=1}^{N} \mu_n \sum_{j=1}^{N_n} p_j g_j \right] + \sum_{n=1}^{N} \mu_n Q_n \tag{9}$$

Thus $L(\mathbf{r}, \mathbf{p})$ can be separate three parts. The first part can be converted to optimal rate sub-problem, the second part can be converted to optimal power sub-problem, and the last one is independent of r, p , for given λ, μ , it is constant.
Sub-problem 1

$$\max \quad L_1(\mathbf{r}) = \left[\sum_{i=1}^{M} \alpha f(r_i) - \sum_{l=1}^{L} \lambda_l \sum_{j \in s(l)} r_i \right] \tag{10}$$
$$\text{s.t.} \quad r_i > r_{\min} i = 1 \cdots M$$

Let $\frac{\partial L_1(\mathbf{r})}{\partial r_i} = 0$, one can get the optimal solution of rate r_i^* , i.e. solving the Eq.(11)

$$\alpha f'(r_i) = \sum_{l=1}^{L} \lambda_l \tag{11}$$

Sub-problem 2

$$\max \quad L_2(\mathbf{p}) = \sum_{i=1}^{M} (1-\alpha) g(p_i) - \beta \sum_{l=1}^{L} \lambda_l c_l - \sum_{n=1}^{N} \mu_n \sum_{j=1}^{N_n} p_j g_j \tag{12}$$
$$\text{s.t.} \quad p_i < p_{\max} i = 1 \cdots M$$

similarlylet $\frac{\partial L_2(\mathbf{p})}{\partial p_i} = 0$ and solve Eq.(13), one can get the optimal power p_i^* .

$$(1-\alpha) g'(p_i) - \beta \sum_{l=1}^{L} \lambda_l c_l' - \sum_{n=1}^{N} \mu_n g_i = 0 \tag{13}$$

Obviously, the above two sub-problems are independent of variable λ, μ . Once the optimal λ, μ are gained, it is easy to get the optimal solution. Next, we analyze the optimal multipliers λ^*, μ^* based on sub-gradient method. At time $t+1$, the multipliers update according to sub-gradient direction, and the rules are as follows.

$$\lambda_l(t+1) = \left[\lambda_l(t) - \delta(t)\frac{\partial L(\lambda, \mu)}{\partial \lambda_l}\right]^+ \tag{14}$$

$$\mu_n(t+1) = \left[\mu_n(t) - \delta(t)\frac{\partial L(\lambda, \mu)}{\partial \mu_n}\right]^+ \tag{15}$$

where, $[\cdot]^+$ denotes the value in the bracket is nonnegative. Once it is smaller than 0, the result of 0. $\delta(n)$ is iterative step. The step has major effect on the convergence rate. Next, we prove that the multiplier can converge the unique optimal point.

4   Simulations

The parameters in the simulation are listed in Table 1. There are 100 nodes are disposed in the interesting region of 200m × 200m . The routing is set up according to clustering algorithm. In general, there are following phases during the process of routing: the phase of the first formation in clustering, the phase of stable operation and the phase of cluster head transfer. The common analysis of clustering algorithm usually focus on the phase of cluster formation and cluster head transfer, and pay more attention to the scale of cluster, energy consumption, lifetime and stability of topology. They are aimed at reducing the cost of routing set-up and maintenance. However, the neglect of adjustment in the phase of stable operation will result in the imbalance among the nodes and affect the cluster stability and lifetime of networks. Here we only investigate the effect on the network performance in the phase of stable operation.

Table 1. Parameters

Parameter	Value
Region of interesting	$200 \times 200 m^2$
Number of nodes	100
Location of base station	(100 m, 100 m)
Initial energy	20 J
Initial multiplier	Random number in(0,1)
Sensing radius	15 m
Available link	3
Attenuation factor	2
Bandwidth	Bandwidth
γ_{min}	20kbps
P_{max}	0.5W
α	0.5

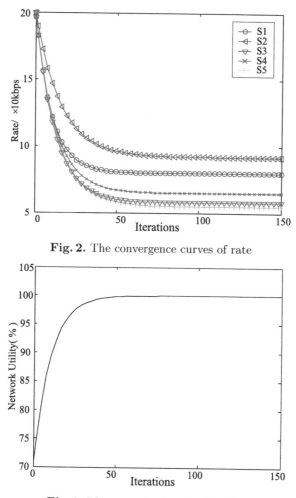

Fig. 2. The convergence curves of rate

Fig. 3. The normalized network utility

Supposed that the nodes are fixed, 100 nodes are devised into five clusters, and the average scale of the cluster is 20. In the phase of stable operation, we first focus on the process of rate adjustment. The adjusting curves of five sensors are given in Fig. 2. One can get that the algorithm has better convergence rate. Now we define the normalized utility of network, $\rho = \frac{U(r,p)}{U(r^*,p^*)} \times 100\%$, which can show the degree of approaching the optimal solution. The curve of network utility is shown in Fig. 3. After clustering, in every round, the algorithm can converge to the optimal point about 50 iterations later.

From the definition of cost function as shown in (6), we can see that the weighted factor can tradeoff the emphasis between rate utility and power utility. For the contradiction between tow performance indexes, it is necessary to balance them. We define the average throughput of a cluster as $\bar{r} = \frac{1}{N_n} \sum_{i=1}^{N_n} r_i.$

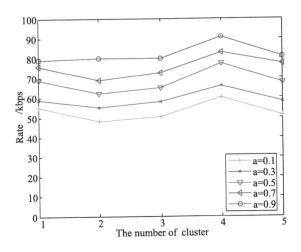

Fig. 4. The average throughput of cluster with different α

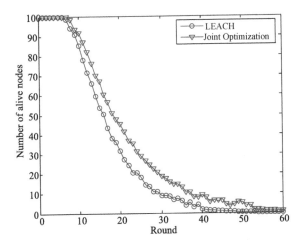

Fig. 5. The comparison of network lifetime

The average throughput with different α is shown in Fig. 4. One can get that the rate utility will be predominate in the whole network utility with the increment of α , and the average throughput also increases. The result show that the improvement of throughput is at the expense of energy consumption. To achieve higher throughput utility, the lifetime of network will decrease.

Next we evaluate the performance of joint optimization, which is based on some typical clustering algorithms, in aspect of energy balance and lifetime prolonging. LEACH is one of the most famous clustering algorithms and is proposed by Heinzelman in MIT. The basic idea of LEACH algorithm is that the cluster head is selected randomly and periodically, the other nodes around the cluster head will join it. Most of the later clustering routing protocols succeed to this idea, and the main attention is paid on the rule of cluster head election. Here we do not change the clustering rules of two algorithms, and adopt the joint optimization strategy in the phase of stable operation. The result is shown in figure 5. For LEACH protocol, the number of alive nodes with joint optimization is more that of primary algorithm.

5   Conclusions

In wireless sensor networks, how to improve network throughput and reduce energy consumption are two important and contradictive indexes in protocol design. In this paper, the frangibility and special particularity of cluster head are considered, and the higher priority is endowed to cluster head. The joint optimization model of power and rate is given and the distributed algorithm is achieved by dual decomposition method. The detail adjusting strategy is presented. The effectiveness of the proposed scheme is validated in simulations.

Acknowledgments. This work was supported partially by the NSFC under Grant 61104033, 61174127, the NSFC key Grant with No. 60934003, the Hebei Provincial Natural Science Fund under Grand F2012203109. All the persons involved in the research projects are thanked for their help.

References

1. Liao, S.B., Yang, Z.K., Cheng, W.Q.: Joint Power Control and Rate Adaptation for Wireless Sensor Networks. Acta Electronica Sinica 36(10), 1931–1937 (2008)
2. Zhao, X.J., Zhuang, Y., Zhao, J., Xue, T.T.: Adaptive Power Control Strategy for Wireless Sensor Networks. Journal of Electronics and Information Technology 32(9), 2231–2235 (2010)
3. Cimatti, G., Rovath, R., Setti, G.: Chaos Based Spreading in DS-UWB Sensor Networks Increases Available Bit Rate. IEEE Transactions on Circuits and Systems-Part I 54(6), 1327–1339 (2007)
4. Reena, J.L.: Joint Congestion and Power Control in UWB Based Wireless Sensor Networks. In: Proceedings of the 32nd IEEE Conference on Local Computer Networks, Dublin, Ireland, pp. 911–918 (2007)
5. Younis, O., Krunz, M., Ramasubramanian, S.: Node Clustering in Wireless Sensor Networks: Recent Developments and Deployment Challenges. IEEE Network 20(3), 20–25 (2006)
6. Liu, A.F., Zhang, P.H., Chen, Z.G.: Theoretical Analysis of the Lifetime and Energy Hole in Cluster Based Wireless Sensor Networks. Journal of Parallel and Distributed Computing 71(10), 1327–1355 (2011)
7. Chandrakasan, A.P., Smith, A.C., Heinzelman, W.B.: An Application Specific Protocol Architecture for Wireless Micro Sensor Networks. IEEE Transaction on Wireless Communications 1(4), 660–669 (2004)
8. Abbas, N., Hamid, S.A.: Performance Modeling of the LEACH Protocol for Mobile Wireless Sensor Networks. Journal of Parallel and Distributed Computing 71(6), 812–821 (2011)

9. Lindsey, S., Raghavendra, C.S.: PEGASIS: Power-efficient Gathering in Sensor Information Systems. In: Proc. of the IEEE Aerospace Conference, pp. 1125–1130 (2002)

10. Younis, Fahmy, S.: HEED: A Hybrid, Energy-efficient, Distributed Clustering Approach for Ad hoc Sensor Networks. IEEE Transactions on Mobile Computing 3(4), 366–379 (2004)

11. Chamam, A., Pierre, S.: A Distributed Energy-efficient Clustering Protocol for Wireless Sensor Networks. Computers Electrical Engineering 36(2), 303–312 (2010)

12. Soro, S., Heinzelman, W.B.: Cluster Head Election Techniques for Coverage Preservation in Wireless Sensor Networks. Ad-Hoc Networks 7(5), 955–972 (2009)

13. Ali, C., Samuel, P.: A Distributed Energy-efficient Clustering Protocol for Wireless Sensor Networks. Computers Electrical Engineering 36(2), 303–312 (2010)

14. Khalil, E.A., Attea, B.A.: Energy-aware Evolutionary Routing Protocol for Dynamic Clustering of Wireless Sensor Networks. Swarm and Evolutionary Computation (2011), doi:10.1016/j.swevo.2011.06004

15. Li, F.M., Liu, X.H., Xu, W.J., Han, P.: Link-stable Clustering and Power Control for Wireless Sensor Networks. Chinese Journal of Computers 31(6), 968–978 (2008)

16. Pan, G.F., Feng, Q.Y.: Optimal Transmission Power Selecting Algorithm for Cluster Based Ultra-wide Bandwidth Wireless Sensor Networks. Journal on Communications 30(11), 79–85 (2009)

17. Kar, K., Sarkar, S., Tassiulas, L.: A Simple Rate Control Algorithm for Maximizing Total User Utility. In: Proceedings IEEE INFOCOM, Anchorage, USA, pp. 39–43 (2001)

Sweep Coverage with Mobile Sensors on Two-Way Road

Xianling Lu[1,2], Si Chen[1], Wenping Chen[1], and Deying Li[1,*]

[1] School of Information, Renmin University of China, Beijing 100872, China
[2] Zhenzhou Information Science and Technology Institute
deyingli@ruc.edu.cn

Abstract. Recently, the sweep coverage has attracted much attention from researchers. There have been some works on the sweep coverage. However, none of them takes into account some constraints of real environment. In this paper, we study the minimum *t-Sweep Coverage with Mobile Sensors on Two-way Road (SCMMSTR)* problem, which is how to schedule mobile sensors' movement to satisfy the requirement of *t*-sweep coverage under the constraints of two-way roads such that the number of used mobile sensors is minimized. We first study the *Minimum Directed Cycles Set (MDCS)* problem to find a set of directed cycles which contains all vertexes such that the total length of these cycles is minimized. A greedy algorithm- *Finding Directed Cycles Set (FDCS) algorithm* is proposed for the *MDCS* problem. Secondly, we study the *Scheduling Mobile Sensors (SMS)* problem which is to schedule mobile sensors along a given set of circles such that the number of required mobile sensors is minimized. We propose the *Scheduling Mobile Sensors(SMS)* algorithm for the *SMS* problem. Based on the *FDCS* algorithm and the *SMS* algorithm, we propose the Computing Minimum Directed Cycle algorithm for the *SCMMSTR* problem. Simulation results demonstrate the performance of our algorithms.

Keywords: Mobile wireless sensor network, t-sweep coverage, two-way road, mobile sensor.

1 Introduction

Wireless sensor networks have been widely used for surveillance in harsh environments. In such applications, there are often special coverage requirements. Most existing works focus on the full coverage and barrier coverage. Full coverage requires that each point of the area is continuously monitored by at least one sensor. In barrier coverage, sensors are deployed to form a barrier for detecting intruders crossing the given strip area. The two kinds of coverage often require dense sensor deployment for critical region.

However, in practice, some applications do not require the entire field or targets to be covered all the time. For example, in the forest surveillance there are some

---

* Corresponding author.

R. Wang and F. Xiao (Eds.): CWSN 2012, CCIS 334, pp. 335–345, 2013.
© Springer-Verlag Berlin Heidelberg 2013

critical points monitoring the hazardous situations which should be checked once in a while. Thus, the workers only need to gather information from those critical points periodically. In such cases, we just need to periodically check the status of critical points. If we use full coverage or barrier coverage in these situations, it will incur prohibitive system cost. Therefore, we may employ another type of coverage called sweep coverage, in which a set of Points of Interests (POIs) but not all points in the monitoring area are periodically monitored instead of continuously monitored. POIs should be scanned once within a given time interval, which is called sweep period. To achieve sweep coverage, the existing works[1],[2],[3] use multiple mobile sensors to periodically cover all POIs. However, the existing works on sweep coverage did not consider some constraints in real situations when they scheduled the movement of mobile sensors. They assumed that mobile sensor can move along a straight line between any two nodes. But in practice, the movement of mobile sensors is usually restricted by roads.

In this paper, we investigate the t-sweep coverage on two-way roads, in which given a two-way road map and POIs, we need to schedule mobile sensors to scan these POIs such that each POI can be scanned at least one time for any t time units and the number of used mobile sensors is minimized. We propose a heuristic algorithm for the problem.

The rest of this paper is organized as follows. Section 2 discusses the existing related works. In Section 3 we present system model and formulate the t-Sweep Coverage with Minimum Mobile Sensors On Two-way Road (SCMMSTR) problem. Section 4 introduces the sweep algorithm to find directed cycle set and set optional positions of mobile sensors. We evaluate the performance of our algorithm in Section 5. Finally we conclude the paper in Section 6.

2   Related Works

Sensor coverage can be considered as a measure of the quality of service of a wireless sensor network. It has been an active and important research topic, evidenced by many research contributions to this field in recent years. The coverage problem can be classified into three categories: full coverage, barrier coverage, and sweep coverage. There have been many existing works on the full coverage[4],[5],[6],[7],[8],[9] and barrier coverage [10],[11],[12],[13],[14].

The problem of sweep coverage comes from the applications without the requirement of continuous coverage. There are some existing works on the sweep coverage problem [1],[2],[3]. Li et al. proposed a centralized algorithm CSWEEP [1], which transformed the sweeping coverage into a traveling salesman problem (TSP), and utilized a PTAS algorithm of traveling salesman problem (TSP) to get an approximate TSP ring. Du et al. [2] proposed two algorithms for two scenarios. In the first scenario, mobile sensors followed the same trajectory in different periods. For this scenario, they proposed a centralized algorithm MinExpand, to gradually deploy more mobile sensors and eventually achieve sweep coverage to all POIs. In the second scenario, the mobile sensors are not restricted to the same trajectory in different periods. The authors designed OSweep for the scenario, which scheduled all the mobile sensors to move along a TSP ring consisting of POIs.

However, none of the above works considered sweep coverage problem in the scenario with real roads. In this paper, we consider the sweep coverage with the real road constraint, which brings two challenges. First, the trajectories of the mobile sensors could not be arbitrarily but be restricted on the real road; Second, the real roads are usually two-way, it means that for any two points A and B, the path from A to B may be different from B to A. To the best of our knowledge, this work is the first to introduce the sweep coverage with the restriction of real roads in sensor networks.

3   Network Model and Problem Formulation

In this section, we introduce the network model and the definition of t-Sweep Coverage with Minimum Mobile Sensors on Two-way Road *(SCMMSTR)* problem.

There are some mobile sensors to monitor m POIs deployed on the given two-way road. The deployments of road and POIs are fixed. We assume that all the mobile sensors move at a constant speed v on the roads. We also assume the sensor radius of a mobile sensor is very small such that a mobile sensor can cover some POI only when the mobile sensor scan this POI.

In this paper, we study the t-sweep coverage problem on two-way road in mobile sensor networks, in which given a two-way road and POIs, we want to schedule some mobile sensors to scan these POIs such that each POI can be scanned at least one time for any given time period and the number of used mobile sensors is minimized.

We give the formal definition of the *T-Sweep Coverage with Minimum Mobile Sensors On Two-way Road (SCMMSTR)* Problem as follows.

Definition 1. *t-Sweep Coverage [1]: A Point Of Interest (POI) is said to be t-sweep coverage by a coverage scheme F if and only if it can be covered at least once for any t time units by the mobile sensors scheduled by F.*

Definition 2. *Restraint t-Sweep Coverage (RTSC): A POI is said to be Restraint t-Sweep Coverage by a coverage scheme F iff it is covered at least once every t time units by a schedule F of mobile sensors movement under the constraints of two-way road.*

Definition 3. *t-Sweep Coverage with Minimum Mobile Sensors on Two-way Road (SCMMSTR) problem: Given a deployment of m POIs on a two-way road, the SCMMSTR problem is how to schedule mobile sensors to meet the requirement of RTSC such that the number of used mobile sensors is minimized.*

Given a two-way road and the deployment of POIs, we construct a directed weight graph $G = (V, A, W)$ to model the relationship of POIs, where $V = \{v_1, v_2, .., v_m\}$ is the set of POIs which distributed at the two sides of two-way road. For any two POIs, if a mobile sensor can travel from v_i to v_j without

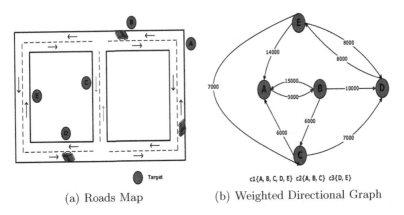

(a) Roads Map   (b) Weighted Directional Graph

Fig. 1. Roads Map and Weighted Directional Graph

passing other POIs on the two-way roads, then there is an arc $\overrightarrow{v_i v_j}$ from v_i to v_j in G. We use w_{ij} to denote the weight of $\overrightarrow{v_i v_j}$ which is the length of the shortest directed path on the two-way roads from v_i to v_j without passing other POIs. Fig. 1(a) shows a two-way road and some POIs. Fig.1(b) is a weighted directed graph corresponding to Fig. 1(a).

A coverage scheme for the *SCMMSTR* problem can be represented by the moving tracks of all mobile sensors. Based on the weighted directed graph, if we can find a set of directed circles which can cover all the POIs, we can get a coverage scheme for the *SCMMSTR* problem. Taking into account the real situation, we assume that G is a union of strong connected component without isolated point. Therefore, it is critical to solve the *SCMMSTR* problem that finding a set of directed cycles which contains all POIs and scheduling mobile sensors under a given set of circles. In the following, we will respectively study the Minimum Directed Cycles Set(MDCS) problem and the Scheduling Mobile Sensors problem, then based on the two subproblems, we propose the Computing Minimum Directed Cycle Algorithm for the *SCMMSTR* problem.

4   The Computing Minimum Directed Cycle Algorithm

It is easy to know that the *SCMMSTR* problem is NP-hard. In this section, we propose an effective greedy algorithm, called as Computing Minimum Directed Cycle *(CMDC)* algorithm to solve the *SCMMSTR* problem. The main idea is first we find a set of directed cycles which cover all vertices and total length is minimized. Then based on the set of directed cycles, we schedule mobile sensors to scan the POIs such that the number of mobile sensors is minimized.

4.1   The Minimum Directed Cycles Set Problem

In this subsection, we first study the Minimum Directed Cycles Set (MDCS) problem: Given an edge weight graph $G = (V, E, w)$, to find a set of directed

cycles which cover all vertexes such that the total length of these cycles is minimized. We will propose an algorithm to solve it.

Before we introduce the *Finding Directed Cycles Set(FDCS)* algorithm, we
give some notations and definitions used in the algorithm. We denote C as the
set of selected cycles. Initially, set $C = \emptyset$. We denote the *unit length coverage*
of a path p as $wd(p)$, $wd(p) = n(p)/d(p)$, where $d(p)$ represents the length of p
and $n(p)$ represents the number of POIs which have not been covered by C in
p. Let $SWP(v_m, v_n)$ denote the maximum weight path among all paths from v_m
to v_n. Let $d^+(v_i)$ and $d^-(v_i)$ denote the out-degree and the in-degree of vertex
v_i respectively.

If some vertices whose *in-degree* and *out-degree* are both equal to 1 which can
form a path of G, they must be contained in a same cycle in G if there is a cycle
containing them. We call this path as $VitalPath$.

Definition 4. *Vital Path:(VP): A path $p(\overrightarrow{v_i v_j ... v_k v_l})$ is called as $VitalPath$ iff
the in-degree of v_i and out-degree of v_l are at least 1, and the out-degree and the
in-degree of other vertexes in path p are 1.*

The *FDCS* algorithm uses a greedy method to select the directional cycle whose
unit length coverage is maximal. The inputs of the algorithm is $G(V, A, W)$. The
output of the algorithm is a set $C = \{c_1, c_2, ..., c_x\}$ of cycles which contains all
vertices in V. In the following, we describe the *FDCS* algorithm in detail.

1 Set $C = \emptyset$ and set all POIs to *uncovered*.
2 Find all VPs from G, and Compute the $SWP(v_n, v_m)$ for each
   VP $p(\overrightarrow{v_m, ..., v_n})$.
3 Construct the set C' of direction cycles which are composed of all VP
   $p(\overrightarrow{v_m ... v_n})$ and $SWP(v_n, v_m)$.
4 Compute the wd of each directed cycle in C'. Then, sort these cycles according to their wd in decreasing order.
5 Select cycle c'_i with the maximal wd in C', and insert c'_i into the set C of
   cycles. Then set all POIs in C to *covered* and remove c'_i from C'. Repeat
   4-5 until all cycles of C' are selected or the set C contains all the vertexes.
6 Split the vertex with the maximal degree among the vertexes which is not
   contained in C. Concretely, split a vertex v_i into v_i^t and v_i^h, and define the
   v_i^t as *arc-head* of these arcs whose *arc-head* is v_i in G, and define the v_i^h as
   arc-tail of these arcs whose *arc-tail* is v_i in G.
7 Repeat 2-4 until C contains all vertexes of V.
8 Remove the redundant cycles from C. Here, the redundant cycles are such
   cycles that if removing from C, C still can contain all vertexes of G.

Theorem 1. *If G is a union of strong connected components without isolated
nodes, then set C resulted by the FDCS algorithm contains all vertices of G.*

Proof: Without loss of generality, we assume the vertex v_i is not contained in
C. Due to G is a union of strong connected components without isolated nodes,
v_j must be included in a strong connected component G_i of G with at least

two vertices. Therefore, there exists an arc $\overrightarrow{v_i v_j}$ in G_i. According to the FDCS algorithm, if C does not contain v_i, then there doesn't exist a path from v_j to v_i in G, which is contradict with that G_i is a strong connected components. The theorem holds.

4.2   The *Scheduling Mobile Sensors(SMS)* Algorithm

In this subsection, we address the Scheduling Mobile Sensors problem: given a set of circles which cover all vertices of V and a constant mobile sensors' moving speed, to schedule mobile sensors' movement such that each node in V can be scanned at least one time for any t time units and the number of used mobile sensors is minimized. Since all the mobile sensors move at a constant speed on given tracking cycles, the schedule of mobile sensors movement can be convert to setting start locations of mobile sensors to minimize the number of used mobile sensors. We will propose a *Scheduling Mobile Sensors(SMS)* algorithm to solve this problem.

Based on the directions of two directed cycles and their sharing arcs and points, we categorize the relations of two directed cycles into intersection, tangency and separation.

Definition 5. *Intersection: Two directed cycles c_i and c_j are called as intersection iff they have at least one common directed arc.*

Definition 6. *Tangency: Two directed cycles c_i and c_j are called as tangency iff they have only one common point.*

Definition 7. *Separation: Two directed cycles c_i and c_j are called as separation iff they are not intersection or tangency.*

In the following, we introduce the SMS algorithm.

Firstly, we deal with the intersecting cycles. Let $ov(c_i, c_j)$ denote a set of common paths shared by cycle c_i and cycle c_j. $ov(c_i, c_j)$ may include more than one path. Let $ov^h(c_i, c_j)$ denote the hth path of $ov(c_i, c_j)$. Let C^t denote a set of directed cycles, initially, $C^t = \phi$. The process is described as follows:

1 First find intersecting directed cycles in C and insert these intersecting cycles into C^t of directed cycles. Then, set $C = C \setminus C^t$.
2 select two intersecting cycles c_i and c_j that the sum of their wd is maximal in C^t, then select the longest path $ov^l(c_i, c_j)$ of $ov(c_i, c_j)$. Assume the wd of c_i is no more than that of c_j.
3 Set the start point of the common path $ov^l(c_i, c_j)$ as the start location of a mobile sensor and evenly set start locations of sensors on the cycle c_i in which the distance between two adjacent sensors is vt.
4 Remove c_i from C^t and remove the common path which contained by c_i and other cycles.

5 Update the wds of cycles in C^t.

6 Repeated 2-5, until there aren't common paths among any two cycles.

7 Set start locations of sensors on the remanent paths in C^t in which the distance between two adjacent sensors is vt.

After the above process, we deal with tangent cycles. First, set $C^t = \phi$ and find tangent cycles in C, then insert these tangent cycles in to C^t. Next, select two tangent cycles c_i and c_j that the sum of their wd is maximal in C^t and set the tangent point as the start location of sensor, then set another sensor every distance of vt according the direction of these cycles and remove the two cycles from C^t. Repeated these processes until there aren't tangent cycles in C^t.

At last, we deal with the separate cycles. For each separate cycle, we evenly deploy sensors on this cycle with distance vt.

4.3 The Computing Minimum Directed Cycle Algorithm

Based on $FDCS$ algorithm and SML algorithm, we propose the Computing Minimum Directed Cycle Algorithm ($CMDC$) to solve the $SCMMSTR$ problem.

The $CMDC$ algorithm contains three steps. The first step is to construct an edge weight directed graph $G = (V, E, W)$ shown in Section 3. The second step is to find a set of directed cycles which contains all vertices in G and the total length of these cycles is minimal. The third is to schedule mobile sensors to scan the POIs based on the set of circles got by the second step.

The pseudocode of the $CMDC$ algorithm is listed in Algorithm 1.

Algorithm 1. CMDC($V, A, W, v, t, \&F$)

1: Let F denote the set of mobile sensors' start locations;

2: construct an edge weight graph G

3: use the algorithm $FDCS(V, A, W, \&C)$ to get a set C of directed cycles which cover all nodes in V.

4: Based on C, use the algorithm $SMS(C, v, t, \&F)$ to get F;

5: use F to schedule the movement of mobile sensors.

The computational complexity of $CMDC$ algorithm is analyzed as follows. Let $|V|$ and $|A|$ denote the cardinalities of V and A respectively. In $FDCS$ algorithm, finding VPs of G takes $O(|A||V|^2)$ time, computing the wd of each VP takes $O(|A||V|^2)$ time, sorting wd of each cycle c'_i in C' takes $O(|A|log|A|)$ time and handling other arcs which aren't included in VPs takes $O(|V|^3)$ time. In SMS algorithm, Finding the inserting cycles and the tangent cycles to form C^I takes $O(|A|^3)$. Let $|C^I|$ denote the number of inserting cycles in C. Sorting the wd of intersecting cycles takes $O(|C^I|^2log|C^I|)$ and computing the longest common path of two intersecting cycles costs $O(|A|^2)$. Computing the start locations on tangent cycles and separate cycles both costs $O(|A|^2)$. Thus, the time complexity of SMS algorithm is $O(|V|^3)$. Therefore, if $|A| > |V|$, the computational complexity of $CMDC$ algorithm is $O(|A|^3)$, else it is $O(|V|^3)$.

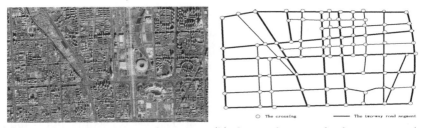

(a) secondary planet map of two-way (b) the topology graph of two-way roads
roads

Fig. 2. The cases of two-way roads

5   Performance Evaluation

In our simulations, we select the real roads in a center region of Beijing city as
the deployment area of POIs. The region is about $7970m \times 5530m$ which includes
82 crossings and 159 two-way road sections. Fig.2(b) is a topology graph of the
roads in Fig.2(a). We randomly select 200 crowded spots at road-sides as POIs
in each simulation scenario, and take the mean values of 20 times of simulations
as the results. Let S denote the number of mobile sensors, v denote the default
moving velocity of mobile sensor, and t denote the required sweep period of each
POIs.

Since none of the previous works about *t-sweep* considers the restrictions of
two-way road, we evaluate the performance of the CMDC algorithm by comparing with randomized scheme (RAND) and a greedy algorithm called Nearest
Neighbor Prior(NNP) algorithm. When simulating $RAND$ and NNP algorithms,
we assume each mobile sensor knows the positions of all POIs in advance. When
determining the next POI to sweep, $RAND$ algorithm randomly chooses a neighboring POI; while NNP algorithm chooses the nearest neighboring POI.

Let S denote the number of mobile sensors, v denote the default moving
velocity of mobile sensor, and t denote the required sweep period of each POIs. In
our simulations, we evaluate the performance of our algorithms with two metrics:
the coverage efficiency and the minimal number of required mobile sensors that
can satisfy the requirement of $RTSC$ under the constraints of v, t and two-way
roads. For simplicity, we call the POIs which meet the t-sweep period requirement
as reliable POIs[2]. Coverage efficiency is defined as the ratio between the reliable
POIs and the total POIs.

5.1   The Minimal Number of Required Mobile Sensors

The goal of the $SCMMSTR$ problem is scheduling the minimum number of mobile sensors such that all POIs meet the requirement of $RTSC$. In Fig.3, we
compare the minimal numbers of mobile sensors required by $RAND$, NNP and
$CMDC$, respectively. Since both $RAND$ and NNP can not guarantee that every
POI meets the sweep period requirement, when the coverage efficiency of $RAND$

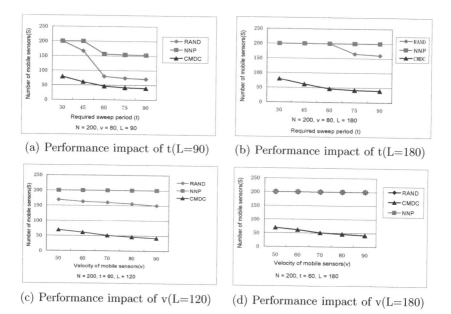

(a) Performance impact of t(L=90)   (b) Performance impact of t(L=180)

(c) Performance impact of v(L=120)   (d) Performance impact of v(L=180)

Fig. 3. The least number of require mobile sensors

and *NNP* is more than 90%, we regard the number of the mobile sensors are eligible on providing the required sweep coverage.

We first study how the required sweep period impact on the performance of all algorithms. As shown in Fig.3(a) and Fig.3(b), the minimal numbers of required mobile sensors of the three algorithms decrease when *t* increases.

We then evaluate how the minimal number of required sensors fluctuate with the velocity *v* of mobile sensor increasing, the results are shown in Fig.3(c) and Fig.3(d). We find that the minimal numbers of required mobile sensors of the three algorithms decrease when *v* increases. Furthermore, under the same constraints, the minimal numbers required by the *CMDC* algorithm in Fig.3(c) and Fig.3(d) are the same, which can be concluded that all POIs can meet the requirement of t-sweep under the minimal number of required sensors in the *CMDC* algorithm whatever the length of running-time is.

From the simulation results shown in Fig. 3(a-d), it is obvious that *CMDC* always outperforms *RAND* and *NNP*. First, the minimal number required by the *CMDC* algorithm is much less than others. Second, the minimal number of required sensors does not vary with the length of running-time.

5.2 Coverage Efficiency

In this subsection, we test and compare the coverage efficiency of the *CMDC* algorithm with that of *RAND*, *NNP*. Fig.4(a) shows how the coverage efficiency varies with the running period. It is obvious that the *CMDC* algorithm significantly outperforms *RAND* and *NNP*. Fig.4(b) shows the impact of velocity of

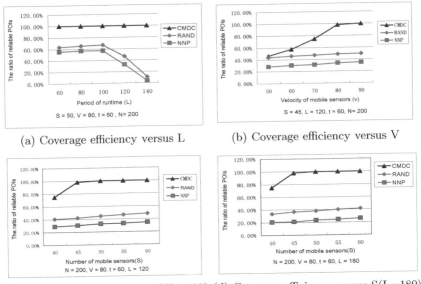

(a) Coverage efficiency versus L   (b) Coverage efficiency versus V

(c) Coverage efficiency versus S(L=120) (d) Coverage efficiency versus S(L=180)

Fig. 4. The ration of reliable POIs and total POIs

sensors on the coverage efficiency. We can observe that the increase slope of the
$CMDC$ algorithm is apparently bigger than that of $RAND$ and NNP.

We also investigate how coverage efficiency varies with the number of mobile
sensors. As illustrated in Fig.4(c), the increase of sensors can improve the performance of all algorithms. Furthermore, we can observe that coverage efficiency
of the $CMDC$ algorithm reaches to 100% quickly with the increasing of the number of used sensors while the ratios of other algorithms increase slowly. The
main reason is that increasing a mobile sensor means that there are additional
POIs on the length of $v * t$ can be covered by $CMDC$. However, because of the
noncooperation of mobile sensors, the performance of $RAND$ and NNP have no
significant improvement when increasing a few mobile sensors.

Comparing Fig.4(c) with Fig.4(d), we can find that the coverage efficiency of
$RAND$ and NNP decrease with the increasing of the running period L. However,
the coverage ratio of CMDC can maintain 100% no matter how the length of
running period varies.

6   Conclusion

We studied how to scheduling minimal mobile sensors movement for the requirements of the t-sweep coverage under the constraints of roads. And proposed a
greedy algorithm $CMDC$ for the $SCMMSTR$ problem. The simulation results
show that $CMDC$ obviously outperforms $RAND$ and NNP in efficiency.

Acknowledgment. Dr. Li was supported in part by the Fundamental Research Funds for the Central Universities, and the Research Funds of Renmin University of China under grant 10XNJ032. This work also was jointly supported in part by National Natural Science Foundation of China under grants 61070191 and 91124001, and Research Fund for the Doctoral Program of Higher Education of China under grant 20100004110001.

References

1. Li, M., Cheng, W., Liu, K., He, Y., Liu, Y., Liao, X.: Sweep Coverage with Mobile Sensors. IEEE Transactions on Mobile Computing 11(10), 1534–1545 (2011)
2. Du, J., Li, Y., Liu, H., Sha, K.: On Sweep Coverage with Minimum Mobile sensors. In: International Conference on Parallel and Distributed Systems (2010)
3. Xi, M., Wu, K., Zhao, J., Liu, Y., Li, M.: Run to Potential: Sweep Coverage in Wireless Sensor Networks. In: International Conference on Parallel Processing (2009)
4. Wang, W., Srinivasan, V., Chua, K.C.: Trade-offs between Mobility and Density for Coverage in Wireless Sensor Networks. In: Proceedings of ACM MobiCom (2007)
5. Balister, P., Bollobas, B., Sarkar, A., Kumar, S.: Reliable Density Estimates for Achieving Coverage and Connectivity in Thin Strips of Finite Length. In: ACM MobiCom (2007)
6. Hefeeda, M., Bagheri, M.: Randomized k-Coverage Algorithms for Dense Sensor Networks. In: IEEE INFOCOM (2007)
7. Liu, H., Chen, W., Ma, H., Li, D.: Energy-Efficient Algorithm for the Target Q-coverage Problem in Wireless Sensor Networks. In: Pandurangan, G., Anil Kumar, V.S., Ming, G., Liu, Y., Li, Y. (eds.) WASA 2010. LNCS, vol. 6221, pp. 21–25. Springer, Heidelberg (2010)
8. Liu, H., Wan, P., Yi, C., Jia, X., Makki, S., Niki, P.: Maximal Lifetime Scheduling in Sensor Surveillance Networks. In: IEEE INFOCOM (2005)
9. Chaudhary, M., Pujari, A.K.: Q-Coverage Problem in Wireless Sensor Networks. In: Garg, V., Wattenhofer, R., Kothapalli, K. (eds.) ICDCN 2009. LNCS, vol. 5408, pp. 325–330. Springer, Heidelberg (2009)
10. Kumar, S., Lai, T.H., Arora, A.: Barrier Coverage with Wireless Sensors. In: ACM MobiCom (2005)
11. Chen, A., Kumar, S., Lai, T.H.: Designing Localized Algorithms for Barrier Coverage. IEEE Transactions on Mobile Computing (2010)
12. Yang, H., Li, D., Zhu, Q., Chen, W., Hong, Y.: Minimum Energy Cost k-barrier Coverage in Wireless Sensor Networks. In: Pandurangan, G., Anil Kumar, V.S., Ming, G., Liu, Y., Li, Y. (eds.) WASA 2010. LNCS, vol. 6221, pp. 80–89. Springer, Heidelberg (2010)
13. Ssu, K.-F., Wang, W.-T., Wu, F.-K., Wu, T.-T.: K-Barrier Coverage with a Directional Sensing Model. International Journal on Smart Sensing and Intelligent Systems (2009)
14. Saipulla, A., Westphal, C., Liu, B., Wang, J.: Barrier Coverage of Line-Based Deployed Wireless Sensor Networks. In: IEEE INFOCOM (2009)

H-Mac: A Hybrid MAC Protocol for VANET

Juan Luo, Junli Zha, Yi Xiao, and Renfa Li

School of Information Science and Engineering,
Hunan University, Changsha 410082, China
{juanluo,zhajunli}@hnu.edu.cn,
xiaoyi567@126.com, lirenfa@vip.sina.cn

Abstract. This paper proposes a Hybrid Mac protocol(H-MAC) that combines reservation and competition mechanisms to solve the sudden burst data flow at link layer of the VANET(Vehicle Ad hoc Network). Based on the entire network time synchronization, H-MAC protocol divides a frame cycle into two parts. The first part is reservation period in which each node has its own slot. Node could send stable data flow such as beacon packets in the slot. The second part is competition period in which burst data could be sent. Therefore, beacon frames and burst data are divided. H-MAC improves the utilization of channels and reduces delays that caused by collision of the burst data. Simulation results show that the proposed H-MAC protocol provides high reliability of broadcast data at MAC layer.

Keywords: VANET, MAC, WAVE, IEEE 802.11p, Broadcast.

1 Introduction

VANET is a technology that uses moving vehicles as nodes to create a mobile network. It composed by the wireless communication module on vehicles and roadside infrastructures [1]. As core part of the intelligent automobiles, VANET have become a more important research and development area. VENET has changing topologies, frequent path loss, short link lifetime and low packet throughput which are caused by high mobility, road environment and volume of traffic. Therefore, traditional MAC layer protocols in Ad hoc network such as IEEE 802.11, RR-ALOHA [2]can not work effectively. It is a challenge for MAC protocol in VANET to ensure efficient, reliable channel access and low delay, high scalability data communication under rapidly changing topologies.

According to different channel allocation methods, MAC protocols for VANET are divided into three categories: competition-based MAC protocol uses CSMA, pre-allocation reservation-based MAC protocol and direction antenna-based MAC protocol.

RR-ALOHA is a typical MAC protocol which based on pre-allocation reservation. RR-ALOHA divides channel by TDMA mechanism, every node that has successfully added into the network would have a fixed time slot which called basic slot. SDMA protocol [3]is a MAC protocol which based on locations of

R. Wang and F. Xiao (Eds.): CWSN 2012, CCIS 334, pp. 346–356, 2013.
© Springer-Verlag Berlin Heidelberg 2013

vehicles to allocate channels [4]. When channel allocation is completed, nodes that utilize reservation-based MAC protocol could send information with no competition. Indeed, collision rate is low, but the dynamic changing topologies would have a greater effect on the effectiveness of channel allocation and limitedness scalability of network. Ray et al. in [5] proposed that road information and speed of vehicles can be used to predict changing topologies and improve the effectiveness of the slot reservation.

Vishnu Navda et al. extend direction-based MAC protocol D-MAC to VANET [6]. From theoretical analysis, directional antenna can greatly improve network performance. However, experiments showed that this protocol has a complex design and implementation. Thus, it is hard to implement this protocol in VANET. Solutions for VANET based on IEEE 802.11 and CSMA algorithm are described in IEEE 802.11p [7]. Even IEEE 802.11p has modified a lot for VANET, there's still a significant decline in network performance under high load environment, particularly for the control channel CCH [8]. In order to improve the security of traffic, the channel of VANET must have a larger number of broadcast frames. However, IEEE 802.11p is similar with IEEE 802.11, so there is no guarantee for the reliability of the broadcast.

In this paper, we newly proposed H-MAC protocol based on the analysis of flow load in VANET. H-MAC protocol combines reservation-based MAC protocol with IEEE 802.11p, to make up for the IEEE 802.11p. Specially, H-MAC protocol is used to solve collision problem in CCH channel in WAVEWireless Access in Vehicular Environment. Each frame period includes appointment section and competition section. In the appointment section, every node has a fixed slot, during which nodes could send fixed load such as beacon frame. In the competition section, CSMA/CA is used for all nodes to compete channels, which is for the nonperiodic sudden load. Separating beacon frame from competition section not only ensure sending success rate of beacon message, but also reduce the collision possibility of the other message in the competition section.

The rest of the paper is organized as follows. Section II reviews IEEE 802.11p for VANET and proposed the problem. The proposed H-MAC protocol is described in section III, while the performance evaluation of the proposed scheme is discussed in section IV. Finally, Section V concludes the paper and presents our plan for future work.

2   Problem Descriptions

2.1   IEEE 802.11p

At present, IEEE 802.11p is the unique communication protocol standard which especially for VANET. IEEE has also developed a protocol clusters matching with the IEEE 802.11p called IEEE 1609.x. The whole IEEE 802.11p/1609.x called WAVE. Figure.1 shows the WAVE protocol stack.

IEEE 802.11p improves traditional IEEE 802.11 from two aspects. Firstly, two communication roles are defined: Provider and User. Simplify the process to establish a data link between two roles, remove a complex data encryption and authentication process. Secondly, entire communication band of the data link layer is divided into a control channel (CCH) and the service channel (SCH), as showed in figure.2. CCH broadcasts beacon messages, security-related messages, service messages and other control messages. SCH is mainly for the other non-security messages. Small number of CCH, large volumes of transmission data and high quality requirement make improvement of CCH performance to be a essential problem in MAC protocol research for VANET.

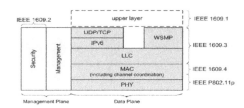

Fig. 1. IEEE 802.11p/1609.x (WAVE) protocol stack

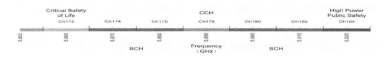

Fig. 2. Channel Assignment of IEEE 802.11p/1609.x (WAVE) protocol

2.2 Shortcoming of IEEE 802.11p

There are two main reasons for the poor performance of data link layer. First, a large number of broadcast data should be transmitted at data link layer. Second, IEEE 802.11p inherited from IEEE 802.11b, so there is no guarantee for reliable broadcast data transmission at data link layer. Carrier sense, RTS / CTS short frame, ACK acknowledgment frame and binary exponential backoff after collision can improve the data transmission reliability. But these mechanisms are only applicable to unicast data frames. Using acknowledgment frame in broadcast frame leads frame collision. Therefore, there is no RTS / CTS and confirmation mechanism in IEEE 802.11p, only CSMA/CA is used to avoid collision. Large numbers of broadcast at data link layer caused high packet loss of the whole network.

$$P_{suc} = \lambda k R p \left(1 - p\right)^{(\lambda k R - 1)}; . \tag{1}$$

Figure.3 shows Psuc changes with packet sent probability in one slot. Apparently, packet success rate is low. The highest packet success rate is only 40%. K.

Bilstrup et al. make the test and results showed that in the worst case, over 80% broadcast frames were discarded for a particular node and about 50% packet were discarded on average[9].

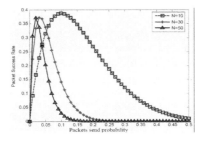

Fig. 3. Packet success rate changes with packets send probability

3   H-MAC

Characteristics of data frames in CCH channel are studied to solve the high packet loss probability of IEEE 802.11p. There are three transmission messages in CCH including beacon frame which sent periodically, service broadcast frame which describes the service and the other security frames. These frames all broadcast in CCH channelcharacteristics are shown in table 1.

Table 1. Characteristics of broadcast frame in CCH

	Delay requirement	Reliability requirement	Load	Sudden
Beacon frames	low	ordinary	high	low
Service broadcast frames	ordinary	ordinary	ordinary	higher
Safety message frames	high	high	low	high

Three broadcast frames send beacon frames periodically to make the vehicle exchange position, speed, type and the other security related messages. Position-based routing protocols such as GPSR [10] relies the beacon frame to update neighbor node information timely. And some other protocols realize security certification based on beacon frame[11]. Beacon frame sending frequency is 10Hz for WAVE, so beacon frame occupies a very heavy proportion of the data link layer load. Literature [12] proposed the distributed cooperative way to reduce sending numbers of beacon frame, but it still can not solve the high collision rate of beacon frames fundamentally. The paper proposed a new MAC protocol for VANET H-MAC (Hybrid-MAC). H-MAC includes three parts: dynamic slot allocation mechanism, cluster fusion mechanism and slot adjustment mechanism. The rest paper will introduce these three mechanisms in details.

3.1   Dynamic Slot Allocation Mechanism

H-MAC protocol divides data link layer channel into multiple discrete sections according to beacon period, which are called BP (Base Period). Figure 4 shows the slot structure of H-MAC protocol. Each Cycle is divided into two parts, RP (Reservation Period) and CP (Competition period). RP is made of many RSs (Reserve Slots) which have the same size. Each node should occupy one RS to send its own beacon frame. In a cycle, except RS is CS. In CS, every node uses CSMA/CA to send its service broadcast frame and security frame. Thus, beacon frame is separated with the other data frames and collision between data frames is reduced.

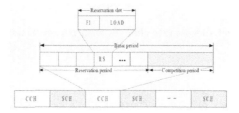

Fig. 4. Slot structure of H-MAC protocol

To allocate RS effectively, each node maintains two data structures, RS allocation table and neighbor node table. RS allocation table records RS allocation that node achieved from neighbor nodes. RS allocation includes how many RSs has been used in the network and each slot is occupied by which node. Neighbor node table records RS number that occupied by one-hop range neighbor node and some other related information.

Proportion of the RP and CP in BP is dynamically changed. Vehicle should monitor for a BP in CCH channel when it opens communication module at the first time. If vehicle does not receive any message, it considered to be the unique node in the network. Then, the node need to initial a network. First, the node should choose the first RS to be its BS (Basic Slot) and update slot allocation table. BS contains beacon frame and FI (Frame Information) frame. FI frame records the RS allocation that the node has observed, including RS that the node and one-hop neighbor node have occupied.

The whole process of a new node joining the network is as follows. Suppose a new node named Node-A is getting into a network. Firstly, Node-A should monitor for a BP and collect other nodes FI frame. Next, Node-A updates RS table and selects a free slot to be its RS. If there is no free slot for it, a new RS should be added to be its applied RS. Then, Node-A sends a RF (Request Frame) in the competition section. MAC address, requested slot number and requested times are included in RF. Nodes that can receive RF frame from Node-A must check whether there is a RS collision. If there is no collision, the requested RS which in RF frame will be allocated to Node-A. Meanwhile, these nodes should update the neighbor node table and RS table. Again, Node-A monitors the channel for a BP. If all FI frames that Node-A has received allocate Node-As requested slot to Node-A, then Node-A appoints the slot successfully. Otherwise, Node-A should request for joining the network again because of collision. To avoid collision again in the next appointment, we set a rule for the node to choose free slot: a new node records the requested times i, the i-th choose a free slot from (0, k) randomly, k is calculated by equation (2).

$$k = \begin{cases} 2^i & 2^i < k_{max} \\ k_{max} & 2^i > k_{max} \end{cases} \tag{2}$$

3.2   Cluster Fusion Mechanism

Nodes in VANET are organized as clusters and the topology of the network changes constantly. Figure.5 shows the example that clusters with slot allocation mechanism would have collisions between reservation slots. As shown in the left part of figure.5, vehicles are apart. Node A and node B are in different clusters, so they would not have a collision. However, as shown in the right side of figure.5, two nodes meet each other. If node A and node B send FI frame at the same time in the same slot, a collision will happen. These two nodes will not receive FI frame from each other. Node can only realize this when they meet node C. A large delay is caused like this and collisions can not solve quickly. The cluster fusion mechanism can solve these problems.

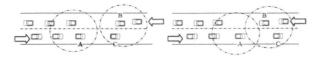

Fig. 5. Clusters collision

Nodes in the network are classified into four roles: normal nodes, cluster heads, cluster tails and signal nodes. Cluster tails are the nodes that have no node behind it in its moving direction. Cluster heads are the nodes that have no node ahead it in its moving direction. Signal nodes are the nodes that have no neighbor. Except these three, the other nodes are called normal nodes. Suppose right to be the positive direction. According to the moving direction, dividing cluster heads to be cluster heads and anti-cluster heads and cluster tails to be cluster tails and anti-cluster tails. The angle between cluster heads ,cluster tails and positive direction vector is(0, 180°)while the angle between anti-cluster heads ,anti-cluster tails and positive direction vector is(−180°, 0). Different roles have their own rules to choose the RS.

Suppose cluster heads, cluster tails, anti-cluster heads and anti-cluster tails select the top four slots in turn. If there is a signal node, it just choosing the first slot. If a little signal nodes exist in the network, then the collision probability will be very low. Because when the other nodes meeting each other, they would be in a different slot in the network and no collision will happen. Meanwhile, they can use FI frame to find the potential collision nodes near them. The prediction way could solve the slot collision when cluster fusion happened effectively and quickly. However, if there are some signal nodes in the network, the performance can not improve so much. But this situation is relatively rare in practical application.

When collisions happened, we should handle them like this. Node updates its own slot allocation table after receiving a FI frame. If there are two nodes have the same slot, then set the slot to be free. The nodes that are in collision will find at least one node set their occupied slot to be free, and then they could realize that they are in collision. After these nodes realizing the collision, they should apply the new slot again.

3.3   Slots Adjustment Mechanical

The size of RP is decided by Smax which is the maximum slot of the two-hop neighbor nodes. Over this slot is the CP. Dynamic changes of topology lead a lot of allocation failures and free slots before Smax. Therefore, lifting occupation of the allocation failure slots and adjusting the free slots should be resolved to reduce the Smax.

Nodes moving between clusters would lead to a lot of allocation failure. When one node leaving the cluster, it should set the slot that occupied to be free. Then, the node need to apply the new slot again in the new cluster.

The following algorithm will be used to adjust the large number of free slots.

(1) At the beginning of the head, node i should check: first, if itself occupied the maximum slot; second, if there is a free slot suit for node i(expect free slot that applied in RF frame).These two demands is satisfied, then go to the step (2).

(2) If there is a suitable slot, then choose a free slot Sf to be the RS. Sending beacon frame and FI frame in BS and RS(the node occupied two slots in FI frame at this time).

(3) Node i monitors for another period T. If all neighbor nodes indicate node i has occupied Sf successfully, node i will make Sf to be its own BS and update its FI. Otherwise, discarding Sf and repeat those three steps again.

H-MAC make efficient channel access by combining dynamic slot allocation mechanism, cluster fusion and slot adjustment mechanism. Compared with IEEE 802.11p, H-MAC can lower the collision rate of beacon frame and reduce the data fame collision.

4   Performance Evaluations

4.1   Simulation Setup

Simulation is performed in a 1km stretch of freeway with a total two lanes where vehicles pass along the road in one way at average speed of 50 mph, under

Nctuns 5.0. We simulate five different traffic density scenarios (from high to low), by varying the number of vehicles from 20 to 100 with the growth rate of 20. Figure 6 shows the simulation scenario.The parameters of the simulation are summarized in table 2.

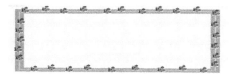

Fig. 6. Simulation scenario

Table 2. Simulation parameters

Parameter	Value
Control channel data rate R	6Mpbs
Packet size	500byte
Beacon frame transmission frequency	10Hz
Communication radius	300m
Data transfer rate	200kbps
Network size	2 lanes, about 1Km
Nodes number	20-100

According to features of the broadcast frame in CCH channel, send delay and packet loss are the most important performance indicators in MAC protocol for VANET. We examined these two indicators. Furthermore, we test effects that vehicle numbers have on. Last, we compared the performance of three protocols, H-MAC protocol, RR-ALOHA and IEEE 802.11p. Results of these examines are as follows.

4.2   Simulation Result

Figure.7 shows that beacon packet loss rate lower than the other broadcast frames apparently. As the other broadcast frames have no collisions avoid mechanism and have a high collision rate, so they have a high packet loss. However, beacon frames send in the pre-applied slot and can avoid collision with the other nodes in the communication range. Furthermore, beacon frame and the other broadcast frame packet loss rate increasing with the increase of the node numbers in the network. To beacon frame, the more the node number, the frequent the topology changed. A frequent change of the topology leads to the large number of the cluster fusion and then increases the packet loss rate. To other broadcast frames, control channel is becoming more crowds with the increasing of the node number, so the collision between nodes increased.

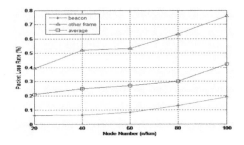

Fig. 7. Packet loss rate changes with node density

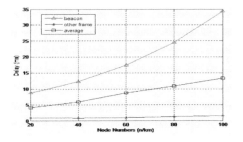

Fig. 8. Delay changes with node density

Data packets send delay changes with node density is shown in figure 8. Beacon frame delay is higher than the other broadcast frame apparently and it increases with the increase of node density. Slot reservation is used for beacon frame to send, each beacon frame must wait until its own slot that it can be sent. While the number of RS is related with the node number that in the communication range. The more the node number, the more slots that beacon frame needs wait to send. So the delay is longer. To the other broadcast frames, CSMA/CA is used for them to be sent. Though collision rate between data frames is high, data packet delay is short, maintaining about 1ms.

Next, we run H-MAC protocol, IEEE 802.11p and RR-ALOHA at the same scenario. Results are shown in figure.9 and figure.10.

Figure.9 shows the beacon frame packet loss rate changes with node density. The packet loss rate increases with the increase of the node density. Packet loss rate of H-MAC and RR-ALOHA lower than IEEE802.11p. In the low node density, it affects not much on H-MAC. In high node density, ratio of node number and slot number that in the neighbor table is close to or over 1, so packet loss rate increased quickly. Meanwhile, topology changes quickly with the increase of the node density. H-MAC protocol slot adjustment is more frequent, so H-MAC packet loss incremental is higher than RR-ALOHA.

Figure.10 shows the other broadcast delay changes with the node density in these three protocols. To normal broadcast frames, IEEE 802.11p and H-MAC

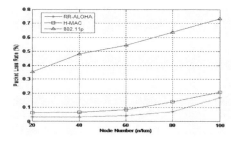

Fig. 9. Beacon frame packet loss rate changes with node density in three protocols

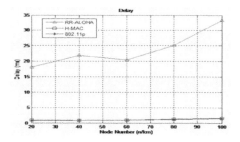

Fig. 10. Delay changes with node density in three protocols

delay is close to each other with the low level. Because RR-ALOHA using slots reservation, so it has longer broadcast delay. Collisions rate in H-MAC and IEEE 802.11p is lower than RR-ALOHA, so node density has less effect on the H-MAC and IEEE 802.11p than RR-ALOHA. Therefore, the delay is less affected by the node density in H-MAC and IEEE 802.11p than in RR-ALOHA.

5   Conclusion

In this paper, we present the Hybrid MAC protocol (H-MAC) that efficiently utilizes separate slots to support sudden burst flow in vehicular network. H-MAC protocol combined competition and reservation mechanisms to reduce the broadcast collisions in WAVE protocol with no effect on the other broadcast frames. Based on time synchronous, H-MAC consists of three parts: slot allocation mechanism, cluster fusion mechanism and dynamic slot adjustment mechanism. Slot allocation mechanism formulates rules for the slot period allocation of each node. Cluster fusion mechanism solves frame collision problem. Dynamic slot adjustment mechanism reduces free reservation slots. We using the Ncuns tools test the performance of H-MAC protocol. Simulation results show that H-MAC outperforms the existing protocols such as IEEE 802.11p and RR-ALOHA, especially in packet delay and packet loss.

Acknowledgements. This work is partially supported by Hunan young core teacher project,Young teacher project from Hunan University.

References

1. Reichardt, D., Miglietta, M., Moretti, L., Morsink, P., Schulz, W.: CarTALK 2000: safe and comfortable driving based upon inter-vehicle-communication. In: IEEE Intelligent Vehicle Symposium, pp. 545–550. IEEE Press, Piscataway (2002)
2. Borgonovo, F., Capone, A., Cesana, M., Fratta, L.: ADHOC MAC: new MAC architecture for ad hoc networks providing efficient and reliable point-to-point and broadcast services. Wireless Networks 10, 359–366 (2004)
3. Bana, S.V., Varaiya, P.: Space division multiple access (SDMA) for robust ad hoc vehicle communication networks. In: Proceedings of 4th IEEE International Conference on ITS (ITSC), pp. 962–967. IEEE Press, NJ (2001)
4. Blum, J.J., Eskandarian, A.: A Reliable Link-Layer Protocol for Robust and Scalable Intervehicle Communications. IEEE Transactions on ITS 8, 4–13 (2007)
5. Lam, R.K., Kumar, P.R.: Dynamic Channel Reservation to Enhance Channel Access by Exploiting Structure of Vehicular Networks. In: Vehicular Technology Conference (VTC 2010-Spring), pp. 1–5. IEEE Press, Berlin (2010)
6. Navda, V., Subramanian, A.P., Dhanasekaran, K., Timm-Giel, A., Das, S.: MobiSteer: using steerable beam directional antenna for vehicular network access. In: Proceedings of the 5th International Conference on Mobile Systems, Applications and Services, pp. 192–205. ACM Press, New York (2007)
7. Jiang, D., Delgrossi, L.: IEEE 802.11p: Towards an International Standard for Wireless Access in Vehicular Environments. In: Vehicular Technology Conference, pp. 2036–2040. IEEE Press, Berlin (2008)
8. Song, K.-J., Lee, C.-H., Woo, M.-S., Min, S.-G.: Distributed Periodic Access Scheme (DPAS) for the Periodic Safety Messages in the IEEE 802.11p WAVE. In: 2011 Third International Conference on Communications and Mobile Computing (CMC), pp. 465–468. IEEE Press, Piscataway (2011)
9. Bilstrup, K., Uhlemann, E., Strom, E.G., Bilstrup, U.: Evaluation of the IEEE 802.11p MAC Method for Vehicle-to-Vehicle Communication. In: Vehicular Technology Conference, pp. 1–5. IEEE Press, Piscataway (2008)
10. Karp, B., Kung, H.T.: GPSR: greedy perimeter stateless routing for wireless networks. In: MobiCom 2000 Proceedings of the 6th Annual International Conference on Mobile Computing and Networking, pp. 243–254. ACM Press, New York (2000)
11. Wei, Y.-C., Chen, Y.-M., Shan, H.-L.: Beacon-based trust management for location privacy enhancement VANETs. In: 2011 13th Asia-Pacific Network Operations and Management Symposium (APNOMS 2011), pp. 1–8. IEEE Press, Piscataway (2011)
12. Schmidt, R.K., Lasowski, R., Leinmuller, T., Linnhoff-Popien, C., Schafer, G.: An approach for selective beacon forwarding to improve cooperative awareness. In: Vehicular Networking Conference (VNC 2010), pp. 182–188. IEEE Press, Piscataway (2010)

Placement and Selection Algorithm of Reference Nodes in WSN Localization

Lin Min[1], Hui Li[2], and Zhengwei Guo[3]

[1] Network Information Center Office, Henan University,
Kaifeng, Henan, 475001, China
[2] Henan University Minsheng College, Kaifeng, Henan, 475004, China
[3] School of Computer and Information Engineering, Institute of Image Processing
and Pattern Recognition, Henan University, Kaifeng, Henan, 475001, China

Abstract. Currently,few studies of wireless sensor network node localization algorithm were focused on the reference nodes, but how to choose and place reference nodes has a great influence on the positioning accuracy. In order to quantitatively study this issue, we proved a theorem, which describes the relationship between the placement of reference nodes and whether the node can be located, then the reference nodes placement method was designed. Finally, a reference nodes selection algorithm was proposed based on the condition number of linear equations, so as to improve the accuracy of range-based localization algorithm.

Keywords: WSN, localization, three dimensional, reference nodes placement, reference nodes selection algorithm.

1 Introduction

Position information of sensor nodes is crucial for application systems in WSN (wireless sensors networks)[1], moreover, localization in 3D space is more practical significance than in 2D plane [2–5]. At present there are few location algorithms about reference nodes placement and selection in 3D space. Literatures [6–8] show that localization is closely relate to the placement method of reference nodes, however, those studies are just based on 2D plane. Literature [9] proves that the placement of reference nodes have a great influence on the location performance, but it lacks further description of how to place reference nodes in 3D indoor environment. This paper proposes a reference nodes placement approach and designs a reference nodes selection algorithm in order to improve the localization accuracy under the same condition.

2 Placement Method of Reference Nodes

Definition 1. *Suppose unknown node X is in three dimensional space. The position of X can be obtained on the basis of measured distance by using at least four reference nodes which are not on a same plane, or cant determine the position of X.*

R. Wang and F. Xiao (Eds.): CWSN 2012, CCIS 334, pp. 357–362, 2013.
© Springer-Verlag Berlin Heidelberg 2013

Proof Is as Follows: Suppose there are n $(n \geq 3)$reference nodes in 3-D space, and their coordinates are $(x_1, y_1, z_1), (x_2, y_2, z_2), ..., (x_n, y_n, z_n)$ separately, the coordinate of unknown node X is (x, y, z), the distance between X and is $(d_1, d_2, ..., d_n)$. We have the following equation set based on space distance formula between two points [11]:

$$
\begin{cases}
(x_1 - x)^2 + (y_1 - y)^2 + (z_1 - z)^2 = d_1^2 \\
(x_2 - x)^2 + (y_2 - y)^2 + (z_2 - z)^2 = d_2^2 \\
\cdots \\
(x_3 - x)^2 + (y_3 - y)^2 + (z_3 - z)^2 = d_3^2
\end{cases}
\tag{1}
$$

For equations set (1), after subtracting the last formula from the first one to the n -1 formula separately, we derive the following nonhomogeneous linear equation set:

$$
\begin{cases}
2(x_1 - x_n)x + 2(y_1 - y_n)y + 2(z_1 - z_n)z = \\
(x_1^2 + y_1^2 + z_1^2) - (x_n^2 + y_n^2 + z_n^2) - (d_1^2 - d_n^2) \\
2(x_2 - x_n)x + 2(y_2 - y_n)y + 2(z_2 - z_n)z = \\
(x_2^2 + y_2^2 + z_2^2) - (x_n^2 + y_n^2 + z_n^2) - (d_2^2 - d_n^2) \\
\cdots \\
2(x_{n-1} - x_n)x + 2(y_{n-1} - y_n)y + 2(z_{n-1} - z_n)z = \\
(x_{n-1}^2 + y_{n-1}^2 + z_{n-1}^2) - (x_n^2 + y_n^2 + z_n^2) - (d_{n-1}^2 - d_n^2)
\end{cases}
\tag{2}
$$

Suppose:

$$
A = \begin{pmatrix}
2(x_1 - x_n) & 2(y_1 - y_n) & 2(z_1 - z_n) \\
2(x_2 - x_n) & 2(y_2 - y_n) & 2(z_2 - z_n) \\
\cdots & & \\
2(x_{n-1} - x_n) & 2(y_{n-1} - y_n) & 2(z_{n-1} - z_n)
\end{pmatrix}
\tag{3}
$$

$$
b = \begin{pmatrix}
(x_1^2 + y_1^2 + z_1^2) - (x_n^2 + y_n^2 + z_n^2) - (d_1^2 - d_n^2) \\
(x_2^2 + y_2^2 + z_2^2) - (x_n^2 + y_n^2 + z_n^2) - (d_2^2 - d_n^2) \\
\cdots \\
(x_{n-1}^2 + y_{n-1}^2 + z_{n-1}^2) - (x_n^2 + y_n^2 + z_n^2) - (d_{n-1}^2 - d_n^2)
\end{pmatrix}
\tag{4}
$$

$$
X = \begin{pmatrix} x \\ y \\ z \end{pmatrix}
\tag{5}
$$

So, (1) When there are n reference nodes on the same plane, for the above equation (3), the rank of matrix A is 2: $rank(A) = 2$, and the rank of the augmented matrix $[A, b]$ (identified as $r[A, b]$)is more than or equal to $r(A)$,namely,$r[A, b] \geq r(A)$. According to the difference value of $(d_1, d_2, ..., d_n)$, when $r[A, b] = r(A) = 2$ the solution of equation set (2) is infinite; if $r[A, b] > r(A)$ equation set (2) has no solution. Therefore, the coordinate of X can not be calculated.

(2) When the n reference nodes are not on a same plane, $r(A) = 3$. According to the difference value of $(d_1, d_2, ..., d_n)$, $r[A, b] \geq 3$.

i) when $r[A, b] = r(A) = 3$equation set (2) has a unique solution, as shown below:

$$\hat{X} = A^+ b \qquad (6)$$

$A^+$is the generalized inverse of matrix A (the Moore-Penrose inverse). A is a matrix of full column rank, so:

$$\hat{X} = A^+ b \qquad (7)$$

Therefor the coordinate of X is

$$\hat{X} = (A^T A)^{-1} A^T b \qquad (8)$$

As we know, equation set (2) has at least 3 equations, and $n - 1 = 3$, so $n = 4$,That is to say, an unknown node's coordinate can be determined when there are at least four reference nodes which are not on a same plane in three-dimensional space. When using four reference nodes, A is a matrix of full column rank, so:

$$\hat{X} = A^{-1} b \qquad (9)$$

ii) When $r([A, b]) \geq 3$, equation set (2) has no solution, that is to say, the coordinate of X can not be determined because of the measured distance $(d_1, d_2, ..., d_n)$. Literature [7] proves that the highest locating accuracy can be acquired when the reference nodes form equilateral triangles in 2-D plane. This conclusion can be extended into 3-D space. Suppose the coordinate of an unknown node X in 3-D space is (x_0, y_0, z_0) .Projecting unknown node X to the x-y plane and y-z plane, so the projection of X to plane xy and plane yz are (x_0, y_0) and (y_0, z_0), so each component of the coordinate of X (x,y and z) can be calculated as same as in 2-D plane. Therefore reference nodes should be arranged to form equilateral triangles in vertical and horizontal planes as many as possible. So one placement method can be shown as figure 1 (the digitals in Figure 1 indicate the serial numbers of reference nodes).

3   Selection Algorithm of Reference Nodes

Even if we select three reference nodes which form an equilateral triangle, there are several selection methods about the fourth reference node. When using 4 reference nodes, the location of one unknown node can be computed with the following equation set:

$$
\begin{cases}
2(x_1 - x_n)x + 2(y_1 - y_n)y + 2(z_1 - z_n)z = \\
(x_1^2 + y_1^2 + z_1^2) - (x_n^2 + y_n^2 + z_n^2) - (d_1^2 - d_4^2) \\
2(x_2 - x_n)x + 2(y_2 - y_n)y + 2(z_2 - z_n)z = \\
(x_2^2 + y_2^2 + z_2^2) - (x_n^2 + y_n^2 + z_n^2) - (d_2^2 - d_4^2) \\
\quad\quad\quad ... \\
2(x_3 - x_4)x + 2(y_3 - y_4)y + 2(z_3 - z_4)z = \\
(x_3^2 + y_3^2 + z_3^2) - (x_4^2 + y_4^2 + z_4^2) - (d_3^2 - d_4^2)
\end{cases}
\qquad (10)
$$

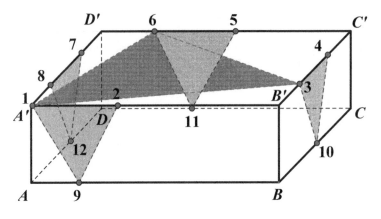

Fig. 1. Placement of Reference nodes

As we can see from equation set (10) , the solution is related to the coordinates of 4 reference nodes, and (d_1, d_2, d_3, d_4) are certain values after measuring, and (d_1, d_2, d_3, d_4) are relate to the 4 reference nodes as well. That is to say, the coordinate of unknown node is influenced by reference nodes' coordinates when distance-measuring error is fixed.

3.1   Condition Number of Linear Equations

When constant vector b has a small disturbance in linear equation set $Ax = b$, then the solution of the equation set(marked as x) has a disturbance (error), identified by Δx.

$$A(x + \Delta x) = b + \Delta b \tag{11}$$

For $Ax = b$,

$$\Delta x = A^{-1} \Delta b \tag{12}$$

Thus

$$\|\Delta x\| \leq \|A^{-1}\| \, \|\Delta b\| \tag{13}$$

Where $\|\Delta x\|$, $\|A^{-1}\|$ and $\|\Delta b\|$ are the spectral norm of Δx, A^{-1} and Δb. And for

$$\|b\| \leq \|A\| \, \|x\| \tag{14}$$

We derive

$$\frac{\|\Delta x\|}{\|x\|} \leq \|A\| \, \|A^{-1}\| \frac{\|\Delta b\|}{\|b\|} \tag{15}$$

Let

$$k(A) = \|A\| \|A^{-1}\| \tag{16}$$

Then $k(A)$ reflects the relationship between the relative error of the solution x of linear equations and the relative error of b. When is fixed, the error of the solution x becomes larger with the increase of $k(A)$. In other words, $k(A)$ is the magnification of relative ranging error. We name $k(A)$ the condition number of solving equation set .

3.2 Selection Algorithm of Reference Nodes

Coefficient matrix A is only related to the coordinates of 4 reference nodes. Therefore, the reference nodes selection algorithm can be listed as follows.

1. Select 3 reference nodes which can form equilateral triangle on horizontal or vertical plane, and recorded as node set N_{s-et}.
2. For the last n-3 nodes, Perform the following steps:
   2.1) for i=1 to n-3
      If (the i-th node is on same plane with N_{s-et})
      Continue judging the next reference node
      Else
         Combined the node with the N_{s-et} and derive the linear equation set about the 4 reference nodes, then calculate the condition number on the linear equation set.
      End if
   End for
   2.2) The reference node corresponded to the minimum $k_i(A)$ is the fourth reference node. If there exist some same value $k_i(A)$, the distance between reference nodes should be as large as possible [10], so in such a case we select the reference node as the fourth reference node which the average distance between the reference node and the other three reference nodes is the largest. It is one of the best reference node sets for locating.
3. Repeat step 1) to step 2), until none reference node form equilateral triangles on horizontal or vertical plane. There will be N node sets for location algorithm if there are N equilateral triangles on horizontal or vertical plane.
4. End.

4 Conclusion

This paper focuses on the placement method and selection algorithm of reference nodes in 3d space. As the precondition of running location algorithm,because they dont participate in coordinate calculating,so it has a certain significance to improve the accuracy of the node localization algorithm based on ranging.

The algorithm we described lay particular emphasis on the locating environment which reference nodes can be placed in advance, such as three dimensional indoor scene. The further research direction is how to choose the best reference nodes set when reference nodes are placed at random(e.g. reference nodes with GPS are sprinkled by airplane).

References

1. Sun, L., Li, J., Chen, Y., et al.: Wireless Sensor Network. Tsinghua University Press, Peking (2005)
2. Yu, N., Wan, J.-W., Ma, W.-X.: Sampling Based Three-Dimensional Localization Algorithm for Wireless Sensor Networks. Journal of Beijing University of Posts and Telecommunications 31(3), 13–18 (2008)
3. Liu, Y., Pu, J., He, Y., Xiong, Z.: Three-dimensional self-localization scheme for wireless sensor networks. Journal of Beijing University of Aeronautics and Astronautics 34(6), 647–651 (2008)
4. Lu, L.-B., Cao, Y., Gao, X., Luo, H.: Three Dimensional Localization Schemes Based on Sphere Intersections in Wireless Sensor Network. Journal of Beijing University of Posts and Telecommunications 29, 48–51 (2006)
5. Zhu, H., Chen, S.: A Novel Distributed and Range-Free Localization Algorithm in Three-Dimensional Wireless Sensor Networks. Chinese Journal of Sensors and Actuators 22(11), 1655–1660 (2009)
6. Noh, A.S., Lee, W.J., Young, J.: Comparison of the mechanisms of the zigbee's indoor localization algorithm. In: Ninth ACIS International Conference on Software Engineering, Artificial Intelligence, Networking, and Parallel/Distributed Computing, Phuket, pp. 13–18 (2008)
7. Guangjie, H., Choi, D., Lim, W.: A novel reference node selection algorithm based on trilateration for indoor sensor networks. In: Seventh International Conference on Computer and Information Technology, pp. 1003–1008 (2007)
8. Bao, R.-X., Zhang, S., Xue, Y.-D.: Research on the Self-localization of wireless sensor networks. In: The 2008 International Conference on Embedded Software and Systems (ICESS 2008), Sichuan, pp. 363–367 (2008)
9. Coluccia, A., Ricciato, F.: On ML estimation for automatic RSS-based indoor localization. In: 2010 5th International Symposium on Wireless Pervasive Computing (ISWPC), pp. 495–502 (2010)
10. Dai, H.: The Theory of Matrices, pp. 169–193. Seience Press, Beijing (2008)

A Distributed Broadcast Protocol of Wireless Sensor Networks Based on Dynamic Multi-channel MAC Protocol

Shaohua Qin[1,2] and Dongyan Chen[1]

[1] The School of Control Science and Engineering of Shandong University
[2] The College of Physics and Electronics of Shandong Normal University
{qsh,dchen}@sdu.edu.cn

Abstract. Multi-channel MAC protocols have recently attracted much attention as it is considered a promising direction for improving the performance of wireless sensor networks. But most of these protocols didnt consider the performance of broadcast. The traditional broadcast is difficult to work in multi-channel wireless sensor networks using dynamic channel assignment. In this letter, we proposed a distributed solution to broadcast by multiple unicast based on a broadcast tree. The tree can be built through sending broadcast training packages several times before broadcast. The simulation results showed that this broadcast protocol has good broadcast latency metric.

Keywords: wireless sensor networks, broadcast, multi-channel.

1   Introduction

Multi-channel MAC protocols were widely employed in wireless sensor networks because of their high throughput and anti-interference ability, dynamic channel assignment MAC protocols among them have better performance with the avoidance of interference and communication collisions between nodes, such as the McMAC [1]and EM-MAC [2]. These protocols focus on reducing the interference between nodes by randomly assigning different channels to different nodes, but this type of channel assignment is a disaster to broadcast. In single channel wireless sensor networks, the node can efficiently distribute the packet to every node within its communication range with the help of the wireless broadcast advantage (WBA). So many applications use the broadcast in wireless sensor networks, for example, the routing and time synchronization, especially for the sink node, the broadcast is important to query information and update programs. But in the multi-channel environment, different nodes use a different channel, so the traditional broadcast is impossible. In the multi-channel environment, a node needs to transmit the same packet multiple to perform a broadcast. So it becomes a problem to perform an efficient broadcast in multi-channel wireless sensor networks using dynamic channel assignment MAC protocols. To our best knowledge, there is no distributed solution to broadcast in multi-channel wireless

R. Wang and F. Xiao (Eds.): CWSN 2012, CCIS 334, pp. 363–370, 2013.
© Springer-Verlag Berlin Heidelberg 2013

sensor networks using dynamic channel assignment MAC protocols. Most of previous multi-channel broadcast protocols are based on static channel assignment. Such as Chun Chou et al. discussed the impact of channel assignment on broadcast in multi-channel environment at [3], he only considered the static channel assignment and presented a centralized solution. Junaid Qadir et al. studied the minimum latency broadcast in multi-channel multi-rate wireless meshes at [4], his solution is also based on the static channel assignment and used the wireless broadcast advantage (WBA) to broadcast. Yanjun Sun et al. studied the broadcast problem in asynchronous networks at [5]. Similar with the multi-channel networks, the node cant use the wireless broadcast advantage (WBA) to broadcast because different node awake in different time in asynchronous networks. They use multiple unicast to perform a broadcast, and add some information about neighbor nodes into the packet to avoid redundant transmission. This distributed method performed the broadcast in asynchronous networks, but the information added to the packet increased the length of the packet, and it also needs the node spending more RAM to store the information about neighbor nodes within two hops. Both of these are a challenge to the limited resource of wireless sensor networks. This paper considered the characteristic of dynamic channel assignment MAC protocols, designed a distributed solution to broadcast in multi-channel wireless sensor networks. Before the broadcast, the source node transmits some broadcast training packets, every node received the packet forwards this packet to all of its neighbor nodes, all of these transmissions are unicast. The neighbor node selects the node which first transmits this packet to it as its father node. We can get a broadcast tree from these father-child relationships. After the broadcast tree has been built, the broadcast packet can be transmitted along the paths of the tree. We call this method as a distributed tree broadcast (DTB) protocol. The contributions of this paper are as follows:

1, We present a first distributed protocol for multi-hop broadcast in multi-channel wireless sensor networks using the dynamic channel assignment MAC protocols.

2, This broadcast tree is built using transmitting broadcast training packets several times through the network, compared with the centralize solution, this method is easy to realize, and meets the limited resource of the node.

3, After the tree has been built, the broadcast packet can be transmitted along the paths of the tree and needs no control overhead.

4, The broadcast tree is flexible to the change of some nodes.

The exponential broadcast tree is introduced in section 2, we discuss our DTB protocol in section 3. Section 4 presents the simulation result. Finally, in section 5 we conclude.

2   The Exponential Broadcast Tree

In wireless sensor networks using the dynamic channel assignment MAC protocol, the node uses different channel at different time. So the node must use multiple unicast to perform a broadcast. As wireless sensor networks are multi-hop networks, if a node wants to perform an efficient broadcast using multiple unicast, the ideal situation is that every node received the broadcast packet forwards this packet to its neighbor nodes without redundant transmissions, i.e. every node in the network received the packet only once. So the number N of nodes received the broadcast packet in the networks and the number M of forwarding meets the exponential relationship in the ideal situation:

$$N = 2^M \tag{1}$$

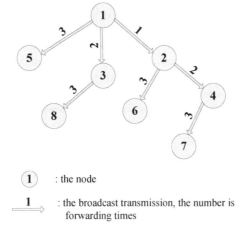

1 : the node

1 : the broadcast transmission, the number is forwarding times

Fig. 1. The ideal exponential broadcast tree

To reach the ideal result, one of the best methods is to build a tree and make the node to forward the packet along the paths of the tree. The quantity of child nodes is different with different parent node, i.e. the sooner the parent node received the broadcast packet, the more its child nodes, on the contrary, the later the parent node received the broadcast packet, the less its child nodes, we call such a tree as an exponential broadcast tree. For example, as shown in Fig.1 the node 1 is the node who wants to broadcast, in order to facilitate the discussion, we assume that all nodes simultaneously awake, but this method is also applicable to the asynchronous network. In the first transmission, the node 1 sends the broadcast packet to the node 2. In the second transmission, the node 1 sends the same packet to the node 3, the node 2 has had this packet at this time, so it can forward this packet to its neighbor node at the same time, i.e. sends to the node 4. Similarly in the third transmission, when the node 1 sends to the node 5, the node 2, 3 and 4 all forward the packet to their neighbor nodes simultaneously. So the quantity of nodes received the broadcast packet increased exponentially with the increasing of forwarding times. In this case, there are eight nodes received the broadcast packet after forwarding three times. If we can build a suitable broadcast tree, and make the node forwarding the broadcast packet along the paths of the tree, we can confirm that the broadcast will cover all the nodes in networks, with low broadcast latency and no redundant transmission. In the fact, the real broadcast tree isnt so ideal limited by the node actual distribution. It needs more times to forward the broadcast packet to every node in networks than the ideal value.

3   DTB Protocol

From section II we can see that the broadcast tree is important to an effective broadcast, but it is difficult to build an exponential broadcast tree or a sub-optimal broadcast tree in wireless sensor networks. The DTB protocol presents a distributed solution to build a broadcast tree in wireless sensor networks using the dynamic channel assignment MAC protocols. Before the broadcast, the source node transmits some broadcast training packets to build a broadcast tree. Every node received the training packet forwards this packet to all of its neighbor nodes , the neighbor node selects a node as its father node which first transmits this packet to it. We can get a broadcast tree from these father-child relationships. The broadcast tree continually optimized with every transmission of the broadcast training packet. Finally, we can build a steady broadcast tree for the broadcast packet to be transmitted effectively. The tree can update when some nodes join or leave the network. This protocol can be divided into three steps, the first is the construction of a broadcast tree, the second is broadcasting, the third is the update of the tree.

3.1   Construction of a Broadcast Tree

Step 1, The source node selects randomly a neighbor node, and sends the broadcast training packet to it through the unicast communication. After received the packet, the neighbor node transmits an ACK packet back to the sender with a flag in it, this flag indicates whether the node received the packet at the first time. If the neighbor node is the first time received the packet, then the sender will add this neighbor node to its forwarding tables. i.e. the sender becomes the father node of this neighbor node.

Step 2, Similar with the source node, every node received the training packet will select randomly a neighbor nodes from its neighbor tables, and forward this packet to its neighbor node until all of its neighbor nodes have been transmitted. The node will add the neighbor node to their forwarding tables if the neighbor node is the first time received this training packet from it.

Step 3, At the end of the transmission, some of the nodes have a forwarding table. All of the forwarding tables of these nodes covered the network and no node appears twice. The node is the father node of the nodes in its forwarding table. From the father-child relationships, a broadcast tree is built in the network.

Step 4, Similar with the first time, the broadcast training packet will be transmitted many times, the difference from the first is some nodes have had a forwarding table after the first training. So the node whose forwarding table isnt empty will transmit the training packet to the node in its forwarding table firstly, then to the rest of neighbor nodes. If the neighbor node is not firstly received the training packet from its father node at this time, it will be removed from the former forwarding table. i.e. there is another node which can transmit the packet to it more rapidly, and it will be added to the new father nodes forwarding table. The father-child relationship will change continuously with the transmission of training packets. And the broadcast tree also be optimized with the change of the father-child relationships.

Step 5, After several training, the forwarding table will be gradually stabilized, and the broadcast tree of the source node will be built in the network.

3.2 Broadcasting

After the tree has been built, when the source node initiates a broadcast, the packet can be transmitted along the paths of the tree. i.e. every node forwards the broadcast packet to the node in its forwarding table in turn. So the packet will cover all the nodes in the network without any redundant transmission.

3.3 Update of the Broadcast Tree

In the wireless sensor network, the topology is constantly changing with some nodes enter or leave the network. The broadcast tree also updates with the changing.

When a node enters the network as a new node, its neighbor nodes will transmit the broadcast packet to it after they finished transmitting the broadcast packet to all nodes in their forwarding tables. The new node will select a neighbor node as its father node which transmitted the packet to it firstly.

When a node leaved the network, its neighbor nodes will remove it from their neighbor tables. If the node is a child node of the neighbor node, it will be removed from its forwarding table; if it is a father node of the neighbor node, the neighbor node will enter the network as a new node to find a new father node.

The DTB protocol needs transmitting broadcast training packets to build a broadcast tree before starting to broadcast. Different source node has different broadcast tree in the network, the router forwards the broadcast packet depending on the source address of the packet. The most overhead of the DTB protocol is the construction of the broadcast tree before the broadcast, but no control information is needed during the process of broadcasting. So the DTB protocol is suitable for the node to broadcast periodically, and it is not worth building a broadcast tree for the broadcast which use the tree only once.

3.4 Pseudocode

This pseudocode shows the procedure of a node i how to build a broadcast tree. The neightable(i) denotes the neighbor table of node i, the forwardtable(i) denotes the forwarding table of node i, the receiveflag(i) in the ACK packet denotes whether the node i is firstly received the broadcast training packet. The pseudocode is as follows:

Example of a node i to build a broadcast tree

```
1:  the node i received a new broadcast training packet
2: IF forwardtable(i) empty
3: FOR every node j forwardtable(i)
4: node i transmits a broadcast training packet to node j
5: node i received an ACK packet from node j
6: IF receiveflag(j)true
7: forwardtable(i)= forwardtable(i)-j
8: END IF
9: END FOR
10: ELSE  IF neightable(i)  empty
11: FOR  every node j (neightable(i) - forwardtable(i))
12: node i transmits a broadcast training packet to node j
13: node i received an ACK packet from node j
14: IF receiveflag(j)=true
15: forwardtable(i)= forwardtable(i)+j
16: END IF
17: END FOR
18: END IF
19: END IF
```

4   Simulation

In wireless sensor networks, there are many metrics to evaluate the performance of a broadcast protocol, some ones are as follows:

1, Coverage, every node in the network should received the broadcast packet.
2, Efficiency, the packet can cover the network with few redundant transmissions and low control overheads.
3, Latency, the time the packet spending to cover the network, in synchronous networks, we can use the forwarding times to evaluate this time.

From the process of the building of the broadcast tree in our DTB protocol, we can see that the tree includes every node in the network, and no node appears twice, and no control overhead is needed in the process of the broadcast. So the DTB protocol is good at the coverage and efficiency metrics.

We use MATLAB [6] to calculate some metrics in our DTB protocol.The scenario is that N nodes randomly located in an area of 100100 m2, the communication range of the node is 40 m, the sender located in the point of (0,0), So the network has three hops from the sender to the farthest node. We assume the nodes randomly select the channel to communicate and dont consider the interference and collision.

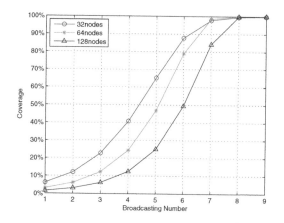

Fig. 2. The relationship of the coverage and broadcasting number

4.1 Coverage and Latency

In the ideal case, the number N of nodes received the broadcast packet in the networks and the number M of forwarding meets the exponential relationship:

$$N = 2^M \tag{2}$$

So the optimal latency is the logarithm of the quantity of the nodes in the network. The DTB protocol cant obtain this optimal value, but the broadcast tree is optimized gradually with the increase of training times, and its latency is close to the optimal value at the end of training. Fig.2 shows the broadcasting coverage of DTB in different sizes networks. We can find that DTB protocol can use small number of broadcasting to cover all the networks, its latency is close to the optimal latency.

4.2 Efficiency

Before broadcasting, the source node need to build the broadcast tree through transmit the training packet. When the construction of a broadcast tree is completed the source node can transmit the broadcast packet along the tree to every node in the network by unicast. So the construction of a broadcast tree is the main overhead of DTB protocol. Fig.3 shows the construction of a broadcast tree, we can see that the construction of a broadcast tree needs to transmit training packet many a time , and the tree continue to be optimized with the transmitting of training packet, the broadcasting latency also continue to be reduced. From the figure we can see that the broadcasting latency is close t the optimal value after 15 training, so the overhead of DTB protocol is little and the efficiency of this protocol is good.

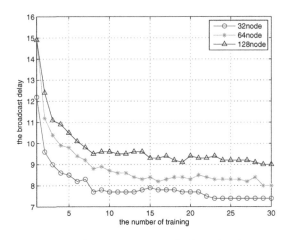

Fig. 3. The construction of a broadcast tree

5   Conclusion

The DTB protocol is a distributed solution for broadcast in wireless sensor networks using dynamic channel assignment. The broadcast tree is built through the training packet in the DTB protocol, the broadcast packet can transmit along the paths of the tree without any control overhead. This protocol has excellent metrics in coverage, efficiency and latency. From the simulation results, we can see that its broadcast latency is close to the optimal value. The DTB protocol is suitable for the node to broadcast periodically in multi-channel wireless sensor works.

References

1. So, H.-S.W., Walrand, J., Mo, J.: McMAC: a parallel rendezvous multi-channel MAC protocol. In: The IEEE Wireless Communications and Networking Conference, pp. 334–339. IEEE Press, Hong Kong (2007)
2. Tang, L., Sun, Y., Gurewitz, O., Johnson, D.: EM-MAC: A Dynamic Multichannel Energy-Efficient MAC Protocol for Wireless Sensor Networks. In: The 12th ACM International Symposium on Mobile Ad Hoc Networking and Computing, pp. 1–11. ACM Press, Paris (2011)
3. Chou, C.T., Qadir, J., Lim, J.G.: Advances and Challenges with Data Broadcasting in Wireless Mesh Networks. IEEE Communications Magazine 45(11), 78–85 (2007)
4. Qadir, J., Chou, C.T., Misra, A., Lim, J.G.: Minimum Latency Broadcasting in Multiradio, Multichannel, Multirate Wireless Meshes. IEEE Transactions on Mobile Computing 8(11), 1510–1523 (2009)
5. Sun, Y., Gurewitz, O., Du, S., Tang, L., Johnson, D.B.: ADB: An Efficient Multihop Broadcast Protocol based on Asynchronous Duty-cycling in Wireless Sensor Networks. In: The 7th ACM Conference on Embedded Networked Sensor Systems, SenSys 2009, pp. 43–56. ACM Press, Berkeley (2009)
6. The MathWorks, Inc., http://www.mathworks.com

Mobile Agent Based Coding Aware Multipath Routing for Wireless Sensor Network

Xing Shao[1,*], Ruchuan Wang[1,2,3], Qiaomin Lin[1], and Haiping Huang[1,2,3]

[1] College of Computer, Nanjing University of Posts and Telecommunications,
XinMoFan Road.66, 210003 Nanjing, China
[2] Jiangsu High Technology Research Key Laboratory for Wireless Sensor Networks,
XinMoFan Road.66, 210003 Nanjing, China
[3] Key Lab of Broadband Wireless Communication and Sensor Network Technology
XinMoFan Road.66, 210003 Nanjing, China
{d0050921,wangrc,qmlin,hhp}@njupt.edu.cn
http://www.springer.com/lncs

Abstract. This paper presents an Mobile Agent based Coding Aware Routing (MA-CAMR) for wireless sensor network, which exploits mobile agent to discovery the routing and coding opportunities, reducing complexity of node design. Besides, the general network coding condition of two cross flows is proposed for coding opportunity discovery. In addition, a novel routing metric, Coding and Energy Aware Routing Metric (CEARM) is proposed, which considers the coding gain, the load and energy of node. MA-CAMR exploits multipath routing and CEARM to balance the network load and energy consumption. Simulation results demonstrate that MA-CAMR could balance network load and energy consumption, reduce energy consumption, and prolong network lifetime.

Keywords: Mobile Agent, Coding Aware, Multipath Routing, Wireless Sensor Network.

1 Introduction

In wireless sensor networks [1], resources and energy of node is limited. Energy efficient routing protocol [2] is significant to wireless sensor networks.

In 2000, Ahlswede et al. first proposed the concept of network coding [3], which changes the mechanism of traditional store/forward, and allows node to perform encoding and decoding operations on received packet. Network coding could reduce the number of transmission, increase network throughput. Though network coding need additional computational overhead, the energy consumption by coding operation can be neglected compared with energy consumption of the saved transmissions [4]. Therefore, network coding is suitable for resource and energy constrained wireless sensor networks.

The capability of network coding in improving the throughput, saving bandwidth, has motivated researchers to propose a series of network coding-based

---

* Corresponding author.

R. Wang and F. Xiao (Eds.): CWSN 2012, CCIS 334, pp. 371–380, 2013.
© Springer-Verlag Berlin Heidelberg 2013

routings [5]. Current network coding-based routings aim to increase network coding opportunities. However, the single pursuit of network coding opportunities increasing could lead to the congregation of routes in area existing coding opportunities, and the uneven distribution of network load [6][7][8]. The other hand, network coding-based routing, didnt take into account the special nature of wireless sensor network, i.e. resources and energy of node is limited [9][10]. In addition, network coding based routings need complex coding opportunities discovery mechanism, which increase the complexity of node design.

Agent refers to a piece of code with certain degree of intelligence, and is able to complete assigned tasks independently. Mobile Agent is a kind of agent that has the ability to move. It is able to decide independently when and where to migrate from one host to another, and complete its task through interacting with other agent or resource. Mobile Agent based routing could balance network traffic, and have been proved its excellent performance in telecommunication networks [11][12].

This paper attempts to exploits mobile agent to resolve the problem of network coding opportunity and routing discovery. Besides, this paper proposes a Mobile Agent based Coding Aware Multipath Routing (MA-CAMR), which is suitable for wireless sensor network. In MA-CAMR, mobile agents migrate in the network and interact with node and other agent to discover routing and network coding opportunities, which reduces the complexity of the node design. Besides, multipath routes discovered by mobile agents could balance network load and energy consumption, and prolong the network lifetime.

2   Mobile Agent Based Coding Aware Routing

2.1   Coding and Energy Aware Routing Metric

Routing metric plays an important role for routing algorithm, since it is used to evaluate the route quality. Considering the demand of wireless sensor networks in energy consumption and the traffic unbalance problem of current coding-aware routing, this paper presents Coding and Energy Aware Routing Metric (CEARM). CEARM is defined as equation (1):

$$CEARM = \sum_{i=1}^{n} ETX_i \times C_i \times E_i \times L_i \times I_i . \tag{1}$$

In equation (1), ETX [13] is the desired number of transmission that a link transmits a packet successfully. C_i is the coding indicator. E_i is the energy factor. L_i is the load factor. L_i is the interference factor.

Starting from the point of view of energy consumption, in wireless sensor network the majority of energy is consumed in transmitting and receiving operations. The ETX value reflects the energy consumption from the side. The smaller the ETX value of a path, the smaller the number of transmission. Then the path will consume less energy.

$$C_i = \begin{cases} 1, \textit{Exist coding opportunity at node } i \\ 0, \textit{Exist no coding opportunity at node } i \end{cases} . \tag{2}$$

Coding indicator C_i, as defined in equation (2), indicates whether there exist coding opportunity at node i. When coding opportunity exists at node i, packet arrives at node i will be coded with other packet and sent, which is like the "Free Ride" phenomenon. Therefore, when coding opportunity exists at node i, C_i is defined 0, to reflect the transmission number decrease due to network coding.

$$E_i = e^{-len} . \tag{3}$$

Energy factor E_i is defined as equation (3), where len is the nodes residual energy ratio. The more residual energy of a node, the less the energy factor of the node.

$$L_i = e^{-lque} . \tag{4}$$

Load factor L_i, as defined in equation (4), where $lque$ is the queue occupancy percentage. The larger is the $lque$, the smaller the load factor.

$$I_i = e^{iload} = e^{\sum_{j=1}^{N_i} cqueue_j} . \tag{5}$$

Interference factor I_i, as defined in equation (5), where $iload$ is the interference load of node i. N_i is the number of interference nodes of node i. $cqueue_j$ is the queue occupancy percentage of interfere node j. In wireless environment, interference has a great impact on routing performance. The interference influence depends on the total interference load. The more interference loads of interfering node, the greater the interference factor. Based on above analysis, the performance of the path with smaller $CEARM$ value is better.

2.2   Agent Structure

MA-CAMR defines two kinds of mobile agents for routing and coding opportunity discovery: Forward of Mobile Agent (FMA) and Backward Mobile Agent (BMA).

FMA owns following fields. *Dst* and *Src* is the destination and source of FMA respectively. *Gen* indicates the generation number of FMA. *Delay* records the delay experienced by FMA since its creation. *FMACode* defines FMAs migration rules. *PathInfo* records the path information traversed by FMA, whose structure is similar with that of Flow Table, including traversed nodes and neighbors of each node.

BMA owns following fields. Compared with FMA, *Gen* and *Delay* are removed. The *PathInfo* records the intermediate node information, including the Coding Indicator, Energy Factor, Load Factor, Interference Factor, as well as the ETX value to the next hop. *BMACode* defines BMA's migration rules.

2.3   Network Coding Condition

The performance coding-aware routing depends on its ability to discover coding opportunities, while the coding opportunity discovery depends on the definition of network coding condition. In COPE [6], the network coding condition is that the next hop of coding node is able to decode correctly. The network coding condition in DCAR[8] considers the network coding condition of two native and intersecting flows at the intersecting node and expands the scope of the coding topology, but it doesnt consider the case of coded flows. This paper proposes the network coding condition of two intersecting general (native or coded) flows. Before delving into the network coding condition, related definitions are introduced in first.

Definition 1 There is a flow form source S to destination D, $f : S \to N_1 \to N_2, \ldots \to N_n \to v \to N_{n+1} \to N_{n+2} \ldots \to N_{n+m} \to D$. $U(v,f)$ denotes the upstream node set of node v in flow f, and $U(v, f) = \{S, N_1, \ldots N_n\}$. $D(v,f)$ is the downstream node set of node v in flow f, and $D(v, f) = \{N_{n+1}, \ldots N_{n+m}, D\}$.

Definition 2 There is a flow form source S to destination D, $f : S \to N_1 \ldots \to N_i \to N_{i+1} \ldots N_n \to v \to N_{n+1} \to N_{n+2} \ldots \to N_{n+m} \to D$. And network coding occurs at node N_i. $UC(N_i, v, f)$ denotes the upstream node set of v, for coding node N_i in flow f. $UC(N_i, v, f) = N_i, N_{i+1} \ldots N_n$.

Theorem 1 Flow f_1 and f_2 intersects at node v. The necessary and sufficient condition for f_1 and f_2 could be coded at v is:

(1) If there is no coding node on f_1, then there exists $d_1 \in D(v, f_1)$, and $d_1 \in N(u_2)$, $u_2 \in U(v, f_2)$; or $d_1 \in U(v, f_2)$. If there is coding node n on f_1, then there exists $d_1 \in D(v, f_1)$, and $d_1 \in N(u_2)$, $u_2 \in UC(n, v, f_2)$; or $d_1 \in UC(n, v, f_2)$

(2) If there is no coding node on f_2, then there exists $d_2 \in D(v, f_2)$, and $d_2 \in N(u_1)$, $u_1 \in U(v, f_1)$; or $d_2 \in U(v, f_1)$. If there is coding node m on f_2, then there exists $d_2 \in D(v, f_2)$, and $d_2 \in N(u_1)$, $u_1 \in UC(m, v, f_1)$; or $d_1 \in UC(m, v, f_1)$

2.4   MA-CAMR Description

In wireless sensor network using MA-CAMR, node S wants to send data to node D, but there is no available routing information to D in its routing table. S generates FMA destined to D. The FMA will migrate to D to explore the routing. At each intermediate node, it will record the information of the current node and store it in its agent structure.

Reaches D, FMA will generate corresponding BMA based on collected path information, and then remove it. BMA will migrate to S along the opposite path. At each intermediate node, BMA will judge the coding opportunity according to network coding condition, and update corresponding field.

$$p_i = \frac{\frac{1}{CEARM_i}}{\sum_{j=1}^{N} \frac{1}{CEARM_j}} . \tag{6}$$

When BMA reaches S, BMA will interact with S and submit the collected path information to S. Then S will calculate CEARM value of each path, select the best N paths, and update the routing table entries. Assume the CEARM value of i-th is $CEARM_i$, the probability that a packet is assigned on path is as equation (6).

3   Simulation and Performance Analysis

3.1   Simulation Parameters

To evaluate the performance of MA-CAMR, simulation is carried out using NS2. The simulation topology consists of 50 nodes, randomly deployed in a 100m*100m square area. IEEE 802.11 protocol is used as MAC protocol. Channel bandwidth is 2Mbps.

Initial energy of each node is 100J. The energy consumption model is the same as that in [14]. To facilitate performance comparison, DCAR, DSR, MA-CAMR-sp is used. MA-CAMR-sp is the single path routing version of MA-CAMR. In the simulation, a data transmission between source and destination is called a session. The rate of each session is 2Kbps. Simulations under different session number are carried out. The network lifetime is the time interval from the beginning to the time one node run out of energy.

To evaluate the load balancing capability of MA-CAMR, the Load Balancing Index is used, which is defined as equation (7). In equation (7), n is the number of the links, x_i is the number of packets transmitted on the link. LBI ranges in [0,1].

$$LBI = \frac{(\sum_{i=1}^{n} x_i)^2}{n \sum_{i=1}^{n} x_i^2} . \tag{7}$$

3.2   Performance Analysis

Fig.1 graphs the throughput under different session number. It can be seen from Fig.1 that, although MA-CAMR-sp is only different from MA-CAMR in single path routing, its throughput is worse than that of MA-CAMR and close to that of DCAR. Since MA-CAMR is multi-path routing, it further increases coding opportunities and its throughput is significantly better than other routings.

Fig.2 depicts coded packets percentage under different session number, which confirms the conclusions of Fig.6 from the side. It is clear from Fig.2 that, the coded packet percentage is higher than that of DCAR and MA-CMAR-sp, and MA-CAMR-sp is slightly higher than DCAR. The reason is that MA-CAMR is multi-path routing, which distribute network traffic evenly, thereby creating more coding opportunities. However, MA-CAMR-sp is single path routing, which limit the increasing of coding opportunities.

Fig.3-5 shows the performance of the four routings in energy consumption. Fig.3 compares the energy consumption of unit bit under different number of sessions. It is obvious from Fig. 5 that, when the session number is less than 14,

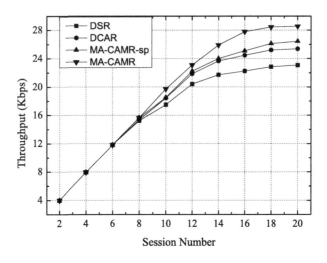

Fig. 1. Throughput under different Session Number

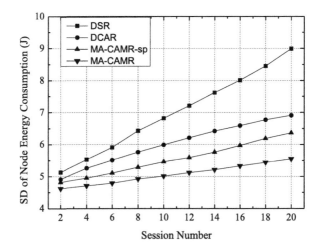

Fig. 2. Coded Packets Percentage under different Session Number

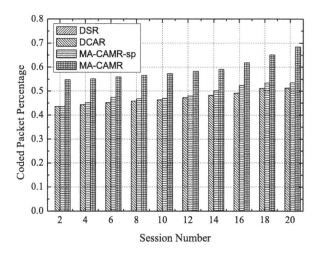

Fig. 3. Energy Consumption per bit under different Session Number

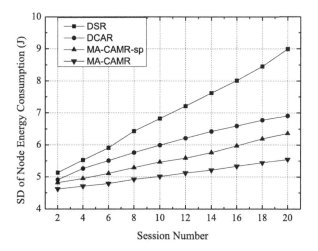

Fig. 4. Standard Deviation (SD) of Node Energy Consumption under different Session Number

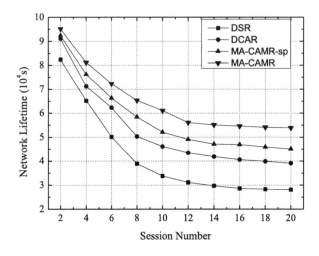

Fig. 5. Network Lifetime under different Session Number

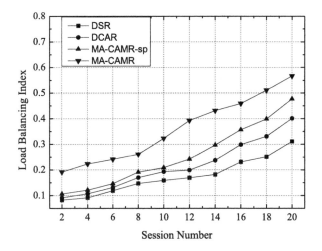

Fig. 6. Load Balancing Index under different Session Number

energy consumption of unit bit of DSR is much smaller than other three coding aware routings, since coding aware routing need additional coding opportunity discovery consuming more energy. With the increase of session number, congestion and retransmission occurs in DSR, which results in the rapid increasing of energy consumption. Coding aware routing could reduce energy consumption and bandwidth resources due to network coding, the energy consumption of unit bit decreases with increase of session number and coding opportunity. But with the growth of traffic, reduce speed reduced.

Fig.4 and Fig.5 illustrate the energy consumption standard deviation and network lifetime respectively. It can be seen from Fig.4 that, since MA-CAMR-sp considers residual energy in route discovery, its energy consumption is more even than that of DCAR, and achieve longer network lifetime than DCAR. MA-CAMR could increase coding opportunity, as well as consider node energy. Therefore, MA-CAMR achieve the best performance in energy consumption standard deviation and network lifetime.

Fig.6 shows Load Balancing Index of four routing under different session number. Due to considering of network load and multipath routing, MA-CAMR could evenly distribute network traffic, and achieve the best performance in LBI. MA-CAMR-sp is better than DCAR in LBI, since it considers node load.

4 Conclusion

This paper presents Mobile Agent based Coding Aware Multipath Routing (MA-CAMR) for wireless sensor network, which exploits mobile agents to explore multipath routing and coding opportunities. Besides, a novel routing metric CEARM is proposed, jointly considering coding gain, load and residual energy of node. Simulation results confirmed that MA-CAMR could save energy consumption, balance traffic distribution and energy consumption, and prolong network lifetime.

Acknowledgments. The subject is sponsored by the National Natural Science Foundation of China (60973139, 61170065, 61171053, 61003039, 61003236, 61103195), Natural Science Foundation of Jiangsu Province (BK2011755), Scientific & Technological Support Project (Industry) of Jiangsu Province (BE2010197, BE2010198, BE2011844, BE2011189), Natural Science Research Major Project of Jiangsu Provincial Colleges (11KJA520001), Jiangsu Provincial research scheme of natural science for higher education institutions (10KJB520013, 11KJB520014, 11KJB520016,12KJB520009), Scientific Research & Industry Promotion Project for Higher Education Institutions (JH2010-14, JHB2011-9), National Postdoctoral Science Foundation (20100480048), Science & Technology Innovation Fund for higher education institutions of Jiangsu Province (CXZZ11-0405, CXZZ11-0406, CXZZ11-0409), Doctoral Fund of Ministry of Education of China (20103223 120007, 20113223110002), Key Laboratory Foundation of Information Technology Processing of Jiangsu Province (KJS1022), The Preponderant Discipline Construction Project of Universities of

Jiangsu Province, Natural Science Key Research Project for Higher Education Institutions in Anhui Province (No.KJ2012A102). Thank anonymous reviewers for their helpful suggestions on the quality improvement of this paper.

References

1. Yick, J., Mukherjee, B., Ghosal, D.: Wireless sensor network survey. Computer Networks 52(12), 2292–2330 (2008)
2. Akkaya, K., Younis, M.: A survey on routing protocols for wireless sensor networks. Ad Hoc Networks 3(3), 325–349 (2005)
3. Ahlswede, R., Cai, N., Li, S.-Y., Yeung, R.W.: Network Information Flow. IEEE/ACM Transactions on Information Theory 46(4), 1204–1216 (2000)
4. Estrin, D.: Wireless Sensor Networks Tutorial Part IV: Sensor Network Protocols. In: Proceedings of Mobicom 2002, pp. 23–28. ACM, USA (2002)
5. Iqbal, M.A., Dai, B., Huang, B., Hassan, A., Yu, S.: Survey of network coding-aware routing protocols in wireless networks. Journal of Network and Computer Applications 34(6), 1956–1970 (2011)
6. Katti, S., Rahul, H., Hu, W., Katabi, D., Medard, M., Crowcroft, J.: XORs in the air: practical wireless network coding. IEEE/ACM Transactions on Networking 16(3), 497–510 (2008)
7. Ni, B., Santhapuri, N., Zhong, Z., Nelakuditi, S.: Routing with opportunistically coded exchanges in wireless mesh networks. In: Proceedings of IEEE WiMesh 2006, pp. 157–159. IEEE Press, New York (2006)
8. Le, J., Lui, J.C.S., Chiu, D.M.: DCAR: Distributed coding-aware routing in wireless networks. IEEE Transactions on Mobile Computing 9(4), 596–608 (2010)
9. Lu, W., Zhu, Y., Chen, G.: Energy Efficient Routing Algorithms Based on Linear Network Coding in Wireless Sensor Networks. Chinese Journal of Electronics 38(10), 2309–2314 (2010)
10. Fu, B., Li, R., Liu, C., Xiao, X.: A Congestion Aware Routing Protocol Based on Network Coding in Wireless Sensor Networks. Chinese Journal of Computer Research and Development 48(6), 991–999 (2011)
11. Wedde, H.F., Farooq, M.: A comprehensive review of nature inspired routing algorithms for fixed telecommunication networks. Journal of Systems Architecture 52(8), 461–484 (2006)
12. Wang, R.-C., Li, Y., Xu, X.-L.: The research of dynamic routing algorithm based on mobile agent. Chinese Journal of Computers 28(3), 420–426 (2005)
13. De Couto, D.S.J., Aguayo, D., Bicket, J., Morris, R.: A high-throughput path metric for multi-hop wireless routing. In: Proceeding of ACM MobiCom 2003, pp. 134–146. IEEE Press, New York (2003)
14. Heinzelman, W.B., Chandrakasan, A.P., Balakrishnan, H.: An application-specific protocol architecture for wireless micro sensor networks. IEEE Transactions on Wireless Communications 1(4), 660–670 (2002)

Maximizing the Lifetime of Unreliable Sensor Networks with Delay Constraint via Genetic Algorithm

Yueyun Shen, Yanjun Li, and Yi-Hua Zhu⋆

School of Computer Science and Technology, Zhejiang University of Technology,
Hangzhou, Zhejiang 310023, China
yueyunshen@gmail.com, {yjli,yhzhu}@zjut.edu.cn

Abstract. Energy saving is a key issue for prolonging the runtime of Wireless Sensor Network (WSN). In real-time applications of WSN, it is required to deliver data to the sink within a delay constraint. It is significant to design a scheme that maximizes the lifetime of WSN and satisfies delay constraint. To meet this requirement, in this paper, we present the Maximizing Lifetime and Delay Aware Scheme (MLDAS) that uses genetic algorithm, in which stochastic ranking (SR) method is applied, to find an Energy and Delay Aware Tree (EDAT) used to gather data in the WSN. Simulation results show that the MLDAS outperforms some existing schemes in terms of network lifetime and data accuracy.

Keywords: Wireless sensor network, network lifetime, delay constraint, data gathering.

1 Introduction

Wireless Sensor Networks (WSNs) are widely used for collecting data. Naturally, the basic operation in a WSN is data gathering that carries the sensed data to the sink (base station) through one or more communication hops.

Most sensor nodes are battery-powered, which makes it significant for the nodes to conserve energy so as to gain a longer run-time. In addition, some real-time applications of WSN require that the sensed data reach the sink within a preset delay constraint. These requirements motivate us to investigate an effective and efficient data gathering scheme that meets the preset delay constraint and saves energy so as to prolong the lifetime of WSN. The main contributions in this paper are as follows:

1) The Maximizing Lifetime and Delay Aware Scheme (MLDAS) is proposed to find the Energy and Delay Aware Tree (EDAT) used to gather data in an energy-efficient manner;

2) The optimization model for the MLDAS, which explicitly accounts for unreliable links and delay constraint is developed to maximize the lifetime of WSN; and

---

⋆ Corresponding author.

R. Wang and F. Xiao (Eds.): CWSN 2012, CCIS 334, pp. 381–392, 2013.
© Springer-Verlag Berlin Heidelberg 2013

3) A Genetic Algorithm (GA) that adopts stochastic ranking (SR) method is presented to find the EDAT.

The remainder of the paper is organized as follows. In Section 2, related works are surveyed. The optimization model is formulated in Section 3 and the MLDAS with its GA-based solution is presented in Section 4. Simulation results and performance analysis are given in Section 5. Section 6 concludes the paper.

2   Related Work

Data gathering schemes for WSN have been extensively investigated in the literature. Tree topology is often adopted in data gathering schemes thanks to its simplicity [1]. To overcome the problem that the Minimum Spanning Tree (MST) based routing protocols probably shorten network lifetime, ERAPL is presented in [2], which can prolong network lifetime.

TEDAS proposed in our previous work [3] can gradually improve the lifetime of WSN by pruning and grafting a sub-tree to a target node repeatedly. However, the main shortcoming in the TEDAS lies in that it may get trapped at a local optimum rather than the global one because a greedy algorithm is used. Noting GA is able to achieve the global optimum [4] at the expense of increasing the computational effort, we, in this paper, present a GA-based scheme, i.e., the MLDAS, to remedy the drawback existing in the TEDAS.

With view of the fact that real deployment of sensor networks has transitional region with highly unreliable links [5], noting that the links in a WSN are prone to losing packets, we consider link quality in MLDAS.

3   System Model and Problem Formulation

We assume that there are $N+1$ nodes in the WSN and Node 0 is the sink.

3.1   Prerequisites

The system is based on the following prerequisites [3].

1) Data aggregation is adopted in intermediate nodes.

2) For each node in the WSN, there exists at least one route to the sink. In fact, the topology of the WSN may change over time due to the link quality fluctuation over time [6]. Hence, network partition may occur in the WSN. If so, MLDAS can be used in each partition to collect all the data to one of the nodes in the partition. And then, the data buffered at the node can be picked by the message ferry [7].

3) Time division multiple access (TDMA) is adopted to arrange nodes for transmitting/receiving data packets.

4) Retransmission and acknowledgement (ACK) mechanisms are used for reliable packet delivery, and ACK packet does not get lost [8].

5) Only the communication (i.e., transmitting and receiving) energy is considered. Measurements show that, compared to the communication cost, energy consumptions for computation, sensing, status switching, and aggregation are stable and negligible [9].

3.2 Lifetime Optimization Problem

The notation $\langle i,j \rangle$ is used for the link that connects node i and node j, where $i \neq j$, i, $j = 0, 1, ..., N$. The Packet Reception Rate (PRR) and the Expected Transmission Count (ETX) of the link $\langle i,j \rangle$ is denoted by $R(i, j)$ and $X(i, j)$, respectively. Hence, $R(i, j) = 1/X(i, j)$. Additionally, ETX of a route is defined as the sum of the ETXs of all the links on the route. Moreover, Link $\langle i,j \rangle$ is said to be a Valid Link (VL) if it satisfies (1), where R_0 is a predefined constant, called link PRR threshold.

$$R(i, j) \geq R_0 \tag{1}$$

We represent the WSN by an undirected graph $G(V, E)$, in which $V = \{0, 1, 2, ..., N\}$ denotes the set of nodes, and E is the set of edges each representing a VL.

Let T be a given spanning tree of $G(V, E)$, rooted at the sink. For node i in tree T, we use $p_T(i)$ to represent its parent node and $C_T(i)$ to represent the set of its child nodes. Thus, if node j is an ancestor of node i, then the ETX of the route from i to j along tree T, denoted by $X_T[i, j]$, is

$$X_T[i, j] = X_T[i, p_T(i)] + X_T[p_T(i), j] \tag{2}$$

which means $X_T[i, j]$ can be obtained by adding the ETX of the link connecting i to its parent to the ETX of the route starting from its parent to j along tree T.

For node $i \in V$, let its initial battery energy be $e(i)$. Assume $e(0) = +\infty$, i.e., the sink has ample energy supply. The energy consumptions for transmitting and receiving a k-bit packet are denoted by $E_{Tx}(k)$ and $E_{Rx}(k)$, respectively, and assume

$$E_{Tx}(k) = \alpha E_{Rx}(k) \tag{3}$$

where α is a constant[10].

Data gathering can be measured by communication rounds. In each round, a node generates a k-bit packet and receives packets from its child nodes, and then these packets are aggregated to form a k-bit ongoing packet to be transmitted.

Let N_{retry} be the maximum number of the transmission/retransmissions specified in the MAC layer. Noting that the number of transmissions Node i performs to transmit a packet to its parent $p_T(i)$ is the ETX of the link $\langle i, p_T(i) \rangle$, i.e., $X_T[i, p_T(i)]$, we obtain the total number of the transmissions node i performs as follows:

$$N_{Tx}(i, T) \equiv \min\{X_T[i, p_T(i)], N_{retry}\} \tag{4}$$

We choose $R_0 \geq 1/N_{retry}$. As only VLs that satisfy (1) are included in $G(V, E)$, we have $X_T[i, p_T(i)] \leq 1/R_0 \leq N_{retry}$. Thus, Eq.(4) turns into

$$N_{Tx}(i, T) = X_T[i, p_T(i)] \tag{5}$$

Similarly, the total number of receptions node i performs is

$$N_{Rx}(i,T) \equiv \sum_{j \in C_T(i)} X_T[i,j] \tag{6}$$

In a round, the energy consumption of node i in tree T, denoted by $E_T(i)$, is the sum of the energy expended for both transmitting a packet to its parent $p_T(i)$ and receiving packets from its child nodes in the set $C_T(i)$. Hence, using (3), (5) and (6), we have

$$
\begin{aligned}
E_T(i) &= N_{Tx}(i,T)E_{Tx}(k) + N_{Rx}(i,T)E_{Rx}(k) \\
&= E_{Rx}(k)\{\alpha X_T[i, p_T(i)] + \sum_{j \in C_T(i)} X_T[i,j]\}
\end{aligned}
\tag{7}
$$

Considering that a leaf node only transmits rather than receives any packet, we introduce the following indicator: $x(i) = 0, i \in V_L; x(i) = 1, i \notin V_L$, where V_L is the set of the leaf nodes in the tree. Thus,

$$E_T(i) = E_{Rx}(k)\{\alpha X_T[i, p_T(i)] + x(i) \sum_{j \in C_T(i)} X_T[i,j]\} \tag{8}$$

Hence, the number of rounds (NoR) node i survives can be expressed in Eq.(9), where $V^* = V - \{0\}$ and the notation $\lfloor \; \rfloor$ is the floor function.

$$L_T(i) = \lfloor \frac{e(i)}{E_T(i)} \rfloor, \; i \in V^* \tag{9}$$

Hitherto, there are various definitions for network lifetime. We define the lifetime of WSN as the time period from the instant when the WSN is put into use to the instant when the first node depletes its energy [1][3]. Moreover, we use NoR to measure lifetime. Thus, according to Eq.(9), with a data gathering tree T, the lifetime of WSN, denoted by $L(T)$, is

$$L(T) = \min_{i \in V^*} L_T(i) \tag{10}$$

In a given tree, we refer to a non-leaf node, exclusive of the sink, as a relay node. Let each relay node use TDMA scheme to collect data packets from its child nodes, which can be realized by letting the relay nodes bound their channel time using superframe structure defined in IEEE 802.15.4 [11]. In each superframe, there are several Guaranteed Time Slots (GTS) each being assigned to a respective child node. Use N_{slot} to denote the number of time slots contained in a superframe and let a GTS only contain one time slot. Thus, a child node can transmit every N_{slot} time slots, i.e., the node finishing one transmission in a time period of σN_{slot}, where σ is the duration of one time slot. Thus, if node i is a child of node j, i.e., $j = p_T(i)$, then, for the lossy link $\langle i,j \rangle$, node i takes a period of

$$D(i,j) \equiv \sigma N_{slot} \lceil N_{Tx}(i,T) \rceil \tag{11}$$

to transmit one packet as the ETX of the link is $N_{Tx}(i, T)$. Here, the notation $\lceil\;\rceil$ stands for the ceil function.

Let $D_{max}(T)$ be the longest delay for a node in tree T to deliver a packet to the sink. $D_{max}(T)$ can be obtained by the Maximum Delay Finding Algorithm (MDFA) given in [3]. Let D_c be the delay constraint. The focus of this paper is to find the spanning tree T that maximizes the lifetime $L(T)$ under the condition that the delay of delivering a packet from any node to the sink must be less than D_c, which is the following Delay Constrained Lifetime Optimization Problem (DCLOP):

$$\max_{T \in \Omega} \min_{i \in V^*} F(T, i) \quad s.t. \; D_{max}(T) \leq D_c \tag{12}$$

where Ω is the set of spanning trees of $G(V, E)$ and the Objective Function (OFun)

$$F(T, i) \equiv \frac{e(i)}{E_{Rx}(k)\{\alpha X_T[i, p_T(i)] + x(i) \sum_{j \in C_T(i)} X_T[i, j]\}} \tag{13}$$

4   GA-Based Solution to DCLOP

In our previous work [3], TEDAS that uses greedy algorithm is presented to solve the DCLOP in Eq.(12). To get rid of the shortcoming of TEDAS that it may get stuck at a local optimum, we present a GA-based method. The basic idea underlying GA is to simulate evolution processes by performing selection, crossover, and mutation operations. A fitness function is used in GA to evaluate individuals. To solve constrained optimization problems, penalty function is often used in GA. With view of the difficulty in finding an appropriate penalty function for the DCLOP, we use stochastic ranking [12] method. Below, we present the GA that solves the DCLOP in details.

4.1   Solution Representation

Tree T is coded into a chromosome represented by a vector $P_T=(p_T(1), p_T(2),..., p_T(i), ..., p_T(N))$, where the i-th element is the parent of node i in $T(i \neq 0)$. For example, assume a WSN has the topology shown in Fig. 1. Then, the trees illustrated in Fig. 2 are possible spanning trees of the WSN. The tree T_1 in Fig. 2(a) is coded into the chromosome $P_{T1} = (5, 3, 0, 0, 2, 3, 4, 4, 7, 7)$ while T_2 in Fig. 2(b) has the chromosome $P_{T2} = (5, 0, 4, 0, 2, 2, 3, 7, 7, 7)$.

4.2   Immune Mechanism

In a given WSN, there may exist leaf nodes, with each having degree of 1. For instance, in the WSN illustrated in Fig. 1, Nodes 1, 9, and 10 are leaf nodes. Noting that removing the Parent of a Leaf Node (PLN) causes network partition, we adopt immune mechanism [13] to vaccinate the gene that corresponds to the PLN so as to protect the PLN from removing. The immune operation aims to avoid performing the crossover and mutation operations on these kinds of genes.

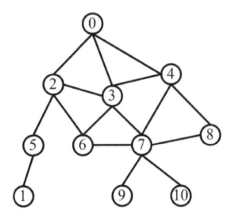

Fig. 1. A WSN with 11 nodes

We use the set S_1 to keep the immune nodes and S_2 for the other nodes. We use M to represent the connection matrix having size of $(N+1) \times (N+1)$, in which the element at the i-th row and j-th column is denoted by $M(i,j)$. For any pair of i and j, if the link $\langle i,j \rangle$ is a VL, then set $M(i,j) = 1$ and $M(j,i) = 1$; otherwise, set $M(i,j) = 0$ and $M(j,i) = 0$. Then, the two sets S_1 and S_2 are formed by the following Immune Node Selecting Algorithm (INSA).

Step 1. Set $S_1=0$ and $S_2 = \{1, 2, ..., N\}$.

Step 2. Let $V_1 = \Phi$ (the empty set); for each $i \in S_2$, if $\sum_{j=1}^{N+1} M(i,j) = 1$, let $V_1 = V_1 + \{i\}$.

Step 3. If $V_1 = \Phi$, go to Step 5.

Step 4. For each $i \in V_1$, let $S_1 = S_1 + \{i\}$, $S_2 = S_2 - \{i\}$, and $M(k,i) = 0$, where Node k is the parent of Node i. Go to step 2

Step 5. End.

For example, for the WSN in Fig. 1, we have $S_1 = \{0, 1, 5, 9, 10\}$ and $S_2 = \{2, 3, 4, 6, 7, 8\}$ when the INSA ends.

It can be clearly seen from S_1 that, apart from the original leaf nodes (i.e., Nodes 1, 9, and 10), the sink node and all the newly-generated leaf nodes after the original leaf nodes are removed (i.e., Node 5) are included in S_1.

It should be stressed that, the crossover and mutation operations are prohibited on the genes in the chromosome that corresponding to immune nodes.

4.3   Initial Population

The population consists of S_p individuals (chromosomes) that represent feasible solutions to the DCLOP. Let $D_v(T)$ be an indicator to identify whether T violates delay constraint or not. That is, $D_v(T) = 1$, if $D_{max}(T) > D_c$; $D_v(T) = 0$, otherwise. To have more diversity in the initial population, we include a chromosome obtained from TEADS [3] and a chromosome from Dijkstra algorithm.

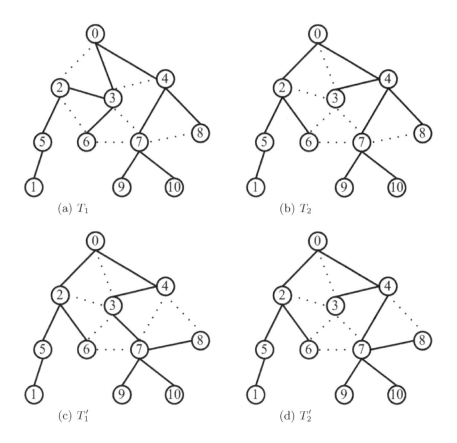

(a) T_1

(b) T_2

(c) T_1'

(d) T_2'

Fig. 2. Spanning trees of the WSN

The other chromosomes are randomly generated spanning trees rooted at the sink with delay limited by $D_c \times C_v$, where $C_v \geq 1$ is a parameter used to tune the delay.

4.4 Fitness Evaluation

We choose the OFun in Eq.(13), i.e., $F(T, i)$, as the fitness function. After the initial population is generated, we compute the fitness value for each chromosome and evaluate the constraints.

4.5 Selection

We use Roulette-Wheel method to select the chromosomes with top fitness values in the current generation, which are then used to create new chromosomes by the crossover and mutation operations.

4.6 Crossover

Crossover operation is performed on the basis of chromosome pair, in which each chromosome is randomly chosen. Assume CH_1 and CH_2 are the two chromosomes in a given pair and they correspond to trees T_1 and T_2, respectively. Randomly choose a node P_c in S_2 as the crossover point and use X_1 and X_2 to hold all the nodes in the subtree rooted at P_c in T_1 and T_2, respectively. Then, for each $k \in X_1$, the k-th gene of CH_1 is replaced with the parent of Node k in T_2. Similarly, for each $k \in X_2$, the k-th gene of CH_2 is replaced with the parent of Node k in T_1. Thus, two new chromosomes is generated.

Now, we give an example to illustrate the crossover operation. Assume the pair of the two trees T_1 and T_2 shown in Fig. 2(a) and Fig. 2(b), respectively, are chosen for crossover operation. They have the chromosomes $CH_1 = (5, 3, 0, 0, 2, 3, 4, 4, 7, 7)$ and $CH_2 = (5, 0, 4, 0, 2, 2, 3, 7, 7, 7)$, respectively.

Suppose node 3 in S_2 is chosen as the crossover point. Thus, the nodes in the subtree rooted at node 3 in T_1 and T_2 are $X_1 = \{1, 2, 3, 5, 6\}$ and $X_2 = \{3, 7, 8, 9, 10\}$, respectively. Since the nodes 1, 2, 3, 5, and 6 in X_1 has parents of 5, 0, 4, 2, and 2 in T_2, respectively, we replace the 1st, the 2nd, the 3rd, the 5th, and the 6-th genes of CH_1 with 5, 0, 4, 2, and 2, respectively, which generates the new chromosome $(5, 0, 4, 0, 2, 2, 4, 4, 7, 7)$ that corresponds to T_1' shown in Fig. 2(c). Similarly, we obtain another new chromosome $(5, 0, 4, 0, 2, 2, 3, 7, 7, 7)$ that corresponds to T_2' shown in Fig. 2(d).

4.7 Mutation

Suppose the gene g is to be mutated. We use $subtree_T(g)$ to represent the subtree rooted at g in tree T. Mutation operation follows the following steps:

Step 1. Randomly choose a node m in S_2 such that $M(g, m) = 1$.

Step 2. If $m \notin subtree_T(g)$, go to Step 9.

Step 3. $T' = T$, $p_{T'}(g) = m$, $V_{loop} = \Phi$

Step 4. For each node i constructing the loop in T', let $V_{loop} = V_{loop} + \{i\}$, $V_{loop} = V_{loop} - g$.

Step 5. If $V_{loop} = \Phi$, go to Step 9.

Step 6. Randomly pick a node x in V_{loop}

Step 7. If there exists a node y that satisfies $M(x, y) = 1$ and $y \notin subtree_T(g)$, replace X's parent with Y in T, and replace g's parent with m in T go to Step 9.

Step 8. Go to Step 5.

Step 9. End.

4.8 Generate New Population

In each generation, we choose S_p chromosomes to make a population for the next generation. These chromosomes are chosen from the population in the current generation and together with the population after selection, crossover and mutation operations, which has totally $2S_p$ chromosomes. To achieve a balance between the OFun and the constraint violation, a probability factor p_{cv} is used to determine whether the fitness or the constraint violation value determines the rank of chromosome. For each chromosome, generate a random number $0 < r < 1$. If $r < p_{cv}$, rank the chromosome based on the fitness value; otherwise, rank the chromosome based on the constraint violation and fitness (the chromosome satisfies $D_v(T) = 0$). The parameter p_{cv} can be a constant or is decreased linearly from 0.475 to 0.025 over generations [14].

The proposed MLDAS progresses as follows: 1) run the above GA; 2) after the GA terminates, the best chromosome that satisfies the delay constraint and has the best fitness value is chosen; and 3) the EDAT is produced from the best chromosome according to the coding scheme in Selection 4.1.

5   Simulation and Performance Analysis

Fix $N = 100$. Distribute the nodes in a 100m×100m field uniformly, where the sink is located at the center and the positions of the other nodes are randomly generated. Each node is assigned an initial energy (in Joule) randomly picked in the interval [1,10] [9]. The link PRR between two nodes are generated according to the model presented in [5], which is built on experimental measures of practical systems with respect to statistics of wireless channel. With the standard non-coherent FSK modulation and Manchester encoding, the PRR of the wireless link $\langle i, j \rangle$ is set according to the following equation [5]:

$$R(i, j) = [1 - \frac{1}{2}exp(-\frac{\gamma(d)}{2}\frac{1}{0.64})]^{8(2f-l)} \tag{14}$$

where d is the distance of nodes i and j; $\gamma(d)$ is the signal-to-noise ratio (SNR); f is the frame size (in octet) including the sizes of preamble payload and frame check sequence; and l is the size of preamble (in octet).

Set $R_0 = 0.1$; $f = 50$ B; $e_{tx} = 0.6$ mJ and $e_{rx} = 0.395$ mJ [10]; $S_p = 50$. The average of 1000 simulation runs, with each mimicking 50 generations, yields Figs. 3-5, where SPTS represents the Shortest Path Tree with Semi-matching presented in [1] and RT stands for the Random Tree (RT) created by letting nodes randomly select their parent [3]. In Fig. 3, there is no delay constraint, i.e., $D_c = \infty$. In Fig. 4, for a given topology of the WSN, we set $D_c = D_{min} + x$, where D_{min} is the minimum delay required for delivering a packet to the sink from any leaf node and x is used for tuning delay constraint.

It can be clearly seen from Fig. 3 that MLDAS achieves the best network lifetime. From Fig. 4, in MLDAS and TEDAS, network lifetime grows as the delay constraint is gradually relaxed, which agrees with our intuition. Besides, with the increase of D_c, MLDAS becomes much better than TEDAS, which indicates that, when D_c is small, only a few spanning trees meet the delay constraint in the DCLOP. Thus, TEDAS gets stuck at a local optimum, but MLDAS can still find the global optimum so that network lifetime is improved.

We define data accuracy as the ratio K/N, where K is the number of nodes whose packets are successfully delivered to the sink in a data gathering round.

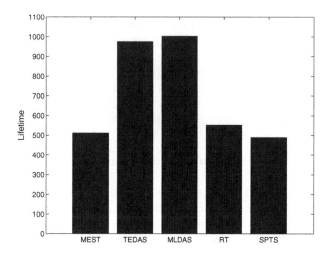

Fig. 3. Comparison of network lifetime, $D_c = \infty$

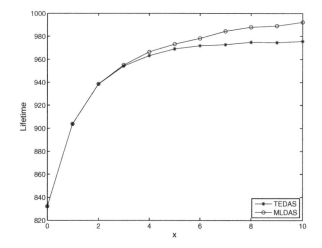

Fig. 4. Impact of delay constraint on WSN's lifetime

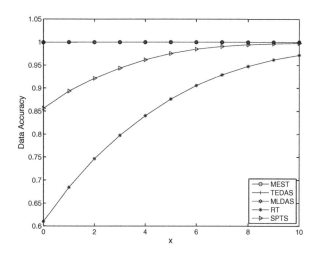

Fig. 5. Data accuracy vs. delay constraint

The data accuracy averaged over both the NoR and the number of the simulation runs (i.e., 1000) is illustrated in Fig. 5. From the figure, we observe that the data accuracy in the proposed MLDAS considerably better than that in the SPTS and the RT and slightly betters than the MEST and TEDAS.

6   Conclusion

In the real-time applications of WSN, it is significant to construct a spanning tree through which data sensed by sensors are gathered to the sink in energy efficient manner while the delay limitation is satisfied. The proposed MLDAS occupies the above features, which is able to prolong lifetime of the WSN with unreliable links under delay constraint.

Acknowledgments. This work was supported by the National Natural Science Foundation of China under Grants No. 61003264 and 61070190, Zhejiang Provincial Natural Science Foundation under Grant No Z1100455 and the Open Project of State Key Lab. of Industrial Control Technology under Grant No. ICT1110.

References

1. Luo, D., Zhu, X., Wu, X., Chen, G.: Maximizing lifetime for the shortest path aggregation tree in wireless sensor networks. In: 30th Conference on Computer Communications, pp. 1566–1574. IEEE Press, Shanghai (2011)
2. Zhu, Y.H., Wu, W., Pan, J., Tang, Y.: An energy-efficient data gathering algorithm to prolong lifetime of wireless sensor networks. Computer Communications 33, 639–647 (2010)

3. Shen, Y., Li, Y., Zhu, Y.H.: Constructing Data Gathering Tree to Maximize the Lifetime of Unreliable Wireless Sensor Network under Delay Constraint. In: 7th International Wireless Communications and Mobile Computing Conference. ACM Press, Cyprus (in press, 2012)

4. Whitley, D.: A genetic algorithm tutorial. In: Statistics and Computing, vol. 4, pp. 65–85. Springer (1994)

5. Zuniga, M., Krishnamachari, B.: Analyzing the transitional region in low power wireless links. In: 1st Communications Society Conference on Sensor, Mesh and Ad Hoc Communications and Networks, pp. 517–526. IEEE Press, California (2004)

6. Cerpa, A., Wong, L.J., Kuang, L., Potkonjak, M., Estrin, D.: Statistical model of lossy links in wireless sensor networks. In: International Conference on Information Processing in Sensor Networks, pp. 81–88. IEEE & ACM Press, California (2005)

7. Zhu, Y.H., Wu, W., Leung, V.C.M.: Energy-efficient Tree-based Message Ferrying Routing Schemes for Wireless Sensor Networks. In: Mobile Networks and Applications, vol. 16, pp. 58–70. Springer (2011)

8. Sang, L., Arora, A., Zhang, H.: On exploiting asymmetric wireless links via one-way estimation. In: 8th ACM International Symposium on Mobile Ad Hoc Networking and Computing, pp. 11–20. ACM Press, Québec (2007)

9. Heinzelman, R.W., Chandrakasan, A., Balakrishnan, H.: Energy-efficient communication protocol for wireless microsensor networks. In: 33rd International Conference on System Sciences, Island of Maui, pp. 10–19 (2000)

10. Lee, M., Wong, V.W.S.: An energy-aware spanning tree algorithm for data aggregation in wireless sensor networks. In: 18th IEEE Pacific Rim Conference on Communications, Computers and Signal Processing, Victoria, pp. 300–303 (2005)

11. IEEE Computer Society. IEEE 802.15.4 Standard for Wireless Medium Access Control (MAC) and Physical Layer (PHY) Specifications for Low-Rate Wireless Personal Area Networks (WPANs) (2006)

12. Runarsson, T.P., Yao, X.: Stochastic ranking for constrained evolutionary optimization. IEEE Transactions on Evolutionary Computation 4, 284–294 (2000)

13. Jiao, L., Wang, L.: A novel genetic algorithm based on immunity. IEEE Transactions on Systems, Man, and Cybernetic 30, 552–561 (2000)

14. Rammohan, M., Ponnuthurai, N.S.: Ensemble of constraint handling techniques. IEEE Transactions on Evolutionary Computation 14, 561–579 (2010)

Wireless Sensor Network Time Synchronization Algorithm Based on SFD

Shanshan Song, Lili He, Yu Jiang, Chengquan Hu, and Yinghui Cao*

College of Computer Science and Technology, Jilin University,
Changchun 130012, China
caoyh@jlu.edu.cn
http://www.springer.com/lncs

Abstract. Time synchronization is an important supporting technology for wireless sensor network (WSN). In most existing WSN time synchronization algorithms, timestamp is recorded by software when sending and receiving synchronization messages, which involving synchronization errors like send time and access time. In this paper, a WSN time synchronization algorithm based on SFD is proposed. In the novel algorithm, timestamp of synchronization message is recorded by SFD hardware capture. It can effectively eliminate send time, access time and other synchronization errors. Experiments based on proposed algorithm have been done to verify the effectiveness and time synchronization errors are analyzed.

Keywords: WSN, Time Synchronization, SFD, CC2530, TIMAC.

1 Introduction

In recent years, wireless sensor network has become an international high-profile emerging discipline. It is widely used in military security, environmental monitoring, medical care, smart home and building status monitoring, etc [1] [2]. Time synchronization is a key technology of wireless sensor network [3]. It guarantees protocol running, sleep together, TDMA scheduling, data integration and positioning for wireless sensor networks [4]. In August 2002, Jeremy Elson and Kay Romer first proposed the research on wireless sensor network time synchronization mechanism and attracted wide attention in HotNets-I [5]. Now we have put forward many time synchronization mechanisms, for example, one-way time synchronization algorithm based on sender/receiver DMTS, two-way time synchronization algorithm based on sender/receiver TPSN and time synchronization algorithm based on receiver/receiver RBS are all widely used synchronization mechanism. WSN time synchronization sources of error include: send time, access time, propagation time and receiver time. Among them, send time is the time to construct a message and send the message to the MAC layer spent at the sender; Access time occurs when a MAC $layer's$ message waiting for wireless

---

* Corresponding author.

R. Wang and F. Xiao (Eds.): CWSN 2012, CCIS 334, pp. 393–400, 2013.
© Springer-Verlag Berlin Heidelberg 2013

communication channel idle spent at the sender, and this period is impacted by channel condition, and extends when the channel is busy [6]. Propagation time is to propagate the message in wireless communication channel from sender to receive, usually can be ignored. Receive time is to receive message from wireless communication channel and restructure message to the upper-layer protocol spent at the receiver. Most WSN time synchronization algorithms use software to record timestamp when send and receive synchronization message, and then compare timestamps to calculate the nodes time difference. The nodes use software to record send/receive message timestamp will inevitably introduce send timeaccess time and receiver time, in particular, access time will unpredictable extend influenced by the channel busy status [7]. To eliminate the impact of these errors, you need hardware to record send/receive message timestamp.

2   Wireless Sensor Network Time Synchronization Algorithm Based on SFD

2.1   Sensor Node Time Model

In a distributed system, each node has its own local clock achieved by a crystal oscillator and a counter [8]. Because of the limitation of factory production technology, the frequency of a sensor nodes crystal oscillator is different from other nodes, and it will vary as time due to electromagnetism, pressure, temperature and other factors [9]. Time model of the sensor nodes can be expressed by formula 1 [10]:

$$T_i(t) = k_i(t) * S_i(t) + b_i(t) . \tag{1}$$

In formula 1, t is a real time variable, b_i is the time offset of node i. Let $k_i = \frac{f_i}{f_0}$ [11], f_i represents node $i's$ crystal oscillator frequency, f_0 represents $node's$ crystal oscillator normal frequency, k_i meets $|k_i - 1| \leq \rho$ and the range of ρ is 1 100ppm (part per million)that is the node will be offset 1 100 microseconds per second. $S_i(t)$ represents system clock function of node i at Time t. $T_i(t)$ represents local clock function of node i at Time t. In this paper, we ignore the difference between nodesfrequency, so we assume $k_i = 1$that is the $node's$ crystal oscillator frequency and normal frequency are the same. Let the local clock offset of node i and j is $T_i(t) - T_j(t) = S_i(t) - S_j(t) + b_i - b_j$. If node j will be synchronous with node i, we can modify the value of b_j making $T_j(t)' = T_i(t)$.

2.2   SFD Signal

The algorithm proposed in this paper is a higher-precision SFD-based WSN time synchronization algorithm, and SFD is the start of frame delimiter. When the $frame's$ SFD domain has already been sent/received, the SFD signal changes from low to high and keeps high until the frame sent/received completely. The capture is the process to capture and lock the signal in communication system. The lock is achieved by hardware when a signal changes. When a signal jumps, the crystal oscillator value of system counter is written to the capture register. Thus, after the capture event occurs, the capture register can keep crystal oscillator value when the signal jumps. SFD hardware capture is the capture of the SFD signal. It occurs once SFD signal of message was sent/received. Because the method of hardware capture recording timestamp does not include the delay produced by software capture recording timestamp, SFD hardware capture exclude send time, access time and receive time. That SFD hardware capture timestamps of sender and receiver are at the same time.

2.3   Algorithm Description

Assuming i is sender, j is receiver, at Time t we get $i's$ local clock $T_i(t)$ and $j's$ local clock $T_j(t)$ and then calculate $\triangle = T_i(t) - T_j(t)$. So the time model of j is $T_j(t)' = T_j(t) + \triangle$. On the basis of formula 1if j will be synchronous with i, then $b'_j = b_j + \triangle$. Later then correct the local clock of j. Algorithm process is as follows:

(1) The sender i sends the first message for time synchronization, called P1, and then records the local time $T_i(t)$ when $P1's$ SFD domain has been sent.
(2) The receiver j receives P1 ,and then records the time when $P1's$ SFD domain has been received.
(3) The sender sends the second message for time synchronization, called P2, the data of P2 carries $T_i(t)$.
(4) The receiver receives P2, gets $T_i(t)$ by the data of P2, then calculates $\triangle = T_i(t) - T_j(t)$, lastly corrects the time offset of the receiver, that $b'_j = b_j + \triangle$.

The time recorded by this algorithm is captured by SFD hardware when SFD signal sent/received, is got by SFD signal which is triggered in communication process, not depend on the software, not affected by channel, excluded the impact of send time, access time and receive time.

3   Algorithm Realization

3.1   Experimental Platform

The hardware used in this paper is CC2530 development kit consists of CC2530EM and SmartRF05EB-M development board, shown in Fig 1. Because protocol stack has its own run time, which can loss the precision of time synchronization, CC2530 runs on no protocol stack. $CC2530's$ Timer 2 provides the basic timing function for IEEE 802.15.4 MAC layer, it consists of a 40 bit register(T2MOVF2, T2MOVF1, T2MOVF0, T2M1 and T2M0). The count of $node's$ crystal oscillator is Timer 2 $register's$ value. It also has the SFD capture function. When detecting SFD signal changing from low to high, the SFD capture function runs, SFD capture register storages the value of Timer 2 on the current.

Fig. 1. CC2530 development kit

3.2   Implementation Process

In order to realize the algorithm in 2.3, to get the sender $i's$ local clock $T_i(t)$ and receiver $j's$ local clock $T_j(t)$, we can just get the value of node $i's$ SFD capture register value N_i and the value of node $j's$ SFD capture register N_j. In 2.1, $S_i(t) = \frac{N_i}{f_i}$, $S_j(t) = \frac{N_j}{f_j}$, so $\triangle = \frac{N_i}{f_i} - \frac{N_j}{f_j} + b_i - b_j$. When initial, time offset of node i and j are both 0. After the first time synchronization, each node records their time offset. We assume that the frequency of nodes i and j are both normal frequency. In order to correct the local clock of node j, we can correct the time offset of node j, $b'_j = b_j + \triangle$, and realize node j and node i synchronous. Communication process for algorithm is shown in Fig. 2.

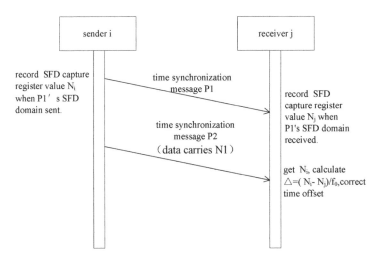

Fig. 2. Communication process for algorithm

In order to make the nodes have a better and longer time function, we constructs a software clock, and the process of software clock is shown in Fig.3. In this paper, we set N to 24, so the time will not be overflow in 100 years.

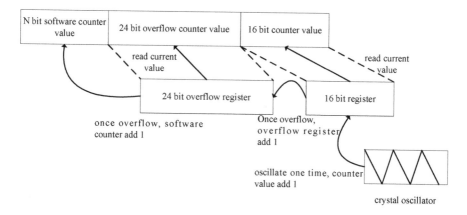

Fig. 3. N bit software clock construction

3.3 Program Flow Chart

Procedure flow chart is shown in Fig.4. Fig.4 (a) is the flow chart of send node. Fig.4 (b) is the program flow chart of receive node.

4 Experimental Results

In this article, we use a third-party node to verify the accuracy of the two sensor nodes which have been time synchronized. The advantage of using third party is to avoid the SFD delay between sender and receiver. After the two nodes synchronized, the third-party node sends a abroad message to the two synchronized nodes. And the two receive the message at the same time, showing their local time stored in SFD register, and then record the time difference between the two nodes. The process is shown in Fig.5.

To stat 50 experimental results, we found that the average of the two synchronized nodes' time difference is about 5.82 microseconds. The statistical results are shown in Fig.6 Based on the above results, also we can see that, in 50 of the experimental results, the min error is 4.84 microseconds, and the max error is 10.25 microseconds. The number of error which is less then 6 microseconds accounts for 72% of the total number. Therefore, the experimental results are stable at 4 to 6 microseconds. By analyzingthe synchronization error is caused by the change of crystal frequency and the difference of the crystal frequency between the nodes. Also there is SFD delay between the sender and receiver, and now we do not know the value of SFD delay. If we can get the value of SFD delay, we will eliminate the SFD delay. The above time synchronization

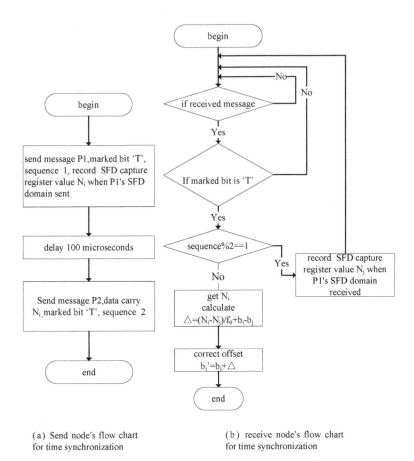

(a) Send node's flow chart
for time synchronization

(b) receive node's flow chart
for time synchronization

Fig. 4. send/receive nodes flow chart for time synchronization

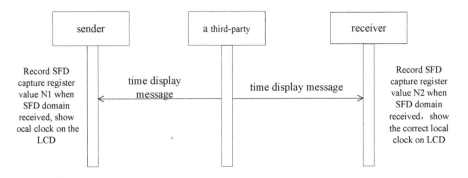

Fig. 5. the validation process of time synchronization results

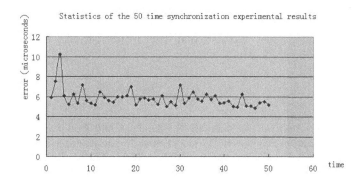

Fig. 6. Statistics of the 50 time synchronization experimental results

algorithm is used for two nodes. For the whole network, you can use the same principle to synchronize. At first we can make the nodes networking, and then sink node send time synchronization messages to all its son nodes. After the son nodes synchronized, they send time synchronization messages to their son nodes, and finally achieve the whole network time synchronization. Through the above experiment data and experimental results, it is proved that WSN time synchronization algorithm based on SFD in this paper has been achieved. Time synchronization error is about 5.82 microseconds, and it has realized higher precision time synchronization. Compared with other traditional WSN time synchronization method, for example, TPSN and RBS, the algorithm proposed in this paper has the advantages of simpler, more accurate [12] . Precision of 11 microseconds has been reached using RBS on Berkeley mote, which is a popular platform. TPSN achieves 16.9 microseconds for the same experimental setup. TPSN and RBS both algorithms were applied on Mica platform. RBS, which is receiver-receiver algorithm, needs 4 messages sent and 3 messages received to synchronize two nodes. TPSN needs 2 messages sent and 2 messages received to synchronize two nodes. But the algorithm proposed in this paper needs only 1 message sent and 1 message received, and it is not depend on some platform, so it is simpler. The precision of it is about 5.82 microseconds less then TPSN and RBS, so it is more accurate. Above all, the algorithm proposed in this paper is better than the traditional WSN time synchronization method.

5   Further Research Plan

The study in this paper ignores the frequency deviation between nodes and frequency change of a node. In the real case, the crystal frequency of the node will offset 1 - 40 microseconds per second. In the subsequent study, a correction for crystal oscillator frequency can be added, and a measuring for SFD delay will be added, achieving a higher precision of time synchronization.

Acknowledgments. We are grateful to the support of Changchun Science and Technology Support Program from Jilin Province, China(grant 11kz23) and Science and Technology Development plan key project of Jilin Province(grant 20090425).

References

1. Rahamatkar, S., Agarwal, A., Kumar, N.: Analysis and Comparative Study of Clock Synchronization Schemes in Wireless Sensor Networks. International Journal on Computer Science and Engineering 02(03), 536–541 (2010)
2. Agre, J., Clare, L.: An integrated architecture for cooperative sensing networks. IEEE Computer 33(5), 106–108 (2000)
3. Schenato, L., Gamba, G.: A distributed consensus protocol for clock synchronization in wireless sensor network. In: 46th IEEE Conference on Decision and Control, pp. 2289–2294. IEEE Press, New Orleans (2007)
4. Benzaid, C., Saiah, A., Badache, N.: Secure Pairwise Broadcast Time Synchronization in Wireless Sensor Networks. In: Distributed Computing in Sensor Systems and Workshops (DCOSS), Barcelona, pp. 1–6 (2011)
5. Liu, D.-X.: Time Synchronization Based on Clock Drift Compensation in Wireless Sensor Network. Journal of Time and Frequency 32(2), 120–128 (2009)
6. Part 15.4: Wireless Medium Access Control and Physical Layer Specications for Low Rate Wireless Personal Area Networks, IEEE Std. 802.15.4 (September 2003)
7. Ramachandran, I., Roy, S.: On the Impact of Clear Channel Assessment on MAC Performance. In: IEEE Global Telecommunications Conference, GLOBECOM 2006, San Francisco, CA, pp. 1–5 (2006)
8. Gao, Q., Xu, B.: Time Synchronization Improvement for Wireless Sensor Networks. In: 1st International Symposium on Pervasive Computing and Applications, Urumqi, pp. 805–810 (2006)
9. Xu, C.-N., Zhao, L., Xu, Y.-J.: A Time Synchronization Improvement Strategy for Wireless Sensor Networks. Chinese Journal of Computers 30(4), 514–523 (2007)
10. Romer, K., Blum, B., Meier, L.: Time Synchronization and Calibration in Wireless Sensor Networks. Wireless Sensor Networks, Algorithms and Architectures (7), 199–237 (2005)
11. Meng, J., Yang, K.: Physical-Layer Time Synchronization for Wireless Sensor Networks Using UWB Signals. In: Communications and Networking, Xian, China, pp. 1–5 (2009)
12. Lasassmeh, S.M., Conrad, J.M.: Time Synchronization in Wireless Sensor Networks: A Survey. In: IEEE SoutheastCon 2010, Concord, NC, pp. 242–245 (2010)

Dynamic Bluetooth Packet Selection Strategy Based on Wi-Fi White-Space Prediction*

Zheng Song, Yongping Xiong, Jian Ma, Ke Zhang, and Wendong Wang

Institute of Networking, Beijing University of Post and Telecommunication,
Xitucheng Str. 10, 100876 Beijing, China
{songzheng,ypxiong,wdwang}@bupt.edu.cn, {majian,zhangke}@mwsn.com.cn

Abstract. In order to coexist Bluetooth with Wi-Fi in mutual interference environment, carrier sensing and traffic forecasting model are
used to optimize the packet selection mechanism in Bluetooth frequency-
hopping process. The probability of collisions of Bluetooth signal and Wi-
Fi signal is gained by baseband layer energy sampling and Wi-Fi traffic
forecasting model. According to the collision probability, the packet types
are selected to achieve maximum throughput of Bluetooth. Simulation
and analysis show that the algorithm can effectively coexist Wi-Fi with
Bluetooth by mean of time divided channel multiplexing in real world
Wi-Fi environment.

Keywords: Wireless Communication, Heterogeneous networks coexistence, Dynamic Packet Selection Strategy, White Space Prediction.

1 Introduction

In recent years, Wi-Fi technology has been widely applied in the field of wireless
communications. Most mobile devices, including notebooks, smart phones and
so on have built-in module supporting Wi-Fi communication. Due to the mobile
devices increasing demand for network access, Wi-Fi hot spots are also in a rapid
growth: the number of global public Wi-Fi hotspots will reach 5.8 million by
2015. Wi-Fi offers high transfer rates and low unit cost for data link, and is widely
used in mobile internet applications, such as Itune, Instagram, Skype, etc. Wi-Fi
technology is occupying the 2.4GHz band in an unprecedented communications
density.

The increasingly intensive Wi-Fi communication promotes interference with
other communications standards working on 2.4GHz frequency band. Bluetooth
is another widely used 2.4GHz protocol which is designed to meet the need
of short-distance voice transmission and data transmission in personal area. In
the emerging Internet of Things architecture, Bluetooth technology is widely

---

* This work was supported in part by the National Natural Science Foundation of
China under Grant No. 61271041, Integrated Project iCore (Internet Connected Ob-
jects for Reconfigurable Eco-systems) under Grant No. 287708, the Natural Science
Foundation of JiangSu Province(Youth Fund) under Grant No. BK2012125.

R. Wang and F. Xiao (Eds.): CWSN 2012, CCIS 334, pp. 401–412, 2013.
© Springer-Verlag Berlin Heidelberg 2013

used as convergence layer of local data collection methods due to its low power consumption and simple protocol stack. Wi-Fi and Bluetooth occupy basically overlapping bands, as shown in Fig. 1. When they send data at the same time on same frequency band, the signals conflict and Bluetooth signal cannot be correctly decoded for Wi-Fi has higher emission energy.

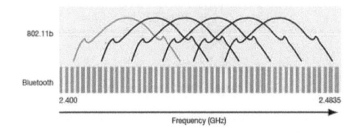

Fig. 1. Bluetooth and Wi-Fi interfering band diagram. The upper part shows the band range of 802.11b and the lower shows the band range of Bluetooth.

However, the intensification of conflict does not come from the limitation of network capacity. Study [1] pointed out that only 5% of network capacity is used in almost any time and any scene. This paper focus on when both Bluetooth and Wi-Fi exist, how to make the best use of the 95% wasted network capacity to avoid interference and improve the transfer rate of Bluetooth network.

In order to resolve the confliction problem, researchers have proposed serveral methods of the following categories: 1) adaptive frequency hopping method (AFH) [2] [3] [4], core idea of which is to minimize the usage of interfered channels in Bluetooths hopping frequency. The method evaluates the channel quality according to packet error rate or channel signal noise rate, and avoids using those channels that Wi-Fi is working on. But if Wi-Fi occupies all three channels and, this method greatly limits the number of optional Bluetooth hopping channels and increases the possibility of confliction between Bluetooth devices; 2) adaptive packet selection method [5], the core the idea of which is to maximize Bluetooth traffic by dynamic packet type selection. This method evaluates the channel quality according to the retransmission rate, assumes that Wi-Fi traffic follows the Gaussian white noise model and calculate the maximum transmission flow of different packet types in a certain retransmission rate; 3) dynamic frequency hopping sequence [6],[7] ,a frequency hopping sequence designing method based on monitoring Wi-Fi traffic and predicting busy-free state of the next time slot by hidden Markov model.

However, method 2) and 3) use Wi-Fi network characteristics in lab network environment to model and to estimate the possibility of confliction with Bluetooth in real- life environment. Research [8] proved that in real-life environment, Wi-Fi traffic distribution is more in line with the Pareto distribution characteristics compared to the Markov model and Gaussian white noise model. More accurate forecasts can be achieved by using Pareto distribution model.

In order to coexist Bluetooth with Wi-Fi in mutual interference environment, carrier sensing and Pareto distribution based traffic forecasting model are used to optimize the packet selection mechanism in the Bluetooth frequency-hopping process. The rest of the paper is organized as follows, Section 2 surveys related work. Section 3 presents detailed description of the system design. Section 4 provides the test-bed evaluation results. Section 5 draws the conclusions.

2   Related Works

Wi-Fi and Bluetooth are the two most commonly used wireless communication protocols working on the same 2.4 to 2.48GHz ISM band. Wi-Fi is based on the CSMA-CA protocol (which means listener to idle channel before send) and features 13 frequency channels on the 2.4 GHz band (in which 5 are non-overlapping). In order to tolerate interference that can rapidly arise in the 2.4GHz ISM band, in Bluetooth system, a frequency hopping (FH) scheme is utilized with terminals cycling through 79 channels at 1600 hops/s. A pseudo-random algorithm is used to select the frequency by same probability and constitute the hopping sequence.

Researchers studied the coexistence of Bluetooth and Wi-Fi from different perspectives [4][5][6][7][8][9][10][11].According to [10], coexistence mechanisms can be classified into two types: collaborative coexistence mechanisms and non-collaborative mechanisms. The collaborative mechanisms rely on communication ability between Bluetooth and 802.11b hardware module, while non-collaborative mechanism does not require two wireless networks to exchange information. Collaborative mechanisms are more common in earlier studies [11][12], and a typical applications is Frequency Nulling from the NST company. With the traffic information of each party known beforehand, coexistence is carried out by ranging the transmissions orthogonal in time domain. Such collaborative coexistence mechanism need to add same physical unit hardware on both device, it is complexity and not usually seen in recent research.

Non-collaborative mechanisms work without any communication between 802.11b and Bluetooth modules. One common approach is the adaptive frequency hopping strategy (AFH). Adaptive frequency hopping strategy was proposed in 2003, the basic idea of which is to avoid using Wi-Fi interfered channels [3].The Bluetooth system gathers channel evaluation information from both master and slave devices. Channels are classified into disturbed channels (Bad Channels) and undisturbed channels (Good channels) and good channels are used to replace bad channels when the hopping frequency sequence is chosen. Taher, T.M. et al.[2] proposed an algorithm to supplement the adaptive frequency hopping (AFH) scheme. It detects APs and their working status and adapts the Bluetooth device to avoid the spectral region occupied by the APs. Seung-Hwan Lee[12] proposed another improvement to AFH, which groups Bluetooth channels according to the channel allocation of WLAN and uses a moving average technique to estimate the status of Bluetooth channels in groups to give a quicker channel evaluation. ISOAFH, proposed by [10], use the bad channels as well, and reduce the transmission on bad channel. All the non-collaborative mechanisms mentioned above share the same basic idea: to reduce transmission on bad channels. However, such mechanisms can not make full use of Wi-Fi-free channel time.

Yang Fan et al.[5] proposed adaptive packet selection strategy based on channel noise. The author derived relationship between ACL packet retransmission probability and the average received SNR, and guide how to choose the right type of packet in different SNR condition to maximum throughput. However, the method is not designed particularly for coexistence with Wi-Fi, and the distribution of Wi-Fi transmission interference is not in line with the Gaussian white noise model in our daily life.

S. Geirhofer improved the existing non-collaborative AFH mechanism in [6] and [7], proposed a cognitive radio based method that can dynamically share the spectrum in the time-domain by exploiting whitespace between the bursty transmissions of Wi-Fi. Continuous-time Markov process is used to model Wi-Fi signal and predict idle time slots, and Bluetooth hopping sequence are selected based on the idle time slots prediction. However, this method does not consider the hopping sequence synchronization problem of the Bluetooth master and slave devices. As the master and slave device may select two different hopping sequences, they must communicate to unify the hopping frequency band before each hop, which causes a great impact on the Bluetooth transmission speed.

Recent research [13] shows that Pareto distribution model fits real-life Wi-Fi traffic distribution better than Gaussian white noise model and the Markov model. In real scenarios with diverse applications, Wi-Fi traffic is highly bursty at a wide range of time scales, the arrival of Wi-Fi frames are clustered together with short intervals, and Pareto model can fit the arrival process of Wi-Fi frame clusters. Based on [13], Jun Huang, et al. [8] proposed a ZigBee segmented transmission method called WISE for Wi-Fi and ZigBee coexistence. WISE gives accurate prediction on blank Wi-Fi time slots, and cut ZigBee frames into pieces that can fit the blank time slots. By maximize the use of Wi-Fi blank slot, WISE can improve ZigBee throughput and achieve desired trade-offs between link throughput and delivery ratio.

Some Bluetooth devices have hardware to measure received signal strength (RSS), which is included in Bluetooth protocol as optional criteria to judge the quality of the channels [14]. We monitor Wi-Fi frames by sampling channel energy using Rss indicator, and use Pareto model to predict the probability of signal collisions (Wi-Fi and Bluetooth both send frames at the same time and on the same frequency band) in a certain moment. Bluetooth packet type on each time slot on each frequency band is dynamically adjusted according to the forecast results. This method can effectively improve the utilization of Wi-Fi blank slot, reduce possibility of collision and increase Bluetooth transmission throughput.

3 Adaptive Packet Selection Strategy Based on White-Space Prediction

The basic idea of the algorithm is shown in Fig. 2.

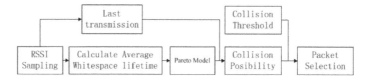

Fig. 2. Packet selection algorithm flowchart

We now discuss the details of implementation of the algorithm:

1) White space sampling and modeling: We scan all 79 channels and record RSSI transients that indicate energy change of Wi-Fi signal. Then we measure the white space between Wi-Fi frame clusters and build Wi-Fi traffic model for each channel.

2) Collision possibility calculating: We continue to read the RSSI transient value and record when Wi-Fi transmission ends. When the frequency hopping sequence of Bluetooth system comes to a frequency band, probability of conflict can be calculated by white space age when a packet is ready to transfer and the Wi-Fi traffic model.

3) Packet selecting: Given the collision probability and default threshold of conflict, we select the packet type, aiming for maximizing throughput efficiency.

3.1 Calculating Collision Probability

First we need to model the white space between Wi-Fi white space. As is mentioned above, in a channel shared by a group of 802.11 devices, the arrival process of Wi-Fi frame clusters has the feature of self-similarity. Pareto model can fit the arrival process of real-life Wi-Fi frame clusters well.

$$P_r(x > t) = \begin{cases} (\frac{\alpha}{t})^\beta, & t > \alpha \\ 1, & \text{otherwise} \end{cases} \tag{1}$$

where α and β are the scale and shape of Pareto model respectively. As time slot in Bluetooth system lasts for 625us, and Bluetooth protocol set very limited additional time listening to the channel before and after each transmission, we set α to 1ms. In other words, our model only accounts for the inter-cluster space that is longer than 1ms, because shorter white spaces cannot be used. In Pareto model, β is given by $\lambda/(\lambda-\alpha)$, where λ is the average inter-arrival time of frame clusters and can be gained by Rssi module.

Then we calculate collision probability. We continue to read the RSSI transient value and record when Wi-Fi transmission ends. When Bluetooth frequency hopping sequence comes to a certain band, data transmission starts if the device detects no Wi-Fi transmission. As Wi-Fi device cannot sense a Bluetooth transmission, a collision appears when Bluetooth transmission is still undergoing and Wi-Fi transmission starts. The collision probability depends on the lifetime and age of the white space upon the start of Bluetooth transmission, where the lifetime is the time interval between two Wi-Fi frame clusters, and the age is the time interval between the start of the white space to the start of the Bluetooth transmission. Define ρ as white space age, and we get the conditional probability of collision:

$$C(\gamma, \rho) = P_r\{t < \rho + \gamma * \rho | \rho\} = 1 - (\frac{\rho}{\gamma * \varphi + \rho})^{\beta} \tag{2}$$

Where γ is number of time slots a packet type occupies, φ is the accurate time of one slot, which is 625 us.

3.2   Packet Selecting Based on Collision Probability

Bluetooth 2.0 + EDR specification defined three link types: synchronous connection-oriented link (SCO), asynchronous connectionless link (ACL) and eSCO link which supports asynchronous retransmission. Different links have different packet types, as shown by Table.1.

Table 1. Packet differences in Bluetooth standards

Packet level	User load	Fec	CRC	Max sending rate
DM1	017	2/3	Y	108.8
DH1	027	Null	Y	172.8
DM3	0121	2/3	Y	387.2
DH3	0183	Null	Y	585.6
DM5	0224	2/3	Y	477.8
DH5	0339	Null	Y	723.2
2-DH1	054	Null	Y	345.6
2-DH3	0367	Null	Y	1174.4
2-DH5	0679	Null	Y	1448.5
3-DH1	083	Null	Y	531.2
3-DH3	0552	Null	Y	1766.4
3-DH5	01021	Null	Y	2178.1
HV1	10	1/3	N	64.0
HV2	20	2/3	N	64.0
HV3	30	Null	N	64.0
DV	10+(0-9)D	2/3D	Y	64.0+57.6D

A Bluetooth frame contains two part, frame header and user data. Headers of different packets are basically the same. The more time slots a packet type occupies, the more throughput we gain. On the other hand, if the collision probability exceeds a threshold, it leads to a rapid raise in retransfer rate, which can holdback throughput. Therefore, the goal of system is to maximize the efficiency of transmission while limiting the collision probability under user requirement. Given a specific collision probability threshold T , the optimization problem of Bluetooth packet adaptation can be formulated as follows:

$$Maximize(\gamma)$$
$$Subject\ to: C(\gamma, \rho) < Threshold, \gamma \in (0, 1, 3, 5) \tag{3}$$

Solving the problem, we obtain the appropriate packet type. A note about γ is, when $\gamma = 0$, it means that the minimum packet type cannot fulfill the collision threshold, so no data is transferred in this particular time slot.

3.3   Algorithm Overview

We further discuss our methods advantages by comparing with AFH method in [5] and adaptive packet selection method in [5]. We set up a scenario, and simplify 79 channels to 3 channels, band 1, 2 and 3. Band 1 carries a heavy Wi-Fi load, band 2 carries a weaker Wi-Fi load, and no load on band 3. As Fig. 3 shows, the blue part indicates Wi-Fi transmission exists, and red part indicates Bluetooth transmission exists. Suppose $T1, T2, T3$ to be three discrete time point. And on all the three time point, the hopping sequence will use band 1 as the next transmission band.

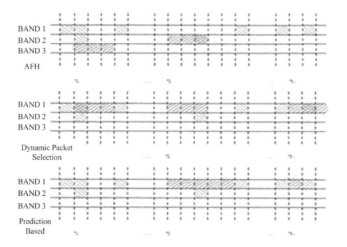

Fig. 3. experimental results of the step-counting algorithm

Assuming that the AFH method works on MODE-L (both good channels and bad channels are used), band 1 will be set to "Bad channel", band 3 will be set to "Good channel", band 2 will be set to "Can work channel". When the Good channels have many competitors, AFH method may hop into "Can work channel". The blind hop is very likely to cause a collision, which is shown in $T2$. There can always be blank time in a bad channel, AFH method will just ignore blank time and hop to another channel, which is shown in $T3$. This method use limited frequency band resources and cause a good chance to crash with Wi-Fi when Wi-Fi transmission is busy.

Adaptive packet selection method analyzes the retransfer rate of band 1, and may select a packet length of 3 time slots. However, the packet may crash in $T1$ and $T3$, and in $T2$, a longer white space appears without being made full use of.

Our method avoids sending Bluetooth package when in $T1$ a Wi-Fi transmission is detected. In $T2$, by predicting the length of white space, we maximize Bluetooth transmission efficiency. In $T3$, we avoid collision by predicting when the next Wi-Fi frame arrives. The method can make best use of interfered channel, maximize throughput as well as avoid collision.

In the next section, we quantitatively analyze the affections to throughput and collision probability by choosing different thresholds. The effectiveness of the algorithm is being measured and simulated.

4   Algorithm Evaluation and Threshold Selection Strategy

Probability of Bluetooth and Wi-Fi conflict is controlled by the conflict threshold selection. A lower threshold can reduce the collision probability and improve throughput. However, the lower threshold can also lead the packet selection strategy tend to use packets with short time slots and lead to lower throughput. We try to figure out relationship between threshold and throughput under given channel conditions. We set:

$$\partial = (1 - Threshold)^{\frac{1}{\beta}} \tag{4}$$

And based on Eq. 3 and Eq. 4., we get:

$$\gamma < \frac{1-\partial}{\partial * \varphi} * \rho \tag{5}$$

To know the probability of the occupied time slots equals 1 or 3 or 5, is to know the probability of $\gamma > n$. Based on Eq. 1, Eq. 5, we get Eq. 6.

$$P\{\gamma = 5\} = P\{\rho > \frac{5*\partial*\varphi}{1-\partial}\} = (\frac{(1-\partial)*\alpha}{5*\partial*\varphi})^{\beta}$$

$$P\{\gamma = 3\} = \begin{cases} (\frac{(1-\partial)*\alpha}{3*\partial*\varphi})^{\beta} - (\frac{(1-\partial)*\alpha}{5*\partial*\varphi})^{\beta} & \frac{(1-\partial)*\alpha}{3*\partial*\varphi} > 1, \partial > 8/23 \\ 1 - (\frac{(1-\partial)*\alpha}{5*\partial*\varphi})^{\beta} & \frac{(1-\partial)*\alpha}{3*\partial*\varphi} < 1, \partial < 8/23 \end{cases}$$

$$P\{\gamma = 1\} = \begin{cases} (\frac{(1-\partial)*\alpha}{1*\partial*\varphi})^{\beta} - (\frac{(1-\partial)*\alpha}{3*\partial*\varphi})^{\beta} & \frac{(1-\partial)*\alpha}{1*\partial*\varphi} > 1, \partial > 8/13 \\ 1 - (\frac{(1-\partial)*\alpha}{3*\partial*\varphi})^{\beta} & \frac{(1-\partial)*\alpha}{1*\partial*\varphi} < 1, \partial < 8/13 \end{cases} \tag{6}$$

$$P\{\gamma = 0\} = \begin{cases} 1 - (\frac{(1-\partial)*\alpha}{3*\partial*\varphi})^{\beta} & \frac{(1-\partial)*\alpha}{1*\partial*\varphi} < 1, \partial > 8/13 \\ 0 & 0 < \partial < 8/13 \end{cases}$$

SCO links are usually used in the real-time transmission of voice and other signals and the transmission delay must meet certain requirements. The ACL links are generally used for data transmission, and the only demand is throughput. We discuss how to choose the threshold in two kinds of links respectively.

4.1 Threshold Selection in SCO Links to Meet Real-Time Transmission Requirement

HV1, HV2 and HV3 are the usually used packet types in SCO links. Every transmission need two time slots: data transmission from master devices to slave devices are done in the odd time slots, and acknowledgement characters are sent from slave devices to master devices in even slots. HV3 is the most commonly used voice sample transmission type, and when it is used to deliver digital voice signal of 64Kb/s sampling rate, a minimized requirement is one packet is send in every six time slots.

When our method is employed in SCO links, the threshold should be low enough to send at least one data packet every six time slots. As one hopping band lasts for two time slots, one transmission must happen in every three hopping band. In reality use, we can use the collision probability of the three hopping bands which has the lowest collision probability as the threshold.

4.2 Threshold Selection in ACL Links to Maximum Throughput

We are free to assume that in real-life, the interference to Wi-Fi signal doesnt cause Wi-Fi retransmission, for Bluetooth signals impact on Wi-Fi signal is so light to notice. However, when collision appears, Bluetooth devices suffer from data lose and are forced to start retransmission. The relationship between total throughput (T_{total}) and real throughput (T_{real})in a period of time can be figured out as :

$$T_{total} = T_{real} + Threshold * T_{real} + Threshold * Threshold * T_{real} + \ldots\ldots \quad (7)$$

Known from geometric series, the relationship is expressed by:

$$T_{real} = (1 - Threshold) * T_{total} \quad (8)$$

In a period of time, the total throughput of Bluetooth system can be expressed by:

$$T_{total} = N_1 * UPL_{DH1} + N_{DH3} * UPL_{DH3} + N_{DH5} * UPL_{DH5} \quad (9)$$

N_1 stands for the number of packets that occupies one time slots and UPL_{DH1} stands for the user payload of such packets. As the occupied time of each packet types sum up to 1 second, we have:

$$1 = (N_{DH1} * 2 + N_{DH3} * 4 + N_{DH5} * 6 + N_{DH0} * 2) * \varphi \quad (10)$$

According to Eq. 5, the relationship between $N_{DH1}, N_{DH3}, N_{DH5}, N_{DH0}$ fits:

$$N_{DH1} : N_{DH3} : N_{DH5} : N_{DH0} = P\{\gamma = 1\} : P\{\gamma = 3\} : P\{\gamma = 5\} : P\{\gamma = 0\} \tag{11}$$

When λ is known, we can figure out the relationship between real throughput and threshold according to (Eq. 6,8,9,10,11.We assume λ to be 5,10,15,20,25,30ms separately and by calculating, we draw the relation as Fig 4 below:

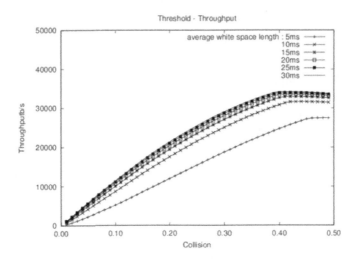

Fig. 4. Relationship between threshold and collision probability in different channel busy status

From the data we conclude: when the channel is busy and the average white space length is less than 15 ms, the throughput is obviously smaller and when the average white space length reaches 20ms, impact of the increment to throughput is few; when the collision probability (threshold) is near 0, data transfer in a very low rate, and the throughput increase quickly with higher threshold; the throughput reaches a top when the threshold is set to 40%-46%. The throughput there can reach 280KB/S, almost half of the max speed Bluetooth (v1.0) can get in a non-interference condition; after that top point, a higher threshold of the collision cannot enhance the transmission performance.

We use the data of [15] to run a evaluation between our method, AFH method[3]. Data set 9 and data set 1 are used to simulate a relatively free load Wi-Fi transmission environment and we also use data set 9 together with dataset 1 to simulate environment with heavy Wi-Fi traffic load. We put the hopping sequence into a random place of the Wi-Fi traffic. We made up a frequency hopping sequence with 10000 random hops, use it directly for our method, used Wi-Fi transmission data as a training set for updating channel status for AFH. Test show, in a relatively free load Wi-Fi traffic environment, our method and

AFH gains almost the same theoretical throughput. However, when the Wi-Fi traffic got busy (experiment 2), our method still got a throughput of 280Kb/s, compared to 50Kb/s of the AFH method.

5   Conclusion

In this paper, we proposed a dynamic Bluetooth packet selection strategy based on Wi-Fi white-space prediction. The probability of collisions of Bluetooth signal and Wi-Fi signal is gained by baseband layer energy sampling and Wi-Fi traffic forecasting model. According to the collision probability, the packet types are selected to achieve maximum throughput of Bluetooth. Simulation and analysis show that the algorithm can effectively co-exist Wi-Fi with Bluetooth by mean of time divided channel multiplexing in real world Wi-Fi environment.

Coexistence of Bluetooth with Wi-Fi is one of the interesting areas in recent years. With the increasing use of Wi-Fi and Bluetooth device, avoiding conflict simply by using distinguished frequency band is less able to solve the problem. A better solution is using the frequency domain and time domain to construct Bluetooth hopping sequence that can fully use the white space of Wi-Fi transmission. The host and slave devices have their own observation about Wi-Fi network statuses, a synchronization procedure must be involved to keep accordant hopping sequence. However, there is still not a reasonable frequency hopping sequence generation mechanism to solve the synchronization problem. Our method uses existing Bluetooth frequency hopping sequence and change usage rate of each hopping point by dynamically modifying the length of the data in each hopping point, is a partial optimization method under present conditions. Therefore, the next step will be to study how the different data transmissions are mapped to different idle channels to maximize the network traffic.

References

1. Tandra, R., Sahai, A.: Fundamental limits on detection in low SNR under noise uncertainty. In: International Conference on Wireless Networks, Communications and Mobile Computing (2005)
2. Taher, T.M., Rele, K., Roberson, D.: Development and Quantitative Analysis of an Adaptive Scheme for Bluetooth and Wi-Fi Co-Existence. In: 6th IEEE Consumer Communications and Networking Conference, CCNC 2009, January 10-13, pp. 1–2 (2009)
3. IEEE. Wireless medium access control (mac) and physical layer (phy) specifications for low-rate wireless personal area networks (lr-wpans). IEEE Standard 802.15.4 (2003)
4. Bamahdi, O.A., Zummo, S.A.: An adaptive frequency hopping technique with application to Bluetooth-WLAN coexistence. In: Proc. of International Conference on Mobile Communications and Learning Technologies, Mauritius (April 2006)
5. Yang, F., Wang, K., Qian, Z.: Performance analysis of Bluetooth packet transmission and adaptive packet selection strategy. Journal on Communications 9, 97–102 (2005)

6. Geirhofer, S., Tong, L., Sadler, B.: Dynamic spectrum access in WLAN channels: Empirical model and its stochastic analysis. In: ACM TAPAS (2006)
7. Geirhofer, S., Tong, L., Sadler, B.: Cognitive medium access: Constraining interference based on experimental models. IEEE Journal on Selected Areas in Communications (2009)
8. Huang, J., Xing, G., Zhou, G., Zhou, R.: Beyond Co-existence: Exploiting Wi-Fi White Space for ZigBee Performance Assurance. In: ICNP (2010)
9. Liang, J.: Proposal for Collaborative Bluetooth and 802.11 b MAC Mechanisms for Enhancing Coexistence, IEEE 802.15-01/080r0 (January 2001)
10. Chek, M.C.-H., Kwok, Y.-K.: Design and Evaluation of Practical Coexistence Management Schemes for Bluetooth and IEEE 802.11b Systems. Computer Networks 51(8) (June 2007)
11. Shellhammer, S.: Collocated collaborative coexistence mechanism: TDMA of 802.11 and Bluetooth, IEEE 802.15-01/025r0 (2001)
12. Lee, S.-H., Lee, Y.-H.: Adaptive frequency hopping for bluetooth robust to WLAN interference. IEEE Communications Letters 13(9), 628–630 (2009)
13. Chlebus, E.: The Pareto or Truncated Pareto Distribution? Measurement-Based Modeling of Session Traffic for Wi-Fi Wireless Internet Access. In: Wireless Communications and Networking Conference, WCNC 2007. IEEE (2007)
14. Specification of the Bluetooth System, pp. 217–221, http://www.bluetooth.org
15. Chandra, R., Mahajan, R., Padmanabhan, V., Zhang, M.: Crawdad, data set microsoft/osdi2006 (v. 2007-05-23) (2007)

An Energy-Aware Routing for Maximum Lifetime in Wireless Sensor Networks

Binhua Wang, Yongrui Chen, and Weidong Yi

Graduate University of the Chinese Academy of Sciences, Beijing
wangbinhua10@mails.gucas.ac.cn,
{chenyongrui,weidong}@gucas.ac.cn

Abstract. Due to the nature of many-to-one or many-to-few traffic patterns in Wireless Sensor Networks (WSNs), some critical nodes overloaded will exhaust their energy fast and will cause the decrease of the network lifetime for WSNs. Typically, routing protocols employ a reliable routing cost metric to avoid the lossy links but cannot balance the energy consumption of different nodes in WSNs. In this paper, we present an energy-aware routing algorithm to maximize the network lifetime of WSNs with the introduction of a new routing cost metric, whose goal is to achieve the best trade-off between energy consumption and routing link selection. We evaluate the performance of our routing algorithm by comparing it with other accessible routing algorithms. And the simulation results show that this energy-aware routing algorithm performs better in network lifetime as well as reliability.

Keywords: WSNs, network lifetime, routing, energy consumption, routing cost, metric, residual energy.

1 Introduction

Wireless Sensor Networks (WSNs) [1] has been applied in a variety of fields, including military surveillance, environmental monitoring, healthcare and disaster rescue etc. In WSNs, sensor nodes are responsible for sensing, processing data and transmitting them to sink node in an autonomous and unattended way. Due to resource con-straints of sensor nodes, low-power WSNs pose significant challenges of achieving trade-off among reliability, energy consumption along with the network lifetime (the network lifetime is commonly defined as the time duration between the start of the network and the moment when the first node dies of energy exhaustion).

Let us consider the network topology in fig.1 where node 1 is the sink node, the other sensor nodes transmit data to sink. In this network, node 2, node 3 and node 4 are all one-hop neighbors of the sink which relay data from other nodes. Assuming the link to sink over node 3 has the best quality among the three, most downstream nodes will choose node 3 as their parent to relay data. As a result, node 3 will drain out of energy fast and causes it unable to transmit data both from itself and other nodes. While node 2 and node 4 still have considerable residual energy, the network is out of function for losing certain important

R. Wang and F. Xiao (Eds.): CWSN 2012, CCIS 334, pp. 413–423, 2013.
© Springer-Verlag Berlin Heidelberg 2013

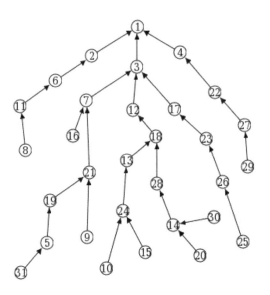

Fig. 1. Example of a sensor network with energy imbalanced

information and the residual energy of the two nodes will be wasted, which is not energy efficient. Thus, during the design of routing protocol, we should pay considerable attention to address this problem.

To balance the energy consumption in WSNs, we propose a new routing cost metric which combines nodes residual energy with link estimation metric ETX (Expected number Transmissions) [6]. With the new metric, we can make relay nodes especially the one-hop neighbors of sink to use energy more efficiently in a balanced way so as to partially solve the problem of network partition caused by some nodes quick death, which therefore, also maximize the lifetime of the sensor network.

In our paper, we evaluate the performance of our routing algorithm with bench-mark of two other routing algorithms: minimum hops routing and routing based on ETX. Simulation results show that this novel routing algorithm performs better in network lifetime, reliability and balance of energy consumption as well.

2   Related Work

The significant resource constraints of low-power WSNs combined with the feature of many-to-one traffic pattern determine that traditional routing protocol designed for ad hoc networks cannot be directly applied to sensor networks. In WSNs, sensor nodes have limited battery power and spend more energy in data transmission or reception than sensing and computation operation. Therefore, it is desired to conserve energy for sensor nodes, especially those critical nodes with more traffic load, and prolong the network lifetime. Despite the numerous research efforts, routing protocol remains a fairly open issue to this day. In the following section, we provide a brief overview of some previous related research work.

Metrics employed by conventional routing protocols can be mainly classified as: hop-based, ETX-based or power-based, although there are a few distinct ones based on geographic information or transmission power [2-4]. The first proposed and most applied routing protocol is the hop-based routing whose representative is minimum-hop routing, such as GBR [5]. In minimum-hop routing protocols, the nodes utilize hop counts as the sole routing cost metric, thereby choosing the path between the source node and sink with the minimum hop counts. Obviously, the link with minimum hops would cost the minimum total energy if we assume the transmission over any hop cost the same energy without considering the possibility of link error.

However, for most sensor network allowing packet retransmissions, hop-based routings cannot minimize the total energy of the network, ignoring the potential cost of retransmissions to achieve reliable packet delivery in the presence of link error. For that reason, another metric which is the expected number of transmissions (ETX) [6] is presented and employed in routings of WSNs: the idea is to estimate the total number of transmissions needed to transmit a packet over a link, and node selects the route with the minimum ETX. It is commonly known that link estimation is an essential and reliable tool for the computation of reliability-oriented route selection metric and ETX has been proved to be a robust and reliable link estimation metric [7]. MintRoute (Mint stands for Minimum Number of Transmissions) [8] is the representative one of ETX-based routing protocol, which uses ETX as the link estimation metric and works with a routing table to manage all potential routings. In MintRoute, nodes will choose its parent with the minimum ETX in order to select a route to sink requiring the minimum total energy.

Since the sensor nodes are mostly powered by battery, efficient utilization of battery is important and has a significant influence on the network lifetime. Although minimum-hop and ETX-based routing, to a certain extent, can reduce the total transmission energy by selecting a high-quality route to sink, they both ignore the importance of individual nodes power level to network lifetime and it may produce the situation of energy imbalance in figure 1. In these cases, if data is transmitted over some links too often, some relay nodes in those links will be overloaded and have a higher energy depletion rate than their peers, which lead to the decrease of network lifetime. In MMBCR and its variant CMMBCR [9-10], the residual power level of individual node is used as routing cost metric. The use of remaining power in determining the routing cost prevents some bottleneck nodes (most drained) from being overloaded, thereby prolonging their battery lifetime and the overall network lifetime.

Besides, during last few years, some new routing protocols [11-13] are proposed, which combine number of hop, geographic information, ETX and nodes residual energy as well as transmission power to get the routing cost metric, aiming to maximize the network lifetime for WSNs.

However, all the algorithms mentioned above are unable to achieve a trade-off among reliability, energy consumption along with the network lifetime for WSNs. Therefore, based on the algorithms above, we propose a novel and simple energy aware routing algorithm (ETXRE) combining the power level of sensor nodes with the link estimation metric ETX in order to achieve maximum network lifetime with reliable routing.

3   Algorithm Description

In this section, we provide in-depth description of our energy-aware routing algorithm for maximizing network lifetime. Overall, the routing protocol architecture can be broken down into two modules: data module and control module.

3.1   Data Module

The data module performs basic functions of data packet buffering and forwarding, limited retransmission as well as data acknowledgement (ACK). Data packets con-tain some necessary information in its header such as the address of source node, its sequence number and source nodes routing cost to sink. If a node sends data packets to its parent, the receiving node will first queue the packet into FIFO buffer and then wait for transmission. Based upon the assumption that all data packets are equally important and no packet should be discarded to favor others, retransmissions are necessary because of the possible link error.Consequently, we adopt limited retransmission with a threshold Nmax. When a node sends a packet to its parent, it should receive ACK from parent which indicates its being successfully received by its parent, otherwise, if it fails to receive an ACK, more retransmissions are performed before the number of retransmission goes up to Nmax. Also, by using ACK, link estimation is easy to implement. Supposing that node k receives an ACK from parent j, then we can use the number of retransmissions to update the link estimation unit in the neighbor table of node k and compute the ETX of (k, j) (link from k to j).

3.2   Control Module

Node uses control module to manage its neighbors and maintain a neighbor table, which is illustrated in table 1. Each slot in the table consist of three items: Node address, Link estimation and Routing cost to sink. In our routing design, nodes broad-cast beacons periodically and collect information of neighbors via receiving beacons from neighbors. To manage the neighbors, all nodes must keep a neighbor table and update the neighbor table when receiving a beacon with related information. In addition, an outgoing beacon from node k includes the following basic information: the address of node k and the routing cost of node k to sink.

Table 1. Neighbor table

Node address	Link estimation uint	Routing cost to sink

3.3   Metric

In ETXRE routing algorithm, the key feature is its combination of residual power of individual node with the reliable link estimation ETX and utilize the combined routing cost metric to select the routing link for node.

ETX. For the link (k ,j), the ETX is the average number of packet retransmissions by k till j receives the packet successfully and sends an ACK back. The link estimation unit is an array storing the number of packet retransmissions and we obtain ETX by computing all the retransmissions number from the array. So ETX can reflect the quality of the routing link, and if ETX has a small value, it means that the corresponding link has a better quality. We define the link estimation of (k, j) as:

$$ETX(k,j) = \frac{\sum_{i=0}^{N-1} TN_i}{N}. \tag{1}$$

Where TNi is the number of packet retransmission and N is the size of the link estimation array. Node starts with the initialization ETX(k, j)=1, which is the best case for (k, j). The purpose of such initialization is to change parent easily when a link failure is detected.

Residual Energy. To prevent the energy consumption imbalance and a partitioned network, we bring the residual energy of sensor node into the routing cost, whose ultimate objective is to prolong the network lifetime. In a network, sensor nodes can be classified into nodes that only transmit locally generated packets and relay nodes which transmit locally generated packets as well as packets from their child nodes. Evidently, the relay nodes will exhaust its energy fast, and the case of fig.1 will occur, when most of high-quality routes to sink contain a certain relay node. Commonly, the node closer to sink has more traffic load and depletes energy faster than others, for example, in fig.1, node 2, 3, 4 as one-hop neighbors of sink have more traffic. The ideal situation for this network is node 2, 3, 4 die of energy exhaustion at the same time so that the network will have a maximum lifetime. In fact, the ideal situation can almost be achieved in ETXRE with the introduction of residual energy to routing cost.

Further, the significant challenge in employing nodes residual energy is how to compute the energy consumption of the nodes correctly. Since relay nodes have larger traffic load, they need to transmit more data packets, and as a result, stay longer in transmitting mode. For that reason, we accumulate the total time that nodes spend on transmitting packets and then compute the total energy consumption at present. We express the residual energy of individual node as:

$$E_{res}(k) = E_{init} - E_{cons}(k) \ . \tag{2}$$

Where Einit is the initial power of nodes that are same for all nodes, Econs(k) is the estimated total energy consumption of node k and Eres(k) is the current residual energy of node k.

Routing Cost Metric. Let p(k) denotes the parent for node k, if k picks node j as its parent , then p(k)=j. We define the routing cost between k and j as Cost(k, j). Also, the routing cost for k to sink is denoted by Cost(k). When k needs to choose a parent, it first looks up its neighbor table and selects node j as its parent so long as the routing cost to sink is minimized if k routes its traffic over j. The selection progress can be shown by the following expression:

$$Cost(k) = \min_{j \in Nei(k)} [Cost(j) + \frac{ETX(k, j)}{E_{res}(k)}] \ . \tag{3}$$

Where Nei(k) is the collection of all neighbors of k. After computing each neighbors routing cost to sink, which considers both ETX and current residual power, we can find the minimum routing cost. As the expression above demonstrates, the more energy a node has and the less ETX is, the less routing cost is, and the more likely the node will be selected as the parent.

3.4   Parent Management

Upon reception of beacon or data packet from node j, node k will do the followings:

(1) If node j is not in the neighbor table of k, add j to the neighbor table with its routing cost Cost(j).
(2) If node j has been in the neighbor table, update the corresponding information of k in neighbor table with the new Cost(j).

On the other hand, k receives an ACK from its current parent p(k) or its secondary parent ps(k) (the neighbor has the minimum routing cost to sink aside from the current parent). In order to get a reliable estimation of links to neighbors, k will send probing packets to its secondary parent if the packet buffer is empty. When k does not receive an ACK within Nmax attempts, link failure will be detected and the routing cost of p(k) will increases to a fixed large value so that the process of changing a parent is necessary and started immediately.
    A node manages its parent through the following steps:

(1) k goes through its neighbor table and selects the best neighbor as its parent when p(k)=null.
(2) Node k has parent p(k)= j, then k scans its neighbor table and find its secondary parent ps(k)=b by computing the probable routing cost Cost(k, b). If ps(k) offers a relatively lower cost reaching sink than p(k) (the difference should beyond certain threshold), k selects ps(k) as its new parent and then p(k)=b.

4   Performance Evaluation

4.1   Methodology

Benchmark. Hop-based routing is the basic routing in WSNs and many routings are modified from it such as MintRoute based on ETX. Among the MintRoute family, different routing protocols use different link estimators to obtain ETX. In our routing protocol, we present another method to estimate ETX and propose a new routing cost metric combining nodes residual energy. Indeed, the main difference between our routing and the other two is the routing cost metric we adopt. Hence, we use different routing cost metrics with the other parts of the protocol being the same to compare their performance using the performance metrics such as network lifetime, energy efficiency (the average residual energy of node) and packet delivery ratio(defined as the ratio of the total number of data packets received by sink to the number of nodes).

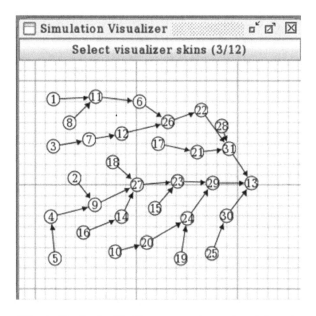

Fig. 2. Testbed with 30 sensor nodes and a sink node

Simulation Environment. We simulated our routing by using Adam Dunkelss Contiki code of Rime communication stack [14] (provided on his website) and the simulation tool Cooja. In our experiments, we use an environment with 30 sensor nodes and a sink node. The 30 sensor nodes are randomly located in an area of 200m200m in fig.2, and sink node 1 is approximately at the position of (210m, 100m). Supposing that every sensor nodes send data packets at s certain rate to sink, we perform a lot of experiments by starting all sensor nodes with an initial energy of (100, 200, 300, 400, 500) except for sink, which is powered with enough energy to make sure it can always work well.

4.2   Simulation Results

Network Lifetime. Fig.3 shows the result of network lifetime by using three different routing cost metrics. Obviously, we can see that ETXRE with ETX and residual energy has the maximum lifetime at the same initial power level, and the lifetime increases with the in-crease of initial energy. Simultaneously, it is presented in fig.3 that the metric of ETX in our new way has a higher performance in the network lifetime than routing protocols based on hop count, since ETX takes into consideration the retransmissions caused by the link error probability.

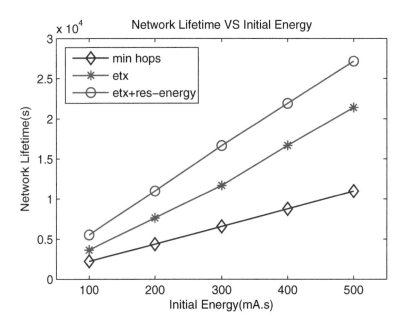

Fig. 3. Network Lifetimw with different initial energy

Packet Delivery Ratio. In fig.4 below, it is shown that ETXRE successfully sends more data packets than the other two routing algorithms and achieves a higher packet delivery ratio (the total number of successfully delivered packets can represent the delivery ratio in fig.4 since the number of nodes is same). On one hand, ETXRE routing certainly can send more data packets and distribute the traffic load in a more fairy manner, since it consider the power levels of all sensor nodes during selecting the routes and can achieve a longer network lifetime. On the other hand, the reason why routing with ETX has more data

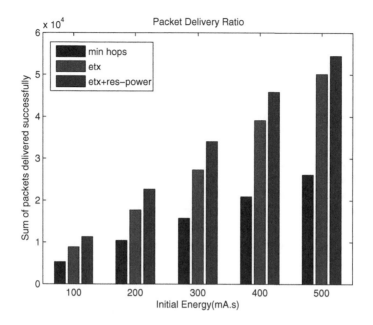

Fig. 4. Sum of packets delivered successfully

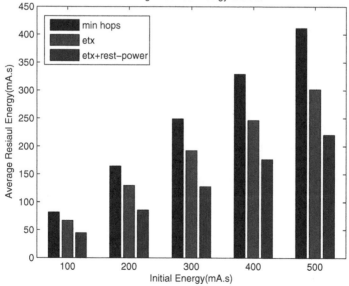

Fig. 5. Average residual energy of nodes

packets delivered than hop-based routing is that taking ETX as link estimation metric can reduce the number of packet retransmissions.

Average Residual Energy of Nodes. As fig.5 demonstrates and confirms, ETXRE has higher energy efficiency and conserve less power when the network is out of function.

As we know, the node closer to sink will have a higher rate of energy consumption; thereby we perform a comparison of the residual energy level of one-hop neighbors of the sink when using the three routing cost metrics. The result is presented by table 2 and it is clearly shown that our routing performs better in energy balancing among one-hop nodes. Therefore, ETXRE can avoid the network partition caused by the death of some critical nodes such as one-hop neighbors of the sink and prolong the network lifetime.

Table 2. Residual energy of one-hop nodes when the first node is dead (initial power is 500)

	Node 29	Node 30	Node 31
Minimum hops	0	422	418
ETX	85	167	0
ETX+residual_energy	1	1	0

5   Conclusions and Future Works

In this paper, we propose ETXRE routing algorithm with a new routing cost metric combining ETX with individual nodes residual energy, aiming to maximize the net-work lifetime for WSNs. Through the simulation results, we can see our design of link estimator is energy efficient and is able to reduce unnecessary retransmissions and thereby has more data packets delivered to sink. In addition, with the introduction of residual energy into routing cost, ETXRE can ensure the network to stay in a more balanced condition of energy consumption and maximize the network lifetime.

Furthermore, we intend to apply our routing protocol into actual sensor network testbeds and perform more experiments to evaluate this routing algorithms performance.

Acknowledgments. This research was supported by the Key Projects of Chinese National Science and Technology (No.2010ZX03006-001) and 2009 NVIDIAs Professor Partnership. This work was also supported by the National Science & Technology Pillar Program during the 12th Five-year Plan Period (NO.2012BAJ24B01) and 100 Talents Program of Chinese Academic of Sciences (No.99T300CEA2).

References

1. Akyildiz, I.F., Su, W., Sankarasubramaniam, Y., Cayirci, E.: Wireless Sensor Networks: A Survey. Computer Networks 38(4), 393–422 (2002)
2. Akkaya, K., Younis, M.: A Survey of Routing Protocols in Wireless Sensor Networks. Ad Hoc Network 3(3), 325–349 (2005)
3. Al-Karaki, J.N., Kamal, A.E.: Routing Techniques in Wireless Sensor Networks: a Survey. IEEE Wireless Communications 11(6), 6–28 (2004)
4. Draves, R., Padhye, J., Zill, B.: Comparison of Routing Metrics for Static Multi-Hop Wireless Networks. In: 4th ACM Annual Conference of the Special Interest Group on Data Communication (SIGCOMM), pp. 133–144 (2004)
5. Schurgers, C., Srivastava, M.B.: Energy Efficient Routing in Wireless Sensor Networks. In: MILCOM Proceedings on Communications for Network-Centric Operations: Creating the Information Force, McLean, VA (2001)
6. De Couto, D.S.J., Aguayo, D., Bicket, J., Morris, R.: A High-Throughput Path Metric for Multi-Hop Wireless Routing. In: ACM Annual International Conference on Mobile Computing and Networking (MOBICOM), pp. 134–146 (2003)
7. Gnawali, O., Yarvis, M.D., Heidemann, J., Govindan, R.: Interaction of Retransmission, Blacklisting, and Routing Metrics for Reliability in Sensor Network Routing. In: Proc. the First International Conference on Sensor and Ad Hoc Communications and Networks (SECON), pp. 34–43 (2004)
8. Woo, A., Tong, T., Culler, D.: Taming the Underlying Challenges of Reliable Multihop Routing in Sensor Networks. In: Proc. ACM SenSys 2003, pp. 14–27. ACM Press, Los Angeles (2003)
9. Singh, S., Woo, M., Raghavendra, C.S.: Power-Aware Routing in Mobile Ad Hoc Networks. In: Proc. ACM Mobicom 1998, Dallas, Texas, pp. 181–190 (1998)
10. Toh, C.K., Cobb, H., Scott, D.A.: Performance Evaluation of Battery-Life-Aware Routing Schemes for Wireless Ad Hoc Networks. In: Proc. IEEE ICC 2001, pp. 2824–2829 (2001)
11. Wang, J., de Dieu, I., Jose, A.D.L.D., Lee, S., Lee, Y.K.: Prolong the Lifetime of Wireless Sensor networks via Hotspot Analysis. In: 10th Annual International Symposium on Applications and the Internet (SAINT), Seoul, Korea, pp. 383–386 (2010)
12. Zhang, H.B., Shen, H.: Energy-Efficient Beaconless Geographic Routing in Wireless Sensor Networks. IEEE Trans. Parallel and Distributed Systems 21, 881–896 (2010)
13. Song, C., Liu, M., Cao, J.N., Zheng, Y., Gong, H.G., Chen, G.H.: Maximizing Network Lifetime Based on Transmission Range Adjustment in Wireless Sensor Networks. Special Issue of Computer Communications on Heterogeneous Networking for Quality, Reliability, Security, and Robustness 32(11), 1316–1325 (2009)
14. Contiki OS, http://www.sics.se/contiki/

Research and Implementation of the System Manager Based on Android Platform for Wireless Sensor Network

Heng Wang*,**, Qiuge Chen, Ping Wang, and Ting Wang

Key Laboratory of Industrial Internet of Things and Network Control,
Chongqing University of Posts and Telecommunications, Chongqing 400065, China
wangheng@cqupt.edu.cn

Abstract. This paper makes a briefly introduction to the background and status of the wireless sensor network and the android platform. It designs and implements the system manager based on android platform for WIA-PA wireless sensor network with combined the advantages of the two techniques, which can provide a real-time, low-cost management manner for wireless sensor network.

Keywords: Wireless Sensor Network, Android, System Manager, WIA-PA.

1 Forward

Wireless sensor network combines the objective physical world and the logic information world together. Human beings can directly perceive the objective world through wireless sensor network, which greatly extends the functionality of the existing network and the cognitive world ability of human beings. Wireless sensor network has been widely used in industrial control, environmental monitoring, military and so on, and the prospect for development of wireless sensor network is very optimistic.

In the industrial field, in order to monitor the operating conditions of wireless sensor network intuitively, there are always specialized equipments to monitor the network to ensure that the network is reliable and stable operation. In this background, the development of system manager for wireless sensor network on android platform can combine wireless sensor network with android platform perfectly, and using mobile phones to replace the traditional wireless sensor network monitoring equipment can not only reduce the cost of the wireless monitoring, but also make the human-computer interaction more convenient and friendly. The open source feature of android platform provides a premise for specific application development.

---

* Corresponding author.
** This work was supported in part by the Foundation for University Youth Key Teacher of Chongqing, the National Science and Technology Major Project of China under Grant 2012ZX03005002 and 2013ZX03005005, and supported by outstanding achievements convertion project of university of CQ KJzh10207.

R. Wang and F. Xiao (Eds.): CWSN 2012, CCIS 334, pp. 424–437, 2013.
© Springer-Verlag Berlin Heidelberg 2013

This development is based on the laboratorys existing wireless sensor network in WIA-PA. It designs and implements system manager for wireless sensor network on android platform, which can achieve the monitoring of the WIA-PA network, schedule and distribute the network communication resources.

2   Function Analysis and Achievement Contrast for WIA-PA System Manager

2.1   WIA-PA Device Type and Logical Role

The WIA-PA standard specifies five types of devices: host configuration computer, gateway device, routing device, filed device and handheld device[1]. The host configuration computer is the device through which users and maintenance/management personnel perform transactions on the WIA-PA network and the management networks. The gateway device connects WIA-PA network to other plant networks. The routing device forwards packets from one WIA-PA device to another in the WIA-PA network. The filed device is one type of device installed in the field, which is connected to or controls the process. The handheld device is a portable device used for provisioning, firmware updating, and device status monitoring. To improve reliability, there may be redundant gateway devices and routing devices in the WIA-PA network, which operate by way of hot backup.

In order to facilitate management, The WIA-PA standard specifies five kinds of logical roles: Gateway, it handles protocol translation and data mapping between the WIA-PA network and other networks[2]; Network manager(NM), it manages and monitors the entire network; Security Manager (SM), it deals with security key management and security authentication of gateway devices, routing devices, field devices, and handheld devices; Cluster head, it manages and monitors field devices and handheld devices. Cluster head also merges and securely forwards packets from local cluster members and other cluster heads; Cluster member, it collects field data and sends the data to its cluster head. The NM and the SM that are used for system management shall reside in a gateway device.

One physical device may perform the functions of several logical roles. In the hierarchical network that combines star and mesh, a gateway device may perform the logical roles of gateway, NM, SM, and cluster head. A routing device shall act as a cluster head. A field device/handheld device shall only act as a cluster member.

2.2   Function Analysis for WIA-PA System Manager

WIA-PA is launched by wireless industry alliance. It is a form of wireless sensor networks in industrial process automation application[3].

The WIA-PA protocol architecture is based on ISO/IEC 7498 OSI Basic Reference Model. The WIA-PA protocol architecture defines the Data Link Sub-Layer, Network Layer and Application Layer[1], as shown in Fig. 1.

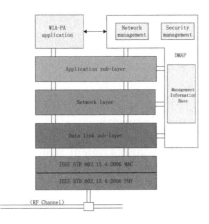

Fig. 1. The WIA-PA protocol architecture

The system management in the WIA-PA network includes both network management and security management. The WIA-PA network supports the hybrid centralized and distributed management scheme. The system management is implemented by the network manager, the security manager, and cluster heads. In the system management process, the network manager and security manager manage the router devices, and the management right to the field device is assigned to router device.

The main management functions of network management are as follows: constructing and maintaining the mesh topology comprised of cluster heads, and star topology comprised of cluster heads and cluster members; allocating communication resources for cluster heads in mesh topology, and allocating communication resources for cluster members to the cluster heads in star topology; monitoring the performance of the WIA-PA network, including device status, path failure, and channel condition.

2.3   Achievement Contrast on Different Platform

The achievement platforms for system management mainly are single-chip platform and computer platform previously, the achievement contrast with android platform is list in Table 1.

3   Software Design for System Manger

3.1   The Development Platform for Hardware and Software

Android software development uses the eclipse platform and it uses java language to program. Developers need to have some java language skills and knowledge of network communication. It needs to fully appreciate the characteristics of the Android platform in the development process, in order to develop simple, beautiful and practical monitoring software.

Table 1. Achievement contrast on different platform

	Advantage	Disadvantage
Single-Chip platform	Low cost,and low power consumption.	Structure is simple ,and the processing capacity is not strong.
Computer platform	Rich in resource, and great processing capability.	It can not be well integrated in gateway device.
Android paltform	Great processing capability, be well integrated in gateway, and great portability.	It has not yet been achieved.

The hardware platform is the laboratory's existing wireless sensor network in WIA-PA. This network has two gateway devices (a redundant gateway), four routing devices and eight filed devices.

3.2 The Software Design Framework

The main function modules of system manager are as follows:

- **Graphical interface module.** It observes the data in the system though different views. For example, the topology view shows the real-time network topology, the historical curve view visually display the history data, the data collection view display the packet received by the current network.
- **Network management module.** This module is the core part of the whole monitoring software, which receives information send by each module and feedback to the module after appropriate analysis. For example, the address and resource allocation module is used to allocate the address and communicate resources, the network status monitoring module monitors the real-time state of the network and make response to the network.
- **Communication module.** It is primarily responsible for sending and receiving data from the physical interface.
- **Network security module.** It is responsible for network device joining the network, communication security and the distribution of the key.

The achieve process for system management is illustrated graphically in Fig. 2.
   The system manager in the android operating system is at the application layer as shown in Fig. 3.

3.3 The Design for Graphical Interface Module

The graphical interface module includes the topology view, the historical curve view and the data collection view.

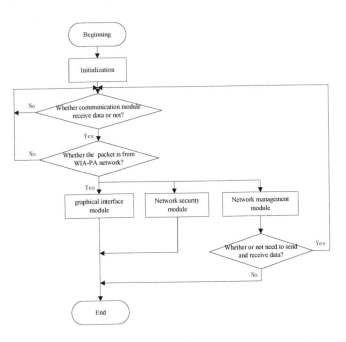

Fig. 2. The achieve process for system management

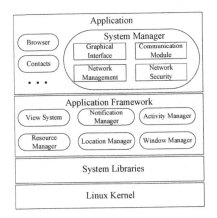

Fig. 3. Android system architecture

The topology view shows the real-time network topology, it is drawn according to the join-network package of the device that has a short address which is four bytes, it can set an area at the view in advance according to the devices short address, set a flag and initial it as false, at the beginning, the picture of device do not display; when the view receiving the join-network packet, the flag changes to true and display the picture of the device which send the join-network packet. The process of topology view is illustrated in Fig. 4

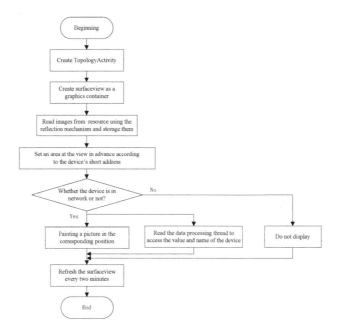

Fig. 4. The process of topology view

The historical curve view creates thread to draw the historical data for each device. It can visually display the operating conditions, which can be used to assess the overall health of the equipment.

The data collection view creates thread to grab the data packet send by the filed devices and display them on the view. There are type flag of data, the device current value, the device address and other information in the packet. When the view receiving the data packet, it stores the data in a buffer, then respectively resolves the data in the buffer and saves them to corresponding variable, and display them in the data collection view.

3.4   Network Management Module

The network management module includes two parts, which are address and communication resource allocation module and the network status monitoring module.

(1) Address and Communication Resource Allocation

In the WIA-PA network, each routing device or field device has a global unique 64Cbit long address and a 16-bit short address. The long address is set by manufacturers according to the IEEE EUI-64 standard. The short address is 16-bit long. The most significant 8 bits of the short address that are assigned by the NM are used to identify different clusters. The least significant 8-bit part of the field devices short address is the intra-cluster address. The intra-cluster address is assigned by the cluster head [1].

In the WIA-PA network, the communication resource consists of timeslots and channels. Allocation of communication resources shall be considered in two dimensions: time and channel[4][5].

The process of communication resource allocation is as follow:

- In the mesh network, the communication resources of the cluster heads are allocated by the NM. The communication resources consist of those used by cluster heads in the mesh network and those allocated by cluster heads to cluster members.
- In the star network, the communication resources are allocated by cluster heads to cluster members. That is, communication resources are bound to cluster members.

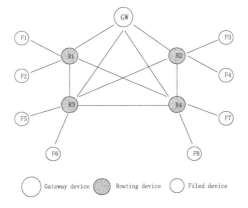

Fig. 5. A resource allocation instance

An example of the resource allocation in the hierarchical network topology that combines star and mesh is shown in Fig. 5, which is the default configuration. First, the NM residing in the GW allocates communication resources to the routing devices R1, R2, R3 and R4. These communication resources are used for communication among R1, R2, R3 and R4, for communication between routing devices and the GW, and for communication between intra-cluster field devices and routing devices. Second, after receiving communication resources from the NM, routing devices allocate some of the communication resources to their intra-cluster field devices, which are used for intra-cluster communications among field devices and their corresponding routing devices. As shown in Figure5, after the NM allocates communication resources for R1, R2, R3 and R4, R1 allocates communication resources for F1 and F2; R2 allocates communication resources for F3 and F4; and R3 allocates communication resources for F5 and F6; and R4 allocates communication resources for F7 and F8.

The communication resources allocation of router devices is as follow: After the routing device joins the network, it shall scan its neighbor devices on each channel and report the neighbor information to the NM. After receiving the neighbor information, the NM shall allocate paths, a superframe, and a block of links to the routing device by using the communication resource allocation services. The information of every routing device superframe is broadcast to its field devices in the beacon frame.

The communication resources allocation of filed devices is as follow: after VCRs of a field device are established successfully, either the routing device or the gateway device allocates timeslots to its field devices by using the communication resource allocation services, which are used in communication between the routing device and the field devices or between the gateway device and the field devices. If the superframes of the routing device and the gateway device are affected by the joining field devices, the routing device and the gateway device shall update their route table, superframe and Link attributes.

(2) The Network Status Monitoring

The network status monitoring module is responsible for monitoring of the device status and channel conditions send by filed device, and the system manager controls the network according to the received reports.

After receiving device status reports from intra-cluster field devices, a routing device reports the health of itself and its field devices to the NM periodically. The NM appraises and diagnoses the network performance according to health information, and replies to the change of network environment timely, as shown in Fig. 6 and Fig. 7. The NM shall detect abnormal conditions in the WIA-PA device, such as low level of battery power and disconnection from neighboring devices. This is realized by setting alarm levels to the WIA-PA devices.

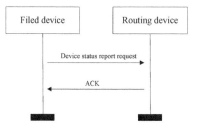

Fig. 6. Device status report process of field device

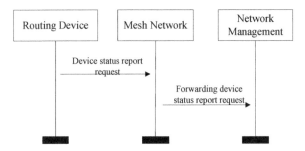

Fig. 7. Device status report process of routing device

The channel condition report is used for the WIA-PA field devices or routing devices to report the channel condition remotely to the NM, as shown in Fig. 8.

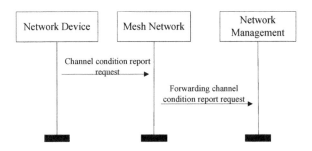

Fig. 8. Process of channel condition report

3.5   Communication Module

Socket programming is used in this module, socket is a very popular programming interface for TCP / IP protocol. A socket is uniquely identified by an IP address and a port. The process of communication module is shown in Fig. 9.

3.6   Network Security Module

The network security module is responsible for authorizing the routing devices and field devices that are attempting to join in the WIA-PA network, Key management, including key generation, key distribution, key recovery, and key update; certified the end-to-end communication.

In this module, when the devices are attempting to join the network, the network security module certified the process of device is safety or not, now the used key is join-network key; when the device is communicating, the network security module detects whether the device is in secure communication, now the used key is application layer key.

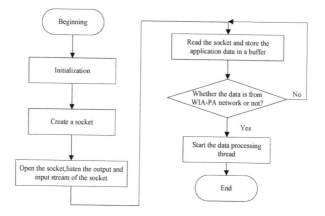

Fig. 9. The process of communication module

4   Test

This system manager is implemented on the android platform. ZTE U880 mobile phone and Lenovo LePad A1-07 panel computer are used in the process of test, which both use android operating system.

After continuous improvement and perfection of the design software, the system manager was tested on the laboratorys existing wireless sensor network in WIA-PA, as shown in Fig. 10 Mobile phones and panel computer display the network topology real-time, which can be seen in the process of test, as shown in Figure 11. This network has two master devices (an android mobile phone and an android panel computer), two gateway devices (one redundant gateway), four routing devices and eight filed devices. The gateway device directly communicate with the master device through the 3G module, the routing device and the filed device transfer data to master device through the gateway, realize the interaction of the data ,complete the joining and communication process of the device. After the network was successfully constructed, the filed device transfers data to master device through the router device, in order to make the user monitor the wireless sensor network real-time and manage the devices in the network.

4.1   The Test of Graphical Interface Module

The WIA-PA network using mesh and star structure, in which the network between router and gateway is mesh structure, and the network between routing device and field device in its cluster is star structure. Fig. 11 is the topology view of the network, it can be seen that in the process of operation of the network, the topology view real-time display the topology of the network with the joining of routing device and field device.

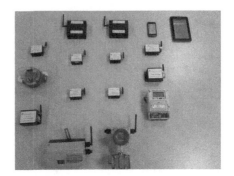

Fig. 10. The test system

In Fig. 11 it can be seen that the interface on the mobile phones and panel computer are the same, so later it only screenshots the interface on the phone, and the view is high-definition without the shell of the mobile phone. The screenshot software is pea pods mobile phone wizard. The Fig. 12(a) is the historical curve view, which will dynamically display the corresponding curve of the data when clicking on the device icon on the interface. The Fig. 12(b) is the data collection view which shows the index number of the packet, the device type and value.

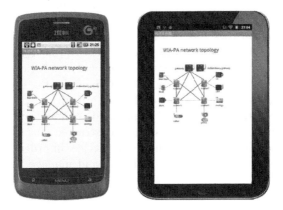

Fig. 11. The topology view

4.2   The Test of Network Management Module

In this module, the user can select the network device and configure it as shown in Fig. 13(a). Now the select device is humiture sensor, configure its address as 0201, the configuration of the superframe and link accordance with section 3.4.

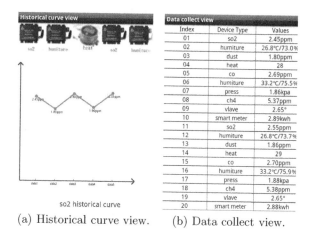

Data collect view		
Index	Device Type	Values
01	so2	2.45ppm
02	humiture	26.8°C/73.0%
03	dust	1.80ppm
04	heat	28
05	co	2.69ppm
06	humiture	33.2°C/75.5%
07	press	1.86kpa
08	ch4	5.37ppm
09	vlave	2.65°
10	smart meter	2.89kwh
11	so2	2.55ppm
12	humiture	26.8°C/73.7%
13	dust	1.86ppm
14	heat	29
15	co	2.70ppm
16	humiture	33.2°C/75.9%
17	press	1.88kpa
18	ch4	5.38ppm
19	vlave	2.65°
20	smart meter	2.88kwh

(a) Historical curve view.   (b) Data collect view.

Fig. 12. The test of graphical interface module

After successful configuration, we can find changes in the topology view, and the short address of humiture sensor changes from 0101 to 0201, now the configuration is successful.

The Fig. 13(b) is the network status monitoring view, from the figure it can be seen that the device status and the channel quality are normal, and in this state the devices can accurately complete communication tasks in real time.

Communication resource allocation		

The select device:

humiture sensor ▼

address	surperframe	channel
0201	default configuration	time slot hopping

Configuration

Network status monitoring view		
decive name	device status	channel status
so2	normal	good
humiture	normal	good
dust	normal	good
heat	normal	good
co	normal	good
humiture	normal	good
press	normal	good
ch4	normal	good
vlave	normal	good
smart meter	normal	good
so2	normal	good
humiture	normal	good
dust	normal	good
heat	normal	good
co	normal	good
humiture	normal	good
press	normal	good
ch4	normal	good
vlave	normal	good
smart meter	normal	good

(a) Address and communi-   (b) Network status moni-
cation resource allocation   toring view.
view.

Fig. 13. The test of network management module

4.3   The Test of Network Security Module

In Fig. 14, the device is in the normal state of communication, the communication condition is security, now the used key is application layer key.

Network security management		
device name	security status	the used key
so2	safety	application ke
humiture	safety	application ke
dust	safety	application ke
heat	safety	application ke
co	safety	application ke
humiture	safety	application ke
press	safety	application ke
ch4	safety	application ke
valve	safety	application ke
smart meter	safety	application ke
so2	safety	application ke
humiture	safety	application ke
dust	safety	application ke
heat	safety	application ke
co	safety	application ke
humiture	safety	application ke
press	safety	application ke
ch4	safety	application ke
valve	safety	application ke
smart meter	safety	application ke

Fig. 14. Network security management view

5   Conclusion

This paper designs and implements the system manager on android platform in the WIA-PA wireless sensor network, which achieves seamless communication between persons and things. The system manager of wireless sensor network integrate in mobile phones, panel computer and other portable devices, which can not only reduce the cost of wireless monitoring and control, but also make the monitoring person monitor the network anywhere. In the background of the rapid development of wireless communications, combining the consumer electronics products such as mobile phones and panel computers with wireless sensor application has great practical significance.

References

1. Industrial communication network-Fieldbus specification - WIA-PA communication network and communication profile, http://www.iec.ch/
2. Zhu, Q., Wang, R., Chen, Q.: IOT Gateway: Bridging Wireless Sensor Networks into Internet of Things. In: 8th International Conference on Embedded and Ubiquitous Computing (EUC), pp. 347–352. IEEE Press, Hong Kong (2010)
3. Tang, Z., Cheng, M., Zeng, P., Wang, H.: Real-time communication in WIA-PA industrial wireless network. In: 3rd IEEE International Conference on Computer Science and Information Technology (ICCSIT), pp. 600–605 (2010)
4. Wang, P., Pan, Q., Wang, H., Xiang, M., Kim, Y.: An improved adaptive channel hopping scheme for WIA-PA industrial wireless networks. In: 3rd International Conference on Advanced Computer Theory and Engineering, pp. 596–600 (2010)

5. Wang, H., Yang, J., Wang, P., Luo, Z., Kim, K.C.: An adaptive deterministic scheme for WIA-PA industrial wireless network. In: 3rd International Conference on Advanced Computer Theory and Engineering (ICACTE), pp. 332–334 (2010)
6. Zhang, X.-L., Liang, W., Zheng, M.: Distributed and dynamic TDMA channel scheduling algorithm for WIA-PA. In: IEEE International Conference on Intelligent Computing and Intelligent Systems, pp. 462–466. IEEE Press, Shanghai (2009)
7. IEC/PAS 62591. Industrial Communication Networks-Fieldbus Specifications-WirelessHART Communication Network and Communication Profile (2008)
8. IEC 62601.8. Wireless Industry Automation Specifications for Process Automation (2011)
9. ISA Std.100.11a. Wireless Systems for Industrial Automation: Process Control and Related Applications (2010)
10. IEEE standard 802.15.4-2006. Wireless Medium Access Control (MAC) and Physical Layer (PHY) Specifications for Low-Rate Wireless Personal Area Networks (2006)

The Key Technologies and Development Research of Chinese Light Industry IOT Application

Jie Wang[1], Dongri Yang[2], Xiangang Liu[3], and Yu Zeng[4]

[1] School of Management, Capital Normal University, Beijing 100089, China
wangjie@cnu.edu.cn
[2] College of Computing & Communication Engineering,
Graduate University of the Chinese Academy of Sciences, Beijing 100049, China
[3] China Electronics Standardization Institute, Beijing 100846, China
[4] Beijing Computing Center, Beijing 100094, China

Abstract. IOT will effectively promote the development of Chinese light industry. In this paper, we firstly introduce the technical architecture of Chinese light industry IOT. Then we analyze the key technologies of it, including the Cloud-Channel-Terminal technology system, identification technology, NFC terminal solutions and architecture technology. We also introduce the key R & D direction of the application of Chinese light industry IOT in the paper. The research in the paper will be helpful for comprehensively promoting the transformation process of Chinese light industry IOT application.

Keywords: Chinese light industry, IOT, Cloud computing, NFC, RFID.

1 Introduction

Currently the Internet of things (IOT) has been the pilot field of countries to construct a new model of economic and remodel of the national long-term competitive-ness [1]. The light industry is the traditional advantage industry of China, and it plays an important role in the economic and social development. The ultimate universal of IOT will be inseparable from the innovation and application in light industry. On the other hand, Chinese light industry is in a critical period of the qualitative leap from the accumulation. To achieve leapfrog development of light industry, we must rely on the new generation of key technologies represented by IOT.

So on the base of full investigation of IOT application of Chinese light industry, we propose the key technologies and research and development (R & D) direction of Chinese light industry IOT application. We propose the technical architecture which takes the RFID and NFC technology as the core, cloud computing technology as a business platform, TD-LTE mobile broadband technology as the neural network, IPV6 as the basis of addressing agreement and NFC module integrated support system for end-use applications.

R. Wang and F. Xiao (Eds.): CWSN 2012, CCIS 334, pp. 438–446, 2013.
© Springer-Verlag Berlin Heidelberg 2013

In the following parts of this paper, we firstly introduce the technical architecture of Chinese light industry IOT. Then we analyze the key technologies of it, including the Cloud-Channel-Terminal technology system, identification technology, NFC terminal solutions and architecture technology. We also introduce the key R & D direction of the application of Chinese light industry IOT in the paper.

2   The Architecture of Chinese Light Industry IOT

Chinese light industry IOT adopts technical architecture as below: using the NFC and RFID technologies as its cores [1], using cloud computing technology as its business platform, using TD-LTE mobile broadband technology as the final neural net-work and NFC module as the end application support.

The business platform is built using SaaS(software as a service) applications as rep-resentative in the cloud; communication channels are based on the existing mature 3G technology [2], and ultimately provide high-speed access by the TD-LTE mobile broadband technology [3]. The architectural design of the terminal is carried out on the base of mature NFC module and two-dimensional code technology and which will realize the technical architecture of industrial chain of the IOT [4] and cloud pipe end applications. Figure 1 describes the technical architecture of Chinese light industry IOT.

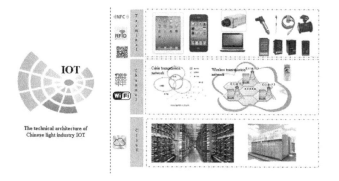

Fig. 1. The technical architecture of Chinese light industry IOT

Based on the architecture, Chinese light industry IOT will establish the core business system of mobile phone information, and crack the combination of labels and terminal products, and also integrate the mobile terminals and NFC module and establish integration programs of construction of public service platform, revenue-sharing system and commercial operation mode. Figure 2 describes the core business architecture of Chinese light industry IOT.

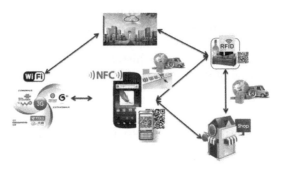

Fig. 2. The technical architecture of Chinese light industry IOT

3   The Key Technologies of Chinese Light Industry IOT Application

3.1   The Cloud-Channel-Terminal Technology System

The Cloud-Channel-Terminal technology system solves the bottlenecks of application of Chinese light industry IOT from business-cloud, the access network–pipe, terminal–terminal.

Cloud computing technology is the business platform of application of Chinese light industry IOT. In this model, shared hardware and software resources and information can be provided to computers and other devices on demand [5]. Cloud computing has two major categories of public clouds and private clouds[6], in the IOT application of China light industry, private and public cloud platform should be effectively integrated.

In the application of Chinese light industry IOT, the channel has far more than the concept of data communications network of the telecommunications industry. As long as it's a channel which can complete the data transmission function, it belongs to the scope of the channel, and this is a true sense of the multi-network integration. In the era of the application of Chinese light industry IOT, higher and higher demands of high bandwidth, low latency, intelligent and easy to access on the channel are required. The TD-LTE, which means TD-SCDMA long term evolution [7], will be used in IOT of China light industry. Internet speed of TD-LIE can be achieved several times faster than the TD-SCDMA technology [8].

Terminal in the application of Chinese light industry IOT does not just mean the mobile terminals in our hands or PC; all equipments connected to channel and as the final tentacles are called terminals, such as various types of sensors, cameras, smart appliances, POS, remote meter, industrial robots and so on. Terminal will gradually develop in personalization and standardization directions.

3.2   Identification Technology (Two-Dimensional Code + RFID)

The main research direction of the identification technology is how to establish a one to one relationship between the items and we usually refer to the unique identifier or unique code (UID) [9]. Identification technology is the primary technical fields of study in the future IOT, and identification technology and the establishment of identification system are the primary prerequisite for the development and construction of future Chinese light industry IOT. The identification technology of IOT covers: framework of a unified identity deployment, unified identity management, identifies coding technology, identifies of encryption / decryption technology, identity verification and storage management technologies of identification and addressing architecture, and creation global identifies the directory lookup and discovery services for networking applications of global architecture objects for mass identifies.

The research of identification technology of Chinese light industry IOT should focus on how to establish a reliable set of identity formation and analytical system platform. Many applications of the IOT will have to consider security risks and privacy issues, identified safety and security technology, such as identity encryption technology and identified by a pseudonym technology. At last, identification is a more critical role of technology as aids search and discovery service. Through the use of identification technology can help Chinese light industry IOT and its application to extract data in a variety of databases and information collection.

Figure 3 describes the RFID used in production-level applications of Chinese light industry IOT. In production-level application, enterprises apply for RFID authorization to the application platform while warehousing the product. Authorization information, product information and manufacturing information write into the label together. Unit of the RFID and operators can achieve service profitability by package unlimited way.

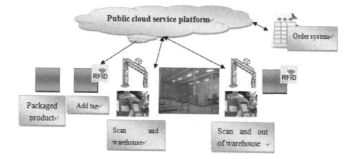

Fig. 3. The technical architecture of Chinese light industry IOT

3.3   NFC Terminal Solutions

NFC (Near Field Communication) is a short-range wireless communication technology [10] and has a lot of applications in Chinese light industry IOT. For example, in the consumer applications of Chinese light industry IOT, when consumers buying a product, you can use the integrated NFC module and mobile devices of mobile phone software (cell phone etc.) to distinguish product information, and return the identify-ing information after reading the information, feedback to public application platform through the mobile Internet. Such application mode is suitable for the rapid consumption of product which has a higher profit of single product. The application mode is describes as below:

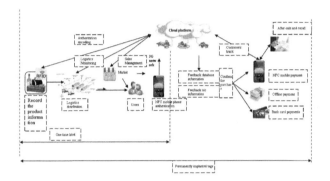

Fig. 4. The application mode example of NFC in Chinese light industry IOT

NFC has taken a unique signal attenuation technology, relative to the RFID, NFC has the characters of near distance, high bandwidth and low power consumption [11]. The hardware architecture of NFC is shown as below:

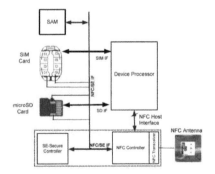

Fig. 5. The hardware architecture of NFC

As shown is figure 5, the function of NFC implementation consists of two parts: the NFC analog front end (NFC Controller with antenna) and security unit. Depending on the application requirements, safety unit is SIM, SD, SAM, or other chips [12].

In addition to NFC, the main short-range wireless communications technology includes Bluetooth, Wi-Fi and Zigbee, we compare these different kinds of short-range wireless communications technology from different aspects. The following table is the comparison of NFC and other short-range wireless technology:

Table 1. NFC and other short-range communication technology

	Zigbee	Bluetooth	UWB	WiFi	NFC
Price	The chipset approximately $4	The chipset approximately $5	The chipset approximately $20	The chipset approximately $25	The chipset approximately $2.5–4
Security	middle	High	high	low	Very high
Transmission speed	10Kbps–250Kbps	1Mbps	53.3–480Mbps	54Mbps	424Kbps
Distance	10m–75m	0–10m	0–10m	0–100m	0–20m
Frequency	Europe:2.4GHz 868MHz USA:915MHz	2.4GHz	3.1GHz–10.6GHz	2.4GHz	13.56MHz
International standard	IEEE 802.15.4	IEEE 802.15.1x	The standard has not yet been set	IEEE802.11b IEEE802.11g	IS0/IEC 18092(ECMA340) ISO/IEC 21481(ECMA352)

In Chinese light industry IOT, NFC will play an important role in payment at the scene, remote payments, parking, electronic posters, cell phone tickets and product information inquiry.

3.4   Architecture Technology of Chinese Light Industry IOT

The architecture technology of Chinese light industry IOT should be able to achieve the flexibility, modular capacity, scalability and interoperability of interaction and application between mass of the vastly different items (things) and between the goods and the environment. On the other hand, the architecture technology of IOT should be able to protect the formation of an open competitive solutions market. From the point of view of architecture system , the future architecture of Chinese light industry IOT will have end-to-end features, interoperability between different systems, neutral access, a clear hierarchical division and resistance to physical network interrupt and interfere with the ability of distributed open architecture, and is based on peer nodes, decentralized, with autonomy architecture. The main research content will cover: cloud computing technology, event-driven system, the lack of operation and data synchronization in the case of network connectivity.

4   The Key R and D Direction of Chinese Light Industry IOT Application

The involved technical scope of the application of Chinese light industry IOT is very widely, and the construction of the system is very difficult. The key R & D direction of the application of Chinese light industry IOT includes the following four aspects:

4.1   The Integration of Electronic Tags and Products

On the basis of the existing thin electronic tag, its necessary to actively promote the integration of the electronic label and product. According to the needs of practical application, and considering the cost advantages, the main choice is the passive RFID tags. In the meanwhile, according to the characteristics and transformation processes, the two level applications of the combination of the one-time integration and permanent integration should be promoted. On the one hand, the primary application of the combination of disposable labels and product packaging should be carried out. On the other hand, the pilot in the permanent integration of the electronic tags on part of the products should be carried out; especially for the products which have higher demand on the after-sales service.

Electronic tag written information ET is defined as: ET= {Product name, brand, model, production date}, and a unified signal range and standard compiled format shall be construed accordingly ET at the same time.

4.2   The Integration of NFC Module and Mobile Terminal

The NFC read module miniaturization design and development should be strengthened, and realize the integrated design of mobile terminal which will promote the industrialization process of the phone's NFC program and ENFC program [13], and will solve the problems of commercial application process such as: loss, viruses, illegal POS, virtual currency, legal and regulatory and other problems. In order to meet the needs of a wide range of users, the combination of NFC technology and home intelligent terminal equipment is recommended to achieve diversity and flexibility of the applications and users selection [14]. The development of application software should be strengthened, as well as the integration and development of CMMB technology.

4.3 The Integration of Reading and Writing Technology and Mobile Payment Technology

The integration and information sharing of reading and writing system and the existing payment system should be solved. The integration and information sharing security test, information written, the purchase payment and sales tracking should also be realized. Phone-based real-name authentication integration system should be built to achieve a fast and convenient payment.

4.4 The Integration of Private and Public Cloud Platform

The unified encoded authorization system of whole country is to be built, and the system should support private cloud computing service and public cloud computing for the majority of small and middle enterprise [15]. The core of the platform is product, and the platform integrates encoding automatic distribution, the security test of queries, direct supply of the product users, monitoring logistics GIS initiative after-sales tracking, and other service functions, and it combines with the industry characteristics to provide low-cost production line transformation technology.

5   Conclusion

Light industry is the traditional advantages of manufacturing in China, this papers research begins from the development status of IOT and China light industry, and then propose the technical architecture which takes the RFID and NFC technology as the core, cloud computing technology as a business platform, TD-LTE mobile broad-band technology as the neural network and NFC module integrated support system for end-use applications. This paper has the reference value for the development of the China Light Industry IOT application. Our research results will be helpful to comprehensively promote the transformation process of Chinese light industry IOT.

Acknowledgments. This work was supported by the National High Technology Research and Development Program of China under contract number 2011AA040502.

References

1. Ning, H., Wang, Z.: Future Internet of Things Architecture. Communications 15(4), 461–463 (2011)
2. Halonen, T., Romero, J., Melero, J.: GSM, GPRS and EDGE Performance - Evolution Towards 3G/UMTS. John Wiley & Sons (2002) ISBN 0470 84457 4
3. Hadden, A.: Mobile broadband-where the next generation leads us Industry Perspectives. Wireless Communications 16(6), 6–9 (2009)

4. Uckelmann, D., Harrison, M., Michahelles, F.: Architecting the Internet of Things, vol. XXXI, p. 351. Springer, Heidelberg (2011)
5. Armbrust, M., Fox, A., Griffith, R., et al.: Above the clouds: A berkeley view of cloudcomputing. Technical report, UCBEECS-2009-28 (2009)
6. Rimal, B.P., Choi, E., Lumb, I.: A Taxonomy and Survey of Cloud Computing Systems. In: Fifth International Joint Conference on INC, IMS and IDC, pp. 44–51 (2009)
7. Chen, S., Wang, Y., Ma, W., et al.: Technical innovations promoting standard evolution: from TD-SCDMA to TD-LTE and beyond. Wireless Communications 19(1), 60–66 (2012)
8. He, H., Dong, H., Yang, T., et al.: Study of TD-LTE Base Station Co-Existence with TD-SCDMA Base Station. Key Engineering Materials 474-476, 888–892 (2011)
9. Brown, I., Russell, J.: Radio frequency identification technology: An exploratory study on adoption in the South African retail sector. International Journal of Information Management 27, 250–265 (2007)
10. Nava, S.W., Hervas, R., Bravojose, J., et al.: Combining RFID and NFC Technologies in an AmI Conference Scenario. In: Eighth Mexican International Conference on Current Trends in Computer Science (2007)
11. Broll, G.: Improving the accessibility of NFC/RFID-based mobile interaction through learnability and guidance. In: Mobile HCI 2009 Proceedings of the 11th International Conference on Human-Computer Interaction with Mobile Devices and Service. ACM, New York (2009)
12. Bravo, J.: From implicit to touching interaction: RFID and NFC approaches. In: Conference on Human System Interactions (2008)
13. Li, P., Zhou, Q.L., Liu, Y., et al.: A Contactless Mobile Payment Method Based on Security TF Card and NFC Technology. Advanced Materials Research 317-319, 1769–1772 (2011)
14. Michahelles, F., Thiesse, F., Schmidt, A., et al.: Pervasive RFID and Near Field Communication Technology. IEEE Pervasive Computing 6(3), 94–96 (2007)
15. Zeng, Y., Wang, J., Wu, X., et al.: The Research and Practice of Industrial Cloud Computing Platform. China Mechanical Engineering 23(1), 69–74 (2012) (in Chinese)

The Research of Routing Forwarding Strategies in DTNs Based on Convergence Point

Luxuan Wang, Lijuan Sun, Fu Xiao, Xiaoguo Ye, and Ruchuan Wang

College of Computer, Nanjing University of Posts and Telecommunications,
Jiangsu High Technology Research Key Laboratory for Wireless Sensor Networks,
Key Lab of Broadband Wireless Communication and Sensor Network Technology,
Ministry of Education Jiangsu Province, Nanjing, 210003, China
{sunlj,xiaof,xgye,wangrc}@njupt.edu.cn

Abstract. DTN is developed as an emerging network technology which is mainly used in network with long waiting time, intermittent connectivity, and other extreme environments network. It has be favored in the military, transportation, marine monitoring, wildlife tracking, satellites communications and have been applied in some aspects. Currently, there is a lot of research about the DTN. The study includes three hot issues: the routing nodes, DTN-based mobility model and the data distribution and retrieval. To better solve the problem of data distribution and retrieval in DTN, an improved routing algorithm is proposed in this paper.

Keywords: DTN, Network protocol, Routing Algorithm, Advanced Probabilistic choose.

1 Introduction

In order to provide communication services in the highly challenged wireless networks that have only intermittent connectivity, such as vehicular ad hoc networks for road safety and commercial applications, sparse sensor networks for wildlife tracking and habitat monitoring, deep-space interplanetary networks and mobile social networks , delay tolerant networks (DTN)[1] were proposed. DTN has a complexity and diversity routing algorithm as it is a class of delay / disruption tolerant networks with significant delay, frequently interrupted, node storage / computing power. In recent years, scholars have developed different algorithms and protocols for different applications in DTN. The study includes three hot issues: the routing nodes, DTN-based mobility model and the data distribution and retrieval. In DTN, there are no end-to-end paths between the communication source and destination. For example, in the vehicular DTN, the nodes are vehicles and they move very quickly. Therefore, the network is highly mobile and frequently disconnected, and it is unrealistic to maintain end-to-end paths between any communication source and destination pairs. Therefore, its routing algorithms are quite different from the Internet and traditional ad hoc networks. The new mechanism for DTN routing is called store-carry-and-forward

R. Wang and F. Xiao (Eds.): CWSN 2012, CCIS 334, pp. 447–457, 2013.
© Springer-Verlag Berlin Heidelberg 2013

and, which exploits the opportunistic contacts between nodes and mobility to relay and carry messages. In store-carry-and-forward routing, if the next hop is not immediately available for the current node to forward a message, the node will store the message in its buffer, carry it along while moving, and forward it to other appropriate nodes until the node gets a communication opportunity which helps to forward this message farther. Therefore, the nodes must be capable of buffering messages for a considerable time. Moreover, to increase the probability of delivery, the messages will be replicated many times in the network due to the lack of complete information about other nodes. For example, in Epidemic routing[4], packets arriving at the intermediate nodes are forwarded to all of their neighbors. [6] Obviously, this new routing mechanism requires the nodes to forward messages in a cooperative and selfless way. For example, every node should utilize its own limited buffer to store the message, carry the message along the movement, and forward the message when it contacts with others to helps to deliver this message. Otherwise, most of the messages would not be transmitted to the destination successfully. However, in real world, most of the nodes exhibit non-cooperative behaviors [8], which would not store messages in their buffer, or even not relaying messages for others in order to conserve the limited buffer and power resources. DTN network was originally proposed for the deep space network, But because of the inconvenience of the simulation, the network gradually evolved to high-altitude HAP structure and spontaneous network model, It features over a network in the convergence layer, and data transmission using a protocol called the bundle[2]. In the platform of DTN or HAP[3], the communication usually uses the Wireless Network. Through the wireless network, it can effectively communicate with relay and run in a relatively stable state. However there is not an end to end path with the traditional sense, the path and lots of hot spots are assigned by the Routing algorithm in the areas which is the problem of wireless network. The characteristic of this class of network is larger RTT, higher packet loss rate.[5] Many researchers have been start of the special research of DTN routing algorithms before. The classical algorithms are Epidemic Routing[4], Probabilistic Routing and Spray and Wait Routing. These routing protocols may be divided into single-copy and multi-copy algorithm. In the single-copy scenario, there is only one node can relay the messages. For example, the copy of message is forwarded based on a utility function when encounter any other node. In the multi-copy scenario, message is allowed to copy several times to spread out. Epidemic Routing and Probabilistic Routing can provide higher delivery probability and reducing delays, they cost too much network traffics. Spray and Wait Routing can reduce the network traffic, but it has low delivery probability and high delay.[6] This paper attempts to use a DTN routing algorithm to change the network's original algorithm, in order to achieve the effect of improving the delivery rate. The routing algorithm should be able to calculate the low-cost communications and computing the path and adapt to real-time network status and network topology routing decisions.

2 DTN Architecture

A Delay Tolerant Networking (DTN)[1] architecture provides an asynchronous service model based on different transport protocols tailored to the specific sublink characteristics and medium-term storage within the network to deal with temporary link outages. In the literature, Performance Enhancing Proxy (PEP) agents are often proposed at the edges of satellite links with the aim to optimize performance. Similarities and differences between PEP and DTN are discussed in depth in presenting results of an extensive test campaign. As a matter of fact, best performance is provided by either PEP or DTN depending on the specific scenario. Nevertheless, the present work focuses only on the DTN application in order to combine performance optimization to the novel approach of DTN to manage packet routing. For this reason, it was suggested that a DTN network architecture for high-altitude satellite network[3]. The target scenario[6] requires the definitions of both a tailored routing and applications compliant with DTN paradigm. Within DTN architecture, a Bundle Protocol[2] is defined to handle application data as a set of "bundles" to be sent in sequence. If the link becomes not available before all the data are entirely received, the already received bundles do not need to be retransmitted once connectivity is restored. As deeply described in, Bundle Protocol manages retransmissions by sending over the new connection only data not received yet. Enabling reactive fragmentation option, even partial received bundles requires retransmission only of the missing part. In this perspective, DTN[7] appears very attractive to complement error recovery functions provided by the lower convergence layer able to efficiently carry bundles across each involved link. A Regional Network[8] is a single network and its protocol applies only where the communication area where is basically the same communications environment. Regional networks cannot communicate with each other due to the use of different protocols. The Internet is a special case of a Regional Network.DTN is a network of Regional Network, which has a Convergence layer above the Regional Network.DTN can communication between the different environments inside and outside Regional Network with each other. DTN[9] is not based on current assumptions on the link, on the contrary, DTN application environment and the DTN nodes within the network makes different from the traditional TCP/IP network features:

Long Delay. For example, Earth and Mars in the nearest time, 4 min of light propagation time is needed and the time between the two farthest one-way propagation time will be more than 20 min. On the Internet, travel time is generally in milliseconds, so such a long delay, many applications, especially those based on TCP / IP applications cannot be achieved[10].

Limited Node. DTN is often located in deep space, lake, battlefield environments and so on, the nodes in size, weight, power or other equipment carried by resource constraints and limited resources necessarily limit the application of performance, which cause the node had to use some strategy to save resources, thus affecting the link performance.

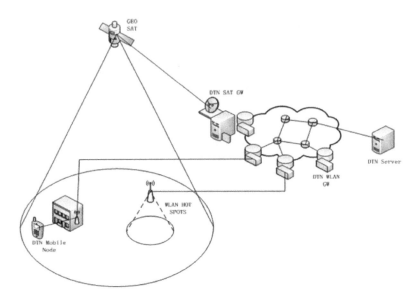

Fig. 1. Application Topolog

Intermittent Connection. DTN intermittent connections caused by many reasons, such as there is no path connecting the two end nodes at present moment; node temporarily turn off the power to conserve resources; movement out of communication range. Network outages can also have certain laws, such as satellite networks[9]; it can be completely random, such as sensor networks.

Asymmetric Data Rate. Asymmetric data rate means that the system data input and output flow rate differences. In the DTN, the bi-directional data transfer rate is often asymmetrical. In the deep-space mission, differences in two-way data rates could be up to 1000 or higher.

DTN architecture design is intended to provide a universal solution to solve the problem of communication in harsh environments, which support regional networks including the Internet and a variety of restricted internal communications network and regional networks of communications and interoperability. Way to interact with store and forward information. In the restricted network conditions due to long delays, non-symmetric channel, intermittent connectivity and high error rate and other issues, Internet information interactively have been inappropriate. To this end, DTN's postal system through the use of a similar store and forward approach to information exchange. [11]This approach requires that each node must have a persistent storage device (eg. hard disk), the persistent storage device requires the ability to store information indefinitely and we called the storage node for Persistent Storage. Information from one node is send to the continued storage of persistent storage to another node for using store and forward approach to information exchange. Bundle Layer[2]. DTN in all regions networks covered a new protocol layer protocol layer that is Bundle on top of the various protocol layers, which is to achieve in every area network interaction. Bundle layer closely linked to a variety of every region of the network and the underlying protocol for supporting within the application and inter-domain communication. Bundle will be used in a variety of network protocol layer, which can work within and through the Bundle of communications networks and interoperability, which formed a DTN. And a variety of network protocols in the Bundles lower layer is unique to the various networks, only to adapt to their environment where the network protocol stacks.

3 The Routing Problem

The best path selection in multi-layer system is an interesting question. Usually the best communication path is through the following aspects in different weights[11]:

1) node capacity
2) destination node of the reach ability
3) end-to-end delay according to the connection constraintsin terms of max-delay and max-Cell-Delay Variation(max-CDV)

The routing algorithms used by this system called Advanced Probabilistic (AP), which is an improvement of ProPHET. It will gradually transfer the message; try to deliver to all networks based on probability and the weight.

3.1 The Routing Strategy

More to say, the routing strategy includes the following four steps:

1) The focal point within the node records the weight, the weight marked convergence point.
2) Each node is updated the scope of the right value when it through the range of the convergence point, the higher the weight the greater the activity of nodes.
3) External node set to the lowest weight, and delivery of the packet is always from the higher weight of the node passed to the lower weight of the node.
4) Delivered in accordance with the probability distribution of probabilistic algorithms, the more occurrences of the probability of message-passing point higher probability to ensure that high-density point to receive the packet.

3.2 Three Principles

AP algorithm is based on three principles: [12]

1) DTN link topology rules
2) The highest probability path is the most active point of the region
3) Try to cover the entire network messaging

Hot links[14] are within the most congested path, or IDL (inter-DTN-link) has the largest usage. The so-called utilization rate means that the range of movement in the point is perhaps only limited coverage in this area, The usual sense of the active point is located in the active range of local convergence point, Therefore, away from the point its efficiency of packet forwarding node is higher than it in the region, The weight of the set is supposed to make the same message, at the expense of a certain amount of network capacity, as far as to send the packet to the global network, in order to achieve delivery rate increase.

3.3   Algorithm Description

To better explain the routing specifications, the following are a few definitions [11]:

Definition 1: P the *IDL* (inter-DTN-link)of Region Network in DTN.

Definition 2: $P_{S \to D}$ P is the path from source S to destination D.

Definition 3: $C_l = 1/vacancy(1)$ C is the cost of each *IDL*, $vacancy(l)$ corresponds to the number of available nodes within the link L.

Definition 4:

$$C\left(P_{S \to D}\right) = \sum_{l \in P_{S \to D}} C_l \tag{1}$$

$C(P)$ means the cost of path P, The formula refers to the sum of all the cost through paths P.

Definition 5: The minimum cost between the source and purpose $minC(P_{S \to D})$, means the smallest cost in all possible paths P from S to D.

Definition 6: The formula of *Packet Delivery Ratio, Network Overhead, Effectiveness Of Delivery* From the terminal end to end by DTN is as follows:

− Packet Delivery Ratio:

$$deliveryprob = \frac{delivery}{created} \tag{2}$$

PacketDeliveryRatio used to calculate the packet delivery capability, this paper packet delivery ratio as a performance evaluation criteria used to evaluate AP algorithm in the DTN network packet transmission capacity.

− Network Overhead:

$$overheadratio = \frac{relayed - delivered}{delivered} \times 100\% \tag{3}$$

Relayed is the numbers of the packets copies in the relay node, delivered is the number of packets transmitted within the network, Thus, the cost of a copy of the packet can be seen as redundancy, The value is to measure the performance of the overall transmission from the routing algorithm. Network *overheadratio* has a close relationship with producing a copy of the packet, so this ratio can be used to represent the cost of the network algorithm.

- Effectiveness of Delivery:

$$\eta = \frac{delivery}{overheadratio} \times 100\% \tag{4}$$

Existing performance indicators C packet delivery ratio, network overhead can only compare one aspect of network performance, and through *effectiveness of delivery* C delivery ratio under the same cost, you can compare the overall DTN advantages and disadvantages between the different algorithms.

Definition 7: SNW means the end to end cost of SNW algorithm from source to the destination across Convergence layer. The cost varies with the packet size.[15] Using the above definition, the formula of the cost of the algorithm from the source to the destination is as follow:

$$\left\{ \begin{array}{l} \min z \\ z = C\left(P_{S \to D}\right) \end{array} \right. \tag{5}$$

$$\Delta T_{end-to-end}\left(P_{S \to D}\right) < \mathrm{SNW} \tag{6}$$

Pseudo code of AP algorithm

```
Node[m] send packet to Point[m];
Node[m].point[m]++
For(i=0;i<N;i++)
Point[m] send packet to {Node[i] which [max]{Node[m].point[m]}}
For(n=1;n<N;n++){
if(Node[i]. point[n]> Node[j]. point[n] & Node[i] has packet & Probability)
Node(i) send packet to Node(j)
}
```

First of all nodes within the coverage in the focal point get a weight and backup, when the node send a packet, the convergence Point backup the copy and send to the node that has the largest weight in this convergence area as its probability. The node forwards the packet in accordance with the weight in descending as each point's probability. Each node will increase the probability and its weight in the coverage area as it update message.

4   The Simulation

In this paper, we select TTL as parameters because it reflected the effect of changes in a certain capacity, under a certain topological well. Parameters for comparison are $delivery_prob, overhead_ratio$ and $effectiveness of delivery$ C η.

Table 1. A comparison of three standard algorithms

Algorithm	The number of packet copies	Packet Delivery Ratio	Delay
Spray And Wait Router	Finitely Many	High	Lower
Prophet Router	Medium	Higher	Low
Epidemic Router	Many	Very high	Very Low

Table 2. Simulation Environment

Network space dimensions	MsgTtl	Simulation time	Map
4500m3400m	6002400s	21600s	Helsinki city

Table 3. Node Environment

Speed range	Buffer size	Wait time	Number	Movement model
0.513.9m/s	4Mb	0120s	120	Random Walk

Table 4. Convergence Point Environment

Transmit range	Speed range	Buffer size	Wait time	Number	Movement model
1000m	710m/s	40Mb	0120s	5	Random Walk

We use ONE (The Opportunistic Network Environment simulator)[13] as the simulation software, which is a DTN-specific simulation software. It use the map of Helsinki, which is the common international standard network environment for testing DTN routing configuration, forward strategy.

This environment is approximately 4500m3400m in Helsinki city. $MsgTtl$ is set from 600s to 2400s. It includes people, vehicles and CP. The simulation time is about 6 hours which is enough to see the results of algorithm. We simulated 10 times for each data, taking the average.

The nodes include peoples and vehicles. The speed of people is 0.5m/s and the vehicle is 13.9m/s. They all have a buffer with a size of 4Mb. The wait time is random from 0s to 120s.There are four kind of nodes with three peoples and a vehicle. There are 30 nodes in each of them. The movement model is set to Random Walk.

There are five convergence points and each of them has a transmit range with 1000m. The speed of CP is random from 7m/s to 10m/s. CPs all has a buffer with a size of 40Mb which is enough for delivery. The wait time is the same with node. The movement model is also set to Random Walk.

Fig.2 presents Epidemic has the best effect in $delivery_p rob$ as it use flooding, AP is better than ProPHET, but the effect is not obvious until the $msgTtl$ is sufficient. SNW has the lowest $delivery_p rob$. As TTL increases, AP algorithm has the fastest delivery growth rate.

As shown in Fig.3, SNW has lowest overhead as it limited the number of copies and prohibits the duplication of packets transmitted. Epidemic has the largest overhead as it using flooding and send packet everywhere and anytime. So nodes distribute packets to every node as they meet. AP has a larger overhead

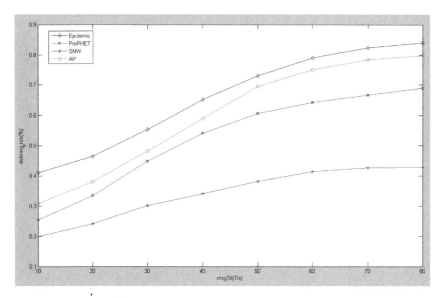

Fig. 2. The *delivery_prob* of four algorithms with different *ttl* periods

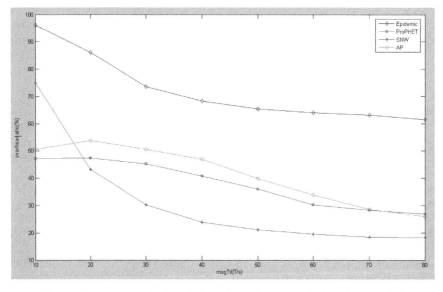

Fig. 3. The *overhead_ratio* of four algorithms with different *ttl* periods

than ProPHET and it doesnt do well in overhead as its copies are more than ProPHET.

In Fig.4, SNW, ProPHET and AP have almost the same effectiveness of η.SNW has a low delivery and a lowest overhead, however AP has a larger delivery and a medium overhead.SNW decreases its delivery to have a low over-head, which is used for low bandwidth and low delay network. AP increase a

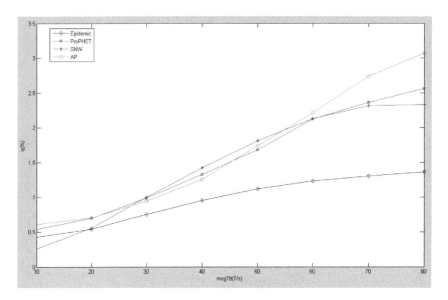

Fig. 4. The η of four algorithms with different *ttl* periods

little overhead to get enough packet copies and have a good delivery. Comparison with AP and ProPHET,AP is better used for a large bandwidth environment.

5   Conclusion

This paper analyzes the Advanced Probabilistic choose in DTNs based on Convergence Point. We chose four algorithms to take a simulation. Simulation results show that SNW decreases its delivery to have a low overhead, which is used for low bandwidth and low delay network. AP use some of the SNW in the basis of the ProPHET, use the probability to send packets and try to cover the convergence area, which avoid the loophole of ProPHET, decrease the redundant packets and increase the delivery.

Acknowledgement. This work is supported in part by the National Natural Science Foundation of China under Grant No. 61003236 and 61171053; the Doctoral Fund of Ministry of Education of China under Grant No. 20113223110002; the Natural Science Major Program for Colleges and Universities in Jiangsu Province under Grant No. 11KJA520001.

References

1. Cerf, V., et al.: Delay-Tolerant Network Architecture, IETF RFC 4838, Informational (April 2007), http://datatracker.ietf.org/doc/rfc4838/
2. Scott, K., Burleigh, S.: Bundle Protocol Specification, RFC 5050 (November 2007), http://datatracker.ietf.org/doc/rfc5050/

3. Caini, C., Cornice, P., Firrincieli, R., Lacamera, D.: A DTN approach to satellite communications. IEEE Journal on Selected Areas in Communications 26(5), 820–827 (2008)
4. Vahdat, A., Becker, D.: Epidemic routing for partially connected ad hoc networks. Technical Report, CS-200006. Duke University, Durham (2000)
5. Caini, C., Firrincieli, R., Livini, M.: DTN Bundle Layer over TCP: Retransmission Algorithms in the Presence of Channel Disruptions. Journal of Communications 5(2), 106–116 (2010)
6. Radenkovic, M., Grundy, A.: Framework for utility driven congestion control in delay tolerant opportunistic networks. In: IWCMC 2011 - 7th International Wireless Communications and Mobile Computing Conference, Article number 5982575, pp. 448–454 (2011)
7. Abdulla, M., Simon, R.: Simulation study of common mobility models for opportunistic networks. In: 41st Annual Simulation Symposium, ANSS 2008, Ottawa, pp. 43–50 (2008)
8. Krishnan, R., Basu, P., Mikkelson, J.M., Small, C., Ramanathan, R.: The SPINDLE disruption-tolerant networking system. In: IEEE Military Communications Conference, Orlando, FL, USA, pp. 1–7 (2007)
9. Lee, K., Yi, Y., Jeong, J., Won, H., Rhee, I., Chong, S.: Max-contribution: on optimal resource allocation in delay tolerant networks. In: Proceedings of IEEE INFOCOM (2010)
10. Caini, C., Cornice, P., Firrincieli, R., Lacamera, D., Livini, M.: Analysis of TCP and DTN retransmission algorithms in presence of channel disruptions. In: Proc. IEEE SPACOMM 2009, Colmar, France (July 2009)
11. Caini, C., Cruickshank, H., Farrell, S., Marchese, M.: Delay- and Disruption-Tolerant Networking (DTN): An Alternative Solution for Future Satellite Networking Applications. Proceedings of the IEEE 99(11), 1980–1997, ISSN: 0018-9219
12. Luglio, M., Roseti, C., Cola, T.D.: A DTN-oriented protocol design for satellite based architectures. In: 2010 5th Advanced Satellite Multimedia Systems Conference and the 11th Signal Processing for Space Communications Workshop, pp. 74–80. IEEE (2010) 978-1-4244-6833-1/10 ?2010
13. The Opportunistic Network Environment simulator, http://www.netlab.tkk.fi/tutkimus/dtn/theone/
14. Xu, F.-L., Liu, M., Gong, H.-G., et al.: Relative distance-aware data delivery scheme for delay tolerant mobile sensor networks. Journal of Software 21(3), 490–504 (2010)
15. Krifa, A., Barakat, C., Spyropoulos, T.: Optimal buffer management policies for delay tolerant networks. In: Proc. of IEEE SECON, San Francisco, pp. 260–268 (2008)

Analysis and Construction of Efficient RFID Authentication Protocol with Backward Privacy

Shaohui Wang⋆, Sujuan Liu, and Danwei Chen

[1] College of Computer, Nanjing University of Posts and Telecommunications,
Nanjing 210046, China
[2] Network and Data Security Key Laboratory of Sichuan Province
{wangshaohui,liusj,chendw}@njupt.edu.cn

Abstract. Privacy of RFID systems is receiving increasing attentions in the RFID community and an important issue required as to the security of RFID system. Backward privacy means the adversary can not trace the tag later even if he reveals the internal states of the tag sometimes before. In this paper, we analyze two recently proposed RFID authentication schemes: Randomized GPS and Randomized Hashed GPS scheme. We show both of them can not provide backward privacy in Juels and Weis privacy model, which allows the adversary to know whether the reader authenticates the tag successfully or not. In addition, we present a new protocol, called Challenge-Hiding GPS, based on the Schnorr identification scheme. The challenge is hidden from the eavesdropping through the technique of Diffie-Hellman key agreement protocol. The new protocol can satisfy backward privacy, and it has less communication overheads and almost the same computation, compared with the two schemes analyzed.

Keywords: RFID, Elliptic Curve Cryptography (ECC), Mutual Authentication, Backward Privacy.

1 Introduction

As Radio Frequency Identification (RFID) systems are becoming more common (for example in access control, product tracking, e-ticketing, electronic passports), managing the associated privacy and security concerns becomes more important. Since RFID tags are primarily used for authentication purposes, 'security' in this context means that it should be infeasible to fake a legitimate tag, and 'Privacy', on the other hand, means that adversaries should not be able to identify, trace, or link tag appearances.

To settle the security and privacy problems, several authentication protocols were presented. Feldhofer et. al. [1] proposed a challenge-response authentication protocol based on AES algorithm; HB+[2] protocol, a very efficient protocol presented by Juels and Weis, is based on the well known LPN problem, but it

---

⋆ Corresponding author.

R. Wang and F. Xiao (Eds.): CWSN 2012, CCIS 334, pp. 458–466, 2013.
© Springer-Verlag Berlin Heidelberg 2013

can not resist man-in-the-middle attack[3], and the subsequent modifications[4,5] all can not resist this attack[6,7]. To measure the privacy level of various RFID protocols, several models for privacy preserving RFID authentication systems have already been proposed, such as Juels and Weis [8](JW model), Burmenster, van Le and de Medeiros [9] and Vaudenay [10]. In the JW model, the adversary has the ability to corrupt the tag and retrieve the internal secrets, and he also knows the authentication result of the reader. Backward privacy, proposed in [11], means that if the adversary reveals the internal state of a tag at some time t, the adversary is not able to tell whether a transaction after time $t + \tau$(for some $\tau > 0$) involves the tag, provided that the adversary does not eavesdrop on the tag continuously after time t.

Usually it is believed public-key cryptography is too slow, complex and power-hungry for RFID. However, recent publications on compact and efficient Elliptic Curve Cryptography (ECC) implementations challenge this assumption [12, 13]. One of the first ECC based authentication protocols is the EC-RAC protocol[14] that has been proposed to address tracking attacks. However, it is shown that EC-RAC is vulnerable to various man-in-the-middle and replay attacks[15-17]. As a result, the EC-RAC protocol has been gradually revised in [18] to tackle the known attacks. In [19], Bringer et.al. have a research on the identification scheme with privacy requirement. They propose a framework which enables to transform some generic ZK scheme into private scheme and they apply as a relevant example this framework to the GPS scheme[20] to propose two efficient schemes(Randomized GPS and Randomized Hashed GPS).

In this paper, we give an analysis of Randomized GPS and Randomized Hashed GPS, and show they can not provide backward privacy in the JW privacy model. Besides we propose an efficient ECC-based authentication protocol for RFID system named Challenge-Hiding GPS scheme, and the scheme can provide backward privacy. In addition, compared with the two schemes in [19], our scheme has less communication overhead and almost the same computation.

The paper is organized as follows: Section 2 gives some preliminaries and recalls the JW privacy model; we present the analysis of Randomized GPS and Randomized Hashed GPS schemes as to a JW adversary in section 3; The Challenge-Hiding GPS scheme which satisfy backward privacy is presented in section 4, and we conclude the paper in section 5.

2   Preliminaries

In this part, we briefly present the preliminaries used in this paper. The schemes we mention are all based upon elliptic curve cryptography(ECC). The security of the ECC lies on the difficulty of solving the elliptic curve discrete logarithm problem (ECDLP), and it can achieve same security as of RSA with the key of fewer bits. Let G denote group of points on an elliptic curve with prime order q, and P is a generator. $+/-$ means elliptic curve point addition/subtraction. $H(\cdot)$ is a collision-resistant hash function. Some mainly used hard problems related to ECC are given below:

Definition 1 (Elliptic Curve Discrete Logarithm Problem (ECDLP)).
Given $P, Q \in G$, it is hard to find the integer $k \in Z_q^*$ such that $Q = kP$.

Definition 2 (Computational Diffie-Hellman Problem (CDHP)). For
any $a, b \in Z_q^*$, given (P, aP, bP), the computation of abP is hard.

Definition 3 (Decisional Diffie-Hellman Problem (DDHP)). For any
$a, b, c \in Z_q^*$, given (P, aP, bP, cP), it is hard to decide whether or not $cP = abP$,
i.e. decide $c \equiv ab \bmod q$ or not.

2.1   RFID Systems

We assume that an RFID system is composed with one reader and many tags.
The reader is not corruptible and all the data stored in reader side are secure.
Only the wireless link established between the reader and the involving tag
during a protocol instance is insecure. Tags are not tamper-proofed.

Definition 2.1 RFID Authentication Scheme. An RFID authentication
scheme is defined by two setup algorithms and the actual protocol.

- SetupReader(1^s) is used to generate the required system public parameters
K_P and reader's private parameters K_S by supplying a security parameter s.

- SetupTag(ID) is used to generate necessary tag secrets key K_{ID} and memory
states S_{ID} by inputting K_P and a custom unique ID. S_{ID} can be updated during
the protocol. Notice that K_{ID} and S_{ID} are not public and are not available to
the adversary unless the tag is corrupted.

- the actual protocol used to identify/authenticate tags with the reader.

The main security objective of an RFID system is to ensure that only legitimate tags are accepted by honest readers (tag authentication). Many application cases additionally require reader to determine the authentic tag identity(tag
identification). Moreover, there are several applications (e.g., electronic tickets)
where reader authentication is a fundamental security property. Here we only
consider tag authentication.

The most deterrent privacy risk concerns the tracking of tag users, which
allows the creation and misuse of detailed user profiles in an RFID system and
an RFID system should provide anonymity (confidentiality of the tag identity)
as well as untraceability (unlinkability of the communication of a tag) even if
the state of a tag has been disclosed.

2.2   JW Privacy Model for RFID Systems

Here we briefly summarize JW privacy model[8], which based on indistinguisha-
bility of tags. The oracles the adversary can access include: $CreatTag(ID)$ allows
the creation of a free tag; $Launch()$ starts a protocol instance at reader's side
and a unique handle π of this instance is returned; $SendReader(m, \pi)$ sends a
message m to the reader for the handle π, and $SendTag(m, \pi)$ sends a message
m to the tag determined by handle π; $result(\pi)$ returns either 1 if the instance
π completed with success or 0 otherwise; $Corrupt(tag)$ returns all the internal
secrets of tag.

Here we give the backward privacy definition based on the notion of indistin-guishability game.

Definition 2.2 Backward Privacy. Backward privacy is defined using the game played between the adversary A and a collection of reader and tag in-stances. A runs the game whose setting is as follows:

First the system is set up, and the adversary A obtains the corresponding public parameters. Then via the learning phase, A can access to all the oracles above. After that, the challenger chooses two tags $\{Tag_0, Tag_1\}$, and both tags can be corrupted by the adversary already. After a randomly bit $b \in \{0, 1\}$ is chosen, the adversary can make a polynomial number of oracle calls to the system, but cannot corrupt the challenged tag Tag_b any more. At last, the adversary outputs a guess bit $b' \in \{0, 1\}$ indicating his guess of the value of b. The success of A in winning the game and thus breaking the notion of backward privacy is quantified in terms of A's advantage in distinguishing $\{Tag_0, Tag_1\}$, i.e. it correctly guesses b.

We say the protocol is considered backward privacy if (ε is negligible):

$$pr(A \text{ guesses } b \text{ correctly}) \leq 0.5 + \varepsilon$$

3   Remarks on Randomized GPS and Randomized Hashed GPS

In this part, we first review the Randomized GPS and Randomized Hashed GPS schemes[19], then we give an impersonate attack on both two schemes, and man-in-the-middle attack on Randomized GPS scheme to show they can not provide backward privacy as to adversary in JW model.

Randomized GPS. The secret/public key pairs of the tag and the reader are $(s, I = sP)$ and $(v, U = vP)$, and the scheme is executed as follows:

1. the tag randomly selects $r_1, r_2 \in Z_q^*$, computes and sends the reader $A_1 = r_1 P$ and $A_2 = r_2 U$;
2. After receiving the messages, the reader randomly picks $c \in Z_q^*$, and sends it to the tag;
3. the tag computes and sends the reader $y = r_1 + r_2 + sc$;
4. reader checks whether the equation $yU = vA_1 + A_2 + cvI$ holds. If it holds, the reader accepts the tag; Otherwise the reader rejects the tag as illegitimate.

Randomized Hashed GPS. The secret/public key pairs of the tag and the reader are the same as the above, and the scheme is executed as follows:

1. the tag randomly selects $r_1, r_2 \in Z_q^*$, computes and sends the reader $z = H(r_1 P, r_2 U)$;
2. the reader randomly picks $c \in Z_q^*$, and sends it to the tag;
3. After receiving the challenge, the tag computes $y = r_1 + r_2 + sc$, and sends the reader $A_1 = r_1 P$, $A_2 = r_2 U$ and y;
4. reader checks whether the equations $yU = vA_1 + A_2 + cvI$ and $z = H(A_1, A_2)$ hold. If they hold, the reader accepts the tag; Otherwise the reader rejects the tag as illegitimate.

As to a JW adversary, he can access to oracle $result(\pi)$, and by definition of oracle $Corrupt(tag)$, the adversary knows the corrupted tag's secret key s. We present an impersonation attack on Randomized (Hashed) GPS scheme and man-in-the-middle attack on Randomized GPS scheme to track the identity of the tag.

Impersonation Attack on Randomized (Hash) GPS Scheme. Assume the adversary has obtained some tag's authentication messages, i.e. $\{A_1, A_2, c, y\}$ in Randomized GPS scheme, in order to test whether the random tag is the corrupted one, the attacker impersonates the tag to have an authentication operation with the reader. The attack is illustrated as follows:

1. the adversary replays the authentication messages A_1 and A_2;
2. the reader randomly picks the challenge $c^* \in Z_q^*$, and sends it to the tag;
3. the tag computes and sends the response $y^* = y - sc + sc^*$.

If the reader accepts the tag as legitimate, the adversary can decide the tag is the corrupted one. Because if both tags are the same, the response $y^* = y - sc + sc^* = r_1 + r_2 + sc^*$ is a right response; Otherwise the correct response should be $r_1 + r_2 + s^*c^*$, where s^* is the secret of the uncorrupted tag, which is not the same as y^*.

Although in Randomized Hashed GPS scheme, the hash function is applied to the first message, and the author claimed Randomized Hashed GPS scheme can enhance privacy, it is easy to see that this scheme can not resist the impersonation attack we present.

Man-in-the-Middle Attack on Randomized GPS Scheme. After the random tag sends the reader $A_1 = r_1P$, $A_2 = r_2U$ with two randomly selected $r_1, r_2 \in Z_q^*$, the adversary executes the man-in-the-middle attack as follows:

1. After obtaining the challenge $c \in Z_q^*$ sent by the reader, the adversary selects a random c^*, computes and sends the tag $c + c^*$;
2. After the adversary gets the tag's response y, he changes it as $y^* = y - c^*s$ with the corrupted tag's secret s. The adversary sends the reader y^* at last.

If the reader accepts the tag as legitimate, the adversary can determine the tag is the same as the corrupted one. Because now the response $y^* = y - c^*s = r_1 + r_2 + cs$ is the right response; Otherwise the changed response is $r_1 + r_2 + (c + c^*)s^* - c^*s$, and the right response should be $r_1 + r_2 + cs^*$, where s^* is the real secret of the tag. These two values are not the same, so the reader will reject the authentication.

4   Our Construction with Backward Privacy

From the analysis in the section 3, we can see if the adversary can not access to $result(\pi)$ oracle, it is difficult to execute many forms of security attacks, because the adversary can not determine the effect of their changes on the communication messages. In this part, we give our construction of the ECC-based authentication scheme with backward privacy in the JW model. We name it as Challenge-Hiding GPS scheme because as to a passive adversary, he can not deduce the real challenge used in the protocol.

4.1   Our Constructions

In our scheme, the secret/public key pairs of the tag and the reader are $(s, I = sP)$ and $(v, U = vP)$, and the scheme is executed as follows:

1. the tag randomly selects $r \in Z_q^*$, computes and sends the reader $A_1 = rP$;
2. the reader randomly picks $c \in Z_q^*$, and sends it to the tag;
3. After receiving the message c, the tag first computes $A_2 = rU$, and the actual challenge $c^* = H(A_2, c)$. At last the tag computes and sends the reader $y = r + sc^*$;
4. When receiving the response y, the reader computes

$$A_2' = vA_1, \quad c' = H(A_2', c)$$

and checks whether there exists tag's public key I satisfying equation $yP = A_1 + c'I$. if the equation holds, the reader accepts the tag; Otherwise the reader rejects the tag.

We can see in our scheme, the real challenge c^* is computed using the message c from the reader and a Diffie-Hellman key agreement value A_2 between the tag and the reader. While in the schemes in section 3 and Schnorr scheme, the challenge is sent by the reader. As to a passive adversary, given A_1 and U, he can not obtain the value of A_2 because of the difficulty of Computational Diffie-Hellman Problem. So, the actual challenge is hiding from the passive adversary.

4.2   Performance and Security Analysis of Our Scheme

Before giving the security analysis of our scheme, we first compare our Challenge-Hiding scheme(CH-GPS) with the Randomized GPS(R-GPS) scheme and Randomized Hashed GPS(RH-GPS) scheme according to computation and communication overhead in the following table 1, where ECPM/ECA means Elliptic Curve point multiplication/addition operation; AM/AA means ordinary arithmetic multiplication/addition operation, Hash means hash function and CO is communication overhead:

From the comparison, we can conclude that our scheme has the best communication overhead just the same as the basic Schnorr identification scheme. As to computation, our scheme is better than the Randomized Hashed GPS

Table 1. The comparison of our scheme with Randomized (Hashed) GPS scheme

Schemes	ECPM	ECA	AM	AA	Hash	CO
CH-GPS(Tag)	2	0	1	1	1	2
R-GPS (Tag)	2	0	1	2	0	3
RH-GPS(Tag)	2	0	1	2	1	4
CH-GPS(Reader)	3	1	0	0	1	1
R-GPS (Reader)	3	2	1	0	0	1
RH-GPS(Reader)	3	2	1	0	1	1

scheme and has more a hash function operation than that of the Randomized GPS scheme.

In the following, we give the security analysis of the authenticity and privacy of Challenge-Hiding GPS scheme proposed.

Theorem 4.1 (Authenticity). Assume $H(\cdot)$ is preimage and collision resistant hash function, and assume the hardness of the DH problem, Challenge-Hiding GPS scheme satisfies Honest-Verifier Zero-knowledge in the random oracle model.

Proof: Honest-Verifier Zero-Knowledge means there exists a simulator Sim able to simulate a protocol instance given the prover's identity I and a challenge c, i.e. $Sim(c; I)$ outputs a pair A and y, such that $[A : c : y]$ is a valid identifying transcript.

The eavesdropping adversary learns the tuple $(A_1 : c : y)$ just as the Schnorr identification scheme. It is easy to see that the random variables A_1, c, y are individually uniformly distributed on their domains. However, the real challenge is not the value c but c^* generated by the scheme. If the verifier publishes his secret key to the simulator, the adversary can deduce the real challenge, and the views of the adversary in our scheme is just the same as in Schnorr scheme.

In the random oracle model, as to a challenge $\tilde{c}$, the simulator Sim can first choose randomly $\tilde{y} \in Z_q$ and $\tilde{c}' \in Z_q$, then computes $\tilde{A} = \tilde{y}P - \tilde{c}'I$, and sets the hash value $H(v\tilde{A}, \tilde{c})$ as $\tilde{c}'$. The tuples $(A_1 : c : y)$ and $(\tilde{A}: \tilde{c}: \tilde{y})$ are then identically distributed.

Theorem 4.2(Backward Privacy). Assume $H(\cdot)$ is preimage and collision resistant hash function, and assume the hardness of the DH and CDH problem, Challenge-Hiding GPS scheme can provide with backward privacy in JW model.

Proof: In the JW security model, the adversary can corrupt the tag and retrieve the secret of the tag, i.e. the value s. In the learning phrase, the adversary can not get the information of the reader's secret key because of the zero-knowledge property.

After selecting the challenged tag Tag_b, the adversary can actively involve in the authentication. He can impersonate the legitimate tag or the reader, but from the CDH problem and the random distribution of the hash function, he can not deduce the real challenge used in each authentication. Here to track the identity of the tag, it is meaningless for the adversary to generate a new commitment A_1 to send when impersonating the tag (In this way, the adversary will know the hiding challenge).

In the equation of $y = r + sc^*$, there must exist two unknown variables r and c^*. And from the verification equation $yP = A_1 + c^*I$, the adversary can not link the identity of the challenge tag with some public key I because of the hardness of DH problem. That is to say, the view of the adversary is uniformly distributed, so the adversary can not have non-negligible advantage to guess the bit b.

Here we show that if there exists an algorithm ALG_1 to break the backward privacy with advantage ε, we can construct an algorithm ALG_2 to break the

DDH problem. The input to the ALG_2 is $(P, P_1 = aP, bP, hP)$, ALG_2 randomly selects $s \in Z_q$ as the secret of the tag, and bP is the public key of the reader, which all send to algorithm ALG_1. To execute the authentication, the ALG_2 can randomly select $r \in Z_q^*$, and sets $A_1 = rP_1$; and as to the challenge c, he can compute the real challenge as $c^* = H(rhP, c)$. We can see if $hP = abP$, then c^* is the correct challenge; otherwise it is not computed correctly. The response of the tag is $y = r + c^* s$, so the verification equation can be modified as $yP_1 = A_1 + c^* sP_1$.

If $hP = abP$ does not hold, the views of the ALG_1 are randomly distributed; while if $hP = abP$ holds, the views of the ALG_1 are real authentication distribution. So we can get:

$$pr(ALG_2 \ win) = pr(ALG_1 \ win/hP = abP + pr(ALG_1 \ win/hP \neq abP)$$

$$= 0.5 * 0.5 + 0.5 * (0.5 + \varepsilon) = 0.5 + 0.25\varepsilon$$

5 Conclusions

Privacy is an important issue required as to the security of RFID system, and backward privacy is a very strong privacy definition. In this paper, we remark on the security of two efficient public key authentication schemes, and show they can not provide backward privacy as to the adversary in JW privacy model. Via hiding the challenge using the technique of Diffie-Hellman key agreement scheme, we present a new scheme satisfying backward privacy, and our scheme has the best communication overheads and the same computation efficiency, compared to these two schemes.

Acknowledgments. This work is supported by the Priority Academic Program Development of Jiangsu Higher Education Institutions(PAPD), National Natural Science Funds (Grant No.60903181) and Nanjing University of Posts and Telecommunications Funds (Grant No.NY208072).

References

1. Feldhofer, M., Dominikus, S., Wolkerstorfer, J.: Strong Authentication for RFID Systems Using the AES Algorithm. In: Joye, M., Quisquater, J.-J. (eds.) CHES 2004. LNCS, vol. 3156, pp. 357–370. Springer, Heidelberg (2004)
2. Juels, A., Weis, S.A.: Authenticating Pervasive Devices with Human Protocols. In: Shoup, V. (ed.) CRYPTO 2005. LNCS, vol. 3621, pp. 293–308. Springer, Heidelberg (2005)
3. Gilbert, H., Robshaw, M., Sibert, H.: An Active Attack Against HB+ - a Provably Secure Lightweight Authentication Protocol. IET Electronic Letters 41(21), 1169–1170 (2005)
4. Bringer, J., Chabanne, H., Dottax, E.: HB++: a Lightweight Authentication Protocol Secure against Some Attacks. In: Security, Privacy and Trust in Pervasive and Ubiquitous Computing, SecPerU 2006, pp. 28–33. IEEE Computer Society (2006)

5. Bringer, J., Chabanne, H.: Trusted-HB: A Low-Cost Version of HB+ Secure Against Man-in-the-Middle Attacks. IEEE Transactions on Information Theory 54(9), 4339–4342 (2008)
6. Gilbert, H., Robshaw, M., Seurin, Y.: Good Variants of HB$^+$ Are Hard to Find. In: Tsudik, G. (ed.) FC 2008. LNCS, vol. 5143, pp. 156–170. Springer, Heidelberg (2008)
7. Frumkin, D., Shamir, A.: Un-Trusted-HB: Security Vulnerabilities of Trusted-HB. In: International Workshop on RFID Security, RFIDsec 2009, pp. 62–71 (2009)
8. Juels, A., Weis, S.A.: Defining strong privacy for RFID. In: PERCOMW, pp. 342–347. IEEE Computer Society (2007)
9. Le, T.V., Burmester, M., de Medeiros, B.: Universally composable and forward-secure RFID authentication and authenticated key exchange. In: ASIACCS 2007, pp. 242–252. ACM (2007)
10. Vaudenay, S.: On Privacy Models for RFID. In: Kurosawa, K. (ed.) ASIACRYPT 2007. LNCS, vol. 4833, pp. 68–87. Springer, Heidelberg (2007)
11. Ohkubo, M., Suzuki, K., Kinoshita, S.: Cryptographic Approach to "Privacy-friendly" Tags. In: Proceedings of RFID Privacy Workshop. MIT (2003)
12. Hein, D., Wolkerstorfer, J., Felber, N.: ECC Is Ready for RFID – A Proof in Silicon. In: Avanzi, R.M., Keliher, L., Sica, F. (eds.) SAC 2008. LNCS, vol. 5381, pp. 401–413. Springer, Heidelberg (2009)
13. Lee, Y.K., Batina, L., Singelee, D., Verbauwhede, I.: Low-Cost Untraceable Authentication Protocols for RFID. In: Proceedings of the 3rd ACM Conference on Wireless Network Security, WiSec 2010, pp. 55–64. ACM (2010)
14. Lee, Y.K., Batina, L., Verbauwhede, I.: EC-RAC (ECDLP based Randomized Access Control): Provably Secure RFID Authentication Protocol. In: IEEE International Conference on RFID 2008, pp. 97–104. IEEE (2008)
15. Bringer, J., Chabanne, H., Icart, T.: Cryptanalysis of EC-RAC, a RFID Identification Protocol. In: Franklin, M.K., Hui, L.C.K., Wong, D.S. (eds.) CANS 2008. LNCS, vol. 5339, pp. 149–161. Springer, Heidelberg (2008)
16. van Deursen, T., Radomirović, S.: EC-RAC: Enriching a Capacious RFID Attack Collection. In: Ors Yalcin, S.B. (ed.) RFIDSec 2010. LNCS, vol. 6370, pp. 75–90. Springer, Heidelberg (2010)
17. Fan, J., Hermans, J., Vercauteren, F.: On the Claimed Privacy of EC-RAC III. In: Ors Yalcin, S.B. (ed.) RFIDSec 2010. LNCS, vol. 6370, pp. 66–74. Springer, Heidelberg (2010)
18. Lee, Y.K., Batina, L., Verbauwhede, I.: Untraceable RFID Authentication Protocols: Revision of EC-RAC. In: IEEE International Conference on RFID, pp. 178–185. IEEE (2009)
19. Bringer, J., Chabanne, H., Icart, T.: Efficient zero-knowledge identification schemes which respect privacy. In: Proceedings of ASIACCS, pp. 195–205 (2009)
20. Girault, M., Poupard, G., Stern, J.: On the fly authentication and signature schemes based on groups of unknown order. J. Cryptology 19(4), 463–487 (2006)

A New TCP Design for Satellite-HAP Networks

Sudan Wang, Lijuan Sun, Fu Xiao, Xiaoguo Ye, and Ruchuan Wang

College of Computer, Nanjing University of Posts and Telecommunications,
Jiangsu High Technology Research Key Laboratory for Wireless Sensor Networks,
Key Lab of Broadband Wireless Communication and Sensor Network Technology,
Ministry of Education Jiangsu Province, Nanjing, 210003, China
{sunlj,xiaof,xgye,wangrc}@njupt.edu.cn

Abstract. In recent years, several new TCP congestion control algorithms have been proposed to improve TCP performance for networks of
high bandwidth delay products. Satellite-HAP networks providing highspeed data transmissions (up to 1 Gb/s). This article aims to show that
the proposed new TCP, as a modification of TCPs congestion control
mechanism, allows it to achieve reasonable performance in Satellite-HAP
networks. In this paper, we implement the performance simulation in NS-
2, and the results demonstrate that the proposed new TCP for Satellite-
HAP networks has a considerable performance improvement comparing
with the other variations of TCP.

Keywords: satellite-HAP, new TCP, NS-2.

1 Introduction

Wireless access to the Internet is becoming extremely popular with the growth
of the Internet. In particular, satellite communication systems are expected as
high speed wireless infrastructures for the next generation global information
networks, since the systems can provide fairly large capacity global networks [1]
. During the last decade, another alternative platform has appeared on the scene:
high-altitude platforms (HAPs), which are aerial unmanned platforms carrying
communications relay payloads and operating in a quasi-stationary position at
altitudes between 15 and 30 km [1,2]. Recent studies have shown the possibility
of utilizing HAPs as an attractive complement or alternative to terrestrial and
satellite systems for telephony and direct access to broadband services [3–5].

TCP(Transmission Control Protocol) is a reliable data transfer protocol used
widely over the Internet for many applications such as FTP and HTTP. Furthermore, TCP is used in the various networks (e.g. optical networks, satellite
networks, cellular networks, and so on) because TCP has been implemented in
many information devices such as computers and cellular phones. However, most
standard TCP implementations perform poorly in the satellite Internet due to
both a high bit error rate and a long propagation delay [6]. Several researches
have proposed the congestion control methods to improve TCP performance in
wireless networks [7,8]. However, these methods have not enough considered the

R. Wang and F. Xiao (Eds.): CWSN 2012, CCIS 334, pp. 467–477, 2013.
© Springer-Verlag Berlin Heidelberg 2013

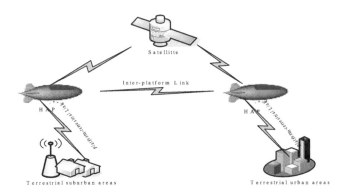

Fig. 1. Satellite-HAPs architecture

satellite communication network which has a long propagation delay and a large bandwidth. In [9–12], the authors proposed two variations of TCP for the satellite Internet. In this paper, our proposed method only requires modification of the TCP module, the performance of the proposal TCP and the difference of its use among the other variations of TCP is analyzed in the satellite-HAP networks conditions. The results of simulation present a distinct strengths of the proposal new TCP. This paper is organized as follows. Section II presents an overview of the current issues faced by TCP in attempting to achieve high performance, and some of the solutions proposed to overcome these obstacles. Section III shows the foundation of New TCP. Section IV discusses the methodology used and the results for the experiments of this study. Section V is dedicated to the conclusion.

2   TCP Performance Problems in Satellite-HAP Networks

Since satellite communications are a topic of great interest, a lot of work investigates its characteristics, and some of the more relevant results for our topics are reported in [13]; in this section we synthesize the characteristics that have heavy effects on TCP connections.

2.1   Delay

Communication based on geostationary orbit satellite links (GEO) are affected by a fixed delay due to the finite speed of light; as reported in [14], considering a distance of the satellite from the earth approximately of 36,000 Km, it correspond to a propagation delay of approximately 239.6 ms for a ground station directly below the satellite and 279.0 ms for a ground station placed at the edge of the view area of the satellite; these delays correspond to a Round Trip Time (RTT) of approximately 558 ms. Obviously this is a lower limit for the RTT, which can be increased by a large number of other factors, such as transmission and propagation times of other links of the network, queuing delays of the base stations and, for satellite equipped with on-board processing hardware, processing times. Its self-evident that the Satellite-HAP networks are the suitable way to optimize the delay.

2.2 Congestion

As for terrestrial communication, radio spectrum is a limited resource, typically controlled by licenses and international agreement, so the amount of band with available for the satellite channel of an heterogeneous network typically is smaller than that of any other transmission resource, so normally the satellite link is the bottleneck of an heterogeneous network.

2.3 Standard TCP

TCPs congestion management is composed of two important algorithms. The slow-start and congestion avoidance algorithms allow TCP to increase the data transmission rate without overwhelming the network. They use a variable called CWND (Congestion Window). TCPs congestion window is the size of the sliding window used by the sender. TCP cannot inject more than CWND segments of unacknowledged data into the network. TCPs algorithms are referred to as AIMD (Additive Increase Multiplicative Decrease) and are the basis for its steady-state Congestion Control. TCP increases the congestion window by one packet per window of data acknowledged, and halves the window for every window of data containing a packet drop. The TCP congestion control can roughly be expressed in the following equations: Congestion Avoidance(ACK:1;DROP:2)

$$cwnd = cwnd + a^*cwnd \tag{1}$$

$$cwnd = cwnd - b^*cwnd \tag{2}$$

Scaling can be applied with any choice of the constants a and b. The choice of a = 1 and b = 0.5 has proven to be very good. Unlike most TCP version, in the design of new TCP we attempts to address all the aforementioned problems in high speed link such as Satellite-HAPs. New TCP is designed to have a different response in environments of very low congestion event rate, and to have the standard TCP response in environments with packet loss rates of at most 10^{-3}. Since, it leaves TCPs behavior unchanged in environments with mild to heavy congestion, it does not increase the risk of congestion collapse. In environments with very low packet loss rates, New TCP presents a more aggressive response function.

3 New TCP

3.1 Variables

The variables used in the problem are:
w(cwnd): current congestion window, short for CWND;

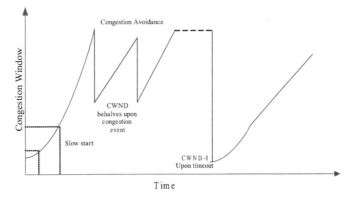

Fig. 2. TCP congestion control

RTT_{base} the minimum RTT measured by the sender;

RTT_{min} the minimum RTT estimated in the current data window of cwnd packets;

RTT_{queue} the current estimated queuing delay, which can be evaluated by equation (3);

G: the useful throughout(goodput);

L : propagation delay that indicates the network congestion level, which can be evaluated by equation (4) ;

Q:the possible number of packets enqueued by the flow, which can be evaluated by equation (5) ;

Q_{max}: the maximum number of packets a single flow is allowed to keep into the buffers;

$1/$ ª: the maximum level of buffer congestion with respect to band delay product;

a(w): the increase parameter, which can be evaluated by equation (11) ;

b(w): the decrease parameter, which can be evaluated by equation (10) ;

W_{high}: the highest congestion window when the phase entered congestion;

W_{low}: the lowest congestion window when the phase entered non-congestion;

p(w): the packet drop rate for congestion window w, which can be evaluated by equation (12) .

3.2   Redefine Congestion

Consequentially, our proposal new TCP assume two different modus non-congestion and congestion modes[10]. During the non-congestion mode, New TCP increment the congestion window according to an aggressive rule which is very simple to implement (according Equation (1-2)). In the congestion mode, its response function is represented by new additive increase and multiplicative decrease parameters. These parameters modify both the increase and decrease parameters according to CWND. Now the problems change to be how to distinguish the two different modus: non-congestion and congestion modes. The state is decided according to the estimated number of packets in the bottleneck queue. Let RTT_{base} be the minimum RTT measured by the sender(i.e. an estimate of the propagation delay) and RTT_{min} the minimum RTT estimated in the current data window of cwnd packets. The current estimated queuing delay is RTT_{queue}. From RTT_{queue} is possible to infer the number of packets enqueued by the flow as,

$$RTT_{queue} = RTT_{base} - RTT_{min} \tag{3}$$

$$L = RTT_{queue}/RTT_{base} \tag{4}$$

$$Q = RTT_{queue} \cdot G = cwnd \cdot \left(\frac{RTT_{queue}}{RTT_{min}} \right) \tag{5}$$

where G is the useful throughout(goodput). We can also evaluate the ratio between the queuing RTT and the propagation delay L , that indicates the network congestion level. Note that RTT_{min} is updated once per window of data. If $Q < Q_{max}$ and $L < 1/^a$, the algorithm is in the non-congestion mode, otherwise it is in the congestion mode. Q_{max} and $1/^a$are two tunable parameters; Q_{max} is the maximum number of packets a single flow is allowed to keep into the buffers and $1/^a$is the maximum level of buffer congestion with respect to band delay product.

$$f = \{ c\,ongestion, \text{if } Q < Q_{max} \,\&\&\, L < 1/^a, non-congestion, \text{else} \tag{6}$$

3.3   Modifying the TCP

During the congestion mode, a precautionary decongestion algorithm is implemented: whenever $Q > Q_{max}$, the congestion window is diminished as follows(ACK:6;DROP:7):

$$cwnd = cwnd + a(w)^*cwnd \tag{7}$$

$$cwnd = cwnd - b(w)^*cwnd \tag{8}$$

Since RTTmin is computed once per RTT, the decongestion granularity is one RTT. This section specifies a(w) and b(w) for New TCP for larger values of CWND. For congestion modes, we have specified a loss rate of p. or from elementary calculations, this requires the following relationship between a(w) and b(w) for current CWND(short for w):

$$a(w) = \frac{W_{high}^2 \cdot p(W_{high}) \cdot 2 \cdot b(w)}{2 - b(w)} \tag{9}$$

We use the parameter De to specify the decrease parameter b(w) for w, and use Equation (6) to derive the increase parameter a(w) for w. Along with P = $10^{-7}$and w = 83000, for example, we specify De= 0.1, specifying that b(83000) = 0.1, giving a decrease of 10% after a congestion event. Equation (6) then gives a(83000) = 72, for an increase of 72 segments, or just under 0.1%, within a round-trip time, for w = 83000. Thus, for W_{high} set to 83000 and p set to 10^{-7}, we get the following response function:

$$W_h igh = \frac{0.12}{p^{0.835}} \qquad (10)$$

Table 1. Parameters of new tcp for congestion avoid

Parameters	value
W_{low}	31
W_{high}	83000
$P(lossrate)$	10^{-7}

This moderate decrease strikes us as acceptable, particularly when coupled with the role of TCPs ACK-clocking in limiting the sending rate in response to more severe congestion. A more severe decrease would require a more aggressive increase in the congestion window for a round-trip time without congestion. In particular, a decrease factor De of 0.5, as in Standard TCP, would require an increase of 459 segments per round-trip time when w =83000. Given decrease parameters of b(w) = 1/2 for w in non-congestion modes, and b(w) = De for w in congestion , we let b(w) vary linearly as the log of w, as follows,

$$b(w) = \frac{(De - 0.5) \cdot (log(w) - log(W_{low}))}{log(W_{high}) - log(w)} + 0.5 \qquad (11)$$

For W_{low} = w in congestion modes and W_{high} = w in non-congestion. The increase parameter a(w) can then be computed as follows:

$$a(w) = \frac{w^2 \cdot p(W) \cdot 2 \cdot b(w)}{2 - b(w)} \qquad (12)$$

For p(w) the packet drop rate for congestion window w. From inverting Equation(9), we get p(w) as follows:

$$p(w) = \frac{0.078}{w^{1.2}} \qquad (13)$$

What is more, if we examine the case when only one TCP flow competes for the link that represents a bottleneck, then Q estimates the excess number of packets in relation to minimum size of the congestion window, which is required in order to exploit the available bandwidth. The specified amount of the packets can be removed from the current congestion window without degradation of useful bandwidth. When the number of the competing flows increase, each flow tries to fill the buffer with the same number of the packets independently of the estimated RTT, achieving internal RTT fairness. Likewise, the preventive reduction of the congestion prevents the queue, which is the bottleneck, to become too large, thereby reducing delays in queues and packet losses duo to the buffer overflow.

Preventive reduction of congestion is optimal only when the flows, which are implementing this, do not compete with greedy sources, such as old version of the TCP protocol. Preventive reduction of congestion is not able to compete with the greedy flows because it tends to leave bandwidth to such flows and to completely run out of the bandwidth [15–17].

4   Results

4.1   Simulation Environment

The experiments were conducted using the NS-2 simulator.

Network Topology: The simulation network topology used was a dumbbell with bottleneck, as shown in Figure 3which the traffic could choose from between the inner link and the Satellite-HAP link. The traffic passed through the bottleneck link whose link bandwidth was 50Mb and the link delay was 50 ms, while the other link bandwidth was 10Mb, the link delay was 2 ms. The simulations used the router queue management, DT (Drop Tail) [18].

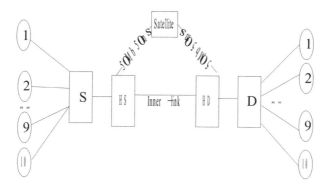

Fig. 3. Topology

TCP Flows Setup: The packet size was 1500 bytes; the maximum window size was large enough to not impose limits; random times between sends were set to avoid phase effects [18]; the flows used a modified version of the Limited Slow-Start algorithm for large congestion windows [9]. The TCP agent used for the sender and the receiver was SACK [19]. FTP was the application used to transmit data through the TCP connections.

Versions of TCP: We choose different versions of TCP to observe the performance among these protocols, TCP vegas, TCP highspeed, TCP reno. We implement them over the Satellite-HAPs using the topology in figure 3.

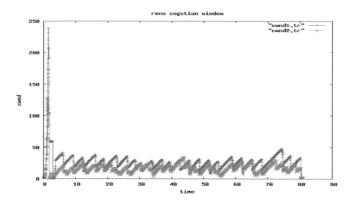

Fig. 4. TCP reno congestion window

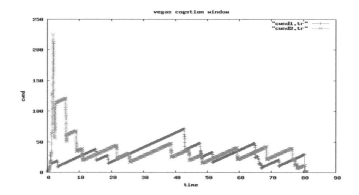

Fig. 5. TCP vegas Highspeed congestion window

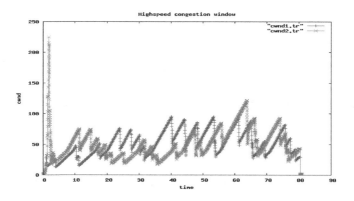

Fig. 6. TCP Highspeed congestion window

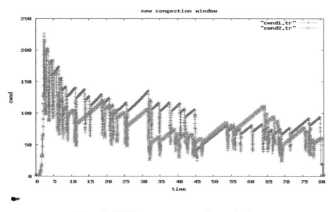

Fig. 7. TCP new congestion window

4.2   Results from the Experiments

This section presents the results of our experiments. All experiments were run with DT queuing policy. In the cases where there is a significant difference in the results, results for each individual queuing policy are presented.

Congestion Window. Figure4,5,6,7 are the result of the simulation, which includes TCP vegas, TCP reno, TCP highspeed and TCP new. The simulation is performed on the NS2 simulator. The Figure 4-7 show the increase of the congestion window (cwnd) in relation to the elapsed time. It may be noted that the New TCP has a large number of cwnd fluctuations, where its value is significantly decreased, and then returned within short time intervals. The results of New TCP, which works in the congestion in case of the congestion networks, and switch to the non-congestion when it comes to the high speed link, reflected in the Figure 7.Acorrding to the principles, we could conclude

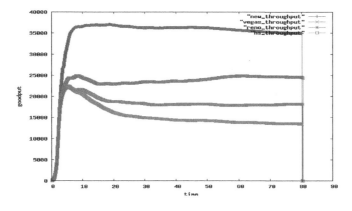

Fig. 8. Goodput of new vs. vegas vs. reno vs. highspeed.

that the New TCP can both work very well in the slow speed networks as well as the high speed links.

Goodput. Based on the simulation result in Figure 8, it is shown that the best results are achieved by the proposed new TCP protocol that is designed accordance with the principles of the combined approach.

5   Conclusion

Networks that operate at satellite-HAPs, represent a special problem for the TCP protocol. We have shown a comparison of many TCP proposals in a simple, parametric large band delay product networking test bed, along with a new yet significant proposal, so called New TCP. Experimental results show that, the conservatism in terms of the speed of increasing the window size and the recovery time after the window reduction due to the congestion. What is more, the throughput of the New TCP has a significant improvement among the other protocols over the high speed networks, as well as in low speed links. Because of this, good prospects exist for the New TCP, which works in the congestion in case of the congestion networks, and switch to the non-congestion when it comes to the high speed link. Further work is required to verify the performance of our proposal in different network scenarios and to formalize analytically some heuristics utilized of the design.

Acknowledgments. This work is supported in part by the National Natural Science Foundation of China under Grant No. 61003236 and 61171053; the Doctoral Fund of Ministry of Education of China under Grant No. 20113223110002; the Natural Science Major Program for Colleges and Universities in Jiangsu Province under Grant No. 11KJA520001.

References

1. Wood, L., Pavlou, G., Evans, B.: Effects on TCP of Routing Strategies in Satellite Constellations. IEEE Communications Magazine 39(3), 172–181 (2001)
2. Karapantazis, S., Pavlidou, F.: Broadband Communications via High-Altitude Platforms: a Survey. IEEE Commun. Surveys & Tutorials 7(1), 1–35 (2005)
3. Pace, P., et al.: An Integrated Satellite-HAP-terrestrial System Architecture: Resource Allocation and Traffic Management Issues. In: Proc. IEEE VTC 2004, Milan, Italy, vol. 5, pp. 2872–2875 (May 2004)
4. Antonini, M., et al.: Stratospheric Relay: Feasibility of New Satellite-High Altitude Platforms Integrated Scenarios. In: IEEE Aerospace Conf., March 8-13 (2003)
5. Avagnina, D., et al.: Wireless Networks based on High-Altitude Platforms for Provision of Integrated Navigation/Communication Services. IEEE Commun. Mag. 40(2), 119–125 (2002)
6. Partridge, C., Shepard, T.: TCP Performance over Satellite Links. IEEE Network 11(5), 44–49 (1997)

7. Sato, N., Kunishi, M., Teraoka, F.: TCP-J: New Transport Protocol for Wireless Network Environments. JPSJ Journal 43(12), 3848–3858 (2002)
8. Casetti, C., Gerla, M., Mascolo, S., Sanadidi, M.Y., Wang, R.: TCP Westwood: Bandwidth Estimation for Enhanced Transport over Wireless Link. In: Proc. International Conference on Mobile Computing and Networking, Mobicom 2001, pp. 287–297 (2001)
9. Baiocchi, A., Castrllani, A.P., Vacirca, F.: YeAH TCP: Yet Another Highspeed TCP. In: International Workshop on Protocols for Future, Large-Scale & Diverse Network Transports (February 2007)
10. Floyd, S.: HighSpeed TCP for Large Congestion Windows. IETF RFC 3649 (December 2003)
11. Allman, M., Glover, D., Sanchez, L.: RFC 2488 Enhancing TCP over Satellite Channels using Standard Mechanism. IETF (January 1999)
12. Abed, G.A., Ismail, M.: A Comparion and Analysis of Congestion Window for HS-TCP, Full-TCP, and TCP-linux in Long Term Evolution System Model. In: IEEE Confrence on Open System, September 25-28 (2011)
13. Mahmoodi, T.: Transport Layer Performance Enhancements over Wireless Networks. University of London (August 2009)
14. Henderson, R.T., Katz, R.H.: Transport Protocols for Internet-Compatible Satellite Networks. IEEE Journal on Selected Areas in Communications 17(2) (February 1999)
15. Stadler, J.S., Gelman, J.: Performance Enhancement for TCP/IP on a Satellite Channel. In: MILCOM 1998, vol. 1, pp. 270–276 (October 1998)
16. Ceco, A.: Performance Comparison of Different TCP Versions Designed for Networks with High Speeds and over Long Distances. In: MIPRO, Opatija, Croatia, May 23-27 (2011)
17. Braden, B., Clark, D., Crowcroft, J., Davie, B., Deering, S., Estrin, D., Floyd, S., Jacobson, V., Minshall, G., Partridge, C., Peterson, L., Ramakrishnan, K., Shenker, S., Wroclawski, J., Zhang, L.: Recommendations on queue management and congestion avoidance in the Internet. Internet Engineering Task Force (April 1998) RFC 2309
18. Floyd, S., Jacobson, V.: On traffic phase effects in packet-switched gateways. Internetworking: Research and Experience 3(3), 115–156 (1992)
19. Fall, K., Floyd, S.: Simulation-based comparisons of Tahoe, Reno and SACK TCP. Computer Communication Review 26(3), 5–21 (1996)

Layered Pre-selection Model Based on the Trust Mechanism for Web Educational Resources

Yang Wang*, Keben You, Yakun Huang, Mengting Wu, and Wenkai Han

Department of Computer Science, Anhui Normal University,
Wuhu, 241000, China
wycap@ustc.edu.cn

Abstract. In order to solve the problem of the credibility on Web educational resources under the current cloud computing platform, we propose a hierarchical pre-selection model of Web educational resources based on trust mechanism. Firstly, a credibility assessment of the Web educational resources was presented. Then the level on pre-selection model by credibility was established. Finally, the resource routing algorithm based on hierarchical pre-selection model was proposed. Simulation results show HPBTA model could ensure that cloud computing Web education resource is availability. In addition, the model provides a solution to pre-selection of cloud computing Web education resources.

Keywords: Trust mechanism, Web educational resource, Hierarchical pre-selection, Rout mechanism.

1   Introduction

With the popularization and development of the open Web internet, how to acquire the Web educational resources under the Cloud computing platform has become challenging problem[1,2]. The utilization of resource and efficiency of services cant be improved effectively. Therefore, establishing a efficient hierarchical model of Web educational resources to solve the pre-selection issue of massive educational resource and reducing the scale and efficiency of candidate services become hotspot during the current research[3].

Rarely in recent years has the research about the management of Web educational resources under the cloud computing been done at home and abroad, however, for the management model of Web resource, there are three following aspects. Firstly, the hierarchical model, such as the resource management model, Globus[4,5,6],Legion[7],Ninf[8] can solve the problems of heterogeneity of the site well. Secondly, the abstract owner model, the agent-based on resource allocation method has many problems in practice. Thirdly, the calculated economic model that combines the ideas of the hierarchical model and the abstract owner model

* This work is supported by the China Postdoctoral Science Foundation(No. 20100480701), The Ministry of education of Humanities and Social Sciences Youth Fund Project (11YJC880119).

R. Wang and F. Xiao (Eds.): CWSN 2012, CCIS 334, pp. 478–489, 2013.
© Springer-Verlag Berlin Heidelberg 2013

can be compatible with the complex network environment well. However, the deficiencies is that the focus on the economic resources management such as the resource management model of NimrodNimrod–G[9,10],JaWS[11]and so on.

Considering the deficiencies of the above models, the paper proposed a hierarchical pre-selection model of Web educational resource based on trust mechanism. Considering the node utilization and availability differences of the dynamic resource node and the requirement of the trust mechanism, we proposed HPBTA model which builds a hierarchical topology according to the affect degree of credible resources.

1.1 Cloud Computing Web Educational Resources

Under the cloud computing platform, the education resources server and provider realized different functions respectively, services will be useroriented directly. The providers need for calculating resource and provide available resources efficiently according to a certain strategy. The Fig1 shows the schematic diagram of the Web educational resources mode under the cloud computing platform.

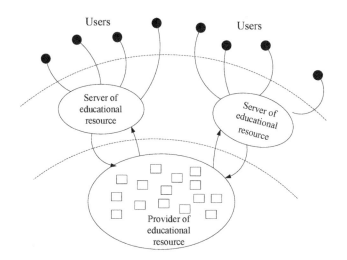

Fig. 1. The management model of Web educational resource

Definition1. Subject, refers to a provider of Web educational resources, Use symbol for S.Resource subject can be video, audio and text content, the resource that the text content allocate.

Definition2. Client, refers to the existence of the object entities, needs to access resources in the Web, Network about education and resource, or other types of networks, The resource users, Use symbol for c.This paper studies the preselected distribution provided by the subject when the Client is working on the visit operations.

Through the definition and description above, The cloud computing of Wed educational resource must be through the service's indirect management, the paper introduces the credibility theory, building a high available model of Web educational resource allocation under the cloud computing platform and relevant theoretical description of the credible resources theory.

1.2   The Affect Degree of Credible Resources

In order to classify and managing resources effectively and to provide the high available resources to the user, we describe the affect degree of credible resources through the two sides: The degree of direct credibility and feedback credibility. Direct credibility can be judged by the credible real time resources, feedback credibility can reduce the accidental error of the credible judgement from the perspective of historical trust

Definition3. The degree of direct credibility.
Assuming that:

d_1 :The number of the other level 1 subject resource nodes that subject resource node is connected, regarded this link acts as the number of this Subject credibility success;
d_2 :The number of the other level 1 subject resource nodes that subject resource node is connected, regarded this link acts as the number of this Subject credibility failure.

Direct credibility is defined as the probability for the Subject resources the first $n + 1$ number of success, the probability of obedience to the beta distribution $d(c, s)$,the derivation obtained according to the density function:

$$d(c, s) = \begin{cases} \frac{d_1+1}{d_1+d_2+2}, & if(d_1, d_2 > 0) \\ 0, & else \end{cases} \tag{1}$$

We can know from the formula, when d_1 equal 0, the node is isolated node; when d_2 equal 0, the node is the trust agent node, without the credible evaluation.

Definition4. Feedback credibility.
The Client resources would make an evaluation and feedback of information to the Subject resources when completing the visit operation to Subject, Including the authenticity accuracy of the provided information, symbol for CF, Generally speaking, there are two factors of the feedback credibility :

(1)The frequency of the current Client's visit to the Subject, visit more often, feedback more credible;
(2)If the similarity between the feedback information of previous Client to the Subject and other Client to the Subject have consistency, the higher consistency, the higher degree of feedback.

Feedback credibility is a direct response to the education of the main historical visit, In order to suppress the attacks of malicious nodes, we require to establish the evaluation to feedback credibility on the basis of the direct credibility and satisfaction evaluation.

The CF formula is given below:

We define visit density Num stands for the number of Client visit Subject influences the feedback credibility object visits the subject of feedback credibility; Assuming N_c stands for the number of Clients visit to the Subject, N_s stands for the total number of visits to Subject.

$$Num(c, s) = \frac{N_c}{N_s} \tag{2}$$

We introduce the description of the consistency factor $Sim(c, s)$; The compare between the feedback TS_c from the current Clients visit and feedback TS_s from all the Clients visit:

$$Sim(c, s) = \frac{TS_c}{TS_s} \tag{3}$$

Taking these two factors, we can define the feedback credibility of CF:

$$CF(c, s) = \delta \cdot Num(c, s) + (1 - \delta) \cdot Sim(c, s) \tag{4}$$

In the formula, we give the percentage between these two, when $CF(c, s)$ meets:

$$CF(c, s) \geq \frac{d(c, s) + A(c, s)}{2}$$

The feedback credibility we have defined could make an effective assessment.

2   Layered Per-selection Model Based on the Mechanism of Trusting Cloud Computing Web Educational Resources

A hierarchical pre-selection model of Web educational resource nodes under the computing platform, we can divide these nodes into three layers: Availability, in general, low available nodes, based on the credibility effects and the capacity area demanded. Generally available nodes around, high available nodes form a new topology dynamically, low available nodes around the generally available nodes form a new topological network. This hierarchal structure model utilizes the efficient features of the structural network research and to ensure the availability of resources at the same time.

2.1   The Hierarchal of Web Educational Resources under the Cloud Computing

Under the Cloud computing platform, the Web educational resources hierarchal model based on credibility theory need to be assessed about the credible degree of influence in the structure of the hierarchal network. Visitors are required to service providers to register when visiting the Cloud resources and then locate and allocate the resources through the server, to complete a visit, and to save the update of the information to the resource.

Here are a hierarchal schematic of Web educational resources:

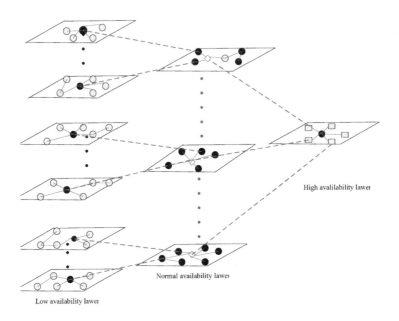

Fig. 2. The hierarchical schematic of Web educational resource

We propose the trust resources available hierarchal algorithm; according to the availability of resources, namely, through making the quantity sort hierarchal management of the direct credibility, Feedback credibility. After initial stratification to the nodes, starting from the low availability node ,form a network topology around the recent general availability of nodes; The general availability of nodes form a topology dynamically around the high available node, high available node form a sufficient star topology from each other.

Web Educational resources hierarchical construction algorithm

```
Data structure:
Web_Res_Net; //Web educational resources library
Web_Sort_List; //Availability sort table of the Web educational resources
Input:
    Web_Res_Net; alpha,beta; //Low available
Output:
    Web_Res_Graph1; Web_Res_Graph2;Web_Res_Graph3;
    //Built in layers of different network topology
Begin
For (Web_Res_Net);
  { Gets  Web _Res; //Take the resource object
```

```
cp capacity(Web _Res); //Calculate the resources availability
if(cp  alpha)
Sort3(Web_Res);//Low available
else if(alpha < cp < beta)
Sort2(Web_Res); //Generally available
else
Sort1(Web_Res); //High available
//To sort by insert according to the availability of the size}
Switch( Sort ){
case: Sort1:
for ( Sort1 )
for ( Sort2 + 1)
{ if(distance(Sort1,(Sort2+1))=0)
 Link(Sort1,Sort2+1); Break; }
 //2 round 1 compared with each other to form a topology
 case: Sort2:
  for ( Sort2 )
   for ( Sort3+ 1)
 { if(distance(Sort2,(Sort3+1))=0)
    Link(Sort2,Sort3+1);Break;}
 //3 round 2 compared with each other to form a topology
 case: Sort3:
  for ( Sort3 )
  { Link(Sort3,Sort3i); Break;}
  //The formation of star topology
 }
End
```

2.2   HPBTA Model Routing Mechanisms

The routing mechanism is the core part of the HPBTA hierarchical pre-selection and makes various designs to the different availability of mode. For the dynamic feature of Web educational resources under the Cloud computing platform. Combination of the above hierarchical model, we constructed a resource route distribution mechanism. This mechanism designated high available and generally available as the active class, low available nodes designated as a general class, different types take different routing algorithms to locate high available information resources provided to the user effectively.

Here are the routing mechanism diagram of HPBTA model :

The schematic of the HPBTA model routing mechanism make the description of the routing mechanism of the different availability of resources layer which has a different entrance and algorithm.

(1)The description of the active class node routing mechanism For the nodes of the active class, Routing and data transmission within the entire network play a supportive role. Its requirements and capabilities are very high. In order to provide efficient location search algorithm, we consider that there are more concentration on the commonly used active resources. It started in the form of hash, trying to make the fast positioning by the Hash function.

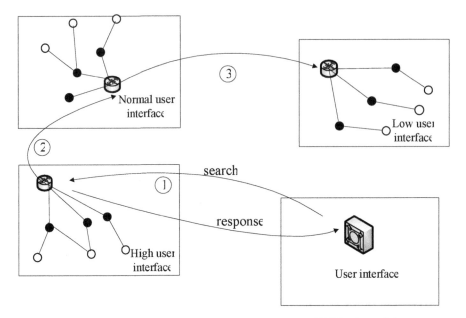

Fig. 3. Schematic of the routing mechanism of HPBTA model

(2)The general class node routing mechanism General class node is a node of the law availability, Easy to know that the probability of these nodes demand is small, less likely to find, we use a linear array to store, Search algorithm by using the linear traverse and give the update mechanism at the same time.

Algorithm Routing preselecting algorithm

```
Input:
      Web_Res_Graph1;Web_Res_Graph2;Web_Res_Graph3;
      //Built in layers of different network topology
      Web_Res_Search; //Need to find resources
Output:
      location of  Web_Res;//Positioning of resources
Begin
      Hash1 ( Web_Res_Graph1 );
      Hash2 ( Web_Res_Graph2 ); //Stored in the form of a hash table
      Direct3(Web_Res_Graph3 ); //Stored in the form of a linear
      For ( Web_Res_Search )
        { Gets  Web_Res;
          if ( Locate ( Hash1) || Locate(Hash2))
          return location;
          else
          for ( Direct3)
          { check ( Web_Res );
            return location;
          }
      Renew (Web_Res);//Update the resources information researched
      }
End
```

2.3 Algorithm Efficiency Analysis

This paper make the analysis in the Hierarchical build algorithms and routing pre-selection time complexity. The constructed algorithm of hierarchical mainly include resources sort dynamically and building the topology dynamically, The sort of resource availability by direct insertion sort, Average time complexity is $O(n^2)$, best case is $O(n)$, higher stability; Dynamically build a topological graph algorithms, mainly through the interaction between the different hierarchical nodes. The time complexity is $O(n^2)$. so the total time complexity of the hierarchical build algorithms is $O(n^2)$, able to meet the requirements under normal circumstances.

Routing pre-selection algorithm uses a hash table and the linear storage, positioning for higher availability of resources in the active class, Hash table look up time complexity is $O(1)$, linear storage find is $O(n)$. Due to the efficiency of hash table which is relevant to the hash function and collision solution, What follows in passage is the problem of collision for hash table.

Theorem1. In a simple and consistent hash, link technology is used to solve the problem of collisions for the hash table, the average seek time is $O(1 + \alpha)$. Proof: To find the keyword is to give possibility of n keywords stored in the table. if insert x_i is the first i element,$i = 1, 2, ...n$ and set $k_i = key[x_i]$. To the keyword k_i and k_j, Define the indicator random variable $X_{ij} = I\{h(k_i) = h(k_j)\}$,so $E(X_{ij}) = 1/m$, During a successful search, The expected number of elements examined is:

$$E[\tfrac{1}{n} \sum_{i=1}^{n} (1 + \sum_{j=i+1}^{n} X_{ij})]$$

$$= \tfrac{1}{n} \sum_{i=1}^{n} (1 + \sum_{j=i+1}^{n} E[X_{ij}])$$

$$= \tfrac{1}{n} \sum_{i=1}^{n} (1 + \sum_{j=i+1}^{n} \tfrac{1}{m}) = 1 + \tfrac{1}{nm} \sum_{i=1}^{n} (n - i)$$

$$= 1 + \tfrac{1}{nm} \sum_{i=1}^{n} (\sum_{i=1}^{n} n - \sum_{i=1}^{n} i) = 1 + \tfrac{1}{nm}(n^2 - \tfrac{n(n+1)}{2})$$

$$= 1 + \tfrac{n-1}{2m} = 1 + \tfrac{\alpha}{2} - \tfrac{\alpha}{2n}$$

The total time of one search is:

$$Theta(2 + \alpha/2 - \alpha/2n) = \Theta(1 + \alpha)$$

3 Simulation Experiments and Results Analysis

In order to evaluate the HPBTA model performance this paper proposed. We simulate the hierarchical pre-selection of the digital library of educational resources. The simulation environment isresources library with 1000 nodes, Based on Mat-lab and VC++6.0 development platform, The simulation results and analysis are given below:

3.1   The Influence of the Hierarchical Threshold α and β.

The experiment results shown that in Figure4,α and β is the control threshold which to make the resource availability layered respectively, We take the average efficienc;

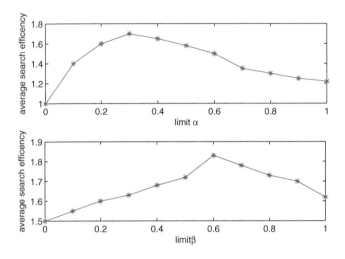

Fig. 4. Influence of hierarchical threshold α and β

Figure 4 can be seen, for the threshold α equal 0.3,the average search efficiency is the largest, When less than 0.3,due to the low number of high available; The high efficiency of the high available search, other node is too many and varied. so the average efficiency is low; When greater than 0.3 with the increase of α,due to the increase in the number of the high available nodes. The time to solve the hash collision is increasing, so the average efficiency is decrease.

The threshold β showing achieve the best results in 0.6 layered, Main reason is when lower than 0.6,low layer available linear search reduce the search efficiency. when higher than 0.6,low available layers are almost nonexistent, Then is, The overhead increase in the system because of all nodes using the hash method to restore and can't filter the information at the same time.

3.2   Hash Positioning Efficiency Analysis

This section is to make the assess to the rote pre-selection algorithm, Figure 5 showsHPBTA model is able to quickly make the appropriate response when located in the access number is low, When the number of discovered access is greater than 50,average search step increase greater because the increasing of the number of the low can be used to find. Increase the overhead, In summary, Hash positioning is able to handle the problem that access a number less well, a certain degree of response.

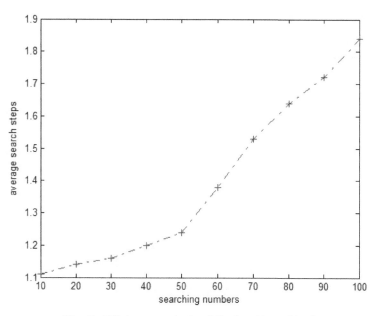

Fig. 5. Efficiency analysis of the location of hash

3.3   Performance Analysis

The Effectiveness of Experiment. The experiment verified the validity of HPBTA to solve practical problems, the algorithm performs CPU overhead, Experiment from the CPU overhead of the service groups of different sizes to verify, It can be seen from figure 6:with increasing the size of resources nodes in the Web education and resource network, It takes the CPU overhead increasing, Overall CPU overhead of less than 0.5,with the extension of the trend, can be drawn from the CPU overhead which can be controlled at a certain effective range, has a certain validity.

The Reliability Experiments. The purpose of this experiment is to validate the model HPBTA to solve the feasibility of the actual resources hierarchical pre-selection compared with the Globus[5] grid system resources hierarchical management model.

Figure 7 shows: Compared the HPBTA model hierarchical management model with the Globus grid system resources, When the nodes are smaller, the time efficiency of the two are less, when a node reaches a larger scale, This article HPBTA model is due to the low available node filtering, The time efficiency is better than Globus model obviously.

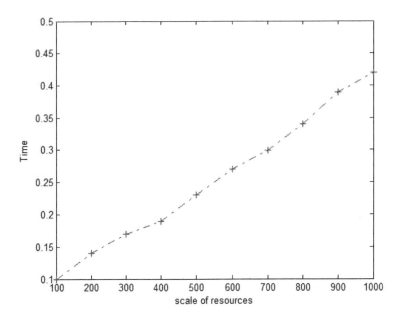

Fig. 6. Average time of different service group

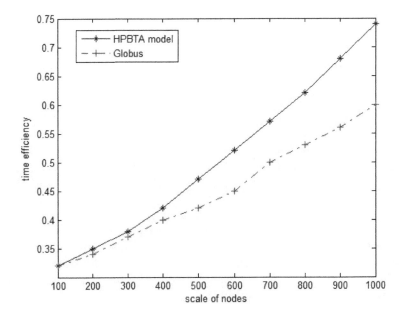

Fig. 7. Contrast of model efficiency

4   Conclusion

Could computing the hierarchical preselection of Web educational resources be an important issue in Web education management. This paper aim to Web distribution of educational resources availability is not high, look low efficiency, According to the dynamic of Web educational resources under the cloud computing platform, heterogeneous characteristic, Put out point of the resource credible Web educational resources based on trust mechanism layered preselection model, Give priority to the user's available resources according to user needs, experiments showed that the model can guarantee the availability of dynamic allocation of resources, improve the utilization of resources Effectively. The next step will combine present work with cloud computing platform to make the actual effect test.

References

1. Rochwerger, B., Breitgand, D., Levy, E., et al.: The Reservoir model and architecture for open federated cloud computing. IBM Journal of Reasearch and Development 53(4), 1–17 (2009)
2. Nurmi, D., Wolski, R., Grzegorczyk, C., et al.: The eucalyptus open-source cloud-computing system. In: Proceedings of the 2009 9th IEEE/ACM Interneational Symposium on Cluster Computing and the Grid, pp. 124–131 (2009)
3. Yang, F.: Ontology-Based Application Framework Education Resources Library, vol. (3), pp. 423–426 (March 2010)
4. Berners-Lee, T., Hendler, J., Lassila, O.: The Semantic Web: A new form of Web content that is meaningful to computers will unleash a revolution of new possibilities. Scientific American, 29–37 (May 2001)
5. Fox, G.: Peer-to-peer Networks. IEEE, Computing in Science and Engineering (3), 75–77 (May 2001)
6. Schollmeier, R.: A definition of p2p networking of the classification of p2p architectures and applications. IEEE, Peer-to-Peer Computing (July 2002)
7. Kelaskar, M., et al.: A study of Discovery Mechanisms for Peer-to-Peer Applications. In: Proceedings of the 2nd IEEE/ACM International Symposium on Cluster Computing and the Grid, CCGRID 2002 (2002)
8. Nakada, H., Takagi, H., Matsuoka, S., Nagashima, U., Sato, M., Sekiguchi, S.: Utilizing the Metaserver Architecture in the Ninf Global Computing System. In: Bubak, M., Hertzberger, B., Sloot, P.M.A. (eds.) HPCN-Europe 1998. LNCS, vol. 1401, pp. 607–616. Springer, Heidelberg (1998)
9. Watts, D.J., Strogatz, S.H.: Collective dynamics of 'small world' networks. Nature 393, 440–442 (1998)
10. Yang, Garcia-Molina: Improving Search in Peer-to-Peer Networks. In: Proc. of the 22nd International Conference on Distributed Computing Systems, ICDCS 2002 (June 2002)
11. Tanenbaum, A.S.: Computer networks, 3rd edn. Prentice Hall (1996)

Cyber-Physical Traffic Systems: Architecture and Implementation Techniques

Zhihua Wang, Yajie Zhang, and Kai Du

School of Electronic Information and Automation,
Chongqing University of Technology, Chongqing 400054, China
zhang_yajie@qq.com

Abstract. To implement the objective of smart traffic system, it is essential to introduce the cutting-edge Information technology, and applied to the transport system. Cyber-physical system (CPS) is a highly complex system that deeply integrates the physical and computing process. Its core is the organic integration of computing, communications and control technology to achieve real-time monitoring, analysis and control of large-scale interconnected physical systems. CPS has broad application prospects. In this paper, the basic framework of the Cyber-Physical traffic System (CPTS) is proposed. The concept and relevant characteristics of the CPS are first introduced. The architecture and key technology of CPTS are then illustrated. Next, Research techniques and methods of future CPTS are discussed in details, from the aspects of system modeling, large-scale information acquisition, optimization and control. The major challenges of CPLS research are finally discussed in details. Finally the future development path of CPTS is simply analyzed.

Keywords: Cyber-physical system, real-time monitoring, large-scale information acquisition.

1 Introduction

Recently, with the constant increasing of traffic congestion, traffic accidents and environmental deteriora- tion, Intelligent Transportation Systems (ITS) has become a very attractive topic of transportation field and academic circles. ITS must have high reliability, safety, economy, comfort and efficiency. To achieve the above-mentioned goals, it will have to introduce new computing, communication and sensing technology, to achieve the much closer integration and cooperation between information system and physical system. Cyber- physical system (CPS) provides a new way to solve these problems.

Based on the existing traffic system and combined with the development of computing and communications, in the paper, cyber-physical traffic system (CPTS) is structured. As the basic framework of future transportation system, CPTS should have various functions that ITS has, such as automatic recognition of vehicles, avoid the collision of intersection, expand driver vision, etc. As a subsystem of the unified CPS, CPTS must be able to realize seamless integration of comput- ation, communication, sensing, control and traffic system, and

R. Wang and F. Xiao (Eds.): CWSN 2012, CCIS 334, pp. 490–500, 2013.
© Springer-Verlag Berlin Heidelberg 2013

can achieve information sharing and collaboration with other subsystems in the unity of the communication and interface standards.

2   Related Work

CPS is a complex system consti- tuted by computing, network and the physical world, which realizes the closer integration of information world with physical world, by the organic integration and depth cooperation of calculation technology, communication technology and control technology[1,2]. In the CPS, the physical world is detected and controlled by the informa- tion world, and provides the human with intelligent efficiency, safety and high quality services. Figure 1 illustrates the interaction principles between them [3].

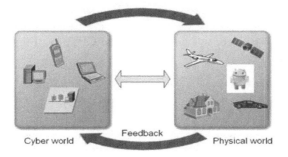

Fig. 1. Interaction diagram of the cyber world and the physical world

CPS has essential differences with traditional embedded system, sensor network system and Internet of Thing (IoT)[4], which aims at overcoming serious problems caused by the separation of information world with physical world. CPS is an integrated system with physical process, economic process and calculation process, which describes the interaction between physical world and human. CPS can achieve the following two goals[3] : Firstly, the features and states of physical world could real-timely, collaboratively, safely and reliably convey to the information world through the networked heterogeneous sensors, which makes the information world accurately analyzes the statuses of the physical world and makes the control decisions instantly. Secondly, the control decisions of the information world real-timely and correctly control the behaviors of the physical world through coordinated implementation of networked Control systems and actuators.

In a word, CPS is high integration of computational resources and physical system, not only has the perception, but can realize control. The long-term development target of CPS is to be the foundation of all large-scale industrial systems. And every industry such as traffic, logistics, manufacturing, energy, health care, etc., will become a subsystem of the unified CPS. Along with the further study on CPS, all systems could be linked to a larger network through the CPS in the near future. Therefore, CPS will become another field technology revolution after Internet.

3   Theory and Realization of CPTS

3.1   CPTS Architecture

There are two goals for constructing CPTS: Firstly, using of all kinds of intelligent technology to realize the global optimization the of traffic system. The targets of optimization mainly include improving traffic efficiency, reduce transportation cost, reduce traffic pollution, etc, which mainly achieve through controlling and coordinating traffic elements such as traffic equipments, transportation nodes, transportation subsystems, etc. The second goal is improving the service level of the whole transport system.Providing intelligent decision-making and optimization control service functions though realizing the control and collaboration of traffic elements. Getting rid of traffic congestion and service level lower of current transport system and improving the traffic system service level. According to the goal of CPTS, referencing the research achievements of Y. Tan[5], we construct the system structure of CPTS, as Figure 2 shows.

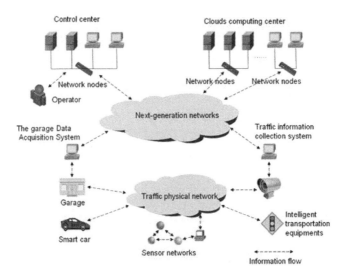

Fig. 2. Architecture of the cyber physical traffic system

3.2   The Compositions of CPTS

The CPTS mainly composes of control center, cloud computing center (distributed computing system, various calculation equipments), traffic net- works (traffic equipments, transport- tation nodes, transport subsystems) and communication networks.

Control Center

Control center is the core of the CPTS, mainly used to control the operation of traffic system. Its functions mainly include collect data of the traffic system acquired by kinds of information detecting devices; set up traffic system simulation model according to the data of the control center, generation system virtual mirror, and constantly updated; analyze the simulation model, and generating control commands based on analysis fruits, control of all kinds of transportation subsystem and transport- ation equipments, and modify the traffic equipments controller parameters when necessary. The control center inter- connects with other traffic subsystems through the communication network in order to realize the whole systems cooperation. In order to get meteoro- logical information related to transport- ation operation, Of course, the control center generally connects with meteoro- logical database through the Internet.

To realize the above functions, control center need exchange inform- ation with information collection system, calculation system and other industry system. Therefore, must have an open system integration platform, which can flexibly access all kinds of complicated heterogeneous system. CPTS has a variety of equipments, only using traditional centralized control methods will bring heavy load to control center, and serious influence the system efficiency. Therefore, we need increase intelligence embedded control equip- ments in the traffic devices to realize local control. Through the coordinate centralized control with distributed control, finally realizes the global optimal control of the traffic system. Finally, because of the control precision of the CPTS always been effected by the accuracy of virtual mirror, once the mirror is error, then control instructions will arise serious deviation with the actual situation. This requires the control center is the ability of the actual synchronization, namely physical systems and virtual image to be automatic mapping, to remain consistent. Therefore, to remain consistent, physical systems and virtual images must be able to automatic mapping.

Cloud Computing Center

Cloud computing center is mainly used to calculate and analyze physics system and simulation model, and provides reference data for traffic optimal control. Usually, computing center and control center is put together as a key processing unit, but because we choose cloud computing model as the computing center of CPTS, a lot of computing devices scattered in the CPS, which arent physically concentrated together, so they are respectively listed as separate part of the system. To realize accurate simulation and control, the data processing ability and calculation of CPTS are amazing, and traditional central calculation mode can't satisfy the requirements. Using cloud computing center[6,7] which based on the large-scale distributed computing technology, we can integrate all kinds of heterogeneous computing devices, get the strong computing power. At the same time cloud computing model has strong scalability, and constantly update and upgrade the computing power to meet the expansion of the transportation system. In addition, the distributed computing model of cloud calculative tallies with the CPTS characteristics that need Combination of Centralized control and distributed control. Completing the analysis of local subsystems and equipments by the dispersed computing devices, realize the distributed control and reduce the load of the control center.

Traffic Physical Network

In the traffic running processes, there are a lot of traffic equipments, transportation nodes and transport subsystems, which make up the traffic physical network. The network also is the data sources and control object of control center. Data of the traffic physical network is mainly acquired through various sensors. For example, using RFID collects information in and out of the garages, using GPS collects the location information of the transportation, using the monitors collect traffic information, etc. The status of the transportation network will changing, transportation equipments, as well as the corresponding sensors access should have flexible and dynamic character- istics. This can achieve by dynamic network of CPS. That is assigned a unique network address for each access to physical devices of the CPS, in order to achieve the automatic search and identification of the physical device. To realize the intelligent control of the traffic physical network, control modules must be embedded in the transportation equipments and intelligent transportation devices must be designed.

Communications Network

CPTS communications network mainly includes three parts of the private network, Internet and wireless networks. Private network used to connect the control center and cloud computing centers, as well as the core of the sensing / control nodes. The private network can significantly reduce communication latency and improve transmission reliability, to meet the real-time requirements of systems analysis and control. Internet network used to connect to real-time less demanding non-critical equipment and systems, such as data backup systems, and customer evaluation system. The wireless network used to connect the activities of transportation equipment such as vehicles and vehicles, vehicles with roadside fixed facilities.

Due to the CPTS communication network contains a variety of different networks, their respective communi- cation protocols are not the same. To achieve a seamless connection between these networks, we must first solve the heterogeneity of the network. Of course, this requires a new network technology to achieve. Currently academia has been proposed for CPS communication protocol stack, the six layers of communication protocol stack, such as the CPS-IP[8] and CPI[5] (Cyber Physical the Internet).

3.3   The Key Technologies of the CPTS

Compared with existing inform- ation systems and physical systems, CPTS will be achieved based on the following key technologies.

Global Optimization and Local Control of Collaborative Technology

CPTS ultimate goal is to achieve global optimal control of the entire system. Control objective is to improve system efficiency, reduce transport costs and reduce environmental pollution, etc. Since the number of devices of the future CPTS will significantly more than the current traffic system and the amount of computation required to achieve optimal control will be very alarming. Therefore, to solve the problem, we can not completely rely on centralized control, but combine centralized control with decentralized control. CPTS local control the physical device through a variety of embedded control systems. Control center can coordinate the whole system by adjust the parameters of the control system and direct control of the physical device where necessary. How to design more flexible and effective control system to achieve optimal coordination of global optimization and local control is the primary technical problem to be solved of the CPTS.

Real-Time Computing and mass- ive Information Processing Technology

In order to ensure the accuracy of the physical system image, on the one hand, requirements of the CPS system has high computing speed and reaction speed, the other hand, requirements of the CPS system acquires and processes of comprehensive and detailed informa- tion of the physical system. These are high demands on computing and information processing capabilities of CPS. Traditional centralized computing platforms is difficult to meet this requirement, new computing technology based on large-scale distributed computing technologies should be considered to build the computing platform of the CPS, such as cloud computing technology.

Dynamic Internet Technology

Due to the flexibility of the physical system, the link between the various components of the CPS is usually dynamic, which is very different from existing physical system fixed networking. CPTS, for example, includes not only the stations, car parks and other stationary facilities, more importantly, also includes moving vehicles. These devices access to the CPS system through the wireless network, but the location of its connection status, and access network will continue to change. Therefore, the dynamic network (Ad-hoc Network)[9] will become important technical foundation of the CPS.

Self-organizing and Adaptive Technology

As mentioned earlier, CPS will be a cover of the giant system of regional and even national, even if the number of access devices in individual sectors CPS systems is still very large, then the implementation of a simple manual management is clearly not feasible. Therefore, the CPS should have the function of self-organization. CPTS, for example, should be able to automatically search for and identify the vehicles that access to the system, when vehicles leave the station or car park, the control center will be able to immediately get the real-time status of the vehicles, and be able to guide the vehicle to choose the best path to destination based on traffic conditions, vehicle route scheduling at any time. In addition, the CPS also should have an adaptive function, that the CPS should have the ability to automatically exclude a variety of system failures (including the failure of the physical system failure and information systems) to ensure the ability of the system during normal operation.

4   Research Techniques and Methods of CPTS

4.1   CPTS Modeling Approach

The depth integration of traffic information systems and traffic opera- tion system is the most significant characteristics of the CPTS, but also the most important technical problems. The current theoretical system is difficult to solve this problem, this is because the information systems general information /event-driven, their theory is based on discrete mathematics. System modeling tools are generally discrete mathematical tools, such as finite state machine (FSM) [10]. The theoretical basis of the traffic operation systems, such as vehicle control systems, vehicle induction systems, etc. are continuous mathema- tics, modeling tools are generally of algebraic equations and differential equations. The significant differences between theoretical basis and modeling approach are the root causes of two areas separated, traffic operations and information systems. In addition, due to the requirements for real-time, Traffic operation system model generally uses the time as an explicit variable to express the order of the transport process. In contrast, due to information system less demands real-time, its Model generally do not explicitly indicates the time, but directly indicates the order of events or computing instructions. Therefore, the most critical and most urgent task to study CPTS is establishes a unified model of information systems and operations systems. New theories and models must adapt to the characteristics of the CPTS that coexistence of continuity and discreteness. New theories and models must be both explicit characterization of the physical system of time-domain information, but also explicit characteri- zation of the execution order of the information system. In CPYS, the system simulation model, the massive information gathering, scheduling algorithms, optimal control research will be built on this new theory.

4.2   Massive Information Collect- ion Technology

Massive information collection is the basis of the CPTS to cognize traffic physical network and build simulation model. The CPTS massive information collection process faces a number of bottlenecks, and future research focuses on how to achieve efficient and real-time traffic information collection. As follows:

Distributed Data Acquisition and Storage

There are a lot of information collection points in the process of vehicle out of the garage, driving and into the garage. If we adopting the traditional centralized acquisition program, always cause some single points of failure and load imbalance. CPTS can adopt distributed information collection and storage mode. Dynamic adjust of the information collection tasks and save the amount of data according to acquisition node load levels to enhance the efficiency of information collection

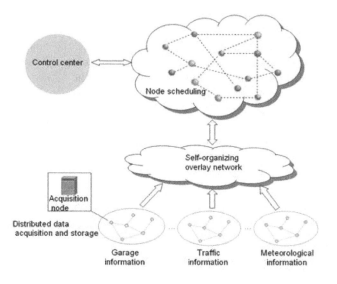

Fig. 3. The framework of traffic information acquisition technology

Self-organizing Overlay Network

Traffic information is usually derived from different types of systems, for example, parking lot information is usually derived from the RFID, vehicle location information is usually derived from the GPS and meteorological information is derived from the Internet. These systems are often heterogeneous. In the future, we need to study how to build self-organizing overlay network with guaranteed quality of service (QOS). The purposes are shielding the underlying heterogeneous network and providing a transparent interface and platform for data acquisition.

Strategic Distribution Technology

In order to adapt to the characteristics of distributed data acquisition, further research is required to research strategic distribution tech -nology under the conditions of complex communications networks, such as the Internet networks, private networks, wireless networks, etc. Ensure that the information acquisition and storage tasks quickly and timely received by the distributed terminal and enhanced real-time data acquisition.

4.3 Optimization Method of CPTS

The role of CPTS optimized method is based on the collected information and the model of CPTS, to obtain the optimal decision-making programs and provide a reference for CPTS controlling traffic system. Traditional transport system optimi- zation methods are mostly used methods such as mathematical programming, operations research, computer simula- tion, which are required improvements and upgrades to accommodate the real- time and dynamic characteristics of CPTS.

Due to the changes of user demand, the uncertainty of the traffic conditions, extreme weather disasters and other reasons, the operation of the transport system has a strong uncertainty. Taking into account of the openness of CPTS various types of transport elements can be flexible access to transport system, so in order to meet system reliability requirements, the future CPTS optimization should be greater use of stochastic.

Conditions of the vast amounts of information, the traditional optimization computation method is not efficient, which needs to spend a lot of time to get the calculated results can not meet the requirements of real-time CPTS. Therefore, the computing model and the algorithm framework need to improve and perfect, even proposing new optimization theories and methods. Due to the superiority of the cloud computing model in the calculation of performance, future researches can focus on the development of distributed optimization methods which suit for the cloud computing model[11].

4.4   Control Technology of CPTS

In CPTS, the control center can choose to directly control each traffic device, and can also choose to indirect control equipments, is only responsible for setting the control parameters and updating the control system, main control tasks completed by human. The control method selected by the level of intelligent transportation equipments. The level of control ability of CPTS is closely related to the intelligence of transport equipments. For an ordinary vehicle, the control center can only complete the simple monitoring and recording, but for a smart car which used GPS technology, the control center is able to complete the complex control , such as out of the garage, vehicle location, route scheduling. To improve control capability of CPTS, the intelligent design and manufacture of transport equipments is an important research direction.

5   The Analysis of CPTS Future Development Path

CPTS will be moving in the direction of the final highly intelligent transport, provide protection for the realization of efficient, economic, modern environmental protection traffic system. With the propulsion and appli- cation of CPS step by step, Transport facilities performance will greatly improve, will basically meet the social demand for transport services growing. The future path development of CPTS will be divided into three stages.

The first stage: Laying soft and hard infrastructure for CPTS develop- ment. Due to the development of China's intelligent transportation is too late, the penetration rate of automation, intelligent technology and equipment is too low. Therefore, to develop CPTS, first and foremost to solve are the developments of soft and hard infrastructure issues. At this stage, accurate acquisition devices and identity devices for transportation information need arranged uniformly. Ensure information exchange and control identify of CPTS. Efforts to resolve the major intelligence algorithms involved in the processing and computing problems as well as the establishment of modern transportation standard revision mechanism. And provide technical supports for the application of CPTS.

The second stage: Promote the healthy development of the industry chain, to build a service business model based on promote. Pre-based bedding, traffic information and standardization will rapidly enhance the initial establishment of related industries layout. After the pre-basis bedding, information and standardization of traffic will be improved rapidly and related industries layout initially established. The main work of this phase is to rely on the Internet and mobile communication network to carry out the testing and application demonstration of the Intelligent Transportation business. Focus on the combination of the introduction of advanced technology and innovation. Promote the absorption and re-innovation for introduction tech- nology. Concentrate on tackling a number of common key technologies that restrict the development of CPTS, efforts to promote the nurturing of the standard system and the industrial chain to form a sound development of commercial models. The goal of this stage is basically established technology R&D and industry development layout of CPTS.

The third stage: Build open and universal intelligent transportation service system. At this stage, the key technical issues of CPTS will be comprehensive broken through and grasped, and independent and controllable intelligent transportation industry chain will be basically taken shape. As the next-generation information network infrastructure is basically formed, at this stage the main work will be building the open universal intelligent transportation system. The global optimization of the whole transport system will be achieved by the combination of intelligent transportation technology, digital technology and networking technology. This stage the development and application of CPTS is basically sound, and the sustainable development of intelligent transportation will be basically realized.

6   Summary

Cyber-physical system (CPS) is a system closely integrated of information world and physical world. Real-time monitoring, analysis and control of large-scale interconnected physical systems are achieved by organic integration and depth collaboration of computing, communications and control. CPS is considered the direction of development of future large-scale industrial systems. The future transpor- tation system should have more functions, more accurate decision-making, better compatibility and scalability. Based on the above considerations, this paper puts forward the basic system of CPTS. On the one hand, the global optimum of the whole transport system is achieved by CPTS controls the physical traffic network. On the other hand, the service level of the whole transport system is enhanced by the realization of the synergy of the transport elements.

CPTS is a new area of research, a large number of theoretical and technical issues to be resolved. This article discusses the important issues to be resolved in the CPTS study, from the aspects of the system model, informa- tion acquisition technology, the system optimization method and the system control technology.

References

1. National Science Foundation of the United States,
   http://www.nsf.gon/pubs/2010/nsf10515/nsf10515.htm
2. Lee, A.: Cyber Physical Systems: Design Challenges. In: 11th IEEE International Symposium on Object Oriented Real-Time Distributed Computing, pp. 363–369 (2008)
3. Li, J.-Z., Gao, H., Yu, B.: Cyber-physical Systems: Concepts, Characteristics, Challenges and Research progress. In: 2009 China Computer Science and Technology Development Report of China Computer Federation Collection, pp. 1–20 (2009)
4. Wang, Z.-J., Xie, L.-L.: Cyber-physical Systems: A Survey. Acta Automatica Sinica 37, 1157–1166 (2011)
5. Tan, Y., et al.: A prototype architecture for Cyber-Physical Systems. ACM SIGBED Review 5, 1–2 (2008)
6. Zhao, J.-H., Wen, F.-S., Xue, Y., et al.: Cloud Computing: Implementing an Essential Computing Platform for Future Power Systems. Automation of Electric Power Systems 34, 1–8 (2010)
7. FOSER I, ZHAO Y, RAICU I, et al: Cloud computing and grid computing 360-degree compared. In: Proceedings of Grid Computing Environments Workshop, pp.1–10. USA (2008)
8. Lin, S., et al.: CPS-IP: Cyber Physical System sinter connection protocol. ACM SIGBED Review 84, 1090–1123 (1996)
9. Koubaa, A., Anderson, B.: A vision of Cyber Physical Internet. In: Proceedings of the Workshop of Real-Time Networks, Dublin, Ireland, pp. 1–6 (2009)
10. Lee, D., Yannakakis, M.: Principles and methods of testing finite state machines-a survey. Proceedings of the IEEE 5, 1–2 (2008)
11. Members of EGEE-II. An EGEE comparative study: grids and clouds-evolution or revolution, http://edms.cern.ch/document/925013/

An Energy Efficiency Evaluation Model Based on the Mechanical Work System⋆

Xianjin Xia, Shining Li, Zhigang Li, and Hao Chen

School of Computer,
Northwestern Polytechnical University,
Xi'an, P.R. China
{jinchenxia,lishining}@mail.nwpu.edu.cn,
lzg.nwpu@yahoo.com.cn

Abstract. Energy efficiency is a key issue in wireless sensor networks. Researches on the energy efficiency evaluation models could promote the development and application of WSN. In this paper, wireless sensor network was modeled as a mechanical work system whose work-efficiency was defined as the metric to measure energy efficiency. In addition, our model introduced a power aggregation function and utility function to filter out application-specific features. Then, based on these models and metrics, we proposed a general framework to evaluate energy efficiency and applied relative energy consumption to measure the operational cost of heterogeneous nodes. Furthermore, we constructed two metrics, average energy discharge rate and energy entropy, to quantitatively measure a systems energy consumption status. The effectiveness of our evaluation model and metrics had been validated by the simulation results.

Keywords: heterogeneous WSN, energy efficiency evaluation, do-work model, energy discharge rate, energy entropy.

1 Introduction

With the capability of data sensing, processing and communicating, WSN can be used to continuously monitor a target area. WSN had experienced a rapid research and development period in the last decade and had been widely applied in areas such as environment monitoring, events detection and target tracking [1]. It exhibited many advantages over traditional network technologies. However, many potential users are reluctant to apply WSNs into their application systems for a lack of effective ways to evaluate WSNs performance [2]. In other words, it is difficult to convince the customers that a specific WSN system can fulfill their application requirements.

Some metrics are needed to quantitatively measure WSNs performance and objectively reflect how well a WSN system fulfills the application requirements.

⋆ This paper is supported by Chinese National Key Science and Technology Special Projects (2012ZX03005007).

R. Wang and F. Xiao (Eds.): CWSN 2012, CCIS 334, pp. 501–515, 2013.
© Springer-Verlag Berlin Heidelberg 2013

Hence, in order to improve a WSN systems energy efficiency, we should concentrate on the performance measurement and evaluation systems (PMES). Generally, a WSN PMES is composed with a couple of metrics and relevant methods to measure and evaluate the system performance.

Article [2] had investigated the challenges and performance issues in WSN applications. The issues were divided into six categories, namely system construction cost, reliability, energy efficiency, interoperability, usability and security. Energy efficiency is a hot research topic, however, most researches were concentrating on energy-saving strategies [3] [4] [5]. The community calls upon systematic approaches to evaluate WSNs energy efficiency.

In this paper, we modeled WSN as a mechanical system and applied a do-work model to analyze its energy efficiency which was measured by the virtual mechanical systems work-efficiency. Then, based on the do-work model, we proposed a general framework to evaluate the energy efficiency of wireless sensor networks. Finally, two simulations were conducted to validate the proposed model and framework. The simulation results can be used as a guidance to effectively deploy a network. Specifically, in order to cope with WSNs energy heterogeneity [10], we introduced relative energy consumption as a uniform metric to measure the operational costs of different nodes. And consequently, the energy consumption status of a WSN system can be indicated by two quantities, energy discharge rate and energy entropy, whose characteristics are demonstrated by the simulation results. The experiment results exhibited that nodes energy discharge rates are approximate to nodes lifetime reciprocals. The results also validate that the energy consumption status of a heterogeneous WSN can be effectively reflected by the networks average energy discharge rate and energy entropy, which can be further applied to analyze the energy efficiency and lifetime of a WSN system.

In the remaining parts of this paper, section 2 reviewed the metrics to measure WSN energy efficiency. The system model is presented in section 3. In section 4, we proposed two quantitative metrics, energy discharge rate and energy entropy, and presented a general framework based on the do-work model to evaluate the energy efficiency of heterogeneous WSN. In section 5 and section 6, two experiments were conducted and the simulation results were presented to validate the proposed energy efficiency metrics and evaluation framework. Finally, we concluded the paper and introduced some further work.

2   Related Works

The energy efficiency of a WSN system can be evaluated with three major approaches namely simulation, experiment measurement and theoretical analysis. And the metrics to measure energy efficiency are the key points of these evaluation methods.

Article [3] and [6] proposed EPUB (energy per useful bit) to measure the energy efficiency of physical protocols. EPUB can be divided into two parts, synchronization cost and load cost per useful bit. The energy costs of communication synchronization are shared with each useful bit. EPUB can guide the design and optimization of physical-layer communication protocols; however, its measurement value depends on the radio hardware.

The impacts of radio circuit power on communication energy costs were investigated in article [7]. In the article, EPTD (energy consumption per unit transmit distance) was proposed to measure the energy efficiency of communication in multi-hop clustered MIMO system and expressed by communication energy consumption and transmit distance. The problem of energy efficient communication was modeled as a two-dimension optimization problem. As with EPUB, EPTD measures the absolute energy consumptions, so, it cannot be applied directly in heterogeneous WSN systems.

In article [8], the operational costs of WSN were described with OCPT (the cost of operation per unit time), which had taken the systems running and maintaining cost into consideration. In the article, nodes operational costs were defined as random variables, and then the systems OCPT can be calculated statistically.

Article [9] reviewed the metrics used to measure the energy efficiency of general information systems. Generally, these metrics were defined by the relation between the whole energy consumption and the effective energy consumption, or by the relation between the energy consumption and achievable system performance. Comparing with the research of green chemistry, article [10] ascertained the limitation and scope of green computing. In the article, factors related to not only the computer system itself, but also the society, people and natural environment were taken into consideration. However, these metrics were only proposed qualitatively, and they were not specifically defined for WSN systems.

Lifetime is a general metric for the measurement of WSN energy performance. It is also constructed as the objective function of many energy efficient strategies. Lifetime is defined with different forms, which are usually application-specific. In article [11], the author presented a general lifetime evaluation framework, which introduced a utility function to measure WSN systems functionality. The utility function was able to define the bounds of network lifetime according to specific application requirements.

Isabel Dietrich surveyed many widely used lifetime definitions in [12]. Additionally, a uniform lifetime definition paradigm was defined based on the formal quantification of criteria affect the network lifetime. In such a definition, the lifetime expression can be applied to various application scenarios by adjusting criteria coefficients.

Article [13] investigated the spatial-temporal distribution of network lifetime to comprehensively explore the energy efficiency of several routing protocols. However, network lifetime spatial-temporal distribution was proposed as an experimental evaluation framework rather than a specific performance metric in the literature.

In general, the energy efficiency metrics presented above are vulnerable to be influenced by the nodes hardware platforms and simulation models, thus they are not suitable to evaluate, especially compare, different strategies energy efficiency. Although lifetime is a general energy performance metric, it is unable to indicate the instant energy consumption status of a WSN system. Moreover, the evaluation of operational energy costs should be independent with nodes hardware platform. In this paper, we take energy heterogeneity into consideration, and measure the operational cost with relative energy values. Additionally, to indicate a WSN systems energy consumption status, we propose two metrics, namely average energy discharge rate and energy entropy, whose effectiveness had been validated by our simulations.

3   System Models

WSNs are usually deployed in or near the physical phenomenon. To complete a monitoring task, senor nodes are collaborated to transmit the sensed data to the sink. Any WSN application systems are composed with software, hardware and a resident environment. Any software operations are finally mapped onto a series of hardware actions; with the execution of these hardware actions, energies are consumed, but the amount of consumed energy is largely influenced by the environment in which the WSN located. So, in a WSN system, energy is directly consumed by the hardware, however, radically, they are determined by software logics.

We assume that the WSN is heterogeneous. Sensor nodes may be equipped with different types of hardware, and consequently, have different power attributes. These nodes are assigned with different tasks and initial energy. In this section, we formally present the WSN system model, which constitute the basis for the energy efficiency evaluation discussed in the next section.

Generally, the hardware components of a node can work in various modes with different power consumption and operational abilities. We denote $HW = \{hw_1, hw_2, \cdots, hw_n\}$ as the set of all the hardware components, each component is associated with several attributes describing the available working modes, the relevant power consumption and operation capability. The attribute can be denoted by $hwp =< M, P, C >$. Then, we introduce the symbol HP, $HP = \{hwp\}$, as the set of all attributes associated with hardware components of nodes in the WSN.

The software running on sensor nodes can be regarded as an operation sequence which is composed by a couple of operation elements. We define OP as the set of all elemental operations, then the software program can be denoted by $SW = \{a\}$, where $a \in OP^*$. SW is the set of languages with alphabet OP.

To deal with the network heterogeneity, we assign each node with an attribute. Then, we introduce PN as the set of all the nodes attributes. So, $PN = \{pn\}$, $pn =< 2^{HW}, SW, HP, E_0, F_m >$, where E_0 is a nodes initial energy; F_m, defined as $F_m : HW \rightarrow 2^{HP}$, associate a hardware component with its hardware attributes.

The WSN system we concerned is composed by n nodes deployed in a target area, and the nodes set can be denoted by $S = \{N_1, N_2, \cdots, N_n\}$. So, finally, the WSN system model is formally defined as $SN =< S, E, T, PN, EC, F_n, F_t >$, where E, $E \subset S \times S$, is the collection of communication links, $F_n : S \rightarrow PN$

assign each node with an attribute, T is the environment where the WSN system resident in. F_t, $F_t : M \times T \rightarrow EC$, defines the impact of environment T on nodes hardware energy consumption, given that the operation cost of a hardware component with mode M can be randomly influenced by the environment and EC is the distribution function family of operational energy consumption.

4   Energy Efficiency Evaluation Model

Based on the system models presented in the previous section, we regard the operational patterns of data sensing and uploading in WSN as a process of doing work in a mechanical system. Thus, we apply the working efficiency of the mechanical system to indicate the WSN systems energy efficiency. In this section, we formally define the energy efficiency evaluation model based on the do-work paradigm, and then introduce several metrics to measure a WSN systems instant energy consumption status. Finally, we integrate the model and metrics, and propose a general energy efficiency evaluation framework.

4.1   Energy Efficiency Model

Maximizing the network lifetime as well as providing the essential system performance is an important principle in WSN energy optimizations. According to this principle, our model evaluates WSNs energy efficiency with a brand-new perspective. The WSN system is modeled as a mechanical work system.

Our model constructs a virtual mechanical work system M for the target WSN. So, WSNs *essential system performance* can be defined as the rated power of M, $P_r(t)$, and then network lifetime T can be mapped to the effective working time of M. As it is equivalent to the work in the virtual mechanical system, the service capability a WSN may provide is defined as the *work of WSN* in the model.

$$W = \int_0^T P_r(t)\mathrm{d}t \tag{1}$$

The expression of $P_r(t)$, which is determined by specific application requirements, can be constructed with criteria such as data sensing rate, real time requirements, network coverage, connectivity, etc. The formula also indicates that the work of WSN can be increased by prolonging the network lifetime T. Application tasks are assigned to each node according to nodes locations and capabilities, then, we define the *rated power* of a node, $P_r(n,t)$, as

$$P_r(n,t) = f(n, P_r(t)) \tag{2}$$

where $n \in S$, $f(\cdot)$is an ideal task assigning function which can minimize WSN's energy consumption.

Given a WSN system sn, $sn \in SN$, $P_s(n,t)$ is the actual working power of node n, then the actual working power of the WSN system is

$$P_s = \oplus_{n \in S} P_s(n,t) \tag{3}$$

where $\oplus$ is a power aggregation rule determined by sn.

In realistic application systems, an excessively high WSN working power $P_s(t)$ contributes little to improve system performance. On the contrary, it means more energy consumption and nodes failure, which leads to the declining of system performance. Similar with WCOT [9], we introduce utility function $U(P_s)$ to uniformly measure the impacts of WSN actual working power P_s on system performances. $U(P_s)$ will be used as a weight function while calculating WSNs effective work.

$$U(P_s) = \begin{cases} 1, & P_s \geq P_r \\ g\left(\frac{P_s}{P_r}\right), & \text{else} \end{cases} \tag{4}$$

where $g(\cdot)$ is an application-specific function valued within $[0, 1]$.

Given T_s denotes the network lifetime of sn, then sn's energy efficiency can be defined as its working efficiency,

$$\eta = \frac{W_r}{W_s} = \frac{\int_0^{T_s} U(P_s) \cdot P_r(t) \mathrm{d}t}{\int_0^{T_s} P_s(t) \mathrm{d}t} \tag{5}$$

where W_r is the effective work being done by sn during its lifetime T_s, W_s is sn's actual energy consumption within T_s.

4.2   Performance Metrics

The software, hardware and environment jointly lead to WSNs energy heterogeneity, which is the major challenge faced in the process of energy efficiency evaluation. To tackle this problem, we introduce relative energy consumption and propose average energy discharge rate, energy entropy as the metrics to indicate WSNs instant energy consumption status.

1) Relative energy consumption

Given a WSN system sn, $sn \in SN$, instead of the absolute energy an operation consumes, we prefer to considering how many operations can be conducted by a node. Thus, we uniformly set each nodes initial energy to 1, and defined the relative energy consumption of operation op as

$$\xi_{op} = \frac{F_t(n.hw.m, env)}{n.e_0} \tag{6}$$

where $F_t(n.hw.m, env)$ represents the energy consumption of op conducted by hw in an environment t, $n.e_0$ is the initial energy of n.

2) Energy discharge rate

We define a nodes accumulated relative energy consumption as

$$E_n(t) = \frac{\int_0^t P_s(n, t) \mathrm{d}t}{n.e_0} = \sum_{i=1}^{N(t)} \xi_{op_i} \tag{7}$$

where $N(t)$ is the number of executed operations within time range $[0, t]$. In order to prolong network lifetime, each node should dissipate its energy in a synchronized pace. So, we introduce energy discharge rate, γ, to indicate a nodes energy consumption status.

$$\gamma_n(t) = \frac{E_n(t)}{t} \tag{8}$$

3) WSNs Energy consumption status

We define the energy consumption status of a WSN system, Ω, as all nodes energy discharge rate at time t.

$$\Omega(t) = (\gamma_1(t), \gamma_2(t), \cdots, \gamma_n(t)) \tag{9}$$

At any time, a nodes energy discharge rate is a random variable, denoted with Γ. Then, a WSN systems energy consumption status can also be represented by the with distribution function of Γ, $F_\Gamma(t)$, where $F_\Gamma(t) \in F_\Gamma^*$, F_Γ^* is the distribution function family of Γ. Thus, $\Omega(t)$ can be regarded as a sampling of Γ at t.

4) Energy entropy

The Expectation and Variance of Γ can also be jointly applied to reflect a WSN systems energy consumption status. In such a circumstance, $E(\Gamma_t)$ is the average energy consumption rate of all nodes in a WSN at t, and $Var(\Gamma_t)$ represents the synchronizing pace of nodes energy discharging rates. In the model, to indicate the degree of energy discharging consistency, we define energy entropy, H, for a WSN system.

$$H(\Gamma_t) = - \sum_{i=1}^{M(\Omega(t))} p(\gamma_{m(i)}) \cdot \ln p(\gamma_{m(i)}) \tag{10}$$

where $M(\Omega(t))$ is the number of mutually different energy consumption rate in $\Omega(t)$, $p(\gamma_{m(i)})$ is the probability of i'th energy consumption rate in the sorted $\Omega(t)$. $E(\Gamma_t)$ and $H(\Gamma_t)$ almost incorporate all the information contained in the three metrics defined previously, so they can jointly indicate the instant energy consumption status of a WSN system.

4.3   Energy Efficiency Evaluation Framework

Applying the proposed models and metrics, we can evaluate the energy efficiency of any WSN systems with the following five steps.

Step 1: measuring a nodes accumulated relative energy consumption

Sensor nodes are usually powered by batteries whose supply voltage can be considered as a constant value. So, the actual working power of n, $n \in S$, can be calculated by $P_s(n, t) = U(n) \cdot I(n, t)$. Hence, the current draw from nodes battery, $I(n, t)$, is the only quantity needed to be physically measured. Then, we can compute the accumulated relative energy consumption with formula 7.

Step 2: calculating the distribution function of Γ

Applying formula 8 and 9 to the raw data get in step 1, we can collect each nodes accumulated relative energy consumption $E_n(t)$, which is the statistical sample of $\Omega(t)$. Furthermore, we can calculate the probability of each Γ's sample value. Thus, the empirical distribution function of Γ, which is the approximate of Γ's distribution function, can be calculated.

Step 3: computing WSNs actual working power P_s

The actual working power of a WSN system can be aggregated from each nodes working power, $P_s(n,t)$, which is contained in $\Omega(t)$. Thus, $P_s(t)$ can be computed as

$$P_s(t) = \Phi\left(E(\Gamma_t), H(\Gamma_t)\right) \tag{11}$$

where $\Phi(\cdot)$ is power aggregation function determined by the application requirements. At any time, WSNs actual working power is a function of average energy discharge rate and energy entropy. For simplicity, we can quantitatively estimate a WSN systems energy consumption status with $E(\Gamma_t)$ and $H(\Gamma_t)$.

Step 4: defining utility function $U(P_s)$

$U(P_s)$, which is determined by the application, expresses the fulfillment degree of a WSN systems actual working power to its application requirements.

Step 5: calculating energy efficiency η

With the former intermediate results, η can be calculated with formula 5 directly.

This framework provides a general energy efficiency evaluation method for WSN systems. Power aggregation function, $\Phi(\cdot)$, and utility function, $U(\cdot)$, are introduced as an abstraction layer to shield the variances features of WSN systems. Usually, the definitions of these two functions, which are application-specific, are provided by experts in the specific field.

In a realistic situation, energy entropy and average energy discharge rate are already sufficient to estimate a WSN systems energy efficiency. Employing an energy aware design methodology, system designers primarily concern how well a design scheme fulfills the requirements, which usually expressed as a predefined network lifetime. Thus, we propose two more metrics to measure such systems energy efficiency status.

$$L(t) = \frac{1}{LT_0} - E(\Gamma_t) \tag{12}$$

$$S(t) = H(\Gamma_t) \tag{13}$$

Formula 12 defines the degree of relaxation between real WSN systems and their requirements; expression 13 can be used to indicate the stability of WSN nodes energy discharge rates. So, $L(t)$ and $S(t)$ are proposed as a WSN systems relaxation component and stability component respectively.

5   Heterogeneous WSN Energy Consumption Analysis Experiments

In this section, a simulation is conducted to analyze a heterogeneous WSN systems energy consumption status applying the two proposed metrics, energy discharge rate and energy entropy. According to the simulation results, two conclusions can be made: 1) in the lifetime, a heterogeneous WSN system may experience several local stable stages which can be divided by the combinational effects of systems average energy discharge rate and energy entropy; 2) a nodes energy discharge rate is the reciprocal of its lifetime. This experiment had validated the effectiveness of applying average energy discharge rate and energy entropy as the quantitative metrics to measure a WSN systems energy consumption status.

5.1 Simulation Settings

In the simulation, a WSN is randomly deployed in a $200 \times 200m^2$ square area, monitoring three types of environment factors. Sink node is located in the center of the area, receiving data packets periodically reported by other nodes. The WSN is composed by three types of sensor nodes, each of which is responsible for a specific environmental factor. These nodes exhibit different energy profiles, which are listed in table 1 in detail.

The simulation employed the communication energy model proposed in article [14]. The model can be simple expressed as

$$E_{tx} = k_1 + k_2 \cdot d^\gamma$$

$$E_{rx} = k_3$$

Where E_{tx} and E_{rx} is the energy consumed while the radio is transmitting and receiving a bit respectively. k_1, k_2, k_3 and r are parameters determined by the radio hardware and the physical layer communication schemes, so they can be treated as a constant. d is the communication distance. The values of these parameters are listed in table 1 in detail.

Table 1. Simulation parameter settings

Parameters	Node1	Node2	Node3
Energy consumption per operation (data sensing) $(10^{-6}J)$	3000	800	100
Packet size (*bits*)	2000	1500	800
k1 $(10^{-6}J/bit)$	0.5	0.2	0.2
k2 $(10^{-6}J/bit/m^2)$	0.0001	0.0001	0.0001
R	2	2	2
k3 $(10^{-6}J/bit)$	0.5	0.2	0.2
Communication radius (M)	80	40	40
Initial energy (J)	4	1	1
Packet report interval (s)	15	15	15

Considering a low communication rate in the environment monitoring application, we assume that no collisions existed in MAC communications. In the simulation, the FLOODING routing protocol is employed to deliver sensed data to the sink. According to the assumptions and parameter settings, a heterogeneous WSN with 40 nodes is simulated by C++ programs, which record each nodes energy statuses. The simulation results are calculated with formulas presented in section 4.

5.2 Results

The distribution of WSN nodes energy discharge rates is exhibited in Fig. 1. In the simulated network, nodes energy consumption levels can be divided into three major categories with an energy discharge rate of 0.025, 0.04 and 0.09 respectively. This property is determined by sensor nodes heterogeneous hardware components.

Fig. 2 exhibit the energy discharge rates of four typical nodes. A nodes energy discharge rate approaches to a fixed value, α, while the node is in stable working states. This property is determined by the periodic operation pattern in the network. Supported by the data listed in table 2, the following conclusion can be made

$$\alpha = \lim_{t \to \infty} \gamma(t) = \frac{1}{T_i} \tag{14}$$

This expression indicates that a nodes energy discharge rate approaches to the reciprocal of its lifetime. This conclusion can be applied to estimate a WSN systems lifetime via the measurement of each nodes energy discharge rate. Fig. 2 also indicates that the failure of one node might affect the energy discharge rates of other active nodes in the WSN, and the impact degree depends on the roles a node plays.

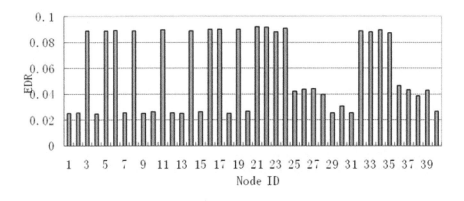

Fig. 1. The energy discharge rates of each node in the WSN

Table 2. A nodes energy discharge rate and its lifetime

Node ID	EDR	lifetime
1	0.025391	39
2	0.090109	11
3	0.030728	32
4	0.046663	21

The curves of average energy discharge rate and energy entropy are showed in Fig. 4 and Fig. 5 respectively. The number of active nodes in the WSN also

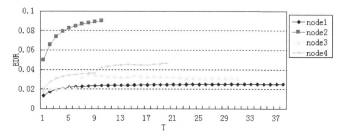

Fig. 2. Node's energy discharge rates vs. time

displays in Fig. 3 as a reference. These results had demonstrated that the WSNs average energy discharge rate was changing in accordance with the number of active nodes. The lifetime of the WSN system had been divided into three major stages by its average energy discharge rate, and the energy entropy of the WSN system is locally convergent in each stage.

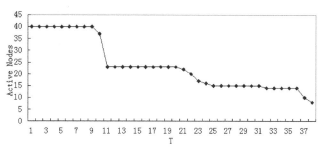

Fig. 3. Active nodes vs. time

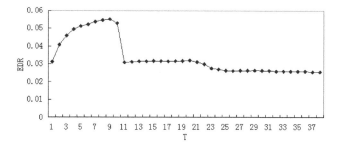

Fig. 4. Energy discharge rate vs. time

Actually, the WSN system exhibited different energy consumption level and service provision capability in each stage. So, average energy discharge rate and energy entropy provided a good criterion for system working stage divisions. As it was shown in the simulation results, the WSN lifetime can be divided into three local stages, range from [1, 10], [11, 24] and [25, 39] respectively. The number of

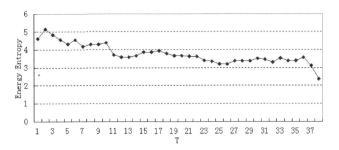

Fig. 5. Energy entropy vs. time

environmental factors the WSN system can be monitored was decreasing from stage to stage. Based on the separated stages, the systems power aggregation function can be defined to evaluate the systems energy efficiency using the model provided in section 4.

6   Energy Efficiency Evaluation Experiments

In this section, we present another simulation applying the do-work model to evaluate the energy efficiency of an environmental monitoring WSN system under different nodes deployment density conditions. The simulation results reveal the relation between energy efficiency and node density and provide guidance for WSN deployments.

6.1   Application Scenario

In the simulation, a WSN was deployed in a target area sized $120 \times 120m^2$ to monitor a single environmental factor. The sink node was located in the center of the area. The sensed data was reported to sink, routed with Gossip protocol, every 15 seconds. The simulation parameters were set by that of Node2 listed in table 1. Every 5 minutes, the application programs conduct a round of computation to estimate the environment status with the data received in the latest time window. The estimation precision is determined by the number of packets received.

Assuming that λ packets are sufficient to achieve the highest estimation precision, the packets received after the essential λ ones make little contribution to the improvement of precision. In this experiment, we define the WSN systems actual working power, P_s, as the number of packets received by sink node within 5 minutes. Thus, the systems power aggregation function can be defined as

$$P_s(t) = \sum_{i=1}^{n} sd(i, t)$$

where $sd(i, t)$ is the number of packets reported to sink by node i during the t'th time slot. Then, we define the utility function as

$$U(P_s) = \begin{cases} 1, & P_s \geq 600 \\ \frac{1}{400}P_s - \frac{1}{2}, & 400 \leq P_s < 600 \\ \frac{1}{80000}P_s^2 - \frac{1}{200}P_s + \frac{1}{2}, & 200 \leq P_s < 400 \\ 0, & P_s < 200 \end{cases}$$

The utility function, $U(P_s)$, is plotted in Fig. 6. According to the energy efficiency model defined in section 4.1, λ is the WSN systems rated working power demanded by the application requirements. Given $\lambda = 600$, then the rated working power is

$$P_r = 600 (packets/5min)$$

The nodes were randomly deployed in the target area. In the experiments, the node density was varied from 0.0007 $(nodes/m^2)$ to 0.006 $(nodes/m^2)$, and the systems energy efficiency was evaluated by the do-work model. We conducted 10 simulations with each simulation settings, and derived the average value to construct the results.

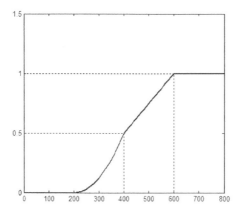

Fig. 6. The utility function, $U(P_s)$

6.2   Results

The relation between energy efficiency and node density is exhibited in Fig. 7, which indicate that the highest energy efficiency is achieved when the node density is around 0.0024 $(nodes/m^2)$. When the node density is less than 0.0024, although the system consumed a small amount of energy, the systems energy efficiency kept low as the sensed data was unable to meet the application demands. And the energy efficiency increased rapidly while the nodes were deployed denser. On the other hand, when the nodes deployed denser than 0.0024 $(nodes/m^2)$, the increased nodes contributed little to the improvement of estimation precision, but brought much more redundant packets which consumed more energy. So, the energy efficiency decreased with the increasing of node density. Hence, in the application scenario, deploying 0.0024 nodes per square meters can not only fulfill the application requirements but also minimize systems energy consumption, and thus yielded best energy efficiency.

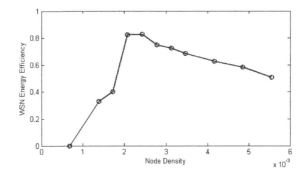

Fig. 7. Energy efficiency vs. nodes density

7   Conclusion

In this paper, we proposed a general energy efficiency evaluating framework applying a do-work model. Our evaluation framework introduced power aggregation function and utility function to shield the application-specific features. To cope with WSNs energy heterogeneity, we defined relative energy consumption, which was independent with nodes hardware platform, to measure the operation cost of different nodes. Then, we proposed two metrics, average energy discharge rate and energy entropy, to quantitatively indicate a WSN systems energy consumption status. The simulation results had demonstrated that the proposed metrics can be employed to identify different system statuses, which can be further applied to the evaluation of energy efficiency.

While applying the do-work model to evaluate a WSN systems energy efficiency, we have to measure each nodes energy discharge rate, which is difficult, almost impossible, to operate in the realistic scenarios. However, the simulation results presented in section 5.2 had demonstrated that each nodes energy discharge rate approaches to the reciprocal of its lifetime. This observation can be used to estimate the network lifetime. In our future work, in order to statistically estimate the network lifetime, we are planning to measure a nodes energy discharge rate in a software-based on-line approach, which is much more operable in the WSN systems.

References

1. Yick, J., Mukherjee, B., Ghosal, D.: Wireless sensor networks survey. Computer Networks 52(12), 2292–2330 (2008)
2. Jang, W.-S., Healy, W.M.: Assessment of Performance Metrics for Use of WSNs in Buildings. In: 26th International Symposium on Automation and Robotics in Construction, ISARC 2009 (2009)
3. Raghunathan, V., Schurgers, C., Park, S., Srivastava, M.B.: Energy-Aware Wireless Microsensor Networks. IEEE Signal Processing Magazine 19(2), 40–50 (2002)

4. Mahfoudh, S., Minet, P.: Survey of energy efficient strategies in wireless ad hoc and sensor networks. In: Seventh International Conference on Networking (2008)
5. Anastasi, G., Conti, M., Di Francesco, M., Passarella, A.: Energy conservation in wireless sensor networks: A survey. Ad Hoc Networks 7(3), 537–568 (2009)
6. Ammer, J., Rabaey, J.: The Energy-per-Useful-Bit Metric for Evaluating and Optimizing Sensor Network Physical Layers. Sensor and Ad Hoc Communications and Networks (2006)
7. Li, B., Wang, W., Yin, Q., Yang, R., Li, Y., Wang, C.: A New Cooperative Transmission Metric in Wireless Sensor Networks to Minimize Energy Consumption per Unit Transmit Distance. IEEE Communications Letters (99), 1–4 (2012)
8. Fonseca Jr., B.J.B., Gubner, J.A.: Operation Cost as a Performance Metric of Wireless Sensor Networks. Statistical Signal Processing (2007)
9. Lin, C., Tian, Y., Yao, M.: Green Network and Green Evaluation: Mechanism, Modeling and Evaluation. Chinese Journal of Computers 34(4), 593–612 (2011)
10. Guo, B., Shen, Y., Shao, Z.-L.: The Redefinition and Some Discussion of Green Computing. Chinese Journal of Computers 32(12), 2311–2319 (2009)
11. Ozgovde, A., Ersoy, C.: WCOT: A utility based lifetime metric for wireless sensor networks. Computer Communications 32(12), 409–418 (2009)
12. Dietrich, I., Dressler, F.: On the Lifetime of Wireless Sensor Networks. ACM Transactions on Sensor Networks 5(1), aticle 5 (2009)
13. Senouci, M.R., Mellouk, A., Senouci, H., Aissani, A.: Performance evaluation of network lifetime spatial-temporal distribution for WSN routing protocols. Journal of Network and Computer Applications (2012)
14. Heinzelman, W.R., Chandrakasan, A., Balakrishnan, H.: Energy-efficient communication protocol for wireless microsensor networks. In: HICSS (2000)

An Energy Efficiency Dynamic Routing Protocol for Farmland Moisture Sensor Networks

Deqin Xiao, Yang Zhang, and Liankuan Zhang

College of Informatics, South China Agricultural University, Guangzhou, 510642, China
{deqinx,yangzhang,zhangliankuan}@scau.edu.cn

Abstract. This article reports an Energy Efficiency Dynamic Routing Protocol for Farmland Moisture Sensor Networks (EEDRP-FMSN) to improve energy efficiency, which combined the characteristics of farmland wireless sensor network deployment model. The EEDRP-FMSN protocol made use of the characteristics that the position of the base station was fixed, and the next hop selection mechanism of the EEDRP-FMSN protocol considered communication quality among nodes, global routing information, residual energy of nodes, and so on. The next hop selection mechanism had the dynamic nature and stronger environmental adaptability to extend the life cycle of network. The EEDRP-FMSN protocol overcomes the shortcoming that capacity and bandwidth of the routing table correspondingly increased with more nodes joining the network. This article also simulated the performance of the EEDRP-FMSN protocol in different conditions and evaluated the performance from energy efficiency, packet energy consumption and packet distribution balance by comparing the EEDRP-FMSN protocol with DSDV, EAP protocols. Simulations indicated that the EEDRP-FMSN had more energy efficiency than the EAP and the DSDV. The EEDRP-FMSN protocol overcame the shortcomings, such as capacity and bandwidth of the routing table increased with more nodes joining the network. It had better scalability, and keeps network loading balance.

Keywords: Computer network, Farmland moisture sensor networks, Dynamic route protocol, Energy efficiency.

1 Introduction

A wireless sensor network (WSN) consists of spatially distributed autonomous sensors to monitor physical or environmental conditions, such as temperature, sound, vibration, pressure, humidity, motion or pollutants and to cooperatively transport their data through the network to a main location. It can acquire a lot of detailed and reliable information at any time, place, and any environmental conditions [1]. Compared to traditional networks, wireless sensor does not require power lines and data lines that it can be applied to many complex areas such as farms, forests, mountains, oceans, and so on [2].

In wireless sensor networks, information is transmitted through the wireless radio channel which is susceptible to signal attenuation, noise, reflection, diffusion, and other factors. These factors result in the signal transmission distance and packet loss rate

R. Wang and F. Xiao (Eds.): CWSN 2012, CCIS 334, pp. 516–524, 2013.
© Springer-Verlag Berlin Heidelberg 2013

and error rate is very unstable, so that the application of wireless sensor networks was subjected to considerable restrictions [3, 4]. Wireless sensor channel was more vulnerable in the external environment than wired networks. Ananstasi's studies confirmed that the communication distance of wireless sensor influenced by rain and fog [5]. The transmission distance of Mica2dot node was 120m in 2.4GHz frequency test, but the transmission distance is only about 10m in fog and heavy rain test. Kang [6] tested the transmission of wireless sensor signals influenced by the weather situation. They pointed out that the wind can make the antenna vibrate, and thus the signal was impacted significantly. Also they pointed out that rain, snow and fog signal cannot be ignored. Information is vulnerable to outside interference in the process of information transmission in the wireless sensor, and an error occurs. Jeong [7] carried out two types of experiments indoor and outdoor, and found the wireless sensor error bit is mostly one and two bits. Also they pointed out that the scheme of 1 and 2-bit linear error-correcting codes is efficient because the multi-hop nature of information transmission in wireless sensor error correction code method the proportion of passes to save energy. Ahn [8] also designed a method of data error correction on FECA algorithm for mobile wireless networks from the packet error rate distance function.

In our first generation sensor networks, we used a simplify energy-efficient static chain routing protocols [9, 10]. It had the fixed next hop node. The data of follow-up nodes couldn't transfer the data to the base station node if a link was disconnected. And the farmland sensor network environment had a lot of uncertain factors, such as poor communication quality, lower correctly rate, and so on. Based on these considerations, this paper drew on the idea of Directed Diffusion protocol and Destination Sequenced Distance Vector (DSDV) protocol. In order to improve network energy efficiency, an Energy Efficiency Dynamic Routing Protocols for Farmland Moisture Sensor Networks (EEDRP-FMSN) was provided basing on the characteristics of farmland wireless sensor network deployment model and the communication quality. EEDRP-FMSN protocol routing has been simplified initialization phase algorithm for its fixed characteristics of the location of the base station node. The EEDRP-FMSN protocol took into account the quality of communication between nodes, the global routing information, the remaining nodes energy, and a number of factors, so that the next hop node had the dynamic and strong environment adaptability for prolonging the network life cycle. The EEDRP-FMSN had better scalability, for no additional energy increase in capacity and bandwidth of the routing tables while more and more nodes joined the network.

2 Systems Engineering Model of EEDRP-FMSN

According to the background of real-time moisture monitoring, and in order to achieve the precise irrigation of farmland, moisture sensor nodes were designed in paper[1]. The main chip of communication module was CC1000. In order to facilitate the description, this paper assumes that the distribution of farmland was a rectangle to ensure that the scope of the coverage-aware and network connectivity. Wireless sensor networks will be deployed in a static grid of rectangular farmlands. Actually, sensor nodes can also be deployed regularly even if in the irregular farmland, so the assumption didn't

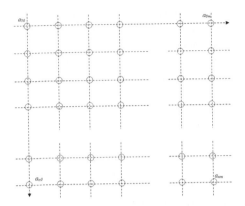

Fig. 1. Deployment model of farmland moisture sensor network

affect the operability. Particularly, all data were sent to the base station eventually. The deployment Topology is shown in Figure 1.

In the figure 1, $a_{i,j}$ was stood an moisture sensor node in FMSN, i was the line number of node, and j was the columns number of node $a_{i,j}$. In which, ($1 \leq i \leq N, 1 \leq j \leq M$), and $a_{0,0}$ was the sink node. According to the background of the practical application environment, there were some other assumptions as follows: (1) the base station was fixed in position $a_{0,0}$; (2) all nodes were loaded with same energy at the beginning; (3) All nodes were static; (4) all nodes knew its own specific location of the network; (5) each node had the ability to calculate data aggregation; (6) sensor networks topology was grid-shaped, each grid had same length x; (7) R was the transmission radius for each sensor node, ($x \leq R$) was required to ensure the routine work.

3 EEDRP-FMSN Routing Protocol Design

3.1 EEDRP-FMSN Routing Protocol Function Modules

There were 6 modules in the EEDRP-FMSN.They were Route Setup Module (RSM), Data Transmission Module (DTM), Next Hop Selection Module (NHSM), Global Route Beacon Module (GRBM), Packet Handle Module (PHM) and Table Handle Module (THM). Figure 2 showed the framework of the EEDRP-FMSN.

EEDRP-FMSN routing protocols layered sensor network in the whole network by flooding Hello packets to establish the gradient field and obtain the node information from a neighbor. The NHSM was the core of the EEDRP-FMSN routing protocols, the module NHSM gave a full consideration to various factors including the status of the quality of communication between nodes, node moisture data packet transmission capacity to the base station node which expressed as the number of global routing beacons, nodes processing ability to send tasks, and probability of node was acted as the next hop node. The DTM stimulated to send moisture packet. When the local node clock Threshold arrived or received water packets from the neighbor, The DTM awaked the next hop, constructed data packets and sent to its next hop. The main function of GRBM was to complete the global routing beacons collections. The base station node would

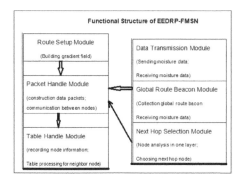

Fig. 2. Functional Structure of EEDRP-FMSN

send a global routing beacon while the water packets reached the base station node, and the beacons were transported reversely along the transmission route of the moisture packets. The PHM was responsible for construction data packets and communication among nodes. The THM was responsible for recording node information and providing data processing for neighbor nodes.

Each round of EEDRP-FMSN routing protocol consisted of two phases of routing updates and data transmission. The establishment of routing and routing updates were built on a gradient field. The base station node didn't require work while EEDRP-FMSN routing protocol processing the abnormal nodes. The NHSM adopted the historical value of the N rounds. The historical value of the abnormal nodes within the past N round would be zero if some node fails. So the NHSM could avoid these abnormal nodes in choosing the next hop. Over a period of time, the terminal could find those abnormal nodes because there was no packets coming from them.

3.2   EEDRP-FMSN Protocol Next Hop Selection Mechanism

Sensor $a_{i,j}$ accorded formula (1) to generate next hop node.

$$A_{one} = \alpha_1 A_{one} + \alpha_2 A_{route} + \alpha_3 E + \alpha_4 C + [\alpha_5] \tag{1}$$

Where, $[\alpha_5]$ was an optional parameter. The first step was computing each node's value P, and then choosing the node of max P. If there were several nodes with the same P, the next hop node was randomly selected from those nodes with same P value. Where, parameters A_{one}, A_{route}, E and C could be calculated separately as follows.

(1)A_{one} was the ratio of the number of the ACK number and the number of total sending packets of node $a_{z,w}$ in N times data packet transmission. The A_{one} reflected their quality of communication channels between two nodes. It showed that the channel quality was relatively poor, or the next hop node was abnormal while A_{one} was relatively small within recent N times. The main reason, we used the last N times transmission instead of using all historical data, was that we could obtain the node changes in a short period. The EEDRP-FMSN routing protocol tried to avoid a node with relatively small A_{one} as a transit node. A_{one} is calculated by the formula (2).

$$A_{one} = \frac{k}{T} \qquad (2)$$

(2) A_{route} was the ratio of the number of beacons and sent packets of the global routing in $a_{z,w}$. Every node recorded the number of global routing beacons from the sink base station node. A_{route} reflected the ability of a node in successful sending. The more A_{route} was, and more possibility for $a_{z,w}$ to select a globally optimal route or close to the global optimum routing. A_{route} was calculated by the formula (3).

$$A_{route} = \frac{s}{t} \qquad (3)$$

Where, s was total number of global routing beacons, t was the number of sent packets.

(3) E was the ratio of $E_{current}$ and E_{init} in node $a_{z,w}$. The node's residual energy represented as an ability of a node in sending packets. The EEDRP-FMSN protocol thought the node which had more residual energy should be responsible for more sending task. E was calculated by the formula (4).

$$E = \frac{E_{current}}{E_{init}} \qquad (4)$$

(4) C was the frequency of next hop nodes of $a_{z,w}$. C was calculated by the formula (5).

$$C = \frac{1}{r} \qquad (5)$$

Where, r was the number of sending packets from node $a_{i,j}$ to node $a_{z,w}$. If $r = 0$, then $C = 1$. The more of r, and the less of C. C showed that the possibility of $a_{z,w}$ was selected.

(5) Each α was a weighting factor according to parameters of A_{one}, A_{route}, E and C.

4   EEDRP-FMSN Routing Protocol Analysis and Test

4.1   Protocol Analysis

Parameter A_{route} influenced by the correct rate of transmission among the nodes; A_{route} influenced by the overall importance in choosing next hop node; E influenced by sending ability of nodes; C influenced by the balance of the node candidate set. The most important work of EEDRP-FMSN routing protocol was provided a transmission selection mechanism for the next hop of. A_{one}, A_{route}, E, C in the formula (1) was on behalf of different influencing factors in EEDRP-FMSN. Combination of weighting factors in the EEDRP-FMSN routing protocol acted as different effects performance.

If A_{one} was the only weight factor, the EEDRP-FMSN could realize the local optimum in figure 3(a). To node $a_{3,3}$, the value A_{one} of node $a_{3,2}$ could ensure the highest success probability between node $a_{3,3}$ and $a_{3,2}$.

The EEDRP-FMSN routing protocol not only considered the single-hop communication ability of sending node and the candidate node, but also the capacity of sending packets from the candidate node to the base station node was considered, so the EEDRP-FMSN ensured that the data packets in the two factors from the sending node

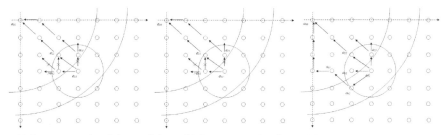

(a) Parameter role of A_{one} and A_{route} (b) Parameter role of E and C (c) Parameter role of α_5

Fig. 3. Role of various parameters in EEDRP-FMSN

to the base station node. Node $a_{2,2}$ was the best next hop of the node $a_{3,3}$ in figure 3 (a). E was the ratio of $E_{current}$ and E_{init} in node $a_{z,w}$. The parameter E was the residual energy of the candidate node, and the parameter C was the number of the sending node. The combination of the two parameters was helpful to choose candidate node in same possibility, so it can balance the network load. For example, $a_{2,2}$ is the best next hop node for $a_{3,3}$ without parameters E and C in Figure 3(b), it resulted in death earlier to $a_{2,2}$ and $a_{1,1}$. $a_{3,2}$ will be the next transfer node of $a_{3,3}$ if parameters E and C were considered, and it can balance the packet distribution. Packet transmission was as far as possible to the edge of the diffusion node under a single hop transmission factor, as shown in Figure 3(c).

4.2   Simulation of Energy Efficiency

In this section, we conducted a performance comparative evaluation among EEDRP-FMSN, DSDV and EAP[11] routing protocol of large-scale network conditions from energy efficiency, the average power consumption of single data packet, the distribution evaluation of the number of packets and the network operating in harsh environments. In this paper, the simulation environment was set to NN nodes in the network that the entire network into a square distribution. The energy of the base station node was supposed to infinite, the wireless sensor networks was sentenced to death after the base station node had no longer received any packet. The simulation results on various aspects of the network were run multiple times. We used the average of the received data by the simulation program. Energy efficiency was expressed by the number of packets which could be handled in a limited energy condition. The most important task in farm-land water sensor networks is to maximize the water data collected from each node. The more packets the base station node have received, the more strong ability the routing protocol had. The numbers of packets received by the base station node were shown in Figure 4 without node abnormalities for three kinds of routing protocol.

From the horizontal view in figure 4, the number of packets received from the base station node was less affected by the size of the network. The packet number of base station node received was about 35,000 under different network size under EEDRP-FMSN routing protocol, the number of receiving packets was about 12000 under DSDV routing protocol, and it was about 29000 under the EAP routing protocol.

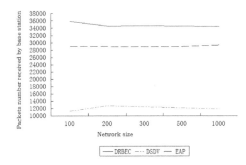

Fig. 4. Amount of packets contrast received by Base station

From the Figure 4, the EEDRP-FMSN route was better than the EAP routing, and EAP route was better than DSDV routing. Additional operating of EEDRP-FMSN routing were the packets of broadcast Hello packets periodically and global routing beacons. Because the EAP routing was a clustering protocol, so it would increase the packet length while data fusion. The Additional consumption operation of the DSDV routing was to exchange routing table among nodes, the larger the network size was, the greater size the routing table was. The EEDRP-FMSN routing took full advantage of the characteristics of the the farmland sensor network. It simplified the network initialization process, deleted the unnecessary operations, and made an additional reduction in energy consumption, So it enhanced the effectiveness of the network energy.

Except for the energy consumption for the normal transmission of moisture packets, there were a series of additional operations, such as the establishment of routing table, packet acknowledgment, packet retransmission, packet transfer, and so on. These additional energy consumptions also related to the performance of the routing protocols. The average energy consumption of a single packet of routing protocols could reflect this performance to some extent, and its formula was given by equation (6).

$$E_{pactet-average} = \frac{E_{total}}{N_{receive}} \qquad (6)$$

Where, $E_{pactet-average}$ was the average packet energy consumption, E_{total} was total energy consumption, $N_{receive}$ was the number of packets received in base station node.

The total energy consumption of the network was the total energy consumption of all nodes until the base station node could not receive any packets in the network.

The average energy consumption of the three routing protocols in a single package was shown in Figure 5 under different network size. The average energy consumption of a variety of routing protocols was increased as the network size increased in Figure 5. The number of packets received by the base station in different network size were shown in Figure 5. Under different network size, the average energy consumption of a single packet in the EEDRP-FMSN route was less than the other two routing protocols. In the case of 1000 nodes, the average energy consumption of the DSDV routing in a single packet rose rapidly, it resulted in the routing table increased rapidly in DSDV routing. This article showed that farmland sensor networks took full advantage of the many-to-one feature to simplify the initialization process than the DSDV routing.

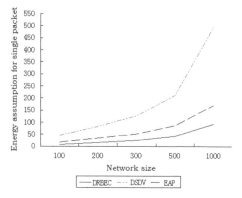

Fig. 5. Average energy consumption comparison in a single packet

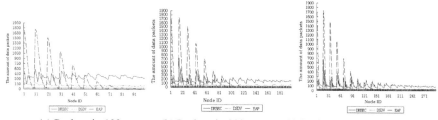

(a) Packets in 100 sensors (b) Packets in 200 sensors (c) Packets in 300 sensors

Fig. 6. Number of data packets distribution

4.3 Packets Distribution Balance

The packet transmission could be guaranteed without error, but the packets by multi-hop transmission were easy to lose.Particularly the data was difficult to reach the base station from the away moisture node, so the packets distribution balance of moisture packets could be used as the routing protocol performance evaluation. The better balance of the routing protocol showed its better network performance. The packet distribution was shown in Figure 6(a), 6 (b), 6 (c) in network size of 100, 200, 300 nodes. In testing, data packet distribution changed greatly in the EAP route, and the DSDV routing changed a little more than the EEDRP-FMSN. This analysis showed that EEDRP-FMSN routing in the node layer within a single hop factors played a role in.

From Figure 6, although the number of packets in the EEDRP-FMSN protocol was less than the EAP protocol, EAP routing protocol packets was over-concentrated in certain node. Most nodes appeared packet loss in the EAP protocol, so its balance was poor. In the farmland sensor network, the EAP routing protocol was the most desirable of the three routing protocols, and the EEDRP-FMSN protocol was better than DSDV protocol under the same conditions. The EEDRP-FMSN protocol extended the network life cycle than the DSDV protocol.

5 Conclusions

The above experiments showed that the routing protocol EEDRP-FMSN maintained a high energy efficiency by reducing the average energy consumption of the data packet, it is very suitable for application farmland moisture sensor network environment.

However, the simulations were supposed to an agreed mode in transmitting power and error rate, and some deviations may be occurred under the real environment. So the next major work of this project is applying the EEDRP-FMSN protocol into the real-world applications. At the same time, we can see from the fifth part of the test, the distribution balance of EEDRP-FMSN routing protocol was not well as DSDV routing, how to further improve the routing protocol balance performance of the EEDRP-FMSN routing protocols are also an important work in the future. In addition, the node selection mechanism of next hop is the most important thing in the EEDRP-FMSN routing, we must adjust the weight ratio of each parameter according to the operation of the network environment to make the EEDRP-FMSN routing in energy efficiency and packet distribution balance in practical applications.

Acknowledgments. The authors would thank the project of the National Key Technology R&D Program (Project Name: Key Technologies for Agricultural Field Information Comprehensive Sensing and Rural Extension, Contact Number: 2011BAD21B01;Project Name: Technology integration and demonstration for Qinghai characteristics of agricultural and livestock products quality and safety traceability, Contact Number:2012BAK17B15).

References

1. Dargie, W., Poellabauer, C.: Fundamentals of wireless sensor networks: theory and practice, pp. 168–183. John Wiley and Sons (2010) ISBN 978-0-470-99765-9
2. Guo, L.Q., Xie, Y., Yang, C.H., et al.: Improvement on LEACH by combining Adaptive Cluster Head Election and Two-hop transmission (2010)
3. Ganesan, D., Krishnamachari, B., Woo, A., et al.: Complex behavior at scale: An experimental study of low-power wireless sensor networks. Technical Report UCLA/CSD-TR (2002)
4. Woo, A., Tong, T., Culler, D.: Taming the underlying challenges of reliable multihop routing in sensor networks (2003)
5. Ananstasi, G., Conti, M., Falchi, A., et al.: Performance Measurements of Mote Sensor networks. ACM (2004)
6. Kang, W., Stankovic, J.A., Son, S.H.: On Using Weather Information for Efficient Remote Data Collection in WSN (2008)
7. Jeong, J., Ee, C.T.: Forward error correction in sensor networks. University of California at Berkeley (2003)
8. Ahn, J., Hong, S., Heidemann, J.: An adaptive FEC code control algorithm for mobile wireless sensor networks. Journal of Communications and Networks 7(4), 489 (2005)
9. Xiao, D.: Study on Paddy field Moisture Sensor Network. South China Agricultural University, Guangzhou (2009) (in Chinese)
10. Xiao, D., Gu, Z., Luo, X., et al.: Paddy-field moisture monitoring sensor networks to optimize the design and testing. Journal of Agricultural Engineering 27(2), 174–179 (2011) (in Chinese)
11. Liu, M., Cao, J., Chen, G., et al.: An energy-aware routing protocol in wireless sensor networks. Sensors 9(1), 445–462 (2009)

A Novel Method for Passive Objective Adaption Localization Using Sensing Link

Tianzhang Xing, Dingyi Fang, Xiaojiang Chen, Liqing Ren,
Jv Wang, and Yuan Zhang

Network and Information Security Laboratory,
Northwest University, Xian 710127, China
{xtz,dyf,xjchen}@nwu.edu.cn

Abstract. The passive object localization problem (POLP) aims to detect the location of the target. This task requires the target does not have any device to receive signal or transfer. For this reason, the data type used for the passive object localization is limited in WSN. The great challenge is how to use rare data to estimate the location in the large area. In this paper, based on our preliminary work, we propose a novel approach to localize objects which is referred as SLAL(Sensing Link Adaptive Localization) in which we can judge the location attribute by the adaption rule, calculate the target position by the diffraction model and point out the area by the RSSI affected. Compared with the traditional methods, our major contribution is that study the diffraction model and the affected degree of RSSI, ensure the localization accuracy with the link length extending. Experimental results demonstrate that the localization accuracy of SLAL outperforms previous methods. Laid the foundation for improve the accuracy in further.

Keywords: WSN, Passive Object Localization, Diffraction Model, RSSI.

1 Introduction

Localization is one of many technologies of wireless sensor networks (WSN). The fundamental requirement of the localization is using the collected data to localize and track, such as battlefield surveillance, patient tracking in a hospital etc.[1]. Generally speaking, localization technology can be divided into two categories: active localization and passive localization, the essential differences of them is whether require the monitored target to carry some devices to transmit signal or receive. Active localization technologies always require the object to carry some devices such that the object can be easily located by other anchor sensor nodes [2-3]. By contrast, passive localization technologies [4-6] assume that the object does not carry any assistant device. Without diversity and sufficient data for position calculation, it brings great difficulties about the feasibility studying and localization accuracy promoting for passive localization.

In this paper, we study the passive localization problem based on RSSI in WSN. We proposed a novel approach based on sensing link adaptive to localize

R. Wang and F. Xiao (Eds.): CWSN 2012, CCIS 334, pp. 525–537, 2013.
© Springer-Verlag Berlin Heidelberg 2013

objects, which is referred as SLAL (Sensing Link Adaptive Localization). Based on the research on the diffraction model, we judge target location's attribution then to define the degree which target influence on the RSSI of the link, finally we take a different approach to achieve the target estimation according to the attribution of location. The key problems are a) How to justify the feasibility about the diffraction model complete the passive localization, b) How to estimated the targets position when it is out of the link. The contributions of this paper have threefold. First, we have intensive study of diffraction model, and confirm it for passive localization feasibility. Second, we can determine the location area by the RSSI affected defined and analyzed. Third, we have designed the unit detecting area to make the SLAL method achieves high localization accuracy.

The rest of this paper is organized as follows. Section 2 introduces the related work. Section 3 describes our SLAL model, it includes the fundamental theory, thinking and processing. Section 4 introduce the experiment condition, then presents the results and the performance evaluation. Section 5 concludes the paper, presents some discussions and future work.

2   Related Work

A number of RF-based localization systems have been proposed in the literature [7]-[13]. LANDMARC is proposed by GreenOrbs in 2004, it is location sensing prototype that uses the Radio Frequency Identification (RFID) technology for indoor localizations. The location of the tracked object is estimated based on the nearest reference tags [9]. MoteTrack is presented by Harvard researcher in 2005. This system and the location of each mobile node is obtained by the received radio signal strength signatures from several beacon nodes, where the signatures database is stored in every beacon node [11]. The other important system is RADRA, designed by Microsoft Research Institute in 2000, update it in 2009. It operates by combining signal strength information at multiple base stations based on empirical measurements [12]. These localization algorithms can obtain a good localization accuracy in different application scenarios. But, the above systems need the target object to carry a wireless device, belong to the active localization, this limits their wide application.

In contrast to the above mentioned, Kaltiokallios work is not necessary for the target object to carry such wireless devices, they use the RSSI signals instead for intrusion detection in 2010 [14]. However, their system cannot localize the object. Another model proposed in Zhangs recent work [4, 5, 15], it is called signal dynamics model based on RSSI to locate, does not require objects carry any devices. The reference nodes are deployed as grid array before,but the communicate distances between nodes are 1 or 2 meters. In Lius work [8], they proposed a approachit do not require the tracked objects to carry any devices as well, but the distance of each tag is 1 meter. When the monitoring region is large, the cost and communication is overhead. These methods belong to the passive localization, they similarity is short link with nodes, ideal and densely deployment policy in monitoring region. These factors result in the methods are not suitable for monitoring large region.

This paper focus on passive localization, presents the SLAL method, by investigating the RSSI affected properties for different link distance.

3   Sensing Link Adaptive Localization

3.1   Diffraction Model of the Wireless Signal

In wireless communication systems, radio waves usually spread in an irregular and non-monolithic environment. If we want to estimate the channel loss, the obstacles on the propagation path need to be considered, such as the topography, buildings, trees, telegraph poles, etc [16]. In different outdoor propagation environment, the link RSSI of the same transceiver is also different, as shown in Fig. 1.

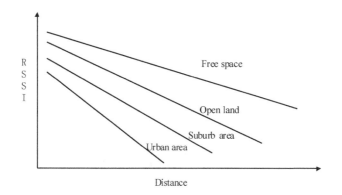

Fig. 1. Radio signal strength attenuation in different environment

RSSI will not only be affected by the link environment, the voltage of the transceiver, the direction of antenna and other conditions will also have a huge impact. In theoretical study, these conditions are treated as constants. When wireless signal is propagating in free space, RSSI is consistent with the normal distribution with the distance [17], it is calculated as follows:

$$PL(dB) = 10\log\frac{P_t}{P_r} = -10\log[\frac{G_tG_r\lambda^2}{(4\pi)^2d^2}]; \qquad (1)$$

$$PL(dB) = 10\log\frac{P_t}{P_r} = -10\log[\frac{\lambda^2}{(4\pi)^2d^2}]; \qquad (2)$$

where $PL(dB)$ denote the path loss, that is, signal attenuation, defined as the difference between effective transmit power and receive power. P_t denote transmit power, P_r denote receive power. G_t denote transmit antenna gain, G_r denote

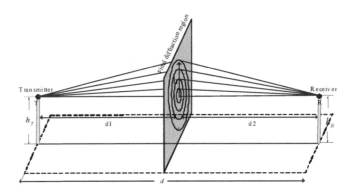

Fig. 2. Boundary of the Fresnel zone in diffraction model

receive antenna gain. λ denote the wireless signal wavelength in meters; d denote the distance between the transmitter and the receiver in meters. Without considering the antenna gain, the antenna gain of the transceiver is set to 1, formula (1) degenerates into formula (2).

The free space transmission is idealized. In the reality of wireless signal transmission, because the transmission environment is uncertain, the communication links will inevitably be blocked, which increases the path loss of wireless signal. The receive field strength will rapidly decline when the link is obscured, but still be able to maintain, this is because of the emergence of the diffraction field. There is path difference when the wireless signal is transmitting in free space and diffraction path, and its corresponding phase. The phase difference is not only a function of the transceivers position, but also a function of the physical location and height of the blocks. The path difference is called the additional paths:

$$\Delta \approx \frac{h^2}{2} \cdot \frac{d_1 + d_2}{d_1 d_2} \qquad d = d_1 + d_2 \qquad (3)$$

The corresponding phase difference:

$$\varphi = \frac{2\pi \Delta}{\lambda} = \frac{2\pi}{\lambda} \cdot \frac{h^2}{2} \cdot \frac{d_1 + d_2}{d_1 d_2} \qquad (4)$$

Diffraction loss has a direct relationship with the additional path, which can be explained by the Fresnel zone. Fresnel zone denote the contact area in which the sub-wave path length from the transmitter to the receiver is $n\lambda/2$ longer than the free space path, as shown in Fig. 2. d_1 denote the distance between the obstacle and the transmitter, d_2 denote the distance between the obstacle and the receiver. Concentric rings are known as Fresnel zone, r_n can be given by the radius of Fresnel zone circle equation as:

$$r_n = \sqrt{\frac{n\lambda d_1 d_2}{d_1 + d_2}}; \qquad (5)$$

Theoretical proof shows that, if an obstacle does not block the 1st Fresnel zone, the diffraction loss will be minimal. In fact, in the design of microwave links, as long as 55% of the Fresnel zone is not blocked, other Fresnel zone will not affect the diffraction loss. Diffraction field strength is usually of sufficient intensity, and its size depends on the diffraction coefficient v

$$v = \alpha \sqrt{\frac{2d_1 d_2}{\lambda(d_1 + d_2)}} ; \tag{6}$$

$$\alpha = \arctan(\frac{h_s - h_T}{d_1}) + \arctan(\frac{h_s - h_R}{d_2}) \approx h(\frac{d_1 + d_2}{d_1 d_2}) \tag{7}$$

where h_s denote the height of the obstacle, h_T denote the height of the transmitter, h_R denote the height of the receiver. Diffracted wave field strength is expressed as:

$$\frac{E_d}{E_o} = F(v) = \frac{(1 + j)}{2} \int_v^\infty \exp(\frac{-j\pi t^2}{2}) dt \tag{8}$$

where E_0 is the free space field strength. $F(v)$ is the Fresnel number, and a function of the diffraction parameter v defined in the formula (6). Contrast to free-space transmission, diffraction gain is expressed as follows:

$$G_d(db) = 20 \log |F(v)| \tag{9}$$

Thus, the diffraction gain of the obstacle somewhere in the link depends on the diffraction coefficient v of the point. When the external environment does not change (the position and height of the transmitter and receiver remains unchanged), the diffraction coefficient v differs with different obstacle position. We know from formula (3) that when the obstacle is in d_1 and d_2 , the diffraction gain of the two points is the same. Therefore, the diffraction gain of each point on a single link must be symmetrical relative to the midpoint, which is called the diffraction symmetry model, as shown in Fig. 3.

We consider the diffraction symmetry model reversely. If the signal attenuation collected by the receiver is all (or most) caused by the obstacle diffraction in the link, we can solve the specific location of the obstacle according to the diffraction gain. Except midpoint location of the link, other locations will be a point of symmetry. After in-depth analysis of the diffraction model, in order to use the diffraction model in passive targeting, the following two questions need to be answered: 1) how to determine the target is in the link? 2) screening select the symmetry point.

3.2   LRA (Link RSSI Affected) Analysis

As the analysis in the previous section, when the monitoring target is located in a communication link, based on the diffraction gain, we can use the diffraction model for position estimation. However, in the actual monitoring environment, it is impossible to guarantee that, in the monitoring region, each location point

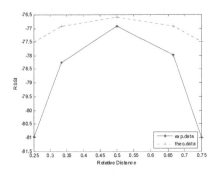
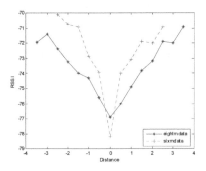

Fig. 3. Diffraction RSSI of each point in 8m link

Fig. 4. RSSI distribution of each point on the main perpendicular bisector of 6, 8 m link

of the target may arise in the communications link. On the contrary, it is more frequent locating outside the communication link. Then further study is needed about the characteristics of the wireless signal transmission model outdoor.

literature[17-18] give out the classic outdoor wireless signal propagation model, such as Longley-Rice model, Durkin model and Okumura model. While Durkin and basic Okumura models applicable frequency do not meet the transmitting frequency of the WSN nodes, and the Longley-Rice is applicable to the communications link above 1km. Therefore, we can only analyze the reason for the attenuation change according to the common characteristics of the wireless signal transmission. The multipath effect caused by reflection and scattering is inevitable, but because the deployment of sensor nodes is relatively fixed, and the natural environment is relatively static, to a fixed communications link, whether or not have objects, or whether far or near to the link, its surrounding environment for reflection and scattering of the signal is denoted as PG. In considering the impact of multipath effect, the received signal strength of a communications link becomes:

$$PL_T(dB) = 10\log\frac{P_t}{P_r} = -10\log[\frac{\lambda^2}{(4\pi)^2 d^2}] + PG \qquad (10)$$

$$PG = P_e + P_o \qquad (11)$$

However, P_e denote the impact of the surrounding physical environment for signal reflection and scattering. If the environment remains unchanged, the size remains the same. P_o denote the reflection and scattering effects due to the target. Because the dynamic nature of the target, we cannot get the accurate angle and the plane of incidence of the radio wave during reflection and scattering. So the analysis of PG is very complex and difficult to calculate accurately. We found some rules through experiments, as shown in Fig. 4.

Easy to draw from the figure, when the target is outside of the communication link, it is a supplemental enhancement to the signal strength. This phenomenon can be attributed to the presence of PG . We also found that, if the distance to the link is different, the RSSI is different and presents a monotone. In this way, we can determine the distance of the target to the link according the targets effect size to the links RSSI. Because the RSSI fluctuation is subtle, we can zoom in it through natural index. It is conducive to the analysis and use of η , the affected degree of RSSI. The links affected degree of RSSI is defined as follows:

$$\eta = \exp(|||PL| - |PL_T|||) \tag{12}$$

The greater of η , the greater impact of the target to the link, the closer from target to link. On the contrary, farther distance from target to link.

3.3   SLAL Model

The above two models are able to reflect target location information in varying degrees, and each have suitable places. Using the diffraction model separately can only locate the target in link orientation, but cannot estimate the location outside the link. The reason is that the obstacle in the link has a negative impact on the link RSSI, and the impact is great (block the first Fresnel zone). The target outside the link has lower impact on the link. So when the target is outside the link, diffraction model is unable to calculate the distance between target and transceiver.

Similarly, its unable to complete the target location in the link, only relying on the affected degree of RSSI. We know from the definition of the affected degree of RSSI, the parameter can only reflect the distance from the target to the link. If the target appears in the link, it is not possible to calculate the specific location of the target.

In summary, we propose a link-aware adaptive passive location method. Link-aware location refers to the analysis, cognition and processing of the RSSI on the communication link. The idea is, adaptively determine the target location attribute firstly, divide the location attribute into two categories, in the link and out of the link; according to the verdict, take the diffraction model or the affected degree of RSSI to fulfill the task of target location. Adaptive criterion can be obtained, relying on the wireless signal transmission characteristics. Links of different length has different criteria, and the parameter change dynamically with the link length.

In the monitoring of the actual target location, just using a link cannot select the symmetric virtual point. When deploying the node, learned from the 2G cellular coverage theory, we can deploy the node by the regular hexagon. The multiple regular hexagon deployment strategy to achieve seamless coverage of the whole monitoring region is shown in Fig. 5. Deploying one more node in the midpoint of each regular hexagon, will divide the regular hexagon into six separate equilateral triangles. Each equilateral triangle is called a unit targeted area. Each unit area has three links,l_1, l_2 and l_3 , and three corresponding nodes P_1, P_2,P_3 as shown in Fig. 6.

The specific locating steps are shown in Fig. 7.

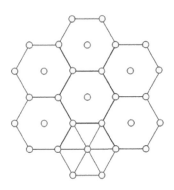

Fig. 5. Cellular coverage the monitoring region.

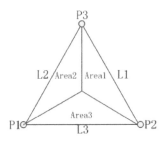

Fig. 6. Unit localized area

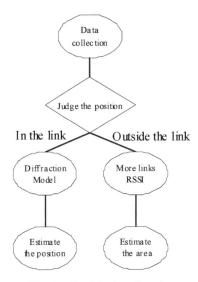

Fig. 7. Positioning flowchart

Determine the target's location attributes

1) Collect the links' PL of free space; 2) Collect the PL_T after the target entering into the monitor area; 3) Adaptive criteria

$$|PL| - |PL_T| = \begin{cases} \geq 0 \to & \textit{target is outside the link} \\ < 0 \to & \textit{target is in the link} \end{cases} \tag{13}$$

Target is in the link

1) Calculate the occlusion point according to the diffraction model, that is, the target location. Except the midpoint of the link, it should be in pairs. 2) Screening select the location point, according to the size of η on the two other links in the unit targeted area.

Target is outside the link

1) Fulfill the granularity division of the unit targeted area, and connect the geometric center of the equilateral triangle with each fixed points, forming three equal areas. 2) Compare the size of $\eta_i(i = 1, 2, 3)$, determine the smallest η_i, then the target is in the region $Area_i$.

4   Experiments and Data Analysis

4.1   Experimental Conditions

The node type we selected is MICAZ, the processing chip is CC2420, the wireless signal frequency is 2.4GHz, the data rate is 2 times/sec. The height of the obstacle (target) is 1.6m, and the height of the transceiver node is 0.95m. In order to reduce the interference of external factors to the link, the selected experimental site is the north square on Changan campus of the Northwest University.

4.2   Experimental Scheme and Results

Experiment 1: Target location on the communication link.

The link length is 4m, 5m, 6m, 8m and 10m, respectively. The height of the obstacle is 1.6m, which stands at the five occlusion points of each link (the relative position L_R to the transmitter is 1/4, 1/3, 1/2, 2/3, 3/4). The standing time is 90 seconds. The diffraction gain $G_d(db)$ of the 5 points is shown in Table 1. The locating result L_E is shown in Table 2.

Table 1. Target location and diffraction gain

Link	1/4		1/3		1/2		2/3		3/4	
length	L_R	$G_d(db)$	L_R	$G_d(db)$	L_R	$G_d(db)$	L_R	$G_d(db)$	L_R	$G_d(db)$
4m	1	-21.986	1.33	-21.613	2	-20.719	2.67	-21.893	3	-22.013
5m	1.25	-22.341	1.67	-20.371	2.5	-20.263	3.33	-20.372	3.75	-21.349
6m	1.5	-20.993	2	-19.809	3	-19.501	4	-19.901	4.5	-20.013
8m	2	-19.381	2.67	-18.901	4	-18.339	5.33	-23.587	6	-19.503
10m	2.5	-19.401	3.33	-18.987	5	-17.617	6.67	-17.790	7.5	-18.929

Note: retention of two or three digits after the decimal point.

Experiment 2: The effect to the link of each point on the vertical line.

The chosen link length is 6m, 8m. Standing on the main perpendicular bisector of the link (on both sides of a link), collect the RSSI of the link affected by the target. The standing point is arranged equidistantly, the interval is 0.5m. The experiment was repeated on the other side of the link. The result is shown in Fig. 4.

Experiment 3: Target location outside the communication link.

Build the unit target area and select the link length as 4m, 5m, 6m, 8m and

Table 2. Location and result

Link	1/4		1/3		1/2		2/3		3/4	
length	L_R	L_E	L_R	L_E	L_R	L_E	L_R	L_E	L_R	L_E
4m	1	0.88	1.33	1.19	2	2.15	2.67	2.81	3	2.89
5m	1.25	0.64	1.67	1.90	2.5	2.31	3.33	2.98	3.75	4.07
6m	1.5	1.17	2	2.29	3	3.13	4	4.17	4.5	4.29
8m	2	1.87	2.67	2.35	4	4.09	5.33	7.13	6	5.98
10m	2.5	1.79	3.33	2.73	5	4.68	6.67	6.17	7.5	8.11

Note: retention of two digits after the decimal point.

10m, respectively. Choose 10 standing position outside the link of the region, the standing time for each point is 90 seconds, collect the signal strength of the three links. Fulfill the regional location by the above methods, and compare the results with the actual standing position to calculate the accuracy rate. Table 3 only lists the links experimental data of 4m. The final positioning accuracy of the experiment is shown in Fig. 8.

Table 3. Experimental data of 4m link

No	Location	η			Estimate Area	Result
		η_1	η_2	η_3		
P1	Area1	20.0856	4.4817	6.6859	Area1	T
P2	Area2	6.0496	2.4596	4.0552	Area1	F
P3	Area1	40.4473	44.7012	2.2255	Area2	F
P4	Area3	33.1155	2.2255	54.5982	Area3	T
P5	Area1	44.7012	6.6859	2.0138	Area1	T
P6	Area3	1.2214	22.1980	134.2898	Area3	T
P7	Area1	3.3201	7.3891	3.0042	Area2	F
P8	Area2	6.0496	54.5982	9.9742	Area2	T
P9	Area3	54.5982	1	148.4132	Area3	T
P10	Area2	1.4918	27.1126	29.9641	Area3	F

Note:η retention of two digits after the decimal point.

4.3   Analysis

The result of experiment 1 show that, when the target is in the link, the coordinates of the target can be calculated, according to the location information of node and the communication signal attenuation with each other. The calculated coordinates can be screening selected according to the RSSI of the three links in the unit targeted area. Experiment 2 and experiment 3 confirmed the feasibility of RSSI for passive targeting. Experiments of different link length in unit targeted area confirmed the accuracy of the method in regional location. The shortcomings are as follows:

1) In experiment 1, with the link length increases, the positioning accuracy cannot be guaranteed. The error amendment requires further study.

2) In experiment 3, with the expansion of unit positioning area, regional positioning accuracy is raised, but failed in calculation of the points coordinates in the experimental region. It also raised new challenges for future research.

3) The standing time of the target is too long. The data type is limited. In order to collect adequate and effective single data, the standing time requirements in each standing point is 90 seconds, brought a great deal of inconvenience to target tracking application relying on the location information.

4) Positioning in extreme positions. In Experiment 3, except 10 regular standing point, we selected several extreme positions (that is, the location near node of two intersect links) in the unit targeted area of each link to test the accuracy rate, but is low.

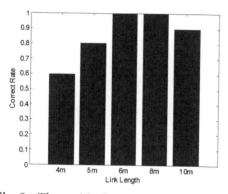

Fig. 8. The positioning accuracy in target area

5 Conclusion and Future Work

In-depth analysis of the characteristics of wireless signal transmission, we proposes a adaptive passive targeting method based on link-aware. The method involves two types of data, one is node location information, and the other is the affected link RSSI by the target. This is fully consistent with the characteristics of lacking location data type in passive location. The location property will be determined adaptively, using different methods to locate the target based on the verdict. The experimental results demonstrate the feasibility of the method, as well as the positioning accuracy. With the continuous expansion application field of WSN, targeting and tracking problem has become a hot topic. This paper just offer some reference to the observations, there are still many room for improvement, as summarized below: 1) Theoretical guidance. Diffraction model solves the problem of positioning target in the link. And if the target is outside the link, we can solve it using the reflection and scattering of signal propagation model. 2) Algorithm. When the target is outside a link, this article has only been able to target the area, but hasnt calculated the position coordinates. 3) Data processing. The standing time is too long for target tracking application, and we did not experiment with different standing time.

Acknowledgments. This research was supported in part by: China NSFC Grants 61070176 and 61170218, the Key Project of Chinese Ministry of Education under Grant No. 211181, the Science and Technology Planning Project of Shaanxi Province, China under Grant No. 2011k06-09.

References

1. Park, J., Curtis, D., Teller, S., Ledlie, J.: Implications of device diversity for organic localization. In: Proceedings of the 30th IEEE International Conference on Computer Communications, INFOCOM 2011, pp. 3182–3190 (2011)
2. Ahmed, N., Dong, Y., Bokareva, T., Kanhere, S., Jha, S., Bessell, T., Rutten, M., Ristic, B., Gordon, N.: Detection and tracking using wireless sensor networks. In: Proceedings of the 5th International Conference on Embedded Networked Sensor Systems, pp. 425–426. ACM (2007)
3. Al-Ali, A.R., Aloul, F.A., Aji, N.R., Al-Zarouni, A.A., Fakhro, N.H.: Mobile rfid tracking system. In: 3rd International Conference on Information and Communication Technologies: From Theory to Applications, ICTTA 2008, pp. 1–4. IEEE (2008)
4. Zhang, D., Ma, J., Chen, Q., Ni, L.M.: An rf-based system for tracking transceiver-free objects. In: Fifth Annual IEEE International Conference on Pervasive Computing and Communications, PerCom 2007, pp. 135–144 (2007)
5. Zhang, D., Ni, L.M.: Dynamic clustering for tracking multiple transceiver-free objects. In: International Conference on Pervasive Computing and Communications, PerCom 2009, pp. 1–8. IEEE (2009)
6. Youssef, M., Mah, M., Agrawala, A.: Challenges: device-free passive localization for wireless environments. In: Proceedings of the 13th Annual ACM International Conference on Mobile Computing and Networking, pp. 222–229 (2007)
7. Zhang, D., Liu, Y., Ni, L.M.: Link-centric probabilistic coverage model for transceiver-free object detection in wireless networks. In: 2010 International Conference on Distributed Computing Systems, pp. 116–125. IEEE (2010)
8. Liu, Y., Chen, L., Pei, J., Chen, Q., Zhao, Y.: Mining frequent trajectory patterns for activity monitoring using radio frequency tag arrays. In: Proceedings of the Fifth IEEE International Conference on Pervasive Computing and Communications, PERCOM 2007, pp. 37–46 (2007)
9. Ni, L.M., Liu, Y., Lau, Y.C., Patil, A.P.: Landmarc: indoor location sensing using active rfid. Wireless Networks, 701–710 (2004)
10. Bahl, P., Padmanabhan, V.N.: Radar: An in-building rf-based user location and tracking system. In: Proceedings of the Nineteenth Annual Joint Conference of the IEEE Computer and Communications Societies, INFOCOM 2000, pp. 775–784 (2000)
11. Lorincz, K., Welsh, M.: MoteTrack: A Robust, Decentralized Approach to RF-Based Location Tracking. In: Strang, T., Linnhoff-Popien, C. (eds.) LoCA 2005. LNCS, vol. 3479, pp. 63–82. Springer, Heidelberg (2005)
12. Bahl, P., Padmanabhan, V.N., Balachandran, A.: Enhancements to the radar user location and tracking system. Microsoft Research (February 2000)
13. Oka, A., Lampe, L.: Distributed target tracking using signal strength measurements by a wireless sensor network. IEEE Journal on Selected Areas in Communications, 1006–1015 (2010)

14. Kaltiokallio, O., Bocca, M., Eriksson, L.M.: Poster abstract: Distributed rssi processing for intrusion detection in indoor environments. In: Proceedings of the 9th ACM/IEEE International Conference on Information Processing in Sensor Networks (2010), doi:10.1145/1791212.1791276
15. Zhang, D., Yang, Y., Cheng, D., Liu, S., Ni, L.M.: Cocktail: An rf-based hybrid approach for indoor localization. In: IEEE International Conference on Communications, ICC 2010, pp. 1–5 (2010)
16. Theodore, S.: Rappaport, Wireless Communications Principles & Practice. Prentice Hall, NJ (1996)
17. Longley, A.G., Rice, P.L.: Prediction of Tropospheric Radio Transmission Loss Over Irregular Terrain: A Computer Method. ESSA Technical Report, ERL 79-ITS 67 (1968)
18. Dadson, C.E., Durkin, J., Martin, E.: Computer Prediction of Field Strength in the Planning of Radio Systems. IEEE Transactions on Vehicular Technology 24(1), 1–7 (1975)
19. Edwards, R., Durkin, J.: Computer Prediction of Service Area for VHF Mobile Radio Networks. IEEE Transactions on Vehicular Technology 26(4), 323–327 (1977)
20. Okumura, T., Ohmori, E., Fukuda, K.: Field Strength and Its Variability in VHF and UHF Land Mobile Service. Review Electrical Communication Laboratory 16(9-10), 825–873 (1968)

Frequency Selection in ECRT-Based Radio Interferometric Ranging

Bing Xu, Wangdong Qi, Yasong Zhu, Li Wei,
Peng Liu, and En Yuan

PLA University of Science and Technology, Nanjing 210007, China
greatbingxu@gmail.com

Abstract. The solution of extended Chinese remainder theorem(ECRT) based radio interferometric ranging (RIR) is in closed form, thus the computational complexity is greatly reduced compared with previous methods. Therefore, ECRT-based RIR shows us the prospects of employing RIR for distributed localization in Wireless Sensor Networks (WSN). But ECRT-based RIR have a tight constraint on the measured frequencies. In this paper, relations between the probabilities of normal error, frequencies available, maximum unambiguous range, the greatest common divisor C and phase noise are given. Then an optimal frequency selection method with computational complexity of $O(N!)$ and a suboptimal frequency selection method with computational complexity of $O(N^2)$ are presented. We can effectively have a tradeoff between noise tolerance, number of frequency available and the maximum unambiguous range in system design. Simulation results corroborate the effectiveness of proposed methods.

Keywords: RIR, ECRT, frequency selection, wireless sensor networks.

1 Introduction

Location service is one of the key implementations in wireless sensor networks, which has attracted extensive research interest in recent years [1][2]. Accuracy of the ranging method is the most crucial factor in determining the positioning performance. Among the common used ranging techniques, TOA(Time of Arrival) requires the tight synchronization between the sending node and receiving node, so high precise clock is a prerequisite for implementation; AOA(Angle of Arrival) requires additional antenna array, increasing the node size and cost, and it is sensitive to the external environment (easy to form the blind fields), so the robustness of it is low; RSSI(Received Signal Strength Indicator) provides a simple ranging method for WSN, but the accuracy of it is extremely low [1].

Maroti and Kusy etc. propose RIR (Radio Interferometric Ranging) in 2005, which achieves high precision and low cost ranging in WSN [3]. The basic unit in RIR is four nodes in which two nodes transmit sine wave simultaneously in slightly different frequencies and the other two measure the phase of the received beat signals [4][6]. The measured phase difference of the beat signals can be used

R. Wang and F. Xiao (Eds.): CWSN 2012, CCIS 334, pp. 538–547, 2013.
© Springer-Verlag Berlin Heidelberg 2013

to obtain a combination of distance (called Q-range) among the four nodes. As the frequency of the beat signal is very low, so it is very easy to measure the phase in low cost node. RIR is phase-based ranging in essence, which has the problem of phase ambiguity. So we usually measure the phase in multi-frequency to get the Q-range. Solving Q-range is a nonlinear problem requiring the grid search process in two dimensions, so the computational complexity is significantly high and the process is usually conducted in a laptop. The high computational complexity in solving Q-range prevents RIR's implementation in distributed localization, which is a common used localization method in WSN.

In order to reduce the computational complexity of RIR, [5] propose the ECRT-based RIR. It has a closed form solution, so the computational complexity is greatly reduced. Therefore, ECRT-based RIR shows us the prospects of employing RIR for distributed localization in WSN. But ECRT-based RIR has a tight constraint on the measured frequencies, and the number of frequencies available is usually small. Therefore, an effective frequency selection process is desiderated, and there is no quantitative analysis of the relations between the probability of normal error in ranging result, the greatest common divisor, maximum unambiguous range and noise tolerance yet.

In this paper, we study the issue of frequency selection in ECRT-based RIR. We first establish the relationship among the probability of normal error in ranging, the greatest common divisor C, maximum unambiguous range and noise tolerance. As the correlation between the frequency f and wavelength λ, the frequency selection problem transformed into the selection of wavelength which are relatively coprime. When C is given, we provide an optimal frequency selection method with the computational complexity of $O(N!)$ and an suboptimal frequency selection method with the computational complexity of $O(N^2)$. The former one is appropriate when the bandwidth is not broad, and the later can be used when the bandwidth is broad, it can't guarantee the optimal solution, but offers an effective solution instead. We can give an effective tradeoff between the greatest common divisor C, noise tolerance, frequency available and the maximum unambiguous range in system design. Simulation results demonstrate the effectiveness of our methods.

This paper is organized as follows: Section 2 briefly describes the theory of RIR; Functional relation formulae and frequency selection method are presented in Section 3; Section 4 demonstrates the simulation result; Section 5 is the conclusion.

2   Radio Interferometric Ranging

RIR calculate the Q-range through measuring the phase difference of the beat signal at multi-frequency, the principle is shown in Fig. 1.

In Fig. 1, A and B are transmitters which transmit sine wave simultaneously at slightly different frequencies; C and D are receivers which measure the phase of the received beat signals. A, B, C and D are the basic unit of RIR and $q_{ABCD} = d_{AD} - d_{BD} + d_{BC} - d_{AC}$, where q_{ABCD} denotes the Q-range and d_{XY}

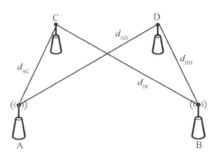

Fig. 1. Radio interferometric ranging

denotes the Euclidean distance between X and Y. They have the correlation of [3][4]

$$q_{ABCD} \bmod \lambda = \frac{\varphi_{CD}}{2\pi} \cdot \lambda \tag{1}$$

where φ_{CD} denotes the phase difference of the beat signal measured by C and D, λ is the average wavelength of the two transmitting sine wave. Due to the phase ambiguity problem, we can't get one unique q_{ABCD}, so measurement in multi-frequency is needed, thus we get

$$q_{ABCD} = n_i \lambda_i + \frac{\varphi_{CD_i}}{2\pi} \lambda_i, i = 1, 2, \cdots, M \tag{2}$$

where M is the number of the frequencies, λ_i, n_i, φ_{CD_i} denote the wavelength, unknown integer and phase difference in the ith frequency.

As the exists of noise in φ_{CD}, we can't get a direct solution of the overdetermined equations in (2). [4] propose the grid search method to get the solution by minimize the residual function, that is

$$\begin{cases} q_{ABCD} = \arg\min_{q \in S^*} \left(\frac{1}{M} \sqrt{\sum_{i=1}^{M} \left(q - n_i \lambda_i - \frac{\varphi_{CD_i}}{2\pi} \lambda_i \right)^2} \right) \\ n = round\left(\left(q - \frac{\varphi_{CD_i}}{2\pi} \lambda_i \right) / \lambda_i \right) \end{cases} \tag{3}$$

where $round(x)$ denotes the rounding of x and S^* denotes the searching range.

3   Frequency Selection for ECRT-Based RIR

3.1   ECRT-Based RIR

ECRT improves the robustness of CRT, extend the application fields of CRT [8]. Unlike CRT, divisors L_i in ECRT have the greatest common divisor $C \geq 1$, that is, $L_i = CP_i, i = 1, \cdots, k$, and $\gcd(P_i, P_j) = 1, i \neq j$. The congruence equations $x \equiv m_i(\bmod L_i)$ has a unique solution when $x < C \prod_{i=1}^{k} P_i$, that is

$$x \equiv Cx_0 + r(\bmod N) \tag{4}$$

where

$$x_0 \equiv \sum_{i=1}^{k} Q_i q_i b_i (\mathrm{mod}\, M), b_i = \lfloor m_i/C \rfloor \tag{5}$$

$\lfloor\,\rfloor$ is the rounding operator, q_i denotes the modular inverse of Q_i, which can be calculated by Euclidean algorithm [7], and $r = m_1 - b_1 \cdot C$.

When the noise is absent, we have the correlation

$$b_i = (m_i - m_1)/C + b_1 \tag{6}$$

When noise exists, we denote m_i as $m_i = m_i^0 + \Delta m_i$, where m_i^0 denotes the true value of m_i and Δm_i is the noise. Then (6) can be expressed as

$$b_i = \frac{m_i^0 - m_1^0}{C} + b_1 + \frac{\Delta m_i - \Delta m_1}{C} \tag{7}$$

where $b_1 = \lfloor m_1/C \rfloor = b_1^0 + \Delta b_1$.

By take the rounding operation of $(\Delta m_i - \Delta m_1)/C$, we get

$$b_i = \frac{m_i^0 - m_1^0}{C} + b_1 + round\left(\frac{\Delta m_i - \Delta m_1}{C}\right) \tag{8}$$

If

$$\left|\frac{\Delta m_i - \Delta m_1}{C}\right| < 0.5, i = 2, \cdots, k \tag{9}$$

Then $round(|\Delta m_i - \Delta m_1| /C) = 0$, b_i will have the equal error as b_1 in (8). Due to the character of ECRT [5][8], the error of x_0 in (5) is Δb_1. Thus the solution is less sensitive to noise. Then $r_i = m_i - b_i \cdot C$, take the average of r_i as the final solution, that is $r = \sum_{i=1}^{k} r_i/k$.

As long as the errors of the remainder $m_1, m_2, \cdots, m_k$ satisfy the condition (9), then we can get the closed-form solution which is robust to noise through (4)-(5).

Formula (1) shows that in multi-frequency RIR, there exists the following corre-lation between q_{ABCD} and φ_{CD_i}

$$q_{ABCD} \equiv \lambda_i \cdot \frac{\varphi_{CD_i}}{2\pi} (\mathrm{mod}\, \lambda_i), i = 1, 2, \cdots, M \tag{10}$$

Let $q = q_{ABCD}$, $\alpha_i = \lambda_i \cdot \frac{\varphi_{CD_i}}{2\pi}$ then

$$q \equiv \alpha_i (\mathrm{mod}\, \lambda_i), i = 1, 2, \cdots, M \tag{11}$$

CRT is discussed in the field of integer, so we should quantize all of the parameters in (11) to integer, let δ denotes the quantization granularity (δ should be smaller than the level of accuracy in ranging, we set $\delta = 10^{-4}$ m herein), and then (11) can be transformed into

$$q^{\mathrm{int}} \equiv \alpha_i^{\mathrm{int}} (\mathrm{mod}\, \lambda_i^{\mathrm{int}}), i = 1, 2, \cdots, M \tag{12}$$

where $q^{\text{int}} = round(q/\delta)$, $\alpha_i^{\text{int}} = round(\alpha_i/\delta)$, and $\lambda_i^{\text{int}} = round(\lambda_i/\delta)$.

Divisor L_i in ECRT corresponds to λ_i^{int} in (12), which requires that the wavelength has the greatest common divisor C. Therefore, our researches should focus on the design of required frequencies (have the greatest common divisor C, hereinafter referred to as coprime).

3.2   Functional Relation Formulae

Suppose the bandwidth is $B = f_l - f_s$, where f_s is the minimum measurement frequency, f_l is the maximum measurement frequency. Let $S_f = \{f_1, f_2, \cdots, f_M\}$ denotes the frequency sequence we select, where M is the number of frequencies and $f_{i+1} < f_i$. As the correlation $\lambda_i = c/f_i$ between the frequency f_i and wavelength λ_i, then the problem transformed into the design of required wavelength sequence $S_\lambda = \{\lambda_1, \lambda_2, \cdots, \lambda_M\}$. In addition to guarantee the coprime of the wavelength, four other factors are also critical: how to guarantee the accuracy in ranging, how to enhance the noise tolerance, how to improve the number of available frequencies and how to extend the maximum unambiguous range.

Let $S_\lambda^{\text{int}} = \{\lambda_1^{\text{int}}, \lambda_2^{\text{int}}, \cdots, \lambda_M^{\text{int}}\}$ denotes the quantification of wavelength S_λ, and equations (12) satisfy

$$\lambda_i^{\text{int}} = C \cdot P_i, i = 1, 2, \cdots, M \tag{13}$$

Then the maximum unambiguous range is

$$T_{Ambiguity}^{\text{int}} = C \cdot \prod_{i=1}^{M} P_i = \prod_{i=1}^{M} \lambda_i \Big/ C^{M-1} \tag{14}$$

In ECRT-based RIR, the condition (9) should be satisfied to guarantee the error in final solution is normal (it is also referred as the error is normal when condition (9) is satisfied), so the issue is focused on the probability that condition (9) is satisfied. After the quantization, condition (9) can be transformed into

$$\left|\Delta\alpha_i^{\text{int}} - \Delta\alpha_1^{\text{int}}\right|/C < 0.5, i = 2, \cdots, M \tag{15}$$

where $\Delta\alpha_i^{\text{int}}$ denotes the error of $\alpha_i^{\text{int}} = round\left(\alpha_i/\delta\right)$. After δ is given, accuracy and noise tolerance are in direct proportion to C. And C is also related to the selection of the frequency sequence.

Let $\varphi_{CD_i} = \varphi_{CD_i}^0 + \Delta\varphi_{CD_i}$ in (10), where $\varphi_{CD_i}^0$ denotes the true value of the phase difference, $\Delta\varphi_{CD_i} \sim N\left(0, \beta^2\right)$ is the phase noise, so $\Delta\alpha_i^{\text{int}} \sim N(0, round((\frac{\beta \cdot \lambda_i}{2\pi \cdot \delta})^2))$, then

$$\left(\Delta\alpha_i^{\text{int}} - \Delta\alpha_1^{\text{int}}\right) \sim N\left(0, 2 \cdot round\left(\left(\frac{\beta \cdot \lambda_i}{2\pi \cdot \delta}\right)^2\right)\right) \tag{16}$$

Then, we can get the probability that condition (9) is satisfied, which is

$$p = \prod_{i=2}^{M} \Phi\left((0.5C) \Big/ \sqrt{2 \cdot round\left(\left(\frac{\beta \cdot \lambda_i}{2\pi \cdot \delta}\right)^2\right)}\right) \tag{17}$$

where $\Phi(\cdot)$ denotes the probability distribution function of standard normal distribution, quantification granularity δ is a constant which is set based on system performance. Through formula (17), we can get the relations between the probability of normal error in ranging, phase noise and the greatest common divisor C.

Note that, formula (17) is different from that in [5]. [5] assumes that Δm_i follows the distribution of zero-mean Gauss noise, then the probability of normal error is derived, and it assumes that condition (9) holds with the same probability in each frequency. Formula (17) is derived from the distribution of phase noise, and the probability is also related to the wavelength of each frequency, so it's more precise.

3.3   Frequency Selection

We can see from formula (15) that the number of frequency selected and the greatest common divisor C are the main factors that determine the noise tolerance. Each frequency should satisfy condition (9), so the probability increases with the decrease of M. The number of frequency available will also decrease with the increase of C, so increasing C is in complete accordance with enhancing noise tolerance.

Increasing the number of frequency available and extending the maximum unambiguous range are also two factors we should consider in system design. As seen from formula (17), the maximum unambiguous range is in direct proportion to the product of each wavelength, so increasing the maximum unambiguous range is in complete accordance with increasing M. Therefore, what we should do is making an effective tradeoff between them.

Frequency Selection When C Is Given. First, we suppose that C is given and discuss the issue of frequency selection. As the most favored way to increase noise tolerance is increasing C, so the issue of noise tolerance is not considered here as well.

As $\lambda_i^{\text{int}} = C \cdot P_i$, $\lambda_l^{\text{int}} < \lambda_i^{\text{int}} < \lambda_s^{\text{int}}$, so $\lceil \lambda_l^{\text{int}}/C \rceil \leq P_i \leq \lfloor \lambda_s^{\text{int}}/C \rfloor$. When C is given, increasing M and extending $T_{ambiguity}$ are the two goals in frequency selection. As they are in accordance with each other, then the problem transformed into: how to select the sequence $S_P = \{P_1, P_2, \cdots, P_M\}$ among $[\lceil \lambda_l^{\text{int}}/C \rceil, \lfloor \lambda_s^{\text{int}}/C \rfloor]$ to maximize M.

Note that a prime is integer that has no positive divisors other than 1 and itself, so we should first select all the primes in integer interval $[\lceil \lambda_l^{\text{int}}/C \rceil, \lfloor \lambda_s^{\text{int}}/C \rfloor]$ as the initial set, and then we move remain elements that satisfy the coprime condition to the set. In order to select the optimal sequence, we should traverse all the set of coprime elements, and then select the set with the maximum elements. The flow chart of optimal frequency selection is shown in Fig. 2.

Fig. 2 demonstrate the optimal method for solving S_P, which can guarantee the maximum M and $\prod_{i=1}^{M} P_i$.

However, as the traverse process, the computational complexity of the method is $O(N!)$, the computational complexity will increase exponentially when the

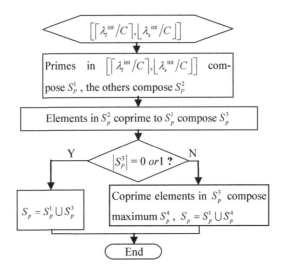

Fig. 2. Optimal method for solving S_P

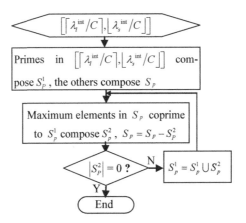

Fig. 3. Suboptimal method for solving S_P

bandwidth increases. If the bandwidth is broad, we can't get the solution in a finite period of time.

In order to select S_P when the bandwidth is broad, Fig. 3 shows an suboptimal method with a computational complexity of $O(N^2)$. This is a heuristic method based on greedy principle; the main rule in it is each time we move the maximum element, which is relatively prime to all the selected elements, to the selected set, the flow chart is shown in Fig. 3. This method can't guarantee the optimal solution, but an effective solution is given, as shown in the analysis of Section 4.

Determining of C. As mentioned above, increasing C is in complete accordance with enhancing noise tolerance, and the most favored way to enhance noise tolerance is increasing C. But they are contradictory to increasing the number of frequency available and extending the maximum unambiguous range, so effective tradeoff between them must be considered.

We can select an initial C in system design, then the frequency available, maximum unambiguous range and noise tolerance can be obtained with the method proposed before. Then we adjust C according to the requirement of the system, adjusting granularity and terminating condition are also due to the requirements. We can have a tradeoff between all the parameters through the methods proposed, which can be seen in in following Section 4.

4 Simulation Results and Analysis

Suppose the bandwidth is $B = 60$MHz, and $f_s = 400$MHz, $f_l = 460$MHz, we set $\delta = 10^{-4}m(0.1\text{mm})$, then $\lambda_s^{int} = 7500$, $\lambda_l^{int} = 6522$. Through the methods in Section 3, we can get the optimal S_P, and efficient $S_P^{efficient}$, as well as the corresponding number of frequency available M, maximum unambiguous range $T_{ambiguity}$ and the probability of normal error when C equals to 100, 200, 300, 400, 500 and 600. The results are shown in Table 1 and Fig. 4.

Table 1. Comparison of S_P and $S_P^{efficient}$

C	100	200	300	400	500	600
S_p	67,71,73,74,75	33,34,35,37	23,24,25	17,18	14,15	11,12
$S_p^{efficient}$	67,71,73,74,75	35,36,37	23,24,25	17,18	14,15	11,12
M	5	4&3	3	2	2	2
$T_{ambiguity}/m$	19272985.5	29059.8&932.4	414	9.18	10.5	7.92

We can see from Table 1 and Fig. 4 that:

- With the increases of C, the number of frequency available decreases or keeps unchanged, the noise tolerance increases.
- The efficient method can get the optimal solution in most cases, it only gives the suboptimal solution when $C = 200$.
- When $C = 100$, the number of frequency available is 5, the maximum unambiguous range is 19272.9855km, which can be used in large deployed fields. But the noise tolerance is low, the probability of normal error is just 61.99% when $\beta = 0.02$.
- When $C = 200$, the number of frequency available is 4, the maximum unambiguous range is 29.0598km, which can be used in km level deployed fields.
- When $C = 300$, the maximum unambiguous range is 414m, which is appropriate for distributed localization in WSN.
- When C increases from 400 to 500, the number of frequency available keeps unchanged; but both the maximum unambiguous range and noise tolerance increases, so we should choose $C = 500$ when both are available.

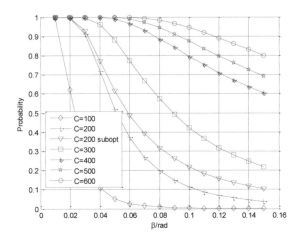

Fig. 4. Probability of Normal Error

– When $C = 400,500$ or 600, the number of frequency available is just 2, and the maximum unambiguous range is about 10m, so it can just be used in limited appliance such as the monitoring of little displacement etc. but the noise tolerance is relatively high.

Then, we compare the accuracy of ECRT-based RIR and original RIR when the error of ECRT-based RIR is normal (the case when $C = 100$ in Table. 1). Suppose $q_{ABCD} = 10000m$, standard deviation of the phase noise is 0.01rad, the region of search is [9900m,10100m], and the search granularity is 0.001m. We perform 100 trials of simulations. The histogram, mean and RMSE of the estimation errors are shown in Fig. 5.

We can see from the simulation result that both the accuracy of ECRT-based RIR and original RIR is high. Therefore, when the noise is low, ECRT-based RIR can be used in resource-limited scenario with an equivalent accuracy to RIR.

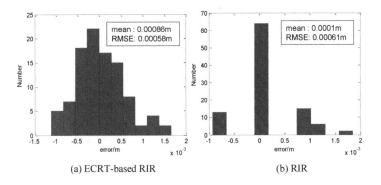

(a) ECRT-based RIR   (b) RIR

Fig. 5. Accuracy Comparison

5   Conclusion

ECRT-based RIR gives a closed form solution for the interforemetric ranging, so the computational complexity is greatly reduced. ECRT-based RIR show us the prospects of using RIR for distributed localization in WSN. This paper gives the frequency selection method for ECRT-based RIR and the relations between parameters, providing an effective guidance for system design, which will also extend the appliance of RIR.

References

1. Zekavat, R., Buehrer, R.M.: Handbook of Position Location: Theory, Practice and Advances. Wiley-IEEE Press (2012)
2. Rudafshani, M., Datta, S.: Localization in wireless sensor networks. In: Proceedings of the 6th International Symposium on Information Processing in Sensor Networks, Cambridge, Massachusetts, USA (2007)
3. Maroti, M., Kusy, B., Balogh, G., et al.: Radio interferometric geolocation. In: Proceedings of the 3rd ACM International Conference on Embedded Networked Sensor Systems, San Diego, California, USA (2005)
4. Kusy, B., Maroti, M., Balogh, G., et al.: Node density independent localization. In: Proceedings of the 5th International Symposium on Information Processing in Sensor Networks, Nashville, Tennessee, USA (2006)
5. Wang, C., Yin, Q.Y., Wang, W.J.: An efficient ranging method on Chinese remainder theorem for RIPS measurement. Sci. China Inf. Sci. 53(6), 1233–1241 (2010)
6. Zhu, Y., Liu, P., Huang, S.: Parameter optimization method to extend deployment area of radio interferometric positioning system. Journal on Communications 31(9A), 47–52 (2010)
7. McIvor, C., McLoone, M., McCanny, J.V.: Improved Montgomery modular inverse algorithm. Electron. Lett. 40, 1110–1112 (2004)
8. Huang, Z.X., Wan, Z.: Range ambiguity resolution in multiple PRF pulse Doppler radars. In: Proc. of IEEE Int. Conf. on Acoustics, Speech, and Signal Processing, Dallas, TX, USA, pp. 1786–1789 (1987)

Design and Implementation of Testing Platform for Middleware of Wireless Sensor Networks

Lipeng Yan[1], Fei Chang[1], Weijun Qin[2], Bo Li[1], and Yan Liu[1]

[1] School of Software and Microelectronics, Peking University, Beijing 102600, China
{yanlipeng,changfei}@is.iscas.ac.cn,
libo1989@pku.edu.cn,
ly@ss.pku.edu.cn
[2] Institute of Information Engineering, Chinese Academy of Sciences,
Beijing 100095, China
qinweijun@iie.ac.cn

Abstract. Middleware for wireless sensor networks (WSNs) is system software between WSNs and applications, which provides a set of common application program interface (API). With the deeper research on the middleware of WSN, the researchers focus on the testing technologies on middleware of WSN and testing platform of middleware of WSN. In this paper, we summarize and propose the standards and common methods of the testing for middleware of WSN, referencing on the ISO/IEC 9126, CSTC and China Mobile standards. We design and implement a testing platform for middleware of WSN based on Web Integration and Eclipse Plug-in technologies, which could conduct the reliability testing, the performance testing and the stress testing for certain specific middleware. The platform provides two common testing methods including the manual way and the automatic way, which aims to efficiently verify the performance, the handling capability of error and the handling capability of concurrent for the middleware of WSN. Finally we give the design details and processes of each software module, and show the experimental evaluation of the testing platform.

Keywords: Wireless Sensor Network, Middleware, Testing Platform, Functional Testing, Performance Testing.

1 Introduction

Wireless sensor network is a Multi-hop self-organizing network system formed by a large number of micro sensor nodes through a wireless network connection, which are deployed in the monitoring area. It has the multiple functions of monitoring, control, and wireless communication[1]. With the sensor network more widely used in the range of application environments, the Application Layer need to interact with the complex, heterogeneous, underlying sensor network flexibly and reliably, in order to fill the gap ,which is about resource constrain, dynamics of network topology, heterogeneous underlying embedded operating system API, between the application layer and the sensor network. To solve these

R. Wang and F. Xiao (Eds.): CWSN 2012, CCIS 334, pp. 548–561, 2013.
© Springer-Verlag Berlin Heidelberg 2013

problems, sensor network researchers and industry have proposed a technology on middleware of WSN. Middleware technology to support multi-sensor network applications has become one of the research topics to be solved in the entire sensor network.

Middleware for wireless sensor networks (WSNs) is system software between WSNs and applications, which provides a set of common application program interface (API) and segregates the difference between the underlying network hardware and reduces the complexity of the distributed environment. The middleware for WSNs can provide standardized services, technologies of adaptive strategies and mechanisms to adapt to the dynamic change of resources and application requirements. Providing a relatively stable high-level application environment for the development of wireless sensor network applications and giving researchers a unified operation platform and friendly development environment [2], [3], [4].

The Middleware for WSNs shields the differences between hardware platforms, software systems and network protocol, which provides a set of common application program interface (API).As shown in Fig. 1, the middleware can be divided into three sub-layer. By the side of sensor node, the middleware provide basic communications functions for nodes, which segregates the difference of communication between un-derlying nodes, the developers no longer focus on the underlying node communication when they develop a upper-layer application. By the side of sensor network, the mid-dleware provide common functions for upper application, such as time synchroniza-tionsecurity mechanismresource management and Location Based Service (LBS). Cooperation and communication are needed between nodes of the sensor network, and gateway to implement these functions or services. Developers can call these services directly through the middleware when developing different kinds of applications, no need to understand the underlying principle of the sensor network.

With the deeper research on the middleware of WSN, the researchers focus on the testing technologies on middleware of WSN and testing platform of middleware of WSN based on sensor nodes. Testing Platform for Middleware of Wireless Sensor Networks related to a lot of features and problems, such as the distribution of Sensor network resource, dynamic changes of network topology, the heterogeneity of nodes. The early research in the area of middleware has provided standards and architecture for the middleware of WSN, however, testing technologies on middleware of WSN has not yet been sufficiently studied. The test for the middleware of WSN is different from the traditional software testing and sensor network testing, as the middleware of WSN must take into account the low energy consumption and communication bandwidth, limited processing and storage capabilities, and dynamic changes in network topology requirements. In order to test and verify the basic functions of the sensor network middleware, such as time synchronization services, location-based services, the re-searchers should concern about the characteristics of the sensor network.

ISO /IEC 9126[6] is a software quality standards, which divides the measurement of software quality into a series of attributes and sub-attributes. ISO/IEC

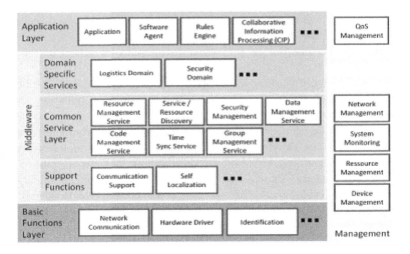

Fig. 1. Middleware of WSN

9126 standard cannot be directly applied to the assessment of the middleware of WSN for the different features of WSN. In this paper, we map ISO / IEC 9126 standard to the assessment for middleware of WSNs, and combine the middleware system testing method of China Mobile[7], we make out the testing standards, testing method and testing contents of the middleware of WSNs. On this basis, we design and implement a testing platform for WSNs, give the framework, design details and processes of each software module. and show the experimental evaluation of the testing platform. Finally, we Put forward the further research prospects of testing for the middleware of WSNs.

2   Testing Standards and Methods for Middleware of WSN

Referencing on ISO/IEC 9126 standard, and combined the middleware system test method of CSTC and China Mobile, we conclude the testing method for Middleware of WSN.

1. *Reliability Testing.* Verifying whether the Middleware System API is able to cooperate with each other and complete the design goal of the middleware system. When we do a reliability test, we mainly consider the following kinds of testing.
   - When the input of legal parameters, verify that the API function can return to the expected correct result.
   - When the input of illegal parameter, verify that the API function correctly handle illegal input parameters.
   - Verify the API function is correct in the local execution.

- Verify the API function is correct when the execution need to cooperate with other middleware.
- Verify whether the middleware runs on different platforms can interact cor-rectly and return the correct results.

2. *Performance Testing.* Performance testing to verify that the performance of software is able to meet the performance indicators when reusing under nor-mal conditions of environment and system. Finding performance bottlenecks in the system and optimizing the system. performance testing include the following kinds of testing:

   - Test the accuracy of data for monitoring and control of sensor network nodes.
   - Test the response time of a single function in the middleware system.
   - Test the Occupancy of the memory resources, CPU resources in certain hardware and software environment.

3. *Security Testing.* The security testing process to verify the application's se-curity services and identify potential security flaws. Security testing include:

   - *Security management mechanism.* Test the Middleware support for the Unified security management mechanism that from the underlying plat-form to Business Application.
   - *Security model.* Test the middleware support for Encryption component like SSLTLSJSR and security model like JAAS.
   - *Security management functions.* Test middleware support for rights man-agement, log management, Security identity and other security manage-ment functions.

4. *Stress Testing.* Test whether a Middleware is able to handle the requests when there are a lot of equipment or large amount of data access in a sim-ulated environment. The researchers also need to test the performance data of Middleware in a concurrent situation.

5. *Compatibility Test.* Test the Middleware support for various hardware config-urations, system compatibility, database compatibility, web server compatibility, Research tool compatibility and other Middleware products compatibilities[7], [8], [9], [10].

This paper designs and implements a testing platform for middleware of wireless sensor network in connection with the above reliability testing, the performance testing and the stress testing. According to the traditional methods of software testing, com-bined with the characteristics of sensor network middleware, we propose tests for the above three test methods.

Reliability testing method. We use the test of the boundary conditions in the black-box testing, which is a supplement of moderate equivalence class analysis. By long-term testing experience that a lot of errors occur on the boundary of the input or output, design test cases for a variety of boundary conditions can detect more errors. Design of possibilities in traverse all the parameters, such as the border demarcation of maximum boundary and minimum boundary of the data type, and border demarcation for the string type, the null type, the non-character string parameter and the maximum length of string parameters.

Performance testing method. For the characteristics of middleware of sensor, we should verify the data process of middleware of sensor network in sensor network environment and the effectiveness of the control of network nodes and other equip-ment. So you need to collect, analyze and process the data of the sensor network environment, the information will be treated as important basis in performance evaluation.

Stress testing method. Stress testing is a basic quality assurance behavior, which is part of every significant software testing. Stress testing resources, including memory, CPU availability, disk space and network bandwidth. Typically, we use testing tools simulate concurrent threads to carry out stress tests.

3 Testing and Verification of Sensor Network Middleware Platform Architecture

Shown in Fig. 2, the overall test platform of middleware of sensor network consists of four parts of the middleware test console, middleware test agent, sensor network data collection procedures and the tested middleware.

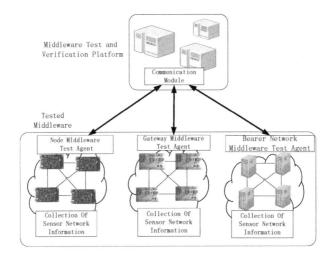

Fig. 2. System framework

Middleware test console is the main section of the platform deployed remotely, which is responsible to generate test cases, and transmit use cases to the test agent which deployed in side of the tested middleware through the communication module. The test agent performs testing functions, and the results reported to the test console. Similarly, the sensor network information collection program has also been deployed in the tested middleware side, collect the data under sensor network environment, and performance testing of the middleware basis for this assessment.

According to the type, middleware test agent can be divided into node middleware test proxy, gateway middleware test agent and bearer network middleware test agent, the test console interact with the communication module and the middleware communication agent. The node-side communication agent supports the Zigbee communication protocol, the gateway side communication agent supports TCP / IP protocol stack and serial read and write, the bearer network side communication agent supports TCP / IP protocol stack. The test agent calls the specified API of tested middleware and returns the result to test and validate console through the communication module.

4   Design and Implementation of Testing Platform for Middleware of Wireless Sensor Networks

4.1   Testing Console

The test console is divided into the following seven functional modules: test case management module, test results analysis module, communication module, the results display module, the history data management module, configuration management and log management module.

Test case management module manages test cases generated from the manual test and automatic test. In manual test, we get the test case file through file uploading then test cases will be transferred to the test agent side through the communication module; In automatic test, we infer to the correct test cases depending on the configuration and rules and write into the test file then the test case transmission to the test agent side through the communication module.

Test result analysis module dose analysis and statistics of test data, for example, the computation of the mean, variance, etc., and reliability fault tolerance test results, the stress test results and performance test results. Communication module connect and communication with test agent through the Mina[11–13], transfer test case file to the test agent side, and receives the test results file from the test agent.

The results display module displays the test result of test data by analysis and sta-tistics in the result interface. A test result of middleware can be subdivided into relia-bility/fault tolerance test results, the stress test results and performance test results. Different test content take a different form of display, the main display form type contains charts, tables and text.

The history data management module is for managing historical data. The log management module record test records of console test middleware, and test results will be shown in the log belongs to the interface the form of log text. Configuration module test console configuration information, and automated test configuration information.

Fig. 3 shows the test console testing process. First, the console initializes each module, and to determine whether the successful launch of the console. After the start of the console, and connect the test agent, the user selects the test mode. If you choose a manual test, you need the user to upload a test file; If you choose automated testing, it will generate test case based reasoning results and write the test file. Then uploading a test file to test the agent side through communication module and listening returned test results. After received the test results from the agent side, analyze test results, and show the result in the page, then the test ends.

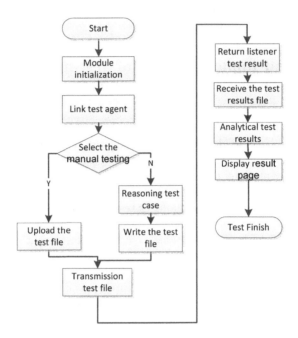

Fig. 3. Flow chart of test console function

4.2   Test Agent

Test agents are deployed on the tested middleware side, which includes communication module, the test case analysis module, the test execution modules and test results management module.

The communication module is used to test console connection and to receive the test case file from console, then send result document in the agency side to the test console. Test case analysis module parse test case file from console into case object, which is for the usage of the test execution module. After resolve the file, it forms a specific test case list of objects, including stress test case list of objects, the performance of the test case list of objects, reliability/fault tolerance test case object list. The test execution module removed test case from the list of use case object and use Junit and other test tools to perform the test. The test execution module is tested middleware reliability/fault tolerance test results, performance test results and the stress test results.

Fig. 4 shows the testing process of test agent. First, the test agent initializes each module, and to determine whether the successful launch of the console. After the start of the console, it will receive communication connect from the console, and receive the test case file. Then, it analyze test case file, if you need to perform a reliability test, it forms a list of reliability/fault tolerance test case. Similarly, according to the need, it forms stress test case list and the performance test case list. After the formation of the test cases, the tested middleware API is called to perform the test and will get the reliability/fault tolerance test results. And for performance test results, you need to open the sensor network data acquisition program, collecting sensor network node information. Finally, the test result is written to the results file, the test results module will send the file to the console side through the communication, then execution finished.

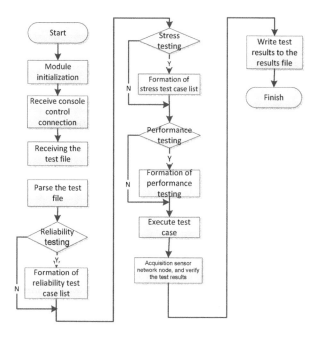

Fig. 4. Flow chart of agent function testing

4.3   Sensor Network Data Acquisition

Sensor network data acquisition program is also deployed in tested middleware side, used to collect data of sensor network, which includes the serial reader module, sensor network data analysis module, and sensor network data management module. After calling tested middleware API, execution result need to be checked that is performance test. Sensor network node data is related to the test of performance of the sensor network middleware, which come from sink node via serial reader module through Zigbee protocol listener. Serial reader module gets the original hexadecimal data and then gets meaningful data after the resolve of the sensor network data through analysis. Sensor network data management module manages the node information from the sensor network data analysis module, leaving only meaningful node data for tested middleware.

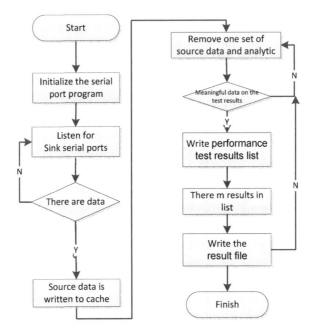

Fig. 5. Flow chart of acquisition sensor network node information

Fig. 5 shows the flow chart of the sensor network information collection. File type is needed during the test of middleware of sensor network to collect corresponding node data. First we should initialize the serial port program, and monitor whether the SINK serial port has data. If it has data, then write the 16 binary source data to cache, another thread removes a source data from the cache each time and resolves the data. If the data is meaningful to the middleware under testing, then write the data to the per-formance test results list, otherwise, just get rid of the data and continue to take out a new data from the cache. Collecting the information needs only m parts, stopping collecting after the list is full of m parts, and then write the results to the performance test results file.

4.4   Design of Testing Methods

According to the testing method of thinking in chapter two, we focus on designing the testing method of the reliability testingthe performance testing and the stress testing. Use the method of equivalence class partitioning method to generate the testing cases of functional testing. In the reliability testing, the tester should give the parameter configuration of the tested API, and for the numeric type parameters, the tester should also list the maximum value and minimum value of the borderboundary overflow exception handingwhether the parameters can be null or notwrong type exception handing and whether the parameters can be zero or not. For the character type parameters, configuration information should contain the maximum length of the characteroverflow exception handingwhether the parameters can be null or not and wrong type exception handing. For the same reason, we can configure other types of parameters. Next, we can get a group of the right parameter sets and a group of the wrong parameter sets through the configuration information of every parameter, the group collection use the border demarcation method of software testing method. Finally, we can traverse the right parameter group and the wrong parameter group of n API parameters, and get the final test case through matching the results.

For the reliability testing, we need to evaluate the performance of the middleware, and the data information of the sensor networks is an important basis for the evaluation. Taking the time synchronization middleware for example, we can get the real time of the node m by using the sensor network information collection program, and at the same time, the system time is n, so the absolute difference of (m-n) is the performance error value of the middleware. Finally, we can get the average error value and the variance by several data.

For the stress test, we use the GroboUtils as the stress testing tool. It extends the function of the JUnit, and can implement a stress test, the stress testing investigate the system memory usage and the CPU usage when concurrent threads call the middle-ware, the appropriate time and whether middleware performance changes or not under the stress testing are another two important bases.

5   Experimental Verification

Focusing on several particular sensor network middleware testing and checking the testing platform, we can take the time synchronization middleware of the sensor networks for example now.

In the experimental verification, the name of the being tested sensor network time synchronization middleware API is Send_Syn_Command, it is packaged by a TinyOs time synchronization package, the function receives a long time parameter called time, and the parameter can synchronize all Zigbee node time. This parameter can be null, and must be between 1300000000 and 1400000000. For example, when we call this time synchronization API to income a parameter 1326785545, the time syn-chronization middleware correct the node time to 2012-02-21,15:58 p.m.

The following shows the results of the manual testing and the automatic testing.

5.1   Manual Testing Experimental Verification

First of all, we should write the testing case file, and then manual design the possible testing case using this file. The form of testing cases are the following, including testing APIincoming parameters and the returned results.

```
<API>Send_Syn_Command</API>
<PARAMETER type="Long">1326785545</PARAMETER>
<EX_RESULT>SUCCESS</EX_RESULT>
```

By using the testing platform, we can get the results as the Fig. 6.

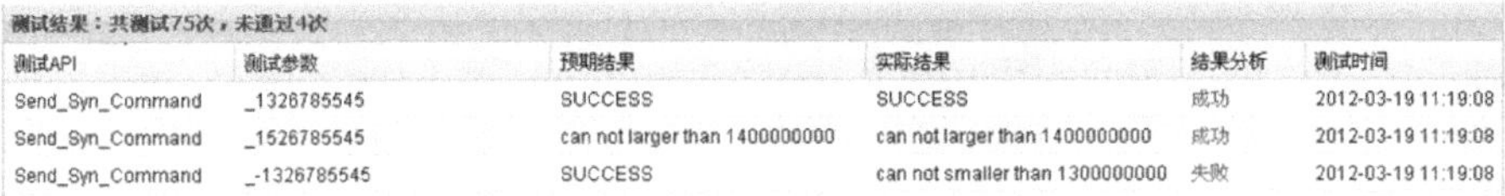

测试API	测试参数	预期结果	实际结果	结果分析	测试时间
Send_Syn_Command	_1326785545	SUCCESS	SUCCESS	成功	2012-03-19 11:19:08
Send_Syn_Command	_1526785545	can not larger than 1400000000	can not larger than 1400000000	成功	2012-03-19 11:19:08
Send_Syn_Command	_-1326785545	SUCCESS	can not smaller than 1300000000	失败	2012-03-19 11:19:08

测试结果：共测试75次，未通过4次

Fig. 6. The interface display of the reliability testing

We can see, there are 75 testing cases, and four of them do not pass, the first three test cases are shown in the figure. In the third testing case, testing parameter is set to -1326785545, according to the real middleware testing we can get the result: "can't smaller than 1300000000", but the intended result of the testing case is "success", so the test is failure.

5.2   Automatic Testing Experimental Verification

First of all, we should configure the testing document, and then explain the perfor-mance of parameters in the time synchronization middlewarethe return value of the testing case and the error handing. Shown in the following figure:

```
<para>
    <ifCanNull>no</ifCanNull>
    <nullerror>input can not be null</nullerror>
    <type>long</type>
    <typeerror>input should be long</typeerror>
    <maxnum>1400000000</maxnum>
    <maxerror>can not larger than 1400000000</maxerror>
    <minnum>1300000000</minnum>
    <minerror>can not smaller than 1300000000</minerror>
    <ifZero>no</ifZero>
    <zeroError>input can not be 0</zeroError>
</para>
```

And then using the testing platform to run a automatic testing, we get results like the Fig. 7, now we can see there are one fail when the parameter is zero, so the middle can't handle the zero parameter error.

测试结果：共测试12次，未通过1次					
测试API	测试参数	预期结果	实际结果	结果分析	测试时间
syntime	_1400000000	SUCCESS	SUCCESS	成功	2012-03-19 15:45:52
syntime	_1300000000	SUCCESS	SUCCESS	成功	2012-03-19 15:45:52
syntime	_1399999999	SUCCESS	SUCCESS	成功	2012-03-19 15:45:52
syntime	_1299999999	can not smaller than 1 300000000	can not smaller than 1300000000	成功	2012-03-19 15:45:52
syntime	_1380151968	SUCCESS	SUCCESS	成功	2012-03-19 15:45:52
syntime	_1394262077	SUCCESS	SUCCESS	成功	2012-03-19 15:45:52
syntime	_1359961659	SUCCESS	SUCCESS	成功	2012-03-19 15:45:52
syntime	_1354411513	SUCCESS	SUCCESS	成功	2012-03-19 15:45:52
syntime	_null	input can not be null	input can not be null	成功	2012-03-19 15:45:52
syntime	_1400000001	can not larger than 1400000000	can not larger than 1400000000	成功	2012-03-19 15:45:52
syntime	_1299999999	can not smaller than 1 300000000	can not smaller than 1300000000	成功	2012-03-19 15:45:52
syntime	_0	input can not be 0	SUCCESS	失败	2012-03-19 15:45:52

Fig. 7. The interface display of the automatic testing

Shown as the Fig. 8, in the results of the automatic performance testing, we have collected six time synchronization data, and the average error of the time synchroni-zation middleware is two seconds.

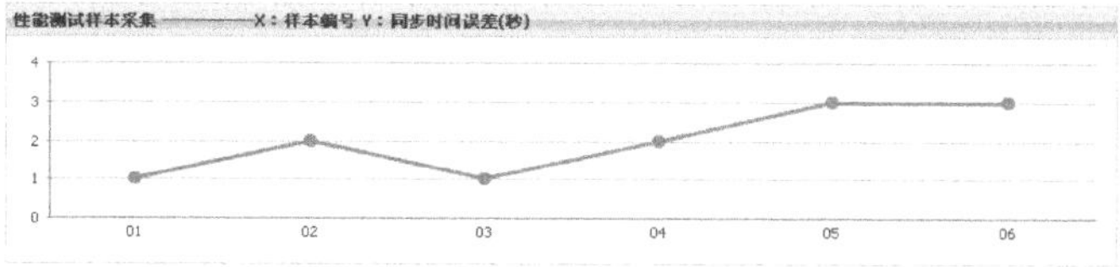

时间同步性能测试结果：平均误差2秒				
编号	测试节点	系统时间	节点时间	误差值
1	13	2012-03-19 11:19:02	2012-03-19 11:19:03	1秒
2	13	2012-03-19 11:19:03	2012-03-19 11:19:05	2秒
3	11	2012-03-19 11:19:03	2012-03-19 11:19:04	1秒
4	13	2012-03-19 11:19:04	2012-03-19 11:19:06	2秒
5	13	2012-03-19 11:19:05	2012-03-19 11:19:08	3秒
6	13	2012-03-19 11:19:06	2012-03-19 11:19:09	3秒

Fig. 8. The interface display of the performance testing

Shown as the Fig. 9, in the automatic stress testing results, we can see the us-age of the memory and the CPU, so we come to a conclusion that the middleware does not support concurrent operations.

6 Conclusion and Further Research

The sensor network middleware can provide a high up in relatively stable appli-cation environment to the wireless sensor network application development, so a sensor network middleware testing platform built by sensor network nodes is a

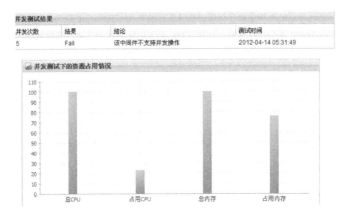

Fig. 9. The interface display of the stress testing

must. This thesis show us some certain methods and standard of sensor network middleware testing, and implements a sensor network middleware testing platform for some specific middleware, it can test the reliabilityperformance and the stress of a middleware by manual testing and automatic testing. Now the testing platform can't test the safetypacket loss and network delay of middleware, so the platform needs to be further strengthened.

Acknowledgement. The work has been funded by National Science and Technology Major Project (2011ZX03005-002) and National Key Technology R&D Program (2012BAH20B03).

References

1. Sun, L.M.: Wireless sensor networks, pp. 6–8. Tsinghua University Press, Beijing (2006)
2. Kormentzas, G., Magedanz, T.: Middleware challenges for next generation networks and services. Computer Network 51(16), 4596–4598 (2007)
3. Masri, W., Mammeri, Z.: Middleware for Wireless Sensor Networks: Approaches, Challenges, and Projects. In: Proc. of IEEE Signal Processing and Communications, pp. 1399–1402. IEEE Press, New York (2007)
4. Molla, M.M., Ahamed, S.I.: A survey of middleware for sensor network and challenges. In: Proc. of Parallel Processing Workshops, pp. 223–228. IEEE Computer Society, NJ (2006)
5. Li, S., Son, S.H., Stankovic, J.A.: Event Detection Services Using Data Service Middleware in Distributed Sensor Networks. In: Zhao, F., Guibas, L.J. (eds.) IPSN 2003. LNCS, vol. 2634, pp. 502–517. Springer, Heidelberg (2003)
6. Correia, J.P., Kanellopoulos, Y., Visser, J.: A Survey-based Study of the Mapping of System Properties to ISO/IEC 9126 Maintainability Characteristics. In: Proc. of IEEE International Conference on Software Maintenance, pp. 61–70. IEEE Press, New York (2009)

7. China Mobile research institute: China Mobile middleware system test code. China Standard Press, Beijing (2006)

8. Dongarra, J.J.: Performance of various computers using standard linear equations software. ACM, SIGARCH Computer 20(3) (1992)

9. Werner-Allen, G., Swieskowski, P., Welsh, M.: A wireless sensor network testbed. In: Proc. of IEEE International Symposium on Information Processing in Sensor Networks, pp. 483–488. IEEE Press, New York (2005)

10. Ertin, E., Arora, A., Ramnath, R., et al.: A testbed for sensing at scale. In: Proc. of IEEE the Fifth International Conference on Information Processing in Sensor Networks, pp. 399–406. IEEE Press, New York (2006)

11. Krechmer, K., Baskin, E.J.: Standards Engineering, p. 2 (2007)

12. Get rewarded for your ideas: Top Shops Contest is offering prizes for the best shop innovations. Successful Farming, 4 (2006)

13. Rossi, K., Molin, K.: Software components-based management of cellular transmission networks, pp. 3–7. IEEE Press, New York (2006)

A Partitioned Link Scheduling Algorithm for Wireless Multimedia Sensor Networks

Guoqiang Yan, Weijun Duan, Chao Ma, and Liang Huang

School of Electronics and Information
Northwestern Polytechnical University, Xi'an, China

Abstract. Link scheduling is one of the main difficulties for a large amount of data real-time and reliable transmission in Wireless Multimedia Sensor Networks. To improve multi-hop transmission performance, MAC layer link scheduling algorithms have received extensive attention. These algorithm allocated slots for every data link. It could lower the number of conflicts and retransmissions. However, as the network size increases, both centralized or distributed scheduling algorithms encounter performance degradation problems. To overcome this problem, a novel scheduling algorithm which based on network partition was proposed. In sparse region, the MAC layer switches to a simple 802.11 mode; In intensive region, the MAC layer switches to queue length based scheduling mode. Emulation study showed that the proposed algorithm had a better performance in both terms of total queue length and average delay.

Keywords: link scheduling, distributed algorithm, MAC, MWSN.

Wireless Multimedia Sensor Networks (WMSNs) is an inheritance of Wireless Sensor Networks (WSN) for its multimedia sensing and high-performance processing abilities. Because its widely applications in military and civilian, it has caused intensive attention of governments and academia [1]. In WMSNs, media data, such as audio, image, video is collected and transported in multi-hop manner. Large amount of data make a big challenge for transport protocols(Multimedia data has 2-3 orders of magnitude than single physical value data). How to enhance throughput and delay performance becomes one of the most important key technology in WMSNs [2].

To the end of transporting large amount of data,*jointly routing and scheduling algorithms* caused intensive attentions [3]. The main idea of these algorithms is taking into account the queue length from the upper layer of networks while scheduling multimedia access. When time is divided into n slots, in every slot, a child set of total link sets which are interfere free is chosen to transmit packets. With this kind of cross-layer design, MAC layer scheduling can allocate media resources more efficiently. In theory, scheduling algorithm has a big enhance for network transport, however, searching an optimal scheduling is hard. For instance, under k-hop interference condition, Maximum Weighted Scheduling (MWS) computing an optimal schedule is NP hard. So R. Preis proposed Greedy Maximal Scheduling (GMS) in [5]. GMS could reduce complexity, and

R. Wang and F. Xiao (Eds.): CWSN 2012, CCIS 334, pp. 562–568, 2013.
© Springer-Verlag Berlin Heidelberg 2013

have 50% provable performance in contrast to MWS. GMS is a centralized algorithm. Literature [6] proposed a distributed version of GMS named Local Greedy Scheduling. In [7], A. Dimakis and J. Walrand studied throughput difference between GMS and MWS, and proposed *local pooling condition*. If the network topology meets local pooling condition, GMS could have the same throughput as MWS.

For purpose of getting more simple and efficient scheduling algorithms, many researchers contributed their efforts. These works could be divided into 4 categories[8]:

1. **Throughput maximal methods**, finding scheduling maximize network throughput against interference constraints, such as GSM[5];
2. **Pick and compare methods**, randomly choosing scheduling until getting the best one;
3. **Carrier Sense based methods**, scheduling choosing based on SNR computation which measured by carrier sense;
4. **Complexity and performance balanced methods**, in this method, a parameter is set to achieve a trade-off between the complexity and performance.

First category algorithms are usually centralized algorithms which can compute upper bound of scheduling performance. For second category, its hard to judge the performance of two scheduling algorithm. And Pick and compare approaches convergence should be carefully considered. Carrier Sense based methods have high complexity for SNR computing. The last category needs locally package exchange, and can make trade-off between the complexity and performance.

In previous studies, scheduling schemas had performance degeneration problem as the network size increased. Although, a distributed algorithm does not require a global coordination node, it still should collect information about the neighbour nodes or the interference nodes around in execution of the algorithm. Therefore, a distributed algorithm cannot fully avoid the complexity when the network size increases. In fact, we found that not all link transmissions in the network need to be scheduled. Only when the node encounters interference and cannot meet traffic demands, it should be scheduled. Base on this understood, we introduced a scheduling algorithm based on network partitioning. In this scheduling, every node has two MAC layer mode. It will switch between random media access mode and queue based scheduling mode depends on if the node locates in sparse or density partition area. By this kind of partitioning scheduling, we can control the complexity while keeping packet forwarding efficiency.

1   Model and Assumptions

1.1   Interference Model

Interference model describes how links interfere with each other. Specifically, different models mean different interfere sets which consist of interfered neighbour nodes. In this paper, a simple interference model as fig.1 shows is employed. In this model, nodes have the same round transmission and interference range. Link 2 interferes link 1, and link 3 does not interfere link 2.

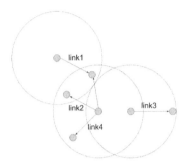

Fig. 1. Interference model

1.2   System Description

We consider a wireless sensor network with N nodes. Let $G(V, E)$ denote the networks, where V denotes node the set of all nodes, E denotes the set of all links. Each sensor node is in charge of both detecting events and relaying packets. If nodes detected an event, they generated a data packet, and delivered to the sink node s via multi-hop relaying.

Due to uneven distribution of network nodes, there are dense or sparse areas in the networks. We assume that every node has two MAC layer mode: CSMA mode and STDMA mode. Nodes in sparse areas are set to work in CSMA mode, and dense areas nodes are set to work in STDMA mode. In both modes, time is divided into mini slots. In CSMA mode, a node randomly chooses back-off slots to communicate if the former transmission is conflicted. In STDMA mode, scheduling node sets which composed of neighbouring or interfering nodes are working in distributed link scheduling manner. The algorithm introduced in our paper is to implement this kind of partitioning and dual MAC scheduling.

2   Network Partition Algorithm

Network partition is the premise of our proposed scheduling algorithm. Network partition should consider not only the density of the distribution of nodes, but also the amount of the node traffic it carries. In this section, a partitioning algorithm based on the idle slot listening is presented. The algorithm is inspired by literature [9] to estimate the number of competition nodes around by idle slot listening. In [9], idle slot listening was used to calculate the density of the network. In this paper, we use idle slot listening to calculate network traffic capacity and decide if a node belongs to the dense or sparse region.

In CSMA, nodes randomly choose a slot to transmit packages. Suppose n nodes compete for m slots. The probability for node j to choose the ith slots is $1/m$. Let random variable X_i denotes the number of nodes who also select the ith slots to transmit. According to binomial distribution,

$$\Pr[X_i = l] = \binom{n}{1}\left(\frac{1}{m}\right)^l\left(1 - \frac{1}{m}\right)^{n-l} \tag{1}$$

Further, expected number of slots which selected by nodes is

$$E[l, n] = m\binom{n}{1}\left(\frac{1}{m}\right)^l\left(1 - \frac{1}{m}\right)^{n-l} \tag{2}$$

Let $l = 0$, we get expected number of free slots,

$$E[0, n] = m\left(1 - \frac{1}{m}\right)^n \tag{3}$$

If m is known, from the above formulation we can estimate the number of competition nodes. Further, we also can use statistical sampling and averaging method to estimate the upper and lower limits of n, by setting confidence probability parameter.

Now, we calculate the actual traffic capacity. Suppose node j chooses the ith slots to transmit and succeed. It means the other n nodes do not select the ith slots, and the probability is $\left(1 - \frac{1}{m}\right)^{n-1}$. Let random variable Y_j denotes the jth transmit event. If transmit succeeded, $Y_j = 1$, others, $Y_j = 0$. With N times sending, $\sum_{j=1}^{N} Y_j$ obeys the binomial distribution $B(N, \left(1 - \frac{1}{m}\right)^{n-1})$.

$$\Pr(\sum_{j=1}^{N} Y_j \geq k) = 1 - \sum_{j=1}^{k}\binom{N}{j}\left(1 - \frac{1}{m}\right)^{(n-1)j}\left(1 - \left(1 - \frac{1}{m}\right)^{(n-1)}\right)^{N-j} \tag{4}$$

The above formulation means, under probability condition, k in N slots can be used to transmit data successfully. The actual transmission rate is $r = R \times k/(N \times m)$. Accordingly, the actual size of the load flow can determine whether the node is the bottleneck node in CSMA mode.

3   Scheduling Algorithm

When the number of competition nodes increases, the performance of the CSMA protocol degrades. In this section, we proposed to use queue based distributed link scheduling algorithms in dense region to keep up transmission performance. The algorithm we employed is derived from the literature [11]. In order to adapt to the dual-MAC work mode operation, the algorithm has been redesigned.

A. Queue length based scheduling

Scheduling can be divided into two phases: *queue length exchange phase* and *data transmission phase*. Each phase is composed of M mini slots. In the first phase, in order to give higher priority to the node with longest queue, each nodes should exchange the queue length information with its neighbour nodes via two-hop broadcasting.

In the second phase, nodes randomly choose a slot from 1,2,?M+1 slots to transmit based on probability computing. If the $M + 1$ slot was selected, nodes rejected to send in this round. By two-hop broadcasting information exchange, each link e knows the queue length of the node in its interfering sets. The probability is calculated as follows,

$$\Pr\{Y = M + 1\} = e^{-P_e}$$
$$\Pr\{Y = m\} = e^{-P_l \frac{m-1}{M}} - e^{-P_l \frac{m}{M}}, \tag{5}$$
$$m = 1, 2, \cdots M.$$

Where $P_e = \alpha \frac{q_e/c_e}{\max_{l \in \varepsilon_e} [\sum_{l \in \varepsilon_e} q_l/c_l]}$, c_e is the queue length constraints for link e, and $\alpha = \log(M)$. For the algorithm is probability-based approach, nodes may still encounter with a conflict in sending packets. So two agreements were made to prevent conflicts: (1)Node exited the current round of transmission if it listened interference from other node in the chosen mini slot, (2) When two nodes happened to conflicted, they both exit the current round of transmission.

B. Compatible with CSMA

In a scheduling node set, the nodes on the edge of the dense and sparse region need to deal with two communication modes, on one hand, participating in the competition on queue length based scheduling, on the other hand, sending or receiving the information to or from CSMA nodes. To make the two protocols compatible, we introduced the concept of *rounds* and *slots* while implementing CSMA protocol. Specifically, channel competition was designed to be slots competition, random back-off was designed to be inround back-off. At the queue length-based scheduling side, CTS / RTS messages were introduced to control media access. Under the protocol interference model, this design can well adapt to partition scheduling.

4   Simulation Results

In this section, we compare the performance of our proposed algorithm with other several scheduling polices, including centralized GMS[6], Q-Sched[11] and CSMA. We measure the total queue lengths and the average scheduling delay in the network changing the traffic loads.

A. Simulation Setup

We generate a network graph on a $100 \times 100m^2$ square area by randomly placing 50 nodes. Two nodes are connected by a link if they are within a distance of $20m$. For each link, we consider single-hop traffic with mean arrival rate either 0 (with probability 0.2), 1 (with probability 0.6), or 2 (with probability 0.2). Packets arrive at links following a Poisson distribution.

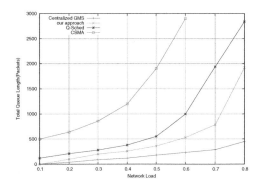

Fig. 2. Queue length sum under different traffic

B. The sum of the node queue

Fig. 2 shows the total queue lengths under centralized GMS, Q-Sched, CSMA, and our proposed algorithm. For the traffic load vector randomly chosen as in the above, we scale the load vector by multiplying a factor. The x-axis represents the scaling factor. We observe that the total queue length rapidly increases over a certain threshold for each scheduling policy. The load at the threshold can be considered as the boundary of the capacity region of the policy, and can be used to measure the performance of the scheduling policy. From the figure, we can see that the performance of our proposed algorithm is between Q-Sched and centralized GMS with a threshold in the range of 0.5 to 0.6.

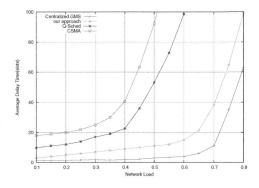

Fig. 3. Average scheduling delay under different traffic

C. Average scheduling delay

Total queue length sum reflects the overall service level of the entire network. Average scheduling delay reflects the average number of time slots for a packet to wait before it is transmitted. As Fig. 3 shows, the proposed algorithm still achieves a good performance close to centralized GMS. The threshold is in the range from 0.6 to 0.7 which is better than Q-sched obviously.

5   Conclusion

Wireless Link scheduling in wireless multimedia sensor networks is a very important issue: (1) finding the optimal scheduling in multi-hop interference has a high computational complexity; (2) centralized scheduling algorithm is difficult to implement in distributed manner; (3) when the network size growing, existing distributed scheduling algorithm performance degraded. This paper proposed partitioned link scheduling algorithm. This algorithm partitioned the network into dense and sparse areas, and made node switch to different schedule policy according the density of the area it belongs. we evaluated the scheduling algorithm under different traffic load in terms of queue length sum and average scheduling delay. The experimental results showed that the proposed algorithm is superior to pure distributed scheduling algorithm, close to centralized GMS algorithm.

References

1. Akyildiz, I.F., Melodia, T., Chowdury, K.R.: Wireless multimedia sensor networks: A survey. IEEE Wireless Communications 14(6), 32–39 (2007)
2. Almeida, J., Grilo, A., Pereira, P.R.: Multimedia Data Transport for Wireless Sensor Networks. In: Next Generation Internet Networks, NGI 2009, July 1-3, pp. 1–8 (2009)
3. Krishnaswamy, D.: Robust Routing and Scheduling in Wireless Mesh Networks under Dynamic Traffic Conditions. IEEE Transactions on Mobile Computing 8(12), 1705–1717 (2009)
4. Avis, D.: A Survey of Heuristics for the Weighted Matching Problem. Networks 13(4), 475–493 (1983)
5. Preis, R.: Linear Time 1/2-Approximation Algorithm for Maximum Weighted Matching in General Graphs. In: Symposium on Theoretical Aspects of Computer Science (1999)
6. Hoepman, J.-H.: Simple Distributed Weighted Matchings, eprint (October 2004)
7. Dimakis, A., Walrand, J.: Sufficient Conditions for Stability of Longest-Queue-First Scheduling: Second-order Properties using Fluid Limits. Advances in Applied Probability 38(2), 505–521 (2006)
8. Joo, C., Shroff, N.B.: Local Greedy Approximation for Scheduling in Multi-hop Wireless Networks. IEEE Transactions on Mobile Computing, 1–14 (2011)
9. Riga, N., Matta, I., Bestavros, A.: DIP: Density Inference Protocol for wireless sensor networks and its application to density-unbiased statistics. Bernoulli, 1–10 (2005)
10. De Couto, D., Aguayo, D., Bicket, J., Morris, R.: High-throughput path metric for multi-hop wireless routing. In: Proceedings of MOBICOM 2003 (2003)
11. Gupta, A., Lin, X., Srikant, R.: Low-Complexity Distributed Scheduling Algorithms for Wireless Networks. Analysis 17(6), 1846–1859 (2009)

Research of Green Moisture Monitoring Node Based on Hardware Modular Design

Dongxuan Yang[1], Yan Chen[*,1], Kedong Wang[1], and Hong Guo[2]

[1] School of Computer and Information Engineering, Beijing Technology and Business University, Beijing 100048
[2] Kunshan Nokisens SAC Co., Ltd 21532
yangdongxuan@yahoo.com.cn, {bjchy2003,wangkdd}@163.com,
guohong@sensors.com.cn

Abstract. The node for building of wireless sensor network to monitor the moisture of urban green space based on the Modular design ideas was designed and implemented. Node is connected together by three separate boards, wireless transceiver, microprocessor and sensor backplane. In order to monitor the vertical distribution of the soil moisture, the sensor base plate is designed that it can access the 8-channel soil moisture sensor at the same time. The node has a time-sharing function. The test results show that the average current is 0.256 mA with the collection frequency of 30 seconds, it is 10 uA in sleeping mode. It can save power consumption than similar products by about 30.

Keywords: Modular design, Soil moisture monitoring node, Low-power, WSN.

1 Introduction

As of the 2011the water for the urban green irrigation is about 100 million cubic meters each year in Beijing.[1] But the water is a serious shortage in Beijing, so it will be a hot topic research about the water-saving how the irrigation systems of the urban green space can be intelligent controlled[2]. The monitoring technology of soil moisture is typically used in the field of agricultural irrigation, there are no more mature results for the research of soil moisture monitoring of urban green space.

There are three popular methods of soil moisture monitoring technology in the agricultural field, such as mobile moisture measurement technology, fixed soil moisture monitoring stations and remote sensing monitoring[3]. For mobile moisture measurement technology it is used of the portable instruments of soil moisture monitoring in different parts of the soil sample monitoring[4]. The expenditure of labor costs will increase for mobile moisture measurement technology with a large number of urban green space in scattered locations. Fixed moisture monitoring stations overcome the shortcomings of the former by establishing fixed monitoring sites within the limited area. But the cost ofestablishing

---

[*] Corresponding author.

R. Wang and F. Xiao (Eds.): CWSN 2012, CCIS 334, pp. 569–577, 2013.
© Springer-Verlag Berlin Heidelberg 2013

fixed soil moisture monitoring stations is too large for each block of the large number of green. Remote sensing soil moisture measurement technology gets the moisture data by deal with surface image which are sent by aviation aircraft or spacecraft[5]. But cities have very different three-dimensional structure compared to farmland, the soil conditions of low-level vegetation can not be collected sometimes, so this method is also not suitable for urban green space.

In addition to the above three kinds of soil moisture measurement method, the research of moisture measurement technology based WSN (Wireless Sensor Network) has relatively popular recently[6-7]. Jin Guang-chao[8], Wang-jian[9] has a more in-depth study of soil moisture monitoring system based on Zig-Bee technology. The main advantages is that wireless sensor nodes is better in terms of low power operation compared to the traditional method of measuring soil moisture and the wireless network can be configured from the network without human intervention routing[10]. The hardware design of soil moisture monitoring node based- WSN has been made more in-depth study, which is designed to realize of a low-power and the high reliability by means of discrete design.

2   Modular Design Ideas

Device type of WSN is divided into three, namely, the coordinator node, the router node, and child nodes[11]. Nodes described in this paper is collectively referred to as router nodes and child nodes. The function of router node will be expanded, it also can collect data.

Common hardware circuit boards of wireless sensor node are integrated design, the capabilities of wireless communication of the RF chip and capabilities of strong data processing of single-chip are integrated into a circuit board, while the circuit board also has a lot of sensor interface[12]. Even though this design is more popular, but its disadvantage is also obvious. The first is that the extension of function is difficult. This type of node is only applicable to monitoring in a single environment, if you get other environments, you can not adapt, Followed by maintenance costs are high, if a part of the circuit fails, then you have to replace the entire node. The most important thing is such a short life cycle of product, because the function has been fixed, not flexible on their own hardware upgrade under the rapid development of electronic technology.

Because the problems faced by the integrated design, a discrete design of circuit hardware is drew up in this paper. Node is grouped into three major components in accordance with the functional, namely, the wireless transceiver module for wireless network communications, microprocessor module is responsible for data collection and processing, as well as the sensor module. A complete circuit board of the node is formed by connecting the circuit of the three different functions. The circuit structure of a node shown in Figure 1.

Compared to the circuit design of the traditional node, discrete design has the following advantages:

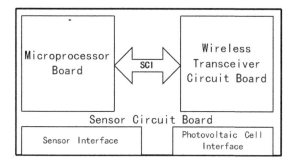

Fig. 1. Node Hardware Structure

1) Be easily upgraded. The wireless transceiver board and microprocessor board can be removed, so if you need a separate upgrade module unnecessary redesigning the entire hardware.

2) Facilitate reuse. The system is based on the ZigBee network now, when radio frequency module is replace, it can also be applied to other wireless communication networks, such as GPRS, 3G, Wi-Fi , Bluetooth and so on.

3) High reliability. As a result of discrete design, if a module is damaged or not working properly, just this board is removed and replaced.

The photo of the node is shown in Figure 2.

Fig. 2. Node circuit photo

3   The Design of Wireless Transceiver and the Microprocessor Board

TI's CC2530 chip is used as the core processing chip of the node's wireless transceiver module, Freescale's 9S12G chips is used as data processing module, ST's M25PE20 chip is used as memory modules.

CC2530 as the core of the RF module has a wireless transceiver module for ZigBee wireless communication protocol, as well as an enhanced 8051 core to help run the ZigBee protocol stack program and some simple data processing procedure. The radio frequency chip with 256KB in-system programmable Flash, 8KB RAM memory. Operating conditions, the power consumption of chip is 24mA when receiving data, the power consumption of chip is 29 mA when sending data, In sleeping mode power consumption is only microampere level.

In the design of the wireless RF module, CC2530 + CC2591 combinations isn't used which is recommended by official, also the design method can effectively enhance the gain of the RF transceiver circuit, to improve the quality of transmission distance and transmission, but the power consumption will be higher. To improve wireless signal quality of the RF transceiver at the same time the power consumption does not be increased, a Balun filter 2450BM15A0002 is used at the interface of antenna instead of discrete band-pass filter circuit. In this way the clutter signal out of the ZigBee communication bands can be effectively filtrated out, while significantly reducing the area of circuit. The CC2530 antenna circuit schematic diagram is showed in Figure 3.

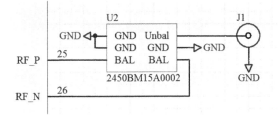

Fig. 3. Antenna circuit schematic diagram

The supply voltage of core processing chip 9S12G of the data processing module is 3.3V as the same as CC2530. The MCU with 1-way CAN transceiver module, 3-way SCI asynchronous serial interface module, 3-way SPI synchronous serial interface module, 8-channel 16-bit counter channels, 12 channels 10 ADC channels. The bus frequency can be multiplied to 64MHz with PLL module, also with a strong computing and controlling output. All the available IO pins are leaded by pin in the form in the data processing module, the module not only can be applied at this stage programs, and more space is provided for the subsequent upgrade program. SCI communication is used for data exchange between the RF processing module and the data processing module.

4   Sensor Backplane Board Design

A bridge for the other board is provided by means of sensor backplane circuit board. In addition, the board also includes a power management module, signal conditioning modules, and data storage module.

4.1 Power Management Module

The power management module includes a voltage regulator circuit and a power switch circuit, the input of the power regulator circuit is provided by photovoltaic modules, low power consumption of the node is determined by the module.

The node need the supply voltage of 3.3V and 4.2V, 3.3V voltage supplies power for the processor module, conditioning modules, memory modules and chips, 4.2V voltage which is the input voltage of the photovoltaic modules supplies power for the soil moisture sensor module directly.

4.2V input voltage is stabilized voltage to 3.3V by using two MIC5205-3.3 chip in the regulator circuit, one of them supplies power for the RF processor module, and the other provide voltage for the remaining modules.

All power switches are controlled by the microprocessor module through the IO port, in addition to the wireless transceiver module. All the rest of the module power are controlled through the P-channel FET, such as memory modules, conditioning modules, and sensor power supply interface. The FET is the IR's IRF7239 dual-channel P-channel FET. The connection diagram of the power management module is shown in Figure 4.

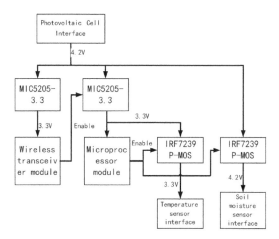

Fig. 4. Power Management Module

4.2 Signal Conditioning Modules

Signal conditioning module is also designed in the sensor base plate. According to the design and planning, each sensor node can be equipped with eight soil moisture sensors and eight temperature sensors. The benefits of this design is that it can reduce the total number of sensor nodes within some green space, more interface means that the sensor node can get more data collection in the horizontal and vertical green space. Therefore the measurement range will be increased by means of multiple sensors collecting in a single node.

According to the traditional design ideas, each sensor interface should be corresponded to the signal conditioning modules, because the output signal of soil moisture sensor and temperature sensor are non-standard voltage, it will be amplified and conditioned to the standard voltage through conditioning circuit. According to the traditional design method, the 16 sensor interface for this program need to take up a lot of area, it will result in large energy loss [13-15].Therefore, the design of this study focus on how to streamline the circuit design and lower power consumption. In this design, the sensor data are collected in the form of the conditioning circuit time-division multiplexing. The output signal of multiple sensors which don't be conditioned is sent t to the op amp circuit through the analog switch. The channel of the analog switch is selected by the data processing module. The standard voltage signal of a single analog channel output which has been amplified and conditioned can access to the analog-digital converter interface of the data processing module. Using TI's CD4051B CMOS as analog switches of analog multiplexers, the input and output of the eight analog channels are controlled by 3 channel control terminal A, B, C.

The device is enabled by INH-side, the four control side, respectively, received the IO port of the data processing module, they are connected to the IO of the data processing module respectively. The analog output of the digital switch accesses the operational amplifier AD623, which is a differential operational amplifier with single supply, high input impedance and simple external circuit. The magnification can be suitable adjusted by means of a high-precision resistor.

The SWR2 soil moisture sensor is used as soil moisture sensor of the sensor node. Its advantages are high accuracy, fast response, little effect of soil quality, good sealing so as to be long buried in the soil from erosion. Its output is a differential signal whose range is from 0V to 2.5V, hence the signal conditioning should be necessary. The schematic of conditioning module is shown in Figure 5.

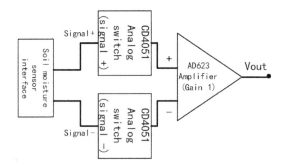

Fig. 5. Soil moisture sensor conditioning modules

The temperature sensor used by the sensor nodes is the PT-1000 platinum resistance sensor. The nominal resistance of the sensor is 1,000 ohms at 0 degree Celsius, the resistance linearly increases with the temperature increases. The output signal needs to be differencing before the sensor access conditioning modules. The method is that the bridge is constituted with temperature sensor and three precision resistors, the voltage of the PT-1000 as a positive signal, signal output of corresponding half-bridge resistance as a negative. The circuit schematic diagram is shown in Figure 6.

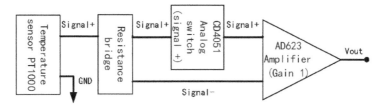

Fig. 6. Temperature sensor conditioning modules

4.3   The Data Storage Module

Flash memory chips M25PE20 with 2MBit data storage space is used the core of data storage module. The chip's supply voltage is 3.3V, SPI synchronous serial communication is used for data storage, update and delete with the inter-processor. The highest clock frequency of communication is up to 75MHz. The page size of the flash chip is 256-byte, the write time of page is 11ms and erase time is 10ms. The current is only 1A when the node deep sleeping. If the amount of data collected of the node is 48 bytes each time, collected once every 10 minutes, the data amount of 37 days can be stored in memory. The actual acquisition frequency is much lower than the frequency, so the chip can store the time will be longer.

5   Analysis of Operating Results

According to design requirements, the current is 42.5mA when the sensor node is in the state of the 4.2V power supply voltage. Status of the work here is that the wireless transceiver module is sending and receiving data, the microprocessor module collecting and processing data, the sensor and the state storage module working on. Typically, each time of collecting and processing of data will be about 9 seconds. In other words, the power consumption of sensor node is 178.5 mW in the working condition.

In order to conveniently monitoring power consumption, the GPS-2303C-type laboratory DC source is used to supply 4.2V DC power instead of photovoltaic module for a sensor node in the network, which is produced by GWINSTEK company. At the same time the GDM-8 145-type desktop digital multi-meter is used to measure current of the node, which also is produced by GWINSTEK company, the measurement accuracy is up to 1uA.

A child node is added to a ZigBee wireless network, the current data which is collected by the current monitoring instruments is real-time output to the computer, and recording in the EXCEL spreadsheet. A wireless sensor network with 12 nodes was built. Nodes in the network had been continuous running for 20 days. Figure 7 shows the current record of the sub-nodes within 3 minutes. Set the operating frequency of the sub-sensor node is 30 seconds.

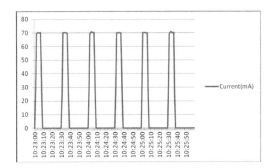

Fig. 7. Current Record

From the figure we can see that the current waveform is the same as the periodic pulse, the current shows this waveform is due to the an average 10uA low power consumption when sensor nodes is in sleep, the current will surge up to about 70 mA when sensor nodes is in state of work. Being analyzed according to the actual measurement data, the average current of the sensor node is 52.89mA in state of work, if the 16-channel sensor is sampled at the same time, not time-sharing, the average current will be 69.13mA,it is increased by about 30

6   Conclusion

The performance of green moisture monitoring nodes based on wireless sensor networks has basically reached the system requirements for reliability and low power consumption which is designed in discrete. The test results show that the power performance is better about 200

References

1. Zhang, G.F., Li, F., J.L.: Beijing Urban Green Space of Rainwater Utilization. Water Saving Irrigation 05, 55–57 (2010) (in Chinese)
2. Song, X.Y., Zang, X.X., Wang, X., Yang, J., Wang, H.: Study on Automatic Monitor and Control of Water-saving Irrigation on Urban Greenbelt. Chinese Agricultural Science Bulletin 27, 317–321 (2011) (in Chinese)
3. Zhu, X.G., Lin, F.C., Gao, H.B.: A Review of Study on Soil Moisture Monitoring. Water Saving Irrigation 11, 53–55, 58 (2011) (in Chinese)
4. Zheng, H.P.: Structure, Design and Application of Mobile Soil Moisture Monitoring System. Anhui Agricultural Science Bulletin 07, 128–129 (2005) (in Chinese)

5. Yang, Q., Wang, C., Zou, A.W.: Typical design method of the northern alpine region moisture Station. Water Resources & Hydropower of Northeast China 12, 49–50 (2010) (in Chinese)
6. Huang, L., Gu, L.: Research on Soil Moisture Monitoring Methods with Remote Sensing Technology. Journal of Capital Normal University (Natural Science Edition) 3, 60–63 (2010) (in Chinese)
7. Hu, P.J., Jiang, T., Zhao, Y.D.: Monitoring system of soil water content based on zigbee wireless sensor network. Transactions of the CSAE 4, 230–234 (2011) (in Chinese)
8. Bogena, H.R., Huisman, J.A., Oberdorster, C., Vereecken, H.: Evaluation of a low-cost soil water content sensor for wireless network applications. Journal of Hydrology 344, 32–42 (2007)
9. Jin, G.C., Peng, C.L., Zhao, D.C., Yang, L.L.: ZigBee-based soil humidity monitoring system. Transducer and Microsystem Technologies 10, 92–94 (2008) (in Chinese)
10. Wang, J., Lei, B.: Design of Zigbee-based soil moisture monitoring system. Electronic Component & Device Applications 2, 35–38 (2009) (in Chinese)
11. Li, K., Wu, X.P., Wu, Y., Jia, H.B.: Dynamic sampling control policy for soil moisture measurements using wireless sensor networks. Journal of Electronic Measurement and Instrument 2, 35–38 (2009) (in Chinese)
12. Li, S., Zhang, H.Y., Lu, H.B.: Research and Design of ZigBee Wireless Sensor Network Management. Journal of Hefei University (Natural Sciences) 4, 37–42 (2011) (in Chinese)
13. Di, X., Zhang, B.H.: Coverage control strategy based on hierarchy for path coverage in wireless sensor networks. Chinese Journal of Scientific Instrument 11, 2416–2423 (2011) (in Chinese)
14. Zhang, Z.L., Yu, X.Q.: Remote Monitoring System for Soil Moisture Based on ZigBee and ARM9. Water Saving Irrigation 7, 54–57 (2011) (in Chinese)
15. Zhang, R.-B., Guo, J.-J., Zhang, L., Zhang, Y.-C., Wang, L.-H., Wang, Q.: A calibration method of detecting soil water content based on the information-sharing in wireless sensor network. Computers and Electronics in Agriculture 76, 161–168 (2011)

Energy-Efficient Multi-hop Routing Algorithm Based on LEACH

He Yang[1,2], Jia Xu[2,3], Ruchuan Wang[2,3], and Liyang Qian[1]

[1] College of Computer, Nanjing University of Posts and Telecommunications
[2] Jiangsu High Technology Research Key Laboratory for Wireless Sensor Networks
[3] Key Lab of Broadband Wireless Communication and Sensor Network Technology
of Ministry of Education, Nanjing 210003, China
yanghe_1987@hotmail.com, wangrc@njupt.edu.cn

Abstract. In order to reduce network energy consumption and prolong the lifetime of wireless sensor networks, this paper improves the LEACH to an energy efficient multi-hop routing algorithm. LEACH in the cluster creation, data transmission, the update phase of the cluster was modified in proposed algorithm. The algorithm updates the cluster head reasonably and adjusts the structure of the cluster to reduce the energy consumption in cluster establishment phrase. In data transmission, it lowers energy consumption by inter-cluster and intra-cluster multi-hop transmission. The simulation runs the algorithm on NS2. The results show that the new algorithm's effectiveness in reducing energy consumption by comparing it with LEACH, LEACH-C,DEEUC.

Keywords: wireless sensor network, intra-cluster, clustering routing algorithm, energy-efficient.

1 Introduction

Wireless sensor network (WSN) is multi-hop and self-organizing network, which is composed of numerous sensor nodes scattered in a certain region by wireless communication. Battery-powered nodes in the network severely resulted in energy constraints because of their large number, wide distribution and complex environment [1]. Generally, the energy of nodes in wireless sensor network is limited and no supplement. In addition, there are lots of nodes while the can only obtain part of topology information to build the routing. Therefore, it needs a better routing algorithm in wireless sensor network to achieve energy optimization.

Low Energy Adaptive Clustering Hierarchy [2] (LEACH) is a kind of routing algorithm in wireless sensor network, which is comparatively mature and commonly used at present. It reduces the energy consumption in data transmission through dynamic clustering, data fusion of cluster members to transfer data to the sink node by cluster head. Combined with multi-hop transmission, this paper puts forward a new algorithm based on LEACH. The new algorithm effectively save energy by adopting methods such as electing cluster heads according to

R. Wang and F. Xiao (Eds.): CWSN 2012, CCIS 334, pp. 578–587, 2013.
© Springer-Verlag Berlin Heidelberg 2013

their residual energy, communicating in clusters through muti-hop and using chain structure in communication between clusters. Simulation shows that new algorithm is superior at aspects of balancing energy consumption of each node, reducing energy consumption of the network and extending the network lifetime to LEACH and other algorithms based on it.

2   Related Research

2.1   LEACH

The basic idea of LEACH is to lower energy consumption and prolong the network lifetime by means of cyclically electing cluster heads at random and evenly distributing the consumption of the network to each node. The process of LEACH is cyclical. At the phrase of establishing clusters in each round, a random number between 0 and 1 can be generated by each node. If the random number is less than the threshold $T(n)$, the node will become a cluster head. $T(n)$ is calculated as follows:

$$T(n) = \begin{cases} \frac{p}{1-p \cdot (r \bmod (\frac{1}{p}))}, & n \in G; \\ 0, & \text{others.} \end{cases} \tag{1}$$

Then, cluster head broadcasts a message that it is a cluster head. According to the intense of radio signal, nodes receiving the message decide which cluster to join in and reply to the cluster head. At the phrase of data transmission, all nodes in cluster send data to the head within the distributed TDMA time slot. Meanwhile, the head fuse data received from other nodes and send fusion to base station. After some time for Stable work, the network begins to start next round of electing cluster heads to rebuild clusters.

The following problems are found after analysis of LEACH.

1) The election of cluster heads

In Formula(1), it is obvious that whether a node can be a cluster head only depends on rCthe random number and no other factors. It will cause some situations that are bad for efficient use of energy in the network. If cluster heads are concentrated in a small area, communication between distant nodes and cluster heads consume more energy. In addition, nodes with low energy which are elected as cluster heads may die soon [3].

2) Energy consumption of communication between clusters

The way of inter-cluster communication in LEACH is that cluster heads directly send data to base station. Because of the random election of cluster heads, it will waste more energy in data transmission for the cluster heads far from base station, which is bound to accelerate the death of them.

3) Energy consumption of rebuilding clusters

In each round, it should reelect cluster heads and create new clusters, which results in larger energy consumption in reconstruction of clusters and is not conductive to prolong the network lifetime.

2.2   Improved Algorithm Based on LEACH

In order to improve quality of cluster, Heinzelman put forward centralized cluster construction algorithm LEACH-C [5]. The basic idea of LEACH-C is that base station collects the position and energy information of all nodes and calculates the average energy while the nodes with energy over the average are able to become cluster heads. As we can see from cluster heads election mechanism, cluster heads are generated under the control of base station in LEACH-C so that cluster heads have more energy and clusters are distributed more evenly to LEACH. However, in LEACH-C base station needs to know the location and energy information of each node resulting in the increase of data amount and energy consumption.

PEGASIS [6] algorithm proposed by Lindsey organizes all nodes in a chain, by which data is fused and transferred to base station. It constructed a chain with greedy algorithm. Due to local optimum of the greedy algorithm, the chain structure isnt the best and there may be a circuity. In addition, it needs to reconstruct the chain once a node is found dead. If constructed chain is too long, a waste of energy is inevitable [7].

Two-stage clustering protocol TPC constructs multi-hop routes in clusters to save energy [8]. Yang Guang proposed a kind of multi-hop routing algorithm [9] by angle limit to further save energy. These methods reduce energy consumption through multi-hop transmission in the cluster. But it is not conducive to the real scene because nodes need to have precise positioning equipment and design of routing algorithm is complex.

3   Energy-Efficient Multi-hop Routing Algorithm Based on LEACH

3.1   Network Model and Energy Model

1) Sensor nodes are randomly distributed in a square area $A(a * a)$
2) There is a unique base station (BS) in a fixed location within the region A.
3) Nodes dont move once deployed. All nodes have a similar capacity, equal status and same limited energy.
4) Nodes can adjust its distance from information source according to the intensity of received signal.
5) Transmission power is controllable so that nodes can adjust it in terms of transmission distance.
6) The energy model adopts multipath fading model.

Energy consumed in sending can be calculated in accordance with Formula (2) while energy consumed in receiving can be calculated in accordance with Formula (3).

$$E_{tx}(k, d) = \begin{cases} k \cdot E_{elec} + k \cdot \varepsilon_{fs} \cdot d^2, & d < d_0; \\ k \cdot E_{elec} + k \cdot \varepsilon_{amp} \cdot d^4, & d \geq d_0. \end{cases} \tag{2}$$

In Formula (2), $E_{tx}(k, d)$ is energy consumed by sending k bit data to receiving node d m far away. E_{elec} is energy consumption of transmission circuit. ε_{fs} and ε_{amp} are different coefficient of amplifier. d_0 represents reference distance.

$$E_{tr}(k, d) = k \cdot E_{elec} \tag{3}$$

In Formula (3), $E_{tr}(k, d)$ is the energy consumed by receiving k bit data from d m away. E_{elec} is energy consumption [8] of receiving circuit.

3.2 Algorithm Description

Through the analysis of LEACH and its improved algorithm, in order to save energy and extend the network life, energy-efficient multi-hop routing algorithm based on LEACH is proposed, which makes improvements in the phrase of establishment of clusters, data transmission and update of cluster.

1) Establishment of clusters

At the beginning of establishment, each sensor node generates a random number (0–1) and compares it with the threshold. If the random number is less than the threshold, the node will be elected as a cluster head. Considering the residual energy of nodes, the energy factor $E_i/E_{average}$ is added into the threshold value, which makes nodes with larger energy become cluster head with more probability. $E_{average}$ can be estimated by the following Formula [10].

$$E_{average} = \frac{E_{total} - r \cdot E_{round}}{N} \tag{4}$$

In Formula (4), $E_{average}$ is the average energy of each node. E_{total} means the total energy of the whole network. E_{round} represents average energy consumption in each round. r is the current round number. N is the amount of living nodes in the network.

$T(n)$ is calculated in accordance with the following Formula.

$$T(n) = \begin{cases} \frac{p}{1 - p \cdot (r \bmod (\frac{1}{p}))} \cdot \frac{E_i}{E_{average}}, & n \in G; \\ 0, & \text{others.} \end{cases} \tag{5}$$

In Formula (5), p is the percentage that a node becomes a cluster head, r is the current round number. G is the collection of nodes which are not cluster heads in the recent $1/p$ round. E_i is the residual energy of node i. $E_{average}$ is average residual energy of all nodes.

Cluster head set H to 0 (H is the hop from the cluster head, $H = 0$ indicates that the node is the cluster head) and CH (cluster heads ID of the cluster) to node ID. Then the head broadcasts the message that it is cluster head ($H = 0$, CH). Assumed that node j receives the clustering broadcast message ($H = 0$, CH) and join the cluster, it sets its own CH to the CH of the message, H_j to $H + 1 = 1$ and PID (ID of its parent node) to $PID = ID_j$. After that, node j continues to broadcast the message (H_j, CH). Similarly, the node receiving node j broadcast message (H_j, CH) sets its own H, CH and PID and keeps on broadcasting.

If a node receives multiple broadcast messages, it should compare the H in messages with its H. Assumed that node p has set its H_p, CH_p and PID_p, it received a message (H_q, CH_q) from node q. If $H_p \leq H_q + 1$, then do nothing; if $H_p > H_q + 1$, then reset H_p to $H_p = H_q + 1$, CH_p to $CH_p = CH_q$, PID_p to $PID_p = ID_q$ and continues to broadcast the messages (H_p, CH_p)

In order to prevent the unlimited broadcasting of the clustering message, the initial value of H of each node should be set to the maximum H_{max} in advance. When broadcast message is received, the node does nothing but stop broadcasting if $H_{max} \leq H + 1$. As nodes are randomly distributed in a square area, the maximum distance between two points of the region is $\sqrt{2}a$ and the distance of single hop communication distance within the cluster is R, then H_{max} can be applied in accordance with the Formula (6).

$$H_{max} = \left\lceil \frac{\sqrt{2} \cdot a}{R} \right\rceil + 1 \qquad (6)$$

Take nodes A, B, C, D, E, F, G, I ,J as examples. Assume that A and I are elected as cluster head, cluster structure are shown in Fig.1 and Fig.2 according to the above method.

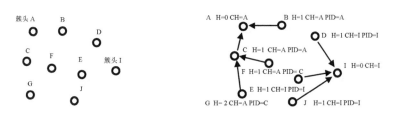

Fig. 1. cluster head selection   **Fig. 2.** clusters after broadcast

2) Data transmission

At the phase of inter-cluster communication, nodes packet their data and remaining energy at regular intervals and sends them to their parent nodes by PID. Parent nodes continue to send packets to their own parent nodes. Eventually the packets reach the cluster head node by multi-hop.

At the phase of communication between clusters, the cluster head node extracts data from the packet, transmits data in chain structure like PEGASIS. It starts from the furthest cluster head away from the base station, chooses the closest cluster head from it as next hop and reaches the base station at last.

3) Update of cluster

Updating cluster is mainly to solve cluster heads update. After a round of data transmission, remaining energy of cluster head may not be sufficient for the next round of data transmission. So cluster head must be replaced to prolong lifetime of the network. Meanwhile, in order to reduce energy consumption caused by cluster reconstruction, it is necessary to choose the node with the most residual energy in the cluster as a candidate cluster head, avoiding re-clustering of the entire network.

Replacement of cluster head node starts after a round of data transmission. It is to find out the node with the most residual energy in nodes which are in the same cluster and never has been cluster head before. The selected node will be cluster head in next round and . When next round begins, the cluster head in last round sets its own H to H_{max} and notify the new cluster head. Then the new cluster head broadcasts message that it is the cluster head to update the cluster structure. After $1/p$ round or all nodes in the cluster have been cluster head, cluster head can be randomly selected according to the threshold and broadcasts clustering message to re-cluster the entire network.

Take node A, B, C, D, E, F, G, I for an example. Assumed that A is the current cluster head, cluster structure is shown in Fig.3. If B is chosen as the new cluster head, updated cluster structures is shown in Fig.4.

Fig. 3. cluster head selection   **Fig. 4.** clusters after broadcast

4   Simulation

This article uses NS2 to simulate the new algorithm and compare it with LEACH, LEACH-C protocol. Simulation scene is set as follows: 100 sensor nodes randomly are deployed in the area of 100m 100m. The base stations location is (50, 50). The initial energy of each node is 2J. The energy loss in sending and receiving data is 50nJ/bit. The energy consumption of data fusion is 5nJ/bit. The size of one packet is 4000 bit. The reference distance d_0 is 87.7m. This paper compares

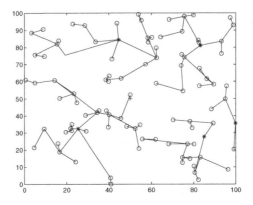

Fig. 5. the network topology structure of new algorithm in first round

the new algorithm with LEACH, LEACH-C and DEEUC in terms of total energy consumption of the network, average energy consumption of each round, the amount of surviving nodes in the network and the amount of data in each round. Fig 5 is the network topology structure of new algorithm in first round ('+' is base stations, '*' is cluster head, 'o' is node in cluster).

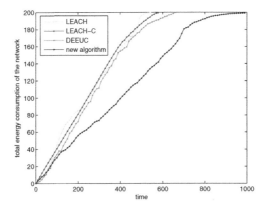

Fig. 6. total energy consumption of the network

It can be seen from Fig.6 that the total energy consumption of LEACH, LEACH-C and DEEUC is almost the same while the total energy consumed by the new algorithm is obviously lower than that of LEACH, LEACH-C and DEEUC. Its main reason is that new algorithm adopts methods of selecting cluster head in LEACH-C and DEEUC to form optimal cluster structure in the cluster. In addition, multi-hop transmission is effective to reduce the cost of communication between cluster heads and base station.

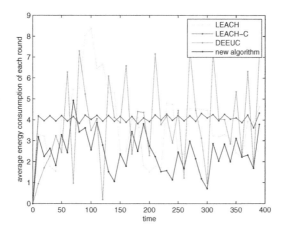

Fig. 7. total energy consumption of the network

In Fig.7, we can see that the energy consumption of LEACH-C in each round is stably kept at about 4. It is mainly because the optimal cluster structure is generated each round according to location and energy information of all nodes. Therefore, energy consumption in each round is relatively balanceable. In LEACH, the energy consumption of each round is between 1 and 9. It is obvious that the scale is relatively large. Because cluster head is randomly selected in LEACH, a poor cluster scheme may be produced, which makes more energy is consumed in communication between some nodes and far cluster heads. And in DEEUC energy consumption of each round is also not very stable. However, the new algorithm keeps energy consumption of each round between 1 and 4, which is relatively stable. It changes little mainly because the new algorithm adopts methods of selecting cluster head of the LEACH-C and updating cluster head. Meanwhile, multi-hop communication saves more energy rather than single-hop communication in LEACH, LEACH-C and DEECU.

Fig.8 shows that some nodes begin to die in LEACH, LEACH-C and DEEUC at the time of about 400. On the contrary, the nodes begin to die in the new algorithm when time is 550. All nodes in LEACH, LEACH-C and DEEUC have been dead respectively at 542, 578 and 667. But in the new algorithm all nodes die at 994. This shows that the new algorithm effectively reduces the energy consumption of the whole network, which avoids premature death of some nodes for overloading and extends the life of the network.

From Fig.9, it can be seen that the amount of data sent in each round in LEACH-C, DEEUC and the new algorithm is relatively stable, while it changes a lot in LEACH. This is mainly because the energy problem is not considered in cluster head election of LEACH. If a low-energy node is elected as a cluster head so that it can not complete communication of a round, it will inevitably lead to small amount of data. However, LEACH-C, DEEUC and the new algorithm take energy factor into consideration when selecting cluster head. Thus the amount of data of communication in each round is relatively stable.

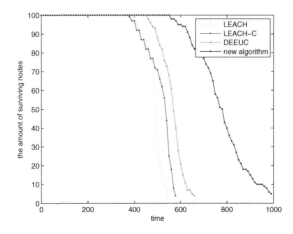

Fig. 8. total energy consumption of the network

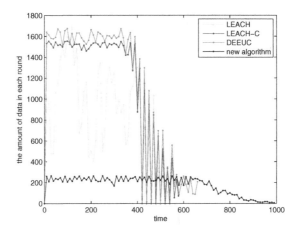

Fig. 9. total energy consumption of the network

5 Conclusion

This paper studies LEACH and its improved algorithm and analyzes their own problems from the perspective of energy consumption. Therefore, in order to save energy and prolong the network lifetime, this paper have made improvements on the phrase of clusters construction, data transmission and clusters update in LEACH, which proposed energy-efficient multi-hop routing algorithm based on LEACH. By replacing the cluster head reasonably and multi-hop transmission in cluster, energy consumption is saved and network lifetime is extended. The simulation experiment on NS2 has proved this point. Meanwhile, it is found in the experiment that the amount of data in communication of each round in new algorithm was relatively low. How to reduce energy consumption while increasing the amount of data will be the next target in research.

Acknowledgement. The subject is sponsored by the National Natural Science Foundation of P.R China (No. 61100199, 61171053), the Natural Science Foundation for Higher Education Institutions of Jiangsu Province(10KJB520014, 12KJA520002) and Scientific and Technological Support Project (Industry) of Jiangsu Province (No.BE2012183).

References

1. Ren, F., Huang, H., Lin, C.: Wireless Sensor Networks. Journal of Software 7, 1282–1291 (2003)
2. Heinzelman, W., Chandrakasan, A., Balakrishnan, H.: Energy-efficient communication protocol for wireless microsensor networks. In: Proceedings of the 33rd Annual Hawaii International Conference on System Sciences, Maui, HI, pp. 1–10 (2000)
3. Zhang, H., Li, L.-Y.: Energy-balancing Routing Algorithm Based on LEACH Protocol. Computer Engineering 37(4), 91–93 (2011)
4. Shang, F., Lei, Y.: Energy Efficient Clustering Algorithm for Wireless Sensor Networks. Journal of Chinese Computer Systems 30(5), 839–842 (2009)
5. Heinzelman, W., Chandrakasan, A., Balakrishnan, H.: An application-specific protocol architecture for wireless micro-sensor networks. IEEE Transactions on Wireless Communications 1(4), 660–670 (2002)
6. Lindsey, S., Raghavendra, C.S.: PEGASIS: Power-efficient gathering in sensor information systems. In: Aerospace Conference Proceedings, pp. 1125–1130. IEEE (2002)
7. Yu, Y.-C., Wei, G.: An Improved PEGASIS Algorithm in Wireless Sensor Network. Acta Electronica Sinica 36(7), 1309–1313 (2008)
8. Choi, W., Shah, P.: A framework for energy-saving data gathering using two-phase clustering in wireless sensor networks. In: Mobile and Ubiquitous Systems: Networking and Services, MOBIQUITOUS 2004, pp. 203–212 (2004)
9. Guang, Y., Guisheng, Y.: Intra-cluster multi-hop routing algorithm based on forwarding restriction angle in WSNs. In: Control and Decision Conference, CCDC 2008, pp. 2035–2039 (2008)
10. Shang, F., Mehran, A., Tadeusz, W.: Distributed energy efficient unequal clustering algorithm for wireless sensor networks. Journal on Communications 30(10), 34–42 (2009)

A Regularity-Based Connectivity Analysis of Three-Dimensional Wireless Sensor Networks*

Huijie Yang, Huibin Wang, and Shufang Xu

College of Computer and Information Engineering,
Hohai University, Nanjing 211100, China
{yanghuijie,hbwang,xushufang}@hhu.edu.cn

Abstract. The connectivity is one of the key issues in the design and application of wireless sensor networks, which is a basic guarantee for the normal operations of networks. In this paper, the region regularity is introduced into the wireless sensor network model for connectivity analysis. By analyzing and simulating the link probability, the average node degree and the node density of networks, we summarize the influence of region regularities on network connectivity. Experimental results show that the connectivity varies with different region regularities and reduces with the decrease of region regularity. Moreover, the energy efficiency and lifetime of the sensor networks can be improved by the analysis of region regularity. To the networks in two-dimensional plane, the proposed methods can also be applied.

Keywords: Three-dimensional Wireless Sensor Networks, Connectivity, Region Regularity.

1 Introduction

Wireless sensor networks (WSN) have been identified as one of the most important technologies in the 21st century. There are a large number of challenge problems in science and engineering of the wireless sensor network area. And connectivity is one of the most fundamental problems as most network functions are predicated upon the network being connected. Although most WSNs are based on two-dimensional (2D) design, such networks are commonly operated in three-dimensions (3D) practically. Since the size (i.e., the length and the width) of the terrestrial networks is significantly larger than the differences in the third dimension (i.e., the height) of the nodes, the 2D assumption is somewhat justified and does not lead to major inaccuracies [1, 2]. However, in some environments, this is not true, such as the underwater, atmospheric, or space communications.

The connectivity is one of the fundamental properties of wireless sensor network that indicates the wireless link between network nodes. Although increasing nodes transmission power will improve network connectivity, too large a power

* This work is supported by Anhui Province Technology Plan of Yangtze River Delta Joint Research Project under Contract 1101c0603055.

R. Wang and F. Xiao (Eds.): CWSN 2012, CCIS 334, pp. 588–597, 2013.
© Springer-Verlag Berlin Heidelberg 2013

level is not feasible as the energy is a scarce resource in wireless sensor networks. Hence, it is crucial to analyze the network connectivity property and identify the minimum node transmission power [3], ensuring network connectivity in high probability. Yu et al. [4] and Han [5] studied the connectivity properties of one-dimensional and two-dimensional networks. Alam et al. [1] derived that the use of the Voronoi tessellation of 3D space to create truncated octahedral cells results in the best strategy for WSN node placement. Vieira et al. [6] and Li [7] studied the geometrical characteristics of three-dimensional MANETs and provided some analytical results of the link probability, node degree and network coverage, assuming nodes are uniformly distributed in a finite cubic region.

In this paper, the region regularity is introduced into our three-dimensional wireless sensor network model. We pay our attention on the connectivity properties of the wireless sensor networks where all the nodes have the same deployment strategies but different region regularities. By analyzing and simulating the link probability, average node degree and node density of the network model, the connectivity of networks could reduce with the decrease of region regularity. Moreover, the energy efficiency and lifetime of sensor networks can be improved by the analysis of region regularity as well. Considering a cubic space region, the proposed methods can also be applied into other terrain shapes, including two-dimensional plane.

2   Preliminaries

In this section, the concept of the region regularity of wireless sensor networks is defined and some background information necessary to explain the problems and our approach are provided.

2.1   Network Model

Real world sensor networks are influenced by many factors. Such as the irregular terrain, asymmetry radio transmission and the radio interference all have serious impact on the operation of the networks. In our study, some assumptions are given to establish a simplified yet reasonable model which in some literatures is called fixed radius model [4]. In three-dimensional wireless sensor networks, the deployment region is usually described by the length, the width and the height. Although in sensor networks node distribution usually presents various structure, to simplify our study, we prefer the assumption that sensor nodes are uniformly distributed in three-dimensional space. Moreover, our parameter model of three-dimensional wireless sensor network $\langle k, r, l, m, n, \sigma \rangle$ is proposed as:

(i) All the sensor nodes are uniformly deployed into a finite three-dimensional space of size $l \times m \times n$, we also assume that the region is perfectly vacant without visible obstacles;

(ii) The number of nodes is k, and all the nodes have the same fixed transmission power and are equipped with omni antenna. That the transmission range of each node is r;

(iii) The regularity of the three-dimensional region is σ, which is the dimensionless ratio of the volume to the surface area.

Our assumption simplifies the radio coverage shape of a node to a perfect ball whose radius is r. The status of link between two nodes is also simplified. A sensor node could only directly communicate with another node when their distance is less than r.

2.2   Regularity

In three-dimensional space, the ratio of the volume to the surface area is a significant feature of the distinction between geometric shapes. The sphere has a smaller surface area than any other irregular space shapes with the same volume. For a three-dimensional cubic space of $l \times m \times n$, the volume is $V = lmn$, the surface area is $S = 2(lm + mn + ln)$, and the ratio γ of the volume to the surface area is written as:

$$\gamma = \frac{V}{S} = \frac{lmn}{2(lm + mn + ln)} \tag{1}$$

For the dimensions of the volume and the surface area are quite different, the ratio is processed with dimensionless method and used as a feature parameter reflecting the degree how close the deployment region is to a regular cube, called *Regularity*. When the region volume V is a constant, the surface area S has a minimum value of $6V^{2/3}$, then γ attains the maximum value of $\sqrt[3]{V}/6$. Nondimensionalize the ratio by dividing by the maximum, the region regularity σ is obtained as follows:

$$\sigma = \frac{\gamma}{\gamma_{max}} = \frac{6V^{\frac{2}{3}}}{S} = \frac{3V^{\frac{2}{3}}}{lm + mn + ln} \tag{2}$$

where V is a constant. Since σ is nondimensional, the following theorem is derived.

Theorem 1: For a three-dimensional space of $l \times m \times n$ $(l > 0, m > 0, n > 0)$ with a constant volume $V = lmn$, if the regularity of the region is defined by:

$$\sigma = \frac{3V^{\frac{2}{3}}}{lm + mn + ln}$$

Then $0 < \sigma \leqslant 1$, and $\sigma_{max} = 1$ at the point $l = m = n$.

Proof: If $l > 0, m > 0$, and $n > 0$, then $\sigma > 0$. For the volume V is a constant, the determination of the maximum value of σ is equivalent to finding the minimum value of $(lm + mn + ln)$. By the Lagrange multipliers, the Lagrange function is established:

$$L(l, m, n, \lambda) = (lm + mn + ln) + \lambda(lmn - V)$$

Taking the partial derivatives of L and setting them equal to 0, we have:

$$\begin{cases} L'_l = m + n + \lambda mn = 0 \\ L'_m = l + n + \lambda ln = 0 \\ L'_n = l + m + \lambda lm = 0 \\ L'_\lambda = lmn - V = 0 \end{cases}$$

The solution to the system above is $(l, m, n, \lambda) = (\sqrt[3]{V}, \sqrt[3]{V}, \sqrt[3]{V}, -2/\sqrt[3]{V})$. So the minimum value of $(lm + mn + ln)$ occurs at $l = m = n = \sqrt[3]{V}$, then σ attains the maximum value of 1. Hence, σ has a maximum value of 1 on its domain at $l = m = n = \sqrt[3]{V}$.

The regularity is a simple but effective parameter for describing the regional features of 3D networks, which also plays an important role in maximizing network connectivity with different deployment regions. According to the meaning of the 3D region regularity, the 2D region regularity could be defined as the nondimensional ratio of the region area to the perimeter in Euclidean plane. Figure 1 shows the dimensionless regularity of three-dimensional regions where $V = 1000$, and σ attains the maximum value of 1 at $l = m = n = 10$.

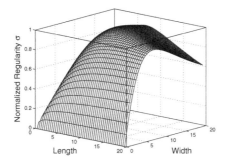

Fig. 1. The normalized regularity of three-dimensional cubic space, where V=1000

3   Regularity and the Network Connectivity

There are many parameters for the connectivity analysis and evaluation of wireless sensor networks, including link probability [6-8], node degree [6, 7], path connectivity and largest component [4] , k-connectivity [9, 10] and so on. Among them, link connectivity probability and node degree are two typical parameters for the description of sensor network's connectivity. In this section, the influence of region regularity on the link probability and the node degree are employed.

3.1   Link Probability

In the wireless sensor network, the link probability is defined as the probability of a direct link between two distinct nodes. Assuming $\langle k, r, l, m, n, \sigma \rangle$ represent a 3D sensor network with k nodes, each node with the communication range r is deployed in the region of $l \times m \times n$. As explained early, the simplified model is employed since only path loss is taken into account. Two nodes have a common link if they are within each other's transmission range. Define any two distinct nodes i and j and whose coordinates are (X_i, Y_i, Z_i) and (X_j, Y_j, Z_j) respectively. Let $U_i = (X_i - X_j)^2$, $V_i = (Y_i - Y_j)^2$, and $W_i = (Z_i - Z_j)^2$ whose p.d.f. are $f(u)$, $g(v)$, and $h(w)$ respectively, and then [6]:

$$\begin{cases} f(u) = \frac{l/\sqrt{u}-1}{l^2}, 0 < u \le l^2 \\ g(v) = \frac{m/\sqrt{v}-1}{m^2}, 0 < v \le m^2 \\ h(w) = \frac{n/\sqrt{w}-1}{n^2}, 0 < w \le n^2 \end{cases} \tag{3}$$

Since u, v and w are independent, their joint p.d.f. is given by Equation 4.

$$t(u, v, w) = \frac{1}{l^2 m^2 n^2}(\frac{lmn}{\sqrt{uvw}} - \frac{lm}{\sqrt{uv}} - \frac{ln}{\sqrt{uw}} - \frac{mn}{\sqrt{vw}} + \frac{l}{\sqrt{u}} + \frac{m}{\sqrt{v}} + \frac{n}{\sqrt{w}} - 1) \tag{4}$$

And the probability of establishing the link of $\langle i, j \rangle$ is :

$$p = P_r[U_i + V_i + W_i \le r^2] = \iiint_{r^2 \in \Omega} t(u, v, w)dwdvdu \tag{5}$$

where Ω represents the interval of this triple integral.

Let $l \ge m \ge n$, the size difference between l^2 and (m^2+n^2) should be discussed in this integral:

(i) When $l^2 \ge (m^2 + n^2)$, the partition of the interval Ω is $0 \le n^2 \le m^2 \le (m^2 + n^2) \le l^2 \le (l^2 + n^2) \le (l^2 + m^2) \le (l^2 + m^2 + n^2) < +\infty$.

(ii) When $l^2 \le (m^2 + n^2)$, the partition of the interval Ω is $0 \le n^2 \le m^2 \le l^2 \le (m^2 + n^2) \le (l^2 + n^2) \le (l^2 + m^2) \le (l^2 + m^2 + n^2) < +\infty$.

Equation 5 gives a model to solve the link probability of the 3D wireless sensor network and indicates that the probability of link $\langle i, j \rangle$ depends on the values of l, m, n and r, not on i, j or k, and all the links have the same probability distribution.

3.2   Regularity and the Link Probability

The effect of region regularity on network link probability is analyzed in this section with the following theorem.

Theorem 2: For a three-dimensional network $\langle k, r, l, m, n, \sigma \rangle$ with a fixed deployment region volume V, the link probability p will raise with the increase of regional regularity, and once σ equals to σ_{max}, the p can attain the maximum.

Proof: To obtain a closed form solution of the link probability, the partitions of interval Ω should be taken into account. For example, take $r \in [0, n)$, we have:

$$p = \iiint_{r^2 \in \Omega} t(u, v, w)dwdvdu = \int_0^{r^2} \int_0^{r^2-u} \int_0^{r^2-u-v} t(u, v, w)dwdudv$$

by Equation 4:

$$p = \frac{1}{l^2 m^2 n^2}[-\frac{1}{6}r^6 + \frac{8}{15}r^5(l + m + n) - \frac{1}{2}\pi r^4(lm + ln + mn) + \frac{4}{3}\pi r^3 lmn]$$

For V is a constant, the equation is written as:

$$p = \frac{r^4}{V^2}[\frac{8}{15}r(l + m + n) - \frac{1}{2}\pi(lm + ln + mn)] + \frac{1}{V^2}[-\frac{1}{6}r^6 + \frac{4}{3}\pi r^3 V]$$

Let $f(l, m, n) = \frac{8}{15}r(l+m+n) - \frac{1}{2}\pi(lm+ln+mn)$, $S_1 = 2(l_1 m_1 + l_1 n_1 + m_1 n_1)$, $S_2 = 2(l_2 m_2 + l_2 n_2 + m_2 n_2)$, $V = l_1 m_1 n_1 = l_2 m_2 n_2$, and assume that $S_1 < S_2$. So it suffices to show that $f(l_1, m_1, n_1) > f(l_2, m_2, n_2)$.

Since $l \geq m \geq n$ and $n > r \geq 0$, it is not hard to get that $f(l_1, m_1, n_1) > f(l_2, m_2, n_2)$.

Furthermore, if $\sigma_1 > \sigma_2$, then $p_1 > p_2$.

Analogously, if r^2 varies through the entire interval Ω, then $p_1 \geq p_2$ (equality holds if $p_1 = p_2 = 1$), and the maximum value of p occurs when $\sigma = \sigma_{max}$.

3.3   Regularity and the Node Degree

In a wireless sensor network, the node degree is defined as the number of a node's neighbors with which the node can communicate directly without any relay, illustrating the local connectivity of the network. Assuming the random variable $L_{i,j}$ is the number of links connecting nodes i and j, $L_{i,j}$ is either 0 or 1 and the node degree of sensor node i is $d_i = \sum_i L_{i,j}$ then.

Corollary 1: In a three-dimensional network $\langle k, r, l, m, n, \sigma \rangle$, the average node degree is $d = (k - 1)p$, and the expected number of links is $k(k - 1)p/2$.

According to Equation 5, the link probability is p, and the number of nodes is k, the average node degree and the expected number of links [6] of a 3D wireless sensor network can be obtained. Corollary 1 illustrates that the average node degree and the expected number of links are proportional to the link probability p, that is $d \propto p$. In a three-dimensional network, if the sensor's transmission power is enhanced, the communication range r, the average node degree d and the expected number of links will be larger and the link probability p will be improved as well.

According to the Theorem 2 and Corollary 1, for the three-dimensional wireless sensor networks $\langle k, r, l, m, n, \sigma \rangle$, if the number of nodes k, the transmission range r and the volume of deployment region V are fixed, the average node degree d will increase with the raise of regional regularity σ. If the ratio of the network's work time to the energy consumption is given as the energy efficiency η of the overall network, the critical transmission range (CTR) [3] which ensures the network's connection would increase with the decrease of region regularity. At the same time, the energy efficiency is falling and the networks are requiring more transmission power for connection.

3.4   Node Density

Node density is defined as the number of nodes in the unit volume, which is an important parameter in the network deployment and application. According to the assumption about the node model in this paper, the radio coverage shape of a node is a spherical region whose radius is r. In a network $\langle k, r, l, m, n, \sigma \rangle$, the average network node density is:

$$D = \frac{k}{V} = \frac{k}{lmn} \cong \frac{k_{negih} + 1}{\frac{4}{3}\pi r^3} = \frac{(k-1)p + 1}{\frac{4}{3}\pi r^3} \tag{6}$$

And then:

$$k \cong \frac{lmn(p-1)}{lmnp - \frac{4}{3}\pi r^3} = \frac{(\sigma S)^{3/2}(p-1)}{(\sigma S)^{3/2}p - 8\sqrt{6}\pi r^3} \tag{7}$$

Equations 6 and 7 reflect the approximate relationship between the link probability, the node density and the number of nodes in a three-dimensional network, and the average node degree is $d = (DV - 1)p$. According to above analysis, the number of nodes and node density can be obtained for a connected network, which has an important significance for the design and deployment of the network.

4   Simulations and Analysis

In this section, the region regularity's impact on the connectivity of three-dimensional wireless sensor networks is simulated. The simulation results show that the regularity is an important parameter for the network's connectivity, and the connectivity analysis with regularity has the ability to improve the energy efficiency effectively.

4.1   The Impact of Regularity on Network Connectivity

Figure 2 shows the link probability with three different region regularities, that the number of nodes k is 20, and the volume of deployment region V is 1000.

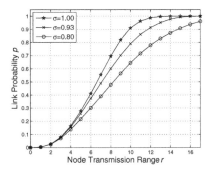

Fig. 2.   Comparison of the link probability with different region regularities of 3D WSNs. The volume of cubic space is 1000.

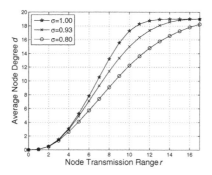

Fig. 3. Comparison of the average node degree with different region regularities. The quantity of nodes is 20. The volume of deployment space is 1000.

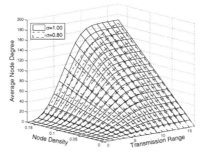

Fig. 4. Comparison of the average node degree and the node density with different region regularities

The uniform distribution of nodes is simulated by 10^8 times, where $l_1 = m_1 = n_1 = 10$, $l_2 = 15, m_2 = 11, n_2 = 6.06$ and $l_3 = 20, m_3 = 12, n_3 = 4.17$, i.e. $\sigma_1 = 1.0, \sigma_2 = 0.93$, and $\sigma_3 = 0.80$. Vieira [6] studied the connectivity properties of wireless ad hoc networks with a specific range in three-dimensional space (the fixed regularity). In contrast, with changing regularities, the link probability decreases with the decline of region regularities and the connectivity of network become worse. When the region regularity takes the maximum 1, the largest average link probability and the best network connectivity will be achieved.

Figure 3 shows the average node degrees with three different region regularities. With the same number of nodes and deployment volume, the average node degree increases with the region regularity and a sensor node can communicate with more neighbors.

According to the analysis results in section 3.4, the relationship between the node density, communication range and the average node degree can be established with different regularities. In Figure 4, $\sigma = 1.0$ or $\sigma = 0.80$, the number of nodes ranges from 0 to 170, and the average node density ranges from 0 to 0.17 per cubic meter. As in the simulation results, it is clear that the deployment region regularity is an important factor to affect the average node degree. With the same node density and transmission range, the higher the regularity is, the greater the average node degree will be. Meanwhile, the lowest node density can be obtained, which can derive the minimal average node degree d (For a connected network, d should not be less than 1). Thus, in the process of network deployment, it is possible to minimize the number of nodes and reduce the costs of the network.

4.2   The Impact of Regularity on the Energy Efficiency

Even with the same range of deployment region, different critical transmission ranges for the networks connection are possibly required for different regularities. Figure 5 shows the impact of region regularity on energy efficiency in three-dimensional wireless sensor networks, where the quantity of nodes is 20 and the volume of deployment region is 1000. Ignoring the region regularity, the energy efficiency of networks is a constant value η_0. Take the impact of region regularity into consideration, instead of setting the critical transmission power for each node, the node transmission power can be reduced for ensuring the connectivity. Numerous simulation results prove that the average energy efficiency of the networks can be improved about 2.92% on the above conditions. Therefore, the employment of regularity gives the connectivity analysis of WSN with the ability to make the network design better and the energy efficiency higher.

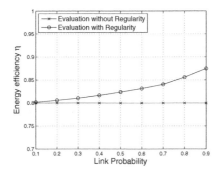

Fig. 5. The influence of the region regularity on evaluating wireless sensor network's energy efficiency is obvious. The curve marked by '*' is the evaluation of the energy efficiency without regularity and that by 'o' is the result evaluated with region regularity.

5   Conclusions

In the paper, the deployment region identity of three-dimensional wireless sensor networks is considered. The region regularity is introduced into our connectivity analysis of sensor networks. After have computed the link probability, the node degree and the node density, we summarize the influence of region regularities on networks. Analysis and simulation results prove that the connectivity is seriously influenced by the region regularity and decreases when it drops. Moreover, the energy efficiency and lifetime of the sensor networks can be improved by the analysis of region regularity. To the plane networks, the proposed methods can also be applied.

References

1. Alam, S., Haas, Z.J.: Coverage and connectivity in three-dimensional networks. In: 12th Annual International Conference on Mobile Computing and Networking, pp. 346–357. ACM, New York (2006)
2. Chee-Yee, C., Kumar, S.P.: Sensor networks: evolution, opportunities, and challenges. Proc. of IEEE, 1247–1256 (2003)
3. Ravelomanana, V.: Extremal properties of three-dimensional sensor networks with applications. IEEE Trans. on Mobile Computing 3(3), 246–257 (2004)
4. Yu, D., Hui, L.: On the definition of ad hoc network connectivity. In: Proc. of the International Conference on Communication Technology, pp. 990–994 (2003)
5. Guang, H.: Connectivity Analysis of Wireless Ad-hoc Networks. University of Maryland, College Park (2007)
6. Vieira, L.F.M., Almiron, M.G., Loureiro, A.A.F.: 3D MANETs: Link Probability, Node Degree, Network Coverage and applications. In: Proc. of the Wireless Communications and Networking Conference, WCNC, Cancun, pp. 2042–2047 (2011)
7. Li, G., Fan, P., Cai, K.: On the geometrical characteristics of three dimensional wireless ad hoc networks and their applications. EURASIP Journal on Wireless Communications and Networking 2006(2), 1–10 (2006)
8. Moltchanov, D.: Distance distributions in random networks. Ad Hoc Networks 10(6), 1146–1166 (2012)
9. Zhang, C., Bai, X., Teng, J., et al.: Constructing Low-Connectivity and Full-Coverage Three Dimensional Sensor Networks. IEEE Journal on Selected Areas in Communiactions 28(7), 984–993 (2010)
10. Pishro-Nik, H., Chan, K., Fehri, F.: Connectivity properties of large-scale sensor networks. Wireless Networks 15(7), 945–964 (2009)

On the Optimum Placement
and Number Selection of Relay Nodes
in Multi-hop Routing for Minimizing
Communication Power Consumption

Pei Yang[1], Le Yang[1,*], Yanbo Xue[2], and Li Peng[1]

[1] Jiangnan University, Wuxi, Jiangsu, China, 214122
[2] McMaster University, Hamilton, ON, Canada, L8S 4K1
le.yang.le@gmail.com

Abstract. The effective use of sensor node battery is crucial for wireless sensor networks (WSNs). Based on a realistic power consumption model for wireless communications, we consider in this paper the low-power-consumption design for multi-hop routing in WSNs. To this end, we first mathematically study the dependence of communication power consumption of a multi-hop route on the relay node placement. Theoretical derivation reveals that in order to minimize the communication power consumption, the relay nodes should be uniformly placed along the line segment connecting the route ends. Utilizing these results, we then proceed to perform a numerical analysis on the relationship between communication power consumption and the number of relay nodes in the route. It is found that the optimum number of relay nodes is almost linearly proportional to the route length from the source node to the sink node. Computer simulations corroborate the theoretical results.

Keywords: Wireless sensor networks, Power consumption model, Multi-hop routing, Optimum inter-node distance, Optimum number of relay nodes.

1 Introduction

Wireless sensor networks (WSNs) are communication networks consisting of a large number of small-sized sensor nodes. The sensor nodes rely on their on-board wireless communication modules to realize inter-connection and inter-node collaboration. In this way, they can cooperatively monitor an area of interest and forward the collected information, possibly after some processing, regarding a physical phenomenon to the network user [1–3]. WSNs have been widely applied in diverse fields such as surveillance, healthcare and environmental monitoring, mainly attributed to their properties of outstanding cost efficiency, scalability, fault tolerance and flexibility in deployment.

---

* Corresponding author.

R. Wang and F. Xiao (Eds.): CWSN 2012, CCIS 334, pp. 598–612, 2013.
© Springer-Verlag Berlin Heidelberg 2013

Sensor nodes are in general small in size and powered by batteries. When the battery power is depleted during operation, the failure of a sensor node occurs, which may affect the coverage, connectivity and the lifetime of the overall WSN [4, 5]. Therefore, the effective use of the limited node battery power becomes one of the important design goals for WSNs.

The wireless communication module of a sensor node is the most power-consuming module. It is responsible not only for transmitting the data generated by the node itself but also for receiving and then relaying the data packets from other nodes to realize the so-called multi-hop communication [4, 5]. In particular, the multi-hop transmission is vital for the successful application of WSNs because it enables data transmission over a large area using nodes with limited communication ranges.

Several power-aware multi-hop routing algorithms, such as those in [6, 7], have been proposed in literatures aimed at minimizing the total transmit power required at the sensor nodes in the route. However, most works did not take into account the battery power spent by the relay nodes in the route on receiving the data packets before forwarding them. It is well-known that the power consumption for data forwarding is proportional to d^r, where d denotes the communication distance and r is the path loss exponent that takes a value between 2 and 4. As a result, increasing d would lead to an exponential increase in transmit power consumption. It is then expected that most existing power-aware routing techniques tend to set up a multi-hop link with a large number of relay nodes so as to reduce the communication distance between two neighbouring relay nodes and decrease the power consumption.

More recently, studies in [8, 9] showed that minimizing the transmit power consumption in a multi-hop link does not necessarily lead to the minimization of the overall communication power consumption if the power consumption from both the data forwarding and reception is considered. In practical WSNs, the power consumption from data packet reception may not be negligible at all, due to, e.g., the dense deployment of sensor nodes. With these observations in mind, [8] investigated the optimum placement of a single relay node between two nodes to achieve a two-hop link with minimum overall communication power consumption. On the other hand, in [9], the problem of optimally determining the number and placement of the relay nodes between two nodes with a known distance to reduce to the maximum level the communication power consumption was considered.

In both [8] and [9], it was assumed that the power consumption for data forwarding between two neighbouring nodes in a multi-hop link is always proportional to d^r, regardless of the value of the inter-node distance d. Nevertheless, in practical wireless communications, the path loss exponent r is functionally dependent on d. In particular, when the inter-node distance d is smaller than a threshold, the signal propagation follows the well-known free-space propagation model and r normally takes the value of 2. When d is beyond the threshold, the signal propagation would be dominated by the multi-path propagation model, where the path loss exponent would take a value of 4 [10, 11]. We argue that the power consumption analysis for a multi-hop route in a WSN should be conducted under such a complicated but realistic dual-mode model.

It is the purpose of this paper to investigate, under the above dual-mode power consumption model, the optimum placement and number selection of relay nodes to minimize the overall communication power consumption in a multi-hop link with its two end nodes having a pre-specified distance. Through rigorous theoretical analysis, we find that

- given the number of relay nodes, the minimum overall communication power consumption is achieved if the relay nodes are uniformly placed between the two end nodes of the multi-hop link, and
- the optimum number of relay nodes in the multi-hop route is approximately proportional to the distance between the route end nodes.

We verify and illustrate the theoretical finding via computer simulations. The results obtained in this paper can serve as part of the guidelines for evaluating the WSN power consumption as well as novel power-aware multi-hop routing algorithm design.

To simplify the derivation and gain insights, we assume as in the previous studies [8, 9] that the relay nodes are placed on a line segment connecting the end nodes of the multi-hop route. In fact, in modern WSNs, the precise evaluation of the route communication power consumption can be more involved and complicated, due to, for example, the use of direct data transmission together with multi-hop transmission in the recently proposed cooperative communications [13, 14]. The choice of the media access control (MAC) protocols can also impact significantly the power consumption level as well. Inclusion of those factors is beyond the scope of this paper but it will be a subject of future researches.

The rest of the paper is organized as follows. Section 2 presents the communication power consumption model adopted in this paper. Section 3 proves that given the number of relay nodes, the uniform placement of them is optimum in the sense of minimizing the overall communication power consumption. Section 4 derives the optimum number of relay nodes in a multi-hop link with a pre-fixed route distance. We conclude the paper in Section 5.

2 System Model

We consider a WSN where there exists two sensor nodes with inter-node distance of D meters. It is assumed for simplicity that all the sensor nodes have identical wireless communication modules so that at any node, the transmit power consumption would be dependent on the communication distance only and the power consumption for data reception, if any, would be the same.

In this paper, the overall communication power consumption is considered, which is the sum of two parts, namely, the transmit power consumption and the data reception power consumption. The battery power spent at a sensor node on forwarding one bit data to another node d meters away is [12]

$$E_{Tx}(d) = \begin{cases} E_{elect} + \varepsilon_{fs} \cdot d^2, & d < d_0 \quad (1a) \\ E_{elect} + \varepsilon_{mp} \cdot d^4, & d \geqslant d_0 \quad (1b) \end{cases} \tag{1}$$

where (1a) and (1b) give the power consumption under the free-space signal propagation mode and the multi-path signal propagation mode, respectively. E_{elect} is the battery power consumed in the data transmit circuitry while ε_{fs} and ε_{mp} are the amount of power consumed due to power amplification under the free-space and multi-path signal propagation modes. The threshold $d_0 = \sqrt{\varepsilon_{fs}/\varepsilon_{mp}}$ is the boundary separating the two power consumption modes. We set that the amount of power consumption from receiving data of one bit is $E_{Rx} = E_{elect}$.

We shall investigate how to determine the number of relay nodes and their placement between two end nodes with a distance of D so that the overall communication power required to transmit one bit over the multi-hop link can be minimized. For sake of simplicity, it is assumed as in [8, 9] that the relay nodes and the end nodes are lying on the same line. To facilitate the theoretical derivation, the following symbols are introduced

$$a = \varepsilon_{fs}, \quad b = \varepsilon_{mp}, \quad E_{elect} = E. \tag{2}$$

From (2) and the definitions of E_{Rx} and d_0, we have

$$E_{Rx} = E, \quad d_0 = \sqrt{a/b} \tag{3}$$

The typical values for the parameters E, a and b from literatures [10, 12] are $E = 50,000PJ/bit$, $a = 10PJ/bit/m^2$ and $b = 0.0013PJ/bit/m^4$. From (3), we can obtain that the threshold d_0 is equal to $d_0 = 87.7m$. Those values will be used in the following sections of this paper to conduct numerical analysis and/or computer simulations aimed at verifying the theoretical findings.

3   Optimum Sensor Placement

We shall consider in this section the use of n relay nodes between two sensor nodes D meters apart to generate an $(n+1)$-hop link. The optimum relay node placement for minimizing the route overall communication power consumption is derived. The theoretical study begins with the simplest case of using a single relay node only (i.e. $n = 1$) and then extends to the more general case of using multiple relay nodes (i.e. $n \geq 2$).

3.1   Two-Hop Link ($n=1$)

Fig. 1 plots the topology of the two-hop link in consideration, where Fig. 1(a) is the link with the position of the relay node deviating from the route midpoint while Fig. 1(b) shows the link with the relay node placed right at the route midpoint. Mathematically, as depicted in Fig. 1(a), the distance between the source node of the link and the relay node (the first hop distance), denoted by d_1, is different from that between the relay node and the sink node of the link (the second hop distance), denoted by d_2, where $d_1 + d_2 = D$. On the other hand, in Fig. 1(b), both distances have the same value of $(d_1 + d_2)/2 = D/2$.

Fig. 1. Topology of a two-hop link. (a) Relay node deviating from the route midpoint, (b) relay node at the route midpoint.

We shall compare the overall communication power consumptions of the above two configurations.

In [8, 9], it has been shown that if either $d_1, d_2 < d_0$ or $d_1, d_2 \geq d_0$ holds, i.e, the communication power consumption of the two hops has the same mode of either (1a) or (1b), putting the relay node at the route midpoint as in Fig. 1(b) would lead to smaller overall communication power consumption than that in Fig. 1(a). We shall proceed to show that the above result remains valid for other choices of d_1 and d_2. Due to the homogeneity of the sensor nodes, only the following two cases need to be considered.

Case I : $d_1 \geq d_0$, $d_2 < d_0$ and $(d_1 + d_2)/2 = D/2 < d_0$

In this case, for the two-hop link in Fig. 1(a), the transmit power consumption in the first hop is governed by the multipath mode (1b) while in the second hop, the transmit power consumption follows the free-space mode (1a). As a result, the overall communication power consumption of the route is

$$E_1 = 4E + bd_1^4 + ad_2^2 \tag{4}$$

where the term $4E$ on the right-hand side includes the power consumption for receiving the data once at the relay node and once at the sink node. Following a similar analysis, the overall communication power consumption for Fig. 1(b) can be expressed as

$$E_2 = 4E + a(d_1 + d_2)^2/2. \tag{5}$$

Subtracting E_2 from E_1 yields

$$E_1 - E_2 = bd_1^4 - ad_1^2 + a(d_1 - d_2)^2/2. \tag{6}$$

Putting $d_1 \geq d_0 > d_2$ and $d_0 = \sqrt{a/b}$ from (3), we have $bd_1^4 - ad_1^2 \geq 0$ and as a result, $E_1 \geq E_2$. In other words, when the route length D is smaller than twice the threshold d_0, placing the relay node at the midpoint would always lead to lower communication power consumption than putting it elsewhere along the link.

Case II : $d_1 \geq d_0$, $d_2 < d_0$ and $(d_1 + d_2)/2 = D/2 \geq d_0$

It can be shown by following the same analytical approach adopted in *Case I* that the overall communication power consumptions for the two configurations are

$$E_1 = 4E + bd_1^4 + ad_2^2 \tag{7a}$$

$$E_2 = 4E + b(d_1 + d_2)^4/8. \tag{7b}$$

Comparing them gives

$$E_1 - E_2 = bd_1^4 + ad_2^2 - b(d_1 + d_2)^4/8 \geq bd_0^4 + ad_0^2 - 2bd_0^4 = 0. \tag{8}$$

Here gain, we arrive at that the placement of the relay node at the route midpoint outperforms putting it away from the route midpoint in reducing the communication power consumption, when the route length is greater than $2d_0$. Summarizing the analytical results presented in this subsection leads to

> Conclusion 1: For a two-hop link with a single relay node, the optimum placement of the relay node for minimizing the overall communication power consumption is to put it at the route midpoint.

We shall verify Conclusion 1 with a computer simulation. In particular, the link length is set to be $D = 120m$ and the values of the power consumption model parameters E, a and b are listed at the end of Section 2. We plot in Fig. 2 as a function of the first hop distance d_1 the overall communication power consumption for the two-hop link. For the purpose of comparison, the overall communication power consumption for direct data transmission without using the relay node is also included. The two sets of results are graphically depicted as solid lines labelled with (1) and (2), respectively.

It can be seen from Fig. 2 that with the use of a single relay node, the two-hop link reaches its minimum overall communication power consumption at $d_1 = 60m$, which indicates, by noting $D = 120m$, that in this case, the relay node is placed at the link midpoint. This is consistent with Conclusion 1.

Another important comment, as made earlier, is that using a relay node between two nodes does not necessarily lead to smaller overall communication power consumption than that of the direct transmission scheme. This is because the introduction of a relay node increases the power consumption on data reception, which may excel the amount of power saving brought by the decrease in the power consumption on data transmission due to the reduction in communication distance. The optimum number of relay nodes for a link with a given length is yet to be discussed in Section 4.

3.2 Multi-hop Link ($n \geq 2$)

We shall generalize Conclusion 1 obtained in the previous subsection to the case of a multi-hop link with n relay nodes. In particular, we shall show that

> Conclusion 2: For an $(n+1)$-hop link with $n \geq 2$ relay nodes, uniformly placing relay nodes along the line segment connecting the route end nodes would minimize the overall communication power consumption.

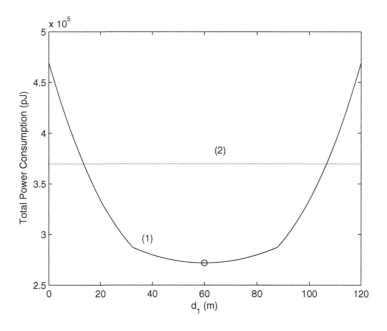

Fig. 2. Effect of relay node placement on the overall communication power consumption in a two-hop link of length $D = 120m$

The proof is based on mathematical induction. First, assume that the above conclusion holds for a n-hop link with $n - 1$ relay nodes ($n \geq 2$). Next, we consider the $(n + 1)$-hop link with n relay nodes. In particular, without loss of generality, we assume the following two-step deployment scheme for the n relay nodes. In the first step, a relay node is placed at the point d_2 meters from the route sink node. In the second step, the remaining $n - 1$ relay nodes are all put left to the relay node just deployed. Clearly, these $n - 1$ relay nodes need to be uniformly distributed with an inter-node distance of d_1, where $nd_1 + d_2 = D$, so as to minimize the overall communication power consumption. This is shown graphically in Fig. 3. At this point, to prove the validity of *Conclusion 2*, we shall only need to show that the overall communication power consumption when $d_1 \neq d_2$ (referred to as the non-uniform relay node placement) would be always higher than that when all the relay nodes are uniformly placed (the inter-node distance here is equal to $(nd_1 + d_2)/(n + 1) = D/(n + 1)$). For this purpose, the following six cases will be considered.

Fig. 3. Topology of the $(n + 1)$-hop link

Case I : $d_1, d_2 < d_0$ and $(nd_1 + d_2)/(n+1) < d_0$

The overall communication power consumptions for the non-uniform and uniform placements of relay nodes are

$$E_1 = n(2E + ad_1^2) + 2E + ad_2^2 \tag{9a}$$

$$E_2 = (n+1) \cdot \left(2E + a\left(\frac{nd_1 + d_2}{n+1}\right)^2\right). \tag{9b}$$

The difference between them is

$$E_1 - E_2 = a\left(\frac{nd_1^2 + nd_2^2 - 2nd_1d_2}{n+1}\right) = \frac{na}{n+1}(d_1 - d_2)^2 \geq 0 \tag{10}$$

which indicates that the link with the uniform placement of relay nodes spends less power in the multi-hop data transmission than the one with the non-uniform deployment scheme.

Case II : $d_1, d_2 \geq d_0$ and $(nd_1 + d_2)/(n+1) \geq d_0$

In this case, the transmit power consumption between any two neighbouring nodes follows the multi-path mode in (1b). After straightforward application of (1b), we can write the overall communication power consumptions for the two relay node placement schemes as

$$E_1 = n(2E + bd_1^4) + 2E + bd_2^4 \tag{11a}$$

$$E_2 = (n+1) \cdot \left(2E + b \cdot \left(\frac{nd_1 + d_2}{n+1}\right)^4\right). \tag{11b}$$

The difference between them is

$$E_1 - E_2 = b\left(nd_1^4 + d_2^4 - \frac{(nd_1 + d_2)^4}{(n+1)^3}\right). \tag{12}$$

Expanding the right-hand side of (12) and applying the geometric inequality $d_1 d_2 \leq (d_1^2 + d_2^2)/2$ yield

$$E_1 - E_2 \geq b\frac{(n^3 + n)}{(n+1)^3}(d_1^2 - d_2^2)^2 \geq 0 \tag{13}$$

which again indicates that the uniform placement of relay nodes leads to less power consumption in the multi-hop data transmission than that of the non-uniform deployment scheme.

Case III : $d_1 \geq d_0$, $d_2 < d_0$ and $(nd_1 + d_2)/(n+1) \geq d_0$

We shall follow the same analytic approach adopted in Case I and Case II. The overall communication power consumptions for the non-uniform and uniform placement of relay nodes can be expressed as

$$E_1 = n(2E + bd_1^4) + 2E + ad_2^2 \tag{14a}$$

$$E_2 = (n+1) \cdot \left(2E + b\left(\frac{nd_1 + d_2}{n+1}\right)^4\right). \tag{14b}$$

The comparison of E_1 and E_2 produces

$$E_1 - E_2 = b\left(nd_1^4 + d_0^2 d_2^2 - \frac{(nd_1 + d_2)^4}{(n+1)^3}\right). \tag{15}$$

Since $d_2 < d_0$, we have

$$E_1 - E_2 \geq b\left(nd_1^4 + d_2^4 - \frac{(nd_1 + d_2)^4}{(n+1)^3}\right) \geq 0 \tag{16}$$

where the last inequality comes from the application of (12) and (13). As such, the same conclusion is reached that the link using the uniform placement of relay nodes would cost less power in the multi-hop data transmission.

Case IV : $d_1 \geq d_0$, $d_2 < d_0$ and $(nd_1 + d_2)/(n+1) < d_0$

In this case, the overall communication power consumptions for the non-uniform and uniform placements of the relay nodes have been derived in (14a) and (9b). Their difference is

$$E_1 - E_2 = b \cdot (n^2 d_1^4 + nd_1^4 + nd_0^2 d_2^2 - n^2 d_0^2 d_1^2 - 2nd_1 d_2 d_0^2)/(n+1).$$

Its non-negativeness can be proven in a straightforward manner.

Case V : $d_1 < d_0$, $d_2 \geq d_0$ and $(nd_1 + d_2)/(n+1) \geq d_0$

Regarding the link with non-uniform placement of relay nodes, its overall communication power consumption is

$$E_1 = n(2E + ad_1^2) + 2E + bd_2^4. \tag{17}$$

On the other hand, the link with uniform placement of relay nodes has an overall communication power consumption given in (11b). Comparing them yields

$$E_1 - E_2 = b \cdot \left(nd_0^2 d_1^2 + d_2^4 - \frac{(nd_1 + d_2)^4}{(n+1)^3}\right). \tag{18}$$

Noting that $d_1 < d_0$, we have $E_1 - E_2 > b \cdot \left(nd_1^4 + d_2^4 - \frac{(nd_1+d_2)^4}{(n+1)^3}\right)$. Again, by applying (12) and (13), we arrive at $E_1 \geq E_2$, which is the desired result that with the uniform placement of relay nodes, the multi-hop link would spend less power on data transmission.

Case VI : $d_1 < d_0$, $d_2 \geq d_0$ and $(nd_1 + d_2)/(n+1) < d_0$

In this case, the overall communication power consumptions for the non-uniform and uniform placements of relay nodes are given in (17) and (14b). Subtracting (14b) from (17) and simplifying, we have

$$E_1 - E_2 \geq \frac{b}{n+1} \left(d_2^4 - d_2^2 d_0^2 + n \cdot d_0^2 (d_1 - d_2)^2 \right) \geq 0. \tag{19}$$

Summarizing the results obtained from the six cases considered above, we notice that, in all cases, the uniform placement of relay nodes always leads to a smaller overall communication power consumption level than its non-uniform counterpart. This completes the proof of *Conclusion 2*. It is worthwhile to point out that authors in [8,9] reached the same conclusion. However, their results were derived on the basis of a single-mode transmit power consumption model $ad^r + c$ with r being the fixed path loss exponent and c being the circuitry power consumption. Different from [8,9], our analysis has taken into consideration that r would increase with the communication distance d, which correspondingly is more practical.

We proceed to verify *Conclusion 2* using a computer simulation set up as follows: Consider the establishment of a multi-hop link between two nodes $800m$ apart using $n = 8$ relay nodes. The relay nodes are arranged as shown in Fig. 3. The power consumption model parameters E, a and b are given at the end of Section 2. We plot as a function of d_2 the overall communication power consumption of the resulting nine-hop link in Fig. 4. The curve reaches its minima at $d_2 = 88.89m$. Using the relation that $D = nd_1 + d_2$, we have $d_1 = d_2$ and this indicates that the relay nodes are uniformly placed along the route, which is expected from *Conclusion 2*.

4   Optimum Number of Relay Nodes

Section 3 reveals that given a certain number of relay nodes, to obtain a multi-hop route with the lowest communication power consumption, a necessary condition is to uniformly place them along the line segment connecting the route ends. However, as shown in Fig. 2 as well as in [8, 9], the use of relay nodes between two nodes to build a multi-hop link does not always lead to power saving in communication over the direct data transmission scheme. It is the purpose of this section to investigate, under the constraint of uniform placement between two nodes of distance D, the optimum number of relay nodes that leads to the lowest power consumption in communication.

The analysis starts with expressing the route length D as

$$D = (m + x)d_0, \tag{20}$$

where $m = \lfloor D/d_0 \rfloor$ is the largest integer smaller than D/d_0 and $x \in [0, 1)$. Suppose n relay nodes are placed between the route end nodes and an $(n + 1)$-hop link is generated. Under *Conclusion 2*, the inter-node distance between any neighbouring node pair would be $d = (m + x)d_0/(n + 1)$. We proceed to prove the following:

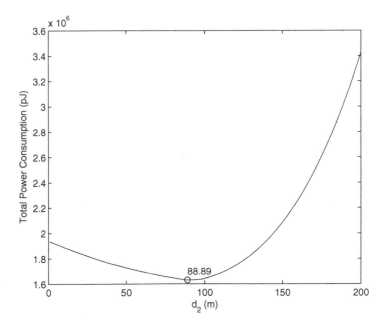

Fig. 4. Effect of relay node placement on the overall communication power consumption in a nine-hop link of length $D = 800m$

<u>*Conclusion 3:*</u> *The multi-hop link of length $D = (m + x)d_0$ would have the lowest possible communication power consumption if the number of relay nodes n is either equal to m or $(m - 1)$ and they are uniformly spaced along the line segment connecting the route end nodes.*

The proof of the above conclusion is achieved via examining the following two cases.

Case I : $n = m + k$ where $k > 0$
We shall verify that the link with $n = m + k$ ($k > 0$) uniformly placed relay nodes has larger overall communication power consumption than the one with $n = m$ equally spaced relay nodes. Under these two configurations, the overall communication power consumptions of the resulting two links are

$$E_1 = (m + k + 1) \left(2E + a \left(\frac{(m + x)d_0}{m + k + 1} \right)^2 \right) \tag{21a}$$

$$E_2 = (m + 1) \left(2E + a \left(\frac{(m + x)d_0}{m + 1} \right)^2 \right) \tag{21b}$$

where the result $(m + x)d_0/(m + j + 1) \leq d_0$ for $j \geq 0$ has been applied. Subtracting E_2 from E_1 yields

$$E_1 - E_2 = 2kE - k\frac{a(m + x)^2 d_0^2}{(m + 1)(m + 1 + k)}. \tag{22}$$

In order to obtain $E_1 \geq E_2$, we need to show equivalently that

$$d_0^2 \leq (2E/a)(m + 1)(m + 1 + k)/(m + x)^2. \tag{23}$$

The above inequality has to be verified via numerical analysis. More specifically, putting the typical values of E and a given at the end of Section 2 and applying the fact that $1 \leq (m+1)(m+1+k)/(m+x)^2$, we can easily arrive at $E_1 \geq E_2$. In other words, it has been shown that under the typical settings for the overall communication power consumption model, using more than m relay nodes to construct a multi-hop link with a length of $D = (m + x)d_0$ would not decrease the overall communication power consumption over the case where only m relay nodes are applied. The reason behind is that increasing the number of relay nodes over m would enhance the power consumed on data reception by an amount which is greater than that of the reduction in transmit power consumption due to the decrease in the inter-node distance.

Case II : $n = m - k - 1$ where $k \geq 0$
In this case, we first note that with $(m - k - 1)$ relay nodes, where $k \geq 0$, the inter-node distance would be $(m + x)d_0/(m - k) \geq d_0$. As a result, every hop of the resulting multi-hop link would have its transmit power consumption given in (1b). We can then write the overall communication power consumption of the $(m - k)$-hop link is

$$E_1 = (m - k)\left(2E + b\left(\frac{m + x}{m - k}d_0\right)^4\right). \tag{24}$$

Differentiating E_1 with respect to k yields

$$E_1' = -2E + \frac{3b(m + x)^4}{(m - k)^4}d_0^4. \tag{25}$$

We can show numerically, after putting the values of E and b given at the end of Section 2, that

$$d_0 \geq \left(\frac{2E}{3b}\right)^{\frac{1}{4}} \times \frac{m - k}{m + x} \tag{26}$$

which leads to the observation that E_1 in (24) is monotonically increasing with respect to k. In other words, for $k \geq 0$, the overall communication power consumption of the $(m - k)$-hop link, i.e., E_1, would reach its minima at $k = 0$. As such, only $m - 1$ relay nodes are used. This result is somewhat expected because reducing the number of relay nodes to a number below $(m - 1)$ would lead to increase in the communication distance and correspondingly the transmit power consumption by an amount larger than that saved from decreasing the number of data reception. We now complete the proof of *Conclusion 3* numerically.

In words, *Conclusion 3* states that the optimum number of relay nodes for minimizing the overall communication power consumption should be proportional to the route distance $D = (m + x)d_0$ and it can take the value of m or $m - 1$. The above ambiguity can be resolved by comparing (21b) and (24) with k set to be zero. In particular, we find after some straightforward manipulations that the optimum number of relay nodes is $(m - 1)$ if the following inequality holds

$$(m+1)x^4+(4m+4m^2)x^3+(6m^2+5m^3)x^2+(4m^3+2m^4)x+m^4-\frac{2E}{bd_0^4}(m+1)m^3 \leq 0 \tag{27}$$

or it is equal to m otherwise.

Putting the values of E, b and d_0 listed at the end of Section 2, we plot the boundary condition on (m, x) that reduces the inequality (27) into an equality in Fig. 5. With Fig. 5, the determination of the optimum number of relay nodes is as follows: Given a route distance D, first express it as $D = (m + x)d_0$. If (m, x) lies below the curve in Fig. 5, the optimum number of relay nodes would be $(m - 1)$. Otherwise, it should be m.

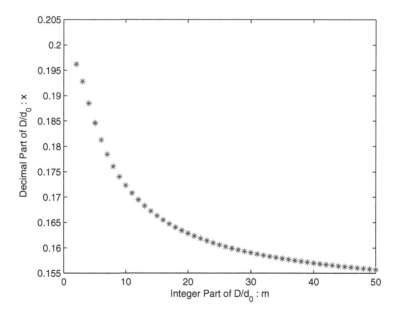

Fig. 5. The boundary condition of (27)

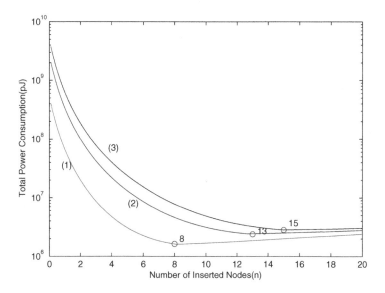

Fig. 6. Effect of the number of relay nodes on the link overall communication power consumption

Finally, to verify *Conclusion 3*, we plot in Fig. 6 as a function of the number of relay nodes the overall communication power consumption of a multi-hop link with a pre-fixed route length. Three sets of results corresponding to $D = 800m$, $D = 1200m$ and $D = 1400m$ are generated and included in the figure as solid lines labelled with (1), (2) and (3). The integers right to the circle symbols denote the optimum numbers of relay nodes in the three simulated scenarios. We can observe that as the link length increases, the optimum number of relay nodes becomes larger, as expected from *Conclusion 3*. Besides, the three curves are all concave with unique minima. This is again consistent with *Conclusion 3* that the use of either more or less than the optimum number of relay nodes does not yield a multi-hop link with low overall communication power consumption.

5   Conclusion

The problem of minimum-power design for multi-hop routes in WSNs is considered. Different from existing literatures, we adopted a more realistic communication power consumption model that takes into account the dependence of the path loss exponent on the communication distance. Under the selected power consumption model, the optimum placement and the number selection of relay nodes in the multi-hop route for minimizing the link communication power consumption were investigated. We proved analytically that the relay nodes need to be uniformly placed along the line segment connecting the route ends to achieve minimum overall communication power consumption. We then conduced a numerical study and revealed that the optimum number of relay nodes for a multi-hop link is proportional to the link length. Computer simulation results supported the theoretical finds.

Acknowledgments. This work is supported by Jiangnan University Startup fund and Youth Foundation of Jiangnan University (Contract No. JUSRP11234).

References

1. Akyildiz, I.F., Su, W.L.: A Survey on Sensor Network. IEEE Commun. Mag. 40, 102–114 (2002)
2. Krishnamachari, B.: Networking Wireless Sensors. Cambridge University Press (2005)
3. Peng, L.: Principles of Wireless Sensor Networks. Publishing House of Metallurgical Industry (2011) (in Chinese)
4. Sai, Y.R.: Coverage-Preserving Routing Protocols for Randomly Distributed Wireless Sensor Networks. IEEE Trans. on Wireless Commun. 6, 1240–1245 (2007)
5. Zhang, H.H., Hou, J.C.: Maintaining Sensing Coverage and Connectivity in Large Sensor Networks. Ad Hoc and Sensor Wireless Networks 1, 89–124 (2005)
6. Catovic, A., Tekinay, S., Otsu, T.: Reducing Transmit Power and Extending Network Lifetime via User Cooperation in the Next Generation Wireless Multi-Hop Networks. J. of Commun. and Networks 4, 351–362 (2004)
7. Monks, J.P., Ebert, J.P., Wolisz, A.: Energy Saving and Capacity Improvement Potential of Power Control in Multi-Hop Wireless Network. Computer Networks 41, 313–330 (2003)
8. Oyman, E.I., Ersoy, C.: Overhead Energy Considerations for Efficient Routing in Wireless Sensor Networks. Computer Networks 46, 465–478 (2004)
9. Stojmenovic, I., Xu, L.: Power-aware Localized Routing in Wireless Networks. IEEE Parallel and Distributed Systems 12, 1122–1133 (2001)
10. Shang, F.J.: Communication Protocols in Wireless Sensor Networks. Publishing House of Electronic Industry (2011) (in Chinese)
11. Sun, Y.J., He, Y.J.: An Energy Efficiency Clustering Routing Protocol for WSNs in Confined Area. Mining Science and Tech. 21, 845–850 (2011)
12. Heinzelman, W.B., Chandrakasan, A.P.: An Application-Specific Protocol Architecture for Wireless Microsensor Networks. IEEE Trans. on Wireless Commun. 1, 660–670 (2002)
13. Laneman, J.N., Tse, D.N., Wornell, G.W.: Cooperative Diversity in Wireless Networks: Efficient Protocols and Outage Behaviour. IEEE Trans. on Information Theory 50, 3062–3080 (2002)
14. Sendonaris, A., Erkip, E., Aazhang, B.: User Cooperation Diversity-Part I: System Description. IEEE Trans. on Commun. 51, 1927–1938 (2003)

AR-HS: Ant Routing Optimized Algorithm on HAPs-Satellite Integrated Networks

Xiaoguo Ye, Huimin Cheng, and Ruchuan Wang

[1] College of Computer, Nanjing University of Posts and Telecommunications,
Nanjing, Jiangsu 210003, China
[2] Jiangsu High Technology Research Key Laboratory for Wireless Sensor Networks,
Nanjing, Jiangsu 210003, China
[3] Key Lab of Broadband Wireless Communication and Sensor Network
Technology(Nanjing University of Posts and Telecommunications), Ministry of
Education Jiangsu Province, Nanjing, Jiangsu 210003, China
xgye@njupt.edu.cn

Abstract. The routing optimized problem in HAPs-Satellite integrated network is focused on this paper. A novel routing algorithm(AR-HS) based on the swarm intelligence by changing the pheromone updating strategy is proposed. In order to build an optimal solution, the proposed algorithm make use of ant agents that consist of probe packets sent on the HAPs-Satellite integrated network that allow to find the optimization problem solution. In this work we have performed a comparison of a classical shortest path algorithm with our the proposed algorithm ,and the simulation results show that our routing algorithm can reduce end to end delay and drop ratio, and improve performance of network.

Keywords: HAPs-Satellite integrated network, routing, QoS.

1 Introduction

As we know, the satellite communication network is playing a key role in the development of future communication systems because of their intrinsic advantages such as available bandwidth and coverage range as well as access broadband communication services. In the last decade, another actor has appeared on the scene: high-altitude platforms (HAPs), which are aerial unmanned platforms carrying communications relay payloads and operating in a quasi-stationary position at altitudes of 15~30km. Recent studies have shown the possibility of utilizing HAPs as an attractive complement or alternative to terrestrial and satellite systems for telephony and direct access to broadband services. Thus, efficient integration of HAP and satellite can lead to a powerful communication infrastructure, with compensating for the weakness of each other[1,2].

An important aspect of communications networks is routing algorithm because it can greatly influence the overall network performance; good routing algorithm can develop a greater throughput or lower average delays and so on. For taking into account the special network characteristics of HAPs-Satellite integrated network such as mobility of terminal and always built in the mountain

R. Wang and F. Xiao (Eds.): CWSN 2012, CCIS 334, pp. 613–622, 2013.
© Springer-Verlag Berlin Heidelberg 2013

area, the routing algorithm should deal with the rapid change of the network topology and it should optimize some quality of service(QoS) parameters in the network.

To solve the routing problem in HAPs-satellites integrated network, we considerate adopting ant colony algorithm. The real ant colony is a dynamic self-built and self-configured system, which is capable of solving its problems efficiently. And the intelligent behavior which emerges from the collection of simple behavior of small agents can be observed easily in nature. They are capable of finding the best path from a food source to their nest by checking pheromone information rather than using visual cues. While walking ants deposit pheromone on the ground, it will determine a link selection probability going through a node in order to define the optimal path towards the destination on the basis of a local heuristic and of the global information of the previous ants that passed in the network, therefore we also call this routing approach called AntNet routing[5].

There already exist many successful adaptations of ant behavior to network routing. AntNet[3,4] introduced by Di Caro and Dorigo, solving routing problem in packet-switching networks, performed better than other conventional algorithms on several packet-switched communications networks in their simulations. The ADRA[5] algorithm is used to improve the convergence rate of ant-based routing in ad hoc network, to reduce the control overhead introduced by a large number of ants, to solve the congestion problem and the shortcut problem quite well, and to balance the network load as well as to reduce the end-to-end delay of packet transmission. ARAMA[6] is also a routing algorithm based on ant colony. It optimized the number of hops and fair energy usage distribution in mobile ad-hoc networks. In [7], multi-constraints routing algorithm based on swarm intelligence is proposed over high altitude platforms, they have considered many constraints such as average delay and available bandwidth and so on, but they treat the network as a static topology ignoring the mobile character of HAPs.

This paper is organized as following: section 2 presents HAPS-Satellite integrated network; in section 3 the Ant colony algorithm is described; section 4 presents the AntRouting algorithm, AR-HS, used in HAPS-Satellite integrated network; in section 5 presents the performance evaluation conducted through an simulator NS-2; At last, the conclusions are summarized.

2   HAPs-Satellite Intergrated Architecture

This architecture is a spatial information network system consisting of high-orbit satellites and high-altitude platforms (HAPs), which brings together ground and space resources. Due to the chip capacity over both high-orbiting satellites and high-altitude platforms, this architecture have capable of macro-control such as scheduling and distribution of resources, thus it is a comprehensive integration network, acting as a background to meet the specific needs of the modern structure. In function aspect, it integrates together communication terminal to complete the task; In practical aspect, it inherits the high bandwidth and large coverage of satellite, and HAPs' advantages of low latency and easy layout. Therefore in this architecture, communication can be more efficiently and accurately completed. The satellites and HAPs integrated network system scenario is shown in figure 1. The top layer is a high-orbit satellite located in the altitude of

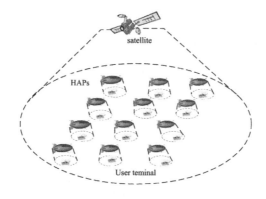

Fig. 1. System scenario

35,786km and responsible to manage and deploy the entire network. The middle layer is the HAPs layer , which locate at 20-50 km high from the ground, between the highest altitude of airspace and the lowest altitude of satellite , this area is called transition zone , which including the atmosphere advection zone ,the middle part of the atmosphere and ionosphere region area. The so-called HAPs, is an aircraft which can perform specific tasks in transition zone, and in the communication field, it can be used as a relay satellite and terrestrial systems. Compared with satellite communications, HAPs has short transmission distance, low transmission loss and delay, and low power requirements. Therefore, HAPs can realize broadband transmission and miniaturization of communication terminals. However, compared with ground relay system, HAPs has a large coverage area more than 100km. The Lowest layer is the layer of ground communications terminals. Because of the advantages of High-orbit satellites and high-altitude platforms (HAPs) network, they are always applied to the remote areas such as the mountains, desert and so on.

3   Ant Colony Algorithm

Currently, there are various forms of ant colony optimization algorithm applying to network routing, and performance well in routing quality, routing costs, congestion control and network adaptability. Because of its self-organizing, auto-optimization and dynamic characteristics, Ant colony routing optimization method is a excellent solution for the HAPs and satellites integrated network.

3.1 Ant Colony Algorithm Mathematical Model

Communications network is described as a directed weighted graph $G = (N, L)$, where N is a collection of all the switching nodes in the graph, and $N = \{n_1, n_2, n_3, \cdots, n_i\}$. L is the set of all edges of the graph, each edge indicates a direct communication path between two adjacent nodes, assumed that there is only one way between two adjacent nodes, and $L = \{L_1, L_2, L_3, \cdots, L_i\}$. Ant colony algorithm is used to find the best path from source node to the destination node in the graph G, each link $L(N_i - N_j)$ has a pheromone value μ_{ij}, which is used to calculate probability to choose the next hop for N_i. The formula for updating the link probability is applied to each link of the HAP crossed by ants and is shown in the following:

$$p_{ij} = \frac{[\mu_{ij}]^\alpha \cdot [\eta_{ij}]^\beta}{\sum [\mu_{ij}]^\alpha \cdot [\eta_{ij}]^\beta} \tag{1}$$

In formula (1), μ_{ij} represents the pheromone quantity released by BANT (backward ant), η_{ij} represents the value of the local heuristic evaluated at the ants traveling, α and β represent respectively the pheromone scale factor and visibility factor associated. While the ant arrives at N_i, it will exploit the probability of every neighbor nodes and then choose which one of them would be the next hop according to formula (2).

$$nextHAP^D = HAP\max(p_{ij}) \tag{2}$$

Where D represents the destination ID, $nextHAP^D$ represents the next HAP to the destination D. Therefore, ant is always forwarded to the nodes which have the maximum probability. In normal, ants can explore multiple paths to find optimum path, according to a probabilistic logic[10].

In addition, the formula (3) shows the pheromone updating method.

$$\mu_{ij}(n + 1) = f(\rho) \cdot \mu_{ij}(n) + g(\rho) \tag{3}$$

With $i, j \in N$ and link is in path $S - D$, pheromone value will be enhanced as formula (3).

$$\mu_{ij}(n + 1) = f(\rho) \cdot \mu_{ij}(n) \tag{4}$$

With $i, j \in N$ and link is not in path $S - D$, pheromone value will be reduced as formula (4).

$\mu_{ij}(n + 1)$ indicates the path grade calculated on the HAP^D, $\mu_{ij}(n)$ is the pheromone value released by the n−th ANT for going towards the j−th HAP from the i−th HAP to the destination D, path $S - D$ is the path from the HAP Source ($HAPS$) to $HAPD$. where f and g are two functions that depend on the path grade.

$$f(\rho) = 1 - \rho \tag{5}$$

$$g(\rho) = \rho^k \tag{6}$$

In particular, function f represents the "vanishing factor" and g represents an "enforcing function", where $0 \leqslant \rho \leqslant 1$, $0 \leqslant f(\rho) \leqslant 1$, $0 \leqslant g(\rho) \leqslant 1$, and

$k \in N$ represents the decaying factor. The higher k, the lower the contribute of enforcement function is, because the path grade is $0 \leqslant \rho \leqslant 1$. In the evaporation and enforcing function the path grade ρ becomes important. The formula (3) and (4) indicate that the pheromone value will be increased in links crossed by FANTs (forward ant) and BANTs, and decreased in other links[9].

3.2 Ant Colony Routing Algorithm Process

Every HAP in the network can be regarded as source node, destination node or intermediate node. Source node will send FANT (forward ants) to search for its destination when it wants to find or maintain a path to a destination. And while FANT travelling in the network, one of their important tasks is to collect paths information and intermediate nodes local information, and they search for the destination according to the intermediate nodes probability routing tables and the local heuristic information .Whole route establishing process is described as two phases: route discovery phase and maintenance and update phase.

1) Route Discovery Phase
In the first one, Route Discovery Phase, new paths are discovered. The creation of new routes requires the use of FANTs (forward ant), which establishes the pheromone track to the source node, and a backward ant (BANT), which establishes the track to the destination node. FANTs are broadcasted by the source node to all its neighbors. Each FANT has a unique sequence number to avoid duplicates. When a node receiving a FANT for the first time, it creates a record (destination address, next hop, pheromone value) in its routing table.
2) Route Maintenance And Update
In the second phase, called Route Maintenance and update, routes are improved during communication. Data packets are used to maintain the path, so no overhead is introduced. Pheromone values of a link are changing as the formula (3) and (4) indicates, that the pheromone values will be increased in links crossed by FANTs and BANTs, and decreased in other links.

4 Antrouting Optimized Algorithm on HAPs-Satellite Integrated Networks

HAPs are responsible to achieve communications relay between terrestrial networks and satellite therefore the routing strategy plays a crucial role for performance of the whole network and is the basis for efficient communication.

4.1 Features of HAPs Network

- there are some ground users moves in high-speed ,so we should conform link handover to continue communication;
- the non-uniformity of distribution of network traffic;
- limited resources of platform.

These characteristics demand routing algorithm of the following conditions:

- rapid changes in network topology;
- the updating rate must be fast enough to detection of the optimal path of the network topology;
- network load balance;
- The algorithm is simple, take up HAP on-chip processing resources less.

4.2   Path Information and Path Grading

The path information may include the nodes local information and global path information. This information should be the parameters we would like to optimize such as Quality of service parameters. We should be very careful in selecting the path information to be collected. The more information collected about the nodes and path, the more close to optimum is the solution. However, the ants sizes will increase, which increases the routing overheads. The calculation of path grading can be done in a distributed way in the intermediate nodes of the path. The path information can be only one field in the FANT, which will be modified as the FANT moves between intermediate nodes. Thus the FANT size is not affected by the amount of information collected.

In this paper we want to optimize the number of hops and the average delay. Minimizing the number of hops can be achieved by calculating the path index of any node as follows:

$$I_1 = 1 - \frac{h_{ij}}{\sum_{j \in N_i} h_{ij}} \tag{7}$$

I_1 is the hops constraints, h_{ij} refers the hop numbers from N_i to N_j on the path to special destination, and N_j is one of the neighbor nodes of N_i. The value I_1 is a good indication taking number of hops into consideration. The fewer the hops number of path $S - D$ is, the value of I_1 will be larger. And I_1 is a good measure of the overall path information. Therefore we can always get the shortest path. As the values of H are smaller than one, the value of I_1 is smaller than the smallest local normalized parameter I_1 along the path.

Then, the average delay information can be achieved by calculating the path index as follows:

$$I_2 = \prod_{i=1}^{L} \frac{\min(PD_{i,j} + DB_{i,j})}{\sum_{j=1}^{N_i}(PD_{i,j} + DB_{i,j})} \tag{8}$$

I_2 is the average delay constraints, $PD_{i,j}$ and $DB_{i,j}$ represent respectively the propagation and the queuing delay for the link $(i,j) \in PathS - D$. Moreover N_i is the set of HAP near to i-th HAP.

Finally, once defined all three metrics we can define a total index that takes into account the minimum hop count metric, average delay metric and the load balancing metric. It is possible to define this total index as follows:

$$\rho = c_1 I_1 + c_2 I_2 \tag{9}$$

Where we define ρ the path grade, and each of these indexes is multiplied for a constant c_i with $i \in [1,2]$. The constant value c_i can assume values in the range [0,1] and it has to satisfy this condition:$c_1 + c_2 = 1$. This constant gives the possibility of taking into account one, two or all three metrics contemporaries, or it gives the possibility of associating a different weight to the metric on the basis of the value that can be assigned to constant c_i.[12]

4.3 Handle Routes Failure

Due to node mobility, a common especially, issue in HAPs-satellites integrated network. AntRouting algorithm recognizes a route failure through a missing acknowledgement. The links are deactivated by setting to 0 the pheromone value. As in most routing table algorithms, AntRouting algorithm provides the source with multiple paths to the destination. Therefore, the node searches for an alternative link. If a second path exists, it is used. Otherwise, neighbors are informed of the new situation.

5 Simulation Results and Analysis

To illustrate performance of the AntRouting algorithm, we use the following network topology and conditions. The whole network is simulated in NS2.33[13].

The network consists of 12 HAPs, due to the characteristics of high-bandwidth long delay of HAPS-satellite integrated communications system we set the maximum bandwidth, B_{max} 50Mbps, and maximum delay D_{max} 2ms. The initial pheromone value is set to 1, information growth factor K is set to 3, the pheromone scale factor α is set to 1 and visibility factor β is set to 0. The following figure 2 is the network simulation topology.

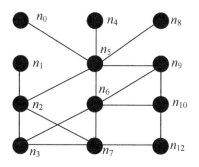

Fig. 2. Network topology

Here, we mainly simulate the implementation of this algorithm and network performance as end to end delay and packet loss rate. At first, we show the routing table of node 2 which is generated after the route discovery phase completes as table 1.

Table 1. Routing Table On Node 2

Destination	Max phenomenon value	Path (S-D)
0	0.84344	2-5-0
1	1	direct
3	1	direct
4	0.947671	2-5-4
5	0.913648	direct
6	0.589107	2-3-6
7	0.640156	direct
8	0.937383	2-5-8
9	0.650684	2-5-9
10	0.444980	2-3-6-10
11	0.569850	2-7-11

From the routing table, we can get the phenomenon value of next hop from node 2 to every node in the network. And by calculating the selection probability then we can know the next hop. For example, when the destination is node 10, the algorithm first calculate the probability value of neighbor nodes 3 and node 7 , we can get $P_{2-10}(3) > P_{2-10}(7)$, so we choose node 3 as the next hop , so the FANT is forwarded to node 3, and finally get the path of $2 - 3 - 6 - 10$.

Then figure 3 and 4 show the comparison of ant routing AR-HS algorithm and SPF algorithm in terms of the average delay and drop rate. The total simulation time is 130s, in order to detect link transitions, we set that the link of $3-6$ is broke in the 60th second.

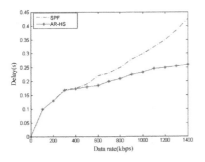

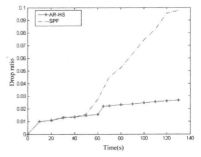

Fig. 3. Average Delay of AR-HS and SPF algorithm

Fig. 4. Drop ratio of AR-HS and SPF algorithm

We compare the end-to-end delay and the packet loss probabilities between the shortest paths (SPF) calculated by the Bellmans shortest path algorithm and the paths created by our routing algorithm AntRouting(AR-HS).

In figure 3, the delay performance of the AntRouting algorithm and the shortest path routing algorithm are depicted. In the first experiment, the CBR date flow sent speed is increased gradually, and the delays are recorded. We can see that when sent speed is smaller than 400kbps,two algorithm perform same in average delay . However ,because SPF algorithm only consider the network topology to find the shortest path , without taking the network load into consideration, it leads to severe congestion on some nodes , and results in a relatively large delay. Hence, along with the increasing of sent speed, the delay of SPF algorithm increase obviously and much larger than AntRouting algorithm. Even when CBR sent speed s higher than 1000kbps, AntRouting algorithm increased very slowly, which conforms that our algorithm optimize the delay performance of network successfully.

In figure 4 In the second experiment, the packet loss probabilities are recorded as the time passing. We can see the drop rate is still very slow before 60s, but the drop rate of SPF algorithm increased much faster than AntRouting algorithm after 60s.. That because we set link broke in 60s, and AntRouting algorithm recovery after some seconds, and drop rate keeps near 2%. This conform that AntRouting algorithm can find other path when the best path can't work, and reduce the packet loss probabilities.

6 Conclusion

In this paper we have proposed a novel algorithm based on ant colony algorithm. We have chosen HAPS-Satellite integrated network architecture in order to take advantage of some useful characteristics such as high bandwidth, lower propagation delay and dynamism. The proposed algorithm has been realized using a novel technique called ant Routing that is based on the ant colony behavior. This algorithm permits to discover minimal length paths that satisfy requirements of end-to-end delay and hops, and can find the suboptimal path when the best is broken. Some simulations have been taken and we performed a comparison between our algorithm with shortest path algorithm. The simulation results show that the performance of ant routing algorithm is better than SPF in average delay and packet loss probability.

Acknowledgment. This work was supported in part by the National Natural Science Foundation of China (No.60903181), Jiangsu Province High-school Natural Science Research Plan (No.09KJB520009), and the Postdoctoral Science Foundation of Jiangsu Province of China (No.1002022B).

References

1. Djuknic, G.M., Freidenfelds, J., Okunev, Y.: Establishing Wireless Communications Services via High-Altitude Aeronautical Platforms: A Concept Whose Time has Come? IEEE Commun. Mag. 35(9), 128–135 (1997)
2. Karapantazis, S., Pavlidou, F.: Broadband Communications via High-Altitude Platforms: a Survey. IEEE Commun. Surveys & Tutorials 7(1), 1–35 (2005)
3. Sun, J., Xiong, S., Guo, F.: A new pheromone update strategy in Ant Colony Optimization. In: Proceedings of 2004 International Conference on Machine Learning and Cybernetics (August 2004)

4. Di Caro, G., Dorigo, M.: AntNet: Distributed Stigmergetic Control for Communications Networks. Journal of Artificial Intelligence Research (JAIR) 9, 317–365 (2011)
5. Zheng, X., Guo, W., Liu, R.: An Ant-Based Distributed Routing Algorithm for Ad-hoc Networks. In: International Conference on Communications, Circuits and Systems, ICCCAS. IEEE (2004)
6. Hussein, O., Sadaawi, T.: Ant Routing Algorithm for Mobile Ad-hoc networks (ARAMA). In: Proceedings of the 2003 IEEE International Performance, Computing, and Communications Conference (2003)
7. De Rango, F., Tropea, M., Provato, A., Santamaria, A.-F., Marano, S.: ANT Based Routing Algorithm over a HAP Network with Integrated Services. In: Gelbukh, A., Morales, E.F. (eds.) MICAI 2008. LNCS (LNAI), vol. 5317, pp. 913–924. Springer, Heidelberg (2008)
8. Dorigo, M., Di Caro, G.: The Ant Colony Optimization (ACO) Meta-Heuristic. In: Corne, D., Dorigo, M., Glover, F. (eds.) New Ideas in Optimization, pp. 11–32. McGraw-Hill, London (1999)
9. Hussein, O.H., Saadawi, T.N., Jong Lee, M.: Probability Routing Algorithm for Mobile Ad Hoc Networks' Resources Management. IEEE Journal on Selected Areas in Communications (2005)
10. Gunes, M., Sorges, U., Bouazizi, I.: ARA - The Ant-Colony Based Routing Algorithm for MANETs. In: Proceedings of International Conference on Parallel Processing Workshops. IEEE, Los Alamitos (2002)
11. Yuan-yuan, Z., Yan-xiang, H.: Ant Routing Algorithm for Mobile Ad-hoc Networks Based on Adaptive Improvement. School of Computer Science, Wuhan University School of Computer and State Key Lab of Software Engineering, Wuhan University Wuhan, Hubei Province, China (2005)
12. De Rango, F., Tropea, M., Provato, A., Santamaria, A., Marano, S.: Multi-Constraints Routing Algorithm based on Swarm Intelligence over High Altitude Platforms. In: NICSO 2007 International Workshop on Nature Inspired Cooperative Strategies for Optimization, Acireale, Italy, November 8-10 (2007)
13. McCanne, S., Floyd, S.: The network simulator: NS-2. 2010-08-15/2008-03-15

R-AODV: A Cognitive AODV Routing Algorithm in Wireless Network

Xiaoguo Ye, Feifei Dong, and Ruchuan Wang

[1] College of Computer, Nanjing University of Posts and Telecommunications,
Nanjing, Jiangsu 210003, China
[2] Jiangsu High Technology Research Key Laboratory for Wireless Sensor Networks,
Nanjing, Jiangsu 210003, China
[3] Key Lab of Broadband Wireless Communication and Sensor Network
Technology(Nanjing University of Posts and Telecommunications), Ministry of
Education Jiangsu Province, Nanjing, Jiangsu 210003, China
xgye@njupt.edu.cn

Abstract. Wireless communication system plays a more and more important role in many fields. Wireless network using traditional AODV algorithm only considers the minimal hop of all routes and can not meet specific QoS requirements. Some network resources will be wasted to some extend using traditional algorithm. A cognitive routing algorithm, R-AODV, which is based on the AODV algorithm, is proposed in this paper. The new proposed algorithm collects network status and chooses different routing strategy to make the best use of network resources. It may collect network status before having routing algorithm and according to different conditions of current network to choose different routing algorithm, which may make the best use of network resources.

Keywords: Cognitive routing, AODV, QoS.

1 Introduction

Wireless sensor network combined with the sensor technology, embedded system technology, distributed information processing technology, and wireless communication technology plays an important role which through the real-time monitoring and data collection information to help people achieve many kinds of objects in many fields management[1,2]. Wireless routing protocol is a key factor of the communication quality in wireless sensor network, because this kind of network has a serious limit, whichs each node have the limit in the energy resources, computing power and bandwidth[3,4]. All this determines the network routing protocol must be able to maximize network resources efficiency.

The traditional routing algorithm only considers a single shortest route or the minimal hop. When a stable routing strategy is deployed, the network would not work well at some special conditions. If a frequency efficiency strategy is chosen, some QoS performances may be limited. If a QoS guarantee routing is deployed, the network resource may be wasted and the congestion may happen. If a load balance routing works in the network, the frequency efficiency and QoS performance

R. Wang and F. Xiao (Eds.): CWSN 2012, CCIS 334, pp. 623–630, 2013.
© Springer-Verlag Berlin Heidelberg 2013

could not be guaranteed. So, the routing in wireless network should select different strategies adaptively based on different network environment, as the grid charges different from the time of use[3]. This paper introduces the cognitive AODV algorithm which is based on the AODV algorithm. Cognitive routing algorithm can prior collect network information and then make a judgment based on the current congestion conditions to send packet to one node.

In this paper, we design the systems with the cognitive routing algorithm in the wireless network. In order to analyzing performance quantitatively with routing algorithm more convenient, we simulate a typical wireless network in NS-2[11]. Cognitive routing algorithm can solve the decline of the utilization which is caused by link choose not balanced in heterogeneous and dynamic network. The remaining of this paper is organized as follows. In Section 2, the cognitive routing algorithm is expanded in detail. In Section 3, the design of wireless communication system in NS-2 with cognitive routing algorithm is described. The simulation results are given Section 4. Finally, Section 5 summarizes and concludes the paper.

2   The Cognitive Routing Algorithm

2.1   Description of Traditional Routing

According to the different classification of routing strategy, the traditional wireless routing protocols can be divided into active routing protocols and passive routing protocol. As wireless network which has dynamic characteristics, active routing protocol used in this network have obvious disadvantages, so often choose passive routing protocol in practice.

AODV routing protocol is one of the most widely used passive routing protocols. AODV routing protocol is a typical on-demand drive routing protocols which is called getting the system by needed. Those nodes which are not active on the path will not hold any related routing information, also won't participate in any cycle of the routing table exchange. In addition, node does not need to find and keep routing to another node unless the two nodes need for communication. The mobile nodes get the local connectivity through several methods, including broadcasting local radio news– Hello message. The main purpose of this algorithm is to send the general topology maintenance packet when there is a need for routing radio. Difference from local connection management (neighbor testing) and general topology maintenance, it needs to send topology information of changes to the mobile neighbor node. AODV using broadcast routing to found information. It relies on the leaf dynamic nodes to set up routing to send a group of packets. In order to maintain the latest routing information between the nodes, AODV lessons the thought from the DSDV of using the serial number, this mechanism can effectively prevent the formation of routing ring. When the source node wants to communicate with the other, and there is no corresponding routing information in the routing table, it will launch routing discovery process. Each node maintains two independent counters: node serial number counter and broadcast marks. Source node broadcasts to its neighbors through RREQ (Route Requests) packet to initiate a mute discovery process.[5]

2.2 Definition of Cognitive Routing Algorithm

Traditional routing is based on the shortest hops, but in wireless communication system, every time, the link status is different, so the traditional routing is not suitable to multi-level satellite communication system.

The proposed cognitive routing algorithm, R-AODV, using several steps, is described as following Algorithm 1.

Algorithm 1. R-AODV using cognitive routing algorithm

//Information collection:
Broadcast the route request;
// the packets carry the current node load information
//Complete the Broadcast, calculate average load of the whole network:
double $avgLoad = (double)load/nodeCount$;
//Judgment:
Calculate hop with the max load;
if $(rt0 \rightarrow rt\_max\_load > avgLoad)$ **then**
  | network_busy;
else
  | network_not_busy;
end
//Transport packets:
if $(network\_not\_busy)$ **then**
  | Choose the route with manual hops;
else
  | Choose another route with lowest load;
end

Cognitive routing algorithm is choosing routing strategies based on the current network status dynamically. When the average load of the network is low, we may choose the routing with the manual hops, but when the load is higher, the routing with manual hops may has a number of packets to send, so the delay may be longer. So we may choose another routing with the lowest load to balance the resource utilization in whole network. Learning the information of load in current network, and making the routing choice by different performance parameter to make sure the current routing is optimal and may utilize the current network resources efficiently.

3 System Design

In this section, some parameters are used to checkout the performance of different routing algorithms. Then, we present our novel cognitive parameters and cognitive routing metric for CBRs that find paths from source node to destination node.

3.1   Classification of Routing Metric

The transmission delay and the hop are the usual additive parameters. The synthesis rule of additive metric is the sum of the parameter of every hop in the link[1].

$$m(p) = \sum_{i=1}^{n} cost(l_i) \tag{1}$$

Where $cost(l_i)$ is the parameter of the l_i hop, $m(p)$ is the metric of the link.

The delivery rate is the usual multiplicative parameters. The synthesis rule of multiplicative metric is the product of the parameter of every hop in the link. The available bandwidth and the remaining buffer are the usual concavity parameters. The synthesis rule of concavity metric is the minimum of the parameter of every hop in the link.

$$m(p) = \prod_{i=1}^{n} delay(l_i) \tag{2}$$

The available bandwidth and the remaining buffer are the usual concavity parameters. The synthesis rule of concavity metric is the minimum of the parameter of every hop in the link.

$$m(p) = \min[bandwidth(l_i)] \tag{3}$$

3.2   Design of R-AODV Routing Metric

Cognitive routing algorithm R-AODV gives priority to different performance requirements according to different network status in routing time[6]. When congestion occurs, the routing will choose the route with minimal hop, while the network is operated at normal heavy load, the route with the lowest load will be chosen. The routing metric is designed as follows:

$$metric(l) = load(l) \cdot hop(l) \tag{4}$$

$metric(l)$ is the routing metric of the lth route, l is the route. $load(l)$ is the load of the lth route, n represents that the lth route has n hops, $hop(l)$ is the total hops of the lth route. To choose different routing cost from by the state of the network, two exponent parameters, a and b, are proposed. The exponent parameters vary adaptive for the congestion status of the network.

$$metric(l) = \sum_{i=1}^{n} [d(l_i)]^b \cdot (\min(l(l_i)))^c \tag{5}$$

In order to measure congestion degree of the network, we introduce a congestive parameter y. The parameter is the ratio of the max load of the current route and the average load of the network in interval time. Through calculating the average ratio, we can estimate the congestion status of networks. Assuming there are n nodes in the network, y can be expressed as

$$y = \max load(l_h)/(\sum_{i=0}^{n} load_i/n) \tag{6}$$

Where $\max load(l_h)$ is the max load of lth route, $load_{avg} = \sum_{i=0}^{n} load_i/n$ is the average load of the whole network. When the average load is bigger than the max load, we may think the whole is congestive in some degree. So, the route will chose the route with lowest load[9,10].

4   Performance Analysis

In this section, we evaluate the performance of the R-AODV routing described in section 3. In order to convenient for the quantitative analysis, we take NS-2 for simulation[11]. The simulation system has many wireless nodes. Setting transmission power as 3.41828e-8W, The simulator apply Quadrature phase-shift keying (QPSK) constellation, white Gaussian noise,802.11DCF of MAC, Simulation topology is described as 500m*500m. In this model experiment, we set different sending rate of the CBR packets, and the performances of through and drop rate is shown in following figures.

As shown in Figure 1, when the load of the network is low, the drop rate is 0 in both AODV and R-AODV routing algorithm. But with the increasing of

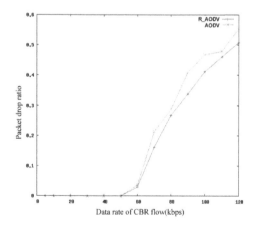

Fig. 1. Drop ratio of R-AODV and AODV in different loads

sending rate, packet loss rates are also on the increase, and at the same rate, the drop rate with the R-AODV routing algorithm is lower than AODV routing algorithm.

Figure 2 shows the throughput of different routing algorithms at the different network load. The horizontal axis is the CBR data rate, the longitudinal axis is throughput. As the results show, when the network load is low, the throughput of R-AODV algorithm is a little higher than AODV algorithm. And when the load is normal, the AODV algorithm have little different in throughput, but when the network load is busy, the performance of the algorithm R-AODV is obviously much better than AODV algorithm. This showed R-AODV routing algorithm can improve the utilization rate of more resources with high load conditions.

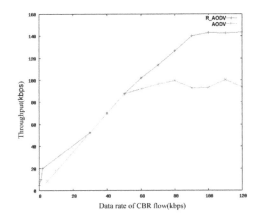

Fig. 2. Throughput of R-AODV and AODV in different load

In addition, we also measured standard deviation of the sample nodes to evaluate the nodal work situation. Standard deviation is $\rho(x) = \sqrt{\sum_{i=0}^{n}(x_i - \bar{x})^2}$. $\bar{x}$ is the average value of the x_i. Variance, used to measure deviation degree from the center data[11,12]. In a group of the data with little difference in average value, the volatility or standard deviation greater means there are some data is far away from average value, otherwise, the whole data is around the average value nearly. Reflected in the network structure is some node has transferred many packets and another nodes with small amount of packets.

Figure 3 shows the standard deviation is smaller with R-AODV routing algorithm than that of AODV algorithm. The routing choice with the AODV routing, the standard deviation is higher, when the rate of CBR packets is higher, the routing is in the same, which may cause some node is busy and the others are free. This is not good use the resource of the free nodes. So, the R-AODV routing algorithm can effectively balance the resources of network, it will not cause the conditions that some nodes are very busy, some are idle.

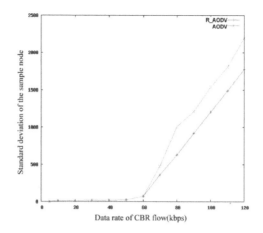

Fig. 3. Standard deviation of R-AODV and AODV in different load

5   Conclusion

In this work, we have designed R-AODV routing algorithm for wireless network and given simulation analysis in network simulator NS-2. From the viewpoints of load balancing and QoS guarantee, a new routing metric based on cognitive information is described in this paper. The metrics is evaluated by simulations. The results can confirm that the proposed multi- strategy routing can improve wireless network performances of packets loss and throughput and achieve resource balance in different network loads.

Acknowledgment. This work was supported in part by the National Natural Science Foundation of China (No.60903181), Jiangsu Province High-school Natural Science Research Plan (No.09KJB520009), the Postdoctoral Science Foundation of Jiangsu Province of China (No.1002022B), and NUPT Research Project (No.NY210034).

References

1. Dai, C., Zhang, Y., Wang, L., Li, Z., Xiao, J.: A Novel Multi-strategy Cognitive Routing, pp. 973–976. IEEE (2011)
2. Akyildiz, I.F., Ekici, E., Bender, M.D.: MLSR: A Novel Routing Algorithm for Multilayered Satellite IP Networks. IEEE/ACM Trans. on Networking 10(3), 411–424 (2002)
3. Khalife, H., Ahuja, S., Malouch, N., Krunz, M.: Probabilistic Path Selection in Opportunistic Cognitive Radio Networks. In: Proceedings of the IEEE GLOBECOM (2008)
4. Zhang, Q.-J., Wu, M.-Q., Zhen, Y., Shang, C.-L.: AODV routing overhead analysis based on link failure probability in MANET. The Journal of China Universities of Posts and Telecommunications 17(5), 109–115 (2010)

5. Wu, S.-L., Lin, C.-Y., Tseng, Y.-C., et al.: A New Multi-Channel MAC Protocol with On-Demand Channel Assignment for Multi-Hop Mobile Ad Hoc Networks. In: IEEE Proceedings of the International Symposium on Parallel Architectures, Algorithms and Networks, pp. 232–237. IEEE Press, Richardson (2000)
6. IEEE Standard for Wireless LAN-Medium Access Control and Physical Layer Specification, P802.11 (1999)
7. Akyildiz, I.F., Wang, X.: Cross-layer design in wireless mesh networks. IEEE Transactions on Vehicular Technology 57(2), 1061–1075 (2008)
8. Bruno, R., Conti, M., Gregori, E.: Mesh networks: Commodity multihop ad hoc networks. IEEE Communications Magazine 43(3), 123–131 (2005)
9. Stojmenovic, I., Giordano, S., Conti, M., Basagni, S.: Mobile Ad Hoc Networks (MANETs): Routing Technology for Dynamic Wireless Networking, pp. 255–259 (2005)
10. Peter, P.P., Sylvie, P.: Performance Analysis of Reactive Shortest Path and Multipath Routing Mechanism with Load Balance. In: Twenty-Second Annual Joint Conference of the IEEE Computer and Communications, March 30-April 3, pp. 251–259 (2003)
11. McCanne, S., Floyd, S.: The network simulator: NS-2. 2010-08-15/2008-03-15

An Overview on Node Behavior Trust Evaluation in Ad Hoc Network

Min Yin[1,*], Jing Feng[1], and Yao Tang[2]

Institute of Meteorology and Oceanography,
PLA Univ. of Sci. and Tech, 211101 Nanjing, China
Institute of Science, PLA Univ. of Sci. and Tech,
211101 Nanjing, China
qqq.yinmin@163.com

Abstract. As a necessary complement to static identity authentication mechanisms in secure applications of ad hoc network, node behavior trust evaluation can solve many security problems effectively. This paper has a general overview on node behavior trust evaluation, analyzes issues of trust model, behavior monitoring, evaluation metrics, trust computation etc., which provides a reference on the future research.

Keywords: trust model, trust evaluation, evaluation metric, ad hoc network.

1 Introduction

Ad Hoc network is an autonomous network composed of mobile nodes. It has wide applications in military and commercial fields. But security problems restrict its popularization. In Ad Hoc network application, static identity-based authentication mechanism has not met the need for dynamic security. The nodes with authentic identity may become defectors and execute interior malicious acts. In order to get better security, it must combine static identity-based authentication mechanism with dynamic behavior-based trust evaluation [1-4].

Trust concept comes from sociology. It has characteristics of subjective and fuzzy. In 1996, Matt Blaze first proposes trust management [5]. According to the class of trust evidence, trust management system is classified as authentication-based trust management and behavior-based trust management [6]. While authentication-based trust management relies on complicated public key computation, absolutely dependable third party and lacks of node behavior evaluation, which make it hard to adapting dynamic Ad Hoc network. In recent years trust management research in Ad Hoc network mainly focuses on behavior-based trust management, which evaluates node trust continuously by direct or indirect observation evidence so as to assign a lower credit for malicious node and isolate it.

---

* This paper is funded by National Science Fund (61070174) and Foundational technology fund of Inst. Meteorology and Oceanography PLAUST.

R. Wang and F. Xiao (Eds.): CWSN 2012, CCIS 334, pp. 631–641, 2013.
© Springer-Verlag Berlin Heidelberg 2013

Node behavior trust evaluation is a very important part in trust model and trust management research. In recent years, more and more scholars are concerned with trust technology applications research in Ad Hoc network [7–9]. This paper has a general overview on the research actualities, including trust model, behavior monitoring, evaluation metrics, trust computation, adaptability in the context etc. It also analyzes existing unresolved problems in node behaviour trust evaluation which provides a reference on the future research. The paper is composed of three parts. First it sums up the concept and category of trust models, then it analyzes and compares existing researches and at last it points out unresolved problems.

2   Trust Model

Trust evaluation is involved in many fields, such as electronic business, P2P network, Ad Hoc network, and sensor network etc. Trust evaluation needs a proper measurable model to compute or estimate node credit, which is called trust model. In the category of network trust is defined as an evaluation based on proper evidence or experience to judge whether an entity obey the regulations. According to the realization manner, network trust models include centralized models and distributed models. In the centralized model node trust value is computed by the absolutely dependable node and it transfers node trust values to each other, for example PKI. In the distributed model, each node computes trust value of the others independently, for example PGP.

In 1998, Abdul-Rahman [10] first proposes a distributed trust model based on the basic trust concept. This trust model aims at open network environment. It first divides trust relations into direct trust and recommended trust. It calculates trust values by a series of discrete value.

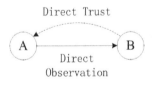

Fig. 1. Direct trust relation

Direct trust relation is illustrated as Figure 1. Entity A forms a trust evaluation on B according to direct observation about Bs behavior. This direct trust can be calculated by the possibility which B can accomplish some service at an A expected success probability or accepted failure probability. This estimation is based on Bs service behavior collected by A in the former period, which is denoted as the number of successful service by B.

Indirect trust relation is illustrated as Figure 2, which is also called recommended trust. Entity A evaluates entity C according to the reliability of

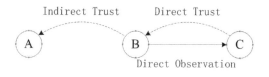

Fig. 2. Indirect trust relation

recommender B, which provides trust value of entity C for A. In indirect trust relations external information and trust value are contents of trust transferring. Transferring external information can reduce subjective effects of the entities along the recommended route, which is propitious to an objective and reasonable trust evaluation. But it also increases processing cost and network overload of the evaluation entity and ignores evaluations of the recommenders. Transferring trust value makes for reasonable trust evaluation according to reliability of the recommenders.

The synthesized trust value of node behavior is usually composed of direct trust value, indirect trust value and historical trust value. Figure 3 illustrates transverse synthesis, which is composed of direct trust value and indirect trust value. Transverse synthesis costs more energy and bandwidth while collecting indirect trust value. Some trust models only consider direct trust value or indirect trust value, which needs much more time to establish credit grade. This leads to slowly credit reduction for malicious node, which can stay in the system for longer time.

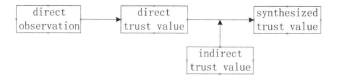

Fig. 3. Transverse synthesis

Figure 4 illustrates vertical synthesis, which synthesizes trust values of different periods. Vertical synthesis considers relations of trust and time. Trust value is only valid in a specific period. The common synthesis method is to assign different weighing coefficients for short-term trust value and historical trust value, which avoids trust aging by assigning a larger weighing coefficient for the short-term trust value. If the historical trust value has a larger weighing coefficient, it will prevent malicious node from counteracting historical misbehaviors by a little operations.

In the trust model with transverse synthesis, there needs trust transferring between nodes each other. According to transferring range it is divided into global trust model and local trust model. In the global trust model, each node

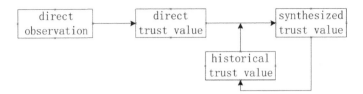

Fig. 4. Vertical synthesis

calculates trust value of another node and transfers this value to others until forms a global trust value. But global trust model ignores private characteristic of the trust, that different nodes may have different trust evaluation for the same node. Also, it costs much more computation. In large scale peer to peer network and rapid dynamic network, it is uncertain whether this cost of network bandwidth and computation is worthy. Local trust model only considers trust transferring within a small range. It has a good timeliness but is weak to defend joint recommended attacks.

In addition, Grandison [11] believes that trust is a certainty of reliable and secure action ability in a specific context. Namely, in different context trust definition is different. According to relations of the context, trust model is divided into universal trust model and application related trust model. They are different from trust evaluation metrics. For example, applications of data sensing, secure routing, admission control need to choose communication, data, energy as the metric separately. Communication factor means that trust value is computed by transmitting ratio. Data factor means to evaluate a node by the data coherence with the other node. Energy factor means that trust is evaluated by the probability for accomplish a mission with the residual energy. If trust model aims at the other application scene, it needs other specific trust metric.

3 Research Issues

Trust model is an integrative framework of node behavior evaluation, including behavior monitoring, metric selection, trust computation etc. A trust model computes credit by direct trust value, indirect trust value and historical trust value, which is illustrated by figure 5. Behavior monitoring module detects node behavior with selected evaluating metric. For example, if forwarding ratio is evaluating metric, forwarding behavior is to be monitored specially. If residual energy is evaluating metric, monitoring of energy management is needed. Trust computation considers direct trust value, indirect trust value, historical trust value, and security measures synthetically. According to practical occasions it allocates weighing coefficients for each factor with mathematics theory.

In recent years, researchers have obtained some primary academic fruit on node behavior trust model of Ad Hoc network. It is discussed as the following.

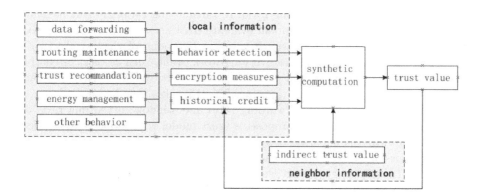

Fig. 5. A trust model example

3.1   Behavior Monitoring

Behavior monitoring module collects information of specific events. It needs continuous monitoring and wastes much of processing cost and storage space, which is the most energy consuming part in trust model. Maarouf I. [12] proposes a new monitoring strategy called an efficient monitoring procedure in a reputation system (EMPIRE), which is a probabilistic and distributed monitoring methodology that tries to reduce the monitoring activities per node while maintaining the ability to detect attacks at a satisfactory level.

In addition, many scholars focus on the relations of trust value and behavior detection time. They believe trust value only reasonable in a specific period as node behavior varying with time. So trust value should be synthesized with the behavior detection results of different time. In the research of synthesized method and trust aging mechanism, a common way is to allocate different weighing coefficients for short-term trust value and historical trust value, which avoids trust aging and prevents malicious node from counteracting historical misbehaviors. Tian Li-Qin [13] put forward a kind of evaluation mechanism on node behavior trust based on sliding windows model. Through various operations on sliding window, it ensures evaluation principles of node behavior trust.

3.2   Evaluation Factors and Metrics

Evaluation factor is the base of trust evaluation. In different context evaluation factors are different, which contains communication factor, data factor, energy factor etc. Communication factor means that trust value is computed by transmitting ratio. Data factor means to evaluate a node by the data coherence with the other node. Energy factor means that trust is evaluated by the probability for accomplish a mission with the residual energy.

Evaluation metric is one of the parameters in the evaluation factors, which denotes numerical trust value of evaluation factor. The common metrics include forwarding ratio [14–15], dropping ratio, retransmitting ratio[16]. But in many context these common metrics cannot evaluate trust accurately, so scholars have to propose other evaluation metrics from respective point of view.

A. Pirzada [17] defines trust as every network event, such as trust of control packet forwarding, trust of data packet forwarding. It evaluates trust value according to the evidence of these metrics. Li X. [15] takes time into consideration of forwarding ratio. He uses forwarding ratio and window forwarding ratio as evaluation metrics. Li Yu [18] proposes a trust model with multiple evaluation factors, including residual energy, delay, delay jitter and others. Karthik, N. [19] uses transmission range, packet loss, energy consumption, latency, path quality, spot of the nodes, hop count, signal to noise ratio, bit error rate etc. when computes node trust value.

3.3 Trust Value Computation

Trust value computation includes steps of formulation, initialization, updating, and synthesis of the trust value [28].

Trust formulation is the mathematic way of scaling trust. Commonly it adopts discrete trust grade or continuous trust region to denote.

Trust initialization assigns initial trust for all of nodes when network is organized. It is increased or decreased along with the trust computation result. In order to get a speedup of trust construction, the same initial value is preassigned, such as Small to medium value, in equivalent and Medium to large value. Xin Jiang [31] considers difference of node trust and proposes a trust model only based on gaming results and history interaction information.

Trust updating means to increase or decrease trust value according to trust computation result. A common computation method is to evaluate by the number of good behavior and bad behavior [20–23]. Although the magnitude of increasing and decreasing can be different, this will also give a chance for bad node, which takes an attack by accumulating trust value. Ishmanov F. [24] proposes a secure trust estimation method which does not allow malicious node to increase its trust value artificially. It calculates trust on nodes based on only a bad behavior. Misbehavior of a node is weighed and based on the weighed misbehavior trust value is decreased. And a node can increase its trust value if it does not misbehave.

Trust computation model, namely synthesis method of trust, is the core of trust computation. It may be denoted by a function as $f(x_1, x_2, ..., x_n)$. Parameters $x_1, x_2, ..., x_n$ are effective factors of behavior. Trust computation models are different from each other as trust models vary. But in general, trust computation depends on direct information, indirect information and historical information. There are kinds of mathematical synthesis method for trust computation, such as simple weighed [26], statistics [27], Bayesian [20], fuzzy logic [21–28], D-S theory [29] , cloud model [30], game theory [31], information entropy [32], semi-ring theory [33] are common computation methods in literature.

Simple weighed method is easy to realize and has a small effect on network throughput and energy consumption. Statistical method mainly calculates weighed mean and weighed square of direct trust values or indirect trust values, by which to evaluate resource consumption. Bayesian method requires node trust obey a supposed prior probability distribution, such as Beta distributionDirichlet distributionGaussian distribution. And then, it speculates posterior probability by Bayesian formula. It is complicated. Fuzzy logic method considers fuzziness and subjectivity of trust. It ratiocinate trust relations with fuzzy theory. D-S theory synthesizes direct trust value and indirect trust value with D-S combination formulas, which is applicable in the case of little evidence conflicts. Cloud model describes trust relation by trust cloud, which is as fuzzy and stochastic as trust relation is. Moreover, Xin Jiang [31] present a trust establishment mechanism for mobile ad hoc networks, which has better adaptability to various situations since it does not need default trust value in the bootstrapping phase of trust establishment. Li Yu[18] uses AHP (Analytic Hierarchy Process) methodology to combine different factors, including transmitting trust, energy trust, delay trust, delay jitter trust. FU Cai [34] propose an trust evaluation method based on grey clustering idea. Marmol[35] uses Ant Colony Algorithm in trust management model.

3.4   Adaptability in the Context

Due to relations between trust model and specific application, some scholars consider model designing from the view of application context [36], such as routing, admission control, public key authentication etc.

S. Ganeriwal [20] first proposes Reputation-Based Framework for High Integrity Sensor Networks (RFSN). In this trust management scheme, each sensor node maintains the reputation for neighboring nodes only. Cheng Weifang [16] proposes a trust-based routing framework, which aims at detecting forwarding invalidation and selective forwarding. Halim I.T.A. [14] points out that to overcome effect of misbehaving nodes the trustworthiness of the network nodes should be considered in the route selection process combined with the hop count. A new protocol based on self monitoring (agent-based) and following the dynamic source routing (DSR) algorithm is presented, which is called Agent-Based Trusted Dynamic Source Routing (ATDSR). Samavati, H. [36] proposes Adaptive Multi Level Trust model (AMLeT), which considers situations and context of the network to work more dynamic and adaptive. It can work dynamically in every network application with different security levels proportionally. Li Yu [18] proposes a trust computation method, in which weighing coefficients are given in accordance with the service differentiation. Because voice and video services often have more restrictive quality requirement on delay and delay jitter than data transfer services such as web browsing have. Huang Tinglei [37] considers misjudging problem of honest node in a bad environment and proposes a scheme to solve this.

4   Problems and Challenges

Although scholars have a primary research on synthesis method and trust model about trust evaluation in Ad Hoc network, there are many problems and challenges to solve.

Trust models limitation of defending more attacks
At present, any trust model cannot deal with all of secure problems [41]. Most of trust evaluation aim at selfish node and selective forwarding. But other than attacks of no forwarding and selective forwarding, there are network attacks of data revision, data forgery, identity imitation, and resource wasting etc., such as DOS attack, Sybil attack, Sinkhole attack, Wormhole attack, Hello flooding attack, selective forwarding attack and so on. Moreover, trust model itself may face attacks of denied recommend, malicious recommend, imitating identity, betrayer, joint recommend etc. When these attacks occur trust evaluation system is very dangerous; because it may give a wrong high trust credit for malicious nodes.

Lack of all-around security-oriented evaluation metrics
In Ad Hoc network applications of sensing data, secure routing, secure data amalgamation, evaluation factors of trust model are different [16], such as communication factor, energy factor, security factor and the other metrics. At present, forwarding ratio is the common evaluation metric. Sometime energy, delay, signal-to-noise ratio, node location are to be evaluation metrics. But forwarding ratio cannot denote characteristics of all kinds of attacks. Also, metric of energy and delay cannot embody network security. Accordingly, it needs to have a deep research on security-oriented trust evaluation metrics for security-oriented trust model.

Trust construction, convergence, reliability in dynamic network
Most trust computation needs indirect information. But how long node needs to wait and how many samples it needs to evaluate correctly are worth detailed researching, which is a convergence problem. Aside this, in rapid dynamic network, both topology change and bad channel quality may lead to a high packet dropping ratio. Also malicious nodes may take recommending attack. Therefore, trust model based on information exchange mechanism may lead to wrong evaluation.

Due to the influence on trust models evaluation efficiency and reliability, it needs to have a deep research on the design of the statistical reliable trust model adapting Ad Hoc network.

Needing research on detection methods of evaluation metric
As forwarding ratio is the common evaluation metric in most of existing literatures, detailed description about metric detection method is lacking. If some other metrics are used, with the limited ability of Ad Hoc network node, it needs to have a deep research on the feasibility and method of obtaining the values of these metrics.

Disorder definition of trust metric leading to hard trust model comparison
Trust relation is the most complicated relation in society. It is some of subjective cognition. Although Sun [23] point out that trust in computer network is different from sociological trust and analyzes their differences, it does not receive extensive agreement. There are still a lot of trust evaluation metrics. At present, existing trust models are based on different application occasions, which have different definitions on attacks, defensive intension, defensive effect, and evaluation metrics. It is hard to make comparisons among trust models and evaluate performance of trust models.

5 Conclusions

As a booming research area, trust evaluation has attracted attentions of researchers, but in general it is underway and has many open subjects for deep research. Solving these pivotal problems is significant to consummating trust management system and solving security issues effectively in Ad Hoc network. And it redounds to promote practical applications of Ad Hoc network. This paper has a general overview on the main issues and research actualities, including trust model, behavior monitoring, evaluation metrics, trust computation, adaptability in the context etc. It also analyzes existing unresolved problems in node behaviour trust evaluation which provides a reference on the future research.

References

1. Zhan, G., Shi, W., Deng, J.: A Resilient Trust Model for WSNs. In: 7th International Conference on Embedded Networked Sensor Systems, Berkeley, California, USA, pp. 411–412 (November 2009)
2. Zhang, M., Yang, B., Qi, Y.: Using Trust Metric to Detect Malicious Behaviors in WSNs. In: 8th ACIS International Conference on Software Engineering, Artificial Intelligence, Networking and Parallel/Distributed Computing, Qingdao, China, pp. 104–108 (2007)
3. Lin, C., Wang, Y., Tian, L.: Development of Trusted Network and Challenges It Faces. ZTE Communications 6(1), 13–17 (2008)
4. Tian, L., Lin, C., Ji, T.: Kind of Quantitative Evaluation of User Behaviour Trust Using AHP. Journal of Computational Information Systems 3(4), 1329–1334 (2007)
5. Blaze, M., Feigenbaum, J., Lacy, J.: Decent Ralized Trust Agement. In: IEEE Symposium on Security and Privacy, Washington, pp. 164–173 (1996)
6. Aivaloglou, E., Gritzalis, S.: Trust Establishment in Sensor Networks: Behaviour-based, Certificate-based and a Combinational Approach. International Journal of System of Systems Engineering 1(1), 128–148 (2008)
7. Boukerche, A., Ren, Y.: A Trust-based Security System for Ubiquitous and Pervasive Computing Environments. Computer Communications 31, 4343–4351 (2008)
8. Boukerche, A.: Algorithms and Protocols for Wireless Sensor Networks. Wiley-IEEE Press (October 2008) ISBN: 978-0-471-79813-2
9. Zhao, X.-B., You, Z.-Y., Zhao, Z.-F.: Availability Based Trust Evaluation Model for MANET. Journal of Communications 31(3), 82–88 (2010)

10. Abdul-Rahman, A., Hailes, S.: A Distributed Trust Model. In: New Security Paradigms Workshop, New York, pp. 48–60 (1998)
11. Grandison, T., Sloman, M.: A Survey of Trust in Internet Appllications. IEEE Communitions Surveys and Tutorials 3(4), 1–15 (2000)
12. Maarouf, I., Baroudi, U., Naseer, A.R.: Efficient Monitoring Approach for Reputation System-based Trust-aware Routing in Wireless Sensor Networks. IET Communications 3(5), 846–858 (2009)
13. Tian, L.-Q., Ni, Y., Lin, C.: Node Behavior Trust Evaluation Based on Behavior Evidence in WSNs. In: 2nd International Conference on Future Computer and Communication (ICFCC), pp. V1-312–V1-317 (2010)
14. Halim, I.T.A., Fahmy, H.M.A., El-Din, A.M.B., El-Shafey, M.H.: Agent-based Trusted On-Demand Routing Protocol for Mobile Ad-hoc Networks. In: 6th International Conference on Wireless Communications Networking and Mobile Computing (WiCOM), pp. 1–8 (2010)
15. Li, X., Jia, Z., Zhang, P., Zhang, R., Wang, H.: Trust-based On-demand Multipath Routing in Mobile Ad Hoc Network. IET Information Security 4(4), 212–232 (2010)
16. Weifang, C., Xiangke, L., Changxiang, S., Shanshan, L., Shaoliang, P.: A Trust-Based Routing Framework in Energy-Constrained Wireless Sensor Networks. In: Cheng, X., Li, W., Znati, T. (eds.) WASA 2006. LNCS, vol. 4138, pp. 478–489. Springer, Heidelberg (2006)
17. Pirzada, A., McDonald, C.: Establishing Trust in Pure Ad-Hoc Nnetworks. In: 27th Australasian Conference on Computer Science (ACSC 2004), pp. 54–63 (2004)
18. Yu, L., Qian, C., Liu, Z., Wang, K., Dai, B.: Ad-hoc Multi-dimensional Trust Evaluation Model Based on Classification of Service. In: 5th International ICST Conference on Communications and Networking in China (CHINACOM), pp. 1–5 (2010)
19. Karthik, N., Dhulipala, V.R.S.: Trust Calculation in Wireless Sensor Networks. In: 3rd International Conference on Electronics Computer Technology (ICECT), pp. 376–380 (2011)
20. Ganeriwal, S., Srivastava, M.B.: Reputation-Based Framework for High Integrity Sensor Networks. In: ACM Workshop Security of Ad Hoc and Sensor Networks (SASN 2004), pp. 66–67 (October 2004)
21. Zhou, Q., Li, L., Wang, S., Xu, S., Tan, W.: A Novel Approach to Manage Trust in Ad Hoc Networks. In: International Conference on Convergence Information Technology, pp. 295–300 (2007)
22. Arijit, U.: Secure Trust Management in Distributed Computing Systems. In: 6th IEEE International Symposium on Electronic Design, Test and Application (DELTA), pp. 116–121 (2011)
23. Sun, Y., Yu, W., Han, Z., Ray Liu, K.J.: Information Theoretic Framework of Trust Modeling and Evaluation for Ad Hoc Networks. IEEE JSAC Special Issue on Security in Wireless Ad Hoc Networks 24(2), 305–317 (2006)
24. Ishmanov, F., Kim, S.W.: A Secure Trust Establishment in Wireless Sensor Networks. In: International Conference on Electrical Engineering and Informatics (ICEEI), pp. 1–6 (2011)
25. Jing, Q., Tang, L.-Y., Chen, Z.: Trust Management in Wireless Sensor Networks. Journal of Software 19(7), 1716–1730 (2008)
26. Yao, Z.Y., Kim, D.Y., Lee, I., et al.: A Securiy Framework with Trust Managent for Sensor Networks. In: 1st IEEE/CREARE-NET Workshop on Security and Qos in Communication Networks, Athens, pp. 190–198 (2005)

27. Probst, M.J., Kasera, S.K.: Statistiical Trust Establishment in Wireless Sensor Networks. In: 13th International Conference on Parallel and Distributed Systems, pp. 1–8 (2007)
28. Ni, Y., Tian, L., Shen, X., Guo, S.: Behavior Trust Evaluation for Node in WSNs with Fuzzy-ANP Method. In: 2nd International Conference on Computer Engineering and Technology (ICCET), pp.V1-299–V1-303 (2010)
29. Chen, S.-L., Zhang, Y.-Q.: Robust Multi-dimensional Trust Model for Improving the Survivability of Ad Hoc Networks. Journal of Communications 31(5), 1–9 (2010)
30. Bin, M.: Cross-layer Trust Model and Algorithm of Node Selection in Wireless Sensor Networks. In: International Conference on Communication Software and Networks, Washington, DC, pp. 812–815 (2009)
31. Jiang, X., Lin, C., Yin, H., Chen, Z., Su, L.: Game-based Trust Establishment for Mobile Ad Hoc Networks. In: WRI International Conference on Communications and Mobile Computing (CMC 2009), pp. 475–479 (2009)
32. Dai, H., Jia, Z., Dong, X.: An Entropy-based Trust Modeling and Evaluation for Wireless Sensor Networks. In: International Conference on Embedded Software and Systems, pp. 27–34 (2008)
33. Theodorakopoulos, G., Baras, S.: On Trust Models and Trust Evaluation Metrics for Ad hoc Networks. IEEE Journal on Selected Areas in Communications 24(2), 318–328 (2006)
34. Fu, C., Hong, L., Peng, B., Han, L.-S., Xu, L.-F.: Incomplete Information Nodes Risk Assessment in Mobile Ad Hoc Networks. Chinese Journal of Computers 32(4), 805–816 (2009)
35. Marmol, F.G., Perez, G.M.: Providing Trust in Wireless Sensor Networks Using a Bio-inspired Technique. In: Networking and Electronic Commerce Research Conference (NAEC 2008), Lake Garda, pp. 25–28 (2008)
36. Samavati, H., Ladani, B.T., Moodi, H.: AMLeT: Adaptive Multi Level Trust framework for MANETs. In: International Symposium on Computer Networks and Distributed Systems (CNDS), pp. 152–157 (2011)
37. Huang, T., Li, X.: An Trust Management Scheme for Sensor Networks. Journal of Guilin University of Electronic Technology 30(5), 428–431 (2010)
38. Maarouf, I., Baroudi, U., Naseer, A.R.: Efficient Monitoring Approach for Reputation System-based Trust-aware Routing in Wireless Sensor Networks. IET Communications 3(5), 846–858 (2009)

Array-Forming Wireless Sensor Network Framework for Target Monitoring and System Scheduling

Ming Yin, Kai Yu, Yuanshi Li, Ji'an Luo, Shengsheng Cai, and Zhi Wang*

State Key Laboratory of Industrial Control Technology, Zhejiang University,
310027 Zhejiang, Hangzhou, China
{yinming1026,kaiyuzju,anjiluo,wangzhizju}@gmail.com

Abstract. Combining wireless sensor network and array signal processing technology, a novel array-forming wireless sensor network framework is presented. Sensor nodes, connected through wireless communication, are grouped to form virtual arrays. Then high-accuracy target positioning can be performed with the help of array signal processing algorithms. Considering real-time target monitoring applications, system performance is modeled in aspects of accuracy, delay and power consumption. To satisfy system performance requirements with inherent contradiction among them, system objective function is built and optimized scheduling is obtained with optimization algorithm. Simulation results verified our performance model and the feasibility of array-forming wireless sensor network framework, and also provide suboptimal solutions for scheduling.

Keywords: wireless sensor network, array signal processing, system scheduling.

1 Introduction

Target monitoring is an important application in environmental, military and other fields. Wireless Sensor Networks(WSN), for its large coverage and flexible deployment, has shown great potential in target monitoring applications. Especially, its stealthiness and low power consumption show great value, which draws much attention from researchers.

Restricted by size and cost, wireless sensor nodes have limited sensing ability. Therefore collaborative sensing within the network becomes a key issue in WSN target monitoring. Most existing studies built relationship between target signal energy and distance based on signal energy attenuation model [1]. But in real applications, difficulties and drawbacks arise: The High precision of attenuation model and signal energy measurement are hard to implement. Also the accuracy of energy-based method is related to nodes distribution density. High-density nodes deployment is inevitable to

---

* This work was supported in part by the National Natural Science Foundation of China(NSFC) under Grant No. 61273079, in part by the Strategic Priority Research Program of the Chinese Academy of Sciences under Grant No. XDA06020300, in part by State Key Laboratory of Industrial Control Technology under Grant No.ICT1206,No.ICT1207, and in part by Key Laboratory of Wireless Sensor Network & Communication of Chinese Academy of Sciences under Grant No.2011001.

R. Wang and F. Xiao (Eds.): CWSN 2012, CCIS 334, pp. 642–654, 2013.
© Springer-Verlag Berlin Heidelberg 2013

achieve high accuracy, which brings many problems to the network, like communication, deployment and cost. Another method, based on signal phase, is to exploit sensor arrays consisting of several closely related sensors. By analyzing the signal phase difference among array elements of the same array, we can find the targets direction. Further positioning and tracking can be performed in the multi-array system. Theoretical and experimental results have been presented in this method [2–4]. Despite its advantages in high-accuracy applications, sensor array has its own drawbacks. First, heavy computation load is required for array signal processing. If processing is done in sensor arrays, high-performance processor is needed, which obviously increase the energy consumption and cost; if raw signal data is sent to the fusion center to be processed, intolerable transmission load will emerge for wireless links, results in large transmission delay and energy consumption. Meanwhile, array sensors are fixed on rods or frames, which restricted the flexibility of measuring as well as bring inconvenience in deployment. In summary, the contradiction between requirements for high-performance and low cost, low energy consumption is the bottleneck for traditional wireless sensor network target monitoring applications.

Considering above issues, a novel array-forming wireless sensor network framework for target monitoring is presented combining traditional WSN and array signal processing technology. On the basis of wireless sensor network, we group a number to form virtual arrays. Then further array signal processing technologies can be adopted to find a rather accurate target direction, as shown in Fig.1.

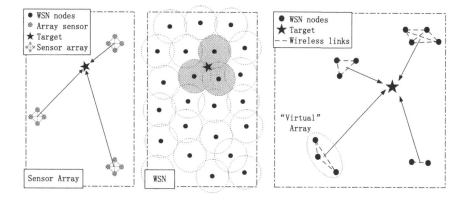

Fig. 1. Sensor array(left), WSN(middle) and array-forming WSN framework (right)

Early-stage exploration on array signal processing based on WSN have been made. In [2, 5], wireless array for target direction finding and positioning is implemented using iPAQ with built-in microphone. This is a prototype for adopting array technology in wireless sensor network. In their work, Wi-Fi is used for wireless for wireless communication, which is enough for transmit raw data and doesnt need consideration on power consumption. In [6], collaborative beamforming and its performance in WSN is studied. These works have shown the feasibility and potential of the combination of WSN and array signal processing. Still one problem remains. WSN aims at building low-cost, long-life platform. The array signal processing algorithms are too complicated for low-cost WSN nodes to perform, meanwhile raw signal are too much for wireless communication. Adding powerful processor or DSP would largely increase the cost of nodes. In our array-forming framework, no complex computation is needed on sensor nodes. Also we cut down transmission load by taking advantage of the novel compressive sampling method [7, 8]. Signal are reconstructed at the fusion center, then array signal processing is down on the reconstructed signal. The process is shown in Fig.2.

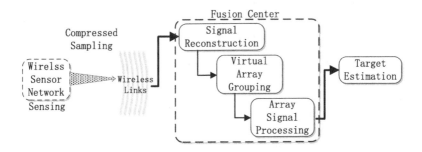

Fig. 2. System process of array-forming wireless sensor network framework

Comparing with traditional target monitoring framework, our new framework combines the advantages of WSN and array sensor. It has deployment flexibility, stealthiness as well as accuracy. As more parameters are involved, system gets flexibility in operation to meet various requirements, while more complex to control with inherent contradiction among different performances. System scheduling, as a key issue in WSN, is introduced to find better parameter set to optimize system performance. Many related researches focus on this issue, like information-driven dynamic sensor collaboration [10] , which considered the influence of nodes scheduling on tracking accuracy and system cost; or network design strategy problem [11], which presented mathematical programming and approximation algorithms, using position estimation as an example. As mentioned, the array-forming WSN framework tries to achieve realtime, high-accuracy target positioning or tracking on low-power, low-cost platform. Therefore, scheduling is crucial in optimizing system performance.

The remainder of this paper is arranged as follows: Section 2 provides motivation with simple simulations. Section 3 presents system performance model for array-forming framework. Section 4 discusses the scheduling issue. Simulation results on influence of each control parameters and scheduling strategies is given in section 5. Conclusion and future work is presented in section 6.

2   Motivation

The main idea of this framework is to move computation load from low-cost nodes to the fusion center, which is able to run more powerful array signal processing algorithm, while using compressed sampling to cut down transmission load, achieving higher accuracy than WSN, better realtime performance and longer system life. In this section, simple simulation is provided to verify the feasibility of this framework, and compare with traditional methods.

We use a 100*100 field in simulation. To show performance of energy based WSN framework, assume sensor nodes are uniformly distributed on this field to form a grid, 121 nodes in total. Each node is 10m away from its four neighbours, and will reports targets existence within its sensing radius. Assume targets randomly appear in this field, uniformly distributed in the square area [30,30,70,70], no noise introduced. Basic Centroid algorithm is used to localize them. Fig.3 give the result from 1000 times simulation for each radius

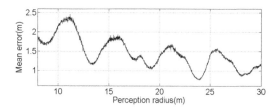

Fig. 3. Mean error against perception radius using centroid algorithm in WSN

In this scenario, WSN can achieve an mean error of about 0.75m with a rather large perception radius. Further improvement could be done by deploy more nodes, which increase cost and deployment difficulty. Also large perception radius would cause higher false alarm rate in noised environment.

Array signal processing methods usually has higher accuracy. Assume four traditional sensor arrays (MUSIC algorithm on raw signal data) are deployed at each corner of an 100*100 square field as shown in Fig.4(left). 100 positions uniformly distributed in the field are picked as samples, for each position, 500 times positioning is performed to get the average error.(Simulation details included in section 5) If the error is larger than three times average error, this data is removed and judged to be a failure. Then a fixed mean error is obtained from the rest. The result is shown in first row of Table 1. Its obvious that sensor array method has higher accuracy than energy-based WSN method, even in a noised environment.

Also, at different position, accuracy differs for array method. Approximation distribution for this scenario is shown in Fig.4(right), which shows that for specific zones, by carefully choosing the position and formation of virtual arrays, better performance could be achieved. But as mentioned, cost, computation load and raw data transmission delay are the bottlenecks for array signal processing on WSN.

Now, our framework, as shown in Fig.2, is used in the same settings as traditional sensor array method. Now MUSIC algorithm is performed on reconstructed signals. Results shown in Table.1. We can see that array-forming framework can achieve similar accuracy as sensor array.(Also similar error distribution) Fixed mean error showed even better performance, which may comes from the noise suppression ability of compressed

Table 1. Accuracy comparison of traditional sensor array and array-forming WSN

	Mean error	Failure rate	Fixed mean error
Traditional sensor array	0.506m	1.2%	0.439m
Array-forming WSN	0.771m	4.6%	0.312m

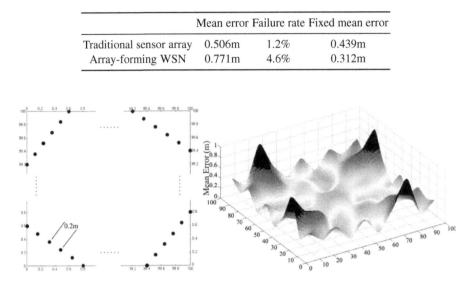

Fig. 4. Node deployment(left) and smoothed mean error distribution(right) in the field

sampling for sparse signal. In energy-based WSN, with 121-nodes grid sensor network, we need perception radius of about 23.7m to achieve 0.77m mean error in noiseless environment. But in array-forming framework, only 24 nodes are needed.

These simple results above showed that array-forming framework has great potential in target monitoring applications. It can achieve better accuracy with much less nodes than WSN, and close accuracy with array sensor but on much lower cost devices. Comparison given in Table.2.

Table 2. Comparison of WSN, sensor array and array-forming WSN

WSN	Sensor Array	Array-forming WSN
Low-cost nodes	High accuracy	High accuracy
Wide coverage	Highest cost	Easy deployment
Easy deployment	Fixed deployment	Fewer nodes needed
Low accuracy	Computation Load	Flexible operation
Too many nodes		

3   System Model and Problem Formulation

As mentioned before, scheduling is crucial in this framework. First we need build system performance model.

3.1   System Modeling

Considering m virtual arrays in the system, each with n_i nodes. Let x_i^j denote the raw data that node j in array i received, $i = 1, 2..., m$. To reduce the amount of data sampled and transmitted, randomly compressed sampling is introduced, and compressed signal y_i^j is sent to the fusion center:

$$y_i^j = F^C(x_i^j + w_i^j). \tag{1}$$

F^C refers to the randomly compressed sampling process, w_i^j refers to noise, which we assume that follows a zero-mean Gaussian distribution: $w_i^j \sim N(0, \sigma_i^j)$. And for different sensor, noises are independent. Randomly compressed sampling [8] is implemented by taking a few signal samples at random intervals, and reconstruct the signal at the receiving end. For signal with sparsity s and length l, which means only s nonzeros in some basis, according to compressive sensing theory, the number of samples needed r is:

$$r = 2s\log_{10}\left(\frac{l}{s}\right) \tag{2}$$

Reconstructed signal $\hat{x}_i^j$ are obtained after compressed signal y_i^j arrived the fusion center. F^R denotes collaborative reconstruction process. Since correlation exists among nodes in the same virtual array, model-based methods [9] can be introduced.

$$\{\hat{x}_i^1, \hat{x}_i^2, ..., \hat{x}_i^n\} = F^R\{y_i^1, y_i^2, ..., y_i^n\} \tag{3}$$

Target direction can be obtained using array signal processing algorithm, then target position can be obtained.

$$\hat{\theta}_i = F^A\{\hat{x}_i^1, \hat{x}_i^2, ..., \hat{x}_i^n\} \tag{4}$$

$$\hat{p}^T = F^P\{\hat{\theta}_1, p_1, \hat{\theta}_2, p_2, ..., \hat{\theta}_m, p_m\} \tag{5}$$

Here F^A refers to array signal processing, which works on reconstructed signals $\{\hat{x}_i^1, \hat{x}_i^2, ..., \hat{x}_i^n\}$. F^P refers to positioning process. p^T is the estimated target position, and $p_1, p_2, ..., p_m$ refers to the position of virtual arrays. In this paper, MUSIC algorithm [12] is adopted in this paper, in which the covariance matrix R of signal from an array is divided into two subspaces: signal subspace and noise subspace:

$$R = U_S \Sigma_S U_S^H + U_N \Sigma_N U_N^H \tag{6}$$

Noise subspace should be Orthogonal to signal vector, the relationship between spatial spectrum and array manifold is:

$$P_{MUSIC}(\theta) = \frac{1}{a^H(\theta)U_N U_N^H a(\theta)} \tag{7}$$

By changing the value of θ step by step, finding the peak of the spatial spectrum, the target direction can be determined. Its obvious that the step size μ, is directly related to angular accuracy. Also, as the number of nodes in an array n_i increase, the array has better performance in noise suppression and signal enhancement.

3.2   System Performance and Scheduling Problem Formulation

To evaluate the system performance, many aspects should be considered. Among them, positioning accuracy, real-time performance and system life are the most important ones. Their corresponding indicators are positioning error δ, time delay τ and power consumption ω. There are complex correlations among all factors, to simplify this scheduling problem, we assume fixed position and all uniform linear arrays to exclude influence from nodes deployment and array formation. In wireless sensor network, wireless communication consumes most of energy. Here we assume wireless communications power consumption has a linear relationship with data transmission amount. With analysis and assumptions above, we reduce control variables to the following three:

r : number of samples in a snapshot. Fewer the samples, better the real-time performance and power consumption, worse the positioning accuracy would fall;
n : number of nodes in a virtual array. With more nodes in an array, accuracy will increase at the expense of real-time performance;
μ : step size in MUSIC algorithm direction finding, in other words, angular resolution. Smaller the step size, better accuracy but worse the real-time performance.

To solve this scheduling system, an objective function should be built at first. Positioning error can be represented as $\delta\left(\phi(r, n, \mu)\right)$, in which $\varphi(r, n, \mu)$ represent the angular error function. Considering the positioning error and angular error has a near-linear relationship when angular error is small, the positioning error can be approximated as:

$$\delta(r, n, \mu) = \sum_{i=1}^{m} \left[\frac{\partial F^P}{\partial \theta_i} \phi_i(r, n, \mu) \right] \tag{8}$$

Delay in the system mainly consists of two parts: transmission delay and computation delay. Transmission delay is proportional to total nodes number and sample numbers. Computational delay mainly comes from direction finding in MUSIC algorithm, proportional to nodes number while inversely proportional to step size. Signal reconstruction is a rather fast procedure and costs nearly fixed time, so we include it in T_{other} with other unmentioned delay in the process. Total delay as follows, in which T_{trans} and T_{comp} represent the transmission delay of data in a node and the time cost on each single direction in MUSIC respectively. N_{angle} Represent the range of possible directions.:

$$\tau(r, n, \mu) = nm \left(T_{trans} r + T_{comp} \frac{N_{angle}}{\mu} \right) + T_{other} \tag{9}$$

Since most power is consumed by wireless transmission, whose power consumption has a linear relationship with the amount of data transmission. We can denote it as follows:

$$\omega(r, n) = \omega_{trans} nmr + \omega_{other} \tag{10}$$

Here ω_{trans} refers to power consumption to transmit a single measured sample on the node.

4 System Scheduling

Since there are three control variables and some performance indicators, the scheduling problem in array-forming wireless sensor network framework can be described as a multi-objective optimization problem. Due to the contradiction among different performance requirements, there is no perfect scheduling strategy to make all performance optimum. Therefore to give a certain scheduling strategy, try turning the multi-objective problem into a single-objective problem according to applications requirements is a possible solution. Two scenarios are considered here:

Scenario 1. We want a balanced and near-optimum performance. In this scenario, the performance indicators are weighted to show its importance. The final objective function is the weighted sum of positioning error, time delay and power consumption. The problem can be described as follows, $[W_\delta, W_\tau, W_\omega]$ is the weight, $[C_\delta, C_\tau, C_\omega]$ is the normalization constant.

$$min \quad f(r, n, \mu) = \frac{W_\delta}{C_\delta}\delta(r, n, \mu) + \frac{W_\tau}{C_\tau}\tau(r, n, \mu) + \frac{W_\omega}{C_\omega}\omega(r, n) \tag{11}$$

$$s.t. \quad r > 0, n > 0, \mu > 0 \tag{12}$$

Here in the above equations, δ, τ and ω is defined in equation (8-10).

Scenario 2. One of the performance indicators has overwhelming importance. The other two are only required to be limited in a given range. Then the chosen performance indicator is set to be the objective function while other two as the constraints. For example, an application has strict requirements for system life while rather loose requirements on accuracy and real-time performance. This scheduling problem can be described similar to (11-12), but objective function is replaced by the following one:

$$min \quad f(r, n, \mu) = \omega(r, n) \tag{13}$$

Then add new constraints:

$$\delta(r, n, \mu) < \delta_{MAX} \quad \tau(r, n, \mu) < \tau_{MAX} \tag{14}$$

For scenario 1, we can turn to method like negative gradient method to search in the feasible solution space. Considering two of the three control parameters are discrete variables(r, n), and its hard to find an analytical expression for $\delta(r, n, \mu)$, we try to obtain a numerical solution by simulation, in which we limit that all three control parameters are discrete. Take objective functions difference against control variable as an indicator, take r as an example:

$$\frac{\Delta f}{\Delta r} = a_1\frac{\Delta\delta}{\Delta r} + a_2\frac{\Delta\tau}{\Delta r} + a_3\frac{\Delta\omega}{\Delta r}$$

$$\Delta f = a_1\left[\delta(r + \Delta r, n, \mu) - \delta(r, n, \mu)\right] + a_2 T_{trans}nm + a_3\omega_{trans}nm \tag{15}$$

Similar expression can be written for n and μ. Since discretization has been introduced, this solution is suboptimal.

For scenario 2, we can introduce penalty into objective function to turn this problem into an unconstrained on. For example, if we want as long system life as possible, consider less about error and time delay, we can add such a penalty:

$$P_{en}(r,n,\mu) = \begin{cases} 0 & \delta(r,n,\mu) < \delta_{\max}, \tau(r,n,\mu) < \tau_{\max} \\ +\infty & other \end{cases} \quad (16)$$

5   Simulation Study

In this section, we use simulation results to: a) verify the feasibility of target positioning in this framework; b) verify our model, find the influence of control variables; c) provide data for system scheduling and give some example strategies.

5.1   Simulation Settings

We use MATLAB on a personal computer with 3.3GHz CPU. In simulation, 340m/s acoustic signal with three sine waves 608Hz,704Hz and 800Hz is used as the target signal. 6 sensor nodes are deployed linearly with constant spacing of 0.2m. When target appears, the signal transmission delay and attenuation to each sensor node is calculated. Delay is used to calculation the phase shift of signals on each nodes. Nodes in the same array receive similar environmental noise of -40db, and each node receives an independent -30db measurement noise, both are white Gaussian noise. Each node get 19 samples in a snapshot, which would be reconstructed using OMP algorithm to an 128 samples length signal at the fusion center. Then 20 snapshots of signal from the same virtual array are processed by MUSIC algorithm to get the direction estimation. Since linear array is used, possible target direction range from 0° to 180°. Step size of direction finding in MUSIC is 0.2°. When considering traditional uniform sampling, we assume a 4096Hz sample rate. In following simulation, this setting is used unless specific declaration is made.

5.2   Influence of Control Variables

In this paper we mainly consider the three control variables. To verify their influence on system performance, we fixed two of then while changing the third in the simulation, using repeated result to obtain mean error and time delay. Power consumption is not included for its rather fixed and clear relationship with these three control variables. Following results in this subsection is obtained under the four arrays field settings in previous subsection.

Number of Samples. To verify the influence of sample numbers, we use a more complex signal, which contains 20 sine waves from 192Hz-800Hz in positioning simulation above. Result is shown in Fig.5 and 6. In Fig.6, DOA mean angular error of two virtual arrays is presented as an example. We can see that as more samples are taken, processing time increases, but in return DOA angular error decrease, leading to smaller positioning error. Also we find that the positioning errors are larger than previous result in Table.1. This indicates clearer and simpler signal composition would lead to better performance.

Also in fig 6, we can see strong relationship exists between DOA error and positioning error. As we are more concerned about target positioning, positioning error is shown in following simulation results.

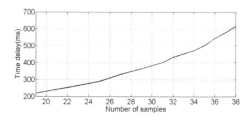

Fig. 5. Time delay against sample numbers

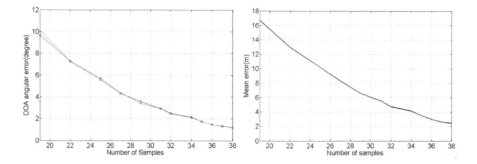

Fig. 6. Mean DOA error of two arrays(left) and positioning error(right) against sample numbers

Step Size in Direction Finding. In simulation ,we used 17 values range from 0.05° to 12°. Results are shown in Fig.7. Results show: a) Positioning accuracy would fall as step size increase. Step size is the dominant factor when its large, but not as important when its small. b) As our model depicted, time delay is inversely proportional to step size. Especially with small step size, step size has overwhelmingly influence on time delay.

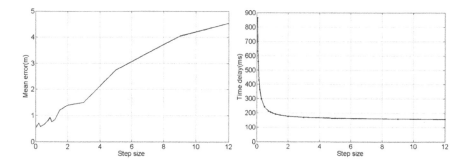

Fig. 7. Mean error (left) and Time delay (right) against step size

Nodes Number in An Array. To exclude the influence of array position, here we use two even-number-nodes array to verify the influence of nodes number. This two arrays lies on x-axis and y-axis respectively. While changing the number in an array, the center

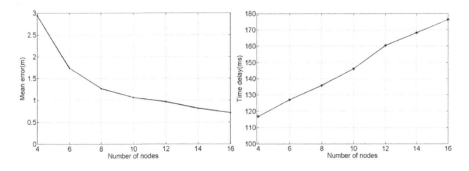

Fig. 8. Mean error (left) and Time delay (right) against number of nodes

of the array is fixed at (15.5,0) and (0,15.5). Nodes have 0.2m spacing and step size is set to be . Result is shown in Fig.8:

As nodes number increase, error decrease and time delay increase, which verified our model. Since only two arrays are included, we can see that time delay is obviously small than previous four array situation. This implies that array number also has its influence, which is beyond the reach of this paper.

Simulation results above is consistent with our system performance model. Since this framework aims at realtime target monitoring, an example is given here: Considering that our sampling time in a single positioning period is 2560 samples long,(128 samples * 20 snapshots) which lasts 625ms at sampling rate 4096Hz. 4 arrays in the System, each has 6 nodes. Each sample is stored using 8-bit data. In each snapshot, we take 19 samples, so 19*20*8*4*6=72960 bit data need to be transmitted. Take Zigbee protocol as example, it cost 292ms at 250Kbps rate. (1967ms if we transmit raw data) From fig 7 we can see that with step size larger than 0.3, time delay would be shorter than 300ms. So the positioning period can cut down to about 1 second, as shown in Fig.9.

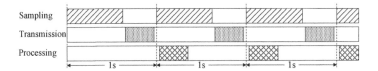

Fig. 9. Timing diagram for a 1 second positioning period

If less snapshots, less arrays are used, or transmit data while sampling for next period, short period can be achieved. This result verified the feasibility of using our new framework in realtime target monitoring applications.

5.3   System Scheduling Strategy

Simulation results in section 5.2 showed that contradiction exists among performances. Here we try to solve this scheduling problem according to different scenarios, giving

Table 3. Available values for control variables

	Available Values
r	{19,22,24,26,28,30,32}
n	{6,8,10}
μ	{0.1,0.3,0.45,0.6,1,2,3,5}

simple strategies to satisfy different application requirements. To simplify this problem, control variable values are limited in given sets according to simulation results in section 5.2.

Scheduling can be dong by solving optimization problem in section 3. For different scenarios or different weights, the solutions are strategies we got, or they can be considered as different system operating mode. Here three solutions are given. First one belongs to scenario 1 in section 3. Latter two belong to scenario 2.

1) Set $[W_{delta}, W_\tau, W_\omega] = \left[\frac{2}{6}, \frac{3}{6}, \frac{1}{6}\right]$, realtime and accuracy performance is emphasized. Scheduling result is $[n, \mu, r] = [6, 3, 32]$, which uses large step size, but more samples to balance.

2) In quick discovery mode, realtime is the first. Scheduling result is $[n, \mu, r] = [6, 5, 22]$, which uses a large step size, and less samples.

3) Low power mode. System life is the first thing. Scheduling result is $[n, \mu, r] = [6, 3, 19]$, which uses least samples. To guarantee accuracy, it uses smaller step size, because MUSIC is operating in the fusion center, doesnt influence nodes power consumption.

6   Conclusion and Future Work

In this paper, combining wireless sensor networks and array signal processing, a novel array-forming wireless sensor network framework is presented. Taking advantage of randomly compressed sampling, it provide new way to achieve high-accuracy target monitoring network. Then the system scheduling issue is considered. Performance model is built in three aspects: accuracy, realtime and power consumption. System scheduling issue is modeled as a multi-objective optimization problem. Simulation results verified the model we built.

As a new framework, many problems are still to be discussed. 1) In this paper, uniform linear array is considered. Influence of array formation and deployment is important and need more attention. 2) To build a real system, more controllable and adjustable factors would bring more potential in performance. Issues like operating mode switching, mobile nodes may be considered. 3) In this paper, transmission is based on Zigbee protocol. To make fully use of array-forming framework, information-driven network technologies need to be studied to achieve high-level interaction within virtual arrays. And network affairs should be included in future works. 4) Currently we discussed the positioning performance. The requirements from realtime tracking and corresponding scheduling problem need to be analyzed.

References

1. Sheng, X., Hu, Y.-H.: Maximum likelihood multiple-source localization using acoustic energy measurements with wireless sensor networks. IEEE Transactions on Signal Processing 53(1), 44–53 (2005)
2. Chen, J.C., Yip, L., Elson, J.: Coherent Acoustic Array Processing and Localization on Wireless Sensor Networks. Proceedings of the IEEE 91(8) (2003)
3. Li, Y., Wang, Z., Bao, M., et al.: Design and experiment for real time multi-target tracking platform based on wireless acoustic array sensor networks. Chinese Journal of Scientific Instrument 33(1), 146–154 (2012)
4. Wang, Z., Luo, J.-A., Zhang, X.-P.: A Novel Location-Penalized Maximum Likelihood Estimator for Bearing-Only Target Localization. IEEE Transactions on Signal Processing (accepted and to appear)
5. Chen, J.C., Yao, K., et al.: Source localization and tracking of a wideband source using a randomly distributed beamforming sensor array. International Journal of High Performance Computing Applications 16(3), 259–272 (2002)
6. Ochiai, H., Mitran, P., et al.: Collaborative beamforming for distributed wireless ad hoc sensor networks. IEEE Transactions on Signal Processing 53(11), 4110–4124 (2005)
7. Candes, E.J., Wakin, M.B.: An Introduction to Compressive Sampling. IEEE Signal Processing Magazine 25(2), 21–30 (2008)
8. Yu, K., Li, Y., Wang, Z., et al.: New method for acoustic signal collection based on compressed sampling. Chinese Journal of Scientific Instrument 33(1), 105–112 (2012)
9. Baraniuk, R.G., Cevher, V., Duarte, M.F., Hegde, C.: Model-Based Compressive Sensing. IEEE Transactions on Information Theory 56(4), 1982–2001 (2010)
10. Zhao, F., Shin, J., Reich, J.: Information-Driven Dynamic Sensor Collaboration for Tracking Applications. IEEE Signal Processing Magazine (2002)
11. Cevher, V., Kaplan, L.M.: Acoustic sensor network design for position estimation. ACM Trans. Sen. Netw. 5(3), 1–28 (2009)
12. Schmidt, R.: Multiple emitter location and signal parameter estimation. IEEE Transactions on Antennas and Propagation 34(3), 276–280 (1986)

A Reliable Congestion Avoidance Protocol for Wireless Sensor Networks

Xiaoyan Yin*, Dingyi Fang, and Xiaojiang Chen

School of Information Science & Technology
Northwest University
Xi'an, 710127, China
{yinxy,dyf,xjchen}@nwu.edu.cn

Abstract. Due to the contradiction between overwhelming traffic and limited bandwidth, congestion is one of the most challenges in wireless sensor networks (WSNs). In this paper, based on network coding and cross-layer optimization, we propose a reliable transmission control scheme to avoid congestion. Our scheme uses network coding to improve the reliability and robustness of system, and applies cross-layer design for suitable rate assignment. Our simulation results and analysis show that our scheme can achieve good performance in terms of reliability and throughput.

Keywords: Wireless Sensor Networks, Congestion Avoidance, Network Coding, Cross-layer Optimization.

1   Introduction

Wireless sensor networks (WSNs) have lots of applications, such as wild animal monitoring, object tracking and intelligent transportation system, etc. In the near future, WSNs are expected to provide support for high data rate applications to transmit multimedia data (i.e., video and audio).

In WSNs, Due to the contradiction between overwhelming traffic and limited bandwidth, congestion is one of the most challenges in wireless sensor networks (WSNs). Congestion occurs at sensors that receive more data than they can forward, and thus results in energy waste, throughput reduction and packet loss. Generally, WSNs work under idle or light network load, and then suddenly turn into active when an event is detected. To report the information about the event, the sensed data, which is very important for integrality of the event, should be transmitted to the sink with reliability. However, the bursty traffic

* This work was supported in part by NSFC (Grant No.61202393, 61272461, 61070176 and 61170218), Educational Commission of Shaanxi Province, China (Grant No.12JK0936, 12JK0937, 2010JK854, 2010JC25 and 2010JC24), SRFDP (Grant No.20106101110018), Natural Science Foundation of Shaanxi Province (Grant No. 2012JQ8038) and the Key Project of Chinese Ministry of Education (Grant No.211181).

R. Wang and F. Xiao (Eds.): CWSN 2012, CCIS 334, pp. 655–664, 2013.
© Springer-Verlag Berlin Heidelberg 2013

exceeds the available bandwidth with high probability, particularly in high-rate applications. Therefore, congestion control is a critical issue in WSNs.

At the same time, reliability is another serious issue because of the lossy nature of WSNs. In WSNs, congestion is not the only reason for packets dropping. Failed sensor nodes or interference also should take responsibility for packets loss. In order to provide better support for all kinds of applications, we should take reliability into account when we design our transmission control protocol in this paper.

In this paper, we propose a new congestion avoidance scheme that can enhance reliability and improve throughput. Our scheme uses network coding to improve the reliability and robustness of system, and applies cross-layer optimization design for suitable rate assignment so as to avoid congestion.

The rest of the paper is organized as follows: in Section 2, we overview the related work; the system model and target problems are described in Section 3; in Section 4, we introduce our congestion avoidance protocol; performance evaluation is carried out in Section 5; finally, we conclude this paper in Section 6.

2   Related Work

In the literature, many researchers have paid more attention to congestion control, congestion mitigation and congestion avoidance in WSNs. ESRT [1] is a centralized congestion control scheme. The sink computes and then allocates transmission rates which can prevent the network from congestion to sensors. The rate in ESRT is the minimum among all the paths and can not adapt to the dynamic network status. Therefore, underutilization is induced by ESRT. Fusion [2] is a distributed congestion control scheme. It measures the congestion level using the queue length and applies three techniques: hop-by-hop flow control, rate control and prioritized MAC. Thus, Fusion can achieve higher throughput and better fairness with heavy network traffic than other congestion control schemes. CODA [3] is a congestion mitigation strategy and uses slightly different strategy from Fusion. It does not take fairness into consideration. The work of Chen et al. [4] is a congestion avoidance strategy using lightweight buffer management. Our previous work [5] categorizes all intermediate sensor nodes into near-source nodes and near-sink nodes, adjusts the sending rate of each flow as early as possible and successfully avoids the congestion. Rangwala et al. [6] proposes a distributed rate allocation scheme, which applies a tree rooted at each sink to transmit all data to achieve fair and efficient rate assignment.

We focus on congestion avoidance based on network coding and cross-layer optimization in this paper. Cross-layer design is getting popular in recent years. Xiao et al. [7] propose a distributed algorithm based on dual decomposition by formulating the problem of simultaneous routing and resource allocation in wireless networks. In [8], a cross-layer optimization scheme of joint rate control and power control for lifetime maximization is proposed in WSNs. Chiang [9] proposes a distributed power control algorithm, which optimizes the end-to-end throughput in a wireless CDMA network with a TCP rate update mechanism. Ahlswede et al. [10] uses network coding to improve system throughput and save bandwidth. AdapCode [11] is a reliable data dissemination protocol and utilizes network coding for code updating in WSNs. The aforementioned schemes based on network coding involved all the intermediate sensor nodes on the path, and thus have higher complexity. In our scheme, network coding is used only at the source sensor nodes and the sink.

3   System Model and Target Problems

3.1   System Model

The sensor network is made up of numerous sensor nodes and a base station, i.e., a sink, which is connected to the control center using an external network. We assume that (1) the transceiver of sensor nodes can run at adjustable rates depending on the different network status; (2) the source and the sink has the capability of encoding and decoding, respectively.

All the sensors share the same wireless medium. The sensor sends packets in a local broadcast manner in the neighborhood. Two sensors are neighbors if they are in the transmission range of each other and can directly communicate with each other. Packets are sent toward the sink from source nodes which can sense the event and produce data packets. All data packets in our system have the same size and the network is not dynamic after deployment. We use IEEE 802.11 as the MAC protocol in this paper because it can ensure that only the intended receiver keeps the packet and other neighbors abandon the packet in the local broadcast range.

We assume that our system consists of N sensor nodes, where each node is labeled by an integer in the range of $[1, N]$. Sensor nodes which can detect the event generate data packets and transmit them towards the sink. The traffic originated by source node i is denoted by the ith flow, r_i is the transmission rate of flow i.

We use the multi-commodity flow to model the WSNs, which represented by a directed graph $G(V, E)$, where V is the set of sensor nodes, and E is the set of logical links. Each sensor node is associated with a utility function $U_n(r_n)$, which reflects the "utility" to the sensor node n when it generates data at rate r_n. We define $N(l)$ as the subset of sensor nodes that are traversing link l. Let $L_{OUT}(n)$ denote the set of outgoing links from node n, $L_{IN}(n)$ the set of incoming links to node n. Thus, in Fig.1, $L_{IN}(a) = \{l_{ba}, l_{ca}, l_{da}\}$, $L_{OUT}(a) = \{l_{ae}, l_{af}\}$.

3.2   Target Problems

Congestion occurs when the total traffic exceeds the available bandwidth. In WSNs, Congestion has an awful influence on network utilization, energy efficiency, packet loss, throughput and reliability. Packets will be dropped because of congestion. When the network load goes beyond the critical point of congestion, fewer packets can be received by the sink with the same amount of resources.

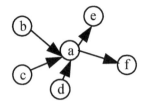

Fig. 1. Traffic analysis for node a

Moreover, packets dropped waste the specious energy of WSNs. Therefore, that is meaningful to assign a suitable rate for every source node so as to avoid congestion. How to calculate and adjust the sending rate for each source node is our first concern.

At the same time, reliability is also one of the most critical issues in WSNs. Due to the energy-exhausted node and/or lossy link and/or interference, packets are dropped unpredictably. Network coding is an effective and helpful way to provide reliable communication in lossy wireless networks, as it naturally offers error recovery and reliable transmission because it comes from erasure coding. Furthermore, throughput will be improved by taking advantage of network coding. Therefore, how to design the strategy of encoding and decoding to achieve the reliable transmission and better throughput is our second concern.

4   Description of Congestion Avoidance Protocol

To avoid congestion that will otherwise cause a waste of resources, and provide reliable transmission at the same time, we take network coding and cross-layer optimization into consideration. Note our objective is not to design the optimal protocol, but a simple and effective one which is suitable to sensor networks. We design corresponding processes for source nodes and the sink, respectively.

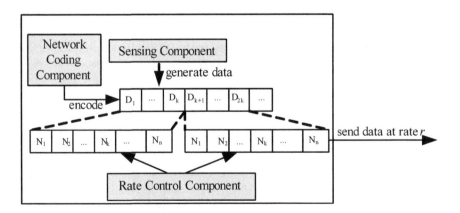

Fig. 2. Process at the source node

At the Side of Source Nodes: firstly, it detects the event and generates data packets; secondly, k packets from the source node will be grouped into an unit and then n new packets are produced; finally, the source node sends packets at rate r calculated by the cross-layer optimization scheme. The detailed process is shown in Fig.2.

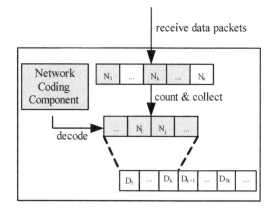

Fig. 3. Process at the sink

At the Side of the Sink: firstly, it receives packets from its upstream sensors; secondly, the sink counts the amount of packets received, denoted by A, and then put these packets into its buffer if A is not less than k (if A is less than k, special process will be needed, the detailed process will be described in 4.1); finally, k packets are selected from A packets and are decoded, and then original k packets are recovered. The detailed process is shown in Fig.3.

4.1   Network Coding Strategy

Network coding can improve greatly the reliability of lossy WSNs. Its implementation includes encoding at the source nodes and decoding at the sink. Note that the linear independency of k encoded packets received at the sink is requisite for decoding successfully.

At the Side of Source Nodes: firstly, k original packets are grouped into an unit; secondly, a $k*1$ Vandermonde matrix $c = [\alpha_1, \alpha_2, ..., \alpha_k]^T$ are selected as our encoding vector; finally, k original packets and the Vandermonde matrix are combined linearly and then a new vector $y = \alpha_1 x_1 + \alpha_2 x_2 + ... + \alpha_k x_k$ is generated. Note that n new packets, where n is not less than k and rests on the quality of link, are indispensable in order to recover those k original packets successfully at the sink.

At the Side of the Sink: firstly, every k packets from the same unit are grouped (the sink sends NACKs for the specific packets and the source retransmits them if the amount of packets received by the sink from the same unit is less than

k, or the sink ignores the unwanted packets if the amount of packets received for the same unit is larger than k); secondly, a new matrix $\mathbf{H}$ is constructed by taking encoding vectors of k encoded packets as column vectors; finally, k original packets are recovered.

The detailed decoding solution is following:

We assume that the corresponding encoding vectors of k encoded packets received by the sink are $[\alpha_{11}...\alpha_{1k}]^T, ..., [\alpha_{k1}...\alpha_{kk}]^T$, we have

$$
\begin{bmatrix} y_1 & y_2 & ...... & y_k \end{bmatrix} = \begin{bmatrix} x_1 & x_2 & ...... & x_k \end{bmatrix} \begin{bmatrix} \alpha_{11} & \alpha_{21} & ...... & \alpha_{k1} \\ \alpha_{12} & \alpha_{22} & ...... & \alpha_{k2} \\ .... \\ \alpha_{1k} & \alpha_{2k} & ...... & \alpha_{kk} \end{bmatrix} = X \bullet H
$$

(1)

We can rewrite Eq. (1) as

$$
\begin{bmatrix} y_1 \\ y_2 \\ ...... \\ y_k \end{bmatrix} = \begin{pmatrix} \alpha_{11} & \alpha_{21} & ...... & \alpha_{k1} \\ \alpha_{12} & \alpha_{22} & ...... & \alpha_{k2} \\ .... \\ \alpha_{1k} & \alpha_{2k} & ...... & \alpha_{kk} \end{pmatrix} \begin{bmatrix} x_1 \\ x_2 \\ ...... \\ x_k \end{bmatrix} \Rightarrow
$$

$$
\begin{bmatrix} x_1 \\ x_2 \\ ...... \\ x_k \end{bmatrix} = \begin{pmatrix} \alpha_{11} & \alpha_{21} & ...... & \alpha_{k1} \\ \alpha_{12} & \alpha_{22} & ...... & \alpha_{k2} \\ .... \\ \alpha_{1k} & \alpha_{2k} & ...... & \alpha_{kk} \end{pmatrix}^{-1} \begin{bmatrix} y_1 \\ y_2 \\ ...... \\ y_k \end{bmatrix}
$$

4.2   Cross-Layer Optimization Strategy

To avoid congestion, suitable rates should be assigned to flows. Our main idea is that rates in total do not exceed the available capacity. In WSNs, the attainable data rates on wireless links is decided by its capacity, and the capacity of link lies on the power control strategy. We can adjust powers used for transmission to obtain different SIR (Signal to Interference Ratios) on the link and then change the attainable capacity on each link. Since the feasible rate region depends on the power, the end-to-end rate optimization problem must be considered in a cross-layer framework, i.e., the rate control strategy must be implemented at both the transport layer and physical layer.

In this paper, the network utility maximization (NUM) framework is conformed and the specific practical concerns are considered. A cross-layer based optimization strategy is proposed by taking advantage of the convex optimization theory.

A. Formulation

We assume that each link has a unity bandwidth and a Shannon capacity c_l, which is approximated as $\log_2(\gamma_l)$, i.e., $c_l = \log_2(\gamma_l)$, $\forall l$, as assumed in [9], where γ_l is the SINR value of link l. we have

$$c_l = \log_2\left(\frac{P_{tx}^l G_{l,l}}{\sum_{k \neq l} P_{tx}^k G_{k,l} + N_l}\right) \tag{2}$$

where P_{tx}^i is the power of link i used for transmission and $G_{m,n}$ is the channel gain between link m and link n. The white Gaussian noise for link l is denoted by N_l. Therefore, the achievable rate on a wireless link is a global function of all the interfering links. In order to avoid congestion at link l, we have the following constraints as

$$\sum_{n:n \in N(l)} r_n \leq c_l \quad \forall l \tag{3}$$

We denote the energy consumption by each sensor node for reliable transmission over link l, for sensing, and for receiving as P_{tx}^l, P_s, P_{rx}, respectively. The total average power consumed by node n is given by

$$P_n^{avg} = \sum_{i:(i,n) \in L_{IN}(n)} r_{in} P_{rx} + \sum_{j:(n,j) \in L_{OUT}(n)} r_{nj} P_{tx}^l + r_n P_s \tag{4}$$

Keeping that in mind, both maximization of the network utility and minimization of the power consumption are our design targets. Therefore, the objective function subjects to Eq. (2), Eq. (3) and Eq. (4), and can be formulated as following:

$$Q1 : \max\left\{\sum_n U_n(x_n) - P_n^{avg}\right\} \tag{5}$$

We acquire the solution using dual decomposition. The detailed process please refers to our previous work [8].

B. Cross-Layer Optimization Strategy

For each sensor node n:

Updates the data rate as

$$r_n(t+1) = \left[\frac{1}{\sum_{l:l \in L(n)} \lambda_l(t)}\right]^+$$

For each link l:

Updates the power as

$$P_{tx}^l(t+1) = [P_{tx}^l(t) + \beta(t)\{\frac{\lambda_l(t)}{\ln 2 P_{tx}^l(t)}$$

$$-(\sum_{i:(i,n) \in L_{IN}(n)} r_{in} + \sum_{j:(n,j) \in L_{OUT}(n)} r_{nj}) - \sum_{j:j \neq l} m_j G_{l,j}\}]^+$$

Updates the message as

$$m_l(t+1) = \frac{\lambda_l(t)\gamma_l(t)}{\ln 2 P_{tx}^l(t)G_{l,l}}$$

and broadcasts it.

Adjusts the link congestion price, λ_l, as

$$\lambda_l(t+1) = [\lambda_l(t) - \beta(t)\{c_l^*(t) - \sum_{n:n\in N(l)} r_n^*(t)\}]^+$$

From the above distributed implementation, our cross-layer optimization scheme hits the original design intention.

5   Performance Evaluation

We evaluate the proposed congestion avoidance scheme in this section. We conduct the simulation using network simulator ns2 version 2.29.

We implement the routing protocols AODV and DD for comparison purposes in our simulations. In what follows, we compare AODV without/with network coding and DD without/with network coding in terms of reliability and throughput. For each data point in the figures, we operate the simulation on 10 randomly created networks and then take the average.

5.1   Reliability Comparison

The first simulation reveals that network coding can improve the reliability of system. As shown in Fig.4, both AODV and DD achieve better reliability by encoding at the source nodes and decoding by the sink. Intuitively, network coding has a tolerance for packet loss. In our scheme, k original packets can be recovered successfully as long as k encoded packets, which belong to the same unit, are received at the sink. Therefore, the system reliability will not be impaired if the amount of dropped packets do not exceeds $(n-k)$. If the probability of packet loss is less than $(n-k)/n$, the system reliability is 1 and the sink can obtain all the original packets.

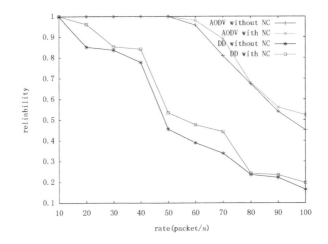

Fig. 4. Reliability with respect to sending rate

5.2   Throughput Comparison

The second simulation verifies that our congestion avoidance scheme obtains higher throughput, as shown in Fig.5. This is because that our scheme can assign the suitable rates to the source nodes so as to the network traffic does not exceed the available bandwidth.

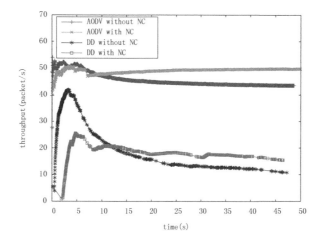

Fig. 5. Throughput over time

6   Conclusion

In this paper, we have proposed a protocol for congestion avoidance in WSNs. This paper has provided a new mechanism to avoid congestion and improve reliability based on network coding and cross-layer optimization in lossy WSNs. We have shown by simulations that our scheme has good performance in terms of reliability and throughput.

References

1. Sankarasubramaniam, Y., Akan, O., Akyildiz, I.F.: ESRT: Event-to-sink reliable transport in wireless sensor networks. In: 4th ACM Int. Symp. Mobile Ad Hoc Netw. Comput., MobiHoc, Annapolis, MD, pp. 177–188 (2003)
2. Hull B., Jamieson K., Balakrishnan H.: Mitigating congestion in wireless sensor networks. In: 2nd ACM Conf. Embedded Netw. Sensys, Baltimore, MD, pp. 134–147 (2004)
3. Wan, C., Eisenman, S., Campbell, A.: CODA: Congestion detection and avoidance in sensor networks. In: 1st ACM Conf. Embedded Netw. Sensys, Los Angeles, CA, pp. 266–279 (2003)
4. Chen, S., Yang, N.: Congestion avoidance based on lightweight buffer management in sensor networks. IEEE Trans. Parallel Distrib. Syst. 17(9), 934–946 (2006)

5. Yin, X., Zhou, X., Huang, R., Fang, Y., Li, S.: A fairness-aware congestion control scheme in wireless sensor networks. IEEE Transactions on Vechicular Technology 58(9), 5225–5234 (2009)
6. Rangwala, S., Gummadi, R., Govindan, R., Psounis, K.: Interference-aware fair rate control in wireless sensor networks. In: SIGCOMM 2006, Pisa, Italy, pp. 63–74 (2006)
7. Xiao, L., Johansson, M., Boyd, S.: Simultaneous routing and resource allocation via dual decomposition. IEEE Transaction on Communications 52(7), 1136–1144 (2004)
8. Yin, X., Zhou, X., Li, Z., Li, S.: Joint rate control and power control for lifetime maximization in wireless sensor networks. Journal of Internet Technology 12(1), 69–78 (2011)
9. Mung, C.: To layer or not to layer: balancing transport and physical layers in wireless multihop networks. In: IEEE INFOCOM 2004, Hong Kong, pp. 2525–2536 (2004)
10. Ahlswede, R., Cai, N., Li, S.R., Yeung, R.W.: Network information flow. IEEE Transaction on Information Theory 46(4), 1204–1216 (2000)
11. Hou, I., Tsai, Y., Abdelzaher, T.F., et al.: AdapCode: Adaptive network coding for code updates in wireless sensor networks. In: INFOCOM 2008, Phoenix, AZ, USA, pp. 1517–1525 (2008)

A Cooperative Routing Algorithm
for Maximizing Network Lifetime

Ji Zhang[1], Dafang Zhang[1], Kun Xie[1], Shiming He[1], Hong Qiao[1], and Bin Zeng[2]

[1] College of Information Science and Engineering
Hunan University, HNU, Changsha, China
[2] China Mobile Group Hunan Company Limited, Changsha, China
{tosky1984,dfzhang,cskxie,smhe,hqiao}@hnu.edu.cn

Abstract. Cooperative communication can send and receive message with virtual MIMO antenna arrays stemming from sharing other users antenna in the network, leading to reducing energy consumption. Cooperative routing is a cross layer routing by using the technology of Cooperative communication in physical layer and routing selection in network layer. For the purpose of maximizing the network lifetime, this paper proposes a weighted power allocation with cooperative transmission by considering various elements, including initial energy of nodes, residual energy, transmission overhead, and designs a cooperative routing algorithm for maximizing network lifetime (MNLCR) which is based on that weighted power allocation. The simulation results show that MNLCR can extend 25% of the network lifetime compared with FACR. *abstract environment.*

Keywords: Wireless Sensor Networks (WSN), cooperative routing, maximizing network lifetime, power allocation.

1 Introduction

Multipath fading decreases channel capacity and network service quality in wireless network. Through multiple antennas equipped in the transmitter and receiver, MIMO [1] (Multiple-Input Multiple-Out-put) can lighten multipath fading and enhance channel capacity significantly. MIMO has become an important technique of wireless communication. In MIMO, the distance between antennas should much larger than wavelength, and the transmission channel between multiple antennas should be independent. However, due to the limited size, weight and energy of mobile terminators, it is unrealistic to install more antennas in a terminator. Hence, although MIMO can run effectively in the cellular base station, its hard to widespread use it in wireless network composed of several mobile terminators.

Due to the broadcasting nature of wireless channel, cooperative communication can form a virtual MIMO antenna arrays by sharing antennas among users to receive and transmit the packet, leading to the reducing energy cost and increasing network throughput. Recently, cooperative communication becomes a

R. Wang and F. Xiao (Eds.): CWSN 2012, CCIS 334, pp. 665–675, 2013.
© Springer-Verlag Berlin Heidelberg 2013

hot spot in wireless network. Cooperative routing is a cross-layer routing selection solution by combining the cooperative communication technique in physical layer and routing technique in network layer. And cooperative routing can be used for saving energy consumption.

Energy-efficient routing algorithm, used for saving nodes' transmission energy, is an important field in wireless sensor network. With the development of routing technique, several energy-efficient cooperative routings are proposed [2-6].

In this paper, according to network nodes' initial energy and remaining energy, a weighted cooperative transmission power allocation method is proposed in order to improve the network lifetime. Furthermore, a cooperative routing algorithm for maximizing network lifetime (MNLCR) is proposed based on the power allocation method. MNLCR is used for choosing a shortest weights routing path and the weight is the nodes' energy consumption. The experimental results show that MNLCR can promote 25% network lifetime.

The rest of this paper is organized as: the section 2 introduces related works; section 3 describes the problem; section 4 explain power allocation method for maximizing network lifetime; section 5 expresses details of MNLCR; section 6 shows the experiments and analyzes the result; the last section summarizes the paper and further work.

2   Related Work

In the multi-hop transmission, nodes that have received the transmitted signal will cooperatively help relaying and form a virtual multi antenna system by using technology of cooperative communication. This virtual multi antenna system achieves significant performance gain as in the MIMO system. According to methods of handling message in nodes, existing cooperative communication protocol can be classified to AF(Amplify and Forward) and DF (Decode and Forward). In AF, nodes just amplify the signal and forward it to receiver; In DF, nodes decode the signal and transmit it to receive after recoding.

The cooperative routing problem can be viewed as a multi-stage decision problem, where at each stage the decision is to pick the transmitting and the receiving set of nodes as well as the transmission power levels among all nodes transmitting in that stage. And the cooperative communication technique in physical layer is used in every stage.

According to different optimal targets, energy-efficient cooperative routing can be classified to two categories: (1) Its target is to minimize the total energy consumption in end-to-end transmission, like PC[2], CAN[2], CSP[3], MPCR[4], GSPRA[5] et. (2) It pursues maximizing the network life time, such as FACR[6] et.

The idea of PC and CAN are the same. They choose the shortest path of traditional routing firstly and then select relay nodes based on the path to transmit packets cooperatively. Although PC saves more energy than CAN, it has much more algorithm complexity. CSP uses the Dijkstra algorithm as the basic structure, and recalculates the shortest path in every step. MPCR is a distributed cooperative routing by using single relay. GSPRA is a distributed cooperative routing based on MIMO.

Above works pay attention to reducing the total energy consumption in end-to-end path. However, because the lifetime of wireless sensor network is determined by the first energy exhausted node, saving the total energy consumption doesn't lead to longer lifetime. Hence, [6] proposes a centralized maximizing lifetime cooperative routing based on FA[7].

Nevertheless, although [6] introduces initial energy and remaining energy into its power allocation method, it doesn't consider how to optimize the power allocation. Besides, FACR[6] is based on shortest path, like most existing cooperative protocol, which can't use cooperative communication sufficiently. So, it is necessary to unify relay selection, power allocation and routing selection in order to maximize the utilization of cooperative communication. Moreover, the minimal energy consumption routing algorithm is not suited for enhancing network lifetime. Hence, in this paper, we propose a weighted power allocation method and a cooperative routing algorithm for maximizing Network Lifetime (MNLCR) based on it.

3   Problem Analysis

In this paper, the network scene is a wireless sensor network, as figure 1. The topology can be described as G=(V, E), where V represents the node sets, E is the set of links, E_i and R_i represents initial energy and remaining energy.

Fig. 1. The Wireless Sensor Networks

The network lifetime is defined as the time interval from the time network start working to the time when the first node exhausts its energy. That is, if there is a node its remaining energy R_i is 0, the network is dead. For a node pair, if the two nodes can communicate with each other by direct mode or cooperative mode, it means there is a link between them and they are neighbors. In the network, any two nodes communicate with each other through multiple hops, and every hop can use direct transmission or cooperative transmission. For every hop, transmitter can dynamically adjust its transmitted power $P_t=|\omega|^2$ and when the signal to noise ratio(SNR) is larger than threshold SNR_{min}, the receiver can receive the packet correctly.

In this paper, we need to solve this problem: how to design a cooperative routing which can maximize the network lifetime under guaranteeing the correct communication.

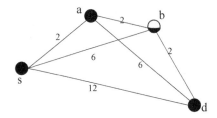

Fig. 2. A simple example of Wireless Sensor Networks

We express our basic idea through an example. In figure 2, we need to transmit the packet from source node s to destination node d. The number beyond the link represents the energy consumption while transmitting a unit packet between the two nodes by direct transmission mode. In figure 2, all nodes have full energy except node b. In traditional routing algorithm, the packet will pass through the path {s→a, a→b, b→d}, and needs consume 6 unit energy for transmitting a unit packet. And node b will exhaust its energy firstly, resulting in the network dead. And common cooperative routings (CAN, PLC, CSP) will select a path{s→a, (s, a)→b, (a, b)→d} to transmit packets, leading to 5 energy consumption.

Compared with direct communication, cooperative communication can reduce energy consumption evidently, leading to enhancing the network lifetime. However, it is not the optimal solution. Firstly, when transmitting the packet through (a,b)→d, it's better to increase node a's transmit power, as well as reducing node bs transmit power. If then, although the total energy consumption will increase compared with CSP, the energy load can be balanced, bringing up the longer network lifetime. Secondly, since cooperative transmission can expand the distance, we can choose the path {s→a, (s, a)→d}, which can avoid node b. Of course, this transmission is limited by the power of node s and node a.

Hence, MNLCR is proposed in this paper to increase network lifetime, and it needs to solve two problems:(1) how to allocate power to nodes according to nodes' initial energy and remaining energy in order to maximize the network lifetime. (2) how to choose the routing path based on power allocation method to maximize the network lifetime

4   Power Allocation Method for Maximize the Network Lifetime

In multi-hop cooperative communication, each hop can have different transmission modes (Figure 3), corresponding to different power allocation and energy consumption. Hence, which transmission is chose plays an important role in network lifetime.

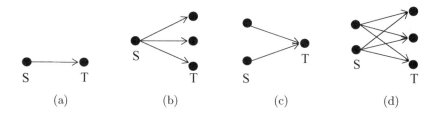

(a)	(b)	(c)	(d)

Fig. 3. Transmission modes:(a) traditional mode;(b) broadcasting mode;(c) cooperative mode;(d) cooperative broadcasting mode.

As figure 3(a), traditional mode is point-to-point, the source node set is S=$\{s_1\}$, the destination node set is T=$\{t_1\}$. As figure 3(b), broadcasting mode is one-to-more, the source node set is S=$\{s_1\}$, the destination node set is T=$\{t_1, t_2, ..., t_m\}$. Broadcasting mode makes use of broadcasting nature of wireless channel, and nodes within the transmission range can receive the signal from source, so the link cost is the largest cost of broadcasting links. Cooperative mode is more-to-one, the source node set is S=$\{s_1, s_2, ..., s_m\}$ the destination node set is T=$\{t_1\}$. MNLCR is based on cooperative mode. As figure 3(d), cooperative broadcasting mode is more-to-more, the source node set S=$\{s_1, s_2, ..., s_m\}$ the destination node set is T=$\{t_1, t_2, ..., t_m\}$.

Recently researches show that cooperative broadcasting mode can increase communication cost, time synchronization cost, interference range obviously stemming from its multiple transmitters and receivers, compared with former three modes. So, currently cooperative routings seldom use this mode. And since cooperative transmission consumes less energy than traditional mode and broadcasting mode, this paper chooses cooperative transmission as the main transmission mode.

In cooperative mode, as figure 3(c), the received signal is described as:

$$r(t) = \sum_{i=1}^{n} \alpha_{i1} |\omega_i| \phi(t) + \eta(t) \tag{1}$$

Where $\phi(t)$ is the unit-power transmitted signal, and $\eta(t)$ is the receiver noise with power P_η. The total transmitted power is $P = \sum_{i=1}^{n} |\omega_i|^2$, and the SNR ratio at the receiver is $|\sum_{i=1}^{n} \omega_i \alpha_{i1}|^2 / P_\eta$.For complete decoding at the receiver, the SNR must be above the threshold value SNR_{min}.

As we know, in wireless sensor networks, multiple source nodes participated in one transmission have different initial energy and remaining energy. It is nature to think that nodes with fewer remaining energy should use fewer energy than nodes with more remaining energy. Hence, the power allocation method should consider the ratio of initial energy to remaining energy instead of pursuing the minimal total energy consumption ($E_i : R_i$). And a novel weighted power allocation method is proposed in this paper. In our method, when two nodes consume the same energy, the higher ratio node will pay more cost. The method details are described as:

$$Min \quad \sum_i^n \left(\frac{E_i}{R_i}\right)^X |\omega_i|^2 \tag{2}$$

$$s.t. \quad \frac{\left|\sum_{i=1}^n \omega_i \alpha_{i1}\right|^2}{P_\eta} \geq SNR_{\min} \tag{3}$$

$$0 \leq |\omega_i| \leq \sqrt{P\gamma_i} \tag{4}$$

$P\gamma_i$ is the node i's rated power. X is the weights parameter, and it defines the weighted relationship between ratio of initial energy E_i to remaining energy R_i and node energy consumption. The larger X value shows that the power allocation method pay more attention to the remaining energy, otherwise, smaller X value represents the method focus more on transmission energy consumption. When X is 0, it means that the method only considers nodes' energy consumption and ignores the nodes' remaining energy, and its effect is the same as CSP. So, X's value has important effect on the reasonability of the power allocation method, we'll discuss it in the simulation experiment part.

The weighted power allocation method is described as a nonlinear programming problem (2)-(4), and can be solved by using Lagrange multiplier method.

$$L(\omega_1, \omega_2 ... \omega_i, \lambda) = \sum_i^n \left(\frac{E_i}{R_i}\right)^X |\omega_i|^2 - \lambda\left(\frac{\left|\sum_{i=1}^n \omega_i \alpha_{i1}\right|^2}{P_\eta} - SNR_{\min}\right) \tag{5}$$

Taking the partial derivatives, we have:

$$\frac{\partial L}{\partial \omega_i} = 2\left(\frac{E_i}{R_i}\right)^X |\omega_i| - 2\frac{\lambda \alpha_{i1}\left|\sum_{i=1}^n \omega_i \alpha_{i1}\right|}{P_\eta} = 0, \forall i \tag{6}$$

$$\frac{\partial L}{\partial \lambda} = \frac{\left|\sum_{i=1}^n \omega_i \alpha_{i1}\right|^2}{P_\eta} - SNR_{\min} = 0 \tag{7}$$

Combining (6) and (7), we get

$$LC(s_i, t_1) = \left|\hat{\omega}_i\right|^2 = \frac{\left(\frac{E_i}{R_i}\right)^X \alpha_{i1}^2 SNR_{\min} P_\eta}{\left(\sum_{i=1}^n \left(\frac{E_i}{R_i}\right)^X \alpha_{i1}^2\right)^2} \tag{8}$$

In one hop cooperative communication, (8) represents the optimal power allocation for transmitter sets S. Weighted power allocation can balance load among transmitter nodes, resulting in increasing network lifetime. Besides, involving initial energy and remaining energy into the cooperative routing can prevent nodes with insufficient energy from participating in forwarding packets. And next section will introduce a maximizing network lifetime cooperative routing algorithm based on the weighted power allocation method.

5   Cooperative Routing Selection

The basic idea of the MNLCR(x) algorithm is:

The network topology can be described as weighted energy consumption graph G=(V, E), where V represents nodes set, E represents links set, E_i and R_i represents node i's initial energy and remaining energy , P_{ij} represents the minimal transmission power from node i to node j through traditional transmission mode respectively. Assuming the weight of link $e_{ij} \in E$ is $(E_i/R_i)^X P_{ij}$. Coop(u,v) represents the weighted cost for transmitting a unit packet from former k-1 nodes to node v. Coop(u, v) can be described as $\sum_{i=1}^{n}(E_i/R_i)^X |\omega_i|^2$ where $|\omega_i|^2$ is calculated by (8) and $(E_i/R_i)^X$ is the weight. And the transmission cost for transmitting a unit packet from source node to destination node v is Cost[u], consisting of two parts: one is the transmission cost from source node to node u, the previous node of node v; another is Coop(u, v), the cost of cooperative transmitting from node u and its previous k-1 nodes to node v.

Algorithm 1. The MNLCR(x) algorithm steps

1: Initially, $S = s$; $U = V - s$;
    For each node i in U
        If node i is neighbor of source s
            Then $Cost[i] = (E_s/R_s)^X P_{si}$
        Else $Cost[i] = \infty$;
2: Select node u with minimal $Cost[u]$ from U,
        add it to S
        $S = S + \{u\}$;
        $U = U - \{u\}$;
3: For every node v in U,
        $Relax(u, v)$;
4: Repeat step 2, 3 until S contains all nodes and U is empty

---

We divide the graph G into two groups. One group is S, containing nodes in the optimal path. Another is U, containing nodes not in optimal path. Initially, S contains only a source node S. Then, at each step, selecting a node u from U with minimal cost transmitting the packet cooperatively from source to u, then add u to set S and remove u from U. Until all nodes are contained in the Set S, the algorithm is finished.

The key part of the algorithm is the relaxation operation. Algorithm 2 gives details of pseudo-code.

Algorithm 2. New relaxation procedure for MNLCR(x) algorithm

1: $Relax(u, v)$
    {
        If $Cost[v] > Cost[u] + Coop(u, v)$ then
        $Cost[v] = Cost[u] + Coop(u, v)$;
        Set node u as node v's previous node;
        Endif
    }
2: //Assume path = $\{t_1, t_2, ..., t_m, u\}$
    $Coop(u, v)$
    {
        If $(m >= k - 1)$
        return PowerAllocation $(t_{m-k+2}, t_{m-k+3}, ..., t_m, u, v)$
        //k cooperative transmitters
        If $(m < k - 1)$
        return $PowerAllocation(t_1, t_2, ..., t_m, v)$
    }
3: $PowerAllocation(t_1, t_2, ..., t_n, v)$
    {

$$LC(s_i, t_1) = \left|\hat{\omega}_i\right|^2 = \frac{\left(\frac{E_i}{R_i}\right)^X \alpha_{i1}^2 SNR_{\min} P_\eta}{\left(\sum_{i=1}^n \left(\frac{E_i}{R_i}\right)^X \alpha_{i1}^2\right)^2}$$

    Return $\sum_{i=1}^n (E_i/R_i)^X |\omega_i|^2$
    }

Since MNLCR(x) is based on Dijkstra algorithm, its calculation complexity is $O(N^2)$, the same with Dijkstrawhere N is node number, and it is easy to implement it in a distributed manner.

6   Simulation Experiment

The section will analyze MNLCR(x) by simulation experiment and compare its performance with mainly existing routing algorithms, including traditional multi-hop routing, FA, CAN, CSP and FACR, all introduced in section 2.

As figure 4, it is assumed that there are N nodes in an 80*80 areas, the power fading factor $\lambda = 2$ and the transmitter node count in cooperative transmission is 2, the longest transmission radius of non-cooperative transmission is $d_{max} = 25$, every node can adjust its transmitting power dynamically, The energy consumed in transmitting a unit packet from node i to its neighbor nodes with traditional mode is normalized to $e_i = (Distance/400)^2$ and nodes initial energy is set to 1. In the experiment, we consider two kinds of scenes. Ones is single flow scenario, which assuming that the source node and destination node is fixed. The other is

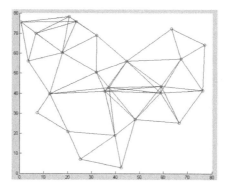

Fig. 4. Random network with 25 nodes in 80 meter by 80 meter area

random flow scenario, which the source node and destination will be randomly selected again after an end-to-end transmission. It is simple to know that node energy consumption is unfair in single flow, leading to the network life is shorter than that of random flow.

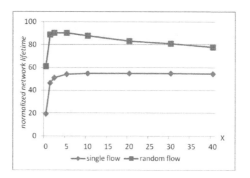

Fig. 5. The normalized network lifetime in different scenes

Figure 5 shows the network lifetime of MNLCR(x) in single flow and random flow scenario respectively, where node number N is 25. In figure 5, the vertical coordinate is normalized network lifetime, horizontal coordinate is x value in MNLCR(x). Overall, network lifetime in random flow scenario is much longer than that of single flow scenario, verifying the conjecture above. When $x = 0$, MNLCR(x) doesn't consider the initial energy and remaining energy and MNLCR(x) is the same as CSP, whose network lifetime is shorter than that of MNLCR(x) where $x \neq 0$. The higher x value represents our algorithm pay more attention on nodes remaining energy while selecting routing path. From figure 5, we can conclude that when x is equal to 2, the network lifetime is longest in single flow scenario and longest network lifetime in random flow scenario is obtained when $x = 5$.

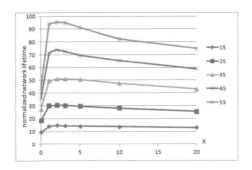

Fig. 6. The normalized network lifetime under different node density

Figure 6 shows the relationship between x and network lifetime under different node density (randomly selecting 15, 25,35,45,55 nodes respectively).In figure 6, vertical coordinate represents network lifetime, horizontal coordinate is x value in MNLCR(x). The experimental results show that the changing trend of network lifetime is the same under different node number. And the higher node density is, the longer network life time is. Besides, in the MNLCR(x), the speed of enhancing network lifetime is faster than that of increasing node number. According to above experimental results, we contend that the longest network lifetime can be gotten when x is equal to 2 under ideal network environment.

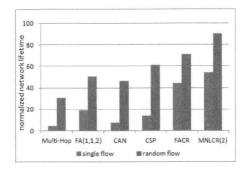

Fig. 7. The normalized network lifetime comparison for different routing algorithms

Figure 7 shows contrast results while comparing MNLCR(x) with other five routing algorithms under single flow scenario and random flow scenario respectively., where node number $N = 25$. Compared with Multi-Hop, FA, CAN, CSP, FARCR respectively, MNLCR(2) extends 1109%, 181%,632%, 293%, 22% of network lifetime in single flow scenario, and 191%,78%,93%, 48%,27% in random flow scenario. Because our goal is to increase the network lifetime, the performance is worse. Although FA is the classical routing for maximizing network lifetime, it performs worse than CSP in random flow scenario for using non-cooperative transmission. However, our MNLCR(2) can extend 25% of network lifetime, compared with FACR which is the real cooperative routing for maximizing network lifetime.

7   Conclusion and Future Work

According to the initial energy and residual energy of each node, this paper proposes a weighted cooperative transmission power allocation method which can balance the energy consumption among cooperative nodes, and then designs a Cooperative Routing Algorithms for Maximizing Network Lifetime MNLCR(x) based on the power allocation method. The simulation experiments conclude that MNLCR(2) is the best in ideal networks. And the results show that MNLCR(2) can extend 25% of the network lifetime compared with FACR.

Furthermore, as we know, the channel quality and topological structure of wireless sensor network changes dynamically, resulting in performance degradation of cooperative routing stemming from channel signaling and synchronization cost. Hence, designing a wireless cooperative routing for maximizing dynamic network lifetime is our future work.

Acknowledgments. This work is supported by the National Natural Science Foundation of China under Grant No. 61003305, 61173168 and 61173167, the National Basic Research Program of China (973) under Grant No. 2012CB315801.

References

1. Gesbert, D., Shafi, M., Shiu, D.-S.: From theory to practice: An overview of MIMO space-time coded wireless systems. IEEE Jour. Select. Areas in Commun. 21(3) (2003)
2. Khandani, A.E., Abounadi, J., Modiano, E.: Cooperative routing in static wireless networks. IEEE Transactions on Communications 55(11) (2007)
3. Li, F., Wu, K., Lippman, A.: Energy-efficient cooperative routing in multi-hop wireless ad hoc networks. In: IEEE International Performance, Computing, and Communications Conference (2006)
4. Ibrahim, A.S., Han, Z., Liu, K.J.R.: Distributed energy-efficient cooperative routing in wireless networks. IEEE Transactions on Wireless Communications 7(10) (2008)
5. Lang, Y., Wubben, D., Dekorsy, A.: Optimal power Routing for End-to-end Outage Restricted Distributed MIMO Multi-hop Networks. In: IEEE International Conference on Communications (2011)
6. Pandana, C., Siriwongpairat, W.P., Himsoon, T.: Distributed cooperative routing algorithm for maximizing network lifetime. In: IEEE Wireless Communications and Networking Conference (2006)
7. Chang, J.-H., Tassiulas, L.: Maximum lifetime routing in wireless sensor networks. IEEE/ACM Transactions on Networking 12(4) (2004)
8. Zhu, Y., Zheng, H.: Understanding the impact of interference on collaborative relays. IEEE Transactions on Mobile Computing 7(6) (2008)

A Dynamic Web Services Selection Algorithm Based on Trust Model for Grid Environment

Lin Zhang*, Zhengbang Liu, Ruchuan Wang, and Haiyan Wang

College of Computer, Nanjing University of Posts and Telecommunications,
Jiangsu High Technology Research Key Laboratory for Wireless Sensor Networks,
Key Lab of Broadband Wireless Communication and Sensor Network Technology,
Ministry of Education Jiangsu Province, Nanjing, 210003, China
zhangl@njupt.edu.cn

Abstract. In order to find the service nodes, which the users are satisfied with, in a high speed and efficiency in open network environment, a new grid-oriented multi-level service selection model is proposed, which is based on the concept of user-similarity group. On this condition, direct trust calculation based on time decay is given and fine-grained recommendation trust calculation is studied, which can distinguish the ability of honesty. In addition, based on activity level of nodes, dynamic weight-allocation method is proposed, which can make the prediction results be closer to the fact. After job-interaction, the update algorithm about honesty ability of recommendation nodes is researched, which will provide more reasonable and reliable reference for the next prediction. Simulation results show that the service selection model and trust calculation methods are reasonable and accurate.

Keywords: grid computing, service selection, trust model, dynamic update, ability of honesty.

1 Introduction

Currently, scholars pay attention to the dynamic trust in open network environment increasingly, many models and programs about trust forecast and update are proposed.Among them, literature[3] proposes a trust evaluation model including the entity risk, literature[7] establishes the feedback mechanism in the authorization system, and dynamically adjusts user roles based on user behaviors. In addition, service selection based on trust metrics has become a popular topic [9-11].In order to find the service nodes which meet user requirements,existing researches were contribution to the rapid development of the trust model, our project team also has done some research work early [12-14], but there are still a number of shortcomings need to be addressed.

1) Many service selection models are not detailed enough and clear in selection level dividing,and waste the limited resources of the system to a certain extent.

---

* Corresponding author.

R. Wang and F. Xiao (Eds.): CWSN 2012, CCIS 334, pp. 676–684, 2013.
© Springer-Verlag Berlin Heidelberg 2013

2) Most service selection models treat the trust value of entity as an important selection evidence,in the calculation of the trust value, however, both the direct trust and recommendation are need to be improved. For example, a simple weighted method to calculate the integrated trust value, this method is not objective, not flexible, not scientific, the focus of this article is to research a dynamic weighted method.

3) The trust value of entity is changing all the time, most of papers pay more attention to the update of the trust value, but less to the real-time updates of the recommended capacity of the recommended node.

Referring to the mentioned problems above, the level of service selection has been meticulously divided to find the service node meeting users need quickly. In the calculation of the integrated trust value, direct trust value and recommended trust value of service nodes use dynamic weighted calculation which is more scientific and flexible. After each job interaction, the trust value of the service node and the recommended capacity of recommended nodes are updated.

The part 2 describes a multi-level services selection model based on the open network, and Part 3 discusses the direct trust value, recommendation trust value, and the trust calculation method based on the dynamic weighted method, part 4 discusses update algorithm of the service node, and the real-time update scheme of the node recommended capacity, part 5 show the experimental results, part 6 is the conclusion.

2   Deployment Scenarios of Service Selection

2.1   Multi-level Service Selection Model

In order to find services more efficient and accurate in a large-scale dynamic grid environment, a multi-level and fine-grained service selection model is presented, as shown in Figure 1.

Service Autonomous Region:Each grid is an autonomous region that contains many services, whose type and quality are different. In order to meet the demand of more services,different services are sorted, at the same time. A service selection machine is set in each type of services to manage the internal service options scheme of this type.

Service Classification Region:The second level is a virtual classified region where the service selection machines from different grids will be unique. Each node can save the number of jobs and each job time records in this region, and it can sort services based on the amount of jobs in each period time. A standard period of time and number of operations requirements are given by users, service selector can lessen the service candidates based on its own information and the recommended information from recommended nodes.

Service Region:The top-level is a user-oriented level, which can render a collection of various service types in the entire network environment.

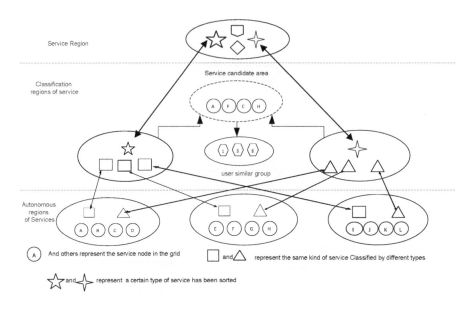

Fig. 1. Multi-level service selection model

2.2   Search Process of the Service Selection

In a huge open network environment, it is important to search effectively, if no efficient search methods, the search process will become very messy. The process of the service selection is as follows:

1) User nodes connect to the grid, query service region, propose the request of the types of services.

2) To access service classification area, where all network nodes that can provide the service were recorded, to get into the fine-grained hierarchical search.

3) The user nodes provide their standard time period parameters and the number of the system operations, service classification area takes the sorting operation according to the types of those services, search service nodes that meet the needs of user nodes.

4) The service candidate area take the sorting operation from high to low , according to the number of interactions of the service node in the recent time period, then the trust value of each node is given by the user evaluation in turn.

5) In order to evaluate the service node, it is necessary to consider both the direct trust value and recommended trust value. Recommendation trust,is need to consider some attributes for recommended, for example, whether they have the same service requests with the current user node in the recent period, or have similar requirements on quality of service. Then, examine the trust information of each node in the user similar group: a. last job interaction time; b.the trust value of the service node evaluation after the last interaction; c.the evaluation

of the Recommended honest ability of the current user from other user nodes; d.the evaluation of the user Recommended honest ability from the current user node.

6)To refer to the computing method on direct trust value recommended trust value and integrated trust value given in part 3, the overall trust value of the service node is gained.And to get the integrated trust value of each candidate service in the same method to refer to this information to choose an effective service node.

7) The user node interacts with the service node, and according to the job completion, the trust value of the service node and the recommendations ability are updated to provide the necessary reference for the next service selection.

3 Trust Value of Service Node

3.1 Calculation of Direct Trust Value

In order to make the direct trust value on a service node closer to the true value, take the nearest N interactions as the basis for calculating of direct trust value on this service node.

Assume a two-dimensional array $< \zeta_1, T_1 >, < \zeta_2, T_2 >, ..., < \zeta_i, T_i >$,every array records the last N interaction time T_i and trust evaluation value ζ_i.As trust value is dynamic, decaying with the time, the direct trust value$\vartheta_0$is as follows:

$$\vartheta_0 = \frac{\sum_{i=1}^{n} \eta_i * \zeta_i}{\sum_{i=1}^{n} \eta_i} \qquad i = 1, ..., n \tag{1}$$

Here, the time attenuation coefficientη_i:

$$\eta_i = \begin{cases} 1 & T_x - T_j \leq T \\ \frac{1}{e^{T_x - T_i - T_r}} & T_x - T_j > T_r \end{cases} \tag{2}$$

If the interval of the current operating time T_x before a operating time is less than a value T_r,it is considered that this trust value is not to be attenuated, the attenuation coefficient is 1.

As can be seen from the above equation, which has taken a conservative approach to the calculation of the trust value, the trust value of the service node must not be raised blindly.

3.2 Calculation of Recommendation Trust Value

A service node will have a plurality of user nodes that had a job interactive with it, these user nodes formed a user similar group to a certain extent, they have the same type of service requirements, and the service demand for quality is similar, so recommended value of those users should be considered.

When it accesses a service node, current user node will query evaluation of the trust values from K nodes which interact with the service node in the recent time.The directly trust values gained by those K nodes on the service node to be

$x_1, x_2, ..., x_k$,which has attenuated by the time. At the same time this K nodes also have a different recommended honesty capability.

Let the comprehensive honesty ability of these recommendation nodes be $K'_1, K'_2, ..., K'_k$, which are provided from nodes of user-similarity group. the ones gained by user node are $K_1, K_2, ..., K_k$, here, K'_i and K_i are less than or equal to 1. Further,ρ_0 is the right weight of the of user-similarity group nodes on honesty ability of the recommendation nodes, ρ_1 is the weight of the current user node itself on these honesty abilities, the recommended trust value ϑ_1 on the service node is as follows:

$$\vartheta_1 = \frac{\sum_{i=1}^{k}(\rho_0 k'_i + \rho_1 k_i) * x_i}{\sum_{i=1}^{k} \rho_0 k'_i + \rho_0 k_i} \tag{3}$$

In this process, the current user node not only refers to its own evaluation about honesty ability of the recommendation node, but also refers to the evaluation of the other nodes in the user-similarity group, This recommendation results fit the exchanges of human society habits better.

3.3   Comprehensive Trust Value Calculation with Dynamical Weight-Allocation

Most of the literature use the expert opinion method or the average weight in computing the trust value method [8-12], resulting in the forecast results with a more subjective component,and being lack of dynamic adaptability.

This article will use a dynamic weight distribution scheme based on node activity to calculate the trust value of the service node.In fact,if an individual is more active in the human society, the quantity of people that communicate with him is more, at the same is his feedback.The recommendation trust value on this person evaluation will be more authentic, this idea also fit human cognitive habits well.

For a service node P_S, it is assumed that within a standard time period T, the quantity of user nodes that have interacted with service node is X, at the same time,number of operations is marked as M, $\beta(P_s)$ is the activity of service node P_S,then:

$$\beta(P_s) = \begin{cases} 1 & X > M \\ \frac{X}{M} & X < M \end{cases} \tag{4}$$

When there are more nodes interacting with the service node in the standard period of time,the value of $\beta(P_s)$ is larger,the trust value of service node will be relatively stable in the open network environment.

4   Trust Update Based on the Mean-Square Deviation

User nodes need to update direct trust value of service nodes after the job interaction completed, and the recommended honest ability of other recommendation nodes.

4.1   Update of Direct Trust Value

After each job interaction, user node holds the value of the trust evaluation of the service node.It is need to re-calculate the trust value of the service node at the next time, using the formula (1) and (2). Thus, user node will have a new cognitive on service node after each job interaction, the cognition is direct.

4.2   Update of Recommended Honesty Ability

For the user node, the recommendation nodes in the user-similarity group which has high credibility are more trustworthy.therefore it is need to distinguish the recommendation honesty ability. When the user nodeP_u and service node P_s completed the job interactions, it is need to update the honest ability of the recommended nodes, according to the actual implementation of the job.

After obtaining the recommendation information of the recommended node,we will do a mean calculation for all of the recommended trust value on the service node,then calculate a mean square deviation about each of the recommended nodes, so that the mean square deviation is larger, the recommended information is more unbelievable, It also shows the honesty ability of the recommended node should be updated in real time, in order to ensure the validity of the recommended information.

Set$M(w_r)$ be the collection of recommendation nodes within the user-similarity group which have interacted with the service nodeP_s,$TR(w_r, P_s)$ expresses the recommended trust value of the service nodeP_s,$|M| = K$,then:

$$E[TR(w_r, P_s)] = \sum_{i=1}^{k} \frac{TR(w_r, P_s)}{k} \tag{5}$$

The relative mean-square deviation of the recommended node w_r is as follows:

$$\delta[TR(w_r, P_s)] = \sqrt{E[(TR(w_r, P_s) - TR(P_u, P_s)^2]) - \mu[TR(w_r, P_s)]^2} \tag{6}$$

$$\mu[TR(w_r, P_s)] = |E[TR(w_r, P_s)] - TR(w_r, P_s)| \tag{7}$$

The update formulas of the honest ability:

$$CH'(w_r, P_s) = \begin{cases} CH(w_r, P_s) + \tau(1 - \varepsilon)CH(w_r, P_s) & \varepsilon < 1 \\ CH(w_r, P_s) - \gamma(1 + 1/\varepsilon)CH(w_r, P_s) & \varepsilon > 1 \end{cases} \tag{8}$$

Here:$0 < \tau < \gamma < 1$,$CH(w_r, P_u)$is the last evaluation of user nodeP_u on the honest ability of recommended node w_r, $CH'(w_r, P_u)$ is the current evaluation on the honest ability after this job interaction ,$CH'(w_r, P_u) \in [0, 1]$.

$$\varepsilon = \frac{||E[TR(w_r, P_s)] - \vartheta(P_u, P_s)| - \mu[TR(w_r, P_s)]|}{\delta[TR(w_r, P_s)]} \tag{9}$$

5   Analysis of Simulation Experiment

5.1   Analysis of Multi-level Service Selection Model

Assume a network environment composed by S autonomous region, There are E service nodes in each autonomous regions and R service types across the grid, Each type of services has the same number of service nodes.During judging on a service node, each user node need determine its type of service firstly.if the service type is suitable, continue to predict the value of trust to obtain satisfactory service node. Set the time to judge the service type of a service node as 1 time unit, and then the time required for calculating a service node trust value as 3 time units.

The model of this article uses a hierarchical thought, and sorts the similar type of services. So when it searches for a satisfactory service node, the user does not need to broadcast-search, but searches rows in the front part of the service node (such as 0.3) to find the goal. And the user searches for a satisfactory service nodes needed for the longest time TS:

$$TS = R + E * \frac{S}{R} * 0.9 \tag{10}$$

Longest time required by the traditional model is longer because they do not adopt such a fine-grained hierarchical thought, so that a user searches for a satisfactory service node:

$$TS' = 4S * E \tag{11}$$

Set $S = 10$, $R = 5$ and E was set $3, 4, 5, 6, 7$, Figure 2 is the experimental comparison chart on search efficiency between a multi-level model of this article and reference model.

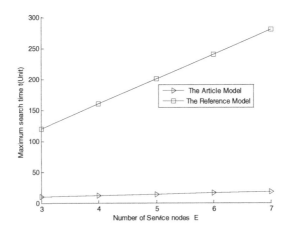

Fig. 2. Experimental comparison chart of the search efficiency

In Figure 2, The maximum time required in querying service nodes in the article model compared with the reference model is much less. That shows that the efficiency of the article model is higher.

5.2 Analysis on Update Honesty Ability

After the job interaction between user node and the service node, not only the direct trust value of service nodes should be updated, but also on the recommended node honest capability, that provide a more effective basis for the next credible projections.

It is considered to be not detailed enough on the update of recommended node honest ability in traditional model, most of them ignore the feedback evaluation of the current user on recommended node recommended capacity, Figure 3 shows the next credible prediction on the service node when the users get different recommended capacity feedback value.

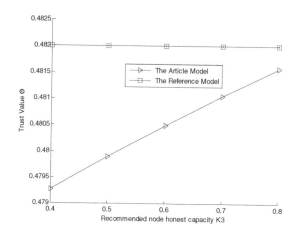

Fig. 3. experimental comparison chart of update of recommended honest ability

Figure 3 shows an update of the current user node on the recommended node honest ability and the recommended node honesty capability are obtained by assigning different weights to different recommended nodes the model of this article model, and thereby its recommended trust value is updated indirectly. Comprehensive update of the recommended node honest ability is not detailed enough in the reference model. Even if a recommended node honest ability has changed, the reference model predicts the overall trust value which is not sensitive enough on the service node. However this article model is more reasonable.

6   Conclusion

In open grid environment, a multi-level and fine-grained service selection model is researched,Thus user nodes can find the service node more efficiently and quickly.Dynamic weight-allocation method based on direct trust value and the recommendation trust value are stressed,And the method fit the habit of human society well,and makes the trust value more credible. The update of direct trust value on service node and honesty ability were researched, after the user node completes the job interaction with the service node,this can provide a more reasonable and reliable reference for the next service selection. Multiple experimental results show the new model is rational and scientific.

References

1. Sun, Y.X., Huang, S.H., Chen, L.J.: Bayesian Decision-Making Based Recommendation Trust Revision Model in Ad Hoc Networks. Journal of Software 20(9), 2574–2586 (2009) (in English)
2. Li, X.Y., Gui, X.L., Mao, Q., Leng, D.Q.: Adaptive Dynamic Trust Measurement and Prediction Model Based on Behavior Monitoring. Chinese Journal of Computers 32(4), 664–674 (2009)
3. Zhang, R.L., Wu, X.N., Zhou, S.Y., Dong, X.S.: A Trust Model Based on Behaviors Risk Evaluation. Chinese Journal of Computers 32(4), 688–698 (2009)
4. Stefan, S., Robert, S.: Fuzzy trust evaluation and credibility development in multi-agent systems. Applied Soft Computing 7(2), 492–505 (2007)
5. Yan, S.R., Zheng, X.L., Chen, D.R.: User-Centric Trust and Reputation Model for Personal and Trusted Service Selection. International Journal of Intelligent Systems 26(8), 687–717 (2011)
6. Wang, Y., Dai, G.P., Jiang, Z.T., Hou, Y.R., Fang, J., Ren, X.T.: A Trust Enhanced Service Composition Scheduling Algorithm. Acta Electronica Sinica 37(10), 2234–2238 (2009)
7. Li, M.C., Yang, B., Zhong, W., Tian, L.L., Jiang, H., Hu, H.G.: Grid Dynamic Authorization Model Based on Feedback Mechanism. Chinese Journal of Computers 32(11), 2187–2199 (2009)
8. Lang, B.: Access control oriented quantified trust degree representation model for distributed systems. Journal on Communications 31(12), 45–54 (2010)
9. Zhang, B., Xiang, Y., Wang, P.: A Novel Capacity and Trust Based Service Selection Mechanism for Collaborative Decision Making in CPS. Computer Science and Information Systems 8(4), 1159–1184 (2011)
10. Pan, Z., Baik, J.: A QoS Enhanced Framework and Trust Model for Effective Web Services Selection. Journal of Web Engineering 9(2), 186–204 (2010)
11. Satsiou, A., Tassiulas, L.: Trust-based exchange of services to motivate cooperation in P2P networks. Peer-to-Peer Networking and Applications 4(2), 122–145 (2011)
12. Zhang, L., Wang, R.C., Zhang, Y.P.: A trust evaluation model based on fuzzy set for grid environment. Acta Electronica Sinica 36(5), 862–868 (2008)
13. Chen, C., Wang, R.C., Zhang, L.: The Research of Subject Trust Model Based on Fuzzy Theoryin Open Networks. Acta Electronica Sinica 38(11), 2505–2509 (2010)
14. Zhang, L., Wang, R.C., Wang, H.Y.: Trust transitivity algorithm based on multiple influencing factors for grid environment. Journal on Communications 32(7), 161–168 (2011)

A Real-Time Micro-sensor Motion Capture System

Zhang Nan[1], Shunyan Sun[1,2], Jiankang Wu[1,2],
Xiaoli Meng[1,2], and Guanhong Tao[1]

[1] Sensor Network and Applications Research Center,
Chinese Academy of Sciences, Beijing, China
[2] China-Singapore Institute of Digital Media, Singapore
zhangnan198711@gmail.com, sunshuy09b@mails.gucas.ac.cn, jkwu@gucas.ac.cn

Abstract. Optical human motion capture system can be applied in commercial use, but require expensive studio-like environments which cannot be fulfilled for daily-life use. We present a substitute system: a real-time motion capture system based on micro sensors, which is ubiquity, low-cost and able to reconstruct human motion almost in any environment in real-time. This system consists of three subsystems: a sensor subsystem, a data fusion subsystem and an animation subsystem. Experiments show that our system can reconstruct motions and render animations in real-time, and reach the accuracy of optical human motion capture system

Keywords: Human motion capture, micro-sensor network, data fusion, real-time motion reconstruction.

1 Introduction

Human Motion capture (Mocap) has wide applications in many areas, such as virtual reality, interactive game, sports training and film-making, etc. It has attracted lots of research interests in the last two decades, and a number of Mocap system have been developed, including optical system, mechanical system, inertial system, magnetic system and hybrid system.

Among all the motion capture techniques, optical Mocap is one of the most mature ones, such as Vicon[1]. In optical Mocap, a subject is asked to wear retro-reflective or light emitting markers. Exact 3D locations of these markers are computed from the images which are recorded by certain number of high resolution surrounding cameras, in order to form the motion of the subject. Optical Mocap systems are of their high accuracy and fast update rates. However, they need multiple high speed and high resolution cameras structured and calibrated in a dedicated studio, which restricts applications into a studio-like environment; the systems are quite complex and have the line-of-sight problem.

Mechanical systems, such as Gypsy[2], employ an exoskeleton which is attached to the articulated body segments to measure joint angles by goniometers

R. Wang and F. Xiao (Eds.): CWSN 2012, CCIS 334, pp. 685–694, 2013.
© Springer-Verlag Berlin Heidelberg 2013

directly. They are transportable and work with any PC for real time performance. However, the main disadvantage of them is that it impedes motion and is uncomfortable to wear for extended time periods[3].

Inertial motion capture systems, such as Verhaert's ALERT system[4], use gyroscopes or accelerometers placed on each body segment to measure orientation. They are portable, and do not have the line-of-sight problem. However, the measurements drift significantly over extended time periods.

Magnetic systems, such as MotionStar[5], use a magnetic field (generated by a magnetic coil or earth magnetic field) to determine both position and orientation of body segments. They can achieve good accuracy in the situation of no interference. However, they have high power consumption and are extremely sensitive to the ferromagnetism in the environment.

Ultrasonic systems, such as Cricket location system[6], employ a set of ultrasonic pulse emitters which are worn by a subject and a set of receivers which are placed at fixed locations in the environment, in order to determine each emitter's location by time-of-flight and triangulation. They are of high tracking accuracy. However, the signal interference is seriously[3,7].

Among all the systems, the research on human motion capture using miniature inertial/magnetic sensors becomes more and more attractive. In Micro-sensor Motion capture (MMocap), miniature inertial and magnetic sensor nodes are attached to body segments. Segment orientation and position can be estimated from the fusion of sensory data. Based on the estimated orientation and position, together with the length of each segment and the arranging relationship between segments, the motion of the whole body can be obtained. MMocap has no line-of-sight requirements, and no emitters to install. Thus, MMocap systems can be applied in a variety of applications almost everywhere. In this paper, we present the design of our ambulatory real-time MMocap system using wearable miniature sensor nodes, which are placed at human body segments. The collected motion signals from micro-sensor nodes are then used to estimate orientations and positions by fusion of sensory data. A sensor data-driven hierarchy human motion model is developed and driven by estimated motion information for real-time motion reconstruction. The experimental results have shown that our motion capture system can capture human motion and drive animation in real-time without drift and delay.

The rest of the paper is organized as follows. Section 2-4 describes the design of the prototype system, including the hardware design and the 3D human motion reconstruction. Particularly, section 4 will discuss the data fusion approach for motion information. And the experimental results will be given in Section 5.

2   Sensor Subsystem

The system of our wearable real-time micro-sensor motion capture is implemented by three subsystems: sensor subsystem, data fusion subsystem and the animation subsystem. As depicted in Figure 1: The sensor subsystem samples and gathers human motion signals, and transmits sensor data to data fusion subsystem. Data fusion subsystem fuses data to obtain the motion information, and sends the motion information to the animation subsystem. The animation subsystem renders animation using an avatar in the 3D virtual space in real-time. The fusion subsystem and the animation subsystem are both implemented in a PC-like terminal which also controls sensor subsystem. The communication between the sensor subsystem and the fusion subsystem is operated wirelessly via Bluetooth or Wi-Fi.

The sensor subsystem is described in this section. Animation subsystem is briefed in section 3. The data fusion subsystem will be discussed in section 4.

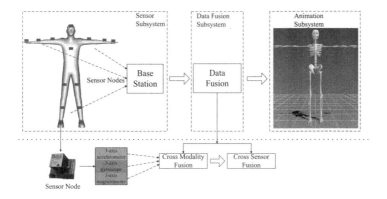

Fig. 1. Our MMocap system contains three subsystems: sensor subsystem, data fusion subsystem and animation subsystem

Sensor subsystem consists of two parts: a base station and certain micro-sensor nodes. Sensor nodes sample human motion signals, and send them to the base station via I²C protocol. On each body segment a sensor node is fixed. Measurement units on node are MEMS micro-sensors including a triad micro accelerometer, a triad micro magnetometer, and a triad micro gyroscope. The accelerometer measures acceleration data which is mixed with human motion acceleration and earth gravity acceleration. The magnetometer measures local earth magnetic field. The gyroscope measures angular rates. The motion information required by animation system can be filtered from those data in the data fusion subsystem detailed in section 4.

Sensor nodes are wired connected to the base station using shielded cables. The sampling rate can be adjusted according to applications, and up to 200Hz. Rechargeable Li-ion battery pack is used to provide power for the sensor subsystem. Taking the range of human activity and exercise level of comfort into account, the system uses wireless communications to send data between the base station and the data fusion subsystem. Depending on different circumstances, the system uses two different wireless communication protocols: Bluetooth and Wi-Fi, while the former one for indoor applications, and the latter one for outdoor applications.

3   Animation Subsystem

The motion information from the data fusion subsystem will be sent to the
animation subsystem to drive an avatar in the 3D virtual space for real-time
human motion reconstruction. During the motion reconstruction, an articulated
anatomic skeleton human model is utilized to represent the subject's body structure. The model is composed of chains of bone segments linked by joints. It
comprises a total of 16 segments. We assume that each bone segment is rigid
and their shape does not change during the motion. Each segment has 6 DOFs
(degree of freedom), three of them represent position and the other three orientation.

The DOF of the articulated body model is represented by a hierarchical structure. In this structure, body segments keep a parent-child hierarchy relationship,
which is maintained by a topological tree as shown in Figure 2. The root of the
tree is the pelvis segment, which is also the Center of Mass (CoM) of the avatar.
Each segment is the child node of the parent segment, except the root segment.
The human model is driven by motion parameters, given by the data fusion subsystem, which results in the real-time animation of human motion. The motion
parameters include orientations and positions of body segments.

Animation system may be rendered using OpenGL or D3D technology, or in
Maya or OGRE.

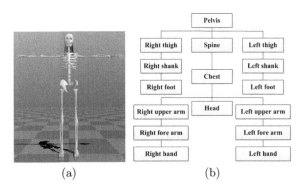

(a)   (b)

Fig. 2. The hierarchical model of the animation subsystem

4   Data Fusion Subsystem

As mentioned above, on each body segment a sensor node is fixed. The data
fusion subsystem receives sensor signals and fuses them to obtain motion information. The motion information mainly includes orientation and position of
each body segment.

The data fusion subsystem first performs cross-modality fusion, which estimates orientation quaternions from the three different modalities of sensors. This
process is accomplished by the orientation estimation. We use a quaternion to

represent the orientation of each body segment. A quaternion consists of a vector part $e = (q_1, q_2, q_3)^T \in \mathbb{R}^3$ and a scalar part $q_4 \in \mathbb{R}$, where the superscript T denotes the transpose of a vector:

$$q = (e^T, q_4)^T = \left(q_1, q_2, q_3, q_4 \right)^T \tag{1}$$

By a unit quaternion q, any given vector $r \in \mathbb{R}^3$ in the reference frame can be rotated into the sensor frame:

$$b = h(q) = C(q)r \tag{2}$$

where $b \in \mathbb{R}^3$ is the representation vector r in the sensor frame, and $C(q)$ is the orientation matrix of the transformation from the reference frame to the sensor frame:

$$C(q) = (q_4^2 - e^T e)I_3 + 2ee^T - 2q_4[e\times] \tag{3}$$

where I_3 denotes 3×3 identity matrix, and the operator $[e\times]$ represents the standard vector cross-product:

$$[e\times] = \begin{pmatrix} 0 & -q_3 & q_2 \\ q_3 & 0 & -q_1 \\ -q_2 & q_1 & 0 \end{pmatrix} \tag{4}$$

Before the analysis it is necessary to define the coordinate systems. First, there exists a Global Coordinate System (GCS) which is earth related and time invariant. GCS is taken as the reference frame. Second, a Body Coordinate System (BCS) is attached to each body segment which is time variant coinciding with segment motion. The origin of each BCS is determined by the anatomical frame and is defined in the center of the functional axes as shown in Figure 3. Third, a Sensor Coordinate System (SCS) is defined by each sensor node itself and also coincides with segment motion. For the convenience of analysis, GCS, BCS, and SCS are also denoted as the reference frame, the body frame and the sensor frame, respectively. The estimated orientation quaternions are between GCS and SCS, denoted as q_t^{GS}. The orientation quaternions employed by the displacement estimation are between GCS and BCS, denoted as q_t^{GB}. The transformation from q_t^{GS} and q_t^{GB} can be performed by the initialization process.

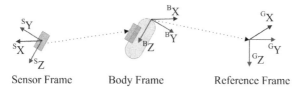

Sensor Frame   Body Frame   Reference Frame

Fig. 3. The relationship between the sensor frame, the body frame and the reference frame

Orientation estimation is a difficult work in micro-sensor based motion capture systems. Li Gang (2009) presents an estimation method[8] using UKF algorithm, but he did not take characteristics of different signal sources into consideration. As a result disturbance from single source may bring huge error for the entire system. In consideration of different characteristics of the three signal source, namely acceleration, angular rate, earth magnetic field, our system use a multi-model orientation estimation method for data fusion[9]. The randomness of human motion brings random motions of sensor nodes, as a result of which could bring different disturbances for different types of sensor node: drift errors for gyroscope; human motion acceleration for accelerometer and iron disturbance for magnetometer. Such errors make degrees of confidence distinct between sensor types. Thus multi-models for orientation estimation should be considered.

Assuming that there are N_d models sharing the same dynamic model, namely $\{M_i\}_{i=1}^{N_d}$, the model probability $P\{M_i\}$ of the N_d models should satisfy: $P\{M_i\} \geq 0$ and $\sum_{i=1}^{N_d} P\{M_i\} = 1$.

In real-time orientation estimation, posterior probability of model M_i in node $j \in \{1, ..., N_s\}$ should be calculated, where N_s is the number of nodes and $i \in \{1, ..., N_d\}$. In our system $N_s = 16$ and $N_d = 4$. Thus the posterior probability of model M_i in node j can be evaluated by equation:

$$\mu_{i,t}^{(j)} = P\left\{M_{i,t}^{(j)}|\mathbf{Y}_t\right\} = \frac{1}{c^{(j)}}\Lambda_{i,t}^{(j)}\sum_{l=1}^{N_d}p_{li}^{(j)}\mu_{l,t-1}^{(j)} \tag{5}$$

$$c^{(j)} = \sum_{i=1}^{N_d}\Lambda_{i,t}^{(j)}\sum_{l=1}^{N_d}p_{li}^{(j)}\mu_{l,t-1}^{(j)} \tag{6}$$

where $i \in \{1, ..., N_d\}$ is index of different models;$j \in \{1, ..., N_s\}$ is node index; $\mathbf{Y}_t = \{\mathbf{y}_1, ..., \mathbf{y}_t\}$, $\mathbf{y}_t$ is the sensor observation in time t ; $M_{i,t}^j$ denotes that node j uses model i at time t . $\mu_{i,t}^{(j)}$ is posterior probability of model M_i in node j ; $p_{li}^{(j)}$ is the transforming probability form model l to model i :

$$p_{li}^{(j)} = P\left\{M_{i,t}^{(j)}|M_{l,t-1}^{(j)}, \mathbf{Y}_{t-1}\right\} \tag{7}$$

$\Lambda_{i,t}^{(j)}$ is the likelihood of model i in node j at time t:

$$\Lambda_{i,t}^{(j)} = P\left\{\mathbf{y}_t^{(j)}|M_{i,t}^{(j)}, \mathbf{Y}_{t-1}\right\} \tag{8}$$

To estimate accurate orientation, the likelihood and posterior probability mentioned above must be obtained. Assuming that orientation of model i in node j at time t is $^{GS}q_{i,t}^{(j)}$ and $i \in \{1, ..., N_d\}$, $j \in \{1, ..., N_s\}$, superscript GS denotes frame transformation from global frame to sensor frame. Quaternion q should satisfy:

$$\frac{d}{dt}\mathbf{q} = \frac{1}{2}\mathbf{\Omega}[\boldsymbol{\omega}]\mathbf{q} \tag{9}$$

where $\boldsymbol{\Omega}[\boldsymbol{\omega}]$ is a 4×4 skew matrix:

$$\boldsymbol{\Omega}[\boldsymbol{\omega}] = \begin{pmatrix} -[\boldsymbol{\omega}\times] & \boldsymbol{\omega} \\ -\boldsymbol{\omega}^T & 0 \end{pmatrix} \tag{10}$$

$\boldsymbol{\omega}$ is the angular velocity:

$$\boldsymbol{\omega} = \left(\omega_x, \omega_y, \omega_z \right)^T \tag{11}$$

operator $[\boldsymbol{\omega}\times]$ represents the standard vector cross-product in equation (4).

Among three type of measurement units, gyroscope measures angular rate mixed with bias and noise, the observation of node $j \in \{1, ..., N_s\}$ is:

$$\boldsymbol{y}_{G,t}^{(j)} = \boldsymbol{\omega}_t^{(j)} + \boldsymbol{h}_{G,t}^{(j)} + \boldsymbol{v}_{G,t}^{(j)} \tag{12}$$

where G, t means gyroscope observation at time t ; $\boldsymbol{v}_{G,t}^{(j)}$ is gyroscope noise, assuming zero-mean Gaussian noise following distribution $N(\boldsymbol{0}, \boldsymbol{\Sigma}_G^{(j)})$ here; $\boldsymbol{h}_{G,t}^{(j)}$ is bias vector. As bias of gyroscope varies slowly with respect to its observation, we model $\boldsymbol{h}_{G,t}^{(j)}$ as a random walk model:

$$\boldsymbol{h}_{G,t}^{(j)} = \boldsymbol{h}_{G,t-1}^{(j)} + \boldsymbol{w}_{h,t}^{(j)} \tag{13}$$

where $\boldsymbol{w}_{h,t}^{(j)}$ is zero-mean Gaussian white noise.

Then we can get dynamic system equation: system state vector $\boldsymbol{x}_{i,t}^{(j)}$ of model i in node j at time t consists of quaternion $^{GS}\boldsymbol{q}_{i,t}^{(j)}$ and bias $\boldsymbol{h}_{G,t}^{(j)}$:

$$\boldsymbol{x}_{i,t}^{(j)} = \begin{pmatrix} ^{GS}\boldsymbol{q}_{i,t}^{(j)} \\ \boldsymbol{h}_{G,t}^{(j)} \end{pmatrix} \tag{14}$$

the state equation is:

$$\begin{aligned} \boldsymbol{x}_{i,t}^{(j)} &= f_{i,t}^{(j)} \left(\boldsymbol{x}_{i,t}^{(j)} \right) + \boldsymbol{w}_{i,t}^{(j)} \\ &= \begin{pmatrix} \exp\left(\tfrac{1}{2}\boldsymbol{\Omega}[\boldsymbol{y}_{G,t}^{(j)} - \boldsymbol{h}_{G,t}^{(j)}]\Delta \right) & \boldsymbol{O}_{4\times3} \\ \boldsymbol{O}_{3\times4} & \boldsymbol{I}_3 \end{pmatrix} \cdot \boldsymbol{x}_{i,t}^{(j)} + \begin{pmatrix} \boldsymbol{w}_{q,i,t}^{(j)} \\ \boldsymbol{w}_{h,t}^{(j)} \end{pmatrix} \end{aligned} \tag{15}$$

The observation of gyroscope is the input of system dynamic model, as a result of which quaternion orientation estimation is updated using real-time observation without any lag.

Among three types of measurement units, magnetometers measure earth magnetic field mixed with noise and magnetic distortion:

$$\boldsymbol{y}_{M,t}^{(j)} = \boldsymbol{B}_{M,t}^{(j)} + \boldsymbol{H}_{M,t}^{(j)} + \boldsymbol{V}_{M,t}^{(j)} \tag{16}$$

where M, t denotes magnetometer observation at time t ; $\boldsymbol{V}_{M,t}^{(j)}$ is observation noise of magnetometers; $\boldsymbol{H}_{M,t}^{(j)}$ is magnetic distortion caused by soft or hard iron disturbances; $\boldsymbol{B}_{M,t}^{(j)}$ is earth magnetic field vector on sensor frame.

Noticed that $\boldsymbol{y}_{M,t}^{(j)}$ consists of magnitude as well as direction information, and only direction useful for orientation estimation. Furthermore, its magnitude information may lead error in orientation estimation. Thus normalization of equation (16) should be performed. Moreover, for the sake of multi-model estimation, bias $\boldsymbol{H}_{M,t}^{(j)}$ should be put into noise:

$$z_{M,i,t}^{(j)} = b_{M,i,t}^{(j)} + v_{M,i,t}^{(j)} \tag{17}$$

where $\boldsymbol{v}_{M,i,t}^{(j)}$ is normalized magnetometer observation noise of model i in node j at time t , which is modeled as Gaussian distribution $N(\mathbf{0}, \boldsymbol{\Sigma}_{M}^{(j)})$; $\boldsymbol{b}_{M,i,t}^{(j)}$ is earth magnetic field vector on sensor frame. Given a quaternion $\boldsymbol{q}_{i,t}^{(j)}$ and earth magnetic field vector on certain frame $\boldsymbol{r}_M$, magnetometer measurement $\boldsymbol{b}_{M,i,t}^{(j)}$ should be evaluated through:

$$b_{M,i,t}^{(j)} = C\left(q_{i,t}^{(j)}\right) \cdot r_M \tag{18}$$

Thus observation equation of magnetometer is:

$$z_{M,i,t}^{(j)} = C\left(q_{i,t}^{(j)}\right) \cdot r_M + v_{M,i,t}^{(j)} \tag{19}$$

Similarly, for accelerometer we have:

$$y_{A,t}^{(j)} = C\left(q_{i,t}^{(j)}\right) \cdot r_A + H_{A,t}^{(j)} + V_{A,t}^{(j)} \tag{20}$$

where A, t denotes accelerometer observation at time t ; $\boldsymbol{V}_{A,t}^{(j)}$ is observation noise of accelerometer; $\boldsymbol{H}_{A,t}^{(j)}$ is human motion acceleration; $\boldsymbol{r}_A$ is earth gravity acceleration measurement on sensor frame.

Noticed that $\boldsymbol{y}_{A,t}^{(j)}$ consists of magnitude as well as direction information, and only direction useful for orientation estimation. Furthermore, its magnitude information may lead error in orientation estimation. Thus normalization of equation (20) should be performed. Moreover, for the sake of multi-model estimation, bias $\boldsymbol{H}_{A,t}^{(j)}$ should be put into noise:

$$z_{A,i,t}^{(j)} = \frac{y_{A,t}^{(j)}}{g} = C\left(q_{i,t}^{(j)}\right)\left(\frac{r_A}{g}\right) + v_{A,i,t}^{(j)} \tag{21}$$

where $\boldsymbol{v}_{A,i,t}^{(j)}$ is normalized accelerometer observation noise of model i in node j at time t , which is modeled as Gaussian distribution $N(\mathbf{0}, \boldsymbol{\Sigma}_{A}^{(j)})$; g is earth gravity acceleration vector on sensor frame.

Then, system observation equation could be conducted. Assume that system observation is $\boldsymbol{z}_{i,t}^{(j)}$:

$$
\begin{aligned}
z_{i,t}^{(j)} = \begin{pmatrix} z_{M,i,t}^{(j)} \\ z_{A,i,t}^{(j)} \end{pmatrix} &= g_{i,t}^{(j)}\left(x_{i,t}^{(j)}\right) + v_{i,t}^{(j)} \\
&= \begin{pmatrix} C(q_{i,t}^{(j)}) & O_{3\times 3} \\ O_{3\times 3} & C(q_{i,t}^{(j)}) \end{pmatrix} \cdot \begin{pmatrix} r_M \\ \frac{r_A}{g} \end{pmatrix} + \begin{pmatrix} v_{M,i,t}^{(j)} \\ v_{A,i,t}^{(j)} \end{pmatrix}
\end{aligned}
\tag{22}
$$

Assuming that $v_{M,i,t}$ does not correlate with $v_{A,i,t}$, system observation noise covariance matrix $R_t = \begin{pmatrix} \Sigma_{M,i,t}^{(j)} & O_{3\times3} \\ O_{3\times3} & \Sigma_{A,i,t}^{(j)} \end{pmatrix}$

Using equation (22) and (15) $\mu_{i,t}^{(j)} = P\left\{M_{i,t}^{(j)}|Y_t\right\}$ could be evaluated. The final orientation $^{GS}q_t^{(j)}$ is estimated through:

$$^{GS}q_t^{(j)} = \sum_{i=1}^{N_d} {}^{GS}q_{i,t}^{(j)} \cdot \mu_{i,t}^{(j)} \tag{23}$$

5   Experimental Results

Experiment investigates the accuracy of our orientation system in contrast with optical motion capture system. As is shown in Fig 4, human lower limbs movements are captured by our MMocap system and Osprey optical system[10]. Osprey optical system captures human motion using six cameras in 2m × 3m space. In our contrast experiment, optical markers and micro-sensors are fixed on human waist, thigh and calf, and both systems capture human motion with 100Hz sample rate. There are three scenes in our experiments:

1. *Scene I:* running forward, backward and jump aside repeatedly with left, right and back turning.
2. *Scene II:* jumping forward repeatedly with back turning.
3. *Scene III:* walking forward, backward and step aside repeatedly with left, right and back turning.

Each scene are sample over 30s for over 5 times. For the convenience of evaluation, quaternions from fusion methods are transformed into degrees. The estimation

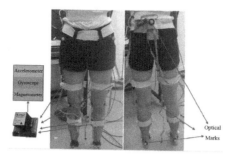

Fig. 4. Contrast experiment between our system and optical system

Table 1. RMSE of MMocap System: mean *pm* standard deviation

Scene	Scene I	Scene II	Scene III
Angle (deg)	2.66 ± 2.56	2.42 ± 1.84	2.44 ± 2.34
Displacement (m)	0.0707 ± 0.0469	0.1673 ± 0.0656	0.0990 ± 0.0374

RMSE of MMocap system to optical system is summarized in Table 1. It can be seen that, unlike other methods, the orientation error of our method does not increase much when the motion acceleration grows. From the comparison of these results, our algorithm has shown its accuracy, stability and efficiency.

Acknowledgement. This paper is supported by the National Natural Science Foundation of China (Grant No. 60932001), and partially supported by CSIDM project 200802.

References

1. Vicon, http://www.vicon.com
2. Gypsy Motion Capture System, http://www.metamotion.com
3. Vlasic, D., Adelsberger, R., Vannucci, G., Barnwell, J., Gross, M., Matusik, W., Popovic, J.: Practical motion capture in everyday surroundings. ACM Transactions on Graphics (TOG) 26(3) (July 2007)
4. Verhaert's ALERT system, http://www.verhaert.com/
5. MotionStar Motion Capture System, http://www.vrealities.com/motionstar.html
6. Priyantha, N., Chakraborty, A., Balakrishnan, H.: The cricket location-support system. In: International Conference on Mobile Computing and Networking, pp. 32–43 (2000)
7. Randell, C., Muller, H.: Low Cost Indoor Positioning System. In: Abowd, G.D., Brumitt, B., Shafer, S.A.N. (eds.) UbiComp 2001. LNCS, vol. 2201, pp. 42–48. Springer, Heidelberg (2001)
8. Li, G., Wu, Z., Wu, J.-K.(n.d.): Micro-sensor driven human model for 3D real-time movement. Journal of Computer Applications 12 (2009)
9. Chen, J., Sun, S., Tao, G., Wu, J. (n.d.): Multi-model Orientation Estimation by Fusion of Micro Sensory Data. Measurement, 4–7
10. Osprey System, http://www.motionanalysis.com/html/movement/osprey.html

Periodic Data Prediction Algorithm in Wireless Sensor Networks

Jijun Zhao*, Hao Liu, Zhihua Li, and Wei Li

School of Information and Electric Engineering,
Hebei University of Engineering, Hebei 056038, China
zjijun@gmail.com, {liuhao.white,li56qi}@163.com, yl_sandy@sina.com

Abstract. Data prediction has been emerged as an important way to reduce the number of transmissions in wireless sensor networks(WSNs). This paper proposes a periodic data prediction algorithm called P-DPA in WSNs. The P-DPA takes the potential law hidden in periodicity as a reference to adjust the data prediction, which helps to improve the accuracy of prediction algorithm. The experiments of temperature, humidity and light intensity based on the dataset which comes from the actual data collected from 54 sensors deployed in the Intel Berkeley Research lab proved that the P-DPA has an obvious enhancement to the existing data prediction algorithms.

Keywords: WSNs, prediction algorithm, auto regression, periodicity.

1   Introduction

Wireless sensor networks (WSNs) consist of a set of autonomous sensor nodes which spontaneously create impromptu communication networks. A sensor node includes a small memory, a low-performance processing unit, several sensors for measuring physical phenomena, a short-range wireless communication device and a limited-power battery [1]. In recent years, WSNs technologies broadly applied in military surveillance and target tracking, ecological habitat monitoring, industrial and agricultural, etc. However, due to the limits of restricted power and computational capabilities, power consumption becomes a major issue in WSNs. Data aggregation has been emerged as a basic approach in order to reduce the number of transmissions of sensor nodes [2].

Data collected from WSNs represent the characteristics of multi-source and multi-attribute with the extending of the scale of WSNs and the increasing of WSNs applications [3]. Multi-source is constituted of information source nodes

---

* Jijun Zhao received his PhD degree in Electromagnetic Field and Microwave Technique from Beijing University of Posts and Telecommunications(BUPT), Beijing, China, in 2003. He was a postdoctoral researcher at the ZTE Corporation(ZTE). He is now a Professor in Hebei University of Engineering, Handan, China. His current research interest includes broadband communication networks and wireless sensor network. He is also a member of ACM.

R. Wang and F. Xiao (Eds.): CWSN 2012, CCIS 334, pp. 695–701, 2013.
© Springer-Verlag Berlin Heidelberg 2013

spatially scattered in the network, and spatially proximal sensor observations are highly correlated due to high density in the network [4]. As such, data aggregation scheduling techniques emerge to exploit the spatial correlation and routing protocol in order to improve the quality of WSNs. Multi-attribute means different types of sensors, in which hidden correlations exist. These correlations inherently exist in nature (e.g. temperature, light and CO_2 mutually affect each other in photosynthesis), or can be calculated and evaluated through mathematical methods [5][6] (e.g. entropy function, covariance function). Besides, the correlation between each consecutive observation of a sensor node constitutes the temporal correlation [4], which is utilized to predict the next time's sample value of a node, the prediction takes a node's historic sample values as input and utilizes a kind of algorithm such as time series algorithms [7]/Gene Expression Programming [8]/BP neutral network [9] to output a prediction value. When the difference between prediction value and actual value is under the threshold, the data transmission is canceled to save energy consumption.

In this work, an algorithm based on a linear regression model called P-DPA(Periodic Data Prediction Algorithm)is proposed, whose main goal is to introduce the potential law hidden in periodicity into the predict algorithm in WSNs. By doing this, P-DPA reduces communication frequency in WSNs and consequently prolong network's lifetime.

The remainder of this paper is broken into parts. In Section 2 we discuss related work and point out the novelty of our approach. In Section 3 we describe P-DPA in detail. In Section 4 we examine the algorithm based on the actual dataset. Finally, the paper ends with conclusions and discussion for future work.

2   Related Works

Temporal-spatial correlation and data aggregation scheduling in WSNs are well studied in recent years. Temporal correlation encourages the research of WSNs prediction technique which already make great breakthrough in reducing energy consumption of WSNs.

For most of WSNs applications, consecutive observations of a single node in WSNs are similar or proximate to a certain extent with time. In [10], Kusuma et al. defined temporal correlation first in 2001: The nature of the energy-radiating physical phenomenon constitutes the temporal correlation between each consecutive observation of a sensor node. After that, Madden et al. proposed a TAG [11] (Tiny AGgregation) framework reducing data transmission by introducing the concept of temporal consistency. As the extension of TAG, TiNA [12] (Temporal coherency-aware In- Network Aggregation) make sensor nodes compare the current sampled-data with that of previous period in each sampling period, and they will not transmit data if the difference less than the threshold defined by users. But it will be effective only when the neighboring sampled data are close to each other. Later, a developed prediction model is proposed in [13], which maintains a pair of dynamic prediction models, one of the model is deployed in the nodes of networks and another is deployed in the base stations. Both models update actual sampled data to keep synchronization when the prediction is failed. However, the algorithm is limited since the probabilistic model is getting more and more complicated with the expansion of network scale. This double prediction model becomes a mature framework of data prediction techniques of WSNs.

Data prediction algorithms have been proposed in some papers to be used as an efficient strategy to reduce the data transmission in WSNs. Several works [7][14][15] are based on time series algorithms including auto regressive prediction algorithm, moving average prediction algorithm and exponential smoothing prediction algorithm. In [7], HUI utilizes seven algorithms in three types to test the success rate of prediction algorithms. The simulation take temperature data collected from environment monitoring network deployed in Palace Museum in three months as input. Results show that auto regressive prediction algorithm has the best performance, whose prediction success rate is 83% when the threshold is 0.5 . Furthermore, in order to improve the accuracy of algorithm, Guo et al. utilize GEP (Gene Expression Programming) algorithm [8] and PSO-BPNN (Particle Swarm Optimization-BP Neural Network) algorithm [9] to predict data in WSNs, in which the performance shows a certain progress but brings high complexity. However, finding out potential laws according to these time-series are valuable for us to research and discuss.

For the issues above, we propose a new data prediction algorithm with potential laws hidden in periodic attributes based on the auto regressive prediction algorithm, and take auto regressive prediction algorithm as a comparison.

3   Our Proposed Algorithm

As we know, temporal correlation is appeared in two sides, one is the data correlation caused by consecutive samplings, which is already defined and widely used in data prediction, the other one is the similarity of data curve shape of adjacent period (e.g. temperature, humidity, light are periodically change by a day), which could be a reference in data prediction and improve the accuracy of algorithm. This improvement is helpful to WSNs systems involved with periodic nature phenomenon. To the best of our knowledge, there is no research taking notice of the periodic temporal correlation.

In this paper, the double prediction model is adopted, one of the models is deployed in the nodes of networks and another is deployed in the base stations, the two models are same. The node does not transmit data to base station when the node's prediction successes while the base station takes its own prediction value which equals to the value of node's prediction. Both models update actual sampled data to keep synchronization when the prediction is failed.

As shown in Fig. 1, in each period, sensor nodes predict new data according to historical data. Our proposed algorithm takes a first-prediction based on auto regression algorithm, and then evaluates the data change direction of current period and previous period. After comparing these two parameters, the piecewise function chooses the manner of adjusting the predictive value and returns it to finish the second-prediction. When nodes get the sampled data, compare the predict one with the actual sampled, if the error of prediction is in the range predefined by users, there is no need to send data to base station, and just wait for the next sampling period; otherwise, update the prediction model and send sampled-data to base station.

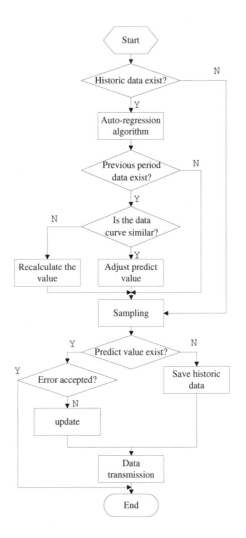

Fig. 1. Algorithm flow chart

The detailed procedure of the algorithm proposed in this paper is as follows. First we define parameters of this algorithm: t is the current time, $t+1$ is the next sampling time. The sampled data sequence of t is normal$\{y_1, y_2, ...y_t\}$, we can use a first-order AR (auto regression) prediction algorithm, so the predicted value of time $t+1$ is:

$$y_{t+1} = \varphi_1 y_t + \alpha_{t+1} \tag{1}$$

And

$$\varphi_1 = \hat{\rho_1} = \frac{N}{N-1} \frac{\sum_{t=2}^{N} y_t y_{t-1}}{\sum_{t=1}^{N} y_t^2} \tag{2}$$

Where $\hat{\rho}$ denotes the sample autocorrelation function and α_{t+1} denotes the stochastic disturbance of $t+1$ sampling time while N denotes the number of historic data.

Next, algorithm chooses the manner of adjusting the predictive value according to the degree of data curve's fitness between current period and previous period. The piecewise function is as bellow:

$$\begin{cases} y_{t+1} = (0.8k + 0.2k') + \alpha_{t+1} \, , \, (k-1)(k'-1) \geq 0 \\ y_{t+1} = k'y_t + \alpha_{t+1} \qquad\qquad , \, (k-1)(k'-1) < 0 \end{cases} \tag{3}$$

Where k denotes the current slope coefficient of data curve and k' denotes slope coefficient of data curve of previous period. The 0.8 and 0.2 is the weight coefficient of k and k' which is fixed by lots of experiment contrast.

4   Experimental Results

This P-DPA algorithm is implemented in MATLAB. We adopt the dataset which comes from the actual data collected from 54 sensors deployed in the Intel Berkeley Research lab. The dataset contains four different attributes: temperature, humidity, light and voltage. We simulate the prediction of temperature, humidity and light intensity but abandon voltage because it is not the environment monitoring target. We compare AR with P-DPA in the algorithm's success rate of different thresholds and different attributes to prove the enhancement of P-DPA as described in Fig. 2. We pick 18 periods' data with 48 data in each period for each attribute.

Obviously, P-DPA has a great enhancement compared with AR in temperature and humidity, and a smaller enhancement in light intensity which clearly exemplifies the advantages of P-DPA. Neither of the prediction algorithms in our paper can efficiently predict the light intensity because of its high variability. But if the dataset is processed with logarithmic functions, P-DPA will be more effective in prediction of light intensity.

Fig. 3 illustrates part of the temperature prediction results, which contains actual value, AR prediction value and P-DPA prediction value. The number of failures of prediction made by P-DPA is less than AR. Fig. 4 illustrates the temperature deviation of AR prediction and P-DPA prediction, as can be seen, the red is closer to the zero-line than the black on the whole. Correspond to Fig.4, the mean deviation of AR is 0.545293 while the mean deviation of P-DPA is 0.422873. This further confirms the enhancement of P-DPA algorithm.

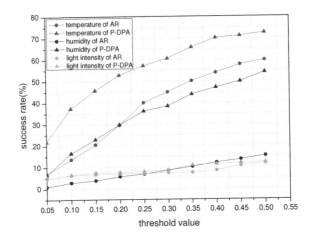

Fig. 2. Comparison of the success rate of prediction results

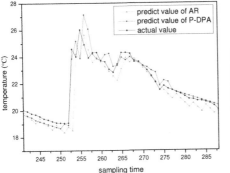

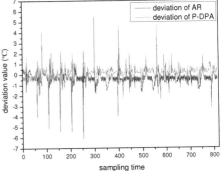

Fig. 3. Part of temperature prediction results

Fig. 4. Temperature deviation of prediction results

5   Conclusions and Discussion

In this paper, we proposed a periodic data prediction algorithm in WSNs, after
the first prediction by AR algorithm, P-DPA takes the useful information of the
potential law hidden in periodicity as a guide to adjust the prediction values. The
experiments based on the data from Intel Berkeley Research lab show that the
proposed algorithm provides a good performance. In the future, we will explore
the attribute correlation and find out how to utilize it in decreasing the energy
consumption.

References

1. Yick, J., Mukherjee, B., Ghosal, D.: Wireless sensor network survey. Computer Networks 52(12), 2292–2330 (2008)
2. Pandey, V., Kaur, A., Chand, N.: A review on data aggregation techniques in wireless sensor network. Journal of Electronic and Electrical Engineering 1(2), 01–08 (2010)
3. Xiang, M., Shi, W.-R.: A cluster data management algorithm based on data correlation of wireless sensor networks. Acta Automatica Sinica 36(9), 1343–1350 (2010)
4. Vuran, M.C., Akan, Ö.B., Akyildiz, I.F.: Spatio-temporal correlation: theory and applications for wireless sensor networks. Computer Networks 45(3), 245–259 (2004)
5. Dong, C., Xiuquan, Q., et al.: Mining data correlation from multi-faceted sensor data in the Internet of Things. China Communications 8(1), 132–138 (2011)
6. Ding, C., Peng, H.: Minimum redundancy feature selection from microarray gene expression data. Journal of Bioinformatics and Computational Biology 3(2), 185–205 (2005)
7. Hui, C.-L., Cui, L.: Forecast-based temporal data aggregation in wireless sensor networks. Computer Engineering and Applications 43(21), 121–125 (2007)
8. Gao, H., Guo, W., et al.: Multi-source temporal data aggregation in wireless sensor networks based on gene expression programming. Computer Engineering & Science 31(9), 28–31 (2009)
9. Guo, W., Xiong, N., Vasilakos, A.V., et al.: Multi-source temporal data aggregation in wireless sensor networks. Wireless personal communications 56(3), 359–370 (2010)
10. Kusuma, J., Doherty, L., Ramchandran, K.: Distributed compression for sensor networks. In: Proc. Image Processing 2001, Thessaloniki, Greece, pp. 82–85 (2001)
11. Madden, S., Franklin, M.J., et al.: Tag: a tiny aggregation service for ad-hoc sensor networks. ACM SIGOPS Operating Systems Review 36(SI), 131–146 (2002)
12. Sharaf, M.A., Beaver, J., Labrinidis, A., et al.: TiNA: a scheme for temporal coherency aware in network aggregation. In: Proc. the Third ACM International Workshop on Data Engineering for Wireless and Mobile Access, San Diego, USA, pp. 69–76 (2003)
13. Chu, D., Deshpande, A., et al.: Approximate data collection in sensor networks using probabilistic models. In: Proc. the 22nd International Conference on Data Engineering, Atlanta, USA, pp. 48–53 (2006)
14. Deligiannakis, A., Kotidis, Y., Roussopoulos, N.: Processing approximate aggregate queries in wireless sensor networks. Information Systems 31(8), 770–792 (2006)
15. Guestrin, C., Bodik, P., Thibaux, R., et al.: Distributed regression: an efficient framework for modeling sensor networks. In: Proc. the Third International Symposium on IPSN, Berkeley, USA, pp. 1–10 (2004)

Filtering Algorithms for Chirp-Spread-Spectrum Ranging

Dong Zheng and Jiuzhen Liang

School of IoT Engineering, Jiangnan University, Wuxi 214122, China
dongzh86@live.cn, jz.liang@yahoo.com.cn

Abstract. The wireless networks based on the IEEE 802.15.4a CSS (chirp-spread-spectrum) PHY are expected to provide accurate ranging. However, the problem is that the measured distances are not only noisy but also biased, which becomes more serious in non-line-of-sight situation. To improve the accuracy of ranging, two methods are used to estimate the positive bias, including state augmentation technique and separate-bias estimation. Then the bias estimation can be used to correct the measured distance. Experiments conducted with Nanotron CSS wireless nodes in indoor-environment validate the algorithm actually. The effectiveness and features of the filtering algorithms are analyzed with the support of the experiment results.

Keywords: IEEE 802.15.4a, ranging, Chirp-spread-spectrum (CSS), positive bias, state augmentation, separate-bias estimation.

1 Introduction

There is much interest within the wireless communications research community in the implementing of real-time locating system (RTLS) which is still a challenging problem, especially indoors where a global positioning system cannot be used. At present, many indoor localization systems have been developed based on different wireless measurements: received signal strength (RSS) [1,2], time of arrival (TOA) [3], and time difference of arrival (TDOA) [4]. Ranging technique, which is used to obtain the distance between two nodes, is the most fundamental and important technology in developing an RTLS system.

Chirp-spread-spectrum (CSS) is defined in the standard IEEE 802.15.4a and is able to measure the distance between a pair of CSS nodes [5,6]. For high precision ranging, the symmetric double-side two-way ranging (SDS-TWR) method has been adopted by the CSS-based wireless networks [5]. SDS-TWR is based on the TOA measurement, and it can effectively reduce the error influence due to the clock frequency error of the wireless network nodes between which the clock synchronization is not required. However, the distance information got by CSS ranging still contains errors owing to other factors such as multipath fading, non-line-of-sight (NLOS) and other phenomenon existed in the radio signals propagation. The mean of these errors is nonzero [5], which leads to the problem that the measured distances are not only noisy but also biased. Because

R. Wang and F. Xiao (Eds.): CWSN 2012, CCIS 334, pp. 702–714, 2013.
© Springer-Verlag Berlin Heidelberg 2013

we do not know the true distance between a pair of CSS nodes, decomposing a measured distance with bias into the true distance and a bias term is hardly possible. However, we can reduce the effect of the bias by using algorithms to estimate the bias term [7].

We conclude three methods to estimate the TOA measurement bias and reduce its effect. Firstly, the bias can be treated totally as NLOS error which can be identified and mitigated by using classic NLOS identification and mitigation method such as in [6,8,9]. Secondly, the bias can be treated as system state with the method of augmented state [7,10]. Thirdly, the measurement bias can be estimated as system output bias with the method of separate-bias estimation.

In fact, in the case of the line of sight (LOS), the TOA measurements based on CSS networks still contain nonzero mean bias [5], which is caused by multipath fading [6].what is more, the bias is positive and time-varying. Based on the above considerations, we used the latter two methods to deal with the positive bias of the ranging values. According to the state augmentation technique, the positive bias could be estimated as an extended state with the self-adaption extended Kalman Filter (EKF), and the changes of bias could be treated as the result of system noise. On the other hand, the positive bias could be estimated as system output bias with separate-bias estimation algorithm, and the changes of bias could be treated as the result of the mismatch in system process models, then the measured distance could be corrected with the estimation of the positive bias.

2   Overview of the Kalman Filter

In this section, we give an overview of the Kalman filter which serves as the base of the filtering algorithms designed in this paper. The notations and equations defined in this section will be used throughout the paper.

The Kalman filter addresses the general problem of trying to estimate the state $x \in R^{n_0}$ of a discrete-time controlled system that is governed by the linear stochastic difference equation

$$x_{n+1} = Ax_n + Bu_{n+1} + w_{n+1} \tag{1}$$

with a measurement $y \in R^{m_0}$ that is

$$y_{n+1} = Hx_{n+1} + v_{n+1} \tag{2}$$

The random variables w_{n+1} and v_{n+1} represent the system and measurement noise respectively, and they are assumed to be uncorrelated zero-mean white noise with autocorrelation matrices Q and R. The $n_0 \times n_0$ matrix A in the difference equation 1 relates the state at the previous time step n to the state at the current step $n+1$ in the absence of either a driving function or system noise. The $n_0 \times l_0$ matrix B relates the optional control input $u \in R^{l_0}$ to the state x. The $m_0 \times n_0$ matrix H in the measurement equation 2 relates the state to the measurement y. The difference equation 1 is a mathematical expression of the target system dynamics, and the measurement equation 2 represents the relationship between the states of the system and measurements generally obtained by sensory devices. The equations for the Kalman filter fall into two groups: time update equations and measurement update equations. Mathematically, the Kalman filter corresponding to equation 1 and 2 is given as recursive update equations for $n = 0, 1, 2, \cdots$:

1. Time update

$$\hat{x}_{n+1}^- = A\hat{x}_n + Bu_{n+1} \tag{3}$$

$$p_{n+1}^- = Ap_n A^T + Q \tag{4}$$

2. Measurement update

$$k_{n+1} = p_{n+1}^- H^T / (Hp_{n+1}^- H^T + R) \tag{5}$$

$$\hat{x}_{n+1} = \hat{x}_{n+1}^- + k_{n+1}(y_{n+1} - H\hat{x}_{n+1}^-) \tag{6}$$

$$p_{n+1} = (I - k_{n+1}H) p_{n+1}^- \tag{7}$$

The vectors $\hat{x}_{n+1}^-$ and $\hat{x}_{n+1}$ are the predicted state vector from the time update and the filtered state from the measurement update. The matrices p_{n+1}^- and p_{n+1}^- are the estimate error covariance of $\hat{x}_{n+1}^-$ and $\hat{x}_{n+1}$, respectively, and they are updated for the calculation of the Kalman gain k_{n+1}.

3   Filtering Algorithm Based on State Augmentation

As mentioned in section 1, in reality, the measured distance obtained from the CSS system contains positive bias. To reduce the estimation errors, it is a common practice to augment the state vector of the original problem by adding additional components to represent the uncertain parameters, which are conveniently designated as bias terms [11]. The filter then estimates the bias terms as well as those of the original problem .

As described above in section 2, the Kalman filter addresses the general problem of trying to estimate the state of a discrete-time controlled system that is governed by the linear stochastic difference equation. When the system to be estimated and (or) the measurement relationship to the system is non-linear, we can linearize the estimation around the current estimate using the partial derivatives of the system and measurement functions to compute estimates even in the face of non-linear relationships, in something akin to a Taylor series. A Kalman filter that linearizes about the current mean and covariance is referred to as an extended Kalman filter.

In this section, we adopt state augmentation technique as well as the extended Kalman filter to design the filter for CSS ranging. Our work of this part is based on the algorithm proposed by Hyeonwoo Cho et al. [7], and we mend their algorithm to improve the performance. We improve the original algorithm as follows:

1. Adjust the autocorrelation matrices of the system noise online according to the bias changes to improve the algorithms robustness.
2. Restrict the estimated value range of the bias to solve the problem that the estimated value would be negative in original algorithm (the bias must be positive in practice).
3. Through lots of CSS ranging experiments, we give a simple but effective method to estimate the initial state according to the initial measurement, since the initial state has a considerable influence on the performance of the state augmentation technique.

3.1   EKF with State Augmentation Technique

When the real distance is a fixed value, following the deduction of [7] the system can be expressed as follows

$$x_{n+1} = Ax_n + w_{n+1} \tag{8}$$

$$y_{n+1} = H_{n+1}x_{n+1} + v_{n+1} \tag{9}$$

where $A = I$ is the state transition matrix, and H is the measurement matrix. The random variables w_{n+1} and v_{n+1} represent the system and measurement noise respectively, and they are assumed to be uncorrelated zero-mean white noise with autocorrelation matrices Q and R. The augmented state vector and system noise are defined as follows:

$$x_n = \begin{bmatrix} d_n \\ r_n \end{bmatrix} \tag{10}$$

$$w_{n+1} = \begin{bmatrix} \delta_n \\ \tau_n \end{bmatrix} \tag{11}$$

where d_n is the distance between the anchor node and mobile node, and δ_n is the system noise of the distance; r_n is the scaling factor, and τ_n is the system noise of the scaling factor. Consequently, the measurement equation 9 can be rewritten as

$$y_n = d_n + r_n d_n + v_n \tag{12}$$

and H_n can be rewritten by linearize the estimation around the current estimate using the partial derivatives of the measurement functions as

$$H_n = [1 + r_n, d_n] \tag{13}$$

3.2   Adjust the Variance of the System Noise

In [7], the system noise of the scaling factor is assumed as zero-mean white noise. However, τ_n is not stationary in fact when the NLOS situation is considered and the inappropriate assumption of τ_n may cause significant performance deterioration. Therefore, we adopt the method similar to the Biased Kalman filter to adjust the variance η of the system noise online to improve the algorithms robustness.

There are two different techniques for variance online-adjustment to choose from and the details of them are described as follows:

1. We can utilize the residual r_n which can be expressed as

$$e_n = \hat{r}_n - \hat{r}_{n-1} \tag{14}$$

then increase variance η if the residual is larger than a threshold

$$\eta = \begin{cases} \eta, & e_n \leq e_{lim} \\ \alpha e_n \eta, & e_n > e_{lim} \end{cases} \tag{15}$$

where e_{lim} is the threshold which can be obtained experimentally and α also can be can be find out experimentally to give a good performance.

2. The second techniques use the standard deviation of the estimation of r_n. The standard deviation θ of the estimation of r_n can be calculated in the floating window. Then according to the value of θ to determine whether and how to change the variance η of the system noise.

$$\eta = \begin{cases} \eta, & \eta/\gamma \leq \theta \leq \eta\gamma \\ \beta\eta, & \theta > \eta\gamma \\ \eta/\beta, & \theta < \eta/\gamma \end{cases} \tag{16}$$

the parameters $\beta > 1, \gamma > 1$, can be find out experimentally, as well as the parameter k which represents the size of the floating window.

3.3   Improve the Performance with Prior Knowledge

The estimated value of the bias r_n would be negative in original algorithm proposed in [7], which does not accord with the facts in any way. Therefore, we can restrict the estimated value range of the bias in a simple manner as follows:

$$\eta = \begin{cases} \hat{r}_n, & \hat{r}_n > 0 \\ 0, & \hat{r}_n \leq 0 \end{cases} \tag{17}$$

Whats more, we give a simple but effective method to estimate the initial state according to the initial measurement, since the initial state has a considerable influence on the performance of the state augmentation technique. Through lots of CSS ranging experiments, we find the relationship between the initial state and the initial measurement:

$$d_0 = \begin{cases} y_0 - 1.85, & y_0 > 3.7 \\ y_0/2, & y_0 \leq 3.7 \end{cases} \tag{18}$$

4   Filtering Algorithm Based on Separate-Bias Estimation

4.1   Estimation of a Constant-Bias Vector

The famous separate-bias estimation algorithm was proposed by Friedland [11] to estimate the state of a linear system influenced by a constant but unknown bias. This class of linear systems can be expressed as follows:

$$x_{n+1} = Ax_n + Bu_{n+1} + w_{n+1} \tag{19}$$

$$b_{n+1} = b_n \tag{20}$$

$$y_{n+1} = Hx_{n+1} + Db_{n+1} + v_{n+1} \tag{21}$$

where A is the state transition matrix, H is the measurement matrix and D is the bias matrix. The random variables w_{n+1} and v_{n+1} represent the system and measurement noise respectively, and are assumed to be uncorrelated zero-mean white noise with autocorrelation matrices Q and R. The vectors x_{n+1} and b_{n+1} represent the system state and the measurement bias, respectively.

First, the estimate of the state is computed as if there were no bias present. The vector μ_{n+1}^- represents the estimate of state regardless of the bias.

$$\mu_{n+1}^- = A\mu_n + Bu_{n+1} \tag{22}$$

project the bias-free error covariance ahead

$$p_{n+1}^- = Ap_n A^T + Q \tag{23}$$

compute bias-free Kalman filter gain

$$k_{n+1} = p_{n+1}^- H^T / (H p_{n+1}^- H^T + R) \tag{24}$$

compute bias-free estimate of state with measurement y_{n+1}

$$\mu_{n+1} = \mu_{n+1}^- + k_{n+1}(y_{n+1} - H\mu_{n+1}^-) \tag{25}$$

update the bias-free error covariance matrix

$$p_{n+1} = (I - k_{n+1}H) p_{n+1}^- \tag{26}$$

Then, the estimate is corrected to account for the bias as follows:

$$\hat{x}_n = \mu_n + \varphi_n \hat{b}_n \tag{27}$$

$$\varphi_{n+1} = (I - k_{n+1}) HA\varphi_n - k_{n+1}D \tag{28}$$

The estimate of the bias can be computed as follows:

$$\hat{b}_{n+1} = \hat{b}_n + g_n(z_{n+1} - C_{n+1}\hat{b}_n) \tag{29}$$

where

$$z_{n+1} = y_{n+1} - H\mu_{n+1}^- \tag{30}$$

$$C_{n+1} = HA\varphi_n + D \tag{31}$$

$$g_n = q_n(Hv_n + D)^T R \tag{32}$$

$$q_{n+1}^{-1} = q_n^{-1} + C_{n+1}^T (Hp_{n+1}^- H^T + R)^{-1} C_{n+1} \tag{33}$$

4.2   Separate-Bias Estimation for Linear Systems with Randomly Time-Variant Bias

The separate-bias estimation algorithm is only suitable for constant-bias situation. However, as described above in section 1, the measured distance obtained from the CSS system contains positive and randomly time-variant bias. A pseudo separated-bias estimation algorithm for time-variant bias changing in large region is proposed by Donghua Zhou et al. [12]. Separated-bias estimation algorithm for linear systems is extended to a class of nonlinear systems with output bias by them. We apply their method to design the filter to estimate the randomly time-variant bias contained in the measured distance.

Now assume that b_n be a randomly time-varying bias subjected to unknown changing law. In this case, following the deduction of [12], equation 33 should be modified as follows:

$$q_{n+1}^{-1} = (\lambda_{n+1} q_n)^{-1} + C_{n+1}^T (Hp_{n+1}^- H^T + R)^{-1} C_{n+1} \tag{34}$$

where λ_{n+1} is the suboptimal fading factor and can be determined as follow:

$$\lambda_{n+1} = \begin{cases} \lambda_0, & \lambda_0 \geq 1 \\ 1, & \lambda_0 < 1 \end{cases} \tag{35}$$

where

$$\lambda_0 = tr(N_{n+1})/tr(M_{n+1}) \tag{36}$$

$$N_{n+1} = L_{n+1} - R \tag{37}$$

$$M_{n+1} = Dq_{n+1}D^T \tag{38}$$

$$L_{n+1} = \begin{cases} s_1 s_1^T, & n = 0 \\ \dfrac{\rho L_n + s_{n+1} s_{n+1}^T}{1+\rho}, & n \geq 1 \end{cases} \tag{39}$$

with $0 < \rho \leq 1$ is the preselect forgetting factor. s_{n+1} represents the filter residual of the positive bias and can be computed as follows:

$$s_{n+1} = y_{n+1} - H\mu_{n+1}^- - D\hat{b}_n \tag{40}$$

5   Experimental Evaluation

5.1   Configuration of the Experiments

To evaluate the performance of filtering algorithms, we conducted realistic experiments in the wireless communication laboratory of IOT School of Jiangnan University which is a typical indoor environment. We used two CSS wireless nodes as anchor node and mobile node, respectively. In addition, in order to simulate the NLOS environment, we placed metal plates at the point of anchor node for blocking the direct path of communication between node pairs. The 802.15.4a CSS ranging hardware is based on the radio frequency chip NA5TR1 [13]. The NA5TR1 transceiver is a low-power highly integrated mixed signal chip with ranging capabilities utilizing Nanotrons wireless CSS communication technology. It provides two kinds of bandwidth mode, 80 MHz and 22 MHz, and the signal duration can be selected as 500 ns, 1000 ns, 2000 ns and 4000 ns [14]. Our experiments used the following CSS transceiver parameter Settings: 80 MHz bandwidth, 1000 ns signal duration, CSMA/CA media access control mode, automatic retransmission 10 times, 10 ms frame confirm overtime time.

As mentioned above, we used two CSS wireless nodes as anchor node and mobile node, respectively. Then, we measured the distance between the anchor node and mobile node with SDS-TWR ranging algorithm. An example time to obtain a ranging value in normal ranging mode between a local and a remote station at 80 MHz and 1000 ns is 6 ms. The information of distance measurement was sent to a PC through RS-232 connector. Then the Kalman Filter (KF), the state augmentation filtering algorithm and the separate-bias filtering algorithm were used in the PC to process the raw ranging data. The settings of the classic Kalman Filter are as follows: $Q = 0.01$, $R = 0.01$. The settings of the state augmentation filtering algorithm are as follows: $r_0 = 1$, $Q = [0.01, 0.1]$, $R = 0.01$, $k = 10$, $\beta = \gamma = 2$. The settings of the separate-bias filtering algorithm are as follows: $Q = 0.01$, $R = 0.01$, $\rho = 0.95$, $b_0 = 0$, $\mu_0 = y_0$.

In order to exclude the influence of the motion model and evaluate the performance of filtering algorithms designed in this paper, the distances were divided into four groups: less than 2 m, 2–5 m, 5–8 m and more than 8m. In every group, a distance value was chosen randomly to represent this group. We finally selected four distance values: 1.80 m, 2.05 m, 6.00 m and 8.09 m, and each of these four groups consists of three cases (LOS, NLOS and mixed LOS/NLOS). So there are 12 subgroups of the ranging data, and each subgroup consists of 400 sample points.

5.2   Results and Discussion

Table 1- Table 3 show the mean squared error (MSE) of three different filtering algorithms results compared with the raw data in LOS, NLOS and mixed LOS/NLOS situation, respectively.

At first, overall, compared to the classic Kalman filtering algorithm, both the state augmentation filter and separate-bias filter can effectively eliminate the

Table 1. MSE in LOS environment

Real distance(m)	Raw data(m)	KF(m)	Augmented-state(m)	Separate-bias (m)
1.80	2.1073	1.9949	0.0542	1.2376
2.05	1.6832	1.6285	0.3039	0.9020
6.00	2.2285	2.1951	0.3806	0.4227
8.09	2.5221	2.4841	1.5865	0.3533

Table 2. MSE in NLOS environment

Real distance(m)	Raw data(m)	KF(m)	Augmented-state(m)	Separate-bias (m)
1.80	7.2922	7.2515	4.8669	5.0711
2.05	5.7420	5.7513	3.9836	4.0290
6.00	4.7955	4.8142	3.5557	2.6013
8.09	4.2830	4.2390	2.7861	1.4643

Table 3. MSE in mixed LOS/NLOS environment

Real distance(m)	Raw data(m)	KF(m)	Augmented-state(m)	Separate-bias (m)
1.80	3.3130	3.0170	0.5465	1.7174
2.05	4.7975	2.9648	0.0816	1.3231
6.00	4.3213	3.9861	0.0891	1.9520
8.09	4.8953	4.5583	1.2181	1.5233

positive bias. In a word, both of two filtering algorithms are effective to improve the accuracy of ranging.Furthermore, comparison among tables shows MSE in table 2 and table 3 are greater than that in table 1, which indicates that these two algorithms work better in the LOS environment. And this result also accord with the knowledge that the positive bias is greater in the NLOS environment.

Fig. 1- Fig. 4 show the estimated distances of the filtering algorithms designed in this paper on each sample point in detail. And each of these figures has three sub graphs. From upper to lower, they are as following in turn: in the situation of LOS, NLOS and mixed LOS/NLOS.

The estimated distance of the state augmentation filter almost keeps unchanged, which has been shown in Fig. 2- Fig. 4. This is because of that in this algorithm the change of observed values is regarded as system process noise completely. The majority of the changes of observed values are regarded as the result from the changes of r_n in equation 10. This assumption is reasonable, and helpful to achieve timely tracking of r_n. On the other hand, it also makes the initial state has a considerable influence on the performance of this filtering algorithm.

Some characteristics of the separate-bias estimation filter are also shown in Fig. 2- Fig. 4. When the measured value changing slowly, the filtering result share the same trend with Kalman algorithm, and are closer to the real value. From

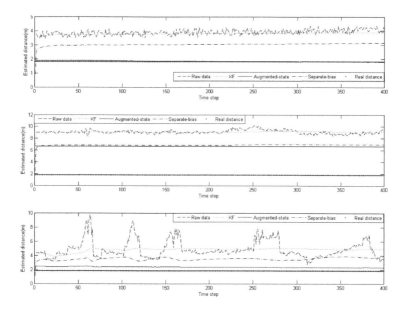

Fig. 1. Experiment results when the real distance is 1.80m

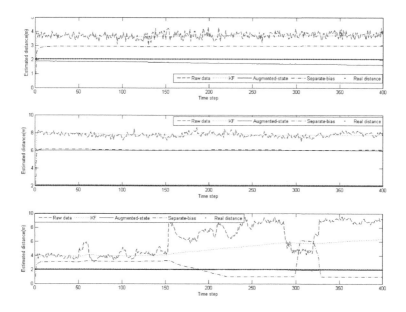

Fig. 2. Experiment results when the real distance is 2.05m

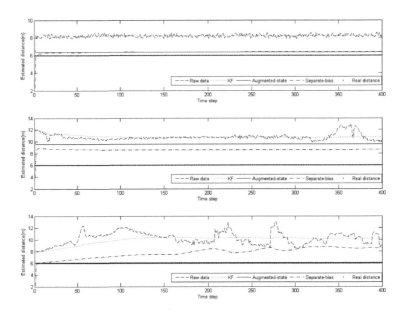

Fig. 3. Experiment results when the real distance is 6.00m

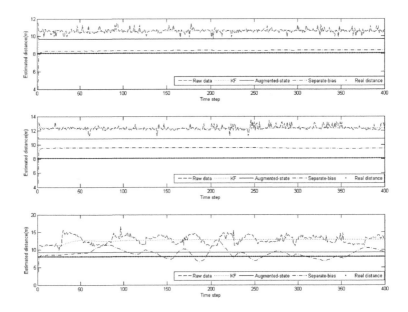

Fig. 4. Experiment results when the real distance is 8.09m

the third sub graph of each figure, it is clearly to learn that when the measured value changing drastically, the filtering result of the separate-bias estimation filter are also affected obviously and appear corresponding fluctuation. Firstly, the estimation of the state is computed by algorithm as if there were no bias present which is similar to the classic Kalman Filter (equation 22- equation 26). Then the bias value is estimated (equation 29- equation 32, equation 34- equation 40), according to the filtering residual computed by the equation 30. Finally, the estimate is corrected to account for the bias (equation 27). When the measured value changing slowly, the bias is regarded to be unchanged, and the trend of the filtering result is similar to that of the Kalman Filter result. But when the measured value changing suddenly, according to equation 40, the residual of the bias will increase suddenly, which makes $\lambda_0 \geq 1$ in the equation 36 , and this situation is regarded as the problem of mismatched model which is the result from the positive deviation changing suddenly. Then the error covariance of bias estimation will be increased (equation 34- equation 35), which leads to the changing of the filtering result. Therefore, the rapidly change of bias can be effectively tracked by the separate-bias estimation filter. But the sudden change of the measured value also leads to the jitter of the filtering result.

6   Conclusion

In this paper, we conclude three approaches to deal with the positive bias in TOA measurement based on the CSS system, and the latter two of them are used to design filters to improve the accuracy of ranging. Experiments conducted with Nanotron CSS wireless nodes in indoor environment validate the algorithm actually. Experiment results illustrate that the filtering algorithms designed in this paper can effectively improve the accuracy of ranging.

References

1. Sen, S., Radunovic, B., Choudhury, R.R., Minka, T.: You are facing the Mona Lisa: spot localization using PHY layer information. In: Proceedings of the 10th International Conference on Mobile Systems, Applications, and Services, pp. 183–196. ACM, Low Wood Bay (2012)
2. Sen, S., Choudhury, R.R., Nelakuditi, S.: SpinLoc: spin once to know your location. In: Proceedings of the Twelfth Workshop on Mobile Computing Systems & Applications, pp. 12:1–12:6. ACM, San Diego (2012)
3. Jhi, H.L., Chen, J.C., Lin, C.H., Huang, C.T.: A Factor-Graph-Based TOA Location Estimator. IEEE Transactions on Wireless Communications 11(5), 1764–1773 (2012)
4. Ho, K.C.: Bias Reduction for an Explicit Solution of Source Localization Using TDOA. IEEE Transactions on Signal Processing 60(5), 2101–2114 (2012)
5. Cho, H., Lee, C.W., Ban, S.J., Kim, S.W.: An enhanced positioning scheme for chirp spread spectrum ranging. Expert Systems with Applications 37(8), 5728–5735 (2010)

6. Rohrig, C., Muller, M.: Indoor location tracking in non-line-of-sight environments using a IEEE 802.15. 4a wireless network. In: Proceedings of the 2009 IEEE/RSJ International Conference on Intelligent Robots and Systems, pp. 552–557. IEEE, St. Louis (2009)

7. Cho, H., Kim, S.W.: Mobile robot localization using biased chirp-spread-spectrum ranging. IEEE Transactions on Industrial Electronics 57(8), 2826–2835 (2010)

8. Wylie, M.P., Holtzman, J.: The non-line of sight problem in mobile location estimation. In: 5th IEEE International Conference on Universal Personal Communications, vol. 2, pp. 827–831. IEEE, Cambridge (1996)

9. Le, B.L., Ahmed, K., Tsuji, H.: Mobile location estimator with NLOS mitigation using Kalman filtering. In: Wireless Communications and Networking, vol. 3, pp. 1969–1973. IEEE, New Orleans (2003)

10. Najar, M., Vidal, J.: Kalman tracking for mobile location in NLOS situations. In: 14th IEEE Proceedings on Personal, Indoor and Mobile Radio Communications, vol. 3, pp. 2203–2207. IEEE, Beijing (2003)

11. Friedland, B.: Treatment of bias in recursive filtering. IEEE Transactions on Automatic Control 14(4), 359–367 (1969)

12. Zhou, D.H., Sun, Y.X., Xi, Y.G., Zhang, Z.J.: Tpseudo Separated–Bias Estimation for a Class of Nonlinear Systems with Output Bias. Information and Control 21(3), 141–145 (1992)

13. nanoloc TRX Transceiver (NA5TR1). Datasheet NA-06-0230-0388-2.00, Nanotron Technologies GmbH (2008)

14. nanoLOC Development Kit User Guide. Technical Report NA-06-0230-0402-1.03, Nanotron Technologies GmbH (2007)

A Secure DV-Hop Localization Algorithm Based on Secure Beacon Nodes

Jinfa Zhong[1], Li Xu[2], Haifeng Hu[1], and A'yong Ye[2]

[1] Computer Department, Min Xi Vocatinal and Technical College,
364021 Longyan Fujian, China
[2] School of Mathematics and Computer Science, Fujian Normal University,
350007 Fuzhou Fujian, China

Abstract. The security problem of beacon nodes is ignored in most existing localization algorithms in Wireless Sensor Networks (WSNs), although beacon nodes' location information is crucial to the process of sensor nodes' localization. Assumed that some of beacon nodes were attacked as a result of the secure vulnerability of WSNs, a secure DV-Hop localization algorithm based on beacons' credits is proposed in the paper. By distributed calculating the credits of beacon nodes, sensor nodes could eliminate the malicious beacon information effectively according to their credits to ensure the correctness of beacon location information they received. Finally, the efficiency and feasibility of proposed algorithm are proved by the performance evaluation results.

Keywords: Wireless Sensor Networks, Localization Algorithm, DV-Hop, Secure Beacon Nodes.

1 Introduction

Most localization algorithms share a common feature in Wireless Sensor Networks (WSNs): there are some beacon nodes, which are assumed to know their own locations (e.g., through GPS receiver or manual configuration). Other nodes' localization based on the beacons provided by the beacon nodes. Broadly speaking, there are two main categories of localization algorithms: range-based and range-free [1]. In range-based localization algorithms, nodes involve measuring physical properties to calculate or measure the distance between itself and the beacon node. The familiar range-based algorithm, such as [2], TDOA [3], RSSI [4] and AOA [5]. In range-free localization algorithms, nodes do not require any measurement of physical distance-related properties, but use the information of networks topology. The familiar range-free algorithm, such as centroid algorithm [6], DV-Hop [7], DV-Distance [7], convex programming algorithm [8], APIT [9] and MDS-MAP [10]. Compared to range-based localization algorithms, range-free ones do not require special hardware to calculate or measure the distance, and their accuracies are thus lower as well. Overall, range-free schemes would be a better choice in WSNs since the cost-effective of the network.

The study on localization Algorithms in WSNs was focused on the precision or accuracy of nodes' localizations and localization algorithm energy-efficiency

R. Wang and F. Xiao (Eds.): CWSN 2012, CCIS 334, pp. 715–724, 2013.
© Springer-Verlag Berlin Heidelberg 2013

formerly [11]. However, it is vulnerable to various attacks in the node localization process, serious consequences may arise by the invalid or wrong location information which released by attacked nodes, especially in some networks whose tasks could be essential, such as battlefield monitor networks [12]. Therefore, how to securely and effectively get the nodes' location information in resource-constrained wireless sensor networks is a challenging issue in nodes' localization algorithms.

The secure localization algorithm proposed in this paper focuses on beacons' security, since it is ignored in most existing localization algorithms in WSNs, beacon nodes' location information is crucial to the process of sensor nodes' localization. It is assumed that some of beacon nodes were attacked as a result of the secure vulnerability of WSNs, so these attacked beacon nodes became malicious beacon nodes. A secure DV-Hop localization algorithm based on beacons' credits is proposed, by distributed calculating the credits of beacon nodes, sensor nodes could effectively eliminate the malicious beacon information to ensure the correctness of beacon location information they received. The beacon nodes in the network make full use of their accurate location information to make verification of the beacons send by other beacon nodes. After calculating the credits of other beacon nodes, the beacon node saves the credits in its credit-list. When the sensor nodes in the network to request the other beacon nodes' credit, the beacon node would get it from its credit-list and send it to the request node. The algorithm not only employs distributed calculating the credits, but also superior in simplicity and effectiveness in WSNs.

2   Related Work

The cost of information's security precautions in wireless networks is greater than cable ones, especially in multi-node collaboration in wireless networks. The same security precaution in WSNs as in wireless networks, some of the security requests in WSNs as follows: Firstly, radio signals easy to be captured or attacked. Since the communicate process between nodes in WSNs employ radio signals as medium, so attacker can make use of it or change the information it received easily, while traditional security technologies or schemes, such as encryption and authentication, would be invalid to come up against such external threats. Secondly, attacker can make use of the deficiency in localization schemes or algorithms in WSNs since thus localization schemes or algorithms ignore the security problems in the process of localization, such as beacon's security. Finally, the secure vulnerability of WSNs is serious because of the nodes employ radio signals to communicate but not cable, nodes were deployed randomly, unattended and resource constrained.

Secure localization has received attention only recently. In [1], the authors listed a few attacks that might affect the correctness of localization algorithms along with a few countermeasures. In [13], the authors assumed beacon nodes as check-nodes to detect and isolate malicious beacon nodes. In the scheme above, each check-node has a check ID, and request information about localization from its neighboring beacon nodes voluntarily, then the check-node makes a verification of the localization result. When detect a malicious beacon node, the check-node would send a warning message and send it to the base station of the network as well, then the base station would isolate the malicious beacon nodes if their warning times are greater than the threshold-times. Compared to these studies, our algorithm employ distributed calculating to calculate the credits, but not use a base station of the network, and superior in simply implementation of the algorithm.

3   Problems and Demand Analysis

3.1   Wormhole Attack to DV-Hop Localization Algorithm

Location information of beacon nodes play an essential role in most localization algorithms in WSNs, especially in range-free algorithms. However, the security of beacons send by beacon nodes was ignored in most existing localization algorithms. Wormhole attack can easily attack the networks which employ range-free algorithms to localization; the wormhole attacker would send the fake location information to another attacker in the network, and they could send the fake message to any node in the network. One technique that may be used to defend against wormhole attacks is to employ packet leashes [14].

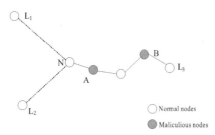

Fig. 1. Wormhole attack to DV-Hop

Fig.1 shows the wormhole attack in DV-Hop localization algorithm. L_1, L_2 and L_3 are normal beacon nodes in the network, N is the normal sensor node in the network, A, B are the malicious nodes (wormhole attackers). When node N calculates the hop counts from itself to the beacon node L_3, malicious node B sends the message which received from L_3 to malicious node A. After received the message, the malicious node A replay it to node N, so node N record the minimum hop counts to L_3 only one. But in an actual fact, the hop counts between them are 4. Therefore, if some the beacon nodes of the network are the malicious nodes, the localization inaccuracy would be great or the sensor node cant be localizable.

3.2   Verification Model of Beacon Nodes Location Information

If some of the beacon nodes in the network are malicious nodes, it will bring a great effect upon the localization accuracy. However, the other beacon nodes in the network have their own accurate location information; they can make full use of the information to verify the beacons sent by other beacon nodes. Some schemes can be used to calculate the other beacon nodes' credits and save them. Fig.2 shows the distance verification scheme according to formula 1.

$$|\sqrt{(x-x')^2 + (y-y')^2} - d| \geq E_{max} \tag{1}$$

Where, E_{max} is the maximum tolerable inaccuracy, (x, y) is the location coordinate value of beacon node v, (x', y') is the location coordinate value sent by beacon node u, d is the given distance between them.

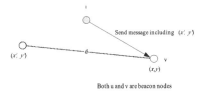

Fig. 2. Distance verification scheme

4   A Secure DV-Hop Localization Algorithm Based on Secure Beacon Nodes

4.1   The Relationship between Node Density and Correction in WSNs

In the process of DV-Hop localization algorithm, beacon nodes calculate the correction value based on both the other beacon nodes' location information and the minimum hop counts between them in the network. Each beacon nodes would calculate their own correction, and then broadcast it to the other nodes in the network. Beacon nodes' correction value are different according to the node density of the network, when the network node density get greater (e.g. more nodes deployed in the fixed network field.), the correction value would be get smaller comparatively. When the network node density get smaller, the correction value would become greater comparatively. Because each beacon node has their own different correction, so the average correction value of all the beacon nodes' correction could be more accurate at the correction value of the network. Our algorithm employs formula 2 to calculate the average correction of the network.

$$correction_{avg} = \frac{1}{m} \sum_{i=1}^{m} (correction_i) \tag{2}$$

Where m is the beacon nodes' total number count, $correction_i$ is the correction value of beacon node i.

Our evaluation parameters as follows: the network simulation field is 500500, set all the nodes' communication radius $R = 100$ in the network. When 50 nodes randomly deployed in the field, the node density was about 5, and the average correction of the network $correction_{avg}$ was about 74.2045. When 100 nodes randomly deployed in the field, the node density was about 9, and the average correction of the network $correction_{avg}$ was about 62.2342. When 200 nodes randomly deployed in the field, the node density was about 17, and the average correction of the network $correction_{avg}$ was about 54.4389. Assume that the probability of the hop counts between any nodes in the network obey the normal distribution with mathematical expectation of $h = D/correction_{avg}$, as show in Fig.3, where, D is the Euclidean distance between them.

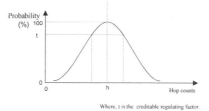

Fig. 3. The probability of the hop counts between nodes

4.2 Hop Counts - Distance Verification in Beacon Nodes

After received the location information including x_i, y_i, h_i sent by beacon node i, the beacon node j would employ formula 3 or formula 4 to make Hop counts - Distance verification to it.

$$HV_{j-i} = \left| \frac{\sqrt{(x_j - x_i)^2 + (y_j - y_i)^2}}{correction_{avg} \times h_{i-j}} - 1 \right| \quad (3)$$

Or

$$HV_{j-i} = \left| \frac{\sqrt{(x_j - x_i)^2 + (y_j - y_i)^2}}{correction_{avg} \times h_{j-i}} - 1 \right| \quad (4)$$

Where, (x_i, y_i) is the location coordinate value of beacon node i, (x_j, y_j) is the location coordinate value of beacon node j, h_{i-j} or h_{j-i} is the hop counts between node i and node j.

$$HV_{j-i} = \begin{cases} \leq \alpha \times h_{j-i} (GoToCreditCalculateStep) \\ > \alpha \times h_{j-i} (MaliciousBeaconNode) \end{cases} \quad (5)$$

Where α is the correction inaccuracy regulating factor.

4.3   Calculate Scheme of Beacon Nodes' Credits

After beacon node j made Hop counts - Distance verification to beacon node i, and the verification meets the hop counts requirements, that means the verification meets formula 6.

$$HV_{j-i} =| \frac{\sqrt{(x_j - x_i)^2 + (y_j - y_i)^2}}{correction_{avg} \times h_{j-i}} - 1 |\leq \alpha \times h_{j-i} \qquad (6)$$

Then beacon node j calculates the credit of beacon node i: C_{j-i}. In our scheme, we defined that: The estimate distance between node j to node i:

$$D_{j-i} = correction_{avg} \times h_{j-i} \qquad (7)$$

The correction inaccuracy between node j to node i:

$$I_{j-i} =| \sqrt{(x_j - x_i)^2 + (y_j - y_i)^2} - D_{j-i} | /h_{j-i} \qquad (8)$$

Beacon node j calculate beacon node i's credit according to formula 9:

$$C_{j-i} = \frac{R}{I_{j-i}} \times t \qquad (9)$$

Where, t is the unit of credit.

Finally, we employ recalculate formula 10 to regulate the credits:

$$C_{j-i} = \begin{cases} 1000t(\frac{R}{I_{j-i}} \times t \geq 1000tOrI_{j-i} = 0) \\ \frac{R}{I_{j-i}} \times t(Others) \end{cases} \qquad (10)$$

4.4   Identify Secure Beacon Scheme

After calculating the other beacon nodes' credits, all the beacon nodes in the network have other beacon nodes' credits in its own credit-list. If any nodes in the network to request the other beacon nodes' credits, the beacon node would get them from its credit-list and send them to the request node.

The process of localization algorithm in our scheme is similar to the other ones, such as DV-Hop localization algorithm. Each sensor node in the network needs at least 3 different beacon nodes' location information to accomplish the localization process. However, some of the beacons the sensor node received might be sent by malicious beacon nodes, they would reduce the accuracy of localization. In our scheme, the sensor nodes fetch the localization reference beacon nodes' credits from other beacon nodes in the network, but not from themselves. In order to avoid beacon nodes' conspire attack, the sensor node select the beacon nodes randomly in the network besides localization reference beacon nodes. After fetching these different credits, the sensor node would calculate the trust degree of the reference beacon node according to formula 11.

$$T_{trust-i} = \frac{1}{k} \sum_{j=1}^{k} (C_{j-i}) \qquad (11)$$

Where, k is number of the beacon node that sent the beacon node is credit value to the sensor node.

5   Performance Evaluation

In our evaluation, we set the parameters as follows: the network simulation field is 500500, all the nodes' communication radius: $R = 100$, 200 nodes were deployed in the fixed network field randomly, and the beacon node ratio was 20% in the network field. By altering the number of malicious beacon nodes in the network to change the ratio of malicious beacon nodes. Sensor nodes localization inaccuracy:

$$I = \frac{\sqrt{(x_i - x_e)^2 + (y_i - y_e)^2}}{R}$$

Where, (x_e, y_e) is the nodes estimated coordinates by our algorithm, while (x_i, y_i) is the nodes real or accurate coordinates.

The malicious beacon nodes sent fake coordinates information to nodes in the network, the fake coordinates could lead to a great inaccuracy, such as greater than the nodes communication radius in the sensor network:

$$E = \sqrt{(x_r - x_d)^2 + (y_r - y_d)^2} \geq R,$$

where, (x_r, y_r) is the malicious beacon nodes real or accurate coordinates, (x_d, y_d) is the malicious beacon nodes fake coordinates.

We set the other evaluation parameters as follows:

The correction inaccuracy regulating factor: $\alpha = 0.2$.

Trust degree: $T_{trust-i} = \frac{1}{k} \sum_{j=1}^{k} (C_{j-i}) \geq 700t$.

In order to get objective evaluation results, we repeat each evaluation scenario 10 times, and the average result of evaluations select as the final result.

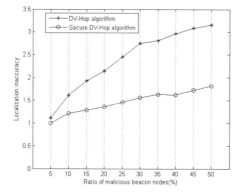

Fig. 4. Relationship between inaccuracy and malicious node ratio

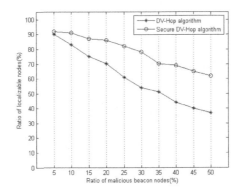

Fig. 5. Relationship between localizable nodes ratio and malicious node ratio

Fig.4 reveals the relationship between the localization inaccuracies according to malicious beacon nodes different ratio in the network. As show in Fig.4, with the increase ratio of malicious beacon nodes, both inaccuracies of DV-Hop localization algorithm and secure DV-Hop localization algorithm were became greater, however, the inaccuracy of secure DV-Hop localization algorithm is obviously smaller than DV-Hop localization algorithm at the same malicious beacon nodes ratio. As the ratio of malicious beacon nodes increase, there were more malicious beacon nodes be eliminated in the secure DV-Hop localization algorithm, it is similar to reduce the effective beacon nodes in the network. This is also the key to greater inaccuracy when malicious beacon nodes ratio rises in secure DV-Hop localization algorithm.

Fig.5 reveals the relationship between the localizable nodes ratio according to malicious beacon nodes different ratio in the network. We defined localizable nodes that the sensor node can get at least 3 beacons sent by different beacon nodes, and the localization result coordinates neither exceed the fixed simulation field nor be negative number values. Localizable nodes have their own location coordinates in the network, since the inaccuracy can examine the localization result. As show in Fig.5, with the increase ratio of malicious beacon nodes, both localizable node ratio of DV-Hop localization algorithm and secure DV-Hop localization algorithm were became smaller, however, the localizable node ratio of secure DV-Hop localization algorithm is greater than DV-Hop localization algorithm at the same malicious beacon nodes ratio. As the ratio of malicious beacon nodes increase, the probability of more malicious beacon nodes around sensor nodes became greater in DV-Hop localization algorithm, so the sensor nodes use more malicious beacons to localization. That leads to localization inaccuracy be great or the node cant be localizable in DV-Hop localization algorithm, it reduce the localizable nodes ratio. In secure DV-Hop localization algorithm, the sensor nodes can eliminate malicious beacons but not use them in the process of localization, so it is similar to reduce the effective beacon nodes in the network. This is also the key to localizable nodes ratio became smaller when malicious beacon nodes ratio rise in secure DV-Hop localization algorithm.

6   Conclusion

Beacon nodes' location information is crucial to the process of sensor nodes' localization. The secure DV-Hop localization algorithm proposed in this paper focused on the beacons' security. Beacon nodes in the network make full use of their accurate location information to make verification of the beacons send by other beacon nodes. By distributed calculating the credits of beacon nodes, sensor nodes could effectively eliminate the malicious beacon according their credits to ensure the correction of beacon location information they received. The algorithm not only employ distributed calculating to calculate the credits, but also superior in simplicity and effectiveness in WSNs. However, it would be better if the lower computational complexity and communication cost between nodes the secure DV-Hop localization algorithm we proposed, therefore, lower computational complexity and communication cost in our secure localization algorithm would be the goals of our further studies.

Acknowledgments. Supported by the National Natural Science Foundation of China under Grant No.61072080, Natural Science Foundation of Fujian Province under Grant NO.2009J01274 and Natural Science Foundation of Min Xi Vocatinal and Technical College under Grant No.MYKJ2011-006.

References

1. Langendoen, K., Reijers, N.: Distributed localization in wireless sensor networks: a quantitative comparison. Comput. Netw. 43, 499–518 (2003)
2. Harter, A., Hopper, A., Steggles, P., Ward, A., Webster, P.: The anatomy of a context-aware application. In: Proceedings of the 5th Annual ACM/IEEE International Conference on Mobile Computing and Networking (MobiCom 1999), pp. 59–68. ACM, New York (1999)
3. Girod, L., Estrin, D.: Robust range estimation using acoustic and multimodal sensing. In: Proc. of the Intelligent Robots and Systems (IROS 2001), vol. 3, pp. 1312–1320. IEEE Robotics and Automation Society, Maui (2001)
4. Girod, L., Bychovkiy, V., Elson, J., Estrin, D.: Locating tiny sensors in time and space: A case study. In: Proc. of the Computer Design: VLSI in Computers and Processors, pp. 214–219. IEEE Computer Society, Freiburg (2002)
5. Priyantha, N.B., Akl, M., Balakrishnan, H., Teller, S.: The cricket compass for context-aware mobile applications. In: Proc. of the 7th Annual Intl. Conf. on Mobile Computing and Networking, pp. 1–14. ACM Press, Rome (2001)
6. Bulusu, N., Heidemann, J., Estrin, D.: GPS-Less low cost outdoor localization for very mall devices. IEEE Personal Communications 7(5), 28–34 (2000)
7. Niculescu, D., Nath, B.: DV based positioning in ad hoc networks. Journal of Telecommunication Systems 22(1/4), 267–280 (2003)
8. Doherty, L., Pister, K.S.J., Ghaoui, L.E.: Convex position estimation in wireless sensor networks. In: Proc. of the IEEE INFOCOM 2001, vol. 3, pp. 1655–1663. IEEE Computer and Communications Societies, Anchorage (2001)
9. He, T., Huang, C.D., Blum, B.M., et al.: Range-Free localization schemes in large scale sensor networks. In: Proc. of the 9th Annual Intl. Conf. on Mobile Computing and Networking, pp. 81–95. ACM Press, San Diego (2003)

10. Shang, Y., Ruml, W., Zhang, Y., Fromherz, M.P.J.: Localization from mere connectivity. In: Proc. of the 4th ACM Intl. Symp. on Mobile Ad Hoc Networking & Computing, pp. 201–212. ACM Press, Annapolis (2003)
11. Wang, F., Shi, L., Ren, F.: Self-Localization Systems and Algorithms for Wireless Sensor Networks. Journal of Software 16(5), 857–868 (2005)
12. Cao, X., Yu, B., Chen, G., Ren, F.: Security Analysis on Node Localization Systems of Wireless Sensor Networks. Journal of Software, 869–877 (2008)
13. Liu, D., Ning, P., Du, W.: Detecting malicious beacon nodes for secure location discovery in wireless sensor networks. In: Proc. of International Conference on Distributed Computing Systems, pp. 609–619. IEEE, Columbus (2005)
14. Hu, Y.C., Perrig, A., Johnson, D.: Packet leashes: a defense against wormhole attacks in wireless networks. In: Proceedings of IEEE Infocom, 1976C–1986C (2003)

Improvement on Localization Error and Adaptability in DV-Hop Algorithm

Ying Zhou, Baojian Gao, Tianzhang Xing,
Xiaojiang Chen, and Dingyi Fang

School of Information Science and Technology,
Northwest University, Xi'an China
Key Laboratory of Culture Heritage Research and Conservation
(Northwest University) Ministry of Education, Xi'an, 710127, China
zhouying953@yahoo.com.cn, esu7031@sina.com, {xtz,xjchen,dyf}@nwu.edu.cn

Abstract. The proliferation of wireless and mobile network has fostered the demand of context aware applications. Location is one of the most basic and significant contexts. An improved DV-HOP localization algorithm based on connectivity of network is proposed in order to decrease the hardware cost and implement in complexity WSN. First of all, by using the weighted least-mean-square error criterion to estimate the network average single hop distance, we can obtain the distance information between any interconnected nodes. Then, the geometric position of the reference nodes affects the localization accuracy; we propose a selective strategy of reference nodes involved in the position calculation process. Finally, based on trusted links to get the location information. The simulation results show that compared with the DV-HOP localization algorithm, the positioning accuracy is improved, and also improves localization performances.

Keywords: wireless sensor network, DV-HOP, Trilateration, GDOP.

1 Introduction

Wireless sensor network, which is made by the convergence of sensor, micro-electro-mechanism system and networks technologies, is a novel technology about acquiring and processing information. Location-aware technology spawns numerous unforeseen pervasive applications in a wide range of living, production, commence, and public services. Making data geographically meaningful, location information is essential for many applications such as environment monitor. Also, location information deeply aids a number of network functions, such as network routing, topology control, coverage, boundary detection, clustering, etc. So it is very intriguing for researchers to discover and design more accurate and cost-effective localization algorithms.

Existing approaches fall into two categories: Range-based approaches [1-4] and Range-free approaches [5-8].Range-based approaches are based on the assumption that through measure one or several electrical parameters of radio signal,

R. Wang and F. Xiao (Eds.): CWSN 2012, CCIS 334, pp. 725–733, 2013.
© Springer-Verlag Berlin Heidelberg 2013

such as amplitude, frequency, phase, Time of Arrive(TOA[1]), Time Difference of Arrival(TDOA[2]), Received Signal Strength Indicator(RSSI[3]), Angle of Arrival(AOA[4]),we can get the distance information between any neighbor nodes and then obtain the localization information of all nods in the network. Range-based approaches have high localization accuracy, but all of TOA, TDOA, and AOA measurement requires hardware devices expensive in both manufacturing cost and energy consumption.

Range-free approaches depend on the connectivity measurements to estimate nodes' localization information. At present, there are many typical positioning algorithm such as DV-HOP [5], Centroid [6], MDS-MAP [7], APIT [8], etc. Due to the hardware limitations and energy constraint of wireless devices, range-free localization is being pursued as a cost-effective alternative to more expensive range-based approaches. And the coarse accuracy is sufficient for most sensor network applications.

2   Problem Statement

DV-HOP is a very important range-free positioning algorithm based on network connectivity. The positioning accuracy is coarse, and is only suitable for isotropic and uniform node deployment networks. In the most practical application scenario and the real geographic shape of region, the network topology is complex and anisotropic. At present, there are a number of further enhanced methods are proposed. In [9], the authors propose the Removing Heavily Curved Path (RHCP) scheme, which takes advantage of selecting the paths which are not heavily affected by the holes to recalculate the location of each unknown node; In [10], the authors propose an error-tolerant localization method, call SISR, to identify automatically "bad nodes" and "bad links" arising from these errors, so that they receive less weight in the localization process. In [11], the authors propose a new localization protocol based on Approximate Convex Decomposition (ACDL). The basic idea is to decompose the network into convex sub-regions. All above the proposed methods can improve location accuracy, but in order to improve the location accuracy and adaptability, there is still need to conduct more research and improve work.

We propose the Trilateration and GDOP DV-HOP (TGDV-HOP) scheme in this paper. The algorithm firstly estimates the average single hop distance based on weighted least-mean-square error criterion. For the sensor nodes are random distribution and there are conflicts in the process of broadcasting, the minimal hop-count between the unknown nodes to anchor nodes has a certain probability bias, and the more hop-count, the greater the deviation. Using the far anchor nodes in position calculation, may reduce the accuracy of positioning, so the position calculation process takes the option of trilateral measurement method. Research [12] shows that the geometric relation of reference nodes significantly affects the localization accuracy, so we propose a selective strategy of reference nodes. And to the participating anchor nodes, long link connection is given smaller credibility, in vice versa, given greater credibility, to optimize the estimation of unknown nodes coordinates.

The paper is organized as follows: The DV-HOP algorithm is presented in the next section. Section 4 gives our improved algorithm. Simulation results are provided in section 5. The last section is to conclude this paper.

3   DV-HOP

DV-HOP approach is developed by Niculescu et al. There are three non-overlapping phases in DV-HOP algorithm (Fig.1). First, all nodes in the network get the minimum hop count values to all beacon nodes. Second, once an anchor gets hop-count value to other anchors, it estimates the average distance of one hop, which is estimated by anchor i using the following formula:

$$C_i = \frac{\sum_{i \neq j} \sqrt{(x_i - x_j)^2 + (y_i - y_j)^2}}{\sum_{i \neq j} hops_{ij}} \qquad (1)$$

Where $(x_i, y_i), (x_j, y_j)$ are coordinates of anchor i and j, hop_{ij} is the hops between anchor i and j. Finally, a non-anchor node is able to estimate its distance to anchors by multiply the average distance of one hop and the short hop-count, and then performs trilateration to estimate its location.

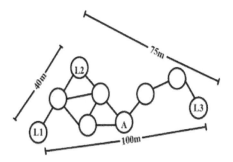

Fig. 1. DV-HOP localization algorithm

To gain more insights of Trilateration, see Fig.2,O is an unknown nodes, A, B and C are the three anchor nodes. Where $(x_1, y_1), (x_2, y_2)$ and (x_3, y_3) are coordinates of anchor nodes. r_1, r_2 and r_3 are the distance between each pair of unknown node and anchor node. The coordinate of O is calculated by the following formulas:

$$\begin{cases} (x - x_1)^2 + (y - y_1)^2 = r_1^2 \\ (x - x_2)^2 + (y - y_2)^2 = r_2^2 \\ (x - x_3)^2 + (y - y_3)^2 = r_3^2. \end{cases} \qquad (2)$$

$$\begin{bmatrix} x \\ y \end{bmatrix} = \begin{bmatrix} 2(x_1 - x_3) & 2(y_1 - y_3) \\ 2(x_2 - x_3) & 2(y_2 - y_3) \end{bmatrix}^{-1} \begin{bmatrix} x_1^2 - x_3^2 + y_1^2 - y_3^2 + r_3^2 - r_1^2 \\ x_2^2 - x_3^2 + y_2^2 - y_3^2 + r_3^2 - r_2^2 \end{bmatrix} \qquad (3)$$

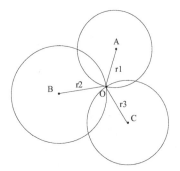

Fig. 2. Trilateration

4   Our Improved Algorithm

There are three main steps in our improved algorithm: 1) Distances estimate between unknown node and anchor node; 2) Anchor nodes selection algorithm; 3) Optimal localization information estimation.

4.1   Distances Estimate Based on Weighted Least-Mean-Square Error Criterion

In the traditional DV-HOP algorithm, based on the unbiased estimate to calculate the average hop distance. In this paper, by using the formula 4, to get the average single hop distance of the whole network.

$$HopSize = \frac{\sum_{i=1}^{n} HopSize_i^N}{n}. \tag{4}$$

The average single hop distance estimate of the anchor node is based on the weighted least-mean-square error criterion (the Formula 5).

$$HopSize_i^N = \frac{\sum_{i \neq j} Hop_{ij} \times d_{ij}}{\sum_{i \neq j} hop_{ij}^2}. \tag{5}$$

Let n be the number of sensor, i and j are anchors, hop_{ij} is the hops between anchor i and j, d_{ij} is the distance between i and j.

From Fig.1, calculate the average single hop distance of the anchor nodes($L1$, $L2$ and $L3$)by using the following formulas:

$$HopSize_{L1}^N = \frac{2d_{L1L2} + 6d_{L1L3}}{(2^2 + 6^2)}. \tag{6}$$

$$HopSize_{L2}^N = \frac{2d_{L1L2} + 5d_{L2L3}}{(2^2 + 5^2)}. \tag{7}$$

$$HopSize_{L3}^N = \frac{6d_{L1L3} + 5d_{L2L3}}{(6^2 + 5^2)}. \tag{8}$$

The average distance of the whole networks calculate by the formula 9:

$$HopSize = \frac{\sum_{i=1}^{3} HopSize_i^N}{3}.$$
(9)

Last, the non-anchor node is able to estimate its distance to anchors by multiply the average single hop distance and the minimum hop-count.

4.2 Anchor Nodes Selection Algorithm

Trilateration is a basic building block of localization. Based on our observation that the geometric relation of reference nodes significantly affects the localization accuracy. When the three anchor nodes are collinear, the localization error is big. When the geometric relation of reference nodes is equilateral triangle, the localization error is small. In the GPS system, Geographic Dilution of Precision (GDOP) [18] which eliminates the impact of ranging errors and amplify the effect caused by the node geometry, expresses the ranging error and the geometric relationship of references and to-be-localized nodes. So it can be an effective selective strategy of anchor nodes. There are m reference nodes $v_1; v_2; \ldots; v_m$ and one node v_0 to be localized. We obtain

$$GDOP = \frac{\sigma_0}{\sigma} = \sqrt{\frac{m}{\sum_{i=1}^{m-1} \sum_{j \neq i}^{m} \sin^2 \alpha_{ij}}}.$$
(10)

Where σ_0 is the variance of the estimate location of v_0, σ is the variance of the ranging error, α_{ij} is the angle between each pair of reference nodes (i, j). Distance estimate based on the weighted least-mean-square error criterion, the ranging error is subject to a Gaussian distribution. When the σ is a constant, the smaller value of GDOP, the higher possibility that the geometric relationship of references is equilateral triangle. Then, we choice the three reference nodes involved in the position calculation process.

To gain more insights of GDOP,we consider a simplified case of trilateration,where the to-be-localized node O is put at the center of a circle and $m = 3$,reference nodes A, B, C lie on the circumference of that circle, setting all references the same distance to O, as shown in Fig.3. Fixing A at $a = 0$, GDOP becomes a function of the locations of B and C, denoted by $a1$, $a2 \in [0, 2\pi]$.We plot the GDOP in Fig.4 and conclude that different geometric forms of trilateration provide different levels of localization accuracy. The impact of node geometry on the accuracy trilateration:

So, let m be the number of anchor sensor in the whole network, there are C_m^3 kinds selection, we choice the three anchor nodes that the geometric relationship is nearly equilateral triangle. The process consists of two parts:

First, through the slope information, exclude the case that the three anchor nodes are collinear;

Second, according to formula 10, calculate the GDOP, then choice the three anchor nodes which make the value smallest to involve in the position calculation process.

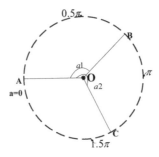

Fig. 3. Node deployment

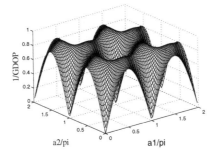

Fig. 4. 3D plot of $1/GDOP$

4.3 Trusted Link Estimation of the Unknown Node Location

In the network, the greater number of hops between nodes, the greater deviation of distance estimate. So, the long link is less reliable and has bad effect on the positioning accuracy when the link takes participation in the position estimation process. For the three links have been selected to participate in the location calculation. Treat the hop-count as the measure index. The longest link receives less credibility and the shortest receive higher credibility in the localization process.

For any two nodes i and j, we obtain:

$$r(i,j) = \widehat{d}_{ij} - d_{ij}. \tag{11}$$

Where $\widehat{d}_{ij}$ is the distance estimated by the coordinate of nodes i and j, d_{ij} is the ranging measurement by the two nodes, $r(i,j)$ is the deviation of estimate distance and the measurement distance. Based on the trust link estimate, we get:

$$s(i,j) = \alpha r(i,j)^2. \tag{12}$$

Different link has different credibility, the method to calculate α is:

$$\alpha_a = \frac{Hop_{abc} - Hop_a}{2 \times Hop_{abc}}. \tag{13}$$

$$\alpha_b = \frac{Hop_{abc} - Hop_b}{2 \times Hop_{abc}}. \tag{14}$$

$$\alpha_c = \frac{Hop_{abc} - Hop_c}{2 \times Hop_{abc}}. \tag{15}$$

$$Hop_{abc} = Hop_a + Hop_b + Hop_c. \tag{16}$$

Where Hop_a, Hop_b and Hop_c are the hop count between the to-be-location node and the three select anchor nodes. Then we obtain:

$$F = \sum_{i,j} s(i,j). \tag{17}$$

By minimizing the objective function F, we can get accuracy location information.

5   Simulation Results

In order to check the performance of TGDV-HOP localization algorithm, we simulate in the Matlab7.0.To quantify the influence made by the factors on localization accuracy, we use Accuracy to denote it:

$$Accuracy = \frac{\sum error}{R} = \frac{\sum \sqrt{(x_i - x_{cal})^2 + (y_i - y_{cal})^2}}{R}. \tag{18}$$

Where (x_i, y_i) is the unknown node's real coordinate, (x_{cal}, y_{cal}) is the calculated coordinate, R is the sensor comunication radius.

We generate networks of 100 nodes randomly distributed in a square area (Fig.5).The size is $200 * 200m^2$. All the statistics reported are averaged over 20 runs for high confidence.

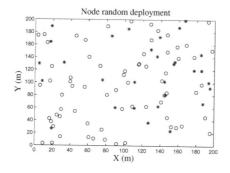

Fig. 5. Node deployment

5.1   Anchor Node Ratio

First, we analyze the impact of anchor node number on the performance of both DV-HOP and TGDV-HOP. In this experiment, we increased the ratio of anchor nodes in the network from 0.05 to 0.4 in step of 0.05. As expected, Fig.6 shows that more anchor nodes help improve the localization accuracy for all methods. More notable is that our method embedding is more effective than traditional method.

5.2   The Communication Radius

Then, we study the impact of transmission range on the performance of both the two algorithms. In this experiment, we increased the communication radius of nodes from 40 to 80 in step of 10m. Fig.7 shows that TGDV-HOP always showed better performance (e.g., about 20% performances gain from DV-HOP respectively).

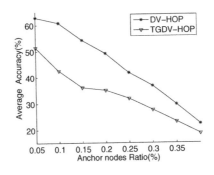

Fig. 6. Simulation Results

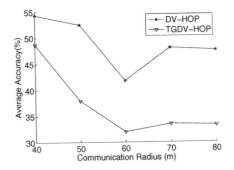

Fig. 7. Simulation Results

6   Conclusion

This paper proposes a new method to improve DV-HOP algorithm localization accuracy and adaptability in the non-uniform node deployment. Via analysis and simulation, the results are conducted to examine the efficiency of the proposed localization approach and significantly outperform previous designs.

Acknowledgments. This work was based on Project 61070176, 61170218, supported by NSFC, SRFDP (20106101110018), the Key Project of Chinese Ministry of Education (211181), Department of Education research project of Shaanxi province, China(2010JK854, 2010JC25, 2010JC24), Science and Technology research project of Shaanxi province(2011K06-07),and supported by Opening Foundation of Key Laboratory of Culture Heritage Research and Conservation(Northwest University), Ministry of Education.

References

1. Liu, Y., Yang, Z., Wang, X., et al.: Location, localization, and localizability. Journal of Computer Science and Technology 25(2), 274–297 (2010)
2. Mao, G., Fidan, B., Anderson, B.D.O.: Wireless sensor network localization techniques. Computer Networks 51(10), 2529–2553 (2007)
3. Ni, L.M., Liu, Y., Lau, Y.C., Patil, A.P.: LANDMARC: indoor location sensing using active RFID. Wireless Networks 10(6), 701–710 (2004)
4. Niculescu, D., Nath, B.: Ad Hoc Positioning System (APS) using AoA. In: IEEE INFOCOM (2003)
5. Niculescu, D., Nath, B.: DV Based Positioning in Ad hoc Networks. Journal of Telecommunication Systems (2003)
6. Bulusu, N., Heidemann, J., Bychkovskly, V., et al.: Density Adaptive Algorithms for Anchor Placement in Wireless Sensor Networks. In: Proc. of the 21st International Conference on Distributed Computing Systems, pp. 489–498 (2001)
7. Shang, Y., Ruml, W.: Improved MDS-Based Localization. In: IEEE INFOCOM (2004)
8. He, T., Huang, C.D., Blum, B.M., et al.: Range Free localization schemes in large scale sensor networks, San Diego, pp. 81–95
9. Fan, Z., Chen, Y., et al.: Removing Heavily Curved Path: Improved DV-HOP Localization in Anisotropic Sensor Networks. In: The 7th International Conference on Mobile Ad-hoc and Sensor Networks (2011)
10. Kung, H.T., Lin, C.K., Lin, T.H., Vlah, D.: Localization with snap-inducing shaped residuals (SISR): Coping with errors in measurement. In: ACM MobiCom, pp. 333–344 (2009)
11. Liu, W., Wang, D., et al.: Approximate Convex Decomposition Based Localization in Wireless Sensor Networks. In: IEEE INFOCOM (2012)
12. Spirito, M.A.: On the accuracy of cellular mobile station location estimation. IEEE Transactions on Vehicular Technology (TVT), 674–685 (2001)

The Chained Mesh-Under Routing (C-MUR) for Improving IPv6 Packet Arrival Rate over Wireless Sensor Networks

Yi-Hua Zhu, Gan Chen, Kaikai Chi, and Yanjun Li

School of Computer Science and Technology, Zhejiang University of Technology,
Hangzhou, Zhejiang 310023, China
yhzhu@zjut.edu.cn, chengan009@163.com, {kkchi,yjli}@zjut.edu.cn

Abstract. The 6LoWPAN protocol is used in delivering IPv6 packet over IEEE 802.15.4 based wireless sensor networks (WSNs). In 6LoW-PAN, adaptation layer is introduced in the protocol stack so that routing can be performed either in the adaptation layer, called mesh-under routing (MUR), or in the network layer, called route-over routing (ROR). To deliver an IPv6 packet over a WSN, the packet has to be divided into multiple fragments, with each being carried in an IEEE 802.15.4 frame, due to the small payload of an 802.15.4 frame. Thus, MUR exhibits the drawback of low packet arrival rate (PAR) when delivering an IPv6 packet over a route consisting of multiple unreliable links in the WSN because the destination node cannot assemble the original IPv6 packet if any fragment of the packet is lost over any link. This drawback is remedied by the proposed chained MUR (C-MUR) scheme, in which some intermediate nodes between the source and the destination are chosen as temporary assembling nodes (TANs), where the received fragments are assembled into the original IP packet and the assembled packet is fragmented again and delivered to the next TAN or the destination node. Experiments show that C-MUR outperforms both MUR and ROR in terms of PAR.

Keywords: 6LoWPAN, route-over routing, mesh-under routing, wireless sensor network.

1 Introduction

Most wireless sensor networks (WSNs) usually adopt IEEE 802.15.4 standard [1], which is defined for the wireless personal area network (WPAN) characterized by low power, small packet size, short communication distance, and low data rate. For instance, the Maximum Transmission Unit (MTU) of a frame in IEEE 802.15.4 is 127 Bytes and the maximum data rate is 250 kbps with 2.5 GHz radio band [1].

It was ever considered to be impossible to use IP protocol in the resource-constrained WPAN. But, this idea has been changed with the advance in microprocessor unit (MPU). In fact, IETF has chartered 6LoWPAN working group

R. Wang and F. Xiao (Eds.): CWSN 2012, CCIS 334, pp. 734–743, 2013.
© Springer-Verlag Berlin Heidelberg 2013

to realize the task of delivering IPv6 packet over low-power and low data rate WPAN. In 6LoWPANs protocol stack, the adaptation layer is introduced, which resides between the network layer and the MAC layer, such that routing can progress either in the network layer (see Fig. 1), called route-over routing (ROR), or in the adaptation layer (see Fig. 2), called mesh-under routing (MUR) [2].

The minimum MTU of IPv6 is 1280 B, which is much larger than the maximum packet size in the 802.15.4 based WSN. As a result, when delivering the packet over the WSN, it is indispensable to fragment an IPv6 packet into multiple small pieces, with each being used as payload of an 802.15.4 MAC frame. Naturally, it is required that the frame size, which includes a MAC header, the payload, and a frame check sequence (FCS), be less than 127 B. Fragmentation, header compression and layer 2 forwarding are three features of 6LoWPAN [3].

```
+-------------------------------+
|       Application Layer        |
+-------------------------------+
|   Transport Layer (TCP/UDP)    |
+-------------------------------+
|  Network        +----------+   |
|  Layer          | Routing  |   |
|  (IPv6)         +----------+   |
+-------------------------------+
|   6LoWPAN Adaptation Layer     |
+-------------------------------+
|        802.15.4 MAC            |
+-------------------------------+
|        802.15.4 PHY            |
+-------------------------------+
```

Fig. 1. Route-over routing [2]

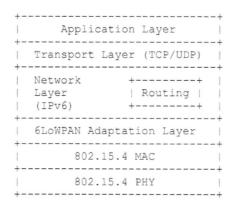

```
+-------------------------------+
|       Application Layer        |
+-------------------------------+
|  Transport Layer (TCP/UDP)     |
+-------------------------------+
|     Network Layer (IPv6)       |
+-------------------------------+
|  6LoWPAN                       |
|  Adaptation                    |
|  Layer          +----------+   |
+----------------| Routing* |-+
| 802.15.4 MAC +----------+   |
+-------------------------------+
|        802.15.4 PHY            |
+-------------------------------+
```

Fig. 2. Mesh-under routing [2]

Hitherto, some 6LoWPAN related problems are investigated in research community. A 6LoWPAN architecture was developed in [4], which enables IPv6 communication over IEEE 802.15.4 links. Lo Piccolo et al. [5] proposed a probably possible practical solution for the problem of how to realize a gateway between the IEEE 802.15.4 LR-WPANs and the IP networks. KIM et al. [6] presented a hierarchical routing over 6LoWPAN (HiLow), in which nodes are classified as parent and child and parent nodes allocate 16-bit short addresses to child ones by a simple formula so as to construct a hierarchical routing tree. Lim et al. [7] presented a mechanism to avoid the bias routing tree resulting from the condition that child nodes dont attach to parent nodes evenly. Chowdhury et al. [8] compared ROR with MUR in terms of the packet/fragment arrival probability, the total number of transmissions, and the total delay between source and destination. In a two-hop network with each hop having distance of 20 cm, Ludovici et al. [9] evaluated the performance of ROR, MUR, and enhanced ROR in terms of latency and energy consumption when transmitting fragmented IP packets.

When the route between two nodes has more than two hops, the processes of packet delivery in ROR and MUR are quite different. In ROR, packet is delivered hop by hop, i.e., the following process repeats before the packet reaches the destination node: the packet is fragmented in a node and is assembled in its neighboring node. In MUR, however, only after all the frames containing the fragments of the packet arrive at the destination, can the packet be assembled into the original packet.

In the case where the route connecting the source and destination nodes has multiple unreliable links, MUR exhibits the shortcoming that the destination node may fail in assembling the packet transmitted by the source node because one or more of the fragments of the packet is lost, which will be illustrated in the next section in details. In order to remedy the problem, we present the Chained MUR (C-MUR). The main contributions in this paper lie in that: 1) the C-MUR together with its algorithms is presented; and 2) the proposed C-MUR is able to improve packet arrival rate (PAR) while controlling packet delay within a preset bound.

The rest of the paper is organized as follows. C-MUR and its implementation are presented in Section 2 and Section 3, respectively. Experimental results are shown in Section 4. Section 5 concludes the paper.

2   The Chained MUR(C-MUR)

We use Fig. 3 to represent the topology for delivering IPv6 packet over a WSN, in which A_0 is a node in an IPv6 network while nodes A_1, A_2, ..., and A_n are in the WSN. When node A_0 intends to deliver packet K to A_n, it fragments this packet into M pieces K_1, K_2, ..., and K_M, which are used as the payloads in M different MAC frames suitable for being delivered in the WSN.

Here, we state the processes of packet delivery in ROR and MUR in details. In ROR, each frame is first transmitted from A_0 to A_1, where the physical (PHY) layer receives the frame and hands it up to the MAC layer, and then the

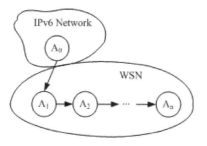

Fig. 3. Packet delivery from IP network to WSN

payload in the frame is further handed up to the network layer if the received frame passes FCS check. After all the fragments K_1, K_2, ..., K_M are gathered in the network layer, node A_1 assembles them to form the original packet K. From the assembled packet, node A_1 obtains the IP address of the destination node, which is then used in making decision on selecting the next-hop node by a routing policy. Upon the next hop is chosen, the packet K is fragmented again by node A_1 to form multiple frames to be transmitted to A_2. This process repeats so that packet K is delivered hop by hop till it reaches A_n.

In MUR, each fragment of packet K goes in the same way as follows. It is transmitted from A_0 to A_1, then to A_2, ..., and finally to A_n. In each hop, local-link address is used to transmit frames. Only when all the fragments of the packet K reach the destination node A_n without any error, can the original packet K be assembled in the destination node. The main difference between ROR and MUR is that, in the former each intermediate node performs fragmentation and assembling whereas in the latter only the source node fragments the packet and the destination node assembles the packet.

We use notation $< A_i, A_{i+1}, ..., A_j >$ to represent the route traversing the nodes A_i, A_{i+1}, ..., and A_j sequentially. Especially, the notation $< A_i, A_j >$ denotes the link that connects nodes A_i and A_j. As links in the WSN are prone to packet loss, we use q_i to represent the packet loss probability of the link $< A_{i-1}, A_i >$ and define $p_i = 1-q_i$, where $i = 1, 2, ...,$ and n. Moreover, let N be the upper bound (i.e., the maximum number) of the frame retransmissions performed in MAC. That is, a loss frame will not be retransmitted after it has been transmitted for N times. Thus, the probability that a frame transmitted by A_{i-1} is not successfully delivered to A_i is as the following:

$$P_i^{(F)} \equiv (q_i)^N, i = 1, 2, ..., n \tag{1}$$

which equals to the probability of the event that the frame has failed in N successive transmission/retransmissions. Hence, the event that the frame is successfully delivered from A_{i-1} to A_i has probability

$$P_i^{(S)} \equiv 1 - P_i^{(F)} = 1 - (q_i)^N, i = 1, 2, ..., n \tag{2}$$

Thus, the event that "the IPv6 packet is successfully delivered to A_1 from A_0" is equivalent to the one that "all the M frames are successfully delivered from A_0 to A_1 ", which has the probability $(P_1^{(S)})^M$. As a result, the probability that the packet fails to reach A_1 is $1 - (P_1^{(S)})^M$.

Clearly, in MUR, the event that " a frame carrying a fragment of the packet is successfully delivered from A_0 to A_n" is equivalent to the one that "the frame is successfully delivered over all the links $< A_0, A_1 >$, $< A_1, A_2 >$, ..., and $< A_{n-1}, A_n >$", which has the probability $\prod_{i=1}^{n} P_i^{(S)}$. Thus, the event that the IPv6 packet is successfully delivered from A_0 to A_n via MUR, i.e., all the M segments reaches A_n, has the probability

$$P_{mu}^{(S)} \equiv (\prod_{i=1}^{n} P_i^{(S)})^M = \prod_{i=1}^{n} [P_i^{(S)}]^M \qquad (3)$$

which leads to the probability that the packet fails to reach A_n via MUR as follows:

$$P_{mu}^{(F)} \equiv 1 - P_{mu}^{(S)} = 1 - \prod_{i=1}^{n} [P_i^{(S)}]^M \qquad (4)$$

Define packet arrival rate (PAR) of a route as the ratio of the number of packets arrived at the destination node to the number of packets transmitted by the source node on the route. Thus, the PAR of MUR is $P_{mu}^{(S)}$.

From (3), we observe that the PAR of MUR decrease as the number of hops, i.e., n, grows due to $[P_i^{(S)}]^M < 1, i = 1, 2, ..., n$. As a result, it is possible that a frame cannot be successfully delivered to the destination if n continues to grow. For example, setting $N = 3$ and assuming the probability of successful delivering a packet over any link of the WSN is the same, which are set to $p = 0.6, 0.7$, and 0.8, respectively, we obtain the relationship between n and PAR according to (3), which is shown in Fig.4. From the figure, we have the following observations: 1) for $p = 0.8$, PAR is less than 0.4 when $n = 20$, but it is above 0.6 when $n = 10$; and 2) for $p = 0.6$, PAR is close to 0 when $n > 10$, which indicates that, under MUR, the destination node nearly has no chance to assemble the IPv6 packet transmitted by the source node on this condition. These observations prompt us to improve the PAR by reducing n, i.e., shortening the length of packet delivery route. In fact, this is the core idea of the proposed C-MUR.

In C-MUR, some intermediate nodes between the source and the destination are chosen as temporary assembling nodes (TANs), where the received fragments are assembled into the original IP packet and the packet is fragmented again to be delivered to the next TAN or the destination node. After TANs are set, the route from the source to the destination is divided into x subroutes $L_1, L_2, ..., L_x(x > 1)$, in which L_i ends at a TAN ($i = 1, 2, ..., x - 1$) while L_x ends at the destination node. For instance, if A_3, A_5, and A_{10} in Fig.3 are TANs, then the route from A_0 to A_n is divided into subroutes L_1, L_2, L_3, and L_4, where $L_1 =< A_0, A_1, A_2, A_3 >, L_2 =< A_3, A_4, A_5 >, L_3 =< A_5, A_6, A_7, ..., A_{10} >$, and $L_4 =< A_{10}, A_{11}, A_{12}, ..., A_n >$.

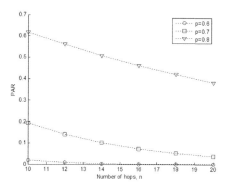

Fig. 4. PAR vs n

Obviously, with C-MUR, the network layer in each TAN is involved in assembling the original IP packet, which introduces extra packet delay. The reason is as follows. First, after all the frames carrying the fragments of the packet are received by a TAN, all the fragments are assembled to form the original packet. Second, the IP address of the destination is extracted in the header of the assembled packet. Third, the IP address of the next hop is determined by searching its routing table. Last, the new packet, in which the destination address is set to the IP address of the determined next hop, is fragmented again and passed down to the adaptation layer whereby to the MAC layer. Therefore, there is a trade-off between PAR and packet delay in C-MUR. Consequently, we introduce θ as the preset lower bound of PAR and D_0 as the preset upper bound of the delay.

Noting that the nodes in the WSN occupy small memory size and weak MPU capacity, for the sake of easy implementation in the WSN, we use the following TAN-finding algorithm (T-FA) to determine TANs for a given x:

Step 1. Let $h = \lceil n/x \rceil$, where $\lceil\ \rceil$ is the ceil function.

Step 2. Starting from the destination, every h-th node, exclusive of the source node, is chosen as a TAN.

Step 3. End.

With T-FA in hand, the core of C-MUR is to find the optimal x, which is determined by the optimization problem shown in (5). The rationale underlying (5) is that the shorter the subroute length, the higher the PAR according to (3).

$$MAX\ x$$

$$st. \begin{cases} \displaystyle\sum_{i=1}^{x} D(L_i) < D_0 \\[2mm] \displaystyle\prod_{i=1}^{|L_j|} [P_i^{(S)}]^M \geq \theta, j = 1, 2, ..., x \\[2mm] 2 \leq x \leq n - 2 \end{cases} \tag{5}$$

where $D(L_i)$ is the delay of delivering a packet along subroute L_i and $|L_j|$ stands for the number of the nodes contained in L_j. The first constraint in (5) indicates that the total delay for delivering a packet along all the subroutes must be less than D_0; and the second constraint requires each subroute has the PAR greater than or equal to θ.

The optimal x in (5) can be easily found by the following algorithm:

Step 1. Let $x = 2$.

Step 2. Determine TANs by T-FA. If the constraints in (5) is met, then go to Step 3; otherwise, go to Step 4.

Step 3. Let $x = x + 1$. If $x > n - 2$, then go to Step 4; otherwise, go to Step 2.

Step 4. End.

C-MUR progresses as follows. First, the optimal x is determined by the above algorithm for given θ and D_0. Second, the TANs are determined by T-FA. Last, the source delivers the packet via MUR to the first TAN, in which the packet is assembled into the original IP packet. Then, the packet is fragmented again and delivered to the next TAN via MUR. The same process repeats till the packet is delivered to the destination.

3   Implementation of the C-MUR

Each node in the WSN computes and stores the frame delivery time (FDT) and the successful transmission probability (STP) for each link connecting to its neighboring node. After a preset period, the source node sends a request packet to collect all the stored FDTs and STPs, which are respectively used to compute $D(L_i)(i = 1, 2, ..., x)$ and $P_i^{(S)}(i = 1, 2, ..., n)$ in the optimization problem (5).

C-MUR is performed in the source node, which is located at the IP network and usually has ample resources, such as memory size, MPU capacity, etc.

4   Experiment

The experiments are based on blip, an open-source TinyOS based 6LoWPAN implementation developed by The University of California at Berkeley. All the motes used in the experiments have the same type as the one shown in Fig. 5. Moreover, we use the linear network shown in Fig. 6, in which the distance between two neighboring motes is set to 2 m and transmission power of each mote is set to 1 mW. In addition, Mote 1 connects to a laptop.

All the IP packets are generated by the laptop. Hence, it is convenient to let the laptop judge whether the packet transmitted by the source node (i.e., Mote 1) is received by the destination node (i.e., mote 6) or not. Therefore, we let each packet first go through the route $< 1, 2, 3, 4, 5, 6 >$ and then go back to the laptop through the route $< 6, 5, 4, 3, 2, 1 >$ after the destination node (i.e., Mote 6) receives the packet. Accordingly, we let the laptop compute two-way PAR (T-PAR), defined as the ratio of the number of transmitted packets to that of the received packets in Mote 1. In addition, the round trip time (RTT) of

Fig. 5. Mote with 802.15.4 wireless transceiver

Fig. 6. A linear network with 6 motes

a packet is the duration from the instant when it is transmitted by Mote 1 to the instant when it is transmitted back to Mote 1. In fact, T-PAR and RTT in this case are respectively equivalent to PAR and the packet delivery time in the following case: the route from the source to the destination consists of 11 motes listed as 1, 2, 3, 4, 5, 6, 5, 4, 3, 2, and 1.

Without considering the constraints of θ and D_0, setting $N = 5$ and $M = 2, 4$, and 6, respectively, after 30,000 packets (each has payload of 101 octets) are transmitted by Mote 1, we obtain Figs. 7 and 8, where "C-MUR" represents the proposed C-MUR scheme in which Motes 2 and Mote 4 are chosen as TANs. It can be clearly seen from the two figures that: 1) round trip time (RTT) and T-PAR in the three schemes grow with M, which agrees with the fact that the

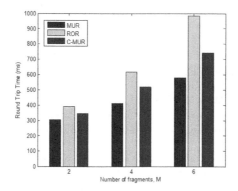

Fig. 7. RTT vs. number of fragments

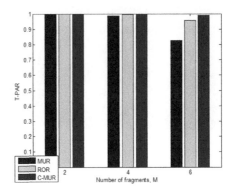

Fig. 8. T-PAR vs. number of fragments

probability of losing packet increases when a packet is fragmented into more pieces; and 2) MUR has the least RTT whereas ROR has the most RTT (see Fig. 7), and the C-MUR achieves the best T-PAR (see Fig. 8) at cost of a little more RTT than MUR. In other words, the proposed C-MUR achieves the aim of improving packet arriving rate.

5   Conclusion

With the advance of MPU, delivering IPv6 packets over WSN becomes increasingly significant. The C-MUR presented in this paper is able to improve the rate of the packets arriving at the destination while delay is controlled within a given bound. The proposed C-MUR is applicable for WSNs.

Acknowledgement. This work was supported by the National Natural Science Foundation of China under grant numbers 61070190, 61001126, and 61003264, and Zhejiang Provincial Natural Science Foundation under grant number Z1100455.

References

1. IEEE Computer Society. IEEE 802.15.4 Standard for Wireless Medium Access Control (MAC) and Physical Layer (PHY) Specifications for Low-Rate Wireless Personal Area Networks (WPANs) (2006)
2. Kim, E., Kaspar, D., Gomez, C., Bormann, C.: Problem statement and requirements for 6LoWPAN routing. Draft-ietf-6lowpan-routing-requirements-10 (November 2011)
3. Hui, J.W., Culler, D.E.: Extending IP to low-power, wireless personal area networks. IEEE Internet Computing 12(4), 37–45 (2008)
4. Hui, J.W., Culler, D.E.: IPv6 in low-power wireless networks. Proc. IEEE 98(11), 1865–1878 (2012)

5. Lo Piccolo, F., Battaglino, D., Bracciale, L., et al.: Towards fully IP-enabled IEEE 802.15.4 LR-WPANs. In: Proc. SECON Workshops 2009, pp. 1–3 (2009)
6. Kim, K., Yoo, S., Lee, J., Mulligan, G.: Hierarchical routing over 6LoWPAN. draft-daniel-6lowpan-hilow-hierarchical-routing-01 (June 2007)
7. Lim, H.J., Chung, T.M.: The bias routing tree avoiding technique for hierarchical routing protocol over 6LoWPAN. In: Proc. NCM 2009, pp. 232–235 (2009)
8. Chowdhury, A.H., Ikram, M., Cha, H.S.: Route-over vs Mesh-under Routing in 6LoWPAN. In: Proc. IWCMC 2009, pp. 1208–1212 (2009)
9. Ludovici, A., Calveras, A., Casademont, J.: Forwarding techniques for IP fragmented packets in a Real 6LoWPAN Network. Sensors 11, 992–1008 (2011), doi:10.3390/s110100992

Compressed Sensing Data Fusion
of Monitoring Cyanobacteria Bloom-Forming

Zhiqiang Zou*, Zeting Li, Hao Zhao, Cunchen Hu, and Fei Zhang

College of Computer, Nanjing University of Posts and Telecommunications,
Nanjing, Jiangsu 210003, China
Jiangsu High Technology Research Key Laboratory for Wireless Sensor Networks,
Nanjing, Jiangsu 210003, China
Key Lab of Broadband Wireless Communication and Sensor Network Technology
(Nanjing University of Posts and Telecommunications),
Ministry of Education Jiangsu Province, Nanjing, Jiangsu 210003, China
zouzq@njupt.edu.cn, memorylzt@yeah.net, wjzhh815@gmail.com,
duihuhu@163.com, zfcsat@126.com

Abstract. Wireless senor networks have more and more applications
while fundamental constraint still exists, such as limited power supply
and bandwidth. When the sensing signal exhibits spare, we can sampling only a part of signal corresponding to nonzero coefficients. Inspired
by recent results in theory of compressive sensing (CS), we propose a
data fusion method based on CS. First, we describe the distributed data
fusion in UWSNs based on CS. Then, we present a monitoring model
of the cyanobacteria bloom-forming (CBF). Finally, we demonstrate the
performance analysis and provide concluding remarks.

Keywords: Compressed Sensing, Underwater Wireless Sensor Networks,
Cyanobacteria Bloom-forming, Monitoring Model, Data Fusion.

1   Introduction

In recent years, wireless sensor networks (WSNs) have achieved great development and are able to collect environment data (e.g. temperature, humidity,
position, salinity), monitor field, prevent disaster and so on. WSNs consist of a
large number of wireless nodes and are responsible for sensing, processing and
monitoring environment data. WSNs can provide great benefits to sensing the
real world smartly [1], [2], [3]. However, there are limitations such as power
consumption, lifetime, bandwidth and delay. Each node of WSNs requires independent energy resources. Therefore, energy efficient method is of particular
importance since battery power is severely limited and re-charging batteries is
difficult in underwater wireless sensor networks (UWSNs).

The emerging theory of compressive sensing (CS) [4], [5], [6], a novel sens-
ing/sampling paradigm that goes against the common wisdom in data acquisition, can elegantly solve the problems of the above limitations. CS theory asserts

---

* Corresponding author.

R. Wang and F. Xiao (Eds.): CWSN 2012, CCIS 334, pp. 744–752, 2013.
© Springer-Verlag Berlin Heidelberg 2013

that one can recover certain signals from far fewer samples or measurements than traditional methods used when the signals meet spatial smoothness of the signal field [7], [8], [9], [10].

The cyanobacteria bloom-forming (CBF) in lake is harmful to our life while lacking effective monitoring and controlling means to solve it. The combination of CS theory with UWSNs holds promising preventing disaster. In order to real-time monitor the underwater environment using a completely decentralized scheme, some quintessential questions must be answered:

(1)How to collect the distributed sensor data?
(2)How to make the data collection method with lower-cost?
(3)How to fuse the heterogeneous data for CBF?

The focus of the paper is to find a data fusion method of monitoring CBF based on compressed sensing theory for solutions to the above questions. In this work, we consider an UWSN that measures a physical phenomenon for CBF monitoring purposes. We assume that the signal of physical phenomenon CBF to be studied is compressible (sparse) in the frequency domain.

1.1   Related Work

The natural phenomena of CBF are sparse [11] so that we can employ compressed sensing to reduce the energy consumption of UWSNs. Authors in [4] give an introduction to compressive sampling. If a signal is known to be compressible, the authors in [5] and [6] find that the number of measurements N to this signal can be dramatically smaller than the size of signal M ($N << M$).Furthermore, near-optimality signal can be recovered from these far fewer measurements, which is very different from the traditional Shannon/Nyquist sampling theorem.

A number of references, such as [7],[8],[9] and [10] focus on the combination of CS theory with WSNs. In [7] authors provide most recent survey of CS theory as it is applied in WSN, especially in describing important parameters in WSNs. A kind of distributed sensor perception based on CS is discussed in [8]. Authors mainly researched on projections of the data and joint method of the sparse signals acquired by multiple sensors. To the best of our knowledge, authors in [10] are the first to introduce the application of compressed sensing in networks. In [10], the authors proposed a distributed joint sourceCchannel communication architecture for energy-efficient estimation of sensor field data and analyzed the corresponding relationships among power, distortion, and latency.

In [9], Fatemeh Fazel, Maryam Fazel and Milica Stojanovic were inspired by the theory of compressed sensing and proposed a distributed energy-efficient sensor network scheme denoted by Random Access Compressed Sensing, which is suitable for long-term deployment of large underwater networks. While some of our work is inspired by and similar in spirit to [9], our work, in contrast, not only extends the results of [9] to the case of monitoring cyanobacteria bloom-forming, but also applies to a broader class of heterogeneous data for CBF and designs new hardware of sensor nodes for UWSNs.

1.2   Organization

The rest of this paper is organized as follows. In Section 2, we describe the distributed data fusion in UWSNs. In particular, we analyze signals sparse representation in Section 2.3 and propose a data fusion method based on compressed sensing theory in Section 2.4. In Section 3, we present a monitoring model based on data fusion method of monitoring CBF in brief. In Section 4, we demonstrate the performance analysis. Finally, we provide concluding remarks in Section 5.

2   Distributed Data Fusion in UWSNs

In order to seek answers to the questions proposed above for monitor CBF, we focus on four main steps. Firstly we review the conventional data fusion method of monitoring CBF. Secondly we characterize the signals of cyanobacteria bloom-forming, which are compressible signals. And then, we introduce the concept of CS and study signals sparse representation, which lay a base of data collection method with lower-cost. At last, we present the data fusion method of monitoring based on compressed sensing theory.

2.1   Conventional Data Fusion Method of Monitoring CBF

In conventional monitoring CBF, multiple wired devices with heterogeneous sensing capabilities can be configured in a network to monitor the CBF in lake.Each sensor node in monitoring point communicates its observations of the field to a central node, named as the Data Fusion Center (DFC) and the DFC uses the management software to remote monitor and local management by using some software.The map of physical field can be reconstructed in DFC. As shown in Fig. 1, there are many sensor nodes communicate with DFC via wired channels, which is a monitoring lake example of Beijing Water & Land Technology CO.,LTD.The infrastructure of conventional monitoring CBF can provide some benefits different from UWSNs, such as power supply by wired communications. However, the cost of this monitoring system is higher than normal UWSNs. Furthermore, the deployment of UWSNs is faster than it. Therefore, UWSNs are adapted for their faster decision making for time-critical applications. In what follows we will focus on UWSNs, while we consider this conventional sensing as a benchmark for comparison.

2.2   Compressible Signals of CBF

Exploiting the fact that most natural phenomena exhibit certain sparsity in either the spatial or frequency domain in an appropriate basis, we take advantage of the emerging CS theory to reduce the energy consumption of UWSNs [9]. The authors in [11] pointed that there many factors in CBF, such as chlorophyll A, temperature, humidity, which are of spatial smoothness. According to the observed value from 2008-05-22 to 2008-09-18 [11], as shown in Table 1, the

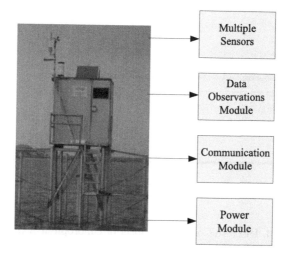

Fig. 1. Conventional Monitoring System

Table 1. Observed Data ChlorophyllA from Sensor Nodes

Logitude	Latitude	Date	Sensing Data
120.296	31.387	2008-05-22	6.16
120.296	31.387	2008-07-03	6.20
120.296	31.387	2008-08-21	7.25
120.379	31.436	2008-05-22	4.30
120.379	31.436	2008-07-03	6.19
120.379	31.436	2008-08-21	12.80

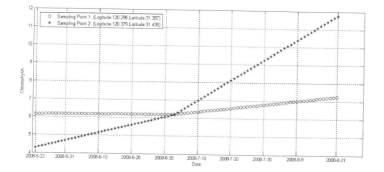

Fig. 2. Original Value of Chlorophyll A Signal

signal of chlorophyll A is compressible. As Fig. 2 and Fig. 3 shown, at sampling point 1, almost 99.96% of the energy of size $N = 92$ is contained in $K = 6$ Fourier coefficients after linear interpolation from Table 1. The results, at sampling point

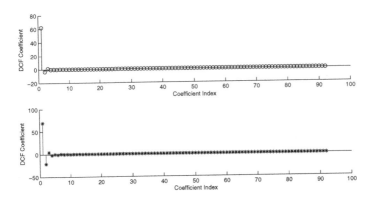

Fig. 3. Discrete Cosine Transform of Chlorophyll A Signal

2, are 99.60% and $K = 10$, which are similar to the value of sampling point 1. Furthermore, from another experiment about the factor temperature, we also can get the similar conclusion that some of main facts of CBF are compressible or sparse.

2.3   Signals Sparse Representation

In general, according to [8] and [9], a signal $S \in R^N$,it is sparse based on some basis φ, i.e.,

$$S = \varphi S_0 \tag{1}$$

where $S_0 \in R^N$, the transformation coefficients of S_0 are zero, $K = ||S_0||$ is called the sparsity of S_0,$K < N$,φ is linear transformation basis. In our work, we use a discrete cosine transform (DCT) as basis $\varphi \in R^{N \times N}$ [8],$\varphi^T \varphi = E$,where

$$\varphi = \sqrt{\frac{2}{N}} \begin{bmatrix} \sqrt{\frac{1}{2}} & \sqrt{\frac{1}{2}} & \cdots & \sqrt{\frac{1}{2}} \\ \cos \frac{1}{2N} \pi & \cos \frac{3}{2N} \pi & \cdots & \cos \frac{2N-1}{2N} \pi \\ \cdots & \cdots & \cdots & \cdots \\ \cos \frac{N-1}{2N} \pi & \cos \frac{3(N-1)}{2N} \pi & \cdots & \cos \frac{(2N-1)(N-1)}{2N} \pi \end{bmatrix} \tag{2}$$

At the same, the signalcan be sensed by formula (3)

$$y = \phi S \tag{3}$$

where y is a smaller set of observations, $y \in R^K$, $\phi \in R^{K \times N}$is the sensing matrix. Let us combination of (1) with (3), we can get the formula (4) as following:

$$y = \phi S = \phi \varphi S_0 \tag{4}$$

If we let $M = \phi \varphi, M \in R^{K \times N}$as measurement matrix, can also get formula (5), which is the simplified version of formula (4), where ϕ must be sufficiently incoherent to the basis φ.

$$y = MS_0 \tag{5}$$

In (5), because the dimensional space of y is lower than S_0, there exist infinitely many solutions that give rise to y. However, the theory of CS states that can be recovered from a small subset of random measurements [8],[9]. Thus taking into account the sparsity of natural phenomena S_0, we can reduce the number of measurements required for field recovery from some K to N by the solution formula (6):

$$min \left\| S_0^0 \right\|_1 \; subject \; to \; y = \phi\varphi \, S_0^0 \tag{6}$$

In short, CS theory provides a means to simultaneously sense and compress the data using just matrix vector multiplication at the edge of the network and the solution to formula (6) can ben computed in literature of convex optimization [5],[12].

2.4 Data Fusion Method Based on Compressed Sensing Theory

CBF disaster prevention is long term complex task with many factors involved. As described in Fig. 3, the distributed observationscorresponding to these factors can be aggregated to DFC. While some of our work is inspired by and similar in spirit to [10], Bajwa, Haupt, Sayeed, and Nowak have primarily studied the case of phase-coherent transmission of data from sensor nodes to the fusion center. Our work, in contrast, not only extends the results of [10] to the case of multiple data fusion centers, but also applies to CBF field. There are some notes about Fig. 3. Note that $S_0^i, 1 \leq i \leq C$ denotes ith signal source; $s_0^{1i}, 1 \leq i \leq N$ denotes ith signal value from ith signal source; $z^{ij}, 1 \leq i \leq C, 1 \leq j \leq N$ denotes the noisy signal from ith signal source jth senor nodes; $y^{ij} = (y_1^{ij}, ..., y_K^{ij}), 1 \leq i \leq C, 1 \leq j \leq N$ denotes observations data vector of k dimensions from ith signal source jth senor nodes based on CS. As Fig. 4 shown, there are main three parts

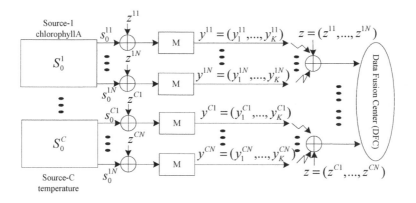

Fig. 4. Data Fusion Scheme Based on CS

in our data fusion scheme based on CS. First part is source sensing part, includes source signal of chorophyll A, temperature and etc. Second part is measurement part, which acquires the observations data y from sensing part. The last part is data fusion part, where multiple observations data and the noisy signal are fused. From this data fusion scheme, we can aggregate the distributed sensor data, which is helpful to faster decision making for CBF field monitoring and disaster prevention.

3   CBF Monitoring Model Based on Data Fusion Method

With regard to the question of fusing the heterogeneous data for CBF, we build a monitoring model based on data fusion method of monitoring CBF. First, we mesh the key water field with grid and deploy the sensor nodes and build the UWSNs to sensing the some key parameters of CBF, such as chlorophyll A and temperature. Consider the balance between input and output of cyanobacteria bloom-forming, we get the monitoring model for CBF based on this balance feature [11], as formula (7),

$$C_i = C_{i-1} + (B_{i-1} - D_{i-1}) + (I_{i-1} - E_{i-1}), i = 1, ..., n \qquad (7)$$

where C_i is the density value of chlorophyll A in one grid of UWSNs at time instant i, and $B_{i-1}, D_{i-1}, I_{i-1}, E_{i-1}$ is the corresponding value of growth, mortality, immigration and emigration, respectively. And these observations vector can be acquired using the method in Fig. 3 based on CS. Although there are many technical problems need to refine in the large scale practical applications of UWSNs, the above model introduces the CS into UWSNs and leads a good start of the study in monitoring CBF.

4   Performance Analysis

In this section, we analyze the performance of our data fusion method. From the above description, it can be seen that there are some distinguished characters from other methods, such as lower power consumption, holding a good approximation of the data from sparse signal and robustness in the face of changing network topology.

Let us first analyze the power consumption and robustness. From the Fig. 3, for the same coverage area, our method offers energy savings of an order of magnitude since we only need fewer sampling than conventional UWSNs. By reducing the energy consumption, our method extends the life-time of the sensor network. We also conclude that, with regard to the robustness, our method need not measure from the whole UWSNs, and instead only uses a small subset of random measurements. If some sensor nodes are failure, they may not be selected in our method at bigger probability.

And then, we will mainly focus on investigating the reconstruction error of our method. The real observation data vector y can be got from the above table in section 2.2. After discrete cosine transform on $y(i)$, the reconstruction data $y(i)\prime$ can be got from formula (6). Formula (8) is general way to compute the reconstruction error. As Fig. 5 shown, the mean of reconstruction error of sampling point 1 is 0.0017 while the result corresponding to sampling point 2 is 0.0159. This result demonstrates that our data fusion method based on CS is suitable in monitoring CBF.

$$e = \sum_{i=1}^{N} [(y(i) - y(i)\prime)/y(i)]/N \qquad (8)$$

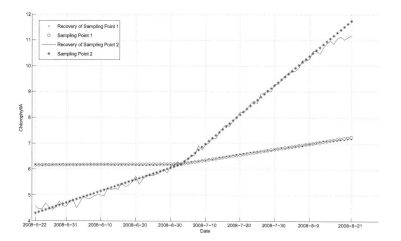

Fig. 5. Reconstruction Error Analyses

5   Conclusion

We described how to combine CS theory with UWSNs for monitoring CBF. The distributed data fusion in UWSNs and a monitoring model based on data fusion method of monitoring CBF are presented. The simulation results show that, in contrast to the conventional data fusion method of monitoring CBF, our data fusion in UWSNs based on CS theory has lower energy consumption, better robustness and smaller reconstruction error. However, this paper only gives a crude framework based on CS for monitoring cyanobacteria bloom-forming and there are still many practical works needed to be done. As our future research, we intend to optimize the CBF Monitoring model in formula (7) and apply our method into monitoring real physical world at large scale in lakes. Our future objective is to help people to make faster decision for preventing disaster (e.g.CBF) in advance.

Acknowledgments. This work is supported by the National Natural Science Foundation of China under Grant No. 61170065 and 61171053; the China Planned Projects for Postdoctoral Research Funds (20100471356); the Open Research Fund from the Key Laboratory of Computer Networks and Information Integration at the Southeast University (K93-9-2010-06); the Project Funded by the Priority Academic Program Development of Jiangsu Higher Education Institutions (yx002001). Finally, we are grateful to the anonymous reviewers for their insightful and constructive suggestions.

References

1. Baronti, P., Pillai, P., Chook, V., Chessa, S., Gotta, A., Hu, Y.: Wireless sensor networks: A survey on the state of the art and the 802.15.4 and zigbee standards. Computer Communications 30, 1655–1695 (2007)
2. Culler, D., Estrin, D., Srivastava, M.: Overview of sensor networks. Computer 8, 41–49 (2004)
3. Al-Karaki, J.N., Kamal, A.E.: Routing techniques in wireless sensor networks: a survey. IEEE Wireless Communications 11, 6–28 (2004)
4. Cands, E., Wakin, M.: An introduction to compressive sampling. IEEE Signal Processing Magazine 25(2), 21–30 (2008)
5. Donoho, D.: Compressed sensing. IEEE Transactions on Information Theory 52(4), 1289–1306 (2006)
6. Donoho, D., Tsaig, Y.: Extensions of compressed sensing. Signal Processing 86(3), 533–548 (2006)
7. Balouchestani, M., Raahemifar, K., Krishnan, S.: Robust Wireless Sensor Networks with Compressed Sensing Theory. In: Benlamri, R. (ed.) NDT 2012, Part I. CCIS, vol. 293, pp. 608–619. Springer, Heidelberg (2012)
8. Yang, A.Y., Gastpar, M., Bajcsy, R., Sastry, S.S.: Distributed Sensor Perception via Sparse representation. Proc. of the IEEE 98(6), 1077–1088 (2010)
9. Fazel, M., Fazel, F., Stojanovic, M.: Random Access Compressed Sensing for Energy-Efficient Underwater Sensor Networks. IEEE Journal on Selected Areas in Communications 29(8), 1660–1670 (2011)
10. Bajwa, W., Haupt, J., Sayeed, A., Nowak, R.: Joint source-channel communication for distributed estimation in sensor networks. IEEE Trans. Inf. Theory 53(10), 3629–3653 (2007)
11. Huang, J.C., Wu, X.D., Gao, J.F., Kong, F.X.: Cyanobacteria bloom prediction model and parameters optimization based on genetic algorithm. Acta Ecologica Sinica 30(4), 1003–1010 (2010) (in Chinese)
12. Cands, E., Romberg, J.: L1-MAGIC: Recovery of sparse signals via convex programming. Technical report, Caltech (2005)

Author Index

CPSIA information can be obtained at www.ICGtesting.com
Printed in the USA
LVOW011744070713

341741LV00005B/50/P